Critical Issues in Educational Psychology

CRITICAL ISSUES IN EDUCATIONAL PSYCHOLOGY

Edited by

Meredith D. Gall

and

Beatrice A. Ward

*Far West Laboratory for
Educational Research
and Development*

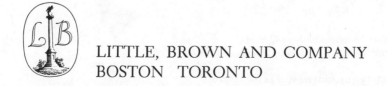

LITTLE, BROWN AND COMPANY
BOSTON TORONTO

Library of Congress Catalog Card No. 73–20936

FIRST PRINTING

Published simultaneously in Canada
by Little, Brown & Company (Canada) Limited

PRINTED IN THE UNITED STATES OF AMERICA

To Walter R. Borg who has greatly influenced our thinking about education.

PREFACE

Students taking courses in educational psychology and related areas increasingly question their instructors about the relevance of course material. They ask how psychological theories can be applied to the real world of schools, teachers, and children. They wonder if research can solve any of the problems besetting education. They doubt that knowledge about teaching and learning is as definitive as their textbooks sometimes seem to imply. Most of all, students question the value of educational psychology in training them for careers as teachers and administrators.

This book of readings was prepared for the instructor in educational psychology or a related area who wishes to respond to the above challenges. We started with the premise that students need to confront the issues and the persons who are generating controversy in education — for example, Jensen's genetic explanation of racial differences in intelligence, Skinner's behavioristic theory of learning, Jencks' research on schools and equal opportunity, Illich's radical alternatives to conventional schooling, Popham's advocacy of behavioral objectives in education, Holt's attack on current grading practices. The typical textbook may help the student acquire knowledge about theory and research in educational psychology, but it does not help him learn how to cope with conflicting views on such issues. Our book of readings is designed to serve this purpose by helping the student analyze the pro and con positions on issues as stated by prominent and sometimes outspoken educators.

The second premise guiding our selection of readings is that most students majoring in education are career-oriented. Therefore, the readings were selected to highlight issues that are likely to concern potential teachers and other educational practitioners: what students should learn in school, whether IQ is really as important as some people think, what the characteristics are of an effective teacher, how important class size is, how open classrooms compare with conventional schooling practices, whether radical steps are necessary for change in education, the case for and against ability grouping, whether schools should be held accountable for the failure of some students to learn, and whether students should be tested and assigned grades.

Our third premise is that the issues and selections should focus on the learning process, which we view as the main concern of educational psychology. The focus on learning is reflected in the titles of the four parts into which the book is organized:

> The learning process.
> Factors that influence learning.
> Ways to help students learn better.
> Ways to evaluate learning.

Some of the issues presented under the above headings have had long histories of research and debate, such as the nature-nurture controversy. Others are newly emerging, such as sex bias in schooling practices. Most of the selections were published in the last five years. Throughout the book we have tried to maintain a balance between research and interpretive articles since both are necessary for developing a firm understanding of the empirical data, ethical considerations, and belief systems which underlie conflicting views on educational issues.

Suggestions for Using This Book

The typical introductory course in educational psychology consists of large lecture presentations. These are accompanied by small-group discussions intended to involve the students in thinking about the lecture and textbook material. This book of readings was designed to serve as the basis for these discussion sessions, although it is not restricted to this use. Each section of the book, which highlights a group of closely related issues, can provide the stimulus for discussions. Since the sections focus on important contemporary issues in educational psychology, the instructor should have no difficulty in assigning a section of readings to complement material presented in the textbook and lectures at any point in the term.

We suggest that, prior to the class discussions, students read the pertinent section introduction and the articles which follow it. For example, if students are reading in their textbooks about IQ measurement, the instructor could assign the introduction for Section 4 and the articles by David Cohen, Lillian Zach, and J. P. Guilford. (The article by Arthur Jensen in Section 3 might also be assigned.) In class, the viewpoints at the end of each section introduction can provide the springboard for discussions.

Referring to the viewpoints on page 171, the instructor might start the discussion with a statement like, "You've all had a chance to read the articles by Cohen, Zach, and Guilford. Some educators think that intelligence tests are useful in planning educational programs geared to the special needs of students. Do you agree with this position?" Sometimes it is helpful to precede the actual discussion by taking a poll of the group to determine how many students agree and disagree with a particular position on an issue. If students see that their peers are not in agreement, this can stimulate them to discuss their reasons for disagreeing.

The success of these discussions depends in large part on the students' interest in the issues and the instructor's skill as a moderator. Some useful techniques in moderating a discussion are:

Use supportive silence in order to promote interaction between the students.

If students react harshly to one of their peers for his stand on an issue, support the right of each person to his own opinion.

State the issue at the beginning of the discussion and restate it, as necessary, to keep the discussion focused.

Paraphrase and summarize occasionally the opinions expressed by participants.

Summarize key areas of agreement and disagreement among participants.

When appropriate, ask a student to clarify what he has said or to give supporting evidence for his opinion.

Call on silent members to involve them in the discussion and to increase the range of opinions on a particular issue.

For their part, students should be encouraged to respond to each other's ideas by agreeing or disagreeing with them, by asking each other to clarify their ideas, and by asking for supporting evidence. Also, the instructor might spend some time with the class talking about techniques that improve discussion climate such as listening carefully to what each person says, acknowledging each other's ideas and avoiding monopolization of the discussion.

The manner in which an instructor ends a discussion may strongly influence what students learn from it. Some useful end-of-discussion techniques are:

Have one or two students review the main points that were made in the discussion.

Ask participants to state viewpoints that differed from their own. (This is a good check on how well students have listened to each other.)

Ask several participants to state their current opinion and how the discussion affected it, if at all.

Spend some time talking about how the ideas brought out in the discussion might affect students' work as professional teachers or administrators.

In addition to their value as a discussion stimulus, the viewpoints that accompany each section introduction can provide ideas for term paper topics. For example, a student might opt to trace the historical development of a particular controversy in educational psychology. Another possibility is for the student to analyze a particular viewpoint, state his agreement or disagreement with it, and present research and theory which supports his position.

Beyond its use in an introductory course in educational psychology, this book of readings has a place in advanced courses. For the advanced student, it brings into focus some timely questions that he must confront as he decides what type of research to conduct or what type of educational program to install. Thus, the book could serve as the primary text for proseminars in areas such as issues and problems in education, teacher education methods, issues in teaching, issues in curriculum development, and instructional decisions facing the school administrator. In courses such as these, each section of readings could serve as the survey material from which the seminar members would conduct an indepth study of the questions raised and conflicting viewpoints expressed by the various authors.

The book also can illustrate what educational research is like. The research reports represent a variety of research approaches and different levels of quality. The instructor and the student, therefore, may analyze and compare examples of research from several viewpoints. Among them are appropriateness of instruments used to measure student learning outcomes and power of the research design. The instructor will find that both the research studies and interpretive articles are useful in stimulating students to think about further research on a specific problem in educational psychology.

Special Learning Aids

This book contains several distinctive learning aids. First is our extensive use of editors' introductions. As we mentioned above, each section in the book starts with an introduction which shows the student how a set of articles relate to each other through their common focus on an important unresolved issue in educational psychology. Also, each article is preceded by an overview of the article's content, viewpoint, and relevance to educational practice. Parts 2 and 3 are preceded by special introductions relating the sections to each other. These introductions are helpful in at least two ways: (1) the instructor does not need to read the entire book in order to determine how to insert each section into his course, since the section introductions provide the necessary information for making this decision; and (2) the section introductions free the student from having to read page after page before he can place an article in perspective or apply it to educational practice.

Although the major goal of each section of readings is to present two or more sides of a critical issue in educational psychology, the articles also contain important information to remember and apply. The questions following each article are designed to help the student check whether he has learned this information. Page references are given to help him quickly locate the answer to each question in the text.

In each section of the book, the comments of one author may relate not only to the issue under consideration but also to research findings and opinions presented in other sections. Furthermore, some comments by an author are especially pertinent to an issue or offer a challenge to which the student should respond. In each instance, we have written special footnotes directing the student to other articles in the book or posing a question for the student to consider.

Use of this book probably will range from beginning students in education to advanced students with several years of training and experience in research. In order to help even the most inexperienced student understand the research procedures and statistics mentioned in the readings, we have prepared a glossary of unfamiliar terms. Such terms appear in the text accompanied by a footnote referring the student to the glossary at the back of the book.

Editing of Articles

We expect the primary readers of this book to be students new to the field of educational psychology. Therefore, we deleted sections of articles referring to sophisticated research techniques that are not essential for understanding the author's viewpoint. Deleted passages in an article are noted by an ellipsis. We also omitted redundant material and material which, in our opinion, digressed from the main points of the article or the issues on which we wish the student to concentrate. These deletions enabled us to include more selections, and consequently a greater range of viewpoints, than would have been possible if some of the lengthier articles had been reprinted intact.

Acknowledgments

We wish to thank the authors for granting us permission to use their articles in this book. Also, we would like to express our appreciation to Lee Schulman of Michigan State University and Steven Owens of the University of Connecticut. They reviewed the manuscript and made many helpful suggestions concerning our editorial devices and selection of articles. As on many other occasions, Carolyn Amable and Ursula Hoffman made our work easier by their expert secretarial assistance in preparing the manuscript. We thank them for their help.

MDG
BAW

CONTENTS

PART TWO
Factors That Influence Learning   105

SECTION THREE
Introduction   107

SECTION FOUR
Social Class, Ethnic Background, and Heredity   115

PART FOUR
Ways To Evaluate Student Learning

SECTION FOURTEEN
Behavioral Objectives

SECTION FIFTEEN
The Accountability Movement

PART ONE

The Learning Process

HOW DOES LEARNING OCCUR?

Introduction

Education has many elements — teachers, administrators, schools, textbooks, teaching methods, curricula, grades, and tests — all directed toward the goal of helping students learn.

What is learning? How does a person learn to define a word, speak a sentence, make polite dinner conversation? How does he learn to count, add and subtract, use higher mathematics to solve complicated problems? These are not just academic questions. Your view of the learning process will influence how you teach and how you go about trying to improve education.

Four major explanations of how learning occurs follow:

1. Behaviorists, particularly B. F. Skinner and his followers, view learning as the acquisition of stimulus-response connections. A teacher shows a picture of a dog (stimulus), says "dog" (response), and then elicits the same response from the child. If the teacher praises or otherwise rewards the child for his correct response, the stimulus-response connection is reinforced, that is, strengthened. Learning has occurred.

2. Such cognitive theorists as Jerome Bruner and David Ausubel believe that the stimulus-response-reinforcement explanation is too simple. For learning to occur, several cognitive processes have to intervene between stimulus and response. These might involve intuition, capacity for processing information, and cognitive structures that provide a context for assimilating new information. Two children might learn different responses to the same stimulus because of differences in the way their minds work.

3. Such learning theorists as Albert Bandura rely on the concept of imitation to explain learning, particularly the learning of social behavior. As a child comes into contact with teachers and other persons, he observes their behavior and gradually adopts their language, mannerisms, problem-solving strategies, and other behaviors. In this

theory the "teacher" is a critical factor in what and how the child learns. In fact, learning can occur even when the teacher is not consciously trying to teach anything.

4. Robert Gagné, a prominent learning theorist, argues that there are different types of learning. The explanation of how learning occurs depends upon the type of learning that is involved. For example, the process by which you acquire a simple verbal association is different from the process by which you learn to solve problems. Gagné also believes that learning does not occur "from scratch," that is, in learning to say "dog" in response to a pictorial representation, the child relies extensively on prior learning. He needs to have learned how to pronounce sounds, focus attention on a picture, and respond to the teacher's request to say the word.

The strongest disagreements have arisen between the behaviorists and the cognitive theorists. The behaviorists claim that a few concepts such as stimulus, response, and reinforcement are sufficient to explain learning. Cognitive theorists argue that these concepts are not sufficient; you need to study the child's perceiving and thinking processes to explain how learning occurs. Another issue concerns the value of theory in explaining learning. Some believe that learning theories provide the best foundation for improving education. However, many educators, including John Holt, believe that these theories are of little value in helping us to understand the mysteries of the learning process.

A third issue concerns individual differences in the learning process. Such theorists as Skinner have searched for learning processes that are shared by everyone, including humans and animals, adults and children. Other theorists like Bruner and Gagné emphasize the differences among learners, particularly between children and adults. They argue that the way a person approaches a learning task is a function of his cognitive maturity and previous learning history.

The following views about the learning process summarize these issues. Which, if any, do you agree with?

Theories of Learning

Pro Theories of learning are useful because they provide explanations of learning, which then can be tested through empirical observation and systematic research.

Con The learning process is a mystery. Theories cannot help us understand it.

Behaviorism

Pro Such behavioristic concepts as stimulus, response, and reinforcement are sufficient to explain how learning occurs. Cognitive concepts are not necessary.

Con To explain learning, we must take into account the cognitive processes and capacities which come into play during learning.

A Unitary Learning Process

Pro   The learning process is essentially the same for all learners, whether child or adult, human or animal.

Con   Human and animal learning differ in fundamental ways.
Human learning involves using cognitive processes not
present in other forms of life. Also, adults learn differently from children because they have different and more
highly developed cognitive capacities.

The following selections present arguments for both sides of
these issues. John Holt criticizes theorists and presents his own insights into the learning process. B. F. Skinner illustrates the basic
concepts of his learning theory by describing how he goes about
teaching animals. Jerome Bruner draws extensively on Piaget's
theory of intelligence to explain how the child's learning capacities
develop. Roger Brown describes research on learning by imitation
and compares this process with learning by reinforcement. Robert
Gagné argues that the answer to the question "How does learning
occur?" must recognize that there are different types of learning.

The Mind at Work

John Holt

> *In contrast to such learning theorists as Skinner and Gagné,*
> *John Holt takes the approach of the poet and novelist. For many*
> *years a schoolteacher, he is a keen observer of human nature, rely-*
> *ing on naturalistic observation and intuitive inference to derive his*
> *insights about how children learn. He argues that most adults, in-*
> *cluding teachers, do not know how to understand the mind of the*
> *child. In this selection Holt shares his insights about his own learn-*
> *ing process and that of children with whom he has worked. From*
> *these experiences comes the following recommendation for helping*
> *children learn: "What is essential is to realize that children learn*
> *independently, not in bunches; that they learn out of interest and*
> *curiosity, not to please or appease the adults in power; and that*
> *they ought to be in control of their own learning, deciding for*
> *themselves what to learn and how they want to learn it." Do you*
> *agree, or do you believe that the child's learning should be carefully*
> *guided by the teacher?*

Reprinted with permission of publisher from *How Children Learn*, New
York: Pitman Publishing Corporation, 1967, pp. 170–189.

One of the puzzles we had in my fifth-grade class was a geometrical puzzle called *Hako*. You began with a number of thin, flat, rectangular plastic pieces arranged a certain way in a shallow box. The aim was to slide them around, without turning them or lifting them out of the box, so as to finish with the largest piece, a square, at the opposite end of the box from which it started. Though I spent many hours on it, I was never able to do it. This exasperated me. What exasperated me even more was that I seemed to be able to prove that the puzzle was impossible — though I knew it was not. Like most people, I began by moving the pieces around in a kind of blind, haphazard way. Before long, and unwisely, I grew impatient with this. There were too many possible moves, this could go on forever. The thing to do was use the brain and figure it out. So, moving the pieces very carefully, and analyzing each move, I deduced that in order to get the large piece from the top to the bottom, certain other things had to happen along the way. There had to be a point at which certain of the pieces were going up past the big piece while it was going down. Then, still carefully analyzing, I showed that this could only happen if certain other pieces moved in certain ways. Finally, I proved that they could not be moved in those ways. Therefore the problem was impossible.

The trouble was, I knew it wasn't impossible. Companies don't sell impossible puzzles; they would be sued, or worse. Besides, the puzzle had been mentioned in the *Scientific American*. Besides that, and worst of all, some students had done it. With all my heart I wanted to believe that they had lied or cheated, but I couldn't convince myself; they weren't the type. I remember thinking furiously, "I suppose anyone could do this puzzle if he were willing to sit in front of it like a nitwit, moving the pieces around blindly, until just by dumb luck he happened to get it. I haven't got time for that sort of thing." More to the point, I felt above that sort of thing.

I went back to the puzzle many times, hoping that I would find some fresh approach to it; but my mind kept moving back into the little groove it had made for itself. I tried to make myself forget my supposed proof that the problem was impossible. No use. Before long I would be back at the business of trying to find the flaw in my reasoning. I never found it. Like many other people, in many other situations, I had reasoned myself into a box. Looking back at the problem, and with the words of Professor Hawkins in my ears, I saw my great mistake.* I had begun to reason too

---

* *David Hawkins is a professor of Philosophy at the University of Colorado. Elsewhere John Holt quotes Hawkins as follows,*

> "... (*in science teaching, and other aspects of elementary education*) *there is a time, much greater in amount than commonly allowed, which should be devoted to free and unguided exploratory work (call it play if you wish; I call it work). Children are given materials and equipment — things — and are allowed to construct,*

soon, before I had allowed myself enough "Messing About," before I had built a good enough mental model of the ways in which those pieces moved, before I had given myself enough time to explore all the possible ways in which they could move. The reason some of the children were able to do the puzzle was not that they did it blindly, but that they did not try to solve it by reason until they had found by experience what the pieces could do. Because their mental model of the puzzle was complete, it served them; because mine was incomplete, it failed me.†

In one of the classes I previously shared with Bill Hull, we worked a good deal with a three-dimensional puzzle named *Soma*, also described and discussed in the *Scientific American*. In this, twenty-seven cubes of wood were glued together to make six four-cube pieces and one three-cube piece. The aim was to use these seven pieces to make various other shapes, beginning with a cube and other simple shapes, and going on to more complicated and difficult shapes such as the Tunnel, the Bathtub, the Castle, etc. It was a splendid puzzle, one of the very best I have ever seen, among other reasons because children can work on it at many different degrees of difficulty.

My first meeting with this puzzle was embarrassing. A person familiar with it can make the cube in less than half-a-minute in any one of several different ways. By the time I started trying to make the cube, a number of the children were able to do it in about fifteen seconds. My first effort took me about fifty minutes. I tried to keep my struggles out of the sight of the children, but there were some pointed questions. Fortunately I was able to avoid falling into the trap of analyzing too soon, perhaps only because I could not see how to. Unable to think of any "sensible" way to proceed, I fiddled with the pieces, trying to fit them this way and that, making mistakes, working myself into dead ends, going back and starting again. One of the frustrating things about this particular puzzle is that if you have it almost right, you know you have it entirely wrong. When you find yourself saying, "If this piece just looked like that piece, I could do it," you have to start almost from the beginning. By many such trials and errors, retrials and corrections, I was finally able, like many of the children, to build up a good mental model of the way these pieces worked. With this model I could tell, without having to try it out, that a certain piece, or even combination of pieces, would not go in a certain spot, and could see several pieces in advance when I was going wrong. Before long I became one of the class experts.

Such experiences suggest a reason why so much that seems to me trivial,

test, probe, and experiment without superimposed questions or instruction. I call this phase 'Messing About.' . . ." (From "Messing About in Science," Science and Children, Feb. 1965).

† *Is this a good explanation? Can you think of another that's equally plausible?*

misleading, or downright false, has been written about child psychology. The psychologists, on the whole, have not done enough of Professor Hawkins' "Messing About." They have not seen enough children in their native habitat — homes, schools, playgrounds, streets, stores, anywhere. They haven't talked or played with enough of them, or helped them, or comforted them, or coerced them, or made them pleased, or excited, or rebellious, or angry. Unless he is very fortunate, a young psychologist is very likely to have his head stuffed full of theories of children before he has had a chance to look at any.* When he does start looking at them, it is likely to be in very special laboratory or testing situations. Like many teachers, he may not recognize the many ways in which children betray anxiety, because he has never seen them in a situation in which they were not anxious. Also, like me trying to do the puzzle, he may be so much a prisoner of his theories that he cannot see anything that does not fit into them.

...My aim ... is not primarily to persuade educators and psychologists to swap new doctrines for old, but to persuade them to *look* at children, patiently, repeatedly, respectfully, and to hold off making theories and judgments about them until they have in their minds what most of them do not now have — a reasonably accurate model of what children are like.

I should add, too, that I am not trying to deny the importance of close, deductive, analytical, logical reasoning. In its proper place, it is a useful, powerful, often essential tool. I am only trying to say that out of its place, it is likely to be not only useless but harmful, and that its place is not everywhere. It works when we have a very limited amount of evidence, all we are going to get, and from it have to reconstruct the past — find out who committed a crime, or how and why an accident took place, or what is ailing in a particular man, or machine. It works when we can limit and isolate, one by one, the variables we have to deal with. Thus the skilled repairman, trying to find out why a machine is working badly, checks its various elements, one by one, until he finds the one that is causing the trouble. Thus the scientist, meeting a new phenomenon in the lab, changes, one by one, the conditions of the experiment until he finds the one that seems to affect the phenomenon. And we use this kind of reasoning to check out hypotheses, our theories or hunches about why things work as they do. We say, "If this theory is true, then certain other things ought to happen," and then we find out whether in fact they do happen. If they do, the theory is confirmed, temporarily, at least. The story is told of Einstein that, after the observations of some astronomers seemed to have confirmed his Theory of Relativity, a woman congratulated him on his theory having been proved right. He said, "Madam, a thousand experiments can never prove me right; a single experiment can prove me wrong." Even when the facts seem to

* *Does this statement apply to the training of teachers, too?*

support our reasoning, we must, like Einstein, not assume that we have found the final truth.

But if there are times and places and conditions where this kind of reasoning is useful, there are others where it does not work at all. If the experience before us is completely new and strange; if there is much new material to be observed, material that doesn't seem to fall into any recognizable pattern or order; if we cannot tell what are the variables that influence the situation, much less isolate them, we will be unwise to try to think like a detective, or a scientist in a laboratory.

Some years ago, some sociologists were trying to draw analogies between the behavior of molecules in a gas and the behavior of human beings in society, and from there between the laws that describe or explain the behavior of gases and comparable laws that would supposedly describe and explain the behavior of human beings in society. This is a very good example of how not to use the scientific method. In such situations, we must use our minds very differently. We must clear them of preconceived notions, we must suspend judgment, we must open ourselves to the situation, take in as much data as we can, and wait patiently for some kind of order to appear out of the chaos. In short, we must think like a little child.

It may be useful to describe a few situations in which I had to, and was able to, make myself think this way. One bright summer day some friends took me to the Haystack School of Arts and Crafts in Maine. There, for the first time, I saw a hand loom. One of the teachers had it out in the sunshine, on one of the many broad, wooden terraces that look down a hill and over the sea. She was setting it up for some weaving, and my hosts gathered around to talk about what she was doing and was planning to do.

After looking at the machine a while, and listening to this informed talk, I felt the faint beginnings of anxiety. A hand loom is a very open machine; all the parts of it can be clearly seen. It seemed to me that after some careful looking and reasoning I ought to be able to figure out how this machine worked. But I couldn't. It looked like nothing but a jumble and confusion of little parts, wires, and scraps of wood. None of it made any sense at all. Nor could I think how to make sense of it. Where to begin?

In such situations we tend to have a defensive reaction, which I began to sense in myself. Confronted with what it cannot grasp, the mind tends to turn away, to shut it out. We say to ourselves, "Oh, well, who cares about looms and weaving, anyway?" We seek the relief of thinking about something that we can grasp and understand. Having learned to recognize this protective and cowardly strategy, I would not allow myself to use it. I thought, "Come on, now, quit acting like a scared kid." I examined the loom more carefully, and began to ask myself intelligent questions. What's this for? Where does this lead? But no use. It remained as much a mystery as ever. The anxiety grew, with a little shame added. Some of this was caused by not being able to make sense of the loom. Some was caused by my feeling that as a supposedly fairly intelligent man I ought to be able to make sense out of it. Like children in school, I was worried by the fear of not being able to live up to my own concept of myself. Finally, I knew that everyone else around me knew how that loom worked, and knew that I didn't. I could almost hear them thinking, "Funny about John, he's usually pretty smart about most things, yet that simple loom, that you would think anyone could understand, is too much for him." Then, to make matters worse, they began to try to help by giving explanations. They spoke with that infuriating mixture of indulgence and impatience with which the expert always explains things to the nonexpert. It is always gratifying to be able to understand what someone else cannot; and more gratifying yet to make yourself his benefactor, by explaining it to him; and still more gratifying — unless you are required to make him understand — if in spite of your explanation he continues not to understand. In this spirit my friends began to say, "It's really very simple; this piece here. . . ."

After a certain amount of this I said, rather sharply, "Please stop talking about it, and just let me look at it." I thought to myself, "Remember what you have learned about learning. Be like a child. Use your eyes. Gag that teacher's mouth inside your head, asking all those questions. Don't try to analyze this thing, look at it, take it in." And shutting out of mind the knowing conversation of the others, I did so. Now and then the voice inside would begin to ask questions. I silenced it, and for some time went on looking.

There were many other things to see: potters, print makers, and most exciting of all, glass blowers. After seeing them all, we started home. And as we drove a most extraordinary thing began to happen. I was not thinking about the loom; as my host was a potter, we were talking mostly about the pottery. But as we talked, a loom began slowly to put itself together in my mind.* There is no other way to describe it. Suddenly, for no reason, the image of a particular part would suddenly appear in my consciousness, but in such a way that I understood what that part was for. When I say "understood," I don't mean that some kind of verbal explanation went along with it. I mean that I could see what the part was for and what it did, I could almost see it doing its work. If I had been building a loom and had had that part in my hand, I would have known where to put it.

This loom-building process was very slow. It would be interesting to have a record of the order in which the parts of this loom appeared and assembled themselves, but I have none. Sensing that something important was happening in the non-verbal, non-conscious part of my mind, I did not want to look too hard at the process, lest I bring it to a stop. Also, I had no way of knowing, at any time, how much further it would go. When the first part of the loom appeared in my surprised consciousness, I had no

* *Have you ever had such an experience?*

reason to believe that other parts would later appear in the same way. However, they did, some during our trip home, others during the rest of the day, some even the following day. By the end of that day, a loom had made itself in my mind. There was a working model of a loom in there. If I had had to build a loom, I would have known at least roughly what parts were needed and where they went. There was much about the loom that I didn't know, but I now knew where knowledge left off and ignorance began; knew the questions I needed to ask; knew enough to be able to make sense of the answers. Some of what people had told me, trying to explain the loom, came back to me, and now I could see what their words meant.

Explanations. We teachers — perhaps all human beings — are in the grip of an astonishing delusion. We think that we can take a picture, a structure, a working model of something, constructed in our minds out of long experience and familiarity, and by turning that model into a string of words, transplant it whole into the mind of someone else. Perhaps once in a thousand times, when the explanation is extraordinarily good, and the listener extraordinarily experienced and skillful at turning word strings into non-verbal reality, and when explainer and listener share in common many of the experiences being talked about, the process may work, and some real meaning may be communicated. Most of the time, explaining does not increase understanding, and may even lessen it.* ...

Jerome Bruner has said that one thing that happens in school is that children are led to believe they don't know or can't do something that they knew, or could do, before they got to school.† I have seen this demonstrated many times, but never as vividly as in the following example, quoted from the prospectus of the Green Valley School, in which George von Hilsheimer writes:

> One of our art associates once conducted an experiment in her art resources classroom. As the children entered the classroom, they found construction paper on the desks. The teacher held up a folded fan — like those you and I have made many times — "Know what this is?"
>
> "Oh, yes!"
>
> "Can you make one?"
>
> "Yes! Yes!"
>
> Every child quickly made the little fan. The teacher then read from the book the instructions on how to make the fan. She read slowly, with proper emphasis and phrasing. The instructions were well designed to be clear to the fifth grade mind. After reading, the teacher asked the children to make the fans again. Not one child could make a fan. The teacher sat at each desk and tried to get the

---

* If teachers shouldn't explain, what should they do?
† Jerome Bruner's views on learning are stated in a selection in this section.

children to go back to the first way they had made the fan (with the fan still lying on the desk). They could not.

There have been many such experiments in educational psychology. Unfortunately, few teachers and even fewer school systems take such evidence seriously. We do.

Such stories make many defenders of the system angry. They say, "But human knowledge is stored and transmitted in symbols. We have to teach children to use them." True enough. But the only way children can learn to get meaning out of symbols, to turn other people's symbols into a kind of reality or a mental model of reality, is by learning first to turn their own reality into symbols. They have to make the journey from reality to symbol many times, before they are ready to go the other way. We must begin with what children see, do, and know, and have them talk and write about such things, before trying to talk to them much about things they don't know. Thus, given children who knew how to make a paper fan, it might not be a bad idea at all to ask them to try to tell someone else how to make one, without using any gestures, as if they were talking over a phone. I used to ask fifth-graders how they would explain over the phone the difference between right and left, to someone who could speak English but did not happen to know those words. Such games are exciting and useful. But when we do what we do most of the time in school — begin with meaningless symbols and statements, and try to fill them with meaning by way of explanations, we only convince most children either that all symbols are meaningless or that they are too stupid to get meaning from them....

Let me sum up what I have been trying to say about the natural learning style of young children. The child is curious. He wants to make sense out of things, find out how things work, gain competence and control over himself and his environment, do what he can see other people doing. He is open, receptive, and perceptive. He does not shut himself off from the strange, confused, complicated world around him. He observes it closely and sharply, tries to take it all in. He is experimental. He does not merely observe the world around him, but tastes it, touches it, hefts it, bends it, breaks it. To find out how reality works, he works on it. He is bold. He is not afraid of making mistakes. And he is patient. He can tolerate an extraordinary amount of uncertainty, confusion, ignorance, and suspense. He does not have to have instant meaning in any new situation. He is willing and able to wait for meaning to come to him — even if it comes very slowly, which it usually does.

School is not a place that gives much time, or opportunity, or reward, for this kind of thinking and learning. Can we make it so? I think we can, and must. In this book I have tried to suggest, very briefly, how we might do it. To discuss this in any detail would take a book in itself. What is essential is to realize that children learn independently, not in bunches; that they learn out of interest and curiosity, not to please or appease the adults in power; and that they ought to be in control of their own learning, deciding for themselves what they want to learn and how they want to learn it.* To such ideas, people react in many ways, but two reactions appear so regularly that they seem worth discussing.

The first is often expressed like this. "Aren't you asking children to discover and re-create, all by themselves, the whole history of the human race?" It would be easy to dismiss the question as silly, except that so many sensible and serious people ask it. What trips them up is this word "discover." They act as if it meant "invent," that is, discover for the first time. But this is not what I mean, or any educators mean, when they talk about the importance of letting children discover things for themselves. We do not ask or expect a child to invent the wheel starting from scratch. He doesn't have to. The wheel has been invented. It is out there, in front of him. All I am saying is that a chid does not need to be *told* what wheels are and what they are for, in order to know. He can figure it out for himself, in his own way, in his own good time. In the same way, he does not have to invent the electric light bulb, the airplane, the internal combustion engine — or law, government, art, or music. They, too, have been invented, and are out there. The whole culture is out there. What I urge is that a child be free to explore and make sense of that culture in his own way.† This is as much discovery as I ask of him, a discovery that he is well able to make.

The second reaction is often expressed like this. "Aren't there certain things that everyone ought to know, and isn't it our job, therefore, to make sure that children know them?" This argument can be attacked on many fronts. With the possible exception of knowing how to read, which in any case is a skill, it cannot be proved that any piece of knowledge is essential for everyone. Useful and convenient, perhaps; essential, no. Moreover, the people who feel that certain knowledge is essential do not agree among themselves on what that knowledge is. The historians would vote for history; the linguists, for language; the mathematicians, for math; and so on. In the words of Jimmy Durante, "Everybody wants to get into the act." Moreover, the knowledge changes, becomes useless, out of date, or downright false. Believers in essential knowledge decreed that when I was in school I should study physics and chemistry. In physics we used a reputable and then up-to-date college text that announced on page 1 that "matter was not created nor destroyed." Of my chemistry, I remember only two or three formulas and a concept called "valence." I mentioned valence to a chemist the other day and he laughed. When I asked what was so funny,

---

* *Carl Rogers expresses a similar view in Section 2.*
† *Key point. Compare with B. F. Skinner's view of learning.*

he said, "Nobody ever talks about valence any more; it's an outmoded concept." But the rate of discovery being what it is, the likelihood that what children learn today will be out of date in twenty years is much *greater* than it was when I was a student.

My real reason, however, for believing that the learner, young or old, is the best judge of what he should learn next, is very different. I would be against trying to cram knowledge into the heads of children, even if we could agree on what knowledge to cram, and could be sure that it would not go out of date, even if we could be sure that, once crammed in, it would stay in. Even then, I would trust the child to direct his own learning. For it seems to me a fact that, in our struggle to make sense out of life, the things we most need to learn are the things we most want to learn.* To put this another way, curiosity is hardly ever idle. What we want to know, we want to know for a reason. The reason is that there is a hole, a gap, an empty space in our understanding of things, our mental model of the world. We feel that gap like a hole in a tooth and want to fill it up. It makes us ask How? When? Why? While the gap is there, we are in tension, in suspense. Listen to the anxiety in a person's voice when he says, "This doesn't make sense!" When the gap in our understanding is filled, we feel pleasure, satisfaction, relief. Things make sense again — or at any rate, they make more sense than they did.

When we learn this way, for these reasons, we learn both rapidly and permanently. The person who really needs to know something, does not need to be told many times, drilled, tested. Once is enough. The new piece of knowledge fits into the gap ready for it, like a missing piece in a jigsaw puzzle. Once in place, it is held in, it can't fall out. We don't forget the things that make the world a more reasonable or interesting place for us, that make our mental model more complete and accurate. Now, if it were possible for us to look into the minds of children and see what gaps in their mental models most needed filling, a good case could be made for giving them the information needed to fill them. But this is not possible. We cannot find out what children's mental models are like, where they are distorted, where incomplete. We cannot make direct contact with a child's understanding of the world. Why not? First, because to a very considerable extent he is unaware of much of his own understanding. Secondly, because he hasn't the skill to put his understanding into words, least of all words that he could be sure would mean to us what they meant to him. Thirdly, because we haven't time. Words are not only a clumsy and ambiguous means of communication, they are extraordinarily slow. To describe only a very small part of his understanding of the world, a man will write a book that takes us days to read.

* *Motivation for learning is important to Holt. How is motivation treated in the selections that follow?*

I think of some good friends of mine. We know each other well, know each other's interests, speak each other's language. We may spend an entire evening talking, each of us intent on gaining a better understanding of the other's thought. At the end of the evening, with luck, we may each have a very slightly better idea about what the other thinks, on a very particular subject. On the other hand, very often an evening of talk, however pleasant and interesting, may only lead us to realize how little we understand the other, how great are the gulfs and mysteries between us.

The human mind is a mystery. To a very large extent, it will probably always be so.* We will never get very far in education until we realize this, and give up the delusion that we can know, measure, and control what goes on in children's minds. To know one's own mind is difficult enough. I am, to quite a high degree, an introspective person. For a long time, I have been interested in my own thoughts, feelings, and motives, eager to know as much as I could of the truth about myself. After many years, I think that at most I may know something about a very small part of what goes on in my own head. How preposterous to imagine that I can know what goes on in someone else's.

In my mind's ear I can hear the anxious voices of a hundred teachers asking me, "How can you tell, how can you be sure what the children are learning, or even that they are learning anything?" The answer is simple. We can't tell. We can't be sure. What I am trying to say about education rests on a belief that, though there is much evidence to support it, I cannot prove, and that may never be proved. Call it a faith. This faith is that man is by nature a learning animal. Birds fly, fish swim; man thinks and learns. Therefore, we do not need to "motivate" children into learning, by wheedling, bribing, or bullying. We do not need to keep picking away at their minds to make sure they are learning. What we need to do, and all we need to do, is bring as much of the world as we can into the school and the classroom; give children as much help and guidance as they need and ask for; listen respectfully when they feel like talking; and then get out of the way. We can trust them to do the rest.

EXERCISE

1. What is the "messing about" process? (p. 7)
2. What recommendation does Holt make to psychologists so that they do not become "prisoners" of their own theories? (p. 8)
3. What does Holt mean by the statement, "the only way children can learn to get meaning out of symbols . . . is by learning first to turn their own reality into symbols"? (p. 12)

* *If the mind is a mystery, why read Holt's views on it?*

4. What does Holt mean when he says that children should be allowed to "discover" things for themselves? (p. 13)

5. What is the child's natural learning style, according to Holt? (p. 12)

6. Why is Holt opposed to education as the imparting of "essential" knowledge? (p. 13)

The Science of Learning and the Art of Teaching

B. F. Skinner

Although written twenty years ago, this article on learning by B. F. Skinner is still remarkably timely. It is a theoretical and research base for such major developments in education as programmed and computer-assisted instruction (see Lindvall and Bolvin, Hall, and Taylor, Section 10) and classroom management using token economies (see Bushell, Section 10). Even the recent emphasis on behavioral objectives to guide instruction (see Section 14) was foreshadowed in this article. According to Skinner, learning is essentially a shaping process. A new behavior pattern is acquired as a series of successive approximations, each of which is rewarded (the technical term is "reinforced") if correct, and extinguished if incorrect. Skinner's learning theory is controversial partly because it was derived primarily from experiments with animals, and also because Skinner has used it here and in several popular books (Walden Two, Beyond Freedom and Dignity) to strongly criticize American schooling and American society. Does the human learning process parallel the learning process which Skinner ascribes to pigeons and other animals? If so, how much? Also, consider how John Holt, Jerome Bruner, and learning-by-imitation theorists would respond to Skinner's theory, which ignores cognitive processes.

Some promising advances have recently been made in the field of learning. Special techniques have been designed to arrange what are called "contingencies of reinforcement" — the relations which prevail between behavior on the one hand and the consequences of that behavior on the

Reprinted with permission of publisher from *Harvard Educational Review*, 24, Spring 1954, 86–97. Copyright © 1954 by the President and Fellows of Harvard College.

other — with the result that a much more effective control of behavior has been achieved. . . .

Recent improvements in the conditions which control behavior in the field of learning are of two principal sorts. The Law of Effect* has been taken seriously; we have made sure that effects *do* occur and that they occur under conditions which are optimal for producing the changes called learning. Once we have arranged the particular type of consequence called a reinforcement,† our techniques permit us to shape up the behavior of an organism almost at will. It has become a routine exercise to demonstrate this in classes in elementary psychology by conditioning such an organism as a pigeon. Simply by presenting food to a hungry pigeon at the right time, it is possible to shape up three or four well-defined responses in a single demonstration period — such responses as turning around, pacing the floor in the pattern of a figure-8, standing still in a corner of the demonstration apparatus, stretching the neck, or stamping the foot. Extremely complex performances may be reached through successive stages in the shaping process, the contingencies of reinforcement being changed progressively in the direction of the required behavior. The results are often quite dramatic. In such a demonstration one can *see* learning take place. A significant change in behavior is often obvious as the result of a single reinforcement.

A second important advance in technique permits us to maintain behavior in given states of strength for long periods of time. Reinforcements continue to be important, of course, long after an organism has learned *how* to do something, long after it has acquired behavior. They are necessary to maintain the behavior in strength. Of special interest is the effect of various schedules of intermittent reinforcement.‡ . . . On the theoretical side we now have a fairly good idea of why a given schedule produces its appropriate performance. On the practical side we have learned how to maintain any given level of activity for daily periods limited only by the physical exhaustion of the organism and from day to day without substantial change throughout its life. . . .

These new methods of shaping behavior and of maintaining it in strength are a great improvement over the traditional practices of professional animal trainers, and it is not surprising that our laboratory results are already being applied to the production of performing animals for commercial purposes. In a more academic environment they have been used for demonstration purposes which extend far beyond an interest in learning as such. For example, it is not too difficult to arrange the complex contingencies which produce many types of social behavior. Competition is exemplified by two pigeons playing a modified game of ping-pong. The pigeons drive

* *The Law of Effect is explained in the glossary.*
† *In nontechnical terms, a reinforcement is equivalent to a reward.*
‡ *Schedules of intermittent reinforcement are explained in the glossary.*

the ball back and forth across a small table by pecking at it. When the ball gets by one pigeon, the other is reinforced. The task of constructing such a "social relation" is probably completely out of reach of the traditional animal trainer. It requires a carefully designed program of gradually changing contingencies and the skillful use of schedules to maintain the behavior in strength. Each pigeon is separately prepared for its part in the total performance, and the "social relation" is then arbitrarily constructed. The sequence of events leading up to this stable state is excellent material for the study of the factors important in nonsynthetic social behavior. It is instructive to consider how a similar series of contingencies could arise in the case of the human organism through the evolution of cultural patterns.

Cooperation can also be set up, perhaps more easily than competition. We have trained two pigeons to coordinate their behavior in a cooperative endeavor with a precision which equals that of the most skillful human dancers.* In a more serious vein these techniques have permitted us to explore the complexities of the individual organism and to analyze some of the serial or coordinate behaviors involved in attention, problem solving, various types of self-control, and the subsidiary systems of responses within a single organism called "personalities." . . .

In all this work, the species of the organism has made surprisingly little difference. It is true that the organisms studied have all been vertebrates, but they still cover a wide range. Comparable results have been obtained with pigeons, rats, dogs, monkeys, human children, and most recently, by the author in collaboration with Ogden R. Lindsley, human psychotic subjects. In spite of great phylogenetic differences, all these organisms show amazingly similar properties of the learning process.† It should be emphasized that this has been achieved by analyzing the effects of reinforcement and by designing techniques which manipulate reinforcement with considerable precision. Only in this way can the behavior of the individual organism be brought under such precise control. It is also important to note that through a gradual advance to complex interrelations among responses, the same degree of rigor is being extended to behavior which would usually be assigned to such fields as perception, thinking, and personality dynamics.

From this exciting prospect of an advancing science of learning, it is a great shock to turn to that branch of technology which is most directly concerned with the learning process — education. Let us consider, for example, the teaching of arithmetic in the lower grades. The school is concerned with imparting to the child a large number of responses of a special sort. The responses are all verbal. They consist of speaking and writing certain words, figures, and signs which, to put it roughly, refer to

* *Does this mean cooperation is learned rather than inborn?*
† *Key point. Do you agree with Skinner's generalization?*

numbers and to arithmetic operations. The first task is to shape up these responses — to get the child to pronounce and to write responses correctly, but the principal task is to bring this behavior under many sorts of stimulus control. This is what happens when the child learns to count, to recite tables, to count while ticking off the items in an assemblage of objects, to respond to spoken or written numbers by saying "odd," "even," "prime," and so on. Over and above this elaborate repertoire of numerical behavior, most of which is often dismissed as the product of rote learning, the teaching of arithmetic looks forward to those complex serial arrangements of responses involved in original mathematical thinking. The child must acquire responses of transposing, clearing fractions, and so on, which modify the order or pattern of the original material so that the response called a solution is eventually made possible.

Now, how is this extremely complicated verbal repertoire set up? In the first place, what reinforcements are used? Fifty years ago the answer would have been clear. At that time educational control was still frankly aversive. The child read numbers, copied numbers, memorized tables, and performed operations upon numbers to escape the threat of the birch rod or cane. Some positive reinforcements were perhaps eventually derived from the increased efficiency of the child in the field of arithmetic and in rare cases some automatic reinforcement may have resulted from the sheer manipulation of the medium — from the solution of problems or the discovery of the intricacies of the number system. But for the immediate purposes of education the child acted to avoid or escape punishment. It was part of the reform movement known as progressive education to make the positive consequences more immediately effective, but any one who visits the lower grades of the average school today will observe that a change has been made, not from aversive to positive control, but from one form of aversive stimulation to another. The child at his desk, filling in his workbook, is behaving primarily to escape from the threat of a series of minor aversive events — the teacher's displeasure, the criticism or ridicule of his classmates, an ignominious showing in a competition, low marks, a trip to the office "to be talked to" by the principal, or a word to the parent who may still resort to the birch rod.* In this welter of aversive consequences, getting the right answer is in itself an insignificant event, any effect of which is lost amid the anxieties, the boredom, and the aggressions which are the inevitable by-products of aversive control.[1]

Secondly, we have to ask how the contingencies of reinforcement are arranged. When is a numerical operation reinforced as "right"? Eventually, of course, the pupil may be able to check his own answers and achieve some sort of automatic reinforcement, but in the early stages the reinforcement of being right is usually accorded by the teacher. The contingencies

Do you think Skinner is setting up a straw man here?

she provides are far from optimal. It can easily be demonstrated that, unless explicit mediating behavior has been set up, the lapse of only a few seconds between response and reinforcement destroys most of the effect. In a typical classroom, nevertheless, long periods of time customarily elapse. The teacher may walk up and down the aisle, for example, while the class is working on a sheet of problems, pausing here and there to say right or wrong. Many seconds or minutes intervene between the child's response and the teacher's reinforcement. In many cases — for example, when papers are taken home to be corrected — as much as 24 hours may intervene. It is surprising that this system has any effect whatsoever.

A third notable shortcoming is the lack of a skillful program which moves forward through a series of progressive approximations to the final complex behavior desired. A long series of contingencies is necessary to bring the organism into the possession of mathematical behavior most efficiently.* But the teacher is seldom able to reinforce at each step in such a series because she cannot deal with the pupil's responses one at a time. It is usually necessary to reinforce the behavior in blocks of responses — as in correcting a work sheet or page from a workbook. The responses within such a block must not be interrelated. The answer to one problem must not depend upon the answer to another. The number of stages through which one may progressively approach a complex pattern of behavior is therefore small, and the task so much the more difficult. Even the most modern workbook in beginning arithmetic is far from exemplifying an efficient program for shaping up mathematical behavior.

Perhaps the most serious criticism of the current classroom is the relative infrequency of reinforcement. Since the pupil is usually dependent upon the teacher for being right, and since many pupils are usually dependent upon the same teacher, the total number of contingencies which may be arranged during, say, the first four years, is of the order of only a few thousand. But a very rough estimate suggests that efficient mathematical behavior at this level requires something of the order of 25,000 contingencies. We may suppose that even in the brighter student a given contingency must be arranged several times to place the behavior well in hand. The responses to be set up are not simply the various items in tables of addition, subtraction, multiplication, and division; we have also to consider the alternative forms in which each item may be stated. To the learning of such material we should add hundreds of responses concerned with factoring, identifying primes, memorizing series, using short-cut techniques of calculation, constructing and using geometric representations or number forms, and so on. Over and above all this, the whole mathematical repertoire must be brought under the control of concrete problems of considerable variety. Perhaps 50,000 contingencies is a more conservative

* The concept of contingency is explained in the glossary.

estimate. In this frame of reference the daily assignment in arithmetic seems pitifully meagre.

The result of all this is, of course, well known. Even our best schools are under criticism for their inefficiency in the teaching of drill subjects such as arithmetic. The condition in the average school is a matter of wide-spread national concern. Modern children simply do not learn arithmetic quickly or well. Nor is the result simply incompetence. The very subjects in which modern techniques are weakest are those in which failure is most conspicuous, and in the wake of an ever-growing incompetence come the anxieties, uncertainties, and aggressions which in their turn present other problems to the school. Most pupils soon claim the asylum of not being "ready" for arithmetic at a given level or, eventually, of not having a mathematical mind. Such explanations are readily seized upon by defensive teachers and parents. Few pupils ever reach the stage at which automatic reinforcements follow as the natural consequences of mathematical behavior. On the contrary, the figures and symbols of mathematics have become standard emotional stimuli. The glimpse of a column of figures, not to say an algebraic symbol or an integral sign, is likely to set off — not mathematical behavior — but a reaction of anxiety, guilt, or fear.

The teacher is usually no happier about this than the pupil. Denied the opportunity to control via the birch rod, quite at sea as to the mode of operation of the few techniques at her disposal, she spends as little time as possible on drill subjects and eagerly subscribes to philosophies of education which emphasize material of greater inherent interest. A confession of weakness is her extraordinary concern lest the child be taught something unnecessary. The repertoire to be imparted is carefully reduced to an essential minimum. In the field of spelling, for example, a great deal of time and energy has gone into discovering just those words which the young child is going to use, as if it were a crime to waste one's educational power in teaching an unnecessary word. Eventually, weakness of technique emerges in the disguise of a reformulation of the aims of education. Skills are minimized in favor of vague achievements — educating for democracy, educating the whole child, educating for life, and so on.* And there the matter ends; for, unfortunately, these philosophies do not in turn suggest improvements in techniques. They offer little or no help in the design of better classroom practices.

There would be no point in urging these objections if improvement were impossible. But the advances which have recently been made in our control of the learning process suggest a thorough revision of classroom practices and, fortunately, they tell us how the revision can be brought about. . . .

---

* These goals are also decried by advocates of behavioral objectives (in Section 14).

In the first place, what reinforcements are available? What does the school have in its possession which will reinforce a child? We may look first to the material to be learned, for it is possible that this will provide considerable automatic reinforcement. Children play for hours with mechanical toys, paints, scissors and paper, noise-makers, puzzles — in short, with almost anything which feeds back significant changes in the environment and is reasonably free of aversive properties. The sheer control of nature is itself reinforcing. This effect is not evident in the modern school because it is masked by the emotional responses generated by aversive control. It is true that automatic reinforcement from the manipulation of the environment is probably only a mild reinforcer and may need to be carefully husbanded, but one of the most striking principles to emerge from recent research is that the *net* amount of reinforcement is of little significance. A very slight reinforcement may be tremendously effective in controlling behavior if it is wisely used.

If the natural reinforcement inherent in the subject matter is not enough, other reinforcers must be employed. Even in school the child is occasionally permitted to do "what he wants to do," and access to reinforcements of many sorts may be made contingent upon the more immediate consequences of the behavior to be established. Those who advocate competition as a useful social motive may wish to use the reinforcements which follow from excelling others, although there is the difficulty that in this case the reinforcement of one child is necessarily aversive to another. Next in order we might place the good will and affection of the teacher, and only when that has failed need we turn to the use of aversive stimulation.

In the second place, how are these reinforcements to be made contingent upon the desired behavior? There are two considerations here — the gradual elaboration of extremely complex patterns of behavior and the maintenance of the behavior in strength at each stage. The whole process of becoming competent in any field must be divided into a very large number of very small steps, and reinforcement must be contingent upon the accomplishment of each step.* This solution to the problem of creating a complex repertoire of behavior also solves the problem of maintaining the behavior in strength. We could, of course, resort to the techniques of scheduling already developed in the study of other organisms but in the present state of our knowledge of educational practices, scheduling appears to be most effectively arranged through the design of the material to be learned. By making each successive step as small as possible, the frequency of reinforcement can be raised to a maximum, while the

---

* *Doesn't learning occur all at once, rather than bit by bit? Compare with modelling theories of learning (Brown, this section).*

possibly aversive consequences of being wrong are reduced to a minimum. Other ways of designing material would yield other programs of reinforcement. Any supplementary reinforcement would probably have to be scheduled in the more traditional way.

These requirements are not excessive, but they are probably incompatible with the current realities of the classroom. In the experimental study of learning it has been found that the contingencies of reinforcement which are most efficient in controlling the organism cannot be arranged through the personal mediation of the experimenter. An organism is affected by subtle details of contingenices which are beyond the capacity of the human organism to arrange. Mechanical and electrical devices must be used.... The simple fact is that, as a mere reinforcing mechanism, the teacher is out of date. This would be true even if a single teacher devoted all her time to a single child, but her inadequacy is multiplied many-fold when she must serve as a reinforcing device to many children at once. If the teacher is to take advantage of recent advances in the study of learning, she must have the help of mechanical devices.

The technical problem of providing the necessary instrumental aid is not particularly difficult. There are many ways in which the necessary contingencies may be arranged, either mechanically or electrically. An inexpensive device which solves most of the principal problems has already been constructed.* It is still in the experimental stage, but a description will suggest the kind of instrument which seems to be required. The device consists of a small box about the size of a small record player. On the top surface is a window through which a question or problem printed on a paper tape may be seen. The child answers the question by moving one or more sliders upon which the digits 0 through 9 are printed. The answer appears in square holes punched in the paper upon which the question is printed. When the answer has been set, the child turns a knob. The operation is as simple as adjusting a television set. If the answer is right, the knob turns freely and can be made to ring a bell or provide some other conditioned reinforcement. If the answer is wrong, the knob will not turn. A counter may be added to tally wrong answers. The knob must then be reversed slightly and a second attempt at a right answer made. (Unlike the flash-card, the device reports a wrong answer without giving the right answer.) When the answer is right, a further turn of the knob engages a clutch which moves the next problem into place in the window. This movement cannot be completed, however, until the sliders have been returned to zero.

* This device has since become known as the teaching machine (see Taylor, Section 10), and it uses the principles of programmed instruction (see Lindvall and Bolvin, Section 10).

The important features of the device are these: Reinforcement for the right answer is immediate. The mere manipulation of the device will probably be reinforcing enough to keep the average pupil at work for a suitable period each day, provided traces of earlier aversive control can be wiped out. A teacher may supervise an entire class at work on such devices at the same time, yet each child may progress at his own rate, completing as many problems as possible within the class period. If forced to be away from school, he may return to pick up where he left off. The gifted child will advance rapidly, but can be kept from getting too far ahead either by being excused from arithmetic for a time or by being given special sets of problems which take him into some of the interesting bypaths of mathematics.

The device makes it possible to present carefully designed material in which one problem can depend upon the answer to the preceding and where, therefore, the most efficient progress to an eventually complex repertoire can be made. Provision has been made for recording the commonest mistakes so that the tapes can be modified as experience dictates. Additional steps can be inserted where pupils tend to have trouble, and ultimately the material will reach a point at which the answers of the average child will almost always be right. . . .

Some objections to the use of such devices in the classroom can easily be foreseen.* The cry will be raised that the child is being treated as a mere animal and that an essentially human intellectual achievement is being analyzed in unduly mechanistic terms. Mathematical behavior is usually regarded, not as a repertoire of responses involving numbers and numerical operations, but as evidences of mathematical ability or the exercise of the power of reason. It is true that the techniques which are emerging from the experimental study of learning are not designed to "develop the mind" or to further some vague "understanding" of mathematical relationships. They are designed, on the contrary, to establish the very behaviors which are taken to be the evidences of such mental states or processes. This is only a special case of the general change which is under way in the interpretation of human affairs. An advancing science continues to offer more and more convincing alternatives to traditional formulations. The behavior in terms of which human thinking must eventually be defined is worth treating in its own right as the substantial goal of education.

Of course the teacher has a more important function than to say right or wrong. The changes proposed would free her for the effective exercise of that function. Marking a set of papers in arithmetic — "Yes, nine and six *are* fifteen; no, nine and seven *are not* eighteen" — is beneath the

* *Do you agree with Skinner, or with the objections?*

dignity of any intelligent individual. There is more important work to be done — in which the teacher's relations to the pupil cannot be duplicated by a mechanical device. Instrumental help would merely improve these relations. One might say that the main trouble with education in the lower grades today is that the child is obviously not competent and *knows it* and that the teacher is unable to do anything about it and *knows that too.* If the advances which have recently been made in our control of behavior can give the child a genuine competence in reading, writing, spelling, and arithmetic, then the teacher may begin to function, not in lieu of a cheap machine, but through intellectual, cultural, and emotional contacts of that distinctive sort which testify to her status as a human being. . . .

There is a simple job to be done. The task can be stated in concrete terms. The necessary techniques are known. The equipment needed can easily be provided. Nothing stands in the way but cultural inertia. But what is more characteristic of America than an unwillingness to accept the traditional as inevitable? We are on the threshold of an exciting and revolutionary period in which the scientific study of man will be put to work in man's best interests. Education must play its part. It must accept the fact that a sweeping revision of educational practices is possible and inevitable. When it has done this, we may look forward with confidence to a school system which is aware of the nature of its tasks, secure in its methods, and generously supported by the informed and effective citizens whom education itself will create.

EXERCISE

1. What does Skinner consider to be two major advances in the field of learning? (pp. 16–17)

2. What does Skinner mean by "aversive control" in the classroom? (p. 19)

3. According to Skinner, what are four deficiencies in the way reinforcements are used in most classrooms? (pp. 19–20)

4. According to Skinner, what are four types of reinforcement that can be used to facilitate the learning process? (p. 22)

5. Why does Skinner advocate use of mechanical and electrical devices in classroom instruction? (p. 23)

6. How does Skinner answer the criticism that mechanical learning devices are dehumanizing? (pp. 24–25)

Readiness for Learning

Jerome S. Bruner

> *This selection is taken from one of the most influential books of the 1960's,* The Process of Education, *by Jerome Bruner, who has taught at Harvard and Oxford. One of Bruner's main arguments, supported by Piaget's research studies, is that the learning process varies depending on the age of the child. A young child learns primarily by taking action; he might learn, for example, that hitting a stack of building blocks causes them to fall down. An older child can learn by thinking about what he has observed. Instead of actually carrying out trial-and-error behavior, he can internalize this operation and do it mentally. In contrast to Skinner, who emphasizes behavior, Bruner studies how the child perceives the world about him, how he organizes these perceptions, and how he acts upon them to generate new learning. Because of his interest in perception and cognitive capacities, Bruner is said to have a "cognitive" theory of learning. This selection is also an illustration of another difference between stimulus-response theorists like Skinner and cognitive theorists. Skinner views learning primarily as the acquisition of behavior patterns. In contrast, Bruner sees learning as the achievement of understanding. A child may learn how to perform simple arithmetic computations by rote, but this does not mean that he understands what he is doing. Bruner claims that teaching for understanding requires different methods than teaching facts.*

We begin with the hypothesis that any subject can be taught effectively in some intellectually honest form to any child at any stage of development. It is a bold hypothesis and an essential one in thinking about the nature of a curriculum. No evidence exists to contradict it; considerable evidence is being amassed that supports it.

To make clear what is implied, let us examine three general ideas. The first has to do with the process of intellectual development in children, the second with the act of learning, and the third with the notion of the "spiral curriculum." . . .

Excerpted by permission of the publishers from pp. 33–40 and 48–54 of *The Process of Education* by Jerome S. Bruner, Cambridge, Mass.: Harvard University Press, Copyright, 1960, by the President and Fellows of Harvard College.

INTELLECTUAL DEVELOPMENT

Research on the intellectual development of the child highlights the fact that at each stage of development the child has a characteristic way of viewing the world and explaining it to himself. The task of teaching a subject to a child at any particular age is one of representing the structure of that subject in terms of the child's way of viewing things. The task can be thought of as one of translation. The general hypothesis that has just been stated is premised on the considered judgment that any idea can be represented honestly and usefully in the thought forms of children of school age, and that these first representations can later be made more powerful and precise the more easily by virtue of this early learning. To illustrate and support this view, we present here a somewhat detailed picture of the course of intellectual development, along with some suggestions about teaching at different stages of it.

The work of Piaget* and others suggests that, roughly speaking, one may distinguish three stages in the intellectual development of the child. The first stage need not concern us in detail, for it is characteristic principally of the pre-school child. In this stage, which ends (at least for Swiss school children) around the fifth or sixth year, the child's mental work consists principally in establishing relationships between experience and action; his concern is with manipulating the world through action. This stage corresponds roughly to the period from the first development of language to the point at which the child learns to manipulate symbols. In this so-called preoperational stage, the principal symbolic achievement is that the child learns how to represent the external world through symbols established by simple generalization; things are represented as equivalent in terms of sharing some common property. But the child's symbolic world does not make a clear separation between internal motives and feelings on the one hand and external reality on the other. The sun moves because God pushes it, and the stars, like himself, have to go to bed. . . .

What is principally lacking at this stage of development is what the Geneva school has called the concept of reversibility.† When the shape of an object is changed, as when one changes the shape of a ball of plasticene, the preoperational child cannot grasp the idea that it can be brought back readily to its original state. Because of this fundamental lack the child cannot understand certain fundamental ideas that lie at the basis of mathematics and physics — the mathematical idea that one conserves

* *Jean Piaget is a famous Swiss psychologist and philosopher who has made many studies of the intellectual functioning of children.*
† *Piaget has conducted most of his research as director of the Jean Jacques Rousseau Institute in Geneva, Switzerland.*

quantity even when one partitions a set of things into subgroups, or the physical idea that one conserves mass and weight even though one transforms the shape of an object. It goes without saying that teachers are severely limited in transmitting concepts to a child at this stage, even in a highly intuitive manner.

The second stage of development — and now the child is in school — is called the stage of concrete operations. This stage is operational in contrast to the preceding stage, which is merely active. An operation is a type of action: it can be carried out rather directly by the manipulation of objects, or internally, as when one manipulates the symbols that represent things and relations in one's mind. Roughly, an operation is a means of getting data about the real world into the mind and there transforming them so that they can be organized and used selectively in the solution of problems. Assume a child is presented with a pinball machine which bounces a ball off a wall at an angle. Let us find out what he appreciates about the relation between the angle of incidence and the angle of reflection. The young child sees no problem: for him, the ball travels in an arc, touching the wall on the way. The somewhat older child, say age ten, sees the two angles as roughly related — as one changes so does the other. The still older child begins to grasp that there is a fixed relation between the two, and usually says it is a right angle. Finally, the thirteen- or fourteen-year-old, often by pointing the ejector directly at the wall and seeing the ball come back at the ejector, gets the idea that the two angles are equal. Each way of looking at the phenomenon represents the result of an operation in this sense, and the child's thinking is constrained by his way of pulling his observations together.

An operation differs from simple action or goal-directed behavior in that it is internalized and reversible. "Internalized" means that the child does not have to go about his problem-solving any longer by overt trial and error, but can actually carry out trial and error in his head. Reversibility is present because operations are seen as characterized where appropriate by what is called "complete compensation"; that is to say, an operation can be compensated for by an inverse operation. If marbles, for example, are divided into subgroups, the child can grasp intuitively that the original collection of marbles can be restored by being added back together again. The child tips a balance scale too far with a weight and then searches systematically for a lighter weight or for something with which to get the scale rebalanced. He may carry reversibility too far by assuming that a piece of paper, once burned, can also be restored.

With the advent of concrete operations, the child develops an internalized structure with which to operate. In the example of the balance scale, the structure is a serial order of weights that the child has in his mind. Such internal structures are of the essence. They are the internalized symbolic systems by which the child represents the world, as in the example of the pinball machine and the angles of incidence and reflection. It is into the language of these internal structures that one must translate ideas if the child is to grasp them.

But concrete operations, though they are guided by the logic of classes and the logic of relations, are means for structuring only immediately present reality. The child is able to give structure to the things he encounters, but he is not yet readily able to deal with possibilities not directly before him or not already experienced. This is not to say that children operating concretely are not able to anticipate things that are not present. Rather, it is that they do not command the operations for conjuring up systematically the full range of alternative possibilities that could exist at any given time. They cannot go systematically beyond the information given them to a description of what else might occur.* Somewhere between ten and fourteen years of age the child passes into a third stage, which is called the stage of "formal operations" by the Geneva school.

Now the child's intellectual activity seems to be based upon an ability to operate on hypothetical propositions rather than being constrained to what he has experienced or what is before him. The child can now think of possible variables and even deduce potential relationships that can later be verified by experiment or observation. Intellectual operations now appear to be predicated upon the same kinds of logical operations that are the stock in trade of the logician, the scientist, or the abstract thinker. It is at this point that the child is able to give formal or axiomatic expression to the concrete ideas that before guided his problem-solving but could not be described or formally understood. . . .

What is most important for teaching basic concepts is that the child be helped to pass progressively from concrete thinking to the utilization of more conceptually adequate modes of thought. But it is futile to attempt this by presenting formal explanations based on a logic that is distant from the child's manner of thinking and sterile in its implications for him. Much teaching in mathematics is of this sort. The child learns not to understand mathematical order but rather to apply certain devices or recipes without understanding their significance and connectedness. They are not translated into his way of thinking. Given this inappropriate start, he is easily led to believe that the important thing is for him to be "accurate" — though accuracy has less to do with mathematics than with computation. Perhaps the most striking example of this type of thing is to be found in the manner in which the high school student meets Euclidian geometry for the first time, as a set of axioms and theorems, without having had some experience with simple geometric configurations and the intuitive means whereby one deals with them. If the child were earlier given the concepts and strategies in the form of intuitive geometry at a level that he could

* *How could you verify or disprove this statement?*

easily follow, he might be far better able to grasp deeply the meaning of the theorems and axioms to which he is exposed later.

But the intellectual development of the child is no clockwork sequence of events; it also responds to influences from the environment, notably the school environment. Thus instruction in scientific ideas, even at the elementary level, need not follow slavishly the natural course of cognitive development in the child. It can also lead intellectual development by providing challenging but usable opportunities for the child to forge ahead in his development. Experience has shown that it is worth the effort to provide the growing child with problems that tempt him into next stages of development. As David Page, one of the most experienced teachers of elementary mathematics, has commented: "In teaching from kindergarten to graduate school, I have been amazed at the intellectual similarity of human beings at all ages, although children are perhaps more spontaneous, creative, and energetic than adults. As far as I am concerned young children learn almost anything faster than adults do if it can be given to them in terms they understand.* Giving the material to them in terms they understand, interestingly enough, turns out to involve knowing the mathematics oneself, and the better one knows it, the better it can be taught. It is appropriate that we warn ourselves to be careful of assigning an absolute level of difficulty to any particular topic. When I tell mathematicians that fourth grade students can go a long way into 'set theory' a few of them reply: 'Of course.' Most of them are startled. The latter ones are completely wrong in assuming that 'set theory' is intrinsically difficult. Of course it may be that nothing is intrinsically difficult. We just have to wait until the proper point of view and corresponding language for presenting it are revealed. Given particular subject matter or a particular concept, it is easy to ask trivial questions or to lead the child to ask trivial questions. It is also easy to ask impossibly difficult questions. The trick is to find the medium questions that can be answered and that take you somewhere. This is the big job of teachers and textbooks." One leads the child by the well-wrought "medium questions" to move more rapidly through the stages of intellectual development, to a deeper understanding of mathematical, physical, and historical principles. We must know far more about the ways in which this can be done. . . .

THE ACT OF LEARNING

Learning a subject seems to involve three almost simultaneous processes.† First there is *acquisition* of new information — often information.

* Holt makes a similar observation earlier in this section.
† Do you think the following is how learning really occurs? How similar is it to John Holt's description?

that runs counter to or is a replacement for what the person has previously known implicitly or explicitly. At the very least it is a refinement of previous knowledge. Thus one teaches a student Newton's laws of motion, which violate the testimony of the senses. Or in teaching a student about wave mechanics, one violates the student's belief in mechanical impact as the sole source of real energy transfer. Or one bucks the language and its built-in way of thinking in terms of "wasting energy" by introducing the student to the conservation theorem in physics which asserts that no energy is lost. More often the situation is less drastic, as when one teaches the details of the circulatory system to a student who already knows vaguely or intuitively that blood circulates.

A second aspect of learning may be called *transformation* — the process of manipulating knowledge to make it fit new tasks. We learn to "unmask" or analyze information, to order it in a way that permits extrapolation or interpolation or conversion into another form. Transformation comprises the ways we deal with information in order to go beyond it.

A third aspect of learning is *evaluation:* checking whether the way we have manipulated information is adequate to the task. Is the generalization fitting, have we extrapolated appropriately, are we operating properly? Often a teacher is crucial in helping with evaluation, but much of it takes place by judgments of plausibility without our actually being able to check rigorously whether we are correct in our efforts.

In the learning of any subject matter, there is usually a series of episodes, each episode involving the three processes. Photosynthesis might reasonably comprise material for a learning episode in biology, fitted into a more comprehensive learning experience such as learning about the conversion of energy generally. At its best a learning episode reflects what has gone before it and permits one to generalize beyond it.

A learning episode can be brief or long, contain many ideas or a few. How sustained an episode a learner is willing to undergo depends upon what the person expects to get from his efforts, in the sense of such external things as grades but also in the sense of a gain in understanding.

We usually tailor material to the capacities and needs of students by manipulating learning episodes in several ways: by shortening or lengthening the episode, by piling on extrinsic rewards in the form of praise and gold stars, or by dramatizing the shock of recognition of what the material means when fully understood. The unit in a curriculum is meant to be a recognition of the importance of learning episodes, though many units drag on with no climax in understanding. There is a surprising lack of research on how one most wisely devises adequate learning episodes for children at different ages and in different subject matters. There are many questions that need answers based on careful research, and to some of these we turn now.

There is, to begin with, the question of the balance between extrinsic rewards and intrinsic ones. There has been much written on the role of reward and punishment in learning, but very little indeed on the role of interest and curiosity and the lure of discovery. If it is our intention as teachers to inure the child to longer and longer episodes of learning, it may well be that intrinsic rewards in the form of quickened awareness and understanding will have to be emphasized far more in the detailed design of curricula. One of the least discussed ways of carrying a student through a hard unit of material is to challenge him with a chance to exercise his full powers, so that he may discover the pleasure of full and effective functioning. Good teachers know the power of this lure. Students should know what it feels like to be completely absorbed in a problem. They seldom experience this feeling in school. Given enough absorption in class, some students may be able to carry over the feeling to work done on their own.

There is a range of problems that have to do with how much emphasis should be placed on acquisition, transformation, and evaluation in a learning episode — getting facts, manipulating them, and checking one's ideas. Is it the case, for example, that it is best to give the young child a minimum set of facts first and then encourage him to draw the fullest set of implications possible from this knowledge? In short, should an episode for a young child contain little new information but emphasize what can be done to go beyond that bit on one's own? One teacher of social studies has had great success with fourth-graders through this approach: he begins, for example, with the fact that civilizations have most often begun in fertile river valleys — the only "fact." The students are encouraged in class discussion to figure out why this is the case and why it would be less likely for civilizations to start in mountainous country.* The effect of this approach, essentially the technique of discovery, is that the child generates information on his own, which he can then check or evaluate against the sources, getting more new information in the process. This obviously is one kind of learning episode, and doubtless it has limited applicability. What other kinds are there, and are some more appropriate to certain topics and ages than others? It is not the case that "to learn is to learn is to learn," yet in the research literature there appears to be little recognition of differences in learning episodes. . . .

The "Spiral Curriculum"

If one respects the ways of thought of the growing child, if one is courteous enough to translate material into his logical forms and challenging enough to tempt him to advance, then it is possible to introduce him at an early age to the ideas and styles that in later life make an educated man. We might ask, as a criterion for any subject taught in primary school,

* *Is this a teaching technique you would use?*

whether, when fully developed, it is worth an adult's knowing, and whether having known it as a child makes a person a better adult. If the answer to both questions is negative or ambiguous, then the material is cluttering the curriculum.

If the hypothesis with which this section was introduced is true — that any subject can be taught to any child in some honest form — then it should follow that a curriculum ought to be built around the great issues, principles, and values that a society deems worthy of the continual concern of its members. Consider two examples — the teaching of literature and of science. If it is granted, for example, that it is desirable to give children an awareness of the meaning of human tragedy and a sense of compassion for it, is it not possible at the earliest appropriate age to teach the literature of tragedy in a manner that illuminates but does not threaten? There are many possible ways to begin: through a retelling of the great myths, through the use of children's classics, through presentation of and commentary on selected films that have proved themselves. . . .

So too in science. If the understanding of number, measure, and probability is judged crucial in the pursuit of science, then instruction in these subjects should begin as intellectually honestly and as early as possible in a manner consistent with the child's forms of thought. Let the topics be developed and redeveloped in later grades. Thus, if most children are to take a tenth-grade unit in biology, need they approach the subject cold? Is it not possible, with a minimum of formal laboratory work if necessary, to introduce them to some of the major biological ideas earlier, in a spirit perhaps less exact and more intuitive?

Many curricula are originally planned with a guiding idea much like the one set forth here. But as curricula are actually executed, as they grow and change, they often lose their original form and suffer a relapse into a certain shapelessness. It is not amiss to urge that actual curricula be reexamined with an eye to the issues of continuity and development referred to in the preceding pages.*. . .

EXERCISE

1. What is the main symbolic achievement that the child experiences in the preoperational stage of development? (p. 27)

2. What is the concept of reversibility? (pp. 27–28)

3. What abilities does the child acquire in the stage of concrete operations? (pp. 28–29)

4. Describe the three aspects of learning identified by Bruner. (pp. 30–31)

* Wouldn't the spiral curriculum result in a highly redundant and limited learning experience?

5. How do the processes of acquisition, transformation, and evaluation work in learning by discovery? (p. 32)
6. What does Bruner mean by "spiral curriculum"? (p. 33)

The Role of Imitation (or Learning by Identification) in Moral Conduct

Roger Brown

> *In this selection Roger Brown argues that learning can occur by either imitation or reinforcement (see the selection by Skinner). Brown's major interest here is the role that imitation plays in learning moral behavior. However, he also discusses research on learning sex-linked behavior by imitating male or female models. Although imitation offers an appealing explanation of how children learn, consider these questions as you read this selection:*
> *Why doesn't the child imitate everything he observes? Usually the child's imitation is not an exact copy of what he has observed. Why? Imitation seems to be dependent upon the ability to observe the behavior of another person. How then do blind children learn? The process of thinking cannot be directly observed. If people learn by imitating others, how do they learn to think?*

Parents who beat their children for aggression intend to "stamp out" the aggression. The fact that the treatment does not work as intended suggests that the implicit learning theory is wrong. A beating may be regarded as an instance of the behavior it is supposed to stamp out. If children are more disposed to learn by imitation or example than by "stamping out" they ought to learn from a beating to beat.* That seems to be roughly what happens. How important in general is imitation for the development of moral conduct?

---

* *What does this imply about violence in television programming for children?*

IMITATION AND LEARNING BY REINFORCEMENT

The analogy between training animals and training children is an obvious one and so the first principle one thinks of using to explain the development of moral conduct is the principle of selective reward and punishment (or positive and negative reinforcement).* In one way or another parents often reward good conduct and punish bad conduct and these rewards and punishments should shape the behavior they follow. Parents will react in terms of their own moral values and so these values should eventually be seen as regularities in the behavior of children. Parents are representative of a larger culture and of subcultures and so the behavior of children after the first year or so varies from one society to another and, within a society, from one socio-economic level to another.

How, in terms of reinforcement, should male children learn to be boys and female children to be girls? Parents do not reinforce the same kinds of behavior in the two sexes; the rules of reinforcement are contingent on the sex of the child. Boys are reinforced for being assertive and girls are not; girls are reinforced for learning to cook and sew and boys are not. Boy and girl roles are two distinct reinforcement programs and so are all sex-typed roles such programs. When the boy and girl become adolescent they assume new roles which is to say that the rules of reinforcement change: Lipstick is approved for teenage girls and driving an automobile for teenage boys.

If sex roles are learned by selective reinforcement the child should have no need of a same-sex model. A woman living away from her husband should be perfectly capable of exerting selection pressures that will cause her son to behave in an ideally masculine fashion. She need only have a correct conception of masculinity and the wish to see her son approximate it. If moral conduct is altogether learned by selective reinforcement a child should have no need of a moral examplar. If the parents have a well-developed conception of what moral behavior is and are guided by it in reinforcing the child they themselves should be able to manifest consistent villainy without doing the child's character any harm. A good example should be of no importance if children do not learn by example but only by direct reward and punishment.

Still there is the fact that parents who beat their children for being aggressive nevertheless have aggressive children, in fact children more aggressive than those of parents who administer no beatings. This is not the way things should go if direct reward and punishment were the only determinants of behavior. It is the way things should go if children learn by example. In addition, Brim (1958) has shown that boys who have a sister for their single sibling manifest more feminine traits than do boys whose single

---

* Reinforcement is discussed also by Skinner in this section.

sibling is a brother. This looks like learning by example again and this time the learning is of sex-typed behavior. . . .

Do children imitate? Of course they do. We even have an experimental demonstration. Bandura and Huston (1961) gave some children, who were busy with a discrimination problem, the opportunity to observe an adult going through various unusual and striking actions unrelated to the child's task. The adult might march about or talk to himself or perhaps knock a small rubber doll off a box. Half of the children saw one set of actions and half saw a different set. Both groups of children later imitated what they had seen and the two groups behaved differently since they had seen different behavior. Bandura, Ross, and Ross (1961) demonstrated that children exposed to aggressive models generalized these aggressive responses to a new setting. In 1963(a) the same authors reported that children who had recently seen aggression in a motion picture reacted aggressively to mild frustration more frequently than did children who had not had the prior exposure to aggressive models. The fact of imitation is established and there is a serious possibility that aggressive children learn by the example of their parents and by the example of aggression shown in the mass media.

Bandura and McDonald (1963) have done an experiment that compares learning by direct reward with learning by imitation and this experiment helps us to understand why a model is important in socialization. . . . [T]he experiment made use of pairs of stories. . . . One story of each pair described a well-intentioned act that resulted in considerable material damage and the other story a selfishly or maliciously motivated act that resulted in trivial damage. The child was to say which act was the naughtier. For the children having an "objective conception" of morality, the younger children, the acts with more serious consequences were the "naughtier" ones. For the children having a "subjective conception" of morality, the older ones, the acts that were selfishly or maliciously motivated seemed the "naughtier" ones.

The initial subjective or objective orientation of each child was determined. Thereafter some of the children listened and watched while adults expressed judgments counter to their own orientation. Other children had no exposure to adults but were themselves directly rewarded whenever they expressed judgments counter to their own original orientation. Finally the orientations of the children were once again determined to see what changes had been produced.

Observation of adults produced much more change than did direct reward.* One probable reason for the inefficacy of the reward training was the very small number of reinforceable responses emitted by the children. For the most part they continued giving the responses of their initial orien-

---

If true, what is its implication for teachers?

tation and so had little experience of reward for giving contrary answers. The desired response had too low a frequency level (too low an operant level) to be selected out by reward.

In the training of animals too one sometimes wants to select out a response that the animal seldom performs. One can often do it by the method of "successive approximations." Perhaps the rat does not initially show any tendency to roll a marble into a cup in the floor of his cage but he can be brought to it. One can begin by giving him a bit of food whenever he moves into the general vicinity of the marble. That will serve to keep him near the marble and will increase the frequency with which he moves the marble. Feed him for that and then for moving in the direction of the cup and at last for dropping the marble into the cup. It is a slow method and it relies on the emission of responses transitional to or in the direction of the response in which we are ultimately interested. Such responses do not always exist. The children chose one story or the other and so long as they were not choosing as the experimenter wished he had no opportunity to reward them.

Apparently once children have attained a certain level of perceptual and motor control they are able to approximate many actions of a model simply from seeing them.* A boy can make a good try at "walking like a man" simply from seeing his father do it. If he had only his mother to reward successive approximations, would he ever learn? Perhaps a girl can look demure once she has seen her mother do it, but her father all alone, rewarding expressions that tend to demureness, might never get her there.

DETERMINANTS OF IMITATION

So the presentation of a model as well as the administration of reward and punishment can cause behavior change in children. In life there are always many models and, from one model, many kinds of behavior so we need to know when imitation is likely to occur and when it is likely not to occur; what are its determinants. Some writers, ambitious for reinforcement theory, have argued that we imitate behavior we have seen reinforced in another. Learning by imitation would then figure as "vicarious reinforcement" (Hill, 1960). . . . Bandura, Ross, and Ross (1963c) have put the idea to a test.†

Children saw films in which someone behaved in a strikingly aggressive way. In one film the very destructive behavior was followed by severe punishment, in another by generous praise and good food, and in a third the behavior had no consequences. In a post-exposure test of imitative behavior

---

* Does this point effectively refute Skinner, who believes learning must be broken down into many small steps?
† The concept of vicarious reinforcement is explained in the glossary.

the children who had seen the figure in the film punished imitated him the least. The children who had seen him rewarded and the children who had seen him experience no consequences imitated him more, but these two groups of children were not different from one another. The idea of vicarious reinforcement would lead us to expect rewarded behavior to be more imitated than punished behavior but not that behavior having no consequences would be imitated as much as rewarded behavior.

Bandura and his associates did not stop with the single post-exposure test of imitation. All of the children were offered attractive incentives for reproducing the behavior they had seen (Bandura and Walters, 1963, pp. 57–58). These incentives completely wiped out the differences previously observed in the performances of the groups. The results compel us to make a distinction between *learning* the behavior of a model and *performing* it. Apparently all three groups had equally well learned the distinctive behavior of the model but those who had seen the behavior punished were less disposed to perform it overtly. Vicarious reinforcement seems to have some differential effect on performance but none whatever on learning.

The distinction between learning the behavior of a model and performing it has also been made by two other theorists — Eleanor Maccoby (1959) and John Whiting (1960) — though they prefer to speak of role-learning and role-performance. Maccoby has argued that a child must necessarily learn his mother's role since that role is complementary to his own. He stands by his highchair and raises his arms, she lifts him just below the armpits and lowers him toward his chair, he slips his legs in and down and lowers his head as she brings the tray over the top. Here is one habit distributed between two nervous systems. Her behavior is matrix to his patrix and so they must learn one another's ways.

Presumably the child runs through his mother's role in his head since that role guides his own behavior. Mother's role includes her judgments of right and wrong, her praise and censure, and Maccoby's theory, therefore, provides for the literal internalization of a parent. It gets us beyond mere conforming behavior and provides for an agency in the mind something like Freud's superego, a voice standing over against the ego telling it what to do and reacting to what it does.

Maccoby's discussion predicts that one will learn the behavior of another whenever that behavior belongs to a role complementary to our own and that certainly happens. However, we also learn roles that are not complementary to our own. An actor in a play certainly learns all the lines of other actors that cue his own lines and he often does say the other actors' lines to himself. A marching soldier certainly learns all the commands the sergeant barks at him and can bark them out himself if he is asked to drill the squad. However, both the actor and the soldier learn more than the roles complementary to their own. The actor may learn the entire play including many lines and actions which are not cues to his own performance. The soldier may learn the role of the sergeant *vis-à-vis* the lieutenant though he himself plays no part in this interaction.

We all have learned how to play many roles not our own and not complementary to our own. A young unmarried man, for example, knows the role of expectant father. He must smoke many cigarettes and pace the floor; he had better not go calmly to the movies. That role was learned by observation alone. There was no necessity for vicarious reinforcement and no necessity that the role be complementary to his own. . . .

In general summary, parents can affect the behavior, the conduct, of children in at least two ways: by direct reward or punishment and by providing a model for imitation. It now looks as if power were the prime factor making a model attractive for imitation though such other factors as nurturance and vicarious rewards may also be important. With two parents to manifest power and administer direct reward and punishment there are many possible kinds of family pattern, many kinds of learning problem presented to children. For some kinds of behavior, for example speaking the local language, all forces work in the same direction. Both parents model English and both reward it. For some kinds of behavior the pattern will be complex, for example assertiveness. Perhaps father manifests considerable assertiveness and has more power in the family than his nonassertive wife. Perhaps both parents reward assertiveness in their son and not in their daughter. Both children might be expected to try out being assertive on the model of their impressive father and the son's performance would be confirmed by approval but the daughter's would not be. Does the daughter perhaps retain a desire to behave assertively, a latent identification with her male parent, that leads her to try out assertiveness in new groups where the reinforcement program may be different? Learning by identification is certainly a complex geometry and it is likely that what we now know is not more than the rudiments.

EXERCISE

1. What are two examples that Brown gives to show that the principles of reward and punishment do not account for all learning? (p. 35)

2. What point about the principle of reinforcement is made by the Bandura and McDonald (1963) experiment? (pp. 36–37)

3. According to Bandura, Ross, and Ross (1963b) and Bandura and Walters (1963), does vicarious reinforcement affect learning? (p. 38)

4. What criticism does Brown make of Eleanor Maccoby's theory that one will imitate the behavior of another person whose behavior is complementary to one's own ? (pp. 38–39)

Domains of Learning

Robert M. Gagné

Robert Gagné, former president of the American Educational Research Association, argues that there is not just one learning process, but rather at least five different types. For example, learning a concept is different from learning an attitude or motor skill. Along with Jerome Bruner, Gagné believes that the person's age makes a difference in how he learns: an adult does not learn the same way that a child does. Both Gagné and Bruner disagree with B. F. Skinner, who believes that some principles of learning are universal and apply equally well for animals and persons of all ages.

Those who profess to study and improve education through methods of research are inevitably concerned with the human activity of learning. It is, after all, the capacity of human beings to learn that makes it possible, and also necessary, for a society to have a set of institutions devoted to education. Educational research may, of course, concern itself rather directly with human learning activity, as when one investigates methods of instruction, modes of communication, or procedures for reinforcing the learner's behavior. Or, such research may be related to the activity of learning in a somewhat less direct way, as when the focus of investigation is the institutions established to bring about learning. Wherever the investigation fits along this broad spectrum, there can be little doubt that it is in some manner ultimately to be related to the question of how human beings learn.

From a dictionary, one can identify two primary meanings for the word "learning." Definition one is "the process of acquiring modifications in existing knowledge, skills, habits, or action tendencies." The second definition is "knowledge or skill that is acquired by instruction or study."*

It is easy enough to identify domains of learning in its second meaning. We do so all the time when we speak of divisions of the curriculum — knowledge about history, society, biology, literature; and skills of language and mathematics. Such domains have been identified in a variety of ways in different periods. The referent is the *content* of learning.

What about the first meaning — the *process* of learning? Are there also

Reprinted from *Interchange: A Journal of Educational Studies*, vol. 3 (1), 1972, 1–8. Published by the Ontario Institute for Studies in Education, Toronto, Canada.

* Do these definitions of learning satisfy you?

domains of learning processes that need to be distinguished, or is it always a single process, to be classified only in terms of its second meaning — the domains of knowledge and skill within which learning occurs? For many years, it would appear, those who conducted research on the learning process proceeded more or less on the assumption that they were searching for a common set of characteristics of the learning process, which would apply whether the learner was engaged in learning to lace a shoe, to define a new word, or to write an essay. Nevertheless, in the course of time, it has evidently become increasingly difficult to deal with the varieties of learning that occur in schools without classifying them in some manner. Accordingly, a number of terms have been invented to differentiate classes of learning, in order to make it possible to think about the learning process more clearly. Such phrases as "cognitive learning," "rote learning," "discovery learning," "concrete vs. symbolic learning," "affective learning," "conceptual learning," and many others, are examples of this strong and demanding tendency.

Each of these categories has some usefulness, of course. However, it also appears that their usefulness is limited — they are not as generally useful as they ought to be. One can readily find examples, for instance, in which learning may be called rote in one situation, conceptual or cognitive in another. Many human performances that may be described as motor from one point of view turn out to be highly symbolic in some other sense. The domains that have been identified for the process of learning are limited in usefulness because they are not well differentiated either by means of the operations required to establish them, or by the consequences to which they lead.

The Need for Domains of the Learning Process

Why should the educational researcher be cognizant of domains of the process of learning? What need do they fulfill? What functions do they serve?

First, they are needed to distinguish the parts of a content area that are subject to different instructional treatments. The learning of science is not simply science learning, and the learning of language is not just language learning. Consider the learning of a foreign language as an example. One part of instruction must typically be concerned with the pronunciation of letters in words. The German word *Gemütlichkeit*, in order to be understood by a hearer, must be said with the proper sound for the umlauted *u*, and for the letter combination *ch* and *ei* — sounds that the student whose native language is English is not used to making. In order to learn to make them, he needs a good deal of practice on these specific letter combinations, as they occur in various words. But what about another part of his foreign language learning, in which he must learn to respond to a German question with a German answer? Is the way to accomplish this to practice a set of

German answers? Of course not, and no teacher of German would imagine that it is so. There are, then, different parts to this single subject that need to be *differentially* handled, so far as instruction is concerned. How shall one describe the different domains of the learning process that apply to the parts of this subject, as they do to the parts of other content areas?

A second need for distinctive domains of the learning process is that of relating the instructional procedures of one subject to those of another. If it is true that one cannot generalize about learning conditions from one part of a subject to another, is it nevertheless also true that similar parts can be found among different content areas? The existence of these comparable parts of different subjects is rather easy to demonstrate. Think of what a student is being asked to learn in mathematics, say, when one asks him to learn to answer the question, "What is a triangle?" We expect that he will be able to define this concept, perhaps by using his own words, but better still by showing how such a figure possesses characteristics of a closed curve and intersections of line segments. Suppose instead the subject is social science, and we want the student to answer the question, "What is a city?" In an entirely comparable way, we expect that he will be able to demonstrate a definition of this concept, by showing that a city possesses the characteristics of concentration of population, commerce, and transportation center. In both these subjects, very different in content, we are dealing with the *use of a definition*, and similar mental activities would be required in any other subject field. In other words, one of the kinds of things students are asked to learn is using definitions, and this is true whether we are dealing with mathematics, foreign language, science, or whatever.

A third reason for identifying domains of learning is that they require different techniques of assessment of learning outcomes. One cannot use a single way of measuring what has been learned. This is, of course, the basic point made by the pioneering work of Bloom (1956), Krathwohl, Bloom, and Masia (1964), and their associates. As this work amply demonstrates, one cannot expect to employ the same kind of test item, or question, to determine whether a student has learned an item of knowledge, on the one hand, or the ability to synthesize several different ideas, on the other hand.* Again, different categories of the learning domain are needed for measurement, regardless of the particular subject matter. They are needed in order to avoid the serious error of assuming that if a student knows something about a topic, that he therefore is part of the way to knowing all he needs to know about that topic. Instead, he can learn many more somethings without ever accomplishing the latter goal; the reason is because he needs to undertake entirely different categories of learning, rather than more of the same. The ways used to measure these different

---

* *Guszak's research deals with this problem (see Guszak, Section 2).*

categories are different, and it is these ways that demonstrate how distinct the mental processes are.

LEARNING DOMAINS

There are, then, a number of reasons for trying to differentiate domains of the learning process that are orthogonal to content, but that at the same time are in opposition to the notion that all learning is the same. From the standpoint of an educational researcher, the search is for domains *within which generalizations of findings can be made*. If the researcher has obtained a result that shows certain conditions to be facilitative of learning, he needs to know how widely this result can be generalized. Does it apply across subject-matter, across age levels, across classrooms? It is this kind of research utilization question to which the differentiation of domains of learning may be most relevant.

I should like here to summarize my conclusions about the desirable distinctions of domains of learning, some of which I have briefly described elsewhere (Gagné, 1971), before going on to discuss their implications for other kinds of distinctions applicable to the learning process. The domains I would distinguish are five, and I call them (1) motor skills, (2) verbal information, (3) intellectual skills, (4) cognitive strategies, and (5) attitudes.*

1. *Motor skills* is a good category to begin with, because it is so generally recognized to be distinctive. These are the capabilities that mediate organized motor performances like tying shoelaces, printing letters, pronouncing letter sounds, using tools and instruments. As everyone knows, learning motor skills takes *practice*, in the sense of repetition of the essential motor act. This requirement, in fact, appears to be one of the main characteristics that distinguish motor skills from other domains of learning. The evidence (Fitts & Posner, 1967, pp. 15–19) is to the effect that motor skills continue to improve with practice over long periods. As for retention, the differences favoring motor skills (Leavitt & Schlosberg, 1944) over verbal materials have often been confirmed.

2. *Verbal information* is a second category, surely of enormous importance for the schools. Facts, principles, and generalizations constitute a large portion of any curriculum, in most subjects. Such information is needed in a specific sense for continued learning within a particular subject area. Larger, organized bodies of information are usually called *knowledge*, and we recognize that people must acquire knowledge not only for further learning within a subject area, but for the lifetime purposes of learning across areas, and for thinking in a very general sense. The learning process

* *In the following description, do you think Gagné gives a better account of the learning process than Holt, Skinner, or Bruner?*

for verbal information appears to be quite different from that of motor skills. Many theorists are now convinced that the repetition provided by successive presentations of word lists on a memory drum is not the factor that causes learning (cf. Battig, 1968).* Instead, the major requirement for learning and retaining verbal information appears to be its presentation within an organized, meaningful context (cf. Mandler, 1962; Rohwer & Levin, 1968), as the work of Ausubel (1968) also suggests.

3. *Intellectual skills* is a third category I would distinguish and I have written about these skills extensively (Gagné, 1970a). They are, most importantly, the discriminations, concepts, and rules that constitute the basic skills of the elementary curriculum, and all of the elaborations of these that occur throughout more advanced subjects. It seems particularly important to distinguish these from verbal information and knowledge. For example, being able to recall and reinstate a definition verbally is quite different from showing that one can use that definition. The latter is what is meant by an intellectual skill, but not the former. Do intellectual skills require practice for their learning? The evidence does not show that practice, in the usual sense of that term, improves them (cf. Gagné, 1970b). Does their learning require an organized, meaningful context? It is doubtful that it does, at least if one attempts to define meaningful context in the same sense as that required for learning verbal knowledge. Most importantly, the learning of intellectual skills appears to require prior learning of prerequisite skills, in a manner that is surely not true for learning verbal information. The absence of a necessity for particular prior learnings is shown in the case of verbal information by studies of programming sequences such as that by Payne, Krathwohl, and Gordon (1967). For these various reasons, it seems essential to consider intellectual skills a domain of learning quite distinct from others.

4. *Cognitive strategies* is the fourth category, a domain that has been particularly emphasized by Bruner (1970; Bruner, Goodnow, & Austin, 1956). In a sense these are also skills, and they are obviously different from verbal knowledge. They are internally organized skills that govern the individual's behavior in learning, remembering, and thinking. Since they are directed toward self-management (cf. Skinner, 1968) of learning and thinking, they are obviously different from intellectual skills, which have an orientation toward the learner's environment. Although they are obviously very different from motor skills, curiously enough they share with them the property of deriving their learned organization from stimuli that arise within the learner. For this reason, they also require a kind of practice. The word is used here, though, mainly to emphasize the analogy; what appears to be required is repeated occasions in which challenges to thinking are presented. It is notable, therefore, that thinking strategies are not

* A *memory drum is a mechanical device used in laboratory studies of learning.*

learned all at once, as intellectual skills may be. Instead, they exhibit continued refinement as the learner continues to encounter situations in which he has to learn, to remember, to solve problems, and to define problems for himself.

5. *Attitudes* constitute the fifth domain of learning. Their learning is obviously different from the other categories. They are not learned by practice. They are by no means dependably affected by a meaningful verbal context, as many studies have shown (Hovland, Janis, & Kelley, 1953; Rosenberg, Hovland, McGuire, Abelson, & Brehm, 1960). One of the most effective ways of changing attitudes would appear to be by means of the human model, and the "vicarious reinforcement" described by Bandura (1969).* In any case, the apparent requirement for involvement of a human person in the process of modifying attitudes makes this kind of learning highly distinctive and different in many respects from the other varieties.

GENERALIZABILITY AND THE DOMAINS OF LEARNING

The suggestion I make, therefore, is that when one deals with learning as a process, rather than as a set of content areas, one needs to distinguish the five domains of motor skills, verbal information, intellectual skills, cognitive strategies, and attitudes.† These domains set the primary limits on generalizability of research findings concerned with learning. One can generalize *within* these areas, regardless of subject matter, with a fair degree of confidence. In contrast, generalizing *across* these domains is at best a highly risky business, and likely to be quite invalid.

Despite the suggestive evidence previously cited concerning the differences among these domains, one can hardly consider them as fully established. My suggestion is that it is these kinds of differences, and these kinds of implications for a generalization, for which the researcher needs to search. One cannot establish domains of learning by means of a few crucial experiments. Instead, conclusions about generalizability or lack of generalizability must be based upon a broad spectrum of findings from many content areas.

Suppose that one is concerned with how learning can be made most effective in a social studies unit on Cities. If the objective is one of having children learn to state the names and locations of major cities of the world, the domain of learning is verbal information. The suggestion is that such an objective will be most readily achieved by providing a meaningful context for each city — for example, the semantic origin of its name, the reasons for its particular location, and so on. But if the objective of the

* *Vicarious reinforcement is explained in the glossary.*
† *Do Gagné's five domains have any implications for the way you would teach children?*

unit on Cities is a different one, say, "deriving a definition of the concept city" (an objective requiring cognitive strategies), or "having a positive interest in visiting a city" (an attitude), the provision of a meaningful context for each city will not accomplish the desired learning. For these latter kinds of learning outcomes, something different is required in each case.

The objective of developing cognitive strategies for application to the defining and solving of problems pertaining to cities must be approached, according to the evidence currently available, by providing a series of learning experiences making possible a variety of opportunities for the student to think out solutions to novel problems, including problems that are not necessarily concerned with cities per se. He might, for example, have been provided with other defining problems, such as those of defining a person, or a group, or a school. But the presentation of meaningful contexts about cities is not what will effect this kind of learning, as it will the contrasted objective of "stating the names and locations of major cities."

Neither will the meaningful context accomplish the job of establishing or changing an attitude toward visiting the city. While one hesitates to say such a context has no effect at all, the evidence is quite substantially lacking that practically significant changes in attitude can be produced in this manner. But they probably can be produced by the modeling of human behavior. Perhaps the teacher, or some other respected person, can show his liking for visiting the city, and the student can observe the pleasure derived from rewarding experiences during such visits.* Or, of course, he may be able to experience such rewards for himself. Both direct and vicarious reinforcement are likely to contribute to the establishment of a positive attitude.

The various objectives that have been described for a unit on Cities are of course all different, and this is the point at issue. Any or all of these might be desired as an outcome of such an instructional unit. The suggestion from research is that these different learning outcomes require different conditions for effective instruction. The question for research is to verify the generalizability, and the absence of generalizability, of learning conditions and learning outcomes across these domains.

Another example may be useful. Suppose one wishes to offer students a science unit on Moments of Force. The likelihood is, in this case, that the major concern is with an intellectual skill such as "demonstrating the equivalence of moments of force about a fulcrum of a body at equilibrium." Such a learning task is best described as the application of a general rule to a specific situation, novel to the learner. Naturally, the learner has to be given specific verbal information (about the body, the fulcrum, etc.) in order to attack the problem. Just as obviously, he may have learned some

---

* *Is this how you would shape students' attitudes?*

ways of defining and approaching such problems that deserve to be called cognitive strategies. But the critically necessary capabilities he must bring to the task are the intellectual skills that include rules for obtaining moments of force, of multiplying specific values of force and distance, of substituting values in statements of equality, and the like.

How are such rules learned? The conditions for their learning are not the same as those for verbal information, nor are they the same as those for cognitive strategies. According to my interpretation of the existing evidence, the critical condition for their learning is the recall of previously learned intellectual skills (subordinate rules, concepts, etc.). As a further consideration, it may be noted that when one attempts to assess the learning of such skills, one does not set about measuring what factual knowledge (verbal information) the student has, nor how well he formulates the problem (cognitive strategies). Instead, one tries to measure the possession of the intellectual skill — whether or not the learner is able to apply the rules he has acquired to this class of problems.

When these five domains are identified as the primary categories that limit the generalizability of conclusions about the learning process, does it not suggest that some other rather obvious human characteristics are being overlooked? For example, is it possible that sex or racial characteristics may impose such limitations even more clearly? Concerning these variables, it seems unlikely to me that they are the kinds of factors that biologically limit the generalizability of propositions about learning, although some investigators wish to explore this possibility (cf. Jensen, 1968). The variable of age, however, may be a good one to consider further in the present context, since it may serve to show not only what the differences in learning are, but why they may be expected to occur.

Age and Learning

Let us consider two students, both of whom are attending school. One is 10 years old, in the fourth grade; the other is 24 years old, and attending graduate school. Is there a difference in the way they learn?

First of all, there are obvious differences in the arrangements made for their instruction. The fourth-grader is learning how to use his langauge, in speaking, reading, and writing. He is learning to use mathematical concepts and to solve quantitative problems. Perhaps he is learning also about different nations and cultures of the world. Many of these things to be learned are prescribed as part of a school curriculum. The graduate student may also have some prescribed subjects to deal with — foreign languages, or statistics, or computer usage. It is perhaps relevant to note that much of what he learns is determined by him, because he sees the need to learn it — the knowledge of how a specialized field is conceptually organized, of its methods, and of its ways of formulating and solving problems.

There are, then, some differences in the kinds of choices that the learner makes, in these two cases, and in the kinds of objectives being pursued, although perhaps not major ones. The 10-year-old is learning how to do some arithmetic, the 24-year-old is learning how to do some statistics. The 10-year-old may have a choice of a South American country whose culture he wishes to explore; the 24-year-old chooses a particular field of research whose findings he wishes to organize. But how do they go about their learning? Are there differences here?

There are, and they are quite striking ones. In the case of the arithmetic, for example, the fourth-grader is responding to a carefully organized plan of instruction, which provides him with illustrations, a rationale or verbal explanation, some chosen examples, and a means for him to check his operations at frequent intervals. He responds to printed text, to some pictorial presentation, and to the oral communications of the teacher. Arrangements are made for spaced reviews, and for application of the principles he learns in a number of verbally described situations. In the case of the statistics, the graduate student meets quite a different set of circumstances. Mainly, he is expected to learn by reading a book chapter by chapter, by following its terse rationale, and by applying what he has learned to problems containing detailed quantitative data. The book does not provide him with many pictorial aids, nor does it furnish lengthy explanations of procedural steps.*

Similar contrasts exist in the learning about a foreign country's culture by the fourth-grader, and the learning of the substance of a field of research by the graduate student. The 10-year-old learns the features of a foreign culture when they are carefully embedded within a meaningful context, which he learns about partly by reading, partly by using audiovisual aids, partly by the teacher's oral communications. Sometimes, in fact, this meaningful context becomes so rich that it is difficult to tell what he is supposed to be learning. The graduate student, in contrast, does a great part of his learning by reading articles in professional journals or technical books. They seldom can include a meaningful context or background since that would require too many pages, and they seldom include diagrams or other pictorial aids, since they cost too much. The sentences and paragraphs he reads tend to be long and densely written, and they refer to many abstract and technical concepts.

Both of these provide examples of learning, and both may be effective learning. Yet if one were to study what made learning effective in the 10-year-old, would one be able to generalize to the 24-year-old? I think not. The difference in the two instances is often summarized by saying that the 24-year-old has become to a large extent a self-learner, whereas the 10-year-

Many graduate students experience considerable difficulty with statistics. Could this be the reason?

old has not yet achieved this state, and has a ways to go before he does.

What might "being a self-learner" mean? What does the graduate student bring to his learning task that differs from what is brought by the fourth-grader? It seems to me that this question can best be answered in terms of the five domains of learning I have described.

The 24-year-old has acquired much complex, highly organized verbal information in his field of study. Accordingly, he is able to supply the meaningful organization required when he reads the journal article that is so concisely written. The 10-year-old has no such store of verbal information about the cultures of foreign countries, or even perhaps about his own country. The meaningful organization he can bring to bear on the learning task is therefore meager, and we must take a variety of means to supply it for him.

The 24-year-old has some highly relevant intellectual skills, which he has used many times, in approaching the study of statistics. He can perform mixed arithmetic operations, interpret graphs and tables, state and solve proportions, use the concepts of area and of limits. In the case of the 10-year-old, one is not so sure he can recall the prerequisite skills to the new operations he is learning in arithmetic. One therefore takes care to arrange the situation so that these intellectual skills are recalled, and also attempts to insure by means of spaced reviews that the new ones he learns will be readily available in the future. Another kind of difference in intellectual skills is exhibited in language usage. The graduate student is able to respond appropriately to the compact and complicated sentences of text he encounters in his reading, whereas the fourth-grader would be confused by these.

The 24-year-old brings to his learning task some highly valuable cognitive strategies, which the 10-year-old has not yet acquired.* The former is probably able to sort out main and subordinate ideas in his attending and in his reading. He may well have some techniques of rehearsal that act in the storage of what is learned, as well as efficient strategies for retrieval of previously learned knowledge and skills. And he almost surely has acquired and refined some ways of approaching problems, defining problems, and weighing alternative solutions to problems — ways that are available only in a primitive form to the 10-year-old.

In terms of these domains alone, there are likely to be enormous differences in the process of learning in the 10-year-old and the 24-year-old individual. These differences exist, not simply because the passage of time has produced a disparity of 14 years in their ages or stage of biological growth and decay. They exist because of a history of learning, which has left in the older person a residue of increased knowledge, a greater repertoire of intellectual skills, a greatly enhanced collection of cognitive strate-

---

* Compare Gagné's analysis with Holt and Bruner, who earlier in this section suggest that children have better learning capacity than adults.

gies, and quite probably a different set of attitudes. All of these capabilities are different in the two instances, and each of them is bound to affect the process of learning, so that a very different problem exists for the design of instruction for these two individuals.

Is it possible that I have distorted these differences by choosing a graduate student as the 24-year-old, rather than an adult who is a high school graduate? The differences may be magnified, surely, but not distorted. If one equates inherent intellectual capacity, the typical adult is likely to outdo the 10-year-old in amount of verbal information he has, either in general or specialized fields. He is very likely to have more powerful cognitive strategies, particularly as these relate to his capabilities of problem-solving and thinking. As for his intellectual skills, these are most likely to display a very uneven picture, since they can rather readily be forgotten unless they are used constantly. For example, unless there are occasions for use in the intervening years, such an adult may well have forgotten how to add fractions, or to find a square root, or to edit written sentences to make verbs agree with subjects. It would not be surprising, therefore, to find a number of specific instances of knowledge or intellectual skill in which the fourth-grader displayed greater capabilities than the young adult. Such instances, however, merely serve to verify the general proposition that the five categories I have described represent the critical dimensions of domains of learning within which generalization is possible. It is of little use to know that some fourth-graders know how to do some things that some adults do not; this is not at all a remarkable fact. But it is of use to know, particularly if one is designing adult education, the nature of the adult's capabilities in the different domains of learning.

It is of some interest to point out some implications of this analysis of age differences in learning. First, it becomes apparent that college and university courses are not good models for the design of instruction for the fourth grade. A laboratory exercise in college chemistry, for example, cannot be made into a suitable learning experience for a child simply by using simpler language. Although the verbal information contained in the exercise may be made understandable to the child, it is quite another matter to attempt to reduce age differences in the domains of intellectual skills and cognitive strategies. The latter capabilities must be learned, and if one sets out to teach them to the fourth-grader, it is likely to take some time, possibly even years of time. A second implication is the reverse of the first: the design of instruction for the 10-year-old is not a good model for college instruction. Suggestions are sometimes made along these lines with reference to the education of teachers. However, as suggested by the previous analysis, the college student brings to his instruction a great variety of knowledge, intellectual skills, cognitive strategies, and attitudes that the 10-year-old simply does not have. If one attempts to design instruction for the college student that assumes that these capabilities are not there, it will surely be perceived as both boring and ridiculous. What is needed instead is a clear recognition of the requirement for different instruction for the fourth-grader and for the college student, based upon expected age differences in the different domains of learning.

Conclusions

The ideas presented in this article are expected to be of primary interest to those who perform research on learning and instruction, and to those who attempt to base instructional procedures upon the findings of such research. An examination of the results of studies of learning, particularly those concerned directly with school subjects, strongly indicates the necessity for recognizing five major domains of learning.* These are here named motor skills, verbal information, intellectual skills, cognitive strategies, and attitudes. It appears likely, on the basis of present evidence, that generalizations about the critical conditions for learning, as well as about the outcomes of learning, can be validly made within these categories (irrespective of specific content), but not across them. Further validation of this proposition must of course come from a great variety of research evidence; therefore, the categories as now formulated may serve as points of emphasis in studies of school-subject learning.

Considerable usefulness can also be foreseen in the application of these categories in instructional design. In such use, the domains are classes of instructional objectives, each of which requires a different set of critical conditions to insure efficient learning, and each of which implies the need for a different sort of situation for its assessment as a learning outcome.

Examples of the generalizability of learning characteristics within domains and their nongeneralizability across domains have been described. An example of age differences in learning between a 10-year-old and a 24-year-old is expanded to clarify the implications of learning domains. The major argument put forth is to the effect that differences in the requirements of instructional design cannot be clearly understood simply by appeal to differences in biological growth or amount of experience. The older and younger learner begin their learning of a new task with particular differences in previously acquired verbal information, intellectual skills, cognitive strategies, attitudes, and motor skills. Depending on what the new learning task is, the younger learner may begin the learning with greater or lesser capabilities than the older learner, in any of these categories. Effective instruction needs to be designed to take full account of the differences within these learning domains.

* *Has Gagné proved his point to your satisfaction?*

EXERCISE

1. According to Gagné, what is misleading about such categories as "language learning," "mathematics learning," or "science learning"? (pp. 41–42)

2. What are three reasons why it is important to distinguish between different domains of the learning process? (pp. 41–43)

3. What five domains of the learning process does Gagné distinguish, and what is at least one characteristic of each domain? (pp. 43–45)

4. In Gagné's example on page 47, what are three differences in the way that a 10-year-old student learns compared to a 24-year-old graduate student? (p. 48)

5. What does Gagné mean by "self-learner"? (pp. 49–50)

6. According to Gagné, why is the design of college instruction not a good model for the design of elementary school instruction? and vice versa? (pp. 50–51)

7. Is it riskier to make generalizations *within* or *between* different domains of the learning process? Explain your answer. (p. 51)

WHAT SHOULD STUDENTS LEARN IN SCHOOL?

Introduction

What do you want students to learn? No matter what professional role you may prepare for in education, this question is one of the most critical you will have to answer. For example, if you become a teacher, you must decide what you want your students to learn so that you can determine appropriate teaching strategies and curriculum content.

The same question arises as you begin to examine issues in educational psychology. For example, many teachers feel that they could help students learn better if class size were reduced. However, research studies show that students in small classes generally do not learn more than students in large classes (see Templeton and Flinker, Section 7). But what type of learning was evaluated in these studies? Usually they concerned fact-learning, measured by performance on paper-and-pencil tests. Perhaps class size does not affect learning facts, but what about learning how to appreciate literature, or to think critically, or to learn on one's own?

Generalizations about factors that influence learning and techniques for improving learning are often based on research which has considered a limited number of learning objectives. Even though a specific factor might not influence one type of learning objective, it could influence another. Therefore, to appraise research in educational psychology properly, you must know the variety of possible learning objectives, and you must decide which you value most. In reviewing the current literature, we have identified these differences of opinion concerning what should be learned by students:

> Some educators believe that the main job of the schools is to impart useful knowledge and skills.

53

Others believe that knowledge and skills quickly become outmoded in our fast-changing society. Thus the school should downplay fact-learning and instead concentrate on broader intellectual skills. That is, they should teach students how to think — how to analyze, synthesize, generalize, or evaluate.

Although such views differ, they both emphasize *cognitive* learning. Some educators feel that schools have the additional responsibility to provide learning experiences that shape the student's personal and social development. For example, they believe that schools should help students learn how to deal with their emotions, to interact effectively with others, to develop favorable attitudes toward ethnic minority groups, to explore career goals, and to develop healthy self-concepts.

Sometimes the issue of what should be learned becomes *who* should decide what is to be learned. Should school boards, teachers, and other educators decide what students are to learn? Or should the students themselves? If the latter, then the effectiveness of the schools should be measured, not by how many specific facts students know, but by how well they have acquired independent learning skills.

Unlike other educational issues, deciding what should be learned can not be resolved by empirical research. It is a value problem. The various groups that make up society, and the individual himself, must each decide what is most important for students to learn. To determine where your values lie, consider whether you agree or disagree with the following views:

Goals of Learning

1. The main job of the schools is to impart useful knowledge and skills.
2. Because knowledge and skills become dated too quickly, the schools should concentrate on training students how to think.
3. The schools should assume the responsibility of teaching skills and attitudes that concern the student's personal and social development.
4. The students, not their teachers, should determine what they will learn in school.

The following selections provide arguments for both sides of these issues. Robert Ebel and Carl Bereiter both argue, for somewhat different reasons, that the schools' only goals should be to impart useful knowledge and skills. Frank Guszak also acknowledges the importance of cognitive learning, but believes the emphasis should be on learning how to think, not just learning and recalling facts. The remaining authors present their case for quite different learning objectives than are currently popular in the schools. James Banks advocates improving society by helping students to understand institutional racism and to acquire skills in political activism, whereas Sidney Marland views career education as the major area for improvement. Harold Bessell is more interested in the individual; he describes ways in which the schools can help students learn about themselves and how they relate to others. Carl Rogers takes perhaps the most radical stance by arguing that all learning objectives should come from the student himself, not from educators.

What Are Schools For?

Robert L. Ebel

Robert L. Ebel, a former president of the American Educational Research Association, takes a strong stand in this selection on what students should learn in school. He favors teaching knowledge, as opposed to teaching intellectual skills, values, or attitudes. He believes in prescribed curricula, not student-selected learning projects. Ebel apparently values "duties" over "feelings," "tradition and stability" over "innovation and change," "the wisdom of age" over "the vigor of youth." These values obviously affect his view of what the schools should teach. Do you think it is possible to subject Ebel's values and beliefs to empirical test through educational research? Or to state the problem differently, is it possible to reconcile Ebel's advocacy of specific learning goals with conflicting views?

When the history of our times is written, it may designate the two decades following World War II as the golden age of American education. Never before was education more highly valued. Never before was so much of it so readily available to so many. Never before had it been supported so generously. Never before was so much expected of it.

But in this eighth decade of the twentieth century public education in this country appears to be in trouble. Taxpayers are revolting against the skyrocketing costs of education. Schools are being denied the funds they

Reprinted with permission of publisher and Robert L. Ebel from *Phi Delta Kappan*, vol. 54, September 1972, pp. 3–7.

say they need for quality education. Teachers are uniting to press demands for higher pay and easier working conditions.

College and high school students have rebelled against what they call "the Establishment," resisting and overturning regulations, demanding pupil-directed rather than teacher-directed education, and turning in some cases to drink, drugs, and delinquency. Minorities are demanding equal treatment, which is surely their right. But when integration makes social differences more visible, and when equality of opportunity is not followed quickly by equality of achievement, frustration turns to anger which sometimes leads to violence.

Surely these problems are serious enough. But I believe there is one yet more serious, because it lies closer to the heart of our whole educational enterprise. We seem to have lost sight of, or become confused about, our main function as educators, our principal goal, our reason for existence. We have no good answer that we are sure of and can agree on to the question, What are schools for?

It may seem presumptuous of me to suggest that I know the answer to this question. Yet the answer I will give is the answer that an overwhelming majority of our fellow citizens would also give. It is the answer that would have been given by most educators of the past who established and operated schools. Indeed, the only reason the question needs to be asked and answered at this time is that some influential educators have been conned into accepting wrong answers to the question. Let me mention a few of these wrong answers:

— Schools are not custodial institutions responsible for coping with emotionally disturbed or incorrigible young people, for keeping nonstudents off the streets or out of the job market.

— Schools are not adjustment centers, responsible for helping young people develop favorable self-concepts, solve personal problems, and come to terms with life.*

— Schools are not recreational facilities designed to entertain and amuse, to cultivate the enjoyment of freedom, to help young people find strength through joy.

— Schools are not social research agencies, to which a society can properly delegate responsibility for the discovery of solutions to the problems that are currently troubling the society.

I do not deny that society needs to be concerned about some of the things just mentioned. What I do deny is that schools were built and are maintained primarily to solve such problems. I deny that schools are good places in which to seek solutions, or that they have demonstrated much success in finding them. Schools have a very important special mission. If they accept responsibility for solving many of the other problems that

* *Harold Bessell (this section) takes the opposite view.*

trouble some young people, they are likely to fail in their primary mission, without having much success in solving the rest of our social problems.

Then what is the right answer to the question, What are schools for? I believe it is that schools are for learning, and that what ought to be learned mainly is useful knowledge.*

Not all educators agree. Some of them discount the value of knowledge in the modern world. They say we ought to strive for the cultivation of intellectual skills. Others claim that schools have concentrated too much on knowledge, to the neglect of values, attitudes, and such affective dispositions. Still others argue that the purpose of education is to change behavior. They would assess its effectiveness by examining the pupil's behavior or performance. Let us consider these three alternatives in reverse order.

If the schools are to be accountable for the performance of their pupils, the question that immediately arises is, What performance? A direct answer to this question is, The performance you've been trying to teach. But that answer is not as simple or as obviously correct as it seems at first glance. Many schools have not been primarily concerned with teaching pupils to perform. They have been trying to develop their pupils' knowledge, understanding, attitudes, interests, and ideals; their cognitive capabilities and affective dispositions rather than their performances. Those who manage such schools would agree that capabilities and dispositions can only be assessed by observing performances, but they would insist that the performances themselves are not the goals of achievement, only the indicators of it. A teacher who is concerned with the pupil's cognitive capabilities and affective dispositions will teach quite differently, they point out, than one whose attention is focused solely on the pupil's performances. And, if performances are not goals but only indicators, we should choose the ones to use in assessment on the basis of their effectiveness as indicators. Clearly we cannot choose them in terms of the amount of effort we made to develop them.

But, if we reject performance goals, another question arises: What should be the relative emphasis placed on affective dispositions as opposed to cognitive capabilities? Here is another issue that divides professional educators. To some, how the pupil feels — his happiness, his interest, his self-concept, his yearnings — are what should most concern teachers. To others the pupil's cognitive resources and capabilities are the main concern. Both would agree that cognition and affect interact, and that no school ought to concentrate solely on one and ignore the other. But they disagree on which should receive primary emphasis.

In trying to resolve this issue it may be helpful to begin by observing that the instructional programs of almost all schools are aimed directly at the cultivation of cognitive competence. Pupils are taught how to read and

* This is the essence of Ebel's position.

to use mathematics, how to write and to express perceptions, feelings, ideas, and desires in writing, to be acquainted with history and to understand science. The pupil's affective dispositions, his feelings, attitudes, interests, etc., constitute conditions that facilitate or inhibit cognitive achievement. They may be enhanced by success or impaired by failure. But they are by-products, not the main products, of the instructional effort. It is almost impossible to find any school that has planned and successfully operated an instructional program aimed primarily at the attainment of affective goals.

That this situation exists does not prove that it ought to exist. But it does suggest that there may be reasons. And we need not look too far to discover what they probably are.

Feelings are essentially unteachable. They can not be passed along from teacher to learner in the way that information is transmitted. Nor can the learner acquire them by pursuing them directly as he might acquire understanding by study. Feelings are almost always the consequence of something — of success or failure, of duty done or duty ignored, of danger encountered or danger escaped. Further, good feelings (and bad feelings also, fortunately) are seldom if ever permanent possessions. They tend to be highly ephemeral. The surest prediction that one can make when he feels particularly good, strong, wise, or happy is that sooner or later he is going to feel bad, weak, foolish, or sad. In these circumstances it is hardly surprising that feelings are difficult to teach.

Nor do they need to be taught. A new-born infant has, or quickly develops, a full complement of them — pain, rage, satiety, drowsiness, vitality, joy, love, and all the rest. Experience may attach these feelings to new objects. It may teach the wisdom of curbing the expression of certain feelings at inappropriate times or in inappropriate ways. And while such attachments and curbings may be desirable, and may be seen as part of the task of the school, they hardly qualify as one of its major missions.

The school has in fact a much more important educational mission than affective education, one which in the current cultural climate and educational fashion is being badly neglected.* I refer to moral education — the inculcation in the young of the accumulated moral wisdom of the race. Some of our young people have been allowed to grow up as virtual moral illiterates. And as Joseph Junell points out elsewhere . . . we are paying a heavy price for this neglect as the youth of our society become alienated, turn to revolt, and threaten the destruction of our social fabric.

This change in our perception of the function of the school is reflected in our statements of educational objectives. A century ago Horace Mann, Herbert Spencer, and most others agreed that there were three main aspects

* Ebel equates "affective" with feelings. What about attitudes and appreciation?

of education: intellectual, moral, and physical. Today the main aspects identified by our taxonomies of objectives are cognitive, affective, and psychomotor. The first and third elements in these two triads are essentially identical. The second elements are quite different. The change reflects a shift in emphasis away from the pupil's duties and toward his feelings.

Why has this come about? Perhaps because of the current emphasis in our society on individual liberty rather than on personal responsibility. Perhaps because we have felt it necessary to be more concerned with civil rights than with civic duties. Perhaps because innovation and change look better to us than tradition and stability. Perhaps because we have come to trust and honor the vigor of youth more than the wisdom of age.

In all these things we may have been misled. As we view the contemporary culture in this country it is hard to see how the changes that have taken place in our moral values during the last half century have brought any visible improvement in the quality of our lives. It may be time for the pendulum to start swinging back toward an emphasis on responsibility, on stability, on wisdom.* Older people are not always wiser people, but wisdom does grow with experience, and experience does accumulate with age.

Schools have much to contribute to moral education if they choose to do so, and if the courts and the public will let them. The rules of conduct and discipline adopted and enforced in the school, the models of excellence and humanity provided by the teachers, can be powerful influences in moral education. The study of history can teach pupils a decent respect for the lessons in morality that long experience has gradually taught the human race. Schools in the Soviet Union today appear to be doing a much more effective job of moral education than we have done in recent years. This fact alone may be enough to discredit moral education in some eyes. But concern for moral education has also been expressed by educational leaders in the democracies.

Albert North Whitehead[1] put the matter this way at the end of his essay on the aims of education:

> The essence of education is that it be religious.
> Pray, what is religious education?
> A religious education is an education which inculcates duty and reverence. Duty arises from our potential control over the course of events. Where attainable knowledge could have changed the issue, ignorance has the guilt of vice. And the foundation of reverence is this perception, that the present holds within itself the complete sum of existence, backwards and forwards, that whole amplitude of time which is eternity.

* *Is such a claim provable? If not, how do we decide whether to use it as a basis for action?*

If these views are correct, moral education deserves a much higher priority among the tasks of the school than does affective education. But it does not deserve the highest priority. That spot must be reserved for the cultivation of cognitive competence. Human beings need strong moral foundations, as part of their cultural heritage. They also need a structure of knowledge as part of their intellectual heritage. What schools were primarily built to do, and what they are most capable of doing well, is to help the student develop cognitive competence.

What is cognitive competence? Two distinctly different answers have been given. One is that it requires acquisition of knowledge. The other is that it requires development of intellectual skills. Here is another issue on which educational specialists are divided.

To avoid confusion or superficiality on this issue it is necessary to be quite clear on the meanings attached to the terms *knowledge* and *intellectual skills*. Knowledge, as the term is used here, is not synonymous with information. Knowledge is built out of information by thinking. It is an integrated structure of relationships among concepts and propositions. A teacher can give his students information. He cannot give them knowledge. A student must earn the right to say "I know" by his own thoughtful efforts to understand.

Whatever a person experiences directly in living or vicariously by reading or listening can become part of his knowledge. It will become part of his knowledge if he succeeds in integrating that experience into the structure of his knowledge, so that it makes sense, is likely to be remembered, and will be available for use when needed. Knowledge is essentially a private possession. Information can be made public. Knowledge cannot. Hence it would be more appropriate to speak of a modern-day information explosion than of a knowledge explosion.

The term *intellectual skills* has also been used with a variety of meanings. Further, those who use it often do not say, precisely and clearly, what they mean by it. Most of them seem not to mean skill in specific operations, such as spelling a word, adding two fractions, diagraming a sentence, or balancing a chemical equation. They are likely to conceive of intellectual skills in much broader terms, such as observing, classifying, measuring, communicating, predicting, inferring, experimenting, formulating hypotheses, and interpreting data.

It seems clear that these broader intellectual skills cannot be developed or used very effectively apart from substantial bodies of relevant knowledge. To be skillful in formulating hypotheses about the cause of a patient's persistent headaches, one needs to know a considerable amount of neurology, anatomy, and physiology, as much as possible about the known disorders that cause headaches, and a great deal about the history and habits of the person who is suffering them. That is, to show a particular intellectual skill a person must possess the relevant knowledge. (Note well at this point that a person cannot look up the knowledge he needs, for knowledge, in the sense of the term as we use it, cannot be looked up. Only information can be looked up. Knowledge has to be built by the knower himself.) And, if he does possess the relevant knowledge, what else does he need in order to show the desired skill?

Intellectual skill that goes beyond knowledge can be developed in specific operations like spelling a word or adding fractions. But the more general (and variable from instance to instance) the operation becomes, the less likely it is that a person's intellectual skills will go far beyond his knowledge.

Those who advocate the development of intellectual skills as the principal cognitive aim of education often express the belief (or hope) that these skills will be broadly transferrable from one area of subject matter to another. But if the subjects are quite different, the transfer is likely to be quite limited. Who would hire a man well trained in the measurement of personal characteristics for the job of measuring stellar distances and compositions?

Those who advocate the cultivation of knowledge as the central focus of our educational efforts are sometimes asked, "What about wisdom? Isn't that more important than knowledge?"

To provide a satisfactory answer to this question we need to say clearly what we mean when we speak of wisdom. In some situations wisdom is simply an alias for good fortune. He who calls the plays in a football game, who designs a new automobile, or who plays the stock market is likely to be well acquainted with this kind of wisdom — and with its constant companion, folly. If an action that might turn out badly in fact turns out well, we call it an act of wisdom. If it turns out badly, it was clearly an act of folly.

But there is more than this to the relation of knowledge to wisdom. C. I. Lewis of Harvard has expressed that relation in this way:

> Where ability to make correct judgments of value is concerned, we more typically speak of wisdom, perhaps, than of knowledge. And "wisdom" connotes one character which is not knowledge at all, though it is quality inculcated by experience; the temper, namely, which avoids perversity in intentions, and the insufficiently considered in actions. But for the rest, wisdom and knowledge are distinct merely because there is so much of knowledge which, for any given individual or under the circumstances which obtain, is relatively inessential to judgment of values and to success in action. Thus a man may be pop-eyed with correct information and still lack wisdom, because his information has little bearing on those judgments of relative value which he is called upon to make, or because he lacks capacity to discriminate the practically important from the unimportant, or to apply his information to concrete problems of action. And men of humble attainments so far as breadth of information goes may still be wise by their correct apprehension of

such values as lie open to them and of the roads to these. But surely wisdom is a type of knowledge; that type which is oriented on the important and the valuable. The wise man is he who knows where good lies and how to act so that it may be attained.[2]

I take Professor Lewis to mean that, apart from the rectitude in purposes and the deliberateness in action that experience must teach, wisdom in action is dependent on relevant knowledge. If that is so, the best the schools can do to foster wisdom is to help students cultivate knowledge.*

Our conclusion at this point is that schools should continue to emphasize cognitive achievements as the vast majority of them have been doing. Some of you may not be willing to accept this conclusion. You may believe some other goal deserves higher priority in the work of the school, perhaps something like general ability to think (apart from any particular body of knowledge), or perhaps having the proper affective dispositions, or stable personal adjustment, or simply love of learning.

If you do, you ought to be prepared to explain how different degrees of attainment of the goal you would support can be determined.† For if you can not do this, if you claim your favored goal is intangible and hence unmeasurable, there is room for strong suspicion that it may not really be very important (since it has no clearly observable concomitants or consequences to render it tangible and measurable). Or perhaps the problem is that you don't have a very concrete idea of what it is you propose as a goal.

Let us return to the question of what schools are for, and in particular, for what they should be accountable. It follows from what has been said about the purposes of schooling, and about the cooperation required from the student if those purposes are to be achieved, that the school should not accept responsibility for the learning achievement of every individual pupil. The essential condition for learning is the purposeful activity, the willingness to work hard to learn, of the individual learner. Learning is not a gift any school can give. It is a prize the learner himself must pursue. If a pupil is unwilling or unable to make the effort required, he will learn little in even the best school.

Does this mean that a school should give the student maximum freedom to learn, that it should abandon prescribed curricula and course content in favor of independent study on projects selected by the pupils themselves? I do not think so. Surely all learning must be done by the learner himself, but a good teacher can motivate, direct, and assist the learning process to

* Don't schools have to teach values, also?
† This is also the view of those who advocate behavioral objectives (see Section 14).

great advantage. For a school to model its instructional program after the kind of free learning pupils do on their own out of school is to abandon most of its special value as a school, most of its very reason for existence.

Harry Broudy and John Palmer, discussing the demise of the kind of progressive education advocated by Dewey's disciple William H. Kilpatrick, had this to say about the predecessors of our contemporary free schools and open classrooms:*

> A technically sophisticated society simply does not dare leave the acquisition of systematized knowledge to concomitant learning, the by-products of projects that are themselves wholesome slices of juvenile life. Intelligence without systematized knowledge will do only for the most ordinary, everyday problems. International amity, survival in our atomic age, automation, racial integration, are not common everyday problems to which common-sense knowledge and a sense of decency are adequate.[3]

Like Broudy and Palmer, I believe that command of useful knowledge is likely to be achieved most rapidly and most surely when the individual pupil's effort to learn is motivated, guided, and assisted by expert instruction. Such instruction is most likely to occur, and to be most efficient and effective, when given in classes, not to individuals singly.

If the school is not held to account for the success of each of its pupils in learning, for what should it be accountable? I would say that it should accept responsibility for providing a favorable learning environment. Such an environment, in my view, is one in which the student's efforts to learn are:

1. guided and assisted by a capable, enthusiastic teacher;

2. facilitated by an abundance of books, films, apparatus, equipment, and other instructional materials;

3. stimulated and rewarded by both formal and informal recognition of achievement; and

4. reinforced by the example and the help of other interested, hard-working students. . . .

Let me now recapitulate what I have tried to say about what schools are for.

1. Public education in America today is in trouble.

2. Though many conditions contribute to our present difficulties, the fundamental cause is our own confusions concerning the central purpose of our activities.

3. Schools have been far too willing to accept responsibility for solving all of the problems of young people, for meeting all of their immediate

* *The open classroom is discussed in Section 10.*

needs. That schools have failed to discharge these obligations successfully is clearly evident.

4. Schools are for learning. They should bend most of their efforts to the facilitation of learning.

5. The kind of learning on which schools should concentrate most of their efforts is cognitive competence, the command of useful knowledge.

6. Knowledge is a structure of relationships among concepts. It must be built by the learner himself as he seeks understanding of the information he has received.

7. Affective dispositions are important by-products of all human experience, but they seldom are or should be the principal targets of our educational efforts. We should be much more concerned with moral education than with affective education.

8. Intellectual skills are more often praised as educational goals than defined clearly enough to be taught effectively. Broadly general intellectual skills are mainly hypothetical constructs which are hard to demonstrate in real life. Highly specific intellectual skills are simply aspects of knowledge.

9. Wisdom depends primarily on knowledge, secondarily on experience.

10. Schools should not accept responsibility for the success of every pupil in learning, since that success depends so much on the pupil's own efforts.

11. Learning is a personal activity which each student must carry on for himself.

12. Individual learning is greatly facilitated by group instruction.

13. Schools should be held accountable for providing a good learning environment, which consists of (a) capable, enthusiastic teachers, (b) abundant and appropriate instructional materials, (c) formal recognition and reward of achievement, and (d) a class of willing learners.

14. Since learning cannot be made compulsory, school attendance ought not to be compulsory either.

Schools ought to be held accountable. One way or another, they surely will be held accountable.* If they persist in trying to do too many things, things they were not designed and are not equipped to do well, things that in some cases can not be done at all, they will show up badly when called to account. But there is one very important thing they were designed and are equipped to do well, and that many schools have done very well in the past. That is to cultivate cognitive competence, to foster the learning of useful knowledge. If they keep this as their primary aim, and do not allow unwilling learners to sabotage the learning process, they are likely to give an excellent accounting of their effectiveness and worth.

---

* Isn't this a matter for research to decide?

EXERCISE

1. What is the main purpose of schools, according to Ebel? (p. 57)
2. Why is Ebel opposed to affective education? (pp. 57–58)
3. What is Ebel's opinion of moral education? (pp. 58–60)
4. Why does Ebel oppose the development of intellectual skills as the principal cognitive aim of education? (pp. 60–61)
5. Why does Ebel believe that "the school should not accept responsibility for the learning achievement of every individual pupil"? (p. 62)
6. What are the four characteristics of a good learning environment, according to Ebel? (p. 63)

A Time to Experiment
with Alternatives to Education

Carl Bereiter

Carl Bereiter criticizes the goal of humanistic education, which is to bring about "the fullest realization of the child's potentialities." Bereiter also deplores some of the concomitants of humanistic education which you will read about elsewhere in this book: teaching for creativity, teaching how to think, the discovery method, nongrading, and individualized instruction. Do you agree with Bereiter's thesis that the humanistic ideal does more harm than good in education? Notice that he does not present any research evidence to support his claims. Can you think of any findings from educational psychology that could be used to refute or support them?

From *Needs of Elementary and Secondary Education for the Seventies. A Compendium of Policy Papers*, compiled by the General Subcommittee on Education of the House of Representatives Committee on Education and Labor, Ninety-First Congress (Washington, D.C.: U.S. Government Printing Office, March 1970), pp. 29–36. Carl Bereiter, "A Time to Experiment with Alternatives to Education," in *Farewell to Schools???* ed. Daniel U. Levine and Robert J. Havighurst (Worthington, Ohio: Charles A. Jones Publishing Company, 1971), pp. 15–24.

THE EDUCATIONAL IDEAL
VERSUS EDUCATIONAL REALITY

In no other institution of our society are the ideal and the reality so far apart as they are in education.

THE IDEAL. The teacher is a sensitive monitor of the child's entire process of growth and development, entering into it in manifold ways, never to hamper, but always to encourage and guide development toward the fullest realization of the child's potentialities. There are other educational purposes (such as a nation's need for technically trained manpower), but no other ideal comes close to all-around acceptability in a free society, and with increasing prosperity and security we should expect that other educational purposes will drop out of competition with this ideal. Thus, when we speak of education in America, we speak of one ideal, shared by almost all educators, even though they differ as to how it should be pursued.*

THE REALITY. Two to three dozen captive children are placed in the charge of a teacher of only modest intellectual ability and little learning, where they spend approximately six hours a day engaged in activities that someone has decided are good for them. In the course of 12 years they acquire a certain amount of worthwhile skill and knowledge, but only on the rarest occasions, if at all, do they encounter anything even remotely resembling the kind of teacher-pupil interaction prescribed as ideal.

IT IS TIME TO QUESTION THE IDEAL

The ideal of humanistic education — "that education in which the primary function of the schools is to cultivate the 'independence' of each 'individual' and to develop each person to the fullest" — has been with us since ancient Greece.[1] Today, it is accepted as virtually beyond question. Educators occasionally accuse one another of holding conflicting ideals, but this is mere mudslinging. Every scheme for educational reform is an attempt, whether misguided or not, to bring reality closer to the humanistic ideal.

Perhaps the humanistic ideal cannot be questioned on ideal grounds, but it can be questioned on practical grounds. The question may be phrased as follows: Is it better to approximate the humanistic ideal as best we can,

* Is this too reductionistic a statement?

regardless of how far we fall short, or is it better to pursue some other ideal more in keeping with the limits imposed by reality? ...

TALENT AS THE LIMITING FACTOR IN EDUCATION

During the seventies it should become clear that lack of money is not the primary factor accounting for the great discrepancy between the educational ideal and reality. If we are unwise, we may learn this lesson through bitter experience. We may invest heavily in electronic and paraprofessional aides in order to free teachers to carry out humanistic education, only to find that they cannot do so any better than they do now. We may extend schooling down into earlier childhood, only to discover that we have spread the supply of competent teachers more thinly than before. We may increase teacher salaries only to find that the quality of teachers remains the same. We may increase the attractiveness of school buildings, equipment, and materials, only to find that students become increasingly disaffected. If, on the other hand, we are wise, we may foresee these results and channel our resources into other kinds of provisions for children that will yield greater social benefits, even though the benefits are not ones that we can properly call educational.

At the bottom of these dismal predictions is the simple premise that humanistic education calls for a supply of teacher talent that cannot possibly be met on the scale for universal education. Educational philosophers, when expounding their particular version of humanistic education, are always ready to admit that the talent required for teachers to bring it off is of a very high level. They seem to feel, however, that the talent can be produced by exhortation, and enormous amounts of educational ink go each year into resounding calls for greatness. If what is required ideally is something more than a Socrates, what is required for even a reasonable approximation is something not much less. Rousseau, who deserves first credit for reestablishing the humanistic ideal in the modern world, was less optimistic: "How can a child be well educated unless by one who is well educated himself? Can this rare mortal be found? I do not know." [2]

The humanistic educator must be continually aware of the growing edge of the child's intellect and character. He must be exceedingly resourceful in seizing upon opportunities of the moment to turn them to educational account. To help the child learn, he must not only know what the child is to learn but know it so thoroughly that he can choose just the right question or demonstration or activity at just the right time. He cannot work from a prepared curriculum but must invent as he interacts with the child. He must at once be a good model and someone who does not force the child to be like himself or as he would like himself to be.

I could go on listing attributes, but let us try to jump from qualitative requirements to ones that can be quantified, realizing that much is lost in the process. It would stand to reason, I think that a minimum requirement for such an educator — a bare minimum, indeed — would be an IQ of 115. Those who would object that some very clever people will earn IQ scores of less than this ought also to agree that their number will be offset by people of higher IQ who are not so clever. By this requirement we limit the potential teaching population to a sixth of the total work force. The other requirements, which have more to do with personality, are not so easily quantified, but we might reasonably judge that no more than half of the people who meet the intelligence requirements would possess the other personal characteristics needed to function adequately as humanistic educators.[3] This reduces the potential supply of educators to a twelfth of the labor force.

Projections of census totals for the labor force and the student population (including those in postsecondary education) into the seventies indicates that about two-thirds as many people will be in school as will be working.[4] Therefore, if everyone who had the minimum talent to teach did teach, we should have a teacher-pupil ratio of one-to-eight. This ratio would be scarcely sufficient to carry on the kind of teacher-pupil interaction required for personalistic education, which is ideally a one-to-one operation. But, of course, we cannot expect that all or even most of the people who could teach would teach, since the qualifications are ones that also fit an increasing number of other careers (including careers in education other than teaching).

Thus, if for no other reason, humanistic education must fail on grounds of a simple shortage of talent. This shortage, moreover, is one that cannot be remedied by any immediate action. Conceivably, better education would produce more people qualified to educate, but such improvement could only come about slowly over generations of students, and for all we know the trend may be downward rather than upward. Educational technology may relieve the teacher of many burdens — it might even be able to take over entirely the teaching of specific skills and knowledge — but what remains for the teacher is the very kind of creative person-to-person activity for which talent is most wanting.

Proposals for reform of the educational system, far from promising to alleviate the strain on talent resources, almost invariably call for more teachers of more exalted caliber. This is true of traditionalist schemes for a return to basic disciplines as it is of radical schemes for the abandonment of definite curricula. It could not be otherwise, for they are all efforts to bring practice closer to the ideal of humanistic education. We must apply to them Daniel P. Moynihan's dictum that "systems that require immense amounts of extraordinarily competent people to run them are not going to run." [5]

THE HUMANISTIC IDEAL
DOES MORE HARM THAN GOOD

Thomas F. Green has claimed that, while educators almost universally claim to be pursuing humanistic education, what they do in reality is not concerned with developing individual potentialities but with training individuals to meet the needs of other institutions in the society.[6] It is no doubt true that what the public mainly expects of the schools is not the development of individual potentials but the teaching of socially useful skills — such as the three R's — and that the schools cannot avoid being responsive to this expectation. I believe it is incorrect, however, to infer from this that the commitment of educators to a humanistic ideology has no practical consequence.

In the first place, the humanistic commitment of educators has an effect — largely negative — on how they carry out their elementary training functions. In teaching reading and arithmetic, for instance, educators do not simply look for the most effective methods of achieving performance criteria. They tend to prefer, on ideological grounds, methods which seem to entail creativity, freedom of choice, discovery, challenges to thinking, democratic processes, and growth of self-knowledge. Moreover, they strive continually to win recognition for these values as more important than objective performance criteria.

In the second place, training in socially required skills does not begin to take up the entire school day. If schools restricted themselves to such training and attempted to do it as efficiently as possible, the school day might have to be only a third as long as it is now, and school costs could be lowered accordingly. Thus it is the addition of many other high-flown purposes, drawn from the humanistic ideal, that serves to justify the vast amount of time and money devoted to schooling and to motivate such costly proposals as year-round schooling and the extension of public education down into the early childhood years.

In the third place, educators are continually pressing for reforms that serve humanistic purposes in education. Nongrading, the open-plan school, the language experience approach, individualized instruction, and innovations of this sort are all reforms which would have the effect of shifting emphasis off training in elementary skills. Indeed, as these approaches come to be assimilated to common educational thinking, it becomes impossible to tell one from the other, because they all consist largely of reassertions of established tenets of humanistic education. And they all involve unrealistic requirements of teacher talent.

In the fourth place, humanistic values subtly infect the ways pupils and teachers are evaluated. Even if correctness and docility are still the attributes most consistently rewarded in students, there is a tendency for the less imaginative, insightful, or independent students to be regarded as failures; and such students are bound to get the message. Such students are put in a very agonizing position, since they are being condemned for failure to learn things that are not actually being taught. Teachers also tend to be evaluated and to evaluate themselves on how well they promote humanistic goals. Since these goals cannot be achieved, teachers are demoralized. Many of them are fine people and could be quite competent in training, but humanistic ideology often forces them to denigrate their own strengths.

This brings us to the last and most ignominious way in which humanistic ideology interacts with the training function of schools. It is that mechanisms of training are applied not only to the skill-learning purposes for which they are appropriate but also to other, humanistically-based purposes for which they are radically unsuited. The result is pseudotraining — ritualistic behavior that has the appearance of training but does not produce any of its desirable results. In social studies, science, and literature, teachers will often claim to be helping students to develop deep understanding, thinking abilities, attitudes, interests, and values. Lacking any definite ways of promoting such development, however, they fall back on memorization, lecture and exhortation, tasks that amount to no more than busy work, and endless practice. Even activities that are less mechanical, such as discussions, "projects," experiments, themes, and field trips, are robbed of what intrinsic merits they might have by efforts to turn them to educational account. Discussions become mealy-mouthed, ill-timed, and pointless; projects become mere copy work; experiments turn into dull problems or the following of recipes; themes become exercises in grammar; and field trips become holidays.

Most of what is so tedious, unprofitable, phony, and "irrelevant" in schooling is done not in the name of training in basic skills but in the name of the highest-sounding humanistic objectives. Radical critics of education find this anomaly perverse, and seem to think that if only educators could get their values straight they would do better. But the anomaly is built into the very structure of mass education. Most teachers cannot educate in the humanistic sense, and of those who can, few are able to do so even sporadically under the pupil loads they bear.

CURRENT MOVEMENTS AWAY FROM EDUCATION

Under the impulse of humanistic ideology, many schools are moving away from the kind of pseudotraining I have described to a type of program in which the pupil is free much of the time to do what he wants. In practice, societal demands for training are usually still recognized, but only limited portions of the day are devoted to meeting them. Individual development is seen as something that will occur pretty much by itself, and the teacher's main job is to refrain from obstructing it. One of the more recent trends is to get away from confining children to school at all, allowing them to pursue their interests in the community at large.*

To the extent that development is truly left up to the child, this type of program amounts to the abandonment of humanistic education in favor of a more simplistic faith in nature. However, these types of programs carry, if anything, an even heavier burden of educational purpose than existing ones. As a result they are even more unrealistic and potentially harmful. The following are some of the disadvantages of this educational approach:

1. Expectations of personal growth in such areas as creativity and understanding are heightened, while the teacher is provided with even less that she can do to bring it about. This can induce a feeling of helplessness in teachers and failure in students.

2. The teacher is expected to monitor the growth process in subtle and unspecified ways, thus to function fully as a humanistic educator, which few teachers are talented enough to do.

3. Since the entire program is carried out under the auspices of the school system, it is continuously vulnerable to pressure from a public which expects something quite different from its schools.

4. The laissez-faire approach is frequently generalized to areas of skill training, where it will likely lead to a deterioration in achievement.

5. A concern to make activities educational is likely to lead to limiting the options open to children and to corruption of activities which they might otherwise enjoy.

6. Such programs are costly, not only because of the need to provide a greater variety of facilities and materials but also because more teachers are required to supervise children when they are all engaged in different activities. When educational programs are extended into the community, there are added costs from the greater demand for community facilities, while teacher costs increase even further.[7]

7. Providing an optimum environment is something that professional educators are not necessarily the best qualified people to do. An enormous variety of specialized talents are applicable, and there is no reason why the utilization of these talents should be centralized. Moreover, as a public institution the school system is barred from partisan, sectarian, or controversial activities that ought to be available to children under a truly open program.

---

* Programs of this type are discussed in Section 11.

WHY NOT ABANDON THE EFFORT
AT HUMANISTIC EDUCATION ALTOGETHER?

I have argued that current and proposed methods of carrying out humanistic education through the schools only make a mockery of it and that such education is impossible to achieve on a mass basis. Current movements away from education, however, suggest a logical next step consisting of the following changes:

1. Restrict the responsibility of the schools entirely to training in well-defined, clearly teachable skills. This should require only about a third of the cost in money, personnel, and time that schooling costs now. What would be lost would be largely good riddance, and with exclusive concentration on training the schools could probably do a much more efficient and pleasing job of it than they do now.

2. Set children free the rest of the time to do what they want, but in doing so get them out from under the authority of the schools. Provide more economical forms of custodial care and guidance, as needed, and do it without educational intent.

3. Use the large amount of money thus saved to provide an enormously enriched supply of cultural resources for children, with which they can spend their new-found free time. These resources may reflect humanistic values to the fullest, but they should not carry any burden of educational intent, in the sense of trying to direct or improve upon the course of personal development. They should simply be resources and activities considered worthy in their own right.

4. Do not restrict children to these publicly sponsored activities. Maintain an open cultural market, in which proponents of diverse activities may compete to attract children to them.

This proposal has, I believe, all of the genuine advantages of the current movements toward freer, more humanistic education, while avoiding the seven faults noted above.* In addition it has the potentiality of enriching the cultural life of our communities in ways by which all citizens would benefit — by increasing the supply of cultural resources, some of which would be of value to adults as well as children, and also by freeing young people to pursue activities through which they could contribute their talents to society.[8]

If humanistic education existed, it would be a shame to lose it; if it could exist we should try to achieve it. When I discuss with people this

* Here's a specific proposal for improving education. Should it be given a try?

proposal to abandon pursuit of humanistic education, I am repeatedly met with personal anecdotes about the one teacher in a person's school career who changed his life, who opened up to him a vision of what he could become and started him on the road to becoming it. These single events are taken as sufficient to offset all the dross that filled most of their school days and to justify the continued largely futile pursuit of the humanistic ideal of education. To this argument I would only reply that such rare encounters, which are indeed the essence of humanistic education, are more likely to occur in a system where children are free to seek their own contacts in the cultural world.* . . .

EXERCISE

1. According to Bereiter, what is the educational ideal and the educational reality? (p. 66)
2. According to Bereiter, what is the main reason why the humanistic ideal in education cannot be achieved? (pp. 67, 68)
3. What are five ways in which Bereiter thinks humanistic ideals have had a negative influence on education? (pp. 69–70)
4. What are three disadvantages that Bereiter sees in student-determined education? (p. 71)
5. What ideal does Bereiter see as the main function of the schools? (p. 72)

* Isn't Bereiter advocating humanistic education, in effect?

Teacher Questioning and Reading

Frank J. Guszak

Frank J. Guszak has investigated the questions that teachers ask in elementary school. His results indicate that teachers emphasize fact questions, which only require the child to recall details of what he has read. According to Guszak, teachers ask too few questions that stimulate the development of higher cognitive processes. His classification of questions is based on Benjamin Bloom's well-known taxonomy of cognitive objectives.

From *The Reading Teacher*, 21, December 1967, 227–234. Reprinted with permission of Frank J. Guszak and the International Reading Association.

Consider the following questions as you read this selection (we've classified them using Guszak's Question-Response Inventory):

In your own words, what was Guszak's study about? (Translation)

What results do you think Guszak would have found if he had included teaching in other subjects besides reading? (Conjecture)

Why don't elementary school teachers ask more conjecture, explanation, and evaluation questions? (Explanation)

Do you think that asking conjecture, explanation, and evaluation questions helps the teacher to achieve important learning objectives? (Evaluation)

In 1917, Thorndike outlined a classic definition of reading in three words when he said, "Reading is thinking." Fifty years later, the conversation on the reading scene is still concerned with reading as thinking with regard to how varied reading-thinking skills can be developed within the classroom. Despite the numerous treatments of such reading-thinking skills as "critical reading skills" in the professional press, contentions abound that classroom teachers are doing little to develop a variety of reading-thinking skills. Rather, according to Austin and Morrison (1964) and Henry (1963), teachers appear to equate reading-thinking skills with the most narrow of literal comprehension skills.

Because standardized reading tests tend to measure literal comprehension skills, it is difficult to make wide assessments of pupils' abilities in various reading-thinking areas. In the absence of such test results, it seems advisable to examine the interaction between teachers and students in the reading circle as they engage in the development of reading-thinking skills. Thus, the current study was initiated in an effort to make determinations about the state of reading-thinking skills development as it occurred in the context of the reading group in the elementary grades. . . .

SUBJECTS AND PROCEDURES

From a population of 106 second, fourth, and sixth grade teachers in a public school system in Texas, a sample of four teachers (and their respective students) at each of these grade levels was randomly selected for the study. The mean class size of the three grades was as follows: second grade, 29.7; fourth grade, 24.7; and sixth grade, 28.5. Three reading-group structures were operant in all of the second and fourth grade classrooms while such a functional structure was found in only one of the sixth grade classrooms. Each reading group in the twelve classrooms was observed and recorded over a three-day period (an average of approximately five hours per classroom). The taped recordings were subsequently transcribed to written protocols and analyzed in accordance with the research questions.

RESULTS

... The initial study task was one of making a determination of what kinds of questions teachers ask about reading assignments.* An extensive survey was made of the following: reading-thinking skills as identified in basal series, reading-thinking skills as identified by reading authors, and representative thinking models. From these sources, the most pertinent conceptualizations of reading-thinking skills were synthesized into the model that subsequently was called the Reading Comprehension Question-Response Inventory. After repeated testing, the instrument was found to possess face validity and reliability when applied to teacher questions and student responses in a pilot study.

Reading Comprehension Question-Response Inventory

RECOGNITION. These questions call upon the students to utilize their literal comprehension skills in the task of locating information from reading context. Frequently, such questions are employed in the guided reading portion of a story, i.e., Find what Little Red Ridinghood says to the wolf.

RECALL. Recall questions, like recognition questions, concern literal comprehension. The recall question calls upon the student to demonstrate his comprehension by recalling factual material previously read. Generally, such activity is primarily concerned with the retrieval of small pieces of factual material, but the size of the pieces may vary greatly. An example of a recall question would be the following where the answer to the question is clearly printed in the text, i.e., What was Little Red Ridinghood carrying in the basket?

TRANSLATION. Translation questions require the student to render an objective, part-for-part rendering of a communication. As such, the behavior is characterized by literal understanding in that the translator does not have to discover intricate relationships, implications, or subtle meanings. Translation questions frequently call upon students to change words, ideas, and pictures into different symbolic form as is illustrated in the following from Bloom (1956).

Translation from one level of abstraction to another; abstract to concrete, lengthy to brief communication, i.e., Briefly re-tell the story of Little Red Ridinghood.

* Guszak seems to imply that teacher questions are important in developing student thinking skills. Do you agree?

Translation from one symbolic form to another, i.e., Draw a picture of the first meeting between Little Red Ridinghood and the wolf.

Translation from one verbal form to another; non-literal statements to ordinary English (metaphor, symbolism).

CONJECTURE. These questions call for a "cognitive leap" on the part of the student as to what will happen or what might happen. As such, the conjecture is an anticipatory thought and not a rationale, i.e., What do you think that Little Red Ridinghood will do in the future when she meets a wolf in the forest?

EXPLANATION. Explanation questions, like conjecture questions, are inferential in nature. However, the inference involved in the explanation situations calls upon the student to supply a rationale. The rationale must be inferred by the student from the context developed or go beyond it if the situation is data-poor in terms of providing a rationale. Instances of explanatory behaviors are found in the following: explanations of value positions, i.e., Explain why you like Little Red Ridinghood best?; conclusions, i.e., Explain why the wolf wanted to eat Little Red Ridinghood.; main ideas, What is the main idea of this story?

EVALUATION. Evaluation questions deal with matters of value rather than matters of fact or inference and are thus characterized by their judgmental quality (worth, acceptability, probability, etc.) The following components of this category are adapted from a classification scheme by Aschner and Gallagher (1965).

Questions calling for a rating (good, bad, true, etc.) on some item (idea, person, etc.) in terms of some scale of values provided by the teacher, i.e., Do you think that this was a good or bad story?

Questions calling for a value judgment on a dimension set up by the teacher. Generally, these are "yes" or "no" responses following questions such as "Would you have liked Tom for a brother?"

Questions that develop from conjectural questions when the question is qualified by probability statements such as "most likely." "Do you think that it is most likely or least likely?"

Questions that present the pupil with a choice of two or more alternatives and require a choice, i.e., "Who did the better job in your opinion, Mary or Susan?"

With the determination of the categories of the Reading Comprehension Question-Response Inventory the first question concerning the kinds of questions asked by teachers was answered. Comparative frequency of the six question types is reported in Table 1.

TABLE 1

Percentages of Each Question Type
in Grades Two, Four, and Six

Grade	Recog.	Recall	Transl.	Conjec.	Explan.	Evalua.
Two	12.3	66.5	.2	5.7	3.8	11.5
Four	16.3	48.4	.6	6.9	7.4	20.4
Six	10.2	47.6	2.4	7.9	8.1	13.8
Total	13.5	56.9	.6	6.5	7.2	15.3

Total questions recorded numbered 1857 — 878 in grade two; 725, grade four; 254, grade six. The teachers spent the greatest portion of their questions on the literal comprehension realms of "recall" and "recognition." Seemingly, the observations tend to support the contention that elementary reading teachers dwell on literal comprehension. It should be added that "dwell" is imprecise as is any determination about what percentage of questions shoud be asked in each category.

Although 15.3 per cent of the teachers' questions were spent on evaluation questions, there seems to be some legitimate doubt about the thinking depth they required. A close inspection of the questions in this category revealed that nearly all called for a simple "yes" or "no" response. Thus, the measure of higher level thinking seemed to be the incidence of questions in the inferential categories of "conjecture" and "explanation." These combined categories accounted for 13.7 per cent of the teachers' questions.

The old adage that "children learn to read in the primary grades and read to learn in the intermediate grades" seems to be borne out if one interprets an increase in inferential questioning as an increase in "reading to learn." There was a pattern of decrease in literal questioning as children reach the higher grade levels. The supplementary observations of the researchers indicated that second grade teachers spent many questions upon the minute, developing details of most story sequences. This close comprehension check is further evidenced by the greater frequency of questioning in the lower grades. . . .

CONCLUSIONS AND IMPLICATIONS

Although the following conclusions and the implications based upon them are aimed specifically at the sample teachers, it is the feeling of the researcher that these items may be keenly appropriate to a much wider group of teachers.

... Conceivably, the expenditure of nearly seventy of a hundred questions in the literal comprehension areas may be justified. Unjustifiable, however, is the involvement of these so-called literal comprehension questions with retrieval of the trivial factual makeup of stories.* In real life reading situations, readers seldom approach reading with the purpose of trying to commit all the minute facts to memory. Rather, the reader is more interested in getting broad understandings of the material, finding out specific things commensurate with his interests or other needs, etc. It would appear, then that much of the recall questioning actually leads the students away from basic literal understandings of story plots, events, and sequences. It seems quite possible that students in these recall situations may miss the literal understanding of the broad text in their effort to satisfy the trivial fact questions of the teachers. Seemingly, if teachers want to get at utilitarian aspects of literal understanding, they would offer many situations (rather than the few evidenced) for translational activities wherein they could really determine the extent to which children were understanding the literal elements. Of course, before teachers can employ more comprehensive questioning patterns, they must be aware of such. Thus, reading series should clearly spell out their comprehension structures in such a way that classroom teachers can have some clear insights into their task in comprehension development....

... If educators want to condition students for irresponsible citizenship, it seems quite appropriate to ask children for unsupported value statements, a practice which is very frequent in the reading circle according to this study. It seems imperative that teachers pattern the all-important "why" questions after students take positions. Until such is the common practice it seems that teachers will condition students to take value positions without the vital weighing of evidence that seems to separate the thinking individual from the mob member. Perhaps the use of a tape recorder would indicate to teachers their patterning practices with regard to such potentially dangerous questioning practices.†

EXERCISE

1. What was Guszak's main purpose in conducting this research project? (p. 74)
2. What was the main finding of Guszak's study? (p. 77)
3. Which categories in the Reading Comprehension Question-Response Inventory require more than literal comprehension? (pp. 75–76)

* Is this practice "unjustifiable"? Can you think of a justification?
† Do you think this research study made a useful contribution to educational practice?

4. As Guszak interpreted his data, what percentage of questions called for true higher-level thinking? (p. 77)

5. What does Guszak recommend that a teacher do after a child gives an unsupported value statement? (p. 78)

Imperatives in Ethnic Minority Education

James A. Banks

James A. Banks argues that all students need to learn about the racial problems in American society. He holds the schools account-able for helping minority students acquire a positive self-concept, knowledge about institutional racism, and skills in political activism. White students, on the other hand, need to acquire positive atti-tudes toward minority groups, an awareness of their cultural ethno-centrism, and knowledge of racism in American history. Banks believes that schools must go beyond their traditional role of impart-ing knowledge; they must also shape attitudes and develop skills of political activism. Do you think educators have the responsibility to undertake such tasks? What is the process by which such attitudes and skills are learned?

As we approach the threshold of the twenty-first century, our nation is witnessing technological progress which has been unparalleled in human history, yet is plagued with social problems of such magnitude that they pose a serious threat to the ideals of American democracy and to man's very survival. Environmental pollution, poverty, war, deteriorating cities, and ethnic conflict are the intractable social problems which Americans must resolve if we are to survive and create a just, humane society. Our society is becoming increasingly polarized and dehumanized, largely be-cause of institutional racism and ethnic hostility. The elimination of con-flicts between the races must be our top priority for the seventies.

One of the founding principles of this nation was that oppressed peoples from other lands would find in America tolerance and acceptance, if not a utopia for the full development of their potential. People who were

From *Phi Delta Kappan*, 53, January 1972, 266–269. Copyright © 1972 by Phi Delta Kappa. Reprinted with permission of Phi Delta Kappa and James A. Banks.

denied religious, economic, and political freedom flocked to the New World in search of a better life. Perhaps more than any nation in human history, the United States has succeeded in culturally assimilating its immigrants and providing them with the opportunity to attain the "good life." The elimination of differences among peoples of diverse nationalities was the essence of the "melting pot" concept.

While the United States has successfully assimilated ethnic groups which shared a set of values and behavior patterns of European origin, it has blatantly denied its black, brown, red, and yellow citizens the opportunity to share fully in the American Dream because they possess physical and cultural characteristics which are non-European. Ethnic minority groups have been the victims of institutional racism in America primarily because of their unique physical traits and the myths which emerged extolling the intrinsic virtues of European civilization and describing non-European peoples as ruthless savages. European and white ancestry have been the primary requisites for full realization of the American Dream. For most colored peoples in the United States, the dream has been deferred. The shattered dream and the denial of equal opportunities to ethnic minority groups have been the sources of acute ethnic conflict within America; it has now reached crisis proportions. The flames that burned in Watts, the blood that ran in Detroit, and now the Attica massacre are alarming manifestations of our inability to resolve conflicts between the majority and ethnic minority groups in America.

No sensitive and perceptive student of American society can deny the seriousness of our current racial problems. In recent years they have intensified as blacks and other powerless ethnic groups have taken aggressive actions to liberate themselves from oppression. Reactions of the white community to the new ethnic militancy have been intense and persisting. A "law and order" cult has emerged to eradicate ethnic revolts. To many white Americans, the plea for law and order is a call for an end to protests by ethnic groups and alienated youths. The fact that many law and order advocates demanded that Lt. Calley go free after a military jury convicted him for killing numbers of civilian colored peoples in Asia indicates that many "middle" Americans do not consistently value law, order, or human life. The law and order movement is directed primarily toward the poor, the colored, and the powerless. One example is the "no-knock" law in Washington, D.C. Although promises to bring law and order to the street often ensure victory in public elections, the most costly and destructive crimes in America are committed by powerful syndicates, corrupted government officials, and industries that pollute our environment, not by the ghetto looter and the petty thief. Also, few constructive actions have been taken by local and national leaders to eliminate the hopelessness, alienation, and poverty which often cause the ghetto dweller to violate laws in order to survive. As our nation becomes increasingly polarized, we are rapidly becoming two separate and unequal societies.[1]

Because the public school is an integral part of our social system, it has been a partner in the denial of equal opportunities to America's ethnic minorities; it has served mainly to perpetuate the status quo and to reinforce social class and racial stratification. Sensitive and perceptive writers such as Kozol and Kohl, and researchers like Pettigrew and Coleman, have extensively documented the ways in which the public schools make the ethnic child feel "invisible," while at the same time teaching the American Dream. Such contradictory behavior on the part of educators makes the ethnic minority child, as Baldwin has insightfully stated, run "the risk of becoming schizophrenic." [2]

Despite the school's reluctance to initiate social change, despite its tendency to reinforce and perpetuate the status quo, whenever our nation faces a crisis we call upon the school to help resolve it. Obviously, this is not because schools have historically responded creatively and imaginatively to social problems. It is because many Americans retain an unshaken faith in the school's *potential* for improving society. *I* share that faith. The school does have potential to promote and lead constructive social change. In fact, it may be the only institution within our society which can spearhead the changes essential to prevent racial wars and chaos in America. I would now like to propose a number of changes which must take place in the school if it is going to exercise a leadership role in eliminating ethnic hostility and conflict in America.

Because the teacher is the most important variable in the child's learning environment, classroom teachers must develop more positive attitudes toward ethnic minorities and their cultures and must develop higher academic expectations for ethnic youths. Teacher attitudes and expectations have a profound impact on students' perceptions, academic behavior, self-concepts, and beliefs. Many teachers do not accept and respect the diverse cultures of ethnic youths, hence ethnic students often find the school's culture alien. The "cultural clash" in the classroom is by now a cliché. Studies by scholars such as Becker, Gottlieb, and Clark indicate that teachers typically have negative attitudes and low academic expectations for their black, brown, red, and poor pupils. Other research suggests that teachers, next to parents, are the most "significant others" in children's lives, and that teachers play an important role in the formation of children's racial attitudes and beliefs. A study by Davidson and Lang indicates that the assessment a child makes of himself is significantly related to the evaluation that "significant" people, such as teachers, make of him.[3]

It is necessary for *all* teachers to view ethnic groups and their cultures more positively, whether they teach in suburbia or in the inner city. The problems in the ghetto are deeply implicated in the larger society. Our future presidents, senators, mayors, policemen, and absentee landlords are taught in suburban classrooms. Unless teachers can succeed in helping these future leaders to develop more humane attitudes toward ethnic minorities, the ghetto will continue to thrive and destroy human lives.

The research on changing teacher attitudes is both sparse and inconclusive. It suggests that changing the racial attitudes of adults is a herculean task. However, the *urgency* of our racial problems demands that we act on the basis of current research. To maximize the chances for successful attitude intervention programs, experiences must be designed specifically for that purpose. Programs with general or global objectives are not likely to be successful. Courses which consist primarily or exclusively of lecture presentations have little impact. Diverse experiences, such as seminars, visitations, community involvement, committee work, guest speakers, movies, multimedia materials, and workshops, combined with factual lectures, are more effective than any single approach. Community involvement and contact (with the appropriate norms in the social setting) are the most productive techniques. Psychotherapy and T-grouping, if led by competent persons, are also promising strategies.[4] *

Teachers must help ethnic minority students to augment their self-concepts, to feel more positively toward their own cultures, to develop a sense of political efficacy, and to master strategies which will enable them to liberate themselves from physical and psychological oppression. There is a movement among ethnic minority groups to reject their old identities, shaped largely by white society, and to create new ones, shaped by themselves. The calls for black, red, brown, and yellow power are rallying cries of these movements. However, despite the positive changes which have resulted from these identity quests, most ethnic minority youths still live in dehumanizing ghettos which tell them that black, brown, and red are ugly and shameful. They have many hostile teachers and administrators who reinforce the negative lessons which they learn from their immediate environment.† Ethnic youths cannot believe that they are beautiful people as long as they have social contacts within the school and the larger society which contradict that belief. While current research is inconclusive and contradictory, the *bulk* of it indicates that recent attempts at self-determination *have not* significantly changed the self-concepts and self-evaluations of most ethnic minority children and youths.[5]

Despite the need for ethnic studies by *all* youths, ethnic content alone

* *Why might these techniques be productive in producing attitude change?*
† *How might the "reinforcement" occur? Compare with Skinner's use of the term (see Skinner, Section 1).*

will not help minority youths to feel more positively about themselves and their cultures, nor will it help them develop a sense of control over their destinies. A school atmosphere must be created which values and accepts cultural differences, and ethnic youths must be taught how they have been victimized by institutional racism. They must become involved in social action projects which will teach them how to influence and change social and political institutions. One of the major goals of ethnic studies should be to help ethnic minority students become effective and rational political activists. We must provide opportunities for them to participate in social action projects so that they can become adept in influencing public policy which affects their lives. We now educate students for political apathy. They are taught that every citizen gets equal protection under the law, that racism only exists in the South, and that if they vote regularly and obey laws our benign political leaders will make sure that they will get their slice of the American Dream pie. The powerlessness and widespread political alienation among blacks, Chicanos, Indians, Puerto Ricans, and other poor peoples are deceptively evaded in such mythical lessons about our political system. We must teach ethnic youths how to obtain and exercise political power in order for them to liberate themselves from physical and psychological captivity. Their liberation might be the salvation of our confused and divided society.

There is also an urgent need for ethnic studies to help white students expand their conception of humanity. Many whites seem to believe that they are the only *humans* on earth. To the extent that a people excludes other humans from their conception of humanity, they themselves are dehumanized. Racism has dehumanized many whites and caused them to exclude ethnic minority groups from their definition of humanity. The differential reactions by the majority of whites to the killings of blacks and whites in recent years indicate how whites often consider blacks and other ethnic groups less than human. During the racial rebellions that broke out in our cities in the early 1900's, the 1940's, and the late 1960's, hundreds of blacks were killed by police because they were protesting against injustices and grinding poverty. Many of these victims were innocent bystanders. In 1969, two black students were shot by police on the campus of a black college in South Carolina. The majority of white Americans remained conspicuously silent during these tragedies; a few even applauded. The tragedy at Kent State evoked strong reactions and protest by many white Americans, but no similarly strong reactions followed the tragedy at Jackson State. Reactions of the majority of white Americans to the My Lai massacre and the Attica incident were not as intense as the reaction to the Kent State tragedy.

Each of these dehumanizing events — the killings of ghetto blacks, the incidents at Kent State and Jackson State, the My Lai massacre, and the

Attica tragedy — should have caused *all* Americans to become saddened, anguished, and outraged. The American dilemma which these incidents illuminated is that Americans are capable of reacting to the killing of human beings differently because of differences in their skin color and social class. While people may start treating others in dehumanizing ways because of their skin color or social class, the dehumanizing process, once started, continues unabated. Unless aggressive efforts are made to humanize white students, future incidents such as Kent State may leave the majority of Americans emotionally untouched. The issue of helping students become more humanized ultimately transcends race and social class. However, helping students see ethnic minorities as fellow humans is imperative if we are to eliminate our racial problems.

Ethnic content can serve as an excellent vehicle to help white students expand their conceptions of humanity and to better understand their own cultures. Since cultures are man-made, there are many ways of being human. The white middle-class life-style is one way; the Spanish Harlem culture is another. By studying this important generalization, students will develop an appreciation for man's great capacity to create a diversity of life-styles and to adapt to a variety of social and physical environments. Most groups tend to think that their culture is superior to all others. Chauvinist ethnocentrism is especially acute among dominant groups in American society. By studying other ways of being and living, students will see how bound they are by their own values, perceptions, and prejudices. The cultures of our powerless ethnic groups, and the devastating experiences of America's oppressed black, brown, red, and yellow peoples, are shocking testimony to the criminal effects of racism on its victims. Ethnic content can serve as an excellent lens to help white America see itself clearly, and hopefully to become more humanized.*

We must construct new conceptions of human intelligence and devise instructional programs based on these novel ideas to improve the education of ethnic minority groups. Brookover and Erickson have summarized the conceptions of human intelligence on which most current educational programs are based: "1) that ability to learn is relatively fixed and unchangeable and 2) that it is predetermined by heredity. . . . These beliefs assume that ability is unaffected by external social forces. Another common assumption is that fixed ability of individuals can be measured with reasonable accuracy by intelligence tests." [6] These pervasive and outmoded assumptions have led to unfortunate practices in our schools. Ethnic minority youths are often placed in low academic tracks, classified as mentally retarded, and exposed to an unstimulating educational environment because they perform poorly on I.Q. and other tests which were standardized on a

---

* Once ethnocentrism has been learned, can it be unlearned this way?

white middle-class population. These practices result in the self-fulfilling prophecy: Teachers assume that these pupils cannot learn, and they do not learn because teachers do not create the kinds of experiences which will enable them to master essential understandings and skills.

The traditional conceptions of human intelligence have been recently defended and popularized by Arthur S. Jensen. Jensen's research is based on unhelpful and faulty assumptions (he maintains, for example, that intelligence is what I.Q. tests measure). His argument is only a hypothesis, and should never have been presented to the general public in a popular magazine such as *Life* (since it is only a hypothesis) in these racially troubled times. I believe that *the hypothesis is immoral, misleading, and irrelevant*. Since we have no reliable and valid ways to determine innate potential, a moral assumption is that *all* students have the ability to master the skills and understandings which educators deem necessary for them to function adequately in our highly technological society; we should search for means to facilitate their acquisition of these skills and understandings and not spend valuable time trying to discover which ethnic group is born with "more" of "something" that we have not yet clearly defined.* As Robert E. L. Faris, the perceptive sociologist, has stated, "We essentially create our own level of human intelligence." [7]

Teachers must obtain a more liberal education, greater familiarity with ethnic cultures, and a more acute awareness of the *racist* assumptions on which much social research is based if they are to become effective change agents in minority education. Social science reflects the norms, values, and goals of the ruling and powerful groups in society; it validates those belief systems which are functional for people in power and dysfunctional for oppressed and powerless groups. Research which is antithetical to the interests of ruling and powerful groups is generally ignored by the scientific community and the society which supports it. [8] Numerous myths about ethnic minorities have been created by white "scholarly" historians and social scientists. Many teachers perpetuate the historical and social science myths which they learned in school and that are pervasive in textbooks because they are unaware of the racist assumptions on which social science research is often based. Much information in textbooks is designed to support the status quo and to keep powerless ethnic groups at the lower rungs of the social ladder.

Teachers often tell students that Columbus discovered America, yet the Indians were here centuries before Columbus. The Columbus myth in one sense denies the Indian child his past and thus his identity. Many teachers believe that Lincoln was the great emancipator of black people; yet he supported a move to deport blacks to Africa and issued the Emancipation Proclamation, in his own words, "as a military necessity" to weaken the

---

* For another view, read Arthur Jensen's paper (Section 4).

Confederacy. Primary grade teachers often try to convince the ghetto child that the policeman is his friend. Many ethnic minority students know from their experiences that some policemen are their enemies. Only when teachers get a truly liberal education about the nature of science and American society will they be able to correct such myths and distortions and make the school experience more realistic and meaningful for *all* students. Both pre- and in-service training is necessary to help teachers to gain a realistic perspective of American society.*

The severity of our current racial problems has rarely been exceeded in human history. The decaying cities, anti-busing movements, escalating poverty, increasing racial polarization, and the recent Attica tragedy are alarming manifestations of the ethnic hostility which is widespread throughout America. Our very existence may ultimately depend upon our creative abilities to solve our urgent racial problems. During the decade which recently closed, much discussion and analysis related to ethnic minority problems occurred, yet few constructive steps were taken to eliminate the basic causes of our racial crisis. Educators must take decisive steps to help create a culturally pluralistic society in which peoples of different colors can live in harmony. Immediate action is imperative if we are to prevent racial wars and chaos and the complete dehumanization of the American man.

EXERCISE

1. What does Banks see as the top priority for the 1970's in education? (p. 79)

2. What evidence does Banks use to document the seriousness of our current racial problems? (p. 80)

3. According to Banks what are at least four things that teachers must do to meet their obligation to reduce ethnic conflict in America? (pp. 81–82)

4. What do the research findings of Becker, Gottlieb, and Clark indicate about teacher attitudes toward ethnic minority children? (p. 81)

5. What does Banks see as the major goal of ethnic study curricula? (p. 83)

6. Why does Banks think that white children should study ethnic cultures? (pp. 83, 84)

7. What criticisms does Banks make of genetic conceptions of intelligence and IQ testing practices? (pp. 84–85)

* *If you plan to teach, would you want to have this training?*

Career Education:
Every Student Headed for a Goal

Sidney P. Marland, Jr.

Sidney Marland, who wrote this article while he was assistant secretary of the Department of Health, Education, and Welfare, suggests that student learning in the schools should emphasize career education. Major learning objectives would be to help the student decide on an occupation from among the 20,000 currently known, and to help him acquire the skills needed for his chosen occupation. Career education of the magnitude described by Marland is not a reality yet, but it is one well-defined direction in which our schools could go. Do you think that career education could serve as an alternative to James Banks's proposal for ethnic minority education? Do you agree with Marland that career education "can embrace within itself the special concerns and special needs of nearly all educational objectives"?

Reduced to its least common denominator, the goal of vocational and technical education is wonderfully simple. It is to educate students for specific types of work.

There is a wonderfully simple way to measure the success of these programs. You find out how many, or what percentage, of the graduates actually get jobs for which they are trained, and whether or not they work at them successfully as well-developed citizens.

Academic programs in high schools also have a simple goal when reduced to least common denominators: to prepare students to enter institutions of higher learning. The success measurement? The percentage of students who are accepted for higher education and who undertake such study with some degree of success. These would be basic and admittedly oversimplified measures that could be refined and elaborated in many ways....

Elementary and secondary education is a field marked by hard-working, dedicated individuals who are currently undertaking serious self-examination in an effort to discover how closely their work approaches the real national needs and the individual needs of the pupils. In the past decade or so, through the impetus of federal funding, an enormous amount of

From *American Vocational Journal*, 47, March 1972, pp. 34–38. Reprinted with permission of publisher, *American Vocational Journal*.

research has been done to improve teaching, to provide new instruments for educating the young, and to obtain accurate evaluations of programs.

In two areas of education we do fairly well if we are working with youngsters who have a reasonable amount of self-discipline and motivation. These areas are the ones I have just described, vocational and technical education on the one hand, and college preparatory education on the other. But the majority of students are not touched by these areas.

FAILING CURRICULUM

The majority of students do not prepare for particular jobs requiring skill training and they are not truly and systematically preparing for higher education, though some may drift in that direction. They are the students in the courses we customarily label "general education."

If we examine by any measure we care to use the accomplishment records of the schools of the nation, we find that the most severe failings can be found in the general education courses and with the young people who are enrolled in them.

Without undertaking a detailed discussion here of its nature and record, we can, nevertheless, say that the general curriculum's failings are self-evident. On paper, the students may or may not fail; in reality, the program fails. While passing grades may be awarded the general education student, his failure resides in his emphasis upon graduation.

We can say with confidence that the program fails because it has no real goals. It doesn't prepare students for a job nor does it prepare them for higher education; therefore we can't use the measures we use for the vocational education and college preparatory programs.

The fact is, no one knows what it is that should be measured in the general curriculum. It seems to be, in some vague way, education for its own sake — or even more euphemistically, "because it's the law." And yet we know that education, as a joint process of teaching and learning, works only when it is conducted for a purpose on the part of the learner, as well as the teacher.

The general curriculum, which engages the largest number of our students and which returns the worst record of failure, lacks the clear purpose which marks the other two areas of reasonable success.

FIRST, A CLEAR PURPOSE

I believe that all education must have a defined, stated purpose and I think we can agree on a statement of purpose for our system of formal elementary and secondary education. The purpose can be stated simply, but again this does not mean that it will be easy to reach:

The purpose of elementary and secondary education in the United States is to prepare all students as well-developed people to enter successfully either a job or some form of post-secondary education, whichever they choose, as soon as they leave the elementary-secondary educational system.*

This is one way to state briefly the overall goal — to develop citizens who function well in society. However, we educate in an imperfect society and under imperfect conditions. Young people, for very legitimate reasons although mostly unfortunate ones, frequently leave school before they are graduated.

I think our goal must include those who, for whatever reason, choose to leave the formal system at any point. In other words, the stated goal is to prepare each student to enter a job or advanced study, successfully, regardless of when he leaves our system.

Entry Ticket for the Dropout

This is not unrealistic. Perhaps we are unrealistic at present to think we can prescribe a "school-leaving age" in universal application. We could be most helpful, while dropouts are a widespread national phenomenon, if we could reduce the crushing effect that dropping out now creates.

If a pupil successfully completes ten grades say, at age 16, and drops out, he is often as ill-equipped to function in society as if he had never gone to school at all, according to present social expectations.

Those ten grades should be meaningful and should represent a level of success that is one grade higher than nine grades of education and one grade lower than eleven grades of education. This should mean an automatic entry ticket to a great many jobs. At present, of course, completion of only ten grades represents failure in our society's stereotype, and it is not an entry ticket to very much at all.

High Priority at USOE

Can we actually set as a national goal for education the preparation of each and every pupil for meaningful work or meaningful higher education lending itself to ultimate career entry and personal fulfillment? Can we keep the options open for *all* young people, so they do not have to choose unalterably at any age between the world of work and the world of continuing education?

Yes, we can, and we have done so. I have proposed, and the U.S. Office of Education has undertaken as a high priority activity, a direct and total confrontation with this concern for purposeful education. We call this new concept "career education."

We are deep into working out the details of how to meet this stated goal. As U.S. Commissioner of Education, I have spent a good deal of

* *Do you think most educators would agree that this is the purpose?*

time around the nation speaking to groups of people with a specific role to play in this new effort. These groups include secondary school administrators, vocational and technical education specialists, school counselors, business and industrial labor representatives.

The response is encouraging because education is a deep concern of people interested in our national development. A feeling of need for substantial change in our educational system pervades much of our profession and our citizenry. They see career education as a rational direction of change.

In the context of this encouragement we are supporting research and the implementation of model programs. These programs and the specifics of their operation remain local, as is all of our elementary and secondary education. The federal role is that of supplying financial support and technical assistance and advice. I will describe some broad ideas that have been put forth, and the stage of development of career education.

Must Be All-Encompassing

In the first place, if career education is to work in terms of the goal I stated, it must encompass the entire school program from kindergarten through secondary school completion. In addition, it should include the post-secondary level and adult and continuing education. This will involve changes in the curriculum as well as in teaching approaches. What we are doing is applying a wholly new concept to the entire system; change, therefore, will be substantial.

Besides encompassing every school year, career education will include all students. They will learn about the wide range of career possibilities in our technologically advanced society. They will learn what is involved in getting a job and holding it. They will receive sound guidance and counseling to help them consider their interests and abilities in relation to potential careers. They will learn of the occupational needs of the nation, as projected.

They will be helped to develop career decision-making skills. They will learn specific job skills. And they will get actual help in finding a job, because if career education is to succeed it cannot merely deliver its graduates to the labor market. There is a destructive gap between school and job, and the way to eliminate it is to bridge it ourselves as teachers.

Fifteen Clusters

To accomplish these things, we think that the curriculum should be built around jobs and work.* Experts have identified more than 20,000

* *Does this subvert education to the goals of employers?*

distinct jobs that people fill. We have had a team of specialists codify these jobs into 15 major groupings which we call career clusters. Some examples are health, marketing and distribution, public service, fine arts and humanities, and manufacturing.

Pupils in the first six grades would become familiar with all of these career clusters through instructional materials and field trips and the kinds of teaching approaches now used to complement courses in basic language, social studies, science, and mathematics.

In Grades 7 and 8, pupils would begin to explore those clusters that most interested them individually. In Grades 9 and 10, a pupil could explore a single cluster of his choice in depth and receive practical experience, even start to develop some specific skills in particular jobs.

In Grades 11 and 12, the student would pursue a selected career area more intensely with three options open to him: he could acquire enough skill to get employment as soon as he left school; he could get a combination of academic and job training courses in preparation for further occupational training at a post-secondary institution; or he could follow a program directed towards enrollment in higher education for a professional degree.

An important aspect of career education would be that opting back into school would be as easy as opting out. Maturity, changing interests, higher aspirations, and increased economic security are among the reasons for returning, and the schools and colleges would be receptive to such re-enrollments.

Out-of-School Models

In order to provide alternative choices, apart from the formal system, three out-of-school models are being developed for career education.

A home-based program would make extensive use of television, correspondence courses, and possibly, tutors. It would combine adult education with vocational education to open career opportunities to adults who have little hope of advancement at present. Women required to be at home would be a special target of this approach, as would handicapped persons.

An employer-based model would rely on industrial firms, businesses, labor, and government agencies to operate work-training programs related to their own varied employment needs. This program, providing basic academic learning along with skill training, would serve students still in school as well as those who might find the alternative more meaningful on a full-time basis.

A rural-residential model would serve entire families who would train together for better employment opportunities. One program based on this model is underway near Glasgow, Montana. It will serve a six-state region.

MAIN THRUST IN THE SCHOOLS

I believe, however, that it is in the established school system and colleges that the greatest number of individuals will be reached, and this is where we will be making our greatest effort. Teachers of all subjects will be encouraged to learn new techniques in relating their work to career education purposes.*

Classes in basic academic subjects will use career-oriented materials. There will be a far stronger role for guidance and counseling than now prevails.

The initial costs will be considerable; we must face this fact. There will be new expenses for planning, for curriculum revision, for training supervisors, counselors, and teachers, and for acquiring new instructional materials.

The best estimates I have indicate that after the "turn-around" costs of the first two or three years, the annual costs of operating such a program would still be slightly higher than current costs. But we would be accomplishing far more than we are at present in terms of developing productive and fulfilled human beings.

WHY CAREER EDUCATION?

One may ask what motivates the Office of Education to move vigorously toward career education as an agent of substantial change in our schools. Some statistics help in illustrating the large problems that confront us as a nation.

Of every ten students in high school, two receive occupational training of some sort and three go to college (although one of these drops out). This means that more than one-half of all students now in high school — 1,500,000 — ought to have opportunities, counseling, and attractive options in occupational training. The system, and the attitudes of young people and their parents, foreclose these conditions in most schools.

Here is another way of looking at the problem. In the 1970–71 school year there were 850,000 elementary and secondary school dropouts. There were 750,000 general education students who graduated from high school but who did not attend college and were not prepared for entering a job. There were 850,000 high school students who entered college (in 1967) but dropped out in 1970.

These three groups comprise an estimated total of 2,450,000 young people who should have had the opportunities for realistic education in

* *Would you want to specialize in teaching career education?*

career development but did not. Education is now the nation's largest enterprise, costing $85 billion a year, a figure surpassing the defense budget. Those 2,450,000 pupils cost us about $28 billion, which is almost one-third of the entire educational expenditure for the nation.

GETTING MORE REALISTIC

For years our secondary schools have been so strongly college-oriented that most of the effort, planning, and aspirations have been directed toward the academic program. And yet the Department of Labor tells us that for now and the foreseeable future, 80 percent of the nation's jobs will be handled by employees with less than a baccalaureate degree.

In some ways we are starting to be more realistic. In fiscal year 1970, one million more secondary school students were enrolled in vocational education courses than the year before, representing a 25 percent increase. Post-secondary vocational and technical education enrollments in fiscal 1970 exceeded one million, an increase of more than 40 percent over 1969.

Local and state governments, exceeding the requirements for matching funds, are spending five dollars on vocational education for every one dollar spent by the federal government.

We have been doing a good job in vocational education and training, and in vocational counseling, but only 12 to 14 percent of all high school students enter these programs. We have attached such emphasis to the baccalaureate degree that we have by implication downgraded other equally worthy options.

Career education would embrace vocational and technical education and go farther and wider. It would help direct every student toward a career goal, including those aiming for professions.

It would, I believe, greatly enhance the quality of learning in the academic subjects as a result of more realistic motivation. And it would enhance the vocational-technical training programs by attaching prestige and attention to the arena that they now occupy alone. That arena is where education is engaged in for a purpose and where a student can see for himself the relevance and usefulness of his efforts.*

CATCHING ON

Career education seems already to have the beginnings of a national movement. We have not consciously sought this degree of consensus,

* *Marland makes many claims for career education. How can they be tested through research?*

believing more time is needed for development and debating the concept among all concerned, especially teachers.

In examining the need for systematic progress, we have, besides developing models, asked each state to undertake plans (with federal funds) for one or more career education projects of its own. Even before this, many states had outstanding local programs in operation — Delaware, Georgia, Mississippi, New Jersey, North Dakota, and Wyoming, for example. . . .

A Focus for All Efforts

This is a time of great ferment and change in education; there is a tremendous amount of sound activity directed toward a great number of goals — universal literacy, raising levels of self-esteem, compensatory programs of all sorts to overcome physical, social, emotional, and cultural handicaps of youngsters in schools. They all have a special concern and a specific population to be reached. Career education is viewed as a new form for all young people in school. It can embrace within itself the special concerns and special needs of nearly all educational objectives.

We can bring these concerns and all of our extra, and very often separate, efforts together in a meaningful way if we have the wisdom, the courage, and the will to find a large new consensus on what the schools might be. Career education can be that goal.

EXERCISE

1. According to Marland, what are two areas of education in which the schools are fairly successful, and one area in which they fail? (p. 88)

2. What does Marland see as the goal of elementary and secondary education? (pp. 88–89)

3. According to Marland, what would be the goals of career education in Grades 1–6, 7–8, 9–10, and 11–12? (p. 91)

4. What are the three nonschool-based models of career education proposed by Marland? (p. 91)

5. What are two reasons that Marland gives for the importance of career education? (p. 92)

Human Development in the Elementary School Classroom

Harold Bessell

> *Harold Bessell, a psychotherapist in private practice, describes the type of curriculum project that Robert Ebel and Carl Bereiter argue against. For example Ebel earlier in this section states, "Schools are not adjustment centers, responsible for helping young people develop favorable self-concepts, solve personal problems, and come to terms with life." In contrast, Bessell believes the schools should take the responsibility for nurturing the personal development of students. He claims that his curriculum, the Human Development Program, and the instructional technique of the Magic Circle are based on sound psychological principles. Also, he believes that they accomplish three important learning objectives — self-awareness, a sense of mastery, and interpersonal communication skills. Bereiter would probably say that the Human Development Program will not work because there are so few trained, capable teachers who can carry out its objectives. Do you agree?*

For most patients, therapy is a painful, expensive, and protracted experience that often comes too late. Encounter group techniques,* as helpful as they can be, invariably labor under this shadow. The damage has been done; pain and guilt have twisted a human life into their own grotesque image. And the therapist must somehow piece this fragile, pain-filled human thing back together. Little wonder that therapy is rarely wholly successful. Our skills and knowedge abound in palliatives, but lasting cures are still rare. Moreover, for every patient we treat, it is an unhappy fact that there are hundreds, even thousands, more who desperately need therapy but cannot afford it or, even if they could, would not be able to find a qualified, let alone effective, therapist available to help them.[1]

These are disturbing truths that must perplex and trouble every therapist as he struggles with his responsibilities. They raise vital, nagging questions for all of us. It was in answer to these questions — and the frustration we

---

From Lawrence N. Solomon and Betty Berzon (eds.) *New Perspectives on Encounter Groups.* San Francisco: Jossey-Bass, 1972, pp. 349–367. Reprinted with permission of publisher and author.

* *The encounter group approach is explained in the glossary.*

all feel at the issues they imply — that the Human Development Program was born.

Simply described, the Human Development Program (HDP) is a curriculum designed for use in schools to foster the positive emotional development of children. Its basic structure consists of a daily encounter group called the Magic Circle, whose purpose is to stimulate and support emotional development. Provocative cues that are significant but nonthreatening are used to open children to a discussion of their feelings and life in such a way as to leave them feeling self-confident and worthwhile — and not eviscerated as many adults feel after intensive sensitivity sessions. Curriculum materials, including a theory manual and curriculum guides which I developed with Uvaldo H. Palomares, spell out the teaching techniques and provide a set of tested and sequenced cues for daily use in pre-school through grade three. . . . While evaluation studies are currently in progress, teachers* nevertheless report highly gratifying results: reduced discipline problems; greater personal involvement; increased verbal expressiveness; higher motivation to learn; greater self-confidence and constructive behavior. Teachers also verify the effect of the program on their own teaching styles and attitudes: They find themselves more flexible and able to cope with teaching problems, more comfortable, and less hostile and distrustful toward children.

The basic premise of the program can be summed up in two words: emotional development. Or to put it another way, the program is designed to prevent emotional problems by developing in each person a set of positive, adaptive skills to cope with problem situations. Therapy certainly has a continuing, useful role to play in treating emotional disorders, as do encounter group techniques. But in the absence of a certain cure for emotional problems, the old canard about an "ounce of prevention" became a challenging imperative. A new strategy was needed, one that focused on the emotional development of children.

Such a program does not spring out of the head of Jove or drop from the heavens; the Human Development Program is no exception. It was the outgrowth of more than seventeen years' experience as a practicing psychotherapist. A selected collection of psychological theories formed its theoretical base, and extensive, continuing research with children in classroom settings gave the program its present form.

The personality-development theory of Karen Horney (1950) provided the major theoretical basis of the program. Horney, who related personal growth to social relationships, concentrates on the basic drives to achieve mastery and to gain approval. Her conviction is that the competent, ap-

---

* *Do you accept teacher reports as valid evidence? Or would you prefer independent evaluation?*

proved child develops a healthy self-concept and the incentive to strive for further self-realization.

In addition, the phenomenon described by Harry Stack Sullivan (1947)* as the "delusion of uniqueness," the notion individuals have that they are different from others and therefore somehow inferior, became a focus for the Magic Circle groups. In these groups, children see and hear that others feel unsure and have fears, and each child can perceive that others in the group are much more like him in their thoughts and feelings than they are different from him.

The basic psychological thrust of the program — its content and organization — grew out of an observation based on years of practical experience. Patients in therapy invariably are deficient in three things: awareness, self-confidence, and an understanding of interpersonal relationships. They are not really aware of the emotional motives that influence their behavior; they lack a real and steady confidence in themselves as whole persons; and they only dimly understand why and how other human beings react to them. Thus, these three main areas of human experience and feeling became the basic themes of the program: awareness (knowing what your thoughts, feelings, and actions are); mastery (knowing what your abilities are and how to use them); and social interaction (knowing other people and how your behavior affects them and influences their behavior toward you).

The theory of awareness is as old as Plato, who discussed feelings and thoughts as they motivate man's behavior. From Plato (Jowett, 1946, pp. 425–434) through Freud (1961) to Bernard Bloom (1956),[2] philosophers and psychologists have arrived at the same notions: Awareness is a major area of human functioning, and a long array of disorders can be associated with insufficient emotional awareness. . . .

Our deepest challenge has been to develop a truly meaningful set of experiences that would stimulate constructive social interactions. We began by setting up simple experiences in which children could learn to talk about how people do nice and mean things to one another. Our goal was to develop a vocabulary for dialogue about feelings and to help children learn to perceive the emotional dynamics of social interaction. The four- and five-year-olds learned the language very quickly and enjoyed the chance to express themselves and to listen to one another. At this juncture the modified encounter group technique we employed demonstrated special value. When the children sat around in a circle, they tended to show and express understanding, kindness, inclusiveness, and helpfulness to a mark-

---

* Karen Horney and Harry Stack Sullivan were psychiatrists who developed theories of personality which stress the role of social relationships in the development of personality.

edly greater extent than they did when they were not seated in a circle arrangement. The children, recognizing this difference in themselves, named the circle sessions the Magic Circle.

To test our basic theories and assumptions, we enlisted the aid of Anna Lord at Twin Trees Nursery School (La Jolla, California). Here we set about to discover a number of vital things: Would children get involved with us, and could a simple vocabulary be devised to enable children to discuss awareness, confidence, and social interaction? The answers were affirmative. Several other practical considerations also became clear. To accomplish any growth, children must be exposed to emotionally maturing experiences every day. Teachers were willing to make this effort, but they needed a daily guide that would name the lesson and its objective, describe the procedure and its rationale, and provide some guidance on how to deal with problem situations. After a year's research testing various lessons, an organized set of lesson plans was devised and published as part of a basic theory manual (Bessell and Palomares, 1967).

The lesson guides were organized to expose children to a series of six-week units on each theme. On the awareness theme, the children devote one week to pleasant feelings, followed by one on pleasant thoughts and another on positive behavior. These same topics are then repeated for further development and reinforcement in the circle process.

On the theme of self-confidence, a six-week program progresses from mastery in naming things to mastery in numbers, motor coordination, performance skills, dress and hygiene, and social comprehension. As the children mature, these six categories are continued in the second semester at a more advanced level. We found that it was crucial to emphasize the fact that they were succeeding at their tasks and to give only secondary emphasis to the actual skill they were achieving. We were not as interested in what the child was learning as we were in the growth of his confidence in himself to cope effectively with any challenge.

On the social interaction theme, the six-week unit treated the following topics: one week each on what we do that people like and dislike; what other people do that we like and dislike; and how to ask for and offer kind behavior. While these six-week units make up a planned program, it is not rigid. Once the focal point of the session is identified by the teacher, the children can discuss it as freely as they wish. . . .

The Magic Circle with its discussion cues and personal interaction is the heart of the Human Development Program; it is the engine that makes it go.* Its basic strategy is to develop affective communication skills in children in their early, formative years while their emotions are still open to positive adaptive development. These skills are learned through daily practice of the two basic ingredients of communication — perception and expression.

What learning processes occur during discussion and interaction?

In essence, the Magic Circle functions as a highly efficient and sophisticated communications system. The circle configuration enables information, both cognitive and affective, to pass among children and the teacher quickly and in all directions. Each child in the circle sends and receives affective information; every day he becomes the focus of vast amounts of instant feedback. For the children this feedback is an impressive experience at receiving attention, praise, or acceptance. Thus, the Magic Circle becomes a vehicle for enlarging the child's emotional experience.

The teacher gently structures this deepening experience so that the child can learn important, adaptive lessons. Like a good facilitator, she generalizes explicitly about the experiences the children relate: "Johnny and Simpson and Fernando and I have all told about a bad dream we had, so you see everybody has them and they're scary, but there's nothing bad about you because everybody has them." In this way, the teacher gives children the support they need to learn important facts about themselves and their experiences.

Much of this information is conveyed verbally, and this in itself represents an important accomplishment. Most people do not really know how to talk about their emotional experience. They have never really learned to name what goes on inside them. The Magic Circle provides children with the opportunity and help to develop an affective vocabulary: "You're teasing me and I don't like it, but it probably means you like me and want to be my friend, so why not be friends."

But verbal comunication is by no means the complete story. People express many of their emotions in nonverbal ways. We tap our feet, bite our nails, blink our eyes, or slump in our chairs. In the Magic Circle, children learn to notice and pay attention to such nonverbal signs and learn to read them so accurately that by the time they are eight years old they can spot and discuss the discrepancies between what a person says he feels and what his behavior implies he feels.

In the Magic Circle, there are no lessons which the children passively absorb. On the contrary, the children are the lessons: Their own experience is the subject matter; their words and feelings, the learning medium. What children learn is what they emotionally want and need to learn — how to be more effective, how to feel better, and how to get along with people. These lessons are learned because the relevant information gets expressed and is then shaped, corrected, and refined by continuous feedback, not only by the teacher but principally from the other children.* . . .

Another important facet of the Magic Circle is to give the children a decision-making role. At an early stage, children are permitted to choose the game or topic of the day. Because they have a stake in this choice and its outcome, they have a natural opportunity to be responsible and com-

---

* Do you see a relationship between feedback and B. F. Skinner's concept of reinforcement (see Section 1)?

mitted. At the same time, they learn to participate in the democratic process through an experience that directly affects them. . . .

In concept and purpose, the Human Development Program is a bold and ambitious undertaking. One of our major tasks was to develop tools that would increase communication between teacher and child; the Magic Circle represents that tool. Its success in classrooms across the country has given us real hope that by teaching adaptive skills to young children we can develop a generation of children capable of becoming truly effective persons and citizens — a generation that will be aware of themselves and others, integrated and effective in their functioning, and humane and constructive in their social relationships. Today that vision is largely a dream. But even as we seek with our children to develop more sophisticated tools to realize such a generation, we know that the first steps have been taken.*

EXERCISE

1. List the main goal and the three subgoals of the Human Development Program and the Magic Circle. (p. 96)

2. How does the Magic Circle help to overcome the individual's "delusion of uniqueness"? (p. 97)

3. What are the topics covered in the six-week unit on social interaction? (p. 98)

4. What is the role of feedback, verbal communication, and nonverbal communication in the Magic Circle? (p. 99)

As a teacher, would you want to use the Human Development Program or a similar curriculum?

Forget You Are
a Teacher

Carl Rogers

> Carl Rogers has made many contributions to the fields of psychology, psychotherapy, and education. In this selection he criticizes education's traditional objective of imparting knowledge to the ex-

Reprinted from *Instructor*, © August/September 1971, The Instructor Publications, Inc., used by permission.

tent of calling it "an almost completely futile, wasteful, overrated function in today's changing world." Rogers does offer a positive alternative, though. He believes that students should learn what they want to learn. The goal of education should be to help students take responsibility for their own learning and to use their freedom constructively. Is Rogers' position on learning and teaching consistent with the goals of ethnic minority education advocated by James Banks and the goals of career education advocated by Sidney Marland in this section?

Not long ago, a teacher asked me, "What changes would you like to see in elementary education?" I answered the question as best as I could at the time, but it stayed with me. Suppose I had a magic wand that could produce only one change in our educational systems. What would that change be?

I finally decided that my imaginary wand would with one sweep cause every teacher at every level to forget that he is a teacher. You would all develop a complete amnesia for the teaching skills you have painstakingly acquired over the years. You would find that you were absolutely unable to teach.

Instead, you would find yourself holding the attitudes and possessed of the skills of a *facilitator of learning*. Why would I be so cruel as to rob teachers of their precious skills? It is because I feel that our educational institutions are in a desperate state; and that unless our schools can become exciting, fun-filled centers of learning, they are quite possibly doomed.

You may be thinking that "facilitator of learning" is just a fancy name for a teacher and that nothing at all would be changed. If so, you are mistaken. There is *no* resemblance between the traditional function of teaching and the function of the facilitator of learning.

The traditional teacher — the *good* traditional teacher — asks himself questions of this sort: "What do I think would be good for a student to learn at his particular age and level of competence? How can I plan a proper curriculum for him? How can I motivate him to learn this curriculum? How can I instruct him in such a way that he will gain the knowledge which he should have? How can I best examine him to see whether he has actually gained this knowledge?"

On the other hand, the facilitator of learning asks questions such as these, not of himself but of his *students:* "What do you want to learn? What things puzzle you? What are you curious about? What issues concern you? What problems do you wish you could solve?" When he has the answers to these questions, he asks himself, "Now how can I help him find the resources — the people, the experiences, the learning facilities, the books, the knowledge in myself — which will help him learn in ways that will provide answers to the things that concern him, the things he is eager to learn?"

The attitudes of the teacher and the facilitator are also at opposite poles. Traditional teaching, no matter how disguised, is based essentially on the mug-and-jug theory. The teacher asks himself: "How can I make the mug hold still while I fill it from the jug with these facts which the curriculum planners.and I regard as valuable?" The attitude of the facilitator has almost entirely to do with climate: "How can I create a psychological climate in which the child will feel free to be curious, will feel free to make mistakes, will feel free to learn from his environment, from fellow students, from me, from experience? How can I help him recapture the excitement of learning which was his in infancy?"*

Once this process of facilitation of wanted learning was underway, a school would become for the child "*my* school." He would feel that he was a living, vital part of a very satisfying process. Astonished adults would begin to hear children say, "I can't wait to get to school today." "For the first time in my life I'm finding out about the things *I* want to know." "Hey, drop that brick! Don't you break the windows in *my* school!"

Beautifully, the same phrases would be used by the retarded child, the gifted child, the ghetto child, the underprivileged child. This is because every student would be working on the problems of real concern and interest to him, at the level at which he could grasp the problem and find a useful solution. He would have a continuing experience of success.

Some educators believe that such individualized learning is completely impractical because it would involve an enormous increase in the number of teachers.† Nothing could be further from the truth. For one thing, when a child is eager to learn, he follows up his own leads and engages in a great deal of independent study on his own. There is also a great saving of the teacher's time because problems of discipline or "control" drop tremendously. Finally, the freedom of interaction which grows out of the climate I have so briefly described makes it possible to use a great untapped resource — the ability of one child to help another in his learning. For John to hear, "John, Ralph is having trouble carrying out the long division which he needs to solve his problem. I wonder if you could help him?" is a marvelous experience for both John and Ralph. It is even more marvelous for the two boys to work together, helping each other to learn, without being asked! John *really* learns long division when he tries to help another learner understand it. Ralph can accept the help and learn because he is not shown up as being stupid, either in public or on a report card.‡

Barbara Shiel tells of her exciting, challenging experiences when, almost

---

* Note the similarity to John Holt's view of teaching and learning (see Section 1).
† This is the view expressed by Carl Bereiter (in this section). Who do you think is correct — Bereiter or Rogers?
‡ For more on peer tutoring, read Herbert Thelen's article (Section 12).

desperate with a difficult sixth grade, she took the risk of trying — with many uncertainties, setbacks, and difficulties — to become a facilitator of learning rather than a teacher. It is such a human, exciting account that I made it the first chapter of my book, *Freedom to Learn* (Merrill, 1969). One of the results which most surprised Miss Shiel was that she had *more* time to spend with each child, not less, when she set each child free to learn.

I cannot stress too strongly how much I wish that someone could wave that magic wand and change teaching to facilitation. I deeply believe that traditional teaching is an almost completely futile, wasteful, overrated function in today's changing world. It is successful mostly in giving children who can't grasp the material a sense of failure. It also succeeds in persuading students to drop out, when they realize that the material taught is almost completely irrelevant to their lives. No one should ever be trying to learn something for which he sees no relevance. No child should ever experience the sense of failure imposed by our grading system, by criticism and ridicule from teachers and others, by rejection when he is slow to comprehend. The sense of failure he experiences when he tries something he wants to achieve that is actually too difficult for him is a healthy one which drives him to further learning. It is very different from a person-imposed failure, which must devalue him as a person.

The most basic of the attitudes that are essential to the facilitation of learning is realness or genuineness in the teacher's relationship with his students. You must take the risk of stepping out from behind your teacher role and becoming a person to your students.

Another outstanding attitude of those who facilitate learning is what I call "prizing" the learner — his feelings, his opinions, his person. It is an acceptance of the other as a person of worth, a basic belief that the other person is fundamentally trustworthy.

A third element is empathic understanding — the ability to understand the way the process of education and learning seems to the student. It is not "I understand what is wrong with you"; it's an attitude that causes the learner to think, "He understands how I feel!"

The methods for you to use in building freedom into your classroom must grow out of direct interaction with your students, and be suited to your own style. What you do *not* do is to set lesson tasks, assign reading, or lecture or expound (unless students ask you to). You do not require examinations or take sole responsibility for grades; you do not evaluate or criticize unless it is requested.

The sort of thing you can do is to draw out from your students their real problems relevant to the course at hand, thus tapping the child's intrinsic motivation. You can provide resources, making them easily available, both practically and psychologically. You can use such techniques as inquiry, simulation games, programmed instruction. You may find student contracts useful to give security and responsibility within an atmosphere of freedom. You will look for ways in which children can express their feelings, work through their own problems, become involved in evaluation of their own learning. You even trust the student's own feelings about himself enough not to force freedom upon him.* However, as the child slowly begins to develop his own value system and becomes less threatened by responsibility, he will be able to accept and use freedom to a greater and greater degree.

Gratifyingly, more and more people are joining me in feeling the urgency of the situation, and a growing number of schools are deeply involved in making educational freedom work. Teachers are forgetting to be teachers; and, in setting their students free to learn, are finding that they have also set themselves free. We have the theories, the methods, and the skills to radically change our whole educational system, and perhaps to rescue our civilization. *Do we have the courage?*

EXERCISE

1. According to Rogers, what are the main differences between a traditional teacher and a "facilitator of learning"? (pp. 101–102)

2. What are three reasons why Rogers believes his goal of individualized learning will not require a great increase in teaching staff? (p. 102)

3. What are three characteristics of Rogers's "facilitator of learning"? (p. 103)

4. According to Rogers, does individualized learning involve giving the student complete freedom? (p. 104)

* *Is Rogers saying that traditional teaching has a legitimate function?*

PART TWO

Factors That
Influence Learning

Section Three.

INTRODUCTION

Individual differences in school achievement are a basic reality for educators. Teachers find that some students learn more than others. District administrators find, too, that some schools have a higher level of scholastic achievement than others, even though the same curriculum is taught in each. Why?

Searching for causes of individual differences in school achievement is important because, first, the discovery of causal factors increases our understanding of the learning process, and second, the increased understanding can be used as a basis for school reform. For example, if some students learn more than others because they are exposed to certain instructional techniques, this knowledge can be used to help all students receive the benefit of these techniques.

Many factors have been suggested as causes of individual differences in school achievement, including the following: the student's background (parents' social class, ethnic culture, genetic determinants), his intelligence, the resources of his school (class size, amount of instruction offered), the quality of teaching to which he is exposed, and his or her sex. The following sections are indications that educators do not agree about the extent to which each factor causes students to do well or poorly in school.

The introductory selection is by Mary Jo Bane and Christopher Jencks, both of whom are affiliated with Harvard University. Unlike the authors of selections that follow, they consider various factors, rather than just one, that might influence school achievement. Their selection is a summary of a much longer study, *Inequality: A Reassessment of the Effect of Family and Schooling in America* (New York: Basic Books, 1972). Like its famous predecessor, the Coleman Report (discussed by Mayeske, Section 4), the study has provoked considerable controversy because of its authors' conclusion that schools have relatively little effect on students' learning of cognitive skills or on their economic success in later life. For example, Bane and Jencks state, "Our research suggests . . . that the character of a school's output depends largely on a single input, the characteristics of the entering children. Everything else — the school budget, its policies, the characteristics of the teachers — is either secondary or completely irrelevant. . . ."

This type of statement is strongly opposed by those who believe that the way to eliminate individual differences is through the schools. If you were a dedicated teacher or school administrator, how would you respond to Bane and Jencks's challenge?

The Schools and Equal Opportunity

Mary Jo Bane and Christopher Jencks

Americans have a recurrent fantasy that schools can solve their problems. Thus it was perhaps inevitable that, after we rediscovered poverty and inequality in the early 1960s, we turned to the schools for solutions. Yet the schools did not provide solutions, the high hopes of the early-and-middle 1960s faded, and the war on poverty ended in ignominious surrender to the *status quo*. In part, of course, this was because the war in Southeast Asia turned out to be incompatible with the war on poverty. In part, however, it was because we all had rather muddleheaded ideas about the various causes and cures of poverty and inequality.

Today there are signs that some people are beginning to look for new solutions to these perennial problems. There is a vast amount of sociological and economic data that can, we think, help in this effort, both by explaining the failures of the 1960s and by suggesting more realistic alternatives. For the past four years we have been working with this data. Our research has led us to three general conclusions.

First, poverty is a condition of relative rather than absolute deprivation. People feel poor and are poor if they have a lot less money than their neighbors. This is true regardless of their absolute income. It follows that we cannot eliminate poverty unless we prevent people from falling too far below the national average. The problem is economic inequality rather than low incomes.

Second, the reforms of the 1960s were misdirected because they focused only on equalizing opportunity to "succeed" (or "fail") rather than on reducing the economic and social distance between those who succeeded and those who failed. The evidence we have reviewed suggests that equalizing opportunity will not do very much to equalize results, and hence that it will not do much to reduce poverty.

Third, even if we are interested solely in equalizing opportunities for economic success, making schools more equal will not help very much. Differences between schools have very little effect on what happens to students after they graduate.

The main policy implication of these findings is that although school reform is important for improving the lives of children, schools cannot contribute significantly to adult equality. If we want economic equality in our society, we will have to get it by changing our economic institutions, not by changing the schools. . . .

SCHOOLING AND OPPORTUNITY

Almost none of the reform legislation of the 1960s involved direct efforts to equalize adult status, power, or income. Most Americans accepted the idea that these rewards should go to those who were most competent and diligent. Their objection to America's traditional economic system was not that it produced inequality but that the rules determining who succeeded and who failed were often unfair. The reformers wanted to create a world in which success would no longer be associated with skin color, economic background, or other "irrelevant" factors, but only with actual merit. What they wanted, in short, was what they called "equal opportunity."

Their strategy for achieving equal opportunity placed great emphasis on education. Many people imagined that if schools could equalize people's cognitive skills this would equalize their bargaining power as adults. Presumably, if everyone had equal bargaining power, few people would end up very poor.

This strategy for reducing poverty rested on a series of assumptions* that went roughly as follows:

1. Eliminating poverty is largely a matter of helping children born into poverty to rise out of it. Once families escape from poverty, they do not fall back into it. Middle-class children rarely end up poor.

2. The primary reason poor children cannot escape from poverty is that they do not acquire basic cognitive skills. They cannot read, write, calculate, or articulate. Lacking these skills, they cannot get or keep a well-paid job.

3. The best mechanism for breaking this "vicious circle" is educational reform. Since children born into poor homes do not acquire the skills they need from their parents, they must be taught these skills in school. This can be done by making sure that they attend the same schools as middle-class children, by giving them extra compensatory programs in

---

* Deutsch (Section 4) presents a strategy for reducing poverty which greatly influenced education reforms of the 1960's. Are Bane and Jencks's assumptions reflected in his article?

school, by giving their parents a voice in running their schools, or by some combination of all three approaches.

Our research over the last four years suggests that each of these assumptions is erroneous:

1. Poverty is not primarily hereditary. While children born into poverty have a higher than average chance of ending up poor, there is still an enormous amount of economic mobility from one generation to the next. A father whose occupational status is high passes on less than half his advantage to his sons, and a father whose status is low passes along less than half his disadvantage. A family whose income is above the norm has an even harder time passing along its privileges; its sons are typically only about a third as advantaged as the parents. Conversely, a family whose income is below average will typically have sons about a third as disadvantaged as the parents. The effects of parents' status on their daughters' economic positions appear to be even weaker. This means that many "advantaged" parents have some "disadvantaged" children and vice versa.

2. The primary reason some people end up richer than others is not that they have more adequate cognitive skills. While children who read well, get the right answers to arithmetic problems, and articulate their thoughts clearly are somewhat more likely than others to get ahead, there are many other equally important factors involved. The effects of I.Q. on economic success are about the same as the effects of family background. This means, for example, that if two men's I.Q. scores differ by 17 points — the typical difference between I.Q. scores of individuals chosen at random — their incomes will typically differ by less than $2,000. That amount is not completely trivial, of course. But the income difference between random individuals is three times as large and the difference between the best-paid fifth and the worst-paid fifth of all male workers averages $14,000. There is almost as much economic inequality among those who score high on standardized tests as in the general population.

3. There is no evidence that school reform can substantially reduce the extent of cognitive inequality, as measured by tests of verbal fluency, reading comprehension, or mathematical skill. Eliminating qualitative differences between elementary schools would reduce the range of scores on standardized tests in sixth grade by less than 3 per cent. Eliminating qualitative differences between high schools would hardly reduce the range of twelfth-grade scores at all and would reduce by only 1 per cent the disparities in the amount of education people eventually get.

Our best guess, after reviewing all the evidence we could find, is that racial desegregation raises black elementary school students' test scores by a couple of points. But most of the test-score gap between blacks and whites persists, even when they are in the same schools. So also: Tracking has very little effect on test scores. And neither the overall level of resources available to a school nor any specific, easily identifiable school policy has a significant effect on students' cognitive skills or educational attainments. Thus, even if we went beyond "equal opportunity" and allocated resources disproportionately to schools whose students now do worst on tests and are least likely to acquire credentials, this would not improve these students' prospects very much.*

The evidence does not tell us why school quality has so little effect on test scores. Three possible explanations come to mind. First, children seem to be more influenced by what happens at home than by what happens in school. They may also be more influenced by what happens on the streets and by what they see on television. Second, administrators have very little control over those aspects of school life that do affect children. Reallocating resources, reassigning pupils, and rewriting the curriculum seldom change the way teachers and students actually treat each other minute by minute. Third, even when the schools exert an unusual influence on children, the resulting changes are not likely to persist into adulthood. It takes a huge change in elementary school test scores, for example, to alter adult income by a significant amount.

EQUAL OPPORTUNITY AND UNEQUAL RESULTS

The evidence we have reviewed, taken all together, suggests that equalizing opportunity cannot take us very far toward eliminating inequality. The simplest way of demonstrating this is to compare the economic prospects of brothers raised in the same home. Even the most egalitarian society could not hope to make opportunities for all children appreciably more equal than the opportunities now available to brothers from the same family. Looking at society at large, if we compare random pairs of individuals, the difference between their occupational statuses averages about 28 points on the Duncan "status scale" (the scale runs from 0 to 96 points). The difference between brothers' occupational statuses averages fully 23 points on this same scale. If we compare men's incomes, the differences between random pairs averaged about $6,200 in 1968. The difference between brothers' incomes, according to our best estimate, probably averaged about $5,700. These estimates mean that people who start off equal end up almost as unequal as everyone else. Inequality is not mostly inherited. It is re-created anew in each generation.

We can take this line of argument a step further by comparing people who not only start off in similar families but who also have the same I.Q. scores and get the same amount of schooling. Such people's occupational

---

* Given this evidence, is the radical reform of the schools proposed by Ivan Illich (Section 11) the only viable way to improve learning?

statuses differ by an average of 21 points, compared to 28 points for random individuals. If we compare their incomes, making the additional assumption that the men have the same occupational status, we find that they differ by an average of about $5,300, compared to $6,200 for men chosen at random.

These comparisons suggest that adult success must depend on a lot of things besides family background, schooling, and the cognitive skills measured by standardized tests. We have no idea what these factors are. To some extent, no doubt, specialized varieties of competence, such as the ability to hit a ball thrown at high speed or the ability to persuade a customer that he wants a larger car than he thought he wanted, play a major role.* Income also depends on luck: the range of jobs available when you are job hunting, the amount of overtime work in your plant, good or bad weather for your strawberry crop, and a hundred other unpredictable accidents.

Equalizing opportunity will not, then, do much to reduce economic inequality in America. If poverty is relative rather than absolute, equalizing opportunity will not do much to reduce poverty, either.

IMPLICATIONS FOR EDUCATIONAL POLICY

These findings imply that school reform is never likely to have any significant effect on the degree of inequality among adults. This suggests that the prevalent "factory" model, in which schools are seen as places that "produce" alumni, probably ought to be abandoned. It is true that schools have "inputs" and "outputs," and that one of their nominal purposes is to take human "raw material" (i.e., children) and convert it into something more "useful" (i.e., employable adults). Our research suggests, however, that the character of a school's output depends largely on a single input, the characteristics of the entering children. Everything else — the school budget, its policies, the characteristics of the teachers — is either secondary or completely irrelevant, at least so long as the range of variation among schools is as narrow as it seems to be in America.

These findings have convinced us that the long-term effects of schooling are relatively uniform. The day-to-day internal life of the schools, in contrast, is highly variable. It follows that *the primary basis for evaluating a school should be whether the students and teachers find it a satisfying place to be.*† This does not mean we think schools should be like mediocre summer camps, in which children are kept out of trouble but not taught anything. We doubt that a school can be enjoyable for either adults or children unless the children keep learning new things. We value ideas and the

* *What type of research could be done to identify these factors?*
† *Key point. Open education (see Rathbone and Madden, Section 10) and some free schools (see Graubard, Section 11) are based on this principle.*

life of the mind, and we think that a school that does not value these things is a poor place for children. But a school that values ideas because they enrich the lives of children is quite different from a school that values high reading scores because reading scores are important for adult success.

Our concern with making schools satisfying places for teachers and children has led us to a concern for diversity and choice. People have widely different notions of what a "satisfying" place is, and we believe they ought to be able to put these values into practice. As we have noted, our research suggests that none of the programs or structural arrangements in common use today has consistently different long-term effects from any other. Since the character of a child's schooling has few long-term effects, and since these effects are quite unpredictable, society has little reason to constrain the choices available to parents and children. If a "good school" is one the students and staff find satisfying, no one school will be best for everyone. Since there is no evidence that professional educators know appreciably more than parents about what is good for children, it seems reasonable to let parents decide what kind of education their children should have while they are young and to let the children decide as they get older.*

Short-term considerations also seem decisive in determining whether to spend more money on schooling or to spend it on busing children to schools outside their neighborhoods. If extra resources make school life pleasanter and more interesting, they are worthwhile. But we should not try to justify school expenditures on the grounds that they boost adult earnings. Likewise, busing ought to be justified in political and moral terms rather than in terms of presumed long-term effects on the children who are bused. If we want an integrated society, we ought to have integrated schools, which make people feel they have a stake in the well-being of other races. If we want a society in which people are free to segregate themselves, then we should apply that principle to our schools. There is, however, no compelling reason to treat schools differently from other social arrangements, including neighborhoods. Personally, we believe in both open housing and open schools. If parents or students want to take buses to schools in other neighborhoods, school boards ought to provide the buses, expand the relevant schools, and ensure that the students are welcome in the schools they want to attend. This is the least we can do to offset the effects of residential segregation. But we do not believe that forced busing can be justified on the grounds of its long-term benefits for students.

This leads to our last conclusion about educational reform. Reformers are always getting trapped into claiming too much for what they propose. They may want a particular reform — like open classrooms, or desegregation, or vouchers — because they think these reforms will make schools more satisfying places to work. Yet they feel obliged to claim that these

* *But do parents know what's best for their children?*

reforms will also reduce the number of nonreaders, increase racial under-standing, or strengthen family life. A wise reformer ought to be more modest, claiming only that a particular reform will not harm adult society and that it will make life pleasanter for parents, teachers, and students in the short run.

This plea for modesty in school reform will, we fear, fall on deaf ears. Ivan Illich is right in seeing schools as secular churches, through which we seek to improve not ourselves but our descendants.* That this process should be disagreeable seems inevitable; one cannot abolish original sin through self-indulgence. That it should be immodest seems equally inevitable; a religion that promises anything less than salvation wins few converts. In school, as in church, we present the world as we wish it were. We try to inspire children with the ideals we ourselves have failed to live up to. We assume, for example, that we cannot make adults live in deseg-regated neighborhoods, so we devise schemes for busing children from one neighborhood to another in order to desegregate the schools. We all prefer conducting our moral experiments on other people. Nonetheless, so long as we confine our experiments to children, we will not have much effect on adult life. . . .

EXERCISE

1. What are the three conclusions that Bane and Jencks reach on the basis of their research findings? (pp. 108–109)

2. What evidence do Bane and Jencks use to support their argu-ment that equality of opportunity will not result in equality of cognitive skills or economic success? (pp. 110–111)

3. According to Bane and Jencks, what should be the goal of school reform? What should not be its goal? (pp. 112, 113)

4. Why do Bane and Jencks make a plea for modesty in school re-form? (pp. 113–114)

* *Ivan Illich presents his views on schooling in Section 11.*

SOCIAL CLASS, ETHNIC BACKGROUND, AND HEREDITY

Introduction

The success of any group of students in the United States, regardless of age or locale, will depend on several known factors. White students generally will be more successful than black students. Students from homes with a high income level generally will be more successful than students from homes with lower incomes. Students with one or more parents who achieved high success in school generally will be more successful than students whose parents had limited success. Of course, some black students will be more successful than whites, some students from low-income homes will perform better than those from high-income homes, and a few students whose parents had limited success in school will outperform other students. However, for the most part, one or more of these characteristics of a student rather accurately predict his success in school.

The problem for educational psychology now is not to determine whether these characteristics make a difference. Numerous research investigations have confirmed that they do. The question to be answered is, Why do ethnic background and social class influence school success? Researchers who have worked on this problem usually attempt to confirm or disprove one of the following theories:

Ethnic minority students or students from low-income homes do not have the same opportunities for preschool and out-of-school learning as students from white middle-class homes. As a result, they come to school less prepared to function successfully.

Parents of ethnic minority students or low-income parents generally have low scholastic attainment and tested intelligence. If intelligence is inherited, their children cannot be expected to have the ability needed to become successful learners.

Students from ethnic minority or low-income backgrounds have many skills that white middle-class students do not have. However, because the schools are designed for white middle-class students, these skills are not usable in school. Before ethnic minority and low-income students can achieve academic success, the schools must be changed to match their learning styles.

These contrasting explanations of social class and ethnic differences are contemporary expressions of the heredity-environment controversy. The controversy is important because of its policy implications: can a system of education advance an individual beyond the success that might be expected from his ethnic background and social class? The controversy also affects potential teachers. How will you explain why some students succeed academically, whereas others do not? As a start toward answering this question, decide whether you agree with the following viewpoints:

Importance of Genetic Factors

Pro   Differences between students in their success as learners are mainly based upon genetic factors over which the schools have no control. The differences should be accepted and schools designed to accommodate them.

Con   Genetic factors only explain a small amount of the differences between students in learning success. Such factors as preschool and out-of-school learning opportunities are more important. When these are lacking or inadequate, the school program can be designed to provide the needed experiences to eliminate differences in students' success.

Adapting Schools to Learner Characteristics

Pro   Students come to school with different skills and different ways of learning. If education were redesigned to match the students being served, differences in learning success based upon ethnicity and social class would be eliminated.

Con   Because one role of the school is to help people fit into a common social framework, everyone should have the same education program. Students whose backgrounds differ from those of white middle-class children should be given special compensatory training so that the white middle-class skills and knowledge they lack are developed. Once this is accomplished, culturally different children will achieve in school.

The selections that follow include arguments and evidence related to these views. George Mayeske presents research data on the relationship between race, social class, and academic achievement. His finding — that social class is more important than race in affecting academic achievement — suggests that heredity (which determines whether one is born white, black, etc.) is not an important determinant of learning ability, unless, as Arthur Jensen asserts, social class itself is determined by hereditary factors. Jensen presents evidence for his theory that heredity has a major influence upon the learning success of individuals and different racial groups. Martin Deutsch and William Labov both discuss language and learning style differences between middle-class white and lower-class black students. Labov's interpretations of these differences and means for dealing with them contrast directly with those presented by Deutsch. However, they both reject genetic explanations of racial-ethnic differences.

On the Explanation of Racial–Ethnic Group Differences in Achievement Test Scores

George W. Mayeske

In this paper George Mayeske analyzes research data to determine what portion of the differences in students' academic achievement can be associated with their membership in six racial ethnic groups (Indian, Mexican-American, Puerto Rican, Negro, Oriental, or white). He suggests that social background factors may be more important than race or ethnic group background in determining school achievement. The data analyzed by Mayeske were taken from the Educational Opportunities Survey, one of the best-known contemporary educational research studies. Its published results are popularly known as the "Coleman Report," in reference to its chief author, James S. Coleman. The Coleman Report has been used in arguments for and against desegregation of schools and for and against increased monetary support for compensatory educational programs. As you read Mayeske's interpretation of the data for sixth-grade students, consider this important point. Mayeske suggests that 24 per cent of the total differences among students in their academic achievement is all that can be explained by racial

Paper presented at the American Psychological Association Convention, Washington, D.C., September 1971. Reprinted with permission of the author.

membership. The other 76 per cent of differences result from other influencing factors. What are these factors? Can you do anything about them? Also, keep in mind that not all researchers accept Mayeske's interpretation of the data. In the following selection, Arthur Jensen presents an alternative interpretation of the findings. Before reading either paper, you might consult the glossary for an explanation of statistical concepts used in them.

INTRODUCTION

My colleagues[1] and I in the U.S. Office of Education have been privileged to be charged with the responsibility for illustrating and documenting the structure and functioning of the American public school system. We could not dream of having such a lofty objective if we did not have at our disposal the most comprehensive body of data ever collected on public schools and their students in the United States. I am, of course, referring to the Educational Opportunities Survey data collected in the fall of 1965 at the direction of Congress in the Civil Rights Act of the prior year. A report utilizing this data to investigate the Equality of Educational Opportunity for various racial and ethnic groups was issued in the fall of 1966 under the principal authorship of James S. Coleman. In this paper I will present excerpts from two reports that utilized this same body of data (Mayeske et al., 1969, 1971)....

THE DATA BASE AND BACKGROUND WORK

The Educational Opportunities Survey entailed the testing and surveying of about 650,000 students in some 4000 public schools throughout the country in grades 1, 3, 6, 9, and 12, together with their teachers, principals, and superintendents. The Survey sample consisted of a 5 per cent sample of schools. The data base is comprehensive in that detailed factual and attitudinal information was collected on the students' home background, attitude toward school, race relations, and the world. A battery of ability and achievement tests was administered at each level. Information was collected from some 60,000 teachers and 4,000 principals concerning their training and experience, their view of the school, etc. The final part of the teacher questionnaire consisted of a 30-item contextual vocabulary test which was intended to be a measure of the verbal facility of the teacher. In addition, the principal provided data on the school's facilities, staff, programs, curricula, etc. For further detailed information on the survey data I will refer you to the report "Equality of Educational Opportunity" (Coleman et al., 1966)....

In this paper I have chosen the sixth-grade students and their schools as the major level of focus. At this grade level the dropout rate is not as severe for many minority group students as it is at the higher grade levels and the number of schools in the sample is quite substantial. However, at the higher grade levels the student indices are more comprehensively measured and the errors in racial–ethnic group identification are less severe than at the lower grade levels, hence some results for these grade levels will also be brought into the discussion. Adequate measures of student attitudes and motivation were not available for grades 1 and 3 and hence these grade levels will not enter further into the discussion.

A Measure of Racial-Ethnic Group Membership

We wanted to incorporate in our analyses a variable that would indicate a student's membership in each of the racial ethnic groups so that we could see how these different groups stood with respect to one another at different points in the analyses. Since these are discrete groups we had to scale or order them in some manner so that a quantitative variable denoting group membership could be incorporated into the analyses.* Our primary dependent variable of interest was achievement and consequently we decided to order the groups according to their mean scores on our achievement composite (ACHV).[2]

Table 1 gives the percentage of students in each of the racial ethnic groups along with the mean ACHV score attained by students who identified themselves as belonging to one of these groups. On a distribution with a mean of 50 and standard deviation of 10 we can see that whites attain the highest score with Orientals following them by about 4 points.† Approximately 5 to 7 points below them lie the Indians, Mexicans, and Negroes with the Puerto Ricans following these groups by another 4 points.

Now when each student is assigned the mean ACHV score attained by members of his racial ethnic group the ordering of these groups is said to be *criterion scaled* (Beaton, 1969). This means that the relationship of our racial–ethnic group membership variable with ACHV is the maximum relationship that can be obtained. No other ordering of these groups will yield a higher relationship. When scores on our racial–ethnic group membership variable, which we shall call RETH [3] from hereon, are correlated with scores on our ACHV composite the correlation obtained will be a maximum.‡ We are particularly interested in what this maximum value might be and how it changes as different social conditions in which these groups are found are first taken into account.

* *Quantitative and dependent variables are explained in the glossary.*
† *Mean and standard deviation are explained in the glossary.*
‡ *Correlation is explained in the glossary.*

TABLE 1

Percentage of Sixth-Grade Students
and Their Average Composite Achievement Score
Classified by Racial–Ethnic Group Membership

Category	Racial–ethnic group	Percentage	Mean achv.
1	American Indian	2.6	44.194
2	Mexican-American	6.1	42.244
3	Puerto Rican	2.0	38.560
4	Negro	15.7	42.513
5	Oriental	0.9	49.391
6	White	69.6	53.181
7	Other	1.4	45.605
8	No response	1.7	43.144
	Total	100.0	50.000 [a]

[a] The total number of students is 123,386. The standard deviation for the total was equal to 10. All figures are weighted for sampling. Later analyses exclude categories 7 and 8.

RACIAL–ETHNIC GROUP DIFFERENCES IN ACHIEVEMENT ADJUSTED FOR SOCIAL BACKGROUND CONDITIONS

Our first question then is: "What is the magnitude of this maximum value?" This is indicated by the squared correlation of RETH with ACHV, which is 24 percent and corresponds to the mean differences in the *none* column of Figure 1.* This is called *none* because none of the background conditions on which these groups differ has yet been taken into account.

Next we may ask, "What is the percent of variation in ACHV associated with RETH after differences among students in their socio-economic status (SES) have been taken into account?" A student with a high score on the SES index has parents who come from the higher educational strata, his father is engaged in a professional, managerial, sales or technical job, there are two to three children in the family, about six to ten rooms in their home, they are more likely to reside in the residential area of the city or the suburbs rather than in the inner city, and there are intellectually stimulating materials accessible in the home such as books, magazines, newspapers, television, and radio. . . . The percentage of ACHV associated with RETH *after* SES has been taken into account is 10.9 percent, which corresponds to the differences among the group means in the SES column of Figure 1.

The percentage of variation in ACHV associated with RETH after other conditions† have been taken into account are:

* Squared correlation is explained in the glossary.
† Does accounting for these conditions support or refute Bane & Jencks's findings?

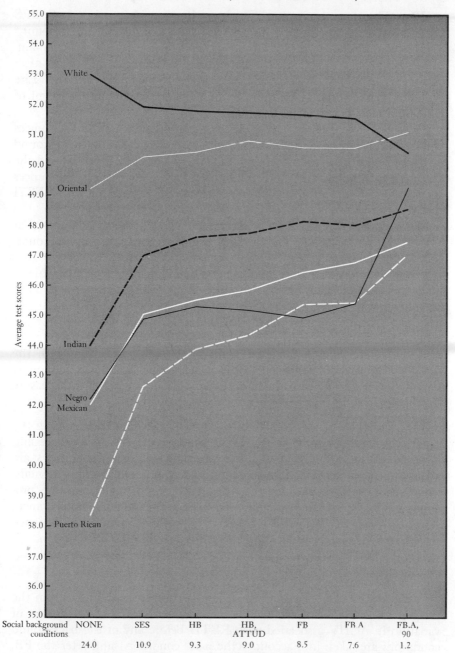

FIGURE 1.

Racial Ethnic Group Achievement Means
Adjusted for Social Background Conditions

HB — These are the mean differences after consideration of both SES and the students' Family Structure (FSS) have been taken into account.[4] They account for 9.3 percent of the differences in ACHV that remain.

HB, ATTUD — These are the magnitude of the mean differences after considerations of SES, FSS, and the students' Attitude Towards Life (ATTUD) have been taken into account.[5] They account for 9 percent of the differences in ACHV that remain.

FB — These are the magnitude of the mean differences after the indices which we felt represented all aspects of the students' Family Background (FB) had been taken into account. These indices were SES, FSS, and the set of four attitudinal and motivational indices. . . . These mean differences account for 8.5 percent of the differences in ACHV associated with RETH that remains.

FB, A — After FB and Area of Residence (A) whether it be South, Far West or North, or Rural-Suburban or Urban have been taken into account, only 7.6 percent remains.

FB, A, SO — After FB, A, and the five school attributes of the achievement and motivational mix of the students one goes to school with have been taken into account, only 1.2 percent remains. This set of five student body variables represents a number of things. By virtue of its high correlations with the comprehensive set of 31 school variables, it represents the aggregate effects of schooling. By virtue of its high correlations with the social background of the student body, as defined by their Socio-Economic, Family Structure, and Racial-Ethnic Composition, it represents a measure of school and residential segregation.

The trend we observe from Figure 1 is that the differences among the racial ethnic groups in their ACHV levels approaches zero as more and more considerations related to differences in their social conditions are taken into account.* This trend is slightly more pronounced for Orientals, whites, and Negroes than for the other groups and might be more pronounced for them if more variables pertinent to their special circumstances were also available. We tried English as opposed to some other language spoken in the home but that did not yield any additional information.

GRADE LEVEL . . . VARIATIONS

We may next ask: "How do these results compare with those from the other grade levels?" For each of the three grade levels the percentage of variation in ACHV associated with RETH before any of the background conditions are taken into account (the *none* condition) and after the FB, A, SO conditions have been accounted for, as these were described in conjunction with Figure 1 are:

* Important finding. It suggests that ethnic background has little influence on what is learned in school.

Grade[a]	None	FB, A, SO*
12	20	1.1
9	22	1.0
6	24	1.2

[a] The numbers of students (N) and schools (n) included in these analyses for grades nine and twelve are, respectively: Ninth, N = 133, 136, n = 923; Twelfth, N = 96, 426, n = 780.

Thus, for each grade level although the percentage before any conditions have been taken into account varies from 24 at the sixth through 22 at the ninth to 20 at the twelfth, they *all* end up at about the same value, namely 1 percent, after a variety of social background conditions (FB, A, SO) have been taken into account. . . .

SUMMARY

This paper has shown that for sixth-grade students, 24 percent of the total differences among students in their academic achievement is the maximum national value that can be associated with their membership in one of six racial ethnic groups (Indian, Mexican, Puerto Rican, Negro, Oriental, or white). This relationship prevails before the allocation of these groups to different social conditions has been taken into account. After a variety of social condition variables have been accounted for such as the social and economic well-being of the family, the presence or absence of key family members, the student's and parents' aspirations for his schooling, their beliefs about how he might benefit from an education, the activities that they engaged in to support these aspirations, one's region of residence, and the achievement and motivational levels of the students one goes to school with, this percentage dropped to 1.2. Similar results were obtained for other grade levels and for each region of the country. Hence, no inferences can be made about the "independent effect" of membership in a particular racial-ethnic group on academic achievement, for that membership, as it relates to academic achievement, is almost completely confounded with a variety of social conditions. . . .

EXERCISE

1. According to Mayeske, why can the data base of the Equal Opportunities Survey be considered to be a comprehensive sample of elementary and secondary education in the United States? (p. 118)

* *Why might the percentage of variation associated with racial-ethnic membership before social conditions are taken into account become less the longer students are in school?*

2. Why did Mayeske choose the sixth grade to study? (p. 119)

3. Which racial ethnic groups come closest to having differences in their achievement levels approach zero as more and more social conditions are considered? (p. 122)

4. What effect did grade level have upon the results of the study? (pp. 122–123)

5. What is the major finding of Mayeske's study? (p. 123)

On "Jensenism":
A Reply to Critics

Arthur R. Jensen

In 1969 a controversial article by Arthur R. Jensen, "How Much Can We Boost IQ and Scholastic Achievement?" was published in the Harvard Educational Review. *Jensen asked whether ethnic differences in school achievement could be attributed solely to social class background and the cultural bias of IQ tests. Instead, he proposed that genetic factors must be considered as partial determinants of social class and racial variations in intelligence. Since 1969, many educators have discussed this article. Others have written more than one hundred articles and books in response to Jensen's comments. Strong views have been expressed in support of and in opposition to Jensen's thesis. The following address was to be given at an educational research convention. However, persons opposed to Jensen's views prevented him from completing the presentation. The text of the address is an updated statement of Jensen's views about the importance of genetic determinants of racial differences in intelligence. Jensen draws on such research as Terman's study of gifted children all with IQ's above 140 and the IQ's of their children; Skodak and Skiels's study of adopted children's IQ's compared with the intelligence levels of their natural mothers; studies of the IQ's of identical twins reared apart; and studies of the intelligence levels of blacks and whites with the same income status. Jensen's research into IQ differences for various ethnic groups and his study of differences in associative, conceptual, and problem-solving learning abilities in various ethnic groups contributed to the conclusions presented in his original article and elaborated in this address. His*

An Address for the American Educational Research Association Annual Convention, Chicago, Illinois, April 7, 1972. Reprinted with permission of the author.

views have been used as arguments in favor of segregated schools and against compensatory education. The need to look at the individual rather than the group when planning education which Jensen emphasizes is often overlooked by those responding to his ideas. Do his statements support such arguments? Also, should the genetic line of inquiry continue to be pursued to explain differential success in learning?

The term "jensenism" occurs in the official program of this 1972 convention of the American Educational Research Association, and therefore I have been invited to say something about "jensenism." Since I did not coin the word, however, I cannot claim to know all the meanings it may have for others or that it may have accrued through popular usage. To the best of my knowledge, "jensenism" was coined by the *Wall Street Journal,* shortly after the publication of my article "How Much Can We Boost IQ and Scholastic Achievement?" in the *Harvard Educational Review* (Jensen, 1969). It has since been used in the popular press and elsewhere (e.g., the *Bulletin of the Atomic Scientists,* March, May 1970) as a term intended to summarize the user's interpretation of one or another aspect of my article: the failure of large-scale compensatory education programs, the theory of the inheritance of mental abilities, the hypothesis that not only individual differences but social class and racial differences in intelligence involve genetic as well as environmental factors, and that mental abilities may be viewed in terms of two broad categories (called Level I and Level II) which are differentially correlated with social class and might have useful implications for instruction in scholastic skills.* Some of my most vehement critics have used the term pejoratively. Professor Lewontin, for example, likened "jensenism" to Jansenism, named after Bishop Jansen in the seventeenth century for his "pernicious heresy ... of total depravity, irresistible grace, lack of free will, predestination, and limited atonement" (Lewontin, 1970; Jensen, 1970).

If "jensenism" has any valid meaning at all, from my own standpoint, what it means is a biological and genetical view of human kind and of human differences — both individual differences and group differences. For me, "jensenism" is the bringing to bear of this genetic viewpoint upon understanding some of the problems of education. The genetic view of man has often been badly misunderstood in this context, and 99 percent of the heated debate I have seen in the three years since the publication of my *Harvard Educational Review* article, I believe, reflects this misunderstanding. Much of the unthinking emotional reaction I attribute to the fact that a generation or more of social scientists and educators have been indoc-

---

* *Correlation is explained in the glossary.*

trinated to ignore genetics, or to believe that genetic factors are of little or no importance in human behavior and human differences, or to think nongenetically or antigenetically.* Any attempt by anyone to introduce into this scene theory and research on genetics as it relates to vital educational and social problems was destined at first to meet hostility and rejection.

The modern genetic view of man calls for a revolution in our thinking, in our whole orientation. It demands on everyone's part an even more drastic reorientation of thinking than was required by other historical revolutions of thought, such as the Copernican, Darwinian, and Einsteinian revolutions. The Mendelian revolution (and Fisher's pioneering extensions of Mendelian genetics to polygenic systems) is already established in biological science, but it has not yet filtered into other domains.† The Mendelian revolution, if it can be called by that, has not yet influenced social scientists on any large scale; it has not characterized the thinking of our social policy makers; and it is totally foreign to the general public, which in terms of thinking genetically in the modern sense is surely at the flat earth stage of scientific sophistication. The educational task that is called for is awesome. It will probably take more than a generation. But at least, perhaps, we have begun. Major revolutions of thought generally are absorbed most slowly and imperfectly. As scientists, researchers, and educators we must take the lead.

The genetic view of man stands in sharp contrast to the prevailing views that dominate most people's thinking. One class of antigenetic view can be characterized as social elitism and racism. These old-fashioned beliefs are quite out of touch with modern genetics; they are now more political and ideological than scientific. . . . They are apparently ignorant of the genetic facts of random segregation and recombination of genes, or of the fundamental principle that the properties of an individual depend upon the state in which he finds himself and not upon the state from which he is derived, or the fact that social classes and races are discrete systems of classification imposed upon what in nature are not at all discrete but rather continuous gene pools which vary statistically. This mistaken typological thinking proclaims "like begets like" but ignores the other half of genetic fact — that "like also begets unlike," due to segregation and recombination of genes in the creation of every individual.‡ In a profound sense, social elitism and racism deny individuality, the very individuality that is in fact ensured by genetic mechanisms.

* *Would Jensen be likely to include Mary Jo Bane, Christopher Jencks, and George Mayeske in this group?*
† *The meaning of the Mendelian revolution is explained in the glossary.*
‡ *Key point. This view affects the three approaches to educational reform which Jensen presents later in this selection.*

There is another class of antigenetic misconceptions, too, which shares many characteristics in common with the first class of erroneous thinking I have just described. It can be called equalitarian environmentalism. Like social elitism and racism, it too ignores the facts of genetics, and it, too, denies individuality if you follow its reasoning all the way. And similarly, it is more political and ideological than scientific. It denies genetic variability, at least with respect to certain characteristics, usually behavioral, and insists that the environment alone — usually the social environment — makes the person and all the behavioral differences among persons. It may at times pay a kind of lip service to genetics, which is often seen as ceasing in importance after the moment of conception, but its conclusions invariably deny the importance of genetic factors in human behavioral differences. It may also wear the guise of "interactionism," based on the truism that the individual is a product of the interaction of genetic and environmental factors, but always with the implication that the genetic factors are more or less totally submerged or obscured by environmental influences.*

Much of the debate and fulmination surrounding my *Harvard Educational Review* article, I submit, is a result of most persons' knowing only these two mistaken views and feeling that their only choice is the one or the other. Most well-intentioned persons have deemed it necessary to put down the first view at all costs and to defend the second. Often it was viewed as the battle of the "good guys" versus the "bad guys." I have been opposed to both these views; "jensenism" is contrary to both. The antidote to both is to *think genetically*, that is to say, in the most fundamental sense to think about yourself, about other persons, and about groups (your own group and other groups, whatever they may be) in ways that are consistent with already well-established principles of modern genetics. In short, I'm saying let's get abreast of the Mendelian revolution.

Just what does this mean? Let's get down to specific points. First and most important, it means that you and everyone else (except monozygotic twins) are genetically unique. The probability that any two sibs (other than MZ twins) will inherit exactly the same genotypes (i.e., the individual's total genetic "blueprint") is less than 1 in 70 trillions.† So if we are to think realistically, in terms of what we know from genetics, we must recognize uniqueness and individuality. A genetic corollary of this is that *you* are not your *parents*. Parents do not transmit their own genotypes to their offspring, but only their genes, and a random selection of only one-half of them at that. Each offspring is a new assortment, a new combination of genetic material, and thus we see great variability among members of the

* *Could Mayeske's study (the previous selection) be classified as an example of "interactionism"?*
† *Genotypes are explained more fully in the glossary.*

same family, probably much greater variability than most persons would like to acknowledge. The average amount of genetic variability *within* families is only slightly less than the genetic variability *between* families. By the same token, nature has seen to it that your children will not be *you*. Perhaps here is the crux of the revolution called for by Mendelism in our thinking and in our attitudes. This is what must sink into our consciousness: the disassociation of our individuality, our genetic uniqueness, from our biological role as mere transmitters of randomly segregating and recombining genetic materials which indeed obey statistical laws but which are not "us." When you have children, you don't make what you want, you take what you get. . . .

This distinction between the individual and the particular gene pool from which the unique combination forming his genotype was derived extends beyond one's family to the racial group with which one is identified and to the social status into which one is born. You are not your race; you are not your group. You are you. That is, if you are talking genetics. . . .

HERITABILITY AND TEACHABILITY

It has been said that the heritability of learning ability or of intelligence is irrelevant to teachability, or as the *Bulletin of the ERIC Information Retrieval Center on the Disadvantaged* (1969, 4, no. 4) printed in boldface: "Teachability is not a function of heritability."* In support of this statement we see it pointed out that a child or a group of children show some response to training, and this is held up as evidence against the heritability of intelligence or learning ability. . . .

The fact that IQ has high heritability surely does *not* mean that individuals cannot learn much. Even if learning ability had 100 percent heritability it would not mean that individuals cannot learn, and therefore the demonstration of learning or the improvement of performance, with or without specific instruction or intervention by a teacher, says absolutely nothing about heritability. But knowing that learning ability has high heritability does tell us this: if a number of individuals are all given *equal* opportunity — the same background, the same conditions, and the same amount of time — for learning something, they will still differ from one another in their rates of learning and consequently in the amount they learn per unit of time spent in learning. That is the meaning of heritability. It does not say that individuals cannot learn or improve with instruction and practice. It says that given equal conditions, individuals will differ from one another, not because of differences in the external conditions but because of differences in the internal environment which is conditioned by genetic factors.

* Heritability is explained in the glossary.

"Teachability" presumably means the ability to learn under conditions of instruction by a teacher. If this is the case, then it is true that heritability has nothing to do with teachability. But was this ever really the question? Has anyone questioned the fact that *all* school children are teachable? The important question has concerned *differences* in teachability — differences both among individuals and among subgroups of the population. And with reference to the question of *differences*, the concept of heritability is indeed a relevant and empirically answerable question. . . .

To dismiss the question of heritability is to dismiss concern with the causes of educational differences and their implications for educational practices. As I read it, what most educators, government officials, and writers in the popular press who discuss the present problems of education are in fact referring to is not primarily dissatisfaction with some *absolute* level of achievement, but rather with the large group *differences* in educational attainments that show up so conspicuously in our educational system — the achievement gaps between the affluent and the poor, the lower-class and the middle-class, the majority and the minority, the urban and the suburban, and so on. Educational *differences*, not absolute level of performance, are the main cause of concern. Whether we like to admit it or not, the problem of achievement differences today is where the action is, where the billions of dollars of educational funds are being poured in, where the heat is on, and where the schools are being torn apart.* Are we not trying to understand more about the causes of these differences? . . .

With respect to IQ, I believe Bereiter (1970) states the situation quite correctly: "What a high heritability ratio implies, therefore, is that changes within the existing range of environmental conditions can have substantial effects on the mean level of IQ in the population but they are unlikely to have much effects on the spread of individual differences in IQ within that population.† If one is concerned with relative standing of individuals within the population, the prospects for doing anything about this through existing educational means are thus not good. Even with a massive redistribution of environmental conditions, one would expect to find the lower quarter of the IQ distribution to be about as far removed from the upper quarter as before" (p. 288). Bereiter goes on to say: "A high heritability ratio for IQ should not discourage people from pursuing environmental improvement in education or any other area. The potential effects on IQ are great, although it still remains to discover the environmental variables capable of producing these effects." . . .

---

* *The Bane and Jencks report (Section 3) was issued a year after this address was written. After reading their findings, do you think these issues still stand?*
† *One way around this problem would be to administer the educational program only to low-IQ students. Is this feasible or desirable?*

HERITABILITY AND GROUP DIFFERENCES

I have been falsely accused of claiming that the high heritability of IQ inevitably means that the mean differences in IQ between social class groups and racial groups must be due to genetic factors. I have never made this incorrect inference. What I have said is this: While it is true, indeed axiomatic, that heritability *within* groups cannot establish heritability *between* group means, high *within* group heritability increases the a priori likelihood that the *between* groups heritability is greater than zero. In nature, characteristics that vary genetically *among* individuals within a population also generally vary genetically *between* different breeding populations of the same species.* Among the genetically conditioned traits known to vary between major racial groups are body size and proportions, cranial size and cephalic index, pigmentation of the hair, skin, and eyes, hair form and distribution on the body, number of vertebrae, fingerprints, bone density, basic metabolic rate, sweating, fissural patterns on the chewing surfaces of the teeth, numerous blood groups, various chronic diseases, frequency of dizygotic (but nonmonozygotic) twinning, male-female birth ratio, ability to taste phenylthiocarbomide, length of gestation period, and degree of physical maturity at birth (as indicated by degree of ossification of cartilage). In light of all these differences, Spuhler and Lindzey (1967) have remarked "it seems to us surprising that one would accept present findings in regard to the existence of genetic anatomical, physiological, and epidemiological differences between the races . . . and still expect to find *no* meaningful differences in behavior between races" (p. 413). The high within-groups heritability of certain behavioral traits, such as intelligence, adds weight to this statement by Spuhler and Lindzey.

In fact, it is quite erroneous to say there is no relationship whatsoever between heritability *within* groups and heritability *between* group means. Jay Lush, a pioneer in quantitative genetics, has shown the formal relationship between these two heritabilities (Lush, 1968, p. 312), and it has been recently introduced into the discussion of racial differences by another geneticist, John C. DeFries (in press). . . .

CONTROLLING FOR SOCIAL CLASS

In the past year two widely publicized studies, one by George W. Mayeske† and the other by Jane Mercer, have claimed that racial differences in intelligence and scholastic achievement can be explained entirely

---

* Here Jensen clarifies a major confusion about the heritability of IQ.
† George Mayeske's findings concerning racial–ethnic group differences in school achievement are presented in the preceding selection.

in terms of the environmental effects of the lower socioeconomic status of Negroes in the United States. They showed that by statistically controlling a large number of social variables associated with socioeconomic status, they were able to "explain" practically all of the achievement gap between Negroes and whites. This procedure is what I have termed the "sociologist's fallacy." It is based on the unwarranted and untenable assumption that all the socioeconomic and environmental variables on which the racial groups have been matched or statistically equated are direct *causal* factors, when in fact they are merely *correlates* of IQ.* If some part of the SES difference within racial groups has a genetic basis, then statistically equating racial groups on social class equates them also to some degree on the genetic factors involved in intelligence. Indeed, it is theoretically conceivable that if one equated racial groups on a large enough number of *correlates* of IQ, one could statistically eliminate all of the IQ differences between them. But it would prove nothing at all about the *causes* of the mean IQ difference between the total populations. Many environmental indices are undoubtedly correlated with genotypes. Educational level of the parents, for example, is often included as an environmental variable affecting the child's development. But it almost certainly includes also some genetic component which is common to both the parents and their children.... Controlling SES thus partials out too much of the difference between the racial groups.† Matching for SES, in short, matches not only for certain environmental factors but also for genetic factors as well. It is interesting also that when such matching is carried out, it is noted that the average skin color of the Negro groups becomes lighter in the higher SES categories, indicating that genetic factors covary with SES, for whatever reason.‡ Genetic SES intelligence differences are firmly established within the white population. Matching Negro and white groups on SES, therefore, is certain to minimize genetic as well as environmental differences. For this reason, studies that control for SES are probably biased in favor of the environmentalist hypothesis and can contribute nothing to elucidating the nature-nurture problem....

ENVIRONMENTALIST HYPOTHESES

Those environmentalist hypotheses of the Negro-white IQ difference which have been most clearly formulated and are therefore subject to empirical tests are the only ones that can be evaluated within a scientific framework. The most frequently cited environmentalist hypotheses which

---

* *The difference between causation and correlation is explained in the glossary.*
† *How does this statement affect your interpretation of Bane and Jencks's and Mayeske's findings?*
‡ *Covariance is explained in the glossary.*

are sufficiently clear to put to an empirical test and which already have been put to a test have not proven adequate to the explanatory function they were intended to serve. A number of lines of such evidence casts serious doubt on purely environmental and cultural theories of the racial IQ difference. . . .

CULTURE-BIASED TESTS. Intelligence tests can be rank-ordered according to certain generally agreed-upon criteria of their cultural loading. Within a given culture, tests are better described as differing in *status fairness*. Environmentalists who criticize intelligence tests usually give as examples those tests which are most obviously loaded with what is presumably white middle-class factual knowledge, vocabulary, and the like,* as contrasted with more abstract figural material such as compose Raven's Progressive Matrices and Cattell's Culture-Fair Tests of g.† Yet it is on the latter type of tests that Negroes perform most poorly, relative to whites and other minority groups. Disadvantaged minorities, such as American Indians and Mexican-Americans, perform on tests showing different degrees of status bias in accord with the environmentalist hypothesis. Negroes do the opposite. "Translation" of tests such as the Stanford-Binet into the Negro ghetto dialect also does not appreciably improve scores.

The scholastic and occupational predictive validity of IQ tests is the same for Negroes as for whites, and item analyses of tests showing large average group mean differences do not reveal significant differences in rank order of item difficulty or in choice of distractors for error responses. Test-taking attitudes and motivational factors appear unconvincing as an explanation of the group difference in view of the fact that on some tests which make equal demands on attention, persistence, and effort, such as various memory tests, Negroes do perform quite well relative to whites. When various diverse tests and test items are ordered in terms of the degree to which they discriminate between Negroes and whites, the one feature which is common to the most discriminating tests and items is the conceptual and abstract nature of the test material. . . .

LANGUAGE DEPRIVATION. This is an unconvincing explanatory hypothesis in view of the fact that Negroes perform best on the most verbal parts of intelligence tests and poorest on the least verbal materials. All other disadvantaged minority groups within the American population show the opposite trend. Children who are born deaf are the most verbally deprived subjects we can study. They show marked verbal deficits on intelligence tests. Yet they perform at an average level on nonverbal tests, thus showing a pattern of abilities opposite to that of Negroes. . . .

* *Compare this statement with Lillian Zach's views in Section 5.*
† *The g factor in intelligence is discussed by J. P. Guilford (Section 5).*

POOR MOTIVATION. There is no consistent evidence that Negroes are less motivated in a test situation than are other groups. Some groups (e.g., Indians) whose general educational aspirations and self-concepts are poorer than those of Negroes actually perform better on tests and in school. Also, on performance tests specially devised to maximize the influence of motivational factors and to minimize the test's dependence upon abstract or complex cognitive functions which would involve g, Negroes do not perform significantly below whites. The "expectancy" or "self-fulfilling prophecy" theory has not been empirically demonstrated, and when put to proper tests it has failed to be substantiated.

NONCOGNITIVE TESTS. Certain perceptual-motor tests such as choice reaction time and pursuit rotor learning (which has a very high heritability) show large Negro-white differences even under very highly controlled experimental conditions, and the results are independent of the race of the tester.* Moreover, the magnitude of the racial difference has been shown to be related to the degree of Caucasian admixture in the Negro sample as assessed by physical indices. If genetic racial differences in behavioral tests other than intelligence tests are admitted, by what principle can one exclude the same possibility for types of tests labeled as measures of intelligence? There is no reason why intelligence tests should be categorically excluded from the possibility of showing genetic race differences when such differences in other physical and behavioral traits can be found.

NUTRITIONAL DEFICIENCIES. The fact that severe malnutrition, especially protein deficiency, during prenatal development and in infancy and childhood can impair mental as well as physical growth is not at issue. Studies from the nutritionally most deprived segments of populations in Africa, Mexico, and South America would support this conclusion. There are no data, however, which would support the hypothesis that malnutrition contributes any appreciable fraction to the average Negro-white IQ difference. In Negro communities where there is no evidence of poor nutrition, the average Negro IQ is still about 1 SD below the white mean.† When groups of Negro children with IQ's *below* the general Negro average have been studied for nutritional status, no signs of malnutrition have been found. Physical evidence of malnutrition found to be correlated with lower IQ's in studies conducted in Africa, Mexico, and Guatemala have not been found even in the poorest and lower IQ segments of the American Negro population. On the basis of present evidence, the hypothesis that lower average Negro IQ is due to poor nutrition is not tenable.

* *Tests of choice reaction time and pursuit rotor learning are described in the glossary.*
† *SD (standard deviation) is explained in the glossary.*

The nutritional and health care status of Indian children, as indicated by much higher rates of infant mortality, is much poorer than that of Negroes; yet Indian children in the first grade in school (age 6) have been found to score about one *SD* above Negroes on nonverbal ability tests.

PRENATAL AND PERINATAL DISADVANTAGES. The higher rate of fetal loss and infant mortality in the Negro population may indicate disadvantages related to prenatal health care of the mother and undesirable conditions attending birth. These conditions prevail in the poorer segment of the Negro population and probably contribute to the incidence of neurological handicaps among Negro children. All of the causes of high fetal loss, however, are not understood, for there are some relatively disadvantaged populations which have shown lower rates of fetal loss than is found in the white majority — Orientals, for example. There is now evidence that the degree of genetic heterogeneity of the fetus' ancestors is directly related to the probability of fetal loss, and thus genetic factors may be involved even in this seemingly environmental phenomenon. Disadvantaging forms of birth trauma such as anoxia, low birth weight, and prematurity are reflected in subnormal performance on infant tests of perceptual-motor development. But large representative samples of Negro children show no depression of scores on these tests and generally perform at slightly higher levels than middle-class white children. Prenatal and perinatal factors, though differing in Negro and white populations, do not begin to account for such phenomena as the six times higher rate of mental retardation (IQ's below 70) in the Negro than in the white population. Unless one hypothesizes the existence of genetic factors, in the vast majority of cases the causes of the mental retardation must be categorized as "unknown" or "unidentified."

EDUCATIONAL IMPLICATIONS

At present, neither I nor anyone else, I'm afraid, has any more than rather general notions concerning the educational implications of the wide range of apparent differences in educability in our population. Since the heredity-environment issue is not likely to reach a general consensus among qualified scientists for quite some time to come and after much more genetical and psychological research has been completed, it is probably wise for educators to assume an openly agnostic position with regard to the genetic issue as it involves racial differences, at the same time recognizing that whatever may be the causes of the difference, we do not at present know of any measures or methods within the power of the schools that will appreciably or permanently diminish either individual or group differences in intelligence or scholastic achievement. There is fundamentally, in my opinion, no difference, psychologically and genetically, between individual differences and group differences. Individual differences often simply get tabulated so as to show up as group differences — between schools in different neighborhoods, between different racial groups, between cities and regions. They then become a political and ideological, not just a psychological, matter. To reduce the social tensions that arise therefrom, we see proposals to abolish aptitude and achievement testing, grading, grade placement, special classes for the educationally retarded and the academically gifted, neighborhood schools, the classroom as the instructional unit, the academic curriculum, and even our whole system of education.* There may be merit in some of these proposals. But I think they are too often aimed at covering up problems rather than coming to grips with them. We can urge doing away with classification and groups, and enforce laws against racial discrimination in educational opportunities and employment and housing; we can and must insist upon considering only persons' individual characteristics rather than their group membership as a basis for educational treatment and in social relations in general. Well and good. I trust there is no disagreement on this. What we may not accomplish by these means, however, is equality of performance in school or in the acquisition of certain skills deemed valuable by society and rewarded accordingly. If we repeatedly look for the causes of differences in ability to acquire an educationally valued skill such as reading, for example, in the external environment and are hard put to find a convincing explanation there, but we also refuse to consider any other than external factors as possible causes of these differences, perhaps we only sow the seeds of a kind of social paranoia — a need to find strictly external causes to blame for the observed differences.

To seek the answers to these questions and yet to worry about their far-reaching implications: surely this is the scientist's moral dilemma. I don't claim to have the solution.

In terms of what we now know in educational research and in terms of what seems immediately feasible, I would suggest further consideration of three main educational approaches. They are not at all mutually exclusive. (The desirability and necessity of eliminating racial discrimination and of generally improving the environmental conditions and educational and occupational opportunities of all disadvantaged persons in the population are taken for granted.) These approaches have nothing to do with race per se, but are concerned with individual differences in those characteristics most relevant to educability. Their success in improving the benefits of education to Negro children, however, may depend in part upon recognizing that racial differences in the distribution of educationally relevant abilities are not mainly a result of discrimination and unequal environ-

* Allen Graubard and Ivan Illich, among others, make such recommendations. See Section 11.

mental conditions. None of the approaches that seem to me realistic is based on the expectation of the schools' significantly changing children's basic intelligence.

SEEKING APTITUDE X TRAINING INTERACTIONS. This means that some children may learn better by one method than by another and that the best method may be quite different for different children, depending on their particular aptitudes or other personological characteristics. It implies that the same educational goals can be accomplished to the same degree for children of different abilities provided the right instructional variations are found. This is merely a hope, and the relevant research so far gives little basis for optimism that such aptitude X training interactions will be found which can overcome to any marked degree the importance of IQ level for educability. But since this type of research has been underway only a few years, it is much too soon to discount the possibilities it may turn up — especially if one expects not miracles, but only positive, if modest, benefits from this approach.

GREATER ATTENTION TO LEARNING READINESS. The concept of developmental readiness for various kinds of school learning has been too neglected in recent educational trends, which have been dominated by the unproved notion that the earlier something can be taught to a child, the better. Forced early learning, prior to some satisfactory level of readiness (which will differ markedly from one child to another), could cause learning blocks which later on practically defy remediation.* The more or less uniform lock-step sequencing of educational experiences may have to be drastically modified for the benefit of many children, but the recent massive insistence on "earliness" and equality of educational treatment of all children has militated against large-scale research on the implications of readiness for children with below-average educability within the traditional school system.

GREATER DIVERSITY OF CURRICULA AND GOALS. Public schools, which aim to serve the entire population, must move beyond narrow conceptions of scholastic achievement to find a greater diversity of ways for children over the entire range of abilities to benefit from their schooling — to benefit especially in ways that will be to their advantage when they are out of school. The academic goals of schooling are so ingrained in our thinking and our values that it will probably call for radical efforts to modify public education in ways such that it will maximally benefit large numbers of children with very limited aptitude for academic achievement. I believe

* William Rohwer (Section 13) makes the same point.

that a well-intentioned but misconceived social egalitarian ideology has prevented public education in the United States from facing up to this challenge.

The belief that equality of educational opportunity should necessarily lead to equality of performance, I believe, is proving to be a false hope. It is the responsibility of scientific research in genetics, psychology, and education to determine the basis for realistic solutions to the problems of universal public education. Though it may be premature to prescribe at present, I venture the prediction that future solutions will take the form not so much of attempting to minimize differences in scholastic aptitudes and motivation, but of creating a greater diversity of curricula, instructional methods, and educational goals and values that will make it possible for children ranging over a wider spectrum of abilities and proclivities genuinely to benefit from their years in school.* The current zeitgeist of environmentalist equalitarianism has all but completely stifled our thinking along these lines. And I believe the magnitude and urgency of the problem are such as to call for quite radical thinking if the educational system is truly to serve the whole of society. We have invested so much for so long in trying to equalize scholastic performance that we have given little or no thought to finding ways of diversifying schools to make them rewarding to everyone while not attempting to equalize everyone's performance in a common curriculum. Recommendations have almost always taken the form of asking what next we might try to make children who in the present school system do not flourish academically become more like those who do. The emphasis has been more on changing children than on revamping the system. A philosophy of equalization, however laudable its ideals, cannot work if it is based on false premises, and no amount of propaganda can make it appear to work. Its failures will be forced upon everyone. Educational pluralism of some sort, encompassing a variety of very different educational curricula and goals, I think, will be the inevitable outcome of the growing realization that the schools are not going to eliminate human differences. Rather than making over a large segment of the school population so they will not be doomed to failure in a largely antiquated elitist-oriented educational system which originally evolved to serve only a relatively small segment of society, the educational system will have to be revamped in order to benefit everyone who is required by the society to attend school. It seems incredible that a system can still survive which virtually guarantees frustration and failure for a large proportion of the children it should intend to serve. From all the indications, public education in such a form will not much longer survive.

But we should not fail to recognize that to propose radical diversity in

* As a teacher, would you want to minimize differences or promote diversity?

accord with individual differences in abilities and interests, as contrasted with uniformity of educational treatment, puts society between Scylla and Charybdis in terms of ensuring for all individuals equality of opportunity for the diversity of educational paths. The surest way to maximize the benefits of schooling to all individuals and at the same time to make the most of a society's human resources is to ensure equality of educational opportunity for all its members. Monolithic educational goals and uniformity of approaches guarantee unnecessary frustration and defeat for many. On the other hand, educational pluralism runs the risk that social, economic, ethnic background or geographic origin, rather than each child's own characteristics, might determine the educational paths available to him. The individual characteristics appropriate for any one of a variety of educational paths and goals are to be found everywhere, in every social stratum, ethnic group, and neighborhood. Academic aptitudes and special talents should be cultivated wherever they are found, and a wise society will take all possible measures to ensure this to the greatest possible extent. At the same time, those who are poor in the traditional academic aptitudes cannot be left by the wayside. Suitable means and goals must be found for making their years of schooling rewarding to them, if not in the usual academic sense, then in ways that can better their chances for socially useful and self-fulfilling roles as adults.

EXERCISE

1. What is the most important genetic characteristic of people that must be recognized? (pp. 127–128)

2. What does it mean to say that "learning ability has high heritability"? (pp. 128–129)

3. What genetically conditioned traits are known to vary between racial groups? (p. 130)

4. Why does Jensen suggest that controlling for socioeconomic status confounds the study of racial differences? (p. 131)

5. How does Jensen respond to the criticism that intelligence tests are culture-biased? (p. 132)

6. What position does Jensen propose that educators take regarding the heredity-environment issue? (p. 134)

7. According to Jensen, what are three approaches that schools might take for dealing with individual differences in intelligence? (pp. 136–137)

Facilitating Development in the Preschool Child: Social and Psychological Perspectives

Martin Deutsch

In this article, Martin Deutsch presents his view of compensatory education, a major school reform during the late 1960's. He feels that the child's social experiences are very influential in his intellectual development. More specifically, Deutsch argues that the experiences of a child from an inner-city, low-income environment are less useful for the development of cognitive skills than those of a child from a middle-class environment. Children from low-income environments, therefore, enter school with a handicap compared to their middle-class peers. One way to eliminate this handicap is to develop special compensatory education programs, as in such projects as Head Start and Follow Through. Current evaluations of these programs indicate that their success has been minimal. (These evaluation studies are discussed by William Rohwer, Jr., Section 13; Mary Jo Bane and Christopher Jencks, Section 3; and Gilbert Austin, Bruce Rogers, and Henry Walbesser, Section 13.) You might find it interesting to relate the reforms recommended by Deutsch in 1964 with those emerging in the 1970's, particularly those discussed in Part 3 of this book. Also, suppose that Martin Deutsch, William Labov, Arthur Jensen, and George Mayeske (all in this section) were discussing causes for differences in learning outcomes of black and white children. What causes, if any, might they agree on? What would be their major areas of disagreement?

A large portion of the following discussion will be the examination of some of the psycho-social highways that criss-cross the early life of the child, and how socio-educational engineering might provide the most facilitating architecture for maximizing human achievement.

Massive evidence makes it clear that a child's social experience is a very influential factor in his development; yet it is also obvious that the relationship between experience and development is an extremely complex one.

From the *Merrill-Palmer Quarterly*, 1964, pp. 249–263. Reprinted with permission of the publisher and author.

A basic assumption of the approach to be presented in this paper is that there is a continual and influential interpenetration of environmental experience and psychological development along a broad front, and that therefore simple cause-effect models can be accurate on only the grossest level.

In a sense, our current social dilemma has the usual contradictions that every period feels are unique to its particular time. Historically, the present era may or may not have more contradictions than other periods. But the rapid development of automated, highly skilled, labor-reducing techniques does have revolutionary consequences for man's relationship to the social order, to work and leisure, and to intellectual activity. Further, the level of our technology, particularly in the field of communication, creates conditions in which these new techniques are rapidly disseminated. Thus, the time within which institutional and structural adjustments can take place is greatly reduced. This necessitates the deliberate and planned manipulation of social conditions in order to avoid, or at least attenuate, the sometimes invidious consequences of rapid change.

In a society of abundance, there is an amazingly large segment of our population living in a subsociety of social, economic, and educational impoverishment. The estimates range from 20 to 40 per cent of our population, depending on criteria. (For example see Harrington, 1963.) The problems associated with marginal employment and crowded, dehumanizing living conditions are, of course, characteristic of the lives of most of the peoples of the world. But here in this country we have the facilities, the productive capacity, and at least some of the knowledge required consciously to reorient social development. A necessary focus for such orientation should be the child, so that he can develop the requisite basic skills for the new technology and changing social institutions.

A thesis presented in this paper is that the behavioral scientist and the educator can facilitate the evolution of the educational institution so that it will be capable of preparing all children for optimal social participation, as the racial, social class, and sex gatekeepers become inoperative. The contemporary problems of education are to some extent a reflection of current technological, racial and urban conflicts inherent in accelerated social change. At the same time, the human sciences (though beset by similar problems) could become major instrumentalities for the resolution of social conflict, since they are among the few systems oriented toward change. For example, the intervention concepts in social psychology and psychiatry are relatively quite new. These disciplines can thus be seen as possible agents for the construction of blueprints to harmonize human needs with cultural transformations.

In general, the human sciences are moving from social and individual diagnosis to remedial therapies. Those sciences are now, in some of the more advanced thinking, concerned with primary prevention, ranging from mental illness and juvenile delinquency to disabilities in learning and socialization. To speculate on a possible avenue of future development, it might be that from this stage an orientation will develop toward assisting the individual to potentiate his intrinsic capacities for productive living and full individual realization.

This is by no means meant to minimize the importance of activities in other disciplines; rather it is an attempt to specify the potential role and contribution of the human sciences. It must also be remarked that the knowledge available in the combined human sciences is still quite limited, and that too frequently formulas have been presented which are insufficiently related to scientific knowledge.

While to a major degree the behavioral sciences and education have run parallel courses, they have insufficiently interacted with and enriched each other. What better place is there to investigate meaningfully the development of learning processes — or of attitudes or of mental health — than in longitudinal studies in the context of the school, from the nursery school through college? It is always surprising to us how many educators are not aware of the exciting investigations of socialization, learning, and cognitive processes in the field of child development. On the other hand, too many social scientists look upon education and work in the educational field as "applied," "atheoretical," and somehow unrelated to the growth of a child into an adult. Just as medicine is the application of physiology, biochemistry, and similar sciences to human problems, so too could education be the application of the human sciences. As medicine discovers principles and laws that are continually being circulated back to its basic sciences, so could education not only evaluate and validate the principles which it derives from the human sciences, but also could lead toward the genesis of methods of influencing and accelerating individual growth.

In order to achieve such integration, a crucial historical difference between education and psychiatry, sociology, and psychology must be recognized. While the latter have the impetus coming from both their newness and their response to challenge, education has the disadvantage of a long and encumbering history. In a sense, the institution of education — the school — is the status quo. Often it must operate through politically oriented bureaucracies that continually inhibit its potential for change and for developing strategies to meet social crises such as those inherent in the new urban America. These bureaucracies are often so large that introduction of meaningful change, even when agreed on by the higher echelons, is limited by the clogging of communication channels with paper, red tape, and assorted other artifacts, and by the constraints under which the average classroom teacher operates.

Somehow, this great gap in the educational hierarchy, separating the educator and his concept from the classroom teacher with her idea, creates a discontinuity that results in much wasted energy and distortion of effort.

A clear educational philosophy can come best from educators who are free enough from bureaucracy to communicate with the classroom teacher as a full professional, and to attenuate the burden of the past while setting up new relationships with the human sciences. Inherent in this approach is the necessity for effective cooperation between educators and behavioral scientists, so as to incorporate the growing knowledge of the socio-psychological development of the child into educational procedures in the interests of facilitating realization of his greatest intellectual and social potential.

The children most in need of help are from the economically and socially marginal and quasi-marginal segments of the community. These groups are the ones most caught in the technological and social changes; in many of our metropolitan areas they are becoming the majority of the center city population. It is in these groups that we find the highest proportion of unemployment, welfare support, and broken families. And it is in their children that we see the highest proportion of learning disabilities and school dropouts. While in the past it was possible to absorb most of such youth in unskilled, low-paying jobs, now the current adult generation is increasingly being replaced in such jobs by machines. With the number of unskilled and semi-skilled jobs decreasing, in order to find any place in the job market youth must now learn more complex functions, for which a successful educational experience is a prerequisite. This is a central problem for the total community, and a challenge for education. How it is met has wide ramifications for other underdeveloped areas outside our large cities and national boundaries.*

There are various avenues of approach to the problem of both preventing learning disabilities and facilitating intellectual growth.

In recent years, there have been major curriculum renovations, enrichment programs, new systems for teaching mathematics and the sciences, programmed courses and teaching machines, as well as a multiplicity of new methods for teaching reading. However, in the disadvantaged, underdeveloped areas of our communities, where there is the large proportion of underachievers, these new methods are probably least applicable, being most often based on an assumption that the child has reached a particular level in skills which underlie them. As will be pointed out later, for the disadvantaged child this is an unwarranted assumption. For the most part, it is a correct assumption for the middle-class child; but here there are other problems. Too often, new methods are seen mainly as more effective techniques to help the child get into college and achieve occupation status goals, and the aim of education along with its innovations becomes narrowly pragmatic. This is not to say that new methods should not be devised and attempted, but rather, that they might be seen neither as solutions to

---

* This is an example of the view that education should be used to alleviate poverty. Compare with Bane and Jencks's view (see Section 3).

underachievement nor as substitutions for the development and encouragement of intrinsic motivation toward intellectual mastery and scholastic achievement.

An approach that combines the preventive with the facilitating — and which would establish a basis for the absorption of new methods — is that of planned intervention at the earlier periods of development of the various components of the intellectual spectrum. Evidence which is accumulating points more and more to the influence of background variables on the patterns of language and cognitive development of the child, and a subsequent diffusion of the effects of such patterns into all areas of the child's academic and psychological performance. Deprived backgrounds thus lead to the inadequacy of such patterns. What is proposed is that experiential inadequacies in the social background can be compensated for by a planned enrichment, channeled through improved schools.*

Reference has been made to the constellation of factors in lower-class life which are associated with a limited range of experiential variability available to the child. Of course, there are probably differing clusters of economic, social and family factors associated with greater or lesser retardation. But the fact remains that lower social class status apparently predisposes to scholastic retardation, even though not all children are equally affected. Therefore, before discussing learning processes in the school it might be helpful to delineate some of the major features of urban slum life.

Geographically, there are crowded and dilapidated tenements quite at variance with the TV image of how people live. If the people are Negro, Puerto Rican, or Mexican-American, or poor mountain white, life is in a more-or-less segregated community. There are likely to be extremely crowded apartments, high rates of unemployment, chronic economic insecurity, a disproportionate number of broken families, and (particularly in the case of the Negro) continual exposure to denigration and social ostracism of varying degrees. The educational level of the adults tends to be quite limited. In the homes, there is likely to be a nearly complete absence of books, relatively few toys, and, in many instances, nothing except a few normal home-objects which may be adapted as playthings. In addition — particularly but not exclusively where relatively new in-migrants are concerned — there is a great deal of horizontal mobility. The result is a pattern of life that exposes a child to a minimum of direct contacts with the central channels of our culture.† The conditions of social inequality, the absence of an accessible opportunity structure, and the frequent non-availability of successful adult male models create an atmosphere that is just not facilitat-

---

* Key point. However, the findings of Bane and Jencks (Section 3) and of Austin et al. (Section 13) suggest that this goal has not been achieved.
† William Labov takes issue with these conclusions in the next selection.

ing to individual development. Moreover, the everyday problems of living, particularly those of economic insecurity and a multiplicity of children, leave minimum time for the adults who may be present to assist the child in exploring the world, to reward him for successful completion of tasks, or to help him in the development of a differentiated self-concept. Even in homes which are not broken, the practical manifestations of economic marginality result in the father sometimes holding two jobs and having little time for interaction with the child. We have found in various studies that children from these circumstances have relatively few shared or planned family activities, again resulting in a narrowing of experience. . . .

Previously, I have said that emphasis on the importance of variety in the environment implies the detrimental effects of lack of variety (Deutsch, 1963). I then postulated that a child from any circumstance, who has been deprived of a substantial portion of the variety of stimuli to which he is maturationally capable of responding, is likely to be deficient in the equipment required for school learning. This does not necessarily imply restriction in the quantity of stimulation; rather, it refers to a restriction in variety — i.e., restriction to only a segment of the spectrum of stimulation potentially available. In addition to such restriction in variety, from the description of the slum environment, it might be postulated that the segments made available to children from that background tend to have poorer and less systematic ordering of stimulation sequences, thereby being less useful to the growth and activation of cognitive potential.

The most promising agency for providing environmental compensations is the school. It is through this institution, which reaches every child, that the requisite stimulation for facilitating learning, psychological maturation, and acculturation can be most efficiently organized and programmed. Yet it is now estimated that up to 60 per cent of lower-class children are retarded two years or more in reading, by the time they leave the elementary school.

Before we place the entire responsibility on the school, however, an important fact must be noted. The overwhelming finding of studies on the relationship between social class and learning, school performance, and the like is that children from backgrounds of social marginality enter the first grade already behind their middle-class counterparts in a number of skills highly related to scholastic achievement. They are simply less prepared to meet the demands of the school and the classroom situation. Conversely, though, the school has failed to prepare to meet their needs. The failure of the educational institution to overcome the children's environmentally determined handicaps too often results in early failure, increasing alienation, and an increasingly greater gap between the lower-class and middle-class youngsters as they progress through school. In other words, intellectual and achievement differences between lower-class and middle-class children are smallest at the first grade level, and tend to increase through the elementary school years. It is here where the interaction between school and early environment, instead of having a facilitating influence, has a negative effect. While the school does not contribute to the initial problem (except through its effects on the previous generation), neither does it contribute to the overcoming of the initial handicaps.

It would seem quite reasonable, in the light of this discussion and its supporting evidence, to better prepare the child to meet the school's demands before he enters the first grade, and before there has been an accumulation of failure experiences and maladaptive behavior.* It would also seem eminently reasonable that the school should accept this responsibility. At the same time, it does not seem reasonable that an institution which so far has generally failed to meet its responsibility to this group should simply be given a mandate, without the incorporation of new and appropriate knowledge and techniques. Here is where the knowledge from the behavioral sciences can be put to its most effective use.

For example, all peoples have difficulties in spanning cultural discontinuities, and the entrance of the child into school for the first time places him in an environment which, in many respects, is discontinuous with his home. This discontinuity is minimal for the middle-class child, who is likely to have had the importance of school imprinted in his consciousness from the earliest possible age. For him, therefore, the school is very central and is continuous with the totality of his life experiences. As a result there are few incongruities between his school experiences and any others he is likely to have had, and there are intrinsic motivating and molding properties in the school situation to which he has been highly sensitized. Further, there is more likely to be contiguity in the school-faculty orientation with his home-family orientation. Failure can be interpreted to him in appropriate and familiar terms, and methods of coping with it can be incorporated, increasing the motivation or offering the necessary rewards, goals, or punishments to effect the desired change in performance.

For the lower-class child there is not the same contiguity or continuity. He does not have the same coping mechanisms for internalizing success or psychologically surviving failure in the formal learning setting. If the lower-class child starts to fail, he does not have the same kinds of operationally significant and functionally relevant support from his family or community — or from the school. Further, because of the differences in preparation, he is more likely to experience failure.

In this context, let us consider White's concept of competence motivation as a primary drive. The middle-class child comes to school prepared for the most part, to meet the demands made on him. The expectations of his teachers are that he will succeed. As he confronts material that is con-

---

* *This and similar views led to establishing the Head Start and Follow Through programs.*

gruent with his underlying skills, he is able to succeed; and thus he achieves the feeling of efficacy which White (1959) points out is so necessary to the "effectance motivation" which promotes continuing positive interaction with the environment. The lower-class child, on the other hand, experiences the middle-class oriented school as discontinuous with his home environment, and further, comes to it unprepared in the basic skills on which the curriculum is founded. The school becomes a place which makes puzzling demands, and where failure is frequent and feelings of competence are subsequently not generated. Motivation decreases, and the school loses its effectiveness.

It is in the transitional years from the pre-school period through the elementary school years that the child is first subject to the influence and the requirements of the broader culture. It is then that two environments are always present for him: the home environment and the school environment. But it is also in these transitional (and especially in the pre-transitional) years that the young organism is most malleable. Thus, that is the point at which efforts might best be initiated to provide a third — an intervention — environment to aid in the reconciliation of the first two. Such reconciliation is required because, especially for the child from a disadvantaged background, there are wide discrepancies between the home and school milieus. In the intervention environment, preventive and remedial measures can be applied to eliminate or overcome the negative effects of the discontinuities....

Scott's (1962) summary of the relevant research information on critical stages in development indicates that the period of greatest plasticity is during the time of the initial socialization. Since the bulk of the literature in this area is on animals, generalizations must be carefully confined. But seemingly, as one ascends the phylogenetic scale, there are greater ranges of time during which the organism has high levels of plasticity and receptivity. There is an insufficient body of data to hypothesize a most critical period for learning in the human child, and there are probably different critical or optimal periods for different functions. However, at about three or four years of age there is a period which would roughly coincide with the early part of what Piaget calls the "preoperational stage." It is then that the child is going through the later stages of early socialization; that he is required to focus his attention and monitor auditory and visual stimuli; and that he learns through language to handle simple symbolic representations. It is at this three- to four-year-old level that organized and systematic stimulation, through a structured and articulated learning program, might most successfully prepare the child for the more formal and demanding structure of the school. It is here, at this early age, that we can postulate that compensation for prior deprivation can most meaningfully be introduced. And, most important, there is considerably less that has to be compensated for at this age than exists when, as a far more complex and at least somewhat less plastic organism, the child gets to the first grade.

This position and its implications for specially organized early stimulation of the child find support in a recent article by Bruner (1961) on cognitive consequences of sensory deprivation. He says: "Not only does early deprivation rob the organism of the opportunity of constructing models of the environment, it also prevents the development of efficient strategies for evaluating information — for digging out what leads to what and with what likelihood. Robbed of development in this sphere, it becomes the more difficult to utilize probable rather than certain cues, the former requiring a more efficient strategy than the latter" (pp. 202–203). Bruner goes on to a discussion of nonspecific transfer of training in which, I think, he provides the most incontrovertible foundation for a structured, systematic pre-school enrichment and retraining program which would compensate, or attempt to compensate, for the deficiencies in the slum environment. His discussion is not of slums or compensation, but in his pointing up the importance of the "normally rich" environment, the serious cognitive consequences of the deprived environment are thrown into relief. Bruner says, " . . . nonspecific or generic transfer involves the learning of general rules and strategies for coping with highly common features of the environment" (p. 203). After pointing out that Piaget " . . . remarks upon the fact that cognitive growth consists of learning how to handle the great informational transformations like reversibility, class identity, and the like" and that Piaget speaks of these as "strategies for dealing with, or better for creating usable information," Bruner proposes: " . . . that exposure to normally rich environments makes the development of such strategies possible by providing intervening opportunity for strategic trial and error" (p. 203).

What Bruner talks about under "trial and error" requires a certain level of motivation and exploratory efforts. I have previously discussed the possible role of early failure experiences in influencing the motivational and goal orientations, and the self-expectancies, of the lower-class child. When the lower-class child gets into first grade, too frequently his cognitive, sensory, and language skills are insufficiently developed to cope with what for him are the complex and confusing stimuli offered by the school. It is the interaction of these motivational and maturational dynamics that makes it extremely important for society, through institutions such as the school, to offer the lower-class child an organized and reasonably orderly program of stimulation, at as early an age as possible, to compensate for possible cognitive deficit.

The focus has been on deficit because of the general hypothesis that the experiential deprivations associated with poverty are disintegrative and subtractive from normative growth expectancies. The extent of academic failure and reading retardation associated with lower-class status — and especially with minority group membership within the lower class — makes it imperative that we study the operational relationship between social conditions and these deficits, and the subsequent failure of the school to reverse the tendency toward cumulative retardation in the primary grades.

Our work has been directed particularly toward delineating the effects of conditions of life on cognitive structures. For an understanding of these relationships and the scientific development of enrichment programs, we have emphasized the role of specific social attributes and experiences in the development of language and verbal behavior, of concept formation and organization, of visual and auditory discrimination, of general environmental orientation, and of self-concepts and motivation; and of all of this to school performance. It is the areas mentioned which apparently are essential to the acquisition of scholastic skills, and around which a basic curriculum for early childhood should be developed. Pragmatically, this must be a program which successfully teaches disadvantaged children.

Examination of the literature yields no explanation or justification for any child with an intact brain, and who is not severely disturbed, not to learn all the basic scholastic skills. The failure of such children to learn is the failure of the schools to develop curricula consistent with the environmental experiences of the children and their subsequent initial abilities and disabilities.*

As has been emphasized previously in this paper, a compensatory program for children, starting at three or four years of age, might provide the maximum opportunity for prevention of future disabilities and for remediation of current skill deficiencies. In addition, such a program might serve to minimize the effect of the discontinuity between the home and school environments, thereby enhancing the child's functional adjustment to school requirements.

For an early enrichment program, one model available is that developed by Maria Montessori (1959) in the slums of Italy. Though her theoretical system need not be critically evaluated here, there is much in her technology that could productively be re-examined and incorporated in compensatory programs. Basically, this includes the organization of perceptual stimuli in the classroom, so that singular properties become more observable, one at a time, without the distraction of competing, overly complex elements. For example, materials used to convey and illustrate the concept of size and size differential are all the same color and shape. This maximizes the attentional properties of size, and minimizes competing elements. Use of such materials should make it possible for size discriminations to be learned more easily. This method is, of course, carried over to many fields, and the availability of such stimuli under the Montessori system gives the

---

* *Compare this statement with the position underlying Jensen's three approaches for improving education (Jensen, this section).*

child an opportunity to select materials consistent with his own developmental capabilities. This makes possible success experience, positive reinforcement, and subsequent enhancement of involvement and motivation. The attention to the minutiae of learning, and the systematic exposure to new learning elements based on prior experience, could allow for the development of individualized learning profiles. This would be particularly appropriate for a compensatory program, where there is a great deal of variation in individual needs.

There is, however, a major variable which is apparently inadequately handled by this method, and that is language.

Language can be thought of as a crucial ingredient in concept formation, problem-solving, and in the relating to and interpretation of the environment. Current data available to the author and his co-workers tend to indicate that class differences in perceptual abilities and general environmental orientation decrease with chronological age, while language differences tend to increase.

In a social-class-related language analysis, Bernstein (1960), an English sociologist, has pointed out that the lower class tends to use informal language and mainly to convey concrete needs and immediate consequences, while the middle-class usage tends to be more formal and to emphasize the relating of concepts.[1] * This difference between these two milieus, then, might explain the finding in some of our recent research that the middle-class fifth grade child has an advantage over the lower-class fifth grader in tasks where precise and somewhat abstract language is required for solution. Further, Bernstein's reasoning would again emphasize the communication gap which can exist between the middle-class teacher and the lower-class child.

One can postulate that the absence of well-structured routine and activity in the home is reflected in the difficulty that the lower-class child has in structuring language. The implication of this for curriculum in the kindergarten and nursery school would be that these children should be offered a great deal of verbalized routine and regulation, so that positive expectations can be built up in the child and then met. It can also be postulated that differences in verbal usage are directly attributable to the level of interaction of the child with the adult, and at this age to a lesser extent, with peers.

In observations of lower-class homes, it appears that speech sequences seem to be temporally very limited and poorly structured syntactically. It is thus not surprising to find that a major focus of deficit in the children's language development is syntactical organization and subject continuity. But in analysis of expressive and receptive language data on samples of

* *Compare this interpretation of Bernstein's research with Labov's criticism (next selection).*

middle- and lower-class children at the first and fifth grade levels, there are indications that the lower-class child has more expressive language ability than is generally recognized or than emerges in the classroom. The main differences between the social classes seem to lie in the level of syntactical organization. If, as is indicated in this research, with proper stimulation a surprisingly high level of expressive language functioning is available to the same children who show syntactical deficits, then we might conclude that the language variables we are dealing with here are by-products of social experience rather than indices of basic ability or intellectual level. This again suggests a vital area to be included in any pre-school enrichment program: training in the use of word sequences to relate and unify cognitions. . . .

Working out compensatory programs is based on the assumption that retardation in achievement results from the interaction of inadequately prepared children with inadequate schools and insufficient curricula.* This in turn is based on the contention that this large proportion of children is not failing because of inferior innate resources. Also implied is the assumption that one does not sit by and wait for children to "unfold," either on the intellectual or behavioral levels. Rather, it is asserted that growth requires guidance of stimulation, and that this is particularly valid with regard to the child who does not receive the functional prerequisites for school learning in the home. Hunt (1961) points out that ". . . the counsel from experts on child-rearing during the third and much of the fourth decades of the twentieth century to let children be while they grow and to avoid excessive stimulation was highly unfortunate" (p. 362). This is particularly true with regard to lower-class children. We have found that, controlling for socio-economic status, children with some pre-school experience have significantly higher intelligence test scores at the fifth grade than do children with no pre-school experience (Deutsch and Brown, 1964).

But it is not necessary to consider special education programs only on the pre-school level, even though that is what has been emphasized here. Rather, to assure stability of progress, it would be desirable to continue special programs for several more years. The construction of a pre-school program does not absolve a community or a school system from the responsibility to construct an effective strategy for teaching the marginal youngster from kindergarten on. In fact, if there is to be a reversal of some of the sequelae associated with poverty discussed in this paper, programs must have continuity, at least through the period of the establishment of the basic scholastic learning skills. This means that it is necessary for the

---

* *This assumption influenced large expenditures under Title I of the Elementary and Secondary Education Act. Does it still apply in the free school movement discussed by Graubard in Section 11?*

community to support kindergartens with reasonable enrollments and adequate equipment, as well as specialized training of staff. As far as the primary grades are concerned, the continuation of special programming through establishment of basic skills would involve probably the time through the third grade year. This level is used, because there is empirical reason to believe that levels of achievement for different social classes start their greatest divergence here. This is probably so because here the work begins to become less concrete and more abstract, more dependent on language symbolization, and, probably most important, more related to good reading skills. For these reasons, it would seem that the child from the pre-school and enriched kindergarten classes might best remain in a special ungraded sequence through the third grade level, a period in which he could be saturated with basic skill training, and not be allowed to move on until he has attained basic competence in the skills required by the higher grades. Such an ungraded school would also be of considerable interest theoretically, inasmuch as the child would be in its program through the preoperational stage delineated by Piaget. This should make it possible to devise a systematic curriculum that is consistent with the actual developmental levels of the child during the early childhood period. . . .

There are those people who seem to fear the word "cognitive," sometimes correctly, because they are reacting to the over-stringent mechanical models of the past. These models are not what is meant. The potentiation of human resources through the stimulation of cognitive growth could represent a primary therapeutic method for developing positive self-attitudes and a meaningful self-realization. For the lower-class child especially, I would postulate that time is extremely valuable if the deficits are not to be cumulative and to permeate the entire functioning of the child.

The overgeneralized influence on some sections of early childhood education of the emphasis in the child guidance movement upon protecting the child from stress, creating a supportive environment, and resolving emotional conflicts has done more to misdirect and retard the fields of child care, guidance, and development than any other single influence. The effect has especially operated to make these fields ineffective in responding to the problems of integrating and educating the non-white urban child. These orientations have conceived of the child as being always on the verge of some disease process, and have assigned to themselves the role of protecting the child in the same manner that a zoo-keeper arranges for the survival of his charges. Too frequently a philosophy of protectiveness that asks only about possible dangers has prevailed over any question of potential stimulation of development. The attitude that perhaps helped to create this policy of protectionism can also be seen in the suburban "mom-ism" that so many sociologists and psychoanalysts have commented on. The child is a far healthier and stronger little organism, with more intrinsic motivation for variegated experience and learning, than the over-protectionists have traditionally given him credit for. . . .

And as Hunt (1961) says: "The problem for the management of child development is to find out how to govern the encounters that children have with their environments to foster both an optimally rapid rate of intellectual development and a satisfying life" (pp. 362–363).

A curriculum as discussed here should serve both for the primary prevention of the social deviancies associated with deprivation and for the stimulation of healthy growth and utilization of individual resources. This orientation would represent one effective method of offering opportunities to all peoples to overcome and break the chains of social and historical limitations that have been externally imposed on them. This of course has immediate significance to the current critical questions in both race relations and education in America.

EXERCISE

1. According to Deutsch, why are economically and socially deprived children most in need of help from the behavioral scientist? (p. 142)

2. Why does Deutsch claim that new curriculum programs and new teaching methods will not help the disadvantaged child? (pp. 142–143)

3. What does Deutsch see as the major features of contemporary urban slum life? (pp. 143–144)

4. Deutsch states that planned intervention in the early years will help the slum child develop his innate abilities to their fullest extent. Why is early intervention important? (pp. 144–145)

5. What is Deutsch's major criticism of the Montessori method as an approach to compensatory education? (p. 149)

6. What major differences in language use by lower-class and middle-class children are described by Deutsch? (pp. 149–150)

7. How long would Deutsch continue a compensatory education program? Why was this termination point selected? (pp. 150–151)

Academic Ignorance
and Black Intelligence

William Labov

*William Labov takes the point of view that differences in learn-
ing outcomes between white and black students result from
teachers' failure to understand and respond to the students' culture.
He presents evidence that black students use an English vernacular
that is grammatically complex and capable of expressing abstract
concepts. However, white teachers and researchers perceive this
form of language as inferior and caused by deficiencies in the students' out-of-school background, a perception shared by Martin
Deutsch in the preceding selection. Labov argues that compensatory
programs designed to overcome these differences only aggravate the
black students' learning problems in school. In short, Labov does
not attribute learning deficiencies to characteristics of the children,
as do Arthur Jensen (genetic inferiority) and Deutsch (lack of basic
skills). Instead, he attributes deficiencies to the way schools treat
children. He suggests that research efforts to identify ways to improve learning have been studying the wrong hypotheses. Rather
than seeking ways to mold the child to the school, educators attempting to improve learning should examine how the school can be
altered to fit the strengths of the child. As an alternative to compensatory education, Labov has several suggestions that, if adopted,
could lead to dramatic changes in education for culturally different
groups of children. How could you apply his findings and point of
view to classroom teaching?*

In the past decade, a great deal of federally sponsored research has been
devoted to the educational problems of children in ghetto schools. To
account for the poor performance of children in these schools, educational
psychologists have tried to discover what kind of disadvantage or defect
the children are suffering from. The viewpoint which has been widely
accepted and used as the basis for large-scale intervention programs is
that the children show a cultural *deficit* as a result of an impoverished

From the Monograph Series on Languages and Linguistics, Number 22,
1969. Georgetown University. Also printed in The Atlantic Monthly, vol.
229, no. 6 (June 1972), pages 59–67. Copyright © 1972 by the Atlantic
Monthly Company, Boston, Mass. Reprinted with permission of publisher
and author.

environment in their early years. A great deal of attention has been given to language. In this area, the deficit theory appears as the notion of "verbal deprivation": black children from the ghetto area are said to receive little verbal stimulation, to hear very little well-formed language, and as a result are impoverished in their means of verbal expression. It is said that they cannot speak complete sentences, do not know the names of common objects, cannot form concepts or convey logical thoughts.

Unfortunately, these notions are based upon the work of educational psychologists who know very little about language and even less about black children. The concept of verbal deprivation has no basis in social reality;* in fact, black children in the urban ghettos receive a great deal of verbal stimulation, hear more well-formed sentences than middle-class children, and participate fully in a highly verbal culture; they have the same basic vocabulary, possess the same capacity for conceptual learning, and use the same logic as anyone else who learns to speak and understand English. The myth of verbal deprivation is particularly dangerous because it diverts the attention from real defects of our educational system to imaginary defects of the child; and as we shall see, it leads its sponsors inevitably to the hypothesis of the genetic inferiority of black children, which the verbal-deprivation theory was designed to avoid.

The deficit theory attempts to account for a number of facts that are known to all of us: that black children in the central urban ghettos do badly on all school subjects, including arithmetic and reading. In reading, they average more than two years behind the national norm. Furthermore, this lag is cumulative, so that they do worse comparatively in the fifth grade than in the first grade. The information available suggests that this bad performance is correlated most closely with socioeconomic status.† Segregated ethnic groups, however, seem to do worse than others: in particular, Indian, Mexican-American, and black children.

We are obviously dealing with the effects of the caste system of American society — essentially a "color-making" system. Everyone recognizes this. The question is, By what mechanism does the color bar prevent children from learning to read? One answer is the notion of "cultural deprivation" put forward by Martin Deutsch and others: the black children are said to lack the favorable factors in their home environment which enable middle-class children to do well in school. These factors involve the development, through verbal interaction with adults, of various cognitive skills, including the ability to reason abstractly, to speak fluently, and to focus upon long-range goals. In their publications, the psycholo-

---

* Deutsch expresses the opposite view in the preceding selection.
† Mayeske's findings (this section) support this statement.

gists Deutsch, Irwin Katz, and Arthur Jensen also recognize broader social factors. However, the deficit theory docs not focus upon the interaction of the black child with white society so much as on his failure to interact with his mother at home. In the literature we find very little direct observation of verbal interaction in the black home; most typically, the investigators ask the child if he has dinner with his parents, and if he engages in dinner-table conversation with them. He is also asked whether his family takes him on trips to museums and other cultural activities. This slender thread of evidence is used to explain and interpret the large body of tests carried out in the laboratory and in the school.

The most extreme view which proceeds from this orientation — and one that is now being widely accepted — is that lower-class black children have no language at all. Some educational psychologists first draw from the writings of the British social psychologist Basil Bernstein the idea that "much of lower-class language consists of a kind of incidental 'emotional accompaniment' to action here and now." Bernstein's views are filtered through their strong bias against all forms of working-class behavior, so that Arthur Jensen, for example, sees middle-class language as superior in every respect — as "more abstract, and necessarily somewhat more flexible, detailed and subtle." One can proceed through a range of such views until one comes to the practical program of Carl Bereiter, Siegfried Engelmann, and their associates. Bereiter's program for an academically oriented preschool is based upon the premise that black children must have a language which they can learn, and their empirical findings that these children come to school without such a language. In his work with four-year-old black children from Urbana, Illinois, Bereiter reports that their communication was by gestures, "single words," and "a series of badly connected words or phrases," such as *They mine* and *Me got juice*. He reports that black children could not ask questions, that "without exaggerating ...these four-year-olds could make no statements of any kind." Furthermore, when these children were asked, "Where is the book?" they did not know enough to look at the table where the book was lying in order to answer. Thus Bereiter concludes that the children's speech forms are nothing more than a series of emotional cries, and he decides to treat them "as if the children had no language at all." He identifies their speech with his interpretation of Bernstein's restricted code: "The language of culturally deprived children ... is not merely an underdeveloped version of standard English, but is a basically non-logical mode of expressive behavior." The basic program of his preschool is to teach them a new language devised by Engelmann, which consists of a limited series of questions and answers such as *Where is the squirrel? / The squirrel is in the tree.* The children will not be punished if they use their vernacular speech on the playground, but they will not be allowed to use it in the school-room. If they should answer the question "Where is the squirrel?" with the illogical vernacular form "In the tree," they will be reprehended by various means and made to say, "The squirrel is in the tree." *

Linguists and psycholinguists who have worked with black children are likely to dismiss this view of their language as utter nonsense. Yet there is no reason to reject Bereiter's observations as spurious: they were certainly not made up. On the contrary, they give us a very clear view of the behavior of student and teacher which can be duplicated in any classroom. Our own research is done outside the schools, in situations where adults are not the dominant force, but on many occasions we have been asked to help analyze the results of research into verbal deprivation in such test situations.

Here, for example, is a complete interview with a black boy, one of hundreds carried out in a New York City school. The boy enters a room where there is a large, friendly, white interviewer, who puts on the table in front of him a block or a fire engine, and says, "Tell me everything you can about this!" (The interviewer's further remarks are in parentheses.)

                    [12 *seconds of silence*]
(What would you say it looks like?)
                    [8 *seconds of silence*]
A spaceship.
(Hmmmmm.)
                    [13 *seconds of silence*]
Like a je-et.
                    [12 *seconds of silence*]
Like a plane.
                    [20 *seconds of silence*]
(What color is it?)
Orange. [2 *seconds*]. An' whi-ite. [2 *seconds*].
An' green.
                    [6 *seconds of silence*]
(An' what could you use it for?)
                    [8 *seconds of silence*]
A je-et.
                    [6 *seconds of silence*]
(If you had two of them, what would you do with them?)
                    [6 *seconds of silence*]
Give one to some-body.
(Hmmm. Who do you think would like to have it?)
                    [10 *seconds of silence*]

* *Is this the type of language program you would expect Bereiter to establish based on his comments in Section 2?*

Cla-rence.
(Mm. Where do you think we could get another one of these?)
At the store.
(Oh-ka-ay!)

We have here the same kind of defensive, monosyllabic behavior which is reported in Bereiter's work. What is the situation that produces it? The child is in an asymmetrical situation where anything he says can literally be held against him. He has learned a number of devices to *avoid* saying anything in this situation, and he works very hard to achieve this end.

If one takes this interview as a measure of the verbal capacity of the child, it must be as his capacity to defend himself in a hostile and threatening situation. But unfortunately, thousands of such interviews are used as evidence of the child's total verbal capacity, or more simply his verbality: it is argued that this lack of "verbality" *explains* his poor performance in school.

The verbal behavior which is shown by the child in the test situation quoted above is not the result of ineptness of the interviewer. It is rather the result of regular sociolinguistic factors operating upon adult and child in this asymmetrical situation. In our work in urban ghetto areas, we have often encountered such behavior. For over a year Clarence Robins had worked with the Thunderbirds, a group of boys ten to twelve years old who were the dominant pre-adolescent group in a low-income project in Harlem. We then decided to interview a few younger brothers of the Thunderbirds, eight to nine years old. But our old approach didn't work. Here is an extract from the interview between Clarence and eight-year-old Leon L.:

CR: What if you saw somebody kickin' somebody else on the ground, or was using a stick, what would you do if you saw that?
LEON: Mmmm.
CR: If it was supposed to be a fair fight —
LEON: I don' know.
CR: You don' know? Would you do anything? . . . huh? I can't hear you.
LEON: No.
CR: Did you ever see somebody get beat up real bad?
LEON: . . . Nope ? ? ?
CR: Well — uh — did you ever get into a fight with a guy?
LEON: Nope.
CR: That was bigger than you?
LEON: Nope.
CR: You never been in a fight?
LEON: Nope.
CR: Nobody ever pick on you?
LEON: Nope.

CR: Nobody ever hit you?
LEON: Nope.
CR: How come?
LEON: Ah 'on' know.
CR: Didn't you ever hit somebody?
LEON: Nope.
CR: [*incredulous*] You never hit nobody?
LEON: Mhm.
CR: Aww, ba-a-a-be, you ain't gonna tell me that.

This nonverbal behavior occurs in a relatively *favorable* context for adult-child interaction, since the adult is a black man raised in Harlem, who knows this particular neighborhood and these boys very well. He is a skilled interviewer who has obtained a very high level of verbal response with techniques developed for a different age level, and has an extraordinary advantage over most teachers or experimenters in these respects. But even his skills and personality are ineffective in breaking down the social constraints that prevail here.

When we reviewed the record of this interview with Leon, we decided to use it as a test of our own knowledge of the sociolinguistic factors which control speech. We made the following changes in the social situation; in the next interview with Leon,* Clarence:

1. Brought along a supply of potato chips, changing the "interview" into something more in the nature of a party.
2. Brought along Leon's best friend, eight-year-old Gregory.
3. Reduced the height imbalance. When Clarence got down on the floor of Leon's room, he dropped from 6 feet, 2 inches to 3 feet, 6 inches.
4. Introduced taboo words and taboo topics, and proved to Leon's surprise that one can say anything into our microphone without any fear of retaliation. It did not hit or bite back. The result of these changes is a striking difference in the volume and style of speech.

[*The tape is punctuated throughout by the sound of potato chips.*]
CR: Is there anybody who says, "Your momma drink pee"?
LEON: [*rapidly and breathlessly*] Yee-ah!
GREG: Yup.
LEON: And your father eat doo-doo for breakfas'!
CR: Ohhh! [*laughs*]
LEON: And they say your father — your father eat doo-doo for dinner!
GREG: When they sound on me, I say "C.B.M."
CR: What that mean?

* *Do these techniques have any implications for the way you would interact with children in an inner-city classroom?*

LEON: Congo booger-snatch! [*laughs*]

GREG: Congo booger-snatcher! [*laughs*]

GREG: And sometimes I'll curse with "B.B."

CR: What that?

GREG: Oh, that's a "M.B.B." Black boy. [*Leon crunching on potato chips*]

GREG: 'Merican Black Boy.

CR: Oh.

GREG: Anyway, 'Mericans is same like white people, right?

LEON: And they talk about Allah.

CR: Oh, yeah?

GREG: Yeah.

CR: What they say about Allah?

LEON: Allah — Allah is God.

GREG: Allah —

CR: And what else?

LEON: I don' know the res'.

GREG: Allah i — Allah is God. Allah is the only God, Allah —

LEON: Allah is the *son* of God.

GREG: But can he make magic?

LEON: Nope.

GREG: I know who can make magic?

CR: Who can?

LEON: The God, the real one.

CR: Who can make magic?

GREG: The son of po' — (CR: Hm?) I'm sayin' the po'k chop God! He only a po'k chop God! [*Leon chuckles*]

The "nonverbal" Leon is now competing actively for the floor; Gregory and Leon talk to each other as much as they do to the interviewer. The monosyllabic speaker who had nothing to say about anything and could not remember what he did yesterday has disappeared. Instead, we have two boys who have so much to say that they keep interrupting each other, who seem to have no difficulty in using the English language to express themselves.

One can now transfer this demonstration of the sociolinguistic control of speech to other test situations, including IQ and reading tests in school. It should be immediately apparent that none of the standard tests will come anywhere near measuring Leon's verbal capacity. On these tests he will show up as very much the monosyllabic, inept, ignorant, bumbling child of our first interview. The teacher has far less ability than Clarence Robins to elicit speech from this child; Clarence knows the community, the things that Leon has been doing, and the things that Leon would like to talk about. But the power relationships in a one-to-one confrontation between adult and child are too asymmetrical. This does not mean that some black children will not talk a great deal when alone with an adult, or that an adult cannot get close to any child. It means that the social situation is the most powerful determinant of verbal behavior and that an adult must enter into the right social relation with a child if he wants to find out what a child can do. This is just what many teachers cannot do.

The view of the black speech community which we obtain from our work in the ghetto areas is precisely the opposite from that reported by Deutsch, Engelmann, and Bereiter. We see a child bathed in verbal stimulation from morning to night.* We see many speech events which depend upon the competitive exhibitions of verbal skills: singing, sounding, toasts, rifting, louding — a whole range of activities in which the individual gains status through his use of language. We see the younger child trying to acquire these skills from older children — hanging around on the outskirts of the older peer groups, and imitating this behavior. We see, however, no connection between verbal skill at the speech events characteristic of the street culture and success in the schoolroom; which says something about classrooms rather than about a child's language.

There are undoubtedly many verbal skills which children from ghetto areas must learn in order to do well in school, and some of these are indeed characteristic of middle-class verbal behavior. Precision in spelling, practice in handling abstract symbols, the ability to state explicitly the meaning of words, and a richer knowledge of the Latinate vocabulary may all be useful acquisitions. But is it true that *all* of the middle-class verbal habits are functional and desirable in school? Before we impose middle-class verbal style upon children from other cultural groups, we should find out how much of it is useful for the main work of analyzing and generalizing, and how much is merely stylistic — or even dysfunctional. In high school and college, middle-class children spontaneously complicate their syntax to the point that instructors despair of getting them to make their language simpler and clearer.

Our work in the speech community makes it painfully obvious that in many ways working-class speakers are more effective narrators, reasoners, and debaters than many middle-class speakers, who temporize, qualify, and lose their argument in a mass of irrelevant detail. Many academic writers try to rid themselves of the part of middle-class style that is empty pretension, and keep the part necessary for precision. But the average middle-class speaker that we encounter makes no such effort: he is enmeshed in verbiage, the victim of sociolinguistic factors beyond his control.

I will not attempt to support this argument here with systematic quan-

---

* Relate these circumstances to Bane and Jencks's statement about the effects of neighborhood experiences on learning (Section 3).

titative evidence, although it is possible to develop measures which show how far middle-class speakers can wander from the point. I would like to contrast two speakers dealing with roughly the same topic: matters of belief. The first is Larry H., a fifteen-year-old core member of another group, the Jets. Larry is being interviewed here by John Lewis, our participant-observer among adolescents in South Central Harlem.

JL: What happens to you after you die? Do you know?

LARRY H: Yeah, I know. (What?) After they put you in the ground, your body turns into — ah — bones, an' *shit*.

JL: What happens to your spirit?

LARRY: Your spirit — soon as you die, your spirit leaves you. (And where does the spirit go?) Well, it all depends. (On what?) You know, like some people say if you're good an' shit, your spirit goin' t'heaven . . . 'n' if you bad, your spirit goin' to hell. Well, *bullshit!* Your spirit goin' to hell anyway, good or bad.

JL: Why?

LARRY: Why? I'll tell you why. 'Cause, you see, doesn' nobody really know that it's a God, y'know, 'cause, I mean I have seen black gods, pink gods, white gods, all color gods, and don't nobody know it's really a God. An' when they be sayin' if you good, you goin' t'heaven, tha's *bullshit*, 'cause you ain't goin' to no heaven, 'cause it ain't no heaven for you to go to.

Larry is a gifted speaker of the Black English vernacular (BEV) as opposed to standard English (SE). His grammar shows a high concentration of such characteristic BEV forms as negative inversion [*don't nobody know*], negative concord [*you ain't goin' to no heaven*], invariant *be* [when they be sayin'], dummy *it* for SE *there* [*it ain't no heaven*], optional copula deletion [*if you're good . . . if you bad*], and full forms of auxiliaries [*I have seen*]. The only SE influence in this passage is the one case of *doesn't* instead of the invariant *don't* of BEV. Larry also provides a paradigmatic example of the rhetorical style of BEV: he can sum up a complex argument in a few words, and the full force of his opinions comes through without qualification or reservation. He is eminently quotable, and his interviews give us a great many concise statements of the BEV point of view. One can almost say that Larry speaks the BEV culture.

It is the logical form of this passage which is of particular interest here. Larry presents a complex set of interdependent propositions which can be explicated by setting out the SE equivalents in linear order. The basic argument is to deny the twin propositions:

(A) If you are good.   (B) then your spirit will go to heaven.
(not A) If you are bad.   (C) then your spirit will go to hell.

Larry denies (B), and allows that if (A) or (not A) is true, (C) will follow. His argument may be outlined:

1. Everyone has a different idea of what God is like.
2. Therefore nobody really knows that God exists.
3. If there is a heaven, it was made by God.
4. If God doesn't exist, he couldn't have made heaven.
5. Therefore heaven does not exist.
6. You can't go somewhere that doesn't exist.

(not B) Therefore you can't go to heaven.
    (C) Therefore you are going to hell.

This hypothetical argument is not carried on at a high level of seriousness. It is a game played with ideas as counters, in which opponents use a wide variety of verbal devices to win. There is no personal commitment to any of these propositions, and no reluctance to strengthen one's argument by bending the rules of logic as in the (2, 4) sequence. But if the opponent invokes the rules of logic, they hold. In John Lewis' interviews, he often makes this move, and the force of his argument is always acknowledged and countered within the rules of logic.

JL: Well, if there's no heaven, how could there be a hell?
LARRY: I mean — ye-eah. Well, let me tell you, it ain't no hell, 'cause this is hell right here, y'know! (This is hell?) Yeah, this is hell right here!

Larry's answer is quick, ingenious, and decisive.* The application of the (3-4-5) argument to hell is denied, since hell is here, and therefore conclusion (not B) stands. These are not ready-made or preconceived opinions, but new propositions devised to win the logical argument in the game being played. The reader will note the speed and precision of Larry's mental operations. He does not wander, or insert meaningless verbiage. It is often said that the nonstandard vernacular is not suited for dealing with abstract or hypothetical questions, but in fact, speakers of the BE vernacular take great delight in exercising their wit and logic on the most improbable and problematical matters. Despite the fact that Larry H. does not believe in God, and has just denied all knowledge of him, John Lewis advances the following hypothetical question:

JL: ... But, just say that there is a God, what color is he? White or black?
LARRY: Well, if it is a God ... I wouldn' know what color, I couldn' say — couldn' nobody say what —

* *Would you have evaluated Larry's answer the same way that Labov did?*

JL: But now, jus' suppose there was a God —

LARRY: Unless'n they say . . .

JL: No, I was jus' sayin' jus' suppose there is a God, would he be white or black?

LARRY: . . . He'd be white, man.

JL: Why?

LARRY: Why? I'll tell you why. 'Cause the average whitey out here got everything, you dig? And the nigger ain't got *shit*, y'know? Y'un-nerstan'? So — um — for — in order for *that* to happen, you know it ain't no black God that's doin' that *bullshit*.

No one can hear Larry's answer to this question without being convinced of being in the presence of a skilled speaker with great "verbal presence of mind," who can use the English language expertly for many purposes.

Let us now turn to the second speaker, an upper-middle-class, college-educated black man being interviewed by Clarence Robins in our survey of adults in South Central Harlem.

CR: Do you know of anything that someone can do, to have some-one who has passed on visit him in a dream?

CHAS. M.: Well, I even heard my parents say that there is such a thing as something in dreams, some things like that, and sometimes dreams do come true. I have personally never had a dream come true. I've never dreamt that somebody was dying and they ac-tually died (Mhm), or that I was going to have ten dollars the next day and somehow I got ten dollars in my pocket. (Mhm.) I don't particuarly believe in that, I don't think it's true. I do feel, though, that there is such a thing as — ah — witchcraft. I do feel that in certain cultures there is such a thing as witch-craft, or some sort of *science* of witchcraft; I don't think that it's just a matter of believing hard enough that there is such a thing as witchcraft. I do believe that there is such a thing that a per-son can put himself in a state of *mind* (Mhm), or that — er — something could be given them to intoxicate them in a certain — to a certain frame of mind — that — that could actually be considered witchcraft.

Charles M. is obviously a "good speaker" who strikes the listener as well-educated, intelligent, and sincere. He is a likable and attractive person — the kind of person that middle-class listeners rate very high on a scale of "job suitability" and equally high as a potential friend. His language is more moderate and tempered than Larry's; he makes every effort to qualify his opinions, and seems anxious to avoid any misstatements or overstate-ments. From these qualities emerges the primary characteristic of this passage — its *verbosity*. Words multiply, some modifying and qualifying, others repeating or padding the main argument. The first half of this extract is a response to the initial question on dreams, basically:

1. Some people say that dreams sometimes come true.
2. I have never had a dream come true.
3. Therefore I don't believe (1).

This much of Charles M.'s response is well directed to the point of the question. He then volunteers a statement of his beliefs about witchcraft which shows the difficulty of middle-class speakers who (a) want to express a belief in something but (b) want to show themselves as judicious, rational, and free from superstitions. The basic proposition can be stated simply in five words:

But I believe in witchcraft.

However, the idea is enlarged to exactly one hundred words, and it is difficult to see what else is being said. The vacuity of this passage becomes more evident if we remove repetitions, fashionable words, and stylistic decorations:

But I believe in witchcraft.
I don't think witchcraft is just a belief.
A person can put himself or be put in a state of mind that is witchcraft.

Without the extra verbiage and the OK words like *science, culture,* and *intoxicate,* Charles M. appears as something less than a first-rate thinker. The initial impression of him as a good speaker is simply our long-conditioned reaction to middle-class verbosity: we know that people who use these stylistic devices are educated people, and we are inclined to credit them with saying something intelligent. . . .

We can isolate six distinct steps in the reasoning which has led to [compensatory] programs such as those of Deutsch, Bereiter, and Engelmann:

1. The lower-class child's verbal response to a formal and threatening situation is used to demonstrate his lack of verbal capacity, or verbal deficit.

2. This verbal deficit is declared to be a major cause of the lower-class child's poor performance in school.

3. Since middle-class children do better in school, middle-class speech habits are said to be necessary for learning.

4. Class and ethnic differences in grammatical form are equated with differences in the capacity for logical analysis.

5. Teaching the child to mimic certain formal speech patterns used by middle-class teachers is seen as teaching him to think logically.

6. Children who learn these formal speech patterns are then said to be thinking logically, and it is predicated that they will do much better in reading and arithmetic in the years to follow.

This article has proved that numbers 1. and 2. at least are wrong. However, it is not too naïve to ask, What is wrong with being wrong? We have already conceded that black children need help in analyzing language into its surface components, and in being more explicit. But there are, in fact, serious and damaging consequences of the verbal-deprivation theory. These may be considered under two headings: (a) the theoretical bias and (b) the consequences of failure.

It is widely recognized that the teacher's attitude toward the child is an important factor in the latter's success or failure.* The work of Robert Rosenthal on "self-fulfilling prophecies" shows that the progress of children in the early grades can be dramatically affected by a single random labeling of certain children as "intellectual bloomers." When the everyday language of black children is stigmatized as "not a language at all" and "not possessing the means for logical thought," the effect of such a labeling is repeated many times during each day of the school year. Every time that a child uses a form of BEV without the copula or with negative concord, he will be labeling himself for the teacher's benefit as "illogical," as a "nonconceptual thinker." This notion gives teachers a ready-made, theoretical basis for the prejudice they may already feel against the lower-class black child and his language. When they hear him say *I don't want none* or *They mine*, they will be hearing, through the bias provided by the verbal-deprivation theory, not an English dialect different from theirs, but the primitive mentality of the savage mind.

But what if the teacher succeeds in training the child to use the new language consistently? The verbal deprivation theory holds that this will lead to a whole chain of successes in school, and that the child will be drawn away from the vernacular culture into the middle-class world. Undoubtedly this will happen with a few isolated individuals, just as it happens in every school system today for a few children. But we are concerned, not with the few but the many, and for the majority of black children the distance between them and the school is bound to widen under this approach.

The essential fallacy of the verbal-deprivation theory lies in tracing the educational failure of the child to his personal deficiencies. At present, these deficiencies are said to be caused by his home environment. It is traditional to explain a child's failure in school by his inadequacy: but when failure reaches such massive proportions, it seems necessary to look

* *Research on self-fulfilling prophecies is reviewed by Brophy and Good in Section 6.*

at the social and cultural obstacles to learning and the inability of the school to adjust to the social situation.*

The second area in which the verbal-deprivation theory is doing serious harm to our educational system is in the consequences of this failure and the reaction to it. As Operation Head Start fails, the interpretations which we receive will be from the same educational psychologists who designed this program. The fault will be found, not in the data, the theory, or the methods used, but rather in the children who have failed to respond to the opportunities offered them. When black children fail to show the significant advance which the deprivation theory predicts, it will be further proof of the profound gulf which separates their mental processes from those of civilized, middle-class mankind.

A sense of the failure of Operation Head Start is already commonplace. Some prominent figures in the program have reacted to this situation by saying that intervention did not take place early enough. Bettye M. Caldwell notes that

> the research literature of the last decade dealing with social-class differences has made abundantly clear that all parents are not qualified to provide even the basic essentials of physical and psychological care to their children.

The deficit theory now begins to focus on the "longstanding patterns of parental deficit" which fill the literature. "There is, perhaps unfortunately," writes Caldwell, "no literacy test for motherhood." Failing such eugenic measures, she has proposed "educationally oriented day care for culturally deprived children between six months and three years of age." The children are returned home each evening to "maintain primary emotional relationships with their own families," but during the day they are removed "hopefully to prevent the deceleration in rate of development which seems to occur in many deprived children around the age of two to three years."

There are others who feel that even the best of the intervention programs, such as those of Bereiter and Engelmann, will not help the black child no matter when they are applied — that we are faced once again with the "inevitable hypothesis" of the genetic inferiority of the black people. Arthur Jensen, for example, in his *Harvard Educational Review* paper (1969), argues that the verbal-deprivation theorists with whom he has been associated — Deutsch, Whiteman, Katz, Bereiter — have been given every opportunity to prove their case and have failed. This opinion forms part of the argument leading to his overall conclusion that the

---

In what ways does the move to accountability in education (in Section 15) indicate that Labov's concerns are being heard?

"preponderance of the evidence is ... less consistent with a strictly environmental hypothesis than with the genetic hypothesis." *

Jensen argues that the middle-class white population is differentiated from the working-class white and black population in the ability for "cognitive or conceptual learning," which Jensen calls Level II intelligence as against mere "associative learning," or Level I intelligence.

Thus Jensen found that one group of middle-class children were helped by their concept-forming ability to recall twenty familiar objects that could be classified into four categories: animals, furniture, clothing, or foods. Lower-class black children did just as well as middle-class children with a miscellaneous set, but showed no improvement with objects that could be so organized.

But linguistic data strongly contradict Jensen's conclusion that these children cannot freely form concepts. In the earliest stages of language learning, children acquire "selectional restrictions" in their use of words. For example, they learn that some verbs take ANIMATE subjects, but others only INANIMATE ones: thus we say *The machine breaks* but not *John breaks*; *The paper tears* but not *George tears*. A speaker of English must master such subtle categories as the things which *break*, like *boards, glasses*, and *ropes*; things which *tear*, like *shirts, paper*, and *skin*; things which *snap*, like *buttons, potato chips*, and *plastic*, and other categories which *smash, crumple*, or *go bust*.

In studies of Samoan children, Keith Kernan has shown that similar rules are learned reliably long before the grammatical particles that mark tense, number, and so on. The experimentation on free recall that Jensen reports ignores such abilities, and defines intelligence as a particular way of answering a particular kind of question within a narrow cultural framework. Recent work of anthropologists in other cultures is beginning to make some headway in discovering how our tests bias the results so as to make normally intelligent people look stupid. Michael Cole and his associates gave the same kind of free recall tests to Kpelle speakers in Liberia. Those who had not been to school — children or adults — could only remember eight or ten out of the twenty and showed no "clustering" according to categories, no matter how long the trials went on. Yet one simple change in the test method produced a surprising change. The interviewer took each of the objects to be remembered and held it over a chair: one chair for each category, or just one chair for all categories. Suddenly the Kpelle subjects showed a dramatic improvement, remembered seventeen to eighteen objects, and matched American subjects in both recall and the amount of clustering by categories. We do not understand this effect, for we are only beginning to discover the subtle biases built

* Compare this summary of Jensen's views with his comments in this section.

in our test methods which prevent people from using the abilities that they display in their language and in everyday life.

Linguists are in an excellent position to demonstrate the fallacies of the verbal-deprivation theory. All linguists agree that nonstandard dialects are highly structured systems; they do not see these dialects as accumulations of errors caused by the failure of their speakers to master standard English.* When linguists hear black children saying *He crazy* or *Her my friend* they do not hear a "primitive language." Nor do they believe that the speech of working-class people is merely a form of emotional expression, incapable of relating logical thought. Linguists therefore condemn with a single voice Bereiter's view that the vernacular can be disregarded.

There is no reason to believe that any nonstandard vernacular is in itself an obstacle to learning. The chief problem is ignorance of language on the part of all concerned. Our job as linguists is to remedy this ignorance: Bereiter and Engelmann want to reinforce it and justify it. Teachers are now being told to ignore the language of black children as unworthy of attention and useless for learning. They are being taught to hear every natural utterance of the child as evidence of his mental inferiority. As linguists we are unanimous in condemning this view as bad observation, bad theory, and bad practice.

That educational psychology should be strongly influenced by a theory so false to the facts of language is unfortunate; but that children should be the victims of this ignorance is intolerable. If linguists can contribute some of their valuable knowledge and energy toward exposing the fallacies of the verbal-deprivation theory, we will have done a great deal to justify the support that society has given to basic research in our field.

EXERCISE

1. What is the verbal-deprivation theory of racial differences in language use? (p. 154)

2. Labov says the defensive, monosyllabic behavior of black students in an interview situation is to be expected. Why do the students perform this way? (p. 157)

3. How does Labov rate Charles M. as compared with Larry as a thinker? (pp. 161, 163, 164)

4. According to Labov, what are the two damaging consequences of adhering to a verbal-deprivation theory to explain racial differences in school achievement? (pp. 165–166)

If nonstandard English dialects are recognized and used in the classroom, what implications would this have for the way such subjects as reading, spelling, and language are taught?

5. What evidence does Labov present to counter Arthur Jensen's research finding that lower-class or black children have poor capability for conceptual learning? (p. 167)

6. In Labov's opinion, what contribution can linguists make to the improvement of education for black students? (p. 168)

INTELLIGENCE

Introduction

Intelligence is considered an important determinant of success in school. Thus, tests of intelligence play a major, although increasingly controversial, role in the educational process.

Researchers have demonstrated convincingly that intelligence tests (at least tests that purport to measure intelligence) predict school achievement with a fair degree of accuracy. They have also shown that children who are poor or black or both earn lower intelligence scores than white middle-class children. Possible reasons for these lower scores are discussed in Section 4. Because such factors as social background and race appear to influence the test scores, several criticisms have been made of the concept of intelligence and the practice of intelligence testing. Many of these criticisms follow the same type of arguments presented by Mayeske and Labov (see Section 4). Among them are:

Intelligence, as typically measured, may only affect the ability to learn in a conventional school setting. Given an appropriate learning environment, any child can learn any subject regardless of his intelligence test score.

Some items on intelligence tests have been demonstrated to be culturally biased; that is, some minority group members, such as blacks, may do poorly on some intelligence test items because they have not been exposed to the experience referred to in the item. In effect, their lower scores reflect a lack of test items relevant to their experience, not a lack of ability to learn.

Intelligence testing promotes segregation. Even in supposedly integrated schools, de facto segregation occurs when children are grouped according to IQ scores. Because blacks generally earn lower scores, most of them are put together in a low-ability group.

Intelligence test scores may be used by teachers, even unconsciously, to type-cast children. If a teacher finds that a student has a low intelligence score, he may *expect* the student to do poorly in school. And as a result of this expectancy, he may act toward the student in such a way that he does in fact do poorly in school. Another possibly harmful effect of intelligence tests is that if a student finds out he has a low intelligence test score, his self-esteem will suffer. Even though he has the ability, he may feel defeated and lose the desire to learn.

Others have argued that intelligence tests have useful functions. Suppose you have designed an educational program that is intellectually challenging. You have many applicants for the program, many more than you can possibly accept. Assuming that intelligence tests do measure the ability to learn, wouldn't they be a useful device for selecting the most promising applicants?

Further, we know that individuals differ in their ability to learn. Not everyone learns at the same rate, and people probably differ in *how* they learn. Might not intelligence tests be useful in helping us to understand these individual differences, and to develop educational programs geared to them? Jensen's theory of different learning types (Section 4) was derived in part from the study of intelligence. If people do, in fact, learn in the different ways Jensen has identified, intelligence tests may help us match the individual with an appropriate educational program.

The following views express some issues about intelligence. Decide how you stand regarding each.

The Validity of Intelligence Scores

Pro   Intelligence, as conventionally measured, is an important determinant of school achievement. Thus, intelligence test scores tell us that "bright" children will profit more from educational opportunities than less bright children.

Con   Conventional intelligence tests measure accurately the ability of white middle-class children only. Scores for any other children are doubtful and thus cannot be used to predict their success in school, particularly when the school is designed to match their particular learning styles.

The Usefulness of Intelligence Scores

Pro   Intelligence tests can be used to plan educational programs geared to the special needs of students. Knowing a student's intelligence score helps him to get the greatest possible benefit from school.

Con   Tests of intelligence help only the students who score high. Low scores result in lowering the student's self-esteem and level of aspiration. Also, teachers expect lower performance from students with low intelligence scores.

The three selections in this section may help you gain more insight into the issues underlying intelligence as it affects learning. David K. Cohen examines how important a factor intelligence is in determining school and occupational success. Lillian Zach defends intelligence testing, and points out ways that these tests have been misused. J. P. Guilford presents research which indicates that traditional concepts and measures of intelligence need to be broadened.

Does IQ Matter?

David K. Cohen

David K. Cohen, a colleague and coworker of Christopher Jencks (see Section 4), analyzes the effect of intelligence on school and occupational success. He concludes that intelligence does have an effect, but not nearly as much as most people believe. For example, Cohen presents evidence indicating that a student's family background (particularly, social class) is almost as important as intelligence in determining whether he goes to college. One way to eliminate the effect of social class is to make college entrance entirely dependent upon IQ scores. The result would be that the poor student with a high IQ would get into college before a rich student with a lower IQ. It would also mean that a high IQ student would get into college before an artistically gifted student with lower IQ. Do you think this would be a good idea?

The last four or five years have not exactly been years of glory for American liberals. Some of the reasons for this — like the war or the President — are ephemeral. At least one other, however — the depressing performance of recent liberal social programs — probably is not. The poor record of the social legislation of the 60's has seriously shaken confidence in traditional liberal reform strategies, and since education has always occupied a favored role in those strategies, it has come in for a good share of the questioning. The apparent failure of programs like Headstart has raised doubts as to whether investment in education for the poor will promote equality.*

Reprinted from *Commentary*, by permission of the publisher and author; copyright © 1972 by the American Jewish Committee.

* *The effectiveness of some compensatory programs is discussed by Austin, Rogers, and Walbesser in Section 13.*

Most commentators have responded to this development in a charac-
teristically American fashion. The failure of earlier programs has been
attributed to inadequate resources, indifferent professionals, or intractable
bureaucracies. Reform can proceed, we are told, only when more money
is spent, or when educational institutions are made more responsive, or
when the professions are made more accountable. In response to apparent
failure a whole new generation of optimistic proposals has sprung up.

A few critics of Great Society programs, however, have been less hopeful. Some ask whether education is in fact the mechanism by which the
distribution of wealth, power, or status has been affected in America. If
schooling has not promoted equality among whites, after all, it would be
a little silly to expect it to do so for blacks. Others have asserted that the
failure of educational programs owes more to the deficiencies of poor
children than to the defects of their schools.* If the sources of school
failure among the poor are either habits of mind imposed by culture or
intellectual barriers imposed by heredity, they argue, it hardly makes sense
to spend money on school-improvement programs that rest on contrary
assumptions.

Each of these two major lines of thought raises serious questions about
received liberal doctrine, because each suggests that institutions or individuals are not as malleable as we have hitherto assumed. But there has
been greater fascination with the question of deficiencies in the poor
than with the possible limits of schooling as an equalizing strategy. A few
years ago, in an essay in the *Harvard Educational Review*, Arthur Jensen
reviewed the evidence on group differences in intellectual ability and
school achievement; everything showed large and consistent gaps among
groups. On the average, children whose families were poor or black did
much less well on tests than children whose families were well-to-do, or
white. Jensen also pulled together a considerable body of research which
suggested that differences in intelligence among individuals seemed to be
caused more by heredity than by environment. And finally he ventured
the idea that heredity may explain intellectual differences among groups
as well as it appears to account for differences among individuals.

More recently H. J. Eysenck, a British psychologist, brought out a book
which purported to subject Jensen's work to a critical assessment.[1] Although there is little indication of such assessment in this pot-boiler, it
does support Jensen's appraisal of the research, as well as his speculation
concerning the genetic sources of racial differences in IQ. Finally, a few
months ago Richard J. Herrnstein, a Harvard psychologist, published an
essay in the *Atlantic Monthly* which generated quite a stir. Herrnstein
broadened, refined, and defended arguments laid down earlier. He maintained that what IQ tests measure is an important and stable human
attribute. He marshaled evidence that IQ differences among individuals

* *Jensen, for one, takes this position in Section 4.*

are mostly accounted for by genes, not by environment.* And he pressed the idea that intelligence is an increasingly powerful influence on the allocation of status, wealth, and power in advanced industrial societies. Although Herrnstein did point out the difficulty of generalizing from individual to group differences, his essay questioned the traditional liberal idea that stupidity results from the inheritance of poverty, contending instead that poverty results from the inheritance of stupidity.

These arguments, of course, are nothing new. The heritability of IQ first became a major public fixation in reaction to the turn-of-the-century deluge of poor European immigrants. It bubbled to the surface once again just after the *Brown* decision in 1954, when racial mixing in public schools seemed to loom on the horizon. And not surprisingly it reemerged when the disappointing results of recent school-improvement programs for the poor became known. As this little chronicle may suggest, recent attention to the subject is not wholly the product of scientific interest. While the heritability of IQ holds a constant fascination for psychologists and demographers, most of the time they are the only people who care enough about the matter even to mention it. Only when there are broader issues involving ethnic or racial minorities — in which the character of the culture, or the allocation of public resources, or the composition of society is at stake — does the relationship between genes and IQ reach the front page of anything other than arcane professional journals.

But while this may help us understand the recent interest in the IQ question as a social phenomenon, it doesn't say much about the arguments themselves. *Does* heredity account for most individual differences in IQ? Does it account for class and racial differences in IQ? Is IQ really a good measure of intelligence, or a good predictor of the things that make for success in America? † . . .

Oddly enough, in most of the arguments about genes and IQ over the past thirty years much greater attention has been paid to the question of the relative importance of circumstances and heredity than to figuring out exactly what IQ means, or what it is good for. Most people with very high IQ's seem very smart, and most people with very low IQ's seem very stupid. But people in between — which is where almost everyone is — are full of surprises. The fact that the tests can distinguish extremes so evident in everyday life inclines one to believe they measure something important. The fact that things get unclear in the middle, however, should make one dubious as to the value of the measuring-stick for most of everyday life.

---

* *This view would be questioned by many psychologists, for example, Mayeske, Deutsch, and Labov, in Section 4.*
† *These questions are at the center of the IQ debate. How does Cohen answer them in the following discussion?*

What do IQ tests measure? Some people naively believe they provide a summary index of a general human ability to cope, but this would appear unlikely: think of the psychologist next door who nearly became unhinged trying to put together a hi-fi kit, or of the university sociologists who lost their shirts running a consulting firm, or of the brilliant computer freak who is incapable of writing an intelligible English sentence.

There are psychologists who believe that IQ tests measure one dimension of some more general and unified underlying intelligence. Perhaps, but at the moment it is hard to know. Psychologists are not in agreement on the elements of this underlying intelligence, and available research shows that sometimes the elements in question are connected only weakly or not at all.* In fact, IQ is about the only thing psychologists *have* learned to measure with much validity or consistency, and as a result good research on the relation between IQ and other aspects of intelligence or personality is not plentiful.

Finally, there are people who think that intelligence is simply the ability to perform well at whatever one's social situation seems to require. This is obviously true in some ways, but in extreme form the notion is not really useful at all. Does it make sense to say that Lewis Strauss was smarter than Robert Oppenheimer? Or to argue that a high-school student who flunked out and then became a successful numbers runner is just as smart as the valedictorian of his high school who couldn't get a job after graduation? Intelligence may not be timeless and unitary, but pushed to the extreme the relativist view dissolves in horrible contortions.

No doubt this debate could go on forever — in fact it probably will — but most people would not wish to pursue it. They assume a social definition of intelligence; they care about not what it is as a psychological construct, but how it works as a phenomenon in society. Indeed, many of those who worry about the proper definition of IQ do so chiefly because they think it is becoming the central criterion for distributing the good things of life. People care about IQ because they regard it as the basis on which society's rewards and punishments are allocated; they believe that America is becoming a society in which status and power are now, and will increasingly be, a function of brains.

This view is so widely held that it has become a sort of secular catechism. It certainly is repeated often enough, and in many different connections. Radicals attack America for allocating rewards on the basis of technical talent rather than need or human value; liberals bemoan the fact that discrimination has kept members of minority groups from competing on their own merits; Jews fear the demise of merit standards in employment and education, and blacks attack the standards themselves as racist.

* Guilford (this section), for example, analyzes intelligence into 120 elements.

Conservatives used to attack merit standards too, on the ground that some things were more important than intelligence, but the fact that this argument no longer has enough credibility to be used in defense of privilege — it is now employed only on behalf of the poor — suggests how widespread is the belief that meritocracy is upon us.

In the light of this concern, the fuss over IQ is indeed as important as Professors Eysenck and Herrnstein believe it to be. However muddy the tests or biased their results, they exist; in a meritocracy of the sort we are said to have, such tests would undoubtedly be a major criterion for the allocation of rewards. The basic question, then, is whether, and how much, IQ counts in America in terms of status and power.*

Perhaps the best place to begin is the schools. Schools, after all, are where IQ is supposed to have its greatest impact, because it is in schools that children get routed on the various educational tracks which are presumed to play a considerable role in their chances for wealth and status later on. Really bright children are supposed to be routed into college preparatory work, and really not-so-bright children into vocational courses. Those in between are assigned to "general," business, or similar curricula. Then everyone graduates and goes to work, or drops out, or goes to college, and moves on to his appointed niche.

This picture is far from being wholly false, but it is by no means as true as most educators make it out to be. Take, for example, what is probably the most critical decision made during a child's school career: the kind of high-school program he will follow. In a perfectly meritocratic system based on IQ this decision would rest exclusively on test scores; in a perfect caste system it would rest exclusively on one's inherited status. In the United States things are much more confused. According to studies of curricula-assignments of high-school students, measured ability is only one among several influential factors; others include the social and economic status of a student's family, his own aspirations for a career, and the degree of encouragement his parents have offered to those aspirations.† The most comprehensive studies suggest in fact that these latter three influences on placement in high school are only slightly less important than measured ability.

Of course, a good deal happens to children in school before they even reach the point where decisions are made about their high-school curriculum. They are graded and grouped from the very beginning, and all of these classification procedures undoubtedly have some impact — if not on how children regard themselves at least on what the teachers think

* How would you answer this question?
† Recall how you selected your high school courses. Which of these factors most influenced your choices?

about them. But the assignment of children to ability groups, like the assignment of curricula, seems to be determined by all sorts of things in addition to IQ. And grades too seem to be influenced as much by the attitudes of the children, their behavior toward authority, and their general demeanor as by their test scores.

But the most important point is that all of these factors together — ability, aspirations, inherited status, etc. — account for less than half of the actual variation in the assignment of students to one high-school track or another. A majority of the differences among students in this respect, in other words, are caused by something other than either status or brains. This is not as odd as it might seem. Some of the differences probably arise from mistakes in assignments — bright children who want to go to college but lose out because of a slip or who are incorrectly assigned because of a perverse teacher. Some of the differences probably are caused by variations in the attitudes and motivation of the family, which seem to have a considerable impact on schooling decisions quite independently of parents' status or children's ability; lots of poor parents push their children very hard, and lots of non-poor parents don't. And some of the differences probably are caused by variations in deportment or motivation, or the encouragement students get from teachers, or other factors that usually go unmeasured. In short, if we consider only measured intelligence or inherited status, we cannot explain most of the variation in placement of students in high school.

What is the relative importance of IQ and inherited status as far as getting into college is concerned? Here, after all, is one of the great divides in American life. A college degree is regarded increasingly as the only sure way to gain access to the good things in this society, and certainly college entrance is the goal toward which so much of the work of the schools is supposed to be aimed. How great a role does IQ play here?

If we look only at the relative influence of tested ability and inherited social and economic status, the available evidence does not show that college entrance is chiefly determined by academic ability. In fact, the relative importance of these two influences seems to be roughly equal. Consider, for example, a high-school senior whose family is in the lowest fifth of the population with respect to both social status and test scores. Not only is this young person less bright than at least 80 per cent of all high-school seniors, but his family is less affluent than at least 80 per cent of American families. In the early 1960's, he had roughly one chance in ten of entering college the year after high-school graduation.

By way of contrast consider his friend down the street, similarly situated with respect to family circumstances, but in the top fifth of the ability distribution. His family is poorer than over 80 per cent of the population, but he is smarter than over 80 per cent of all high-school seniors. He had roughly six chances in ten of entering college the year after graduating high school.

A comparison of these two seniors reveals that among poor students, when family circumstances are roughly the same, more brains means a much better chance of going to college.

What about more advantaged students — do IQ and status operate in the same way? Consider two seniors who come from families in the upper fifth of the distribution of social advantages and economic status. If one of them fell in the bottom fifth of the ability distribution, he would have roughly four chances in ten of going to college. If the other fell in the top fifth of the ability distribution, he would have nine chances in ten of going to college. This comparison reveals that brains are a help at the top of the social pyramid, just as at the bottom: rich boys and girls with high IQ's go to college more often than rich boys and girls with low IQ's.

But now a comparison of the first pair of students with the second pair reveals that getting rich (moving from the bottom to the top of the social pyramid), is nearly as big a help in increasing a student's chances of going to college as getting smart (moving from the bottom to the top of the IQ distribution). More precise analyses of the data on college-going confirm the impression gained from these examples: measured intelligence is of slightly greater influence on college attendance than inherited status. This is a great deal different from a world in which going to college is wholly determined by family position, but it is far from a world in which going to college is wholly determined by intellectual ability.

Once again, however, these comparisons do not reveal what must be the most important fact — namely, that ability and status combined explain somewhat less than half the actual variation in college attendance. As in the case of curriculum placement, we must turn to other factors — motivation, luck, discrimination, chance, and family encouragement or lack of it — to find likely explanations. Existing research provides support for the idea that these other factors do play a role (although it does not afford comprehensive estimates of their relative importance).[2]

Thus, while academic ability or intelligence is important to educational success, other factors, measured and unmeasured, seem to have at least as much weight in determining who gets ahead in the world of American schools.* But this in turn raises an absolute swarm of problems. If test scores are only moderately important, should steps be taken to increase their influence? Or would relying more heavily on test scores in order to lessen the influence of social inheritance leave less room for people to be selected on other criteria, such as motivation? If the influence of inherited status on selection ought to be reduced, how great should the reduction

* *This statement summarizes the research findings discussed thus far by Cohen.*

be? In a perfect meritocracy, after all, the objective would be to remove the effect of any social advantages parents had achieved on the life-chances of their children — but what sort of society would that be? Would it be consistent with a society of nuclear families? Does anyone want a society in which every child has an equal chance to be a clamdigger or a cardiac surgeon, subject only to IQ differences? The idea seems bizarre, for it suggests a social rat-race which would make the Great American Status Scramble look like a party game for retired schoolmarms. And if a perfect meritocracy seems like a perfect neurotic nightmare, then just how much, or how little, of an educational advantage would we want families to be able to pass along to their children?

Anyone who thinks about these questions for more than ten seconds will realize that no easy answers are available. More equality in education would be a good thing, and it is sensible to suppose that this implies some effort to reduce the influence of social and economic inheritance on school success. But the questions reveal that we have no well-formed conception of how much the impact of families ought to be reduced, or how much of a role IQ ought to have in reducing it. Nor, indeed, is it clear that IQ should bear that burden at all. Distributing rewards in accordance with IQ scores, after all, is not the only known device for reducing social and economic differences, even in education.

Of course, one's view on these last issues will depend in part on the role one thinks intelligence actually plays in the allocation of adult status and power. If it turned out that IQ was crucial, it would be hard to maintain that it ought not to be the principal means for discriminating among school children. So before going any further with these questions about meritocracy in schools, it might be wise to find out just how important IQ is once people get out of them. I will deal with occupational status first, because that is what seems to fascinate most writers on the subject.[3]

One way of looking at this question — as Eysenck and Herrnstein did — is by pointing to the evidence on the average IQ's of people in different occupations. Thus, manual laborers turn out to have much lower IQ's than professors of theology, and this is assumed to mean that IQ is an entry requirement for these occupations. But simply presenting the gross differences begs all the basic questions. First, the averages don't reveal the considerable dispersion of IQ's within occupational groups, which reveals that there are lots of people in working-class jobs whose IQ's are in the same range as those in higher-status occupations, and vice versa. But more significantly, listing IQ differences among occupations only tells us that differences exist; it does not tell us how important IQ was in getting people into those occupations.

A satisfactory account would indeed require that we know the IQ's of people in different occupations, but it would require other information as well. We would need to know, for example, how far people got in school and what social and economic advantages their parents had, because these might have had a real impact on their own occupational status as adults to say nothing of their IQ's. Armed with evidence of this sort — which is hard to come by because it covers almost the entire life-cycle — we could compare the relative importance of IQ and other influences on the sorts of jobs adults wind up with. Now we do in fact have a good deal of research which shows that people who stay in school longer wind up on the average with higher status jobs, and that on the average people who begin life with more social and economic advantages wind up with more of them as adults.* But when researchers try to assess the relative importance of education and social inheritance they begin to part company. Some argue that staying in school is a considerably more important influence on occupational attainment than inherited status; others find the opposite to be true. The former category of researchers also tend to think of America as a relatively open society, in which schooling serves as a vehicle of social mobility from one generation to another. Researchers in the second category tend to think of America as a relatively closed society, in which the schools mostly transmit the same status from parents to children. Since both judgments are manifestly true to some degree, and since the evidence is not entirely adequate to resolve the matter, the argument will continue for some time. But what is important for our purposes is not how much mobility there is, or to what extent schooling contributes to it; rather we want to know whether IQ has an effect on occupational status which is *independent* of these two influences.

The available evidence suggests that it does not. IQ seems to have little or no independent effect on the sorts of jobs people wind up with as adults, all other things being equal.† IQ does help moderately and indirectly, because it has a moderate influence on how long people stay in school, and the length of their stay in school affects the sorts of jobs they get. But once the influence of schooling is taken into account, IQ appears to have no independent relation to occupational success. If a meritocracy is a society in which intelligent people do well regardless of their parents or their schooling, America is not such a society.

To make this concrete, consider several adults who differ in every aspect under discussion here — jobs, IQ's, length of stay in school, and social and economic backgrounds. The differences in their inherited status and in the length of time they stayed in school account for a fair proportion (somewhat less than half) of the differences in the status of their jobs. Since those who have higher IQ's will have stayed in school somewhat longer,

---

* *Refer to Bane and Jencks for a discussion of this research.*
† *If IQ has such a limited relation to future employment, why do we try to measure it?*

IQ can be said to have a moderate effect on occupational status. But when people with equal amounts of schooling are considered, differences in their IQ's turn out to account for none of the differences in the status of their jobs. Having a higher IQ is no help in getting a higher status job for people who have the same educational attainment and the same social and economic background. In addition, there is an abundance of studies showing that the grades of college students are not related either to their income or to their occupational status once they get out of college; similarly, research on what differentiates good from bad workers (within broad occupational categories) shows that workers who produce more or who are rated highly by their supervisors generally do not have higher test scores, although they do tend to have "better" attitudes, greater "motivation," better "deportment" — in effect, more of the attributes which also seem to make for success in school.

Thus, the process of selection to occupations in America does not appear to be more than mildly dependent on IQ. And here too, as in the case of high-school placement and college entrance, recent research has shown that IQ, schooling, and inherited status together account for less than half of the variation in the occupational attainment of American males. More than half of the differences in the job status of American men is explained neither by their IQ, nor by how long they went to school, nor by the social and economic advantages (or burdens) they inherited. Some of these unexplained differences are undoubtedly due to errors in the ways sociologists measure things, but others are probably due to such imponderables as enterprise, motivation, the luck of the draw, and preferences unrelated either to brains or to economic background.

That, however, is not the end of the matter. Whatever the evidence may suggest about the modest influence IQ presently exerts on occupational selection, the popular mythology is that it is much greater now than it was fifty years ago.* America, we are told, is a "knowledge society"; we are moving into a post-industrial age, in which talent will rule. Yet when we turn to historical evidence concerning the role of IQ in occupational selection, once again we find little support for such claims. If IQ were becoming a more important force in occupational selection we would expect the IQ averages of people in any occupation to have become more similar over time: the IQ's of professional people should have grown more nearly equal as merit selection proceeded, and the same would be true of blue-collar workers. But the fragmentary evidence we have suggests this is not true: the dispersion of IQ's within occupational categories for native American whites seems to have remained pretty stable over the last four or five decades. Similarly, if IQ were becoming more important we might

* *Does this mythology have any merit?*

expect the intellectual level of intellectually demanding occupations to rise, and the level of undemanding jobs to fall. But no such development seems to have taken place. Finally, if IQ were becoming more important to adult success, we would imagine that the main instrument by which IQ makes itself felt in America — schooling — would have become more important to getting a job. But according to the historical evidence concerning the effect of schooling on occupational attainment over the past four or five decades, education seems to bear no more powerful relationship to the job one gets today than it did earlier in the century.

Now all of this evidence is partial, and subject to a variety of caveats. But the striking thing is that nowhere can we find any empirical support for the idea that brains are becoming increasingly more important to status in America. Of course, this by itself is not incompatible with the observation that "knowledge" is an increasingly central aspect of life. For one thing, measures of occupational status are based on opinion surveys in which random samples of the American people are asked about the relative prestige of occupations. Thus, the "importance" of intellectual work would appear to change only if people thought its prestige was changing. But in general public attitudes toward the relative prestige of various occupations have changed very little over time, so that paradoxically intellectual work may in fact be becoming more important even though this is not reflected in the measures used by sociologists. No one has ever actually set out to measure how much more important technological and scientific work is now than in 1920, and probably no one ever will.

But even if we assume that brains *are* becoming more important or powerful (a moot point in my view), other things are changing as well. Fifty years ago most Americans never finished high school, and only a tiny percentage went on to college. Now almost everyone finishes high school, and more than one third go on to some form of post-secondary education. This means that lots of ordinary people who would never have had the chance fifty years ago to be doctors or teachers or engineers, have the chance today. If brains are becoming more powerful at the same time as schooling becomes more universal (and thereby opens up opportunity through the power of certification), the two tendencies may cancel each other out. Of course I am speculating here, but observed evidence would tend to support this view, and to suggest also how complicated the relationship among intelligence, status, and power can be; some social forces may be acting to intensify the connection at the same time as others are weakening it.

If, then, we measure adult status by way of occupational prestige rankings, and merit by IQ, America does not appear more than mildly meritocratic. Nor is there reason to believe that IQ has grown more important to individual success during the past five or six decades. This does not mean that the symbols of learning — or its apparatus — have not become more important. Indeed, it is clear that the length of time one stays in school is more relevant to occupational attainment than is raw IQ. Rather than a social hierarchy based on intellect, we may be creating a "schoolocracy." But the importance of schooling to occupational status may itself be based on a variety of non-intellectual factors. Employers use the school system as an elaborate behavior-screening mechanism, on the theory that certain kinds of work require certain kinds of personalities. This would explain why schools place so much stress on deportment, and why they screen out youngsters who have a hard time sitting still for long periods of time, or who don't have the right appearance; these tend to get tracked to lower-status school work and to lower-status jobs. Students who have "better" manners, who behave "properly," who accept authority, and who look the way they should, tend to be routed into higher-status school work and occupations. This screening system may or may not accord with the actual behavior which is required in various sorts of occupations, but it does seem to fit what people *think* is appropriate behavior.

Another cause of the connection between schooling and adult success may be that schools are becoming the principal vehicle for "professionalizing" occupations. Especially in the marginal and semi-marginal professions, adding educational requirements for certification and licensing is a way of enhancing the standing and respectability of a given line of work in the eyes of its practitioners and clients. It also is a way of persuading people that the occupation in question is up-to-date, modern, and in touch with the latest wisdom. And it often is a way (as with teachers, for example) of getting a bigger paycheck. But whatever the explanation, the additional educational requirements cannot be said to have much relation to job performance.*

When schooling becomes necessary to later occupational standing for essentially non-intellectual reasons, various unhappy consequences can result. One such consequence is the subversion of the legitimate purposes of educational institutions, and the breeding of contempt for what they do; another is the creation of an occupational selection system in which the ability to remain glued to the seat of a chair for long periods of time becomes a prime recommendation for advancement. (The ability to sit still is useful for many purposes, but especially among children it may not be related to the ingenuity, enterprise, and cleverness which any lively society would want to promote.) Under such a system of occupational selection, we are as likely to produce an unhealthy accumulation of boredom

* Is Cohen implying that schools should not directly prepare students for careers? Compare with Sidney Marland's position (Section 2).

and discontent as we are to create a dangerous maldistribution of intellect.

Developments like these are the more distressing because of the greater uniformity they promise, both in what people do and in how they think about it. Such uniformity has not always characterized American society. There is fairly convincing evidence, for example, of ethnic differences in the role that schools have played in promoting occupational mobility. Studies of European ethnic groups show that during this century all of them made substantial increases in occupational status, but that they did so in rather different ways. The children of Russian immigrants (which means Jews for the most part) completed more years of school, on the average, than children from other groups. In addition, educational attainment had a much stronger relationship to the later occupational attainment of these children than it did for children from other groups — which probably means that a disproportionate number of Jews went into occupations which had substantial educational requirements. Not all nationalities had the same experience; Italian and Polish children, for example, tended to complete fewer years of school than those of some other groups. But for Italians and Poles educational differences were not in themselves an important influence as far as later occupational status was concerned.

The history of ethnic variations in the importance of schooling suggests in turn the underlying differences in the avenues that various ethnic groups have taken to achieve higher social and economic status. And these different avenues probably reflect cultural and historical differences from group to group with regard to the sorts of work which were known and esteemed in the parent country. They even may have been indicative of ethnic differences in the "talent for school," for there were very considerable IQ differences among the European immigrant groups which roughly corresponded to their success or failure in school. But the important point is that to the extent that schooling is made an unavoidable requirement for occupational entry or advancement, it may close off genuine cultural differences in occupational values, and irrationally stifle alternatives which might otherwise flourish.* To the extent that success in a homogeneous system of schooling becomes the *sine qua non* of entry to occupations, cultural diversity in conceptions of success and worthy work may be diminished. It is hard to think of any good which could possibly come from that situation.

In a sense, however, all the attention to the relative status of occupations is misleading. It is easy to understand why intellectuals might be obsessed with the question, but it is important in the discussion of meritocracy only because of the assumption that jobs which require brains wield more power than jobs which don't. If it turned out that people

---

* In this view, should we be trying to eliminate or to tolerate individual differences in IQ?

with high IQ's did not really have more power than ordinary folks, there wouldn't be very much left for one to argue about.

Normally when intellectuals write about this question they bemoan the fact that people like themselves have *little* power and influence. Indeed, they have mourned this situation for so long that most Americans who read what intellectuals write probably concluded long ago that anyone who has power is either a knave or a fool. As a result, it comes as something of a surprise to hear that intellectuals are in danger of having too much power. But if holding political office, for instance, is an index of power, it is hard to see any cause for alarm, for there certainly is no evidence of an undue concentration of raw IQ among the ranks of government officials. Indeed, it is hard to imagine why anyone would think government officials should have unusually high IQ's. After all, the motives which lead men and women into public life probably have more to do with the desire for power, or money, or recognition, than with the need to exercise a restless and powerful intellect.

Politics, however, is only one of the several sources of power and influence in America; great wealth is another. Here again, it should come as no great surprise to learn that a high IQ is not the main requirement for having lots of money. People with more schooling do tend to have somewhat higher incomes, but the relationship between the two is not even as strong as the relationship between schooling and occupational status. Partly this is due to the fact that lots of jobs with rather high status — preaching, teaching, and the like — don't come with cushy salaries, and lots of jobs with rather low status, like being a plumber or a machinist, do. There also is the fact that spending decades in school is a condition of employment in most of the high-status but low-paying jobs, but not a condition of tenure in the others. And finally, doing well in school is not yet a prerequisite for inheriting money.

Then there are the other ways of attaining power, or at least influence. The people who write for newspapers and talk on television offer one example, and the "experts" who work for Congressional committees and executive agencies offer another. And university professors who spend half their lives traveling to consultations with government officials or corporate managers offer yet another. Still, one is at a loss to imagine why journalists should be either brighter or more influential than they were fifty years ago, and a modest stint of watching television would not lead anyone to conclude that the medium is in peril of being taken over by people with dangerously high IQ's. Finally, anyone who imagines that "experts" with high IQ's have a great future in public life ought to visit his nearest government agency and see how it works. Most important government business turns not on the technical skills that experts do monopolize, but on ethical and political considerations. Experts have had to relearn this lesson every few years since the Progressive era.

Let us try to summarize, in general form, the conclusions of all this.

First, America is not a meritocracy, if by that we mean a society in which income, status, or power are heavily determined by IQ. All the evidence suggests that IQ has only moderate impact on adult success, and that this impact is exerted only through the schools.

Second, America seems on balance not to have become more meritocratic in the course of the 20th century. All the evidence suggests that the relationship between IQ and income and status has been perfectly stable. While opportunity has opened up for great segments of the population, the criteria for advancement seem to have involved many things in addition to, and other than, IQ.

Third, something we often incorrectly identify with IQ — namely schooling — seems to be a much more important determinant of adult success than IQ. If getting through school is a mark of merit, then America is moderately meritocratic. But then, in a society in which education is an increasingly universal experience, such a conception of merit begins to lose its meaning.

And finally, among all the many factors which lead to a situation in which some people are poor or hold low-status jobs, lower intellectual ability is not a terribly important one. Being stupid is not what is responsible for being poor in America.

EXERCISE

1. What does Cohen mean when he states that most people assume a social definition of intelligence? (p. 175)

2. According to Cohen, how important is IQ in determining what high school program a student will enter? (p. 176)

3. According to Cohen, how important is IQ in determining which students will enter college? (pp. 177–178)

4. According to Cohen, how important is IQ in determining adult occupational status? (pp. 179–180, 181)

5. How important does Cohen think IQ is in determining one's power or wealth? (184–185)

The IQ Debate

Lillian Zach

Lillian Zach contends that intelligence testing does have value. For example, according to Zach, IQ tests were useful for screening men for the armed forces in World War I. They are also useful for describing the child's current level of intellectual functioning. However, Zach observes that the intent of such original test developers as Alfred Binet and Wilhelm Stern has been changed by many who have used intelligence tests. Originally, the tests were designed to measure what general intellectual skills an individual possessed at a particular time. Measuring inborn capacity was not the purpose of the tests. Several articles in this book (for example, Arthur Jensen, Section 4, and David Cohen, preceding selection) illustrate how psychologists and educators have moved from this original position. Zach finds the greatest number of problems in the use of test results, not in the tests themselves: "The failure lies not in the mental tests themselves, but in the perversion of the test results by investigators and social philosophers who use numbers in support of particular far-reaching positions." As a positive alternative, Zach proposes several ways to use intelligence tests to improve education. Would you use the tests as she suggests or would you recommend simply that they be abandoned by the schools?

Intelligence testing from basis to implications, continues to be the center of heated debate. Despite a history which is almost three quarters of a century long and despite the fact that the IQ is by now a household term in America, mental tests are still reeling under the impact of criticisms which term them, among other things, invalid, misleading, and based upon false assumptions of human development.

In a highly controversial article published in December 1969, Arthur Jensen, a professor at the University of California at Berkeley, proposed that compensatory education failed to raise the IQ of black children because of a biological difference in the way these children learn. The topic became incendiary; psychological, educational, political, and racist groups began interpreting the data to suit their views. Arguments and criticisms continue. Yet, unquestionably, the Stanford-Binet, the Wechsler Scales,

From *Today's Education*, 61, 1972, pp. 40ff. Reprinted with permission of publisher and author.

and certain group tests do provide useful information, and the tests remain the most relied-on source for sorting children according to their presumed learning ability. Is it any wonder that teachers are uncertain what to believe about intelligence testing?

Binet's original intent was to develop an instrument to determine which children in Paris were retarded and in need of special education. In 1905, he produced the first Binet scale, designed to measure a retarded child's intelligence and compare it to the intelligence of normal children the same age. There was no attempt to determine whether the child's retarded learning was genetic or curable.

In 1912, German psychologist Wilhelm Stern suggested that one could express the developmental level, or mental age, of a given child as the age at which the average child achieved equivalent ability. If mental age (MA) were used as a ratio to the child's chronological age (CA), one could arrive at a brightness index, now called the Intelligence Quotient (IQ).

Like Binet, Stern did not claim that the test measured inborn capacity. In 1914, he wrote, "No series of tests, however skillfully selected it may be, does reach the innate intellectual endowment, stripped of all complications, but rather this endowment, in conjunction with all influences to which the examinee has been subjected up to the moment of testing. And it is just these external influences that are different in the lower social classes.* Children of higher social status are much more often in the company of adults, are stimulated in manifold ways, are busy in play and amusement with things that require thinking, acquire a totally different vocabulary, and receive better school instruction. All this must bring it about that they meet the demands of the test better than children of the uncultured classes."

But H. H. Goddard, who brought the test to America in 1910, had a very different viewpoint. Dr. Goddard translated the test into English for use at the Vineland Training School for the mentally defective. Perhaps it was an act of fate that the man who brought mental testing to this country was someone who emphasized the importance of heredity on human behavior.

Goddard was working with grossly defective children, and one can speculate that he was probably not convinced they could be educated. (Further, the chances are they were biologically defective as well as mentally retarded.) Goddard became intrigued with the notion that, being able to measure innate intelligence, we had the means for a sweeping program of social reform, with every man working on his own mental level. Soon, mental testing was adopted in every training school and teachers college in the country. Few stopped to consider that perhaps the innate intelli-

* *Although this statement was made in 1914, note its similarity to the views expressed about compensatory education in the 1960's (see Deutsch, Section 4).*

gence which Goddard postulated and the intelligence measured by the test were not the same. Shortly thereafter, in 1916, L. M. Terman revised the Binet Scale at Stanford University to give birth to the Stanford-Binet, the standard of today's intelligence test. The test was revised and updated in 1937 and 1960. The rapid growth of compulsory education in the United States required some means to identify the intellectual capacities of pupils in the schools, and the Stanford-Binet seemed to fill the bill.

When the intelligence test is evaluated in terms of its value to meet specifically defined, immediate situations, its usefulness has proven itself. A good case in point can be seen in its use since the start of World War I to screen men for the armed forces. In these instances, the mental test has provided the means for appraising what an individual could do, here and now, as the product of his biological inheritance and his training and background.

But as testing proliferated, some problems became apparent. Testing in America was growing along two separate paths. One was in the real world of the school, the armed forces, and the industrial plant. The other was in the halls of academe, where the basic theoretical issues of intelligence were not yet settled. This lack of a universally accepted theoretical framework led to the anomolous situation in which intelligence is defined as that which intelligence tests test.

Herein lies a dilemma: Intelligence was only vaguely defined by the test maker, but the tests were used to define intelligence.* This is perhaps the greatest failure of the testing movement in the United States. The pragmatic value of the mental test is undiminished. Test scores are good indicators of functioning abilities as long as their limitations are clearly understood, but these scores should not be used outside of their immediate significance. The failure lies not in the mental tests themselves, but in the perversion of the test results by investigators and social philosophers who use numbers in support of particular far-reaching positions. It is unfair both to the person tested and to the test itself to say that the scores of any one individual represent support for broad statements concerning human development.

There is nothing inherently wrong with practical definitions as long as they are clearly understood. The tests, after all, were developed to measure those aspects of human behavior which correlate well with scholastic achievement. In order to succeed in school, an individual must demonstrate certain types of abilities. If we develop tests to measure these abilities and if they prove to be valid and reliable instruments, we are measuring some form of intellectual ability. But if we lose sight of what we are measuring and if we claim for the test qualities for which it was never intended, we can be led into invalid implications.

* *Is this perhaps the heart of the IQ controversy?*

The IQ, like the MA, is nothing but a score. The IQ indicates a child's performance on a test in the same way that a score of 80 on an arithmetic test does, except that intelligence tests purport to measure more general learning skills. Further, the scores merely reflect the child's performance on a specific test at a given time. The difference between the IQ and other test scores is that intelligence tests are standardized. Standardization means that the same test items are developed and revised on a large group, representative of the population for whom the test is designed — U.S. elementary school students, for example. Standardization also requires that the same test be administered under the same carefully controlled conditions to all who take the test. This means that a given child's score can be compared with scores obtained by other children of the same age on whom the test was originally standardized. It also permits prediction of the chances that in later testing a given child will obtain a score which is close to the original score, and further, to what extent a given child's performance is the result of the construction of the test rather than his own ability.

In order to interpret the results of standardized tests, certain fundamental assumptions are implicit. It is assumed, for example, that test norms are fair, since they are based on a representative national sampling of children. But this does not take into consideration the fact that the national sample is weighted heavily by average white children.

Since the mental test purports to measure basic learning capacities, it is also assumed that the items which make up the test are of two types — information which for the most part all children have been exposed to or situations to which no one has been exposed.

For items based upon supposedly equal opportunities of exposure, it is possible to reason that a child who has learned what he has been exposed to is bright; one who has not done so is not bright. Observation tells us that this does not have to be true.

In my own testing experiences, I found that many black children who had just come North gave as response to the question, "Who discovered America?" the answer, "Abraham Lincoln." The response is obviously wrong and adds no points to the IQ score.* But does this response mean that this child has no ability to learn or does it merely reflect the child's background? In certain ways, the answer could be considered a meaningful and pertinent response.

For items to which no one has been exposed and which therefore demand "on the spot" learning, similar problems arise. Usually, tests try to utilize nonverbal materials like blocks and puzzles as a way of minimizing factors like education and experience. But these are not equally novel

---

* *What is the correct response? If "Columbus" is scored as correct, this reflects another cultural bias in the test.*

experiences for all children. Many youngsters are familiar with educational toys long before they enter school. (Even more important, and less easy to identify, are factors related to "learning to learn" and test-taking abilities.)

Another assumption is that the mental test is a sampling of behaviors which directly reflect the general capacity for learning. Actually, all available intelligence tests are direct measures only of achievement in learning.* We wrongly equate the inferences from scores on IQ tests to some native inherent trait. Many persons think of intelligence as a discrete dimension existing within the individual and believe that different people have different amounts of it. In a certain sense this is true, but one's intelligence is not a characteristic of a person so much as it is a characteristic of the person's behavior. We can only hope to measure or observe manifestations of it.

It is also not possible to add up the elements of someone's intelligence in the same way that you can count the number of fingers on his hand. Although two people can have the same IQ score, they may demonstrate quite different abilities by virtue of the fact that they succeeded on different parts of the test. All too often, undue weight is given to an IQ score, although numerical assignment of a child to a man-made concept, untied to real characteristics of the child, tells us very little. Even more unfortunate, parents and some teachers are led to believe that the IQ concept has deeper significance than its meaning as a score.

Unquestioning faith in descriptive concepts reaches the height of absurdity in the notion of overachievers — a word used to describe children whose classroom performance is higher than their IQ scores would predict. The concept makes no sense at all because it says, in effect, that although these children are achieving, they do not have the ability to do so. Their success is laid to other factors, such as motivation. It's like telling the child who had the highest batting average in the Little League that, on the basis of batting practice, he's really a very poor hitter. He only did it because he wanted to.

The danger in a meaningless concept like overachieving is that children so designated may not receive as positive a recommendation for college as other children with the same grades but higher IQ scores. Few stop to consider that the methods used to judge ability must have been inadequate and that terms like IQ, MA, and overachievement are man-made.

In view of all the drawbacks, one might reasonably ask, then, why do we continue using mental tests? Even though many have argued for abandoning them, most psychologists still feel that they have value. In most cases, we can describe, evaluate, and even predict certain kinds of behavior much better with tests than without them. The paradox exists that most

* *Is Zach implying that intelligence tests are equivalent to achievement tests?*

psychologists, who were responsible for the tests, have never given them as much weight as those in schools and industries who use and misuse them.

While various practical problems were being confronted, the academic world of psychology was still trying to resolve many basic issues about intelligence testing. One of these, the focus of several decades of research, concerned the whole heredity-environment controversy — the battle over nature versus nurture.*

Not all psychologists in America were convinced that the IQ was the highly predictive, hereditarily determined measure it was held to be by Goddard and his followers. It wasn't long before studies were reported which demonstrated that not only was the IQ not fixed but that it could be altered with training, experience, and changes in adjustment patterns.

Although research was reported from all over the nation to support one or the other position, two distinct battle camps could be located. One group, at the University of Iowa, came to be known as the environmentalists. The other, at Stanford University, supported the significance of heredity. After a while, it seemed as if the heredity-environment controversy had settled down into a comfortable compromise: Most people were content to accept the notion that the IQ is the result of the interaction between the gene structure and the environment.

Everyone knew that the argument was not settled, however, probably because people were asking the wrong kinds of questions. Instead of asking how *much* is contributed by heredity and environment respectively, they should have been asking *how* each makes its particular contributions.

For example, in our present state of knowledge, nothing will enable a child who is born deaf to hear. How differences in environment can affect his future development, however, is a terribly significant factor: With appropriate educational procedures he can develop into a literate, communicating adult; without them, he can remain illiterate and uncommunicative. Concentrating on heredity versus environment obscures the more important problem of determining how education can help each child best use what he has at his disposal.†

In recent years, the black community has become more and more vociferous in its objections to the mental test as being biased against them. The outcry has been especially strong against group testing because these tests depend almost entirely on the child's ability to read. Since the child has to read the questions in order to answer them, blacks question whether the test measures capacity to learn or ability to read. They also argue that IQ tests are self-fulfilling predictions.‡ A child with a low IQ score is placed

---

* Again, the heredity versus environment issue appears.
† Do you agree that it's fruitless to debate the heredity-environment issue?
‡ Research evidence concerning this point is presented by Jere Brophy and Thomas Good (Section 6) and by Glen Heathers (Section 13).

in slow learning classes, where he learns less, thereby supporting the original score. Prompted by such arguments, many major school systems abandoned group intelligence testing. Individual tests like the Stanford-Binet and the Wechsler Scales are less subject to criticism, since, hopefully, the trained psychologist ensures that the test is administered properly under an optimum testing climate, and is able to evaluate better to what extent a given child's performance is influenced by emotional, motivational, educational, and socioeconomic factors. . . .

A peculiar characteristic of American education is that, although we give lip service to meeting the needs of individual children, we seldom follow through with concrete actions. We meet the needs of individual children as long as they respond to the existing curriculum, but when a child fails to learn under the existing structure, we assume there is something wrong with him. If "meeting the needs of individual children" is to become meaningful, we should consider the possibility that perhaps a particular teaching method is all wrong for a particular child.*

Certainly, we can't make wholesale prescriptions for black children as if they were all alike. A black child who is not doing well in school may be more like a white child who is similarly unsuccessful than he is like an achieving black child. The problem of understanding learning deficiencies and of locating appropriate pedagogy for overcoming them is not something we know too much about. The storm over the Jensen article may provide the impetus toward working for a true understanding of education and individual differences.

A first step might well be to define our aims and come to grips with why we test. Are we concerned with measuring the amount of cognitive ability an individual is born with, or do we wish to appraise, by sampling performance, the level of adaptive capacities at his disposal?

Do we seek to predict, by way of one or several tests, what an individual will do 20 years from now? Or do we seek to know how and at what stage educational circumstances might be arranged for the individual to achieve his highest level of intellectual functioning ability? Piaget, among others, has never been impressed with standard IQ tests because they do not lead to an understanding of how intelligence functions.† His work is not based on predictions, but rather on assessments of the presence or absence of the essential abilities related to intellectual functioning.

Schools must decide what is the purpose of testing. If all we wish is to separate the bright child from the dull child, the brain-damaged from the neurologically intact, the retarded learner from the gifted, and to attach labels to the children in our schools, we can go on using tests the way we

---

* Many educational psychologists speak on this point, for example, Jensen and Labov (Section 4), Domino (Section 13), and Block (Section 15).
† Piaget's theory of intellectual functioning is presented in Bruner's article in Section 1.

always have, and the argument over genes will continue. But if we mean what we say about meeting individual needs, we can put tests to better use.

The intelligence test, not the IQ score, can tell us the level of the child's functioning in a variety of tasks which measure general intelligence and which are intimately correlated with classroom learning. The goal of testing then becomes to describe the developmental level the child has attained.* The next step requires that educators and psychologists together formulate the educational environment necessary to raise the child to the next developmental level.

EXERCISE

1. What was the original intent of Binet's measure of intelligence? (p. 188)

2. Did Binet and Stern see IQ tests as measures of innate intellectual ability or of the individual's current intellectual functioning? (p. 188)

3. What does Zach consider to be the greatest failure of the IQ testing movement in the United States? (p. 189)

4. What are two reasons why the black community has been opposed to intelligence testing in the schools (pp. 192–193)

5. According to Zach, how can IQ tests be used to meet the needs of individual students? (pp. 193–194)

* Would criterion-referenced tests be better for this purpose than intelligence tests? See Millman, Section 16.

Intelligence Has Three Facets

J. P. Guilford

J. P. Guilford has been one of the chief critics of traditional intelligence tests, mainly because they measure a limited range of abilities and sum them up in a single IQ score. As Lillian Zach

From *Science*, Vol. 160, 10 (May 1968), 615–620. Copyright 1968 © by the American Association for the Advancement of Science. Reprinted with permission of publisher and author.

*explained in the preceding article, test developers and test users
often rely on a vague, general notion of intelligence. Guilford's research indicates that intelligence is composed of a great many independent abilities — at least 120 and perhaps more. His concepts
of "convergent" and "divergent" production abilities have become
household terms in education. In convergent thinking, a person
searches for one correct answer or response to a problem situation.
In divergent thinking, the person is free to produce many possible
responses. Many educators believe that the schools overemphasize
activities which develop convergent production abilities and under-
emphasize those which develop divergent production abilities. The
view of intelligence developed by Guilford has many implications
for education. For example, suppose you are a teacher of two of the
students described in Guilford's Table 1: the student with a high
IQ (140–149) and high divergent production score (50–59), and the
student with the same high IQ but a low divergent production
score (10–19). Would you teach these students the same way? How
might you individualize their educational programs?*

Many a layman who has taken a psychologist's intelligence test, especially if he did not do as well as he thought he should, has the conviction
that a score, such as an IQ, does not tell the whole story regarding intelligence.* In thinking so, he is absolutely right; traditional intelligence tests
fall far short of indicating fully an individual's intellectual status. Just how
far short and in what respects have not been well realized until very recent
years during which the whole scope of human intelligence has been in-
tensively investigated.

This is not to say that IQ tests are not useful, for they definitely are,
as years of experience have demonstrated. Intelligence-quotient tests were
originated more than 60 years ago for the purpose of determining which
children could not learn at normal rates. This meant that the content of
IQ tests weights heavily those intellectual abilities that are pertinent to
school learning in the key subjects of reading and arithmetic, and other
subjects that depend directly upon them or are of similar nature psychologically. IQ tests (and also academic-aptitude tests, which are essentially
similar) predict less well at educational levels higher than the elementary
grades, for at higher levels subject matter becomes more varied. Even at
the elementary level, predictions of achievement have been poor in connection with the *initial* stages of learning to read, in spelling, and in the
arts. The defender of the IQ test might say that intelligence is not involved in such subjects. But he would not only be wrong, he would also
be dodging problems.

* *Zach would agree with this statement, but for different reasons. Why would
she say the tests fall short?*

ONE INTELLIGENCE, OR MANY ABILITIES?

The father of IQ tests, Alfred Binet, believed firmly that intelligence is a very complex affair, comprising a number of different abilities, and he manifested this conviction by introducing tests of many kinds into his composite scale. He did not know what the component abilities are, although he suggested that there are several different kinds of memory, for example. He went along with the idea of using a single, overall score, since the immediate practical goal was to make a single administrative decision regarding each child.

Test-makers following Binet were mostly unconcerned about having a basic psychological theory for intelligence tests, another example of technology running far in advance of theory.* There was some concern about theory in England, however, where Charles Spearman developed a procedure of factor analysis by which it became possible to discover component abilities.[1] † Spearman was obsessed with a very restricting conception that there is a universal g factor that is common to all tests that have any claim to the label of "intelligence tests," where each test has its own unique kind of items or problems. His research, and that of others in his country, found, however, that correlations between tests could not be fully accounted for on the basis of a single common factor.[2] They had to admit the existence of a number of "group" factors in addition to g. For example, sets of tests having verbal, numerical, or spatial material, respectively, correlated higher within sets than with tests in other sets. The extra correlation among tests within sets was attributed to additional abilities each of limited scope....

DISCOVERY OF MULTIPLE ABILITIES

Only a few events in discovering factors by the Thurstone approach will be mentioned. In Thurstone's first major study[3] as many as nine common factors were thought to be sufficiently interpretable psychologically to justify calling them "primary mental abilities." A factor is interpreted intuitively in terms of the apparent human resource needed to do well in the set of tests loaded strongly together on the mathematical factor. A distinction between mathematical factors and psychological factors is important. Surface features of the tests in the set may differ, but examinees have to perform well in some unique way in all of them. For example, Thurstone designated some of the abilities as being visual-perceptual,

---

* Could this same accusation be made about other "advances" in educational technology?
† See the glossary for an explanation of factor analysis.

inductive, deductive, numerical, spatial, and verbal. Two others dealt with rote memory and word fluency. Thurstone and his students followed his 1938 analysis with others that revealed a few additional kinds of abilities.

Another major source of identified intellectual abilities was the research of aviation psychologists in the U.S. Army Air Force during World War II.[4] More important than the outcome of adding to the number of intellectual abilities that called for recognition was the fact that where Thurstone had found one spatial ability, there proved to be at least three, one of them being recognized as spatial orientation and another as spatial visualization. Where Thurstone had found an inductive ability, there were three, including visual memory. In some of these cases a Thurstone factor turned out to be a confounding of two or more separable abilities, separable when more representative tests for each factor were analyzed together and when allowance was made for a sufficient number of factors. In other cases, new varieties of tests were explored — new memory tests, space tests, and reasoning tests.

The third major event was in the form of a program of analyses conducted in the Aptitudes Research Project at the University of Southern California since 1949, in which attention was first concentrated on tests in the provisional categories of reasoning, creative thinking, planning, evaluation, and problem-solving.[5] Nearly 20 years later, the number of separate intellectual abilities has increased to about 80, with at least 50 percent more predicted by a comprehensive, unified theory. The remainder of this article is mainly concerned with that theory.

The Structure-of-Intellect Model

Two previous attempts to put the known intellectual abilities into logical schema had been made by Burt [6] and Vernon,[7] with similar results. In both cases, the models were of hierarchical form, reminiscent of the Linnaeus taxonomic model for the animal kingdoms. Following the British tradition of emphasis upon g, which was placed at the apex of the system, there were broad subdivisions under g and under each subdivision some sub-subcategories, on down to abilities that are regarded as being very narrow in scope.

My first attempts[8] found that the hierarchical type of model had to be discarded for several reasons. First, there had to be a rejection of g itself, for reasons mentioned earlier. Furthermore, most factors seemed to be of somewhat comparable level of generality where generality is operationally defined in terms of the number and variety of tests found to represent each ability. There did appear to be categories of abilities, some concerned with discovery or recognition of information, productive thinking, and evaluation, with a number of abilities in each category, but there are other ways of organizing categories of abilities. The most decisive observation was that there were a number of parallels between abilities, in terms of their common features.*

Some examples of parallels in abilities will help. Two parallel abilities differ in only one respect. There was known to be an ability to see relations between perceived, visual figures, and a parallel ability to see relations between concepts. An example of a test item in the first case would be seeing that one figure is the lower-left half of another. An item in the second case might require seeing that the words "bird" and "fly" are related as object and its mode of locomotion. The ability to do the one kind of item is relatively independent of the ability to do the other, the only difference being that of kind of information — concrete or perceived in the one case and abstract or conceived in the other.

For a pair of abilities differing in another way, the kind of information is the same for both. One of the abilities pertains to *seeing* class ideas. Given the set of words footstool, lamp, rocker, television, can the examinee grasp the essence of the nature of the class, as shown by his naming the class, by putting another word or two into it, or by recognizing its name among four alternatives? The ability pertains to discovery or recognition of a class concept. In another kind of test we ask the examinee to *produce* classes by partitioning a list of words into mutually exclusive sets, each with a different class concept. These two abilities are relatively independent. The one involves a process of understanding and the other a process of production. These processes involve two psychologically different kinds of operation.

A third kind of parallel abilities has pairs that are alike in kind of information involved and in kind of operation. Suppose we give the examinee this kind of test item: "Name as many objects as you can that are both edible and white." Here we have given the specifications for a class and the examinee is to produce from his memory store some class members. The ability involved was at first called "ideational fluency." The more of appropriate members the examinee can produce in a limited time, the better his score. In a test for a parallel ability, instead of producing single words the examinee is to produce a list of sentences. To standardize his task for testing purposes and to further control his efforts, we can give him the initial letters of four words that he is to give in each of a variety of sentences, for example: W——— c——— s——— d———.†
Without using any word twice, the examinee might say, "Why can't Susan dance?," "Workers could seldom deviate," or "Weary cats sense destruction." The ability was first called "expressional fluency." The kind of in-

* *Gagné's domains of learning (see Section 1) include some abilities similar to those discussed here. Where is the overlap?*
† *Is this task too artificial to tell you anything meaningful about students' ability levels?*

formation in both these tests is conceptual, and the kind of operation is production.

But the kind of operation in the last test is different from that for the classifying test mentioned before. In the classifying test, the words given to the examinee are so selected that they form a unique set of classes and he is so told. The operation is called "convergent production." In the last two tests under discussion, there are many possible responses and the examinee produces alternatives. The operation is called "divergent production." It involves a broad searching or scanning process. Both operations depend upon retrieval of information from the examinee's memory store.

The difference between the two abilities illustrated by the last two tests is in the nature of the things produced. In the first case they are single words that stand for single objects or concepts. The thing produced, the "product," is a *unit* of information. In the second case, the product is an organized sequence of words, each word standing for a concept or unit. This kind of product is given the name of "system."

In order to take care of all such parallels (and the number increased as time went on and experience grew), a matrix type of model seemed called for in the manner of Mendeleev's table of chemical elements. The differences in the three ways indicated — operation (kind of processing of information), content (kind of information), and product (formal aspect of information) — called for a three-dimensional model. Such a model has been called "morphological." [9] The model as finally completed and presented in 1959 [10] is illustrated in Figure 1. It has five categories of operation, four categories of content, and six categories of product.

It is readily seen that the theory calls for $5 \times 4 \times 6$, or 120, cubical cells in the model, each one representing a unique ability, unique by virtue of its peculiar conjunction of operation, content, and product. The reader has already been introduced to three kinds of operation: cognition (discovery, recognition, comprehension), divergent production, and convergent production. The memory operation involves putting information into the memory store and must be distinguished from the memory store itself. The latter underlies all the operations; all the abilities depend upon it. This is the best logical basis for believing that the abilities increase with experience, depending upon the kinds of experience. The evaluation operation deals with assessment of information, cognized or produced, determining its goodness with respect to adopted (logical) criteria, such as identity and consistency.

The distinction between figural and semantic (conceptual) contents was mentioned earlier. The distinguishing of symbolic information from these two came later. Symbolic information is presented in tests in the form of letters or numbers, ordinarily, but other signs that have only "token" value or meaning can be used.

OPERATIONS
Evaluation
Convergent production
Divergent production
Memory
Cognition

PRODUCTS
Units
Classes
Relations
Systems
Transformations
Implications

CONTENTS
Figural
Symbolic
Semantic
Behavioral

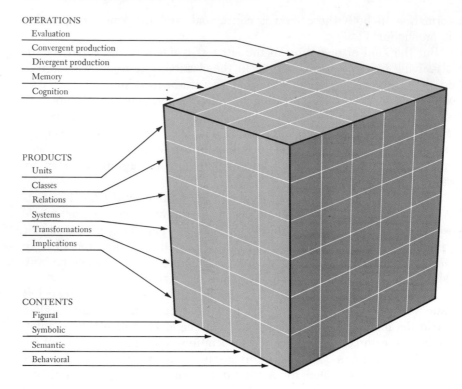

FIGURE 1.

The Structure-of-Intellect Model

The category of behavioral information was added on the basis of a hunch; no abilities involving it were known to have been demonstrated when it was included. The basis was E. L. Thorndike's suggestion[11] many years ago that there is a "social intelligence," distinct from what he called "concrete" and "abstract" intelligences. It was decided to distinguish "social intelligence" on the basis of kind of information, the kind that one person derives from observation of the behavior of another. Subsequent experience has demonstrated a full set of six behavioral-cognition abilities as predicted by the model, and a current analytical investigation is designed to test the part of the model that includes six behavioral-divergent-production abilities. In a test for cognition of behavioral systems, three parts of a four-part cartoon are given in each item, with four alternative parts that are potential completions. The examinee has to size up each situation, and the sequence of events, correctly in order to select the appropriate part. As a test for divergent production of behavioral systems, the examinee is given descriptions of three characters, for example, a jubilant man, an angry woman, and a sullen boy, for which he is to construct a number of alternative story plots involving the characters and their moods, all stories being different.

The reader has already encountered four kinds of products: units, classes, relations, and systems, with illustrations. The other two kinds of products are transformations and implications. Transformations include any kind of change: movement in space, rearrangement or regrouping of letters in words or factoring or simplifying an equation, redefining a concept or adapting an object or part of an object to a new use, revising one's interpretation of another person's action, or rearranging events in a story. In these examples the four kinds of content are involved, from figural to behavioral, illustrating the fact that all six kinds of products apply in every content category.

Implied information is suggested by other information. Foresight or prediction depends upon extrapolating from given information to some naturally following future condition or event. If I make this move in chess, my knight will be vulnerable. If I divide by X, I will have a simpler expression. If it rains tonight, my tent will leak. If I whistle at that girl, she will turn her head. The "If . . . then" expression well describes an instance of implication, the implication actually being the thing implied.

Some Consequences of the Theory

The most immediate consequence of the theory and its model has been its heuristic value in suggesting where to look for still undemonstrated abilities.* The modus operandi of the Aptitudes Research Project from the beginning has been to hypothesize certain kinds of abilities, to create new types of tests that should emphasize each hypothesized ability, then factor analyze to determine whether the hypothesis is well supported. With hypotheses generated by the model, the rate of demonstration of new abilities has been much accelerated.

At the time this article was written, of 24 hypothesized abilities in the category of cognition, 23 had been demonstrated. Of 24 expected memory abilities, 14 were recognized. In the other operation categories of divergent production, convergent production, and evaluation, 16, 13, and 13 abilities, respectively, were accounted for, and in all these categories 17 other hypotheses are under investigation. These studies should bring the number of demonstrated abilities close to the century mark. It is expected that the total will go beyond the 120 indicated by the model, for some cells in the figural and symbolic columns already have more than one ability each. These proliferations arise from the differences in kind of sensory input. Most known abilities are represented by tests with visual input. A

* Are there immediate practical consequences, also? Does the model have meaning for you as a potential teacher?

few have been found in tests with auditory input, and possibly one involving kinesthetic information. Each one can also be placed in the model in terms of its three sources of specification — operation, content, and product. . . .

The structure of intellect, as such, is a taxonomic model; it provides fruitful concepts. For theory that accounts for behavior, we need operational models, and they can be based on SI concepts. For example, I have produced such a model for problem-solving.[12]

There is no one problem-solving ability. Many different SI abilities may be drawn upon in solving a problem, depending upon the nature of the problem.* Almost always there are cognitive operations (in understanding the nature of the problem), productive operations (in generating steps toward solution), and evaluative operations (in checking upon both understanding and production). Memory operations enter in, to keep a record of information regarding previous steps, and the memory store underlies all.

There is something novel about producing solutions to problems, hence creative thinking is involved. Creative thinking depends most clearly upon divergent-production operations on the one hand, and on transformations on the other. Thus, these two categories have unique roles in creative problem-solving. There is accordingly no one unique ability to account for creative potential. Creative production depends upon the area in which one works, whether it is in pictorial art, music, drama, mathematics, science, writing, or management. In view of the relative independence of the intellectual abilities, unevenness of status in the various abilities within the same person should be the rule rather than the exception. Some individuals can excel in more than one art form, but few excel in all, as witness the practice of having multiple creative contributors to a single motion picture.

The implications of all this for education are numerous. The doctrine that intelligence is a unitary something that is established for each person by heredity and that stays fixed through life should be summarily banished.† There is abundant proof that greater intelligence is associated with increased education. One of education's major objectives should be to increase the stature of its recipients in intelligence, which should now mean stature in the various intellectual abilities. Knowing what those abilities are, we not only have more precise goals but also much better conceptions of how to achieve those goals.

For much too long, many educators have assumed, at least implicitly,

---

* Consider how you approach a problem. Do you use all these intellectual abilities?

† Key statement. Assuming Guilford is right, does it mean that the research of Jensen (Section 4) and Cohen (this section) is misguided?

that if we provide individuals with information they will also be able to use that information productively. Building up the memory store is a necessary condition for productive thinking, but it is not a sufficient condition, for productive abilities are relatively independent of cognitive abilities. There are some revealing findings on this point.[13] In a sample of about 200 ninth-grade students, IQ measurements were available and also the scores on a large number of tests of various divergent-production (DP) abilities. Table 1 shows a scatter diagram with plots of DP scores[14] as a function of IQ. The striking feature of this diagram pertains to the large proportion of high-IQ students who had low, even some very low, DP scores. In general, IQ appears to set a kind of upper limit upon DP performance but not a lower limit. The same kind of result was true for most other DP tests.

TABLE 1
Scatterplot of Expressional Fluency (One Aspect of Divergent Production) Scores in Relation to CTMM (California Test of Mental Maturity) IQ.

DP score	Intelligence quotient								
	60–69	70–79	80–89	90–99	100–109	110–119	120–129	130–139	140–149
50–59						1	3		1
40–49						2	4	1	
30–39			2	3	4	11	17	6	2
20–29			1	3	10	23	13	7	
10–19	1	5	3	9	11	19	7	3	1
0– 9	1	3	1	4	10	11	2		

On the basis of present information, it would be best to regard each intellectual ability of a person as a somewhat generalized skill that has developed through the circumstances of experience, within a certain culture, and that can be further developed by means of the right kind of exercise. There may be limits to abilities set by heredity, but it is probably safe to say that very rarely does an individual really test such limits. There is much experimental evidence, rough though it may be, that exercise devoted to certain skills involved in creative thinking is followed by increased capability.[15] Although special exercises have their demonstrated value, it is probably better to have such exercises worked into teaching, whatever the subject, where there are opportunities. Informing individuals regarding the nature of their own intellectual resources, and how they enter into mental work, has also been found beneficial.

There is not space to mention many other problems related to intelligence — its growth and its decline, its relation to brain anatomy and brain functions, and its role in learning. All these problems take on new aspects, when viewed in terms of the proposed frame of reference. For too long, many investigators have been handicapped by using a single, highly ambiguous score to represent what is very complex but very comprehensible. . . .

SUMMARY

In this limited space I have attempted to convey information regarding progress in discovering the nature of human intelligence. By intensive factor-analytic investigation, mostly within the past 20 years, the multi-factor picture of intelligence has grown far beyond the expectations of those who have been most concerned. A comprehensive, systematic theoretical model known as the "structure of intellect" has been developed to put rationality into the picture.

The model is a cubical affair, its three dimensions representing ways in which the abilities differ from one another. Represented are: five basic kinds of operation, four substantive kinds of information or "contents," and six formal kinds of information or "products," respectively. Each intellectual ability involves a unique conjunction of one kind of operation, one kind of content, and one kind of product, all abilities being relatively independent in a population, but with common joint involvement in intellectual activity.

This taxonomic model has led to the discovery of many abilities not suspected before. Although the number of abilities is large, the 15 category constructs provide much parsimony. They also provide a systematic basis for viewing mental operations in general, thus suggesting new general psychological theory.

The implications for future intelligence testing and for education are numerous. Assessment of intellectual qualities should go much beyond present standard intelligence tests, which seriously neglect important abilities that contribute to problem-solving and creative performance in general. Educational philosophy, curriculum-building, teaching procedures, and examination methods should all be improved by giving attention to the structure of intellect as the basic frame of reference.* There is much basis for expecting that various intellectual abilities can be improved in individuals, and the procedures needed for doing this should be clear.

EXERCISE

1. Did the work of Spearman, Thurstone, and others support the notion of intelligence as a single ability or as a complex of many abilities? (p. 196)

* Are there any new developments in education (see Part III) which do this?

2. According to Guilford, what are the three dimensions which can be used to characterize and group all intellectual abilities? (p. 199)

3. What is the distinction between convergent production and divergent production? (p. 199)

4. According to Guilford, what are the abilities involved in problem-solving? (p. 202)

5. What is the main implication of the structure-of-intellect model for education? (p. 202)

QUALITY
OF TEACHING

Introduction

The teacher is the mainstay of education in the Western world. Currently, nearly two million are in direct contact with students most of each school day in this country. With this amount of teacher-student interaction, it is easy to understand why many people believe that the teacher is the most important factor that influences student learning. Students instructed by skilled teachers should make significantly greater learning gains than students instructed by ineffective teachers. Has research in educational psychology substantiated this claim?

Unfortunately, despite a great amount of research on teacher effectiveness, few positive results have been obtained. Many teaching practices that appear to have a logical relationship to the learning goals presented in Part I of this book have been investigated — asking thought-provoking questions, establishing rapport with students, showing warmth, emphasizing discussion rather than lecture, and adapting instruction to the individual student's learning needs. However, teachers who use such techniques generally do not bring about greater student learning, as measured by gains on standard achievement tests, than teachers who do not use them. Why?

One view which has become popular recently is that teachers cannot make much of a difference, through no fault of their own. Subscribers to this view cite the Coleman report and other studies (see Mayeske, Section 4; Bane and Jencks, Section 3; and Husen, Section 7), which indicate that individual differences in student achievement are mostly caused by differences in intelligence, learning outside of school, and social background factors. The influence of these factors is so strong that the teacher cannot overcome them to any significant degree. Identifying what constitutes a "good" teacher or training teachers to make them more effective has little effect.

Another view is that teachers do not make a difference because they are too concerned with *process*; that is, they are preoccupied with maintaining classroom control, being kind and interested, covering content, or giving tests. Instead, teachers should concentrate on *product*, that is, in helping students achieve specific instructional objectives. Proponents of this view believe that if teachers can be trained to consciously teach for specific learnings, then we will find that they can make a difference. This view of teaching has led to the recent emphasis on behavioral objectives and accountability discussed in Part 4 of this book.

Still another view of this problem is provided by educators who believe that too much emphasis has been placed on judging teachers in terms of their effectiveness in promoting the type of learning usually measured by standard achievement tests. They point to studies which show that teachers can affect student *attitudes* toward school and learning. These relationships are not clearly understood, however. Much more research is needed.

To clarify these issues about teacher effectiveness, we present the following views. Do you agree or disagree with them?

Effects of Skilled Teachers

Pro Teachers who can use a variety of teaching strategies with a high level of skill can improve students' learning. The important factor is to train teachers in those skills that most directly relate to the learning goals of school and society and the learning characteristics of children.

Con Quality of teaching has little effect on student learning. Most bright students will learn despite a bad teacher. Most dull students will learn little despite the efforts of a skilled teacher.

Using Achievement Test Scores to Measure Teacher Influence on Student Learning

Pro Achievement test scores represent basic skills and knowledge that students must acquire. Teachers should be expected to teach students these skills. Teacher performance, therefore, should affect student learning as measured by achievement tests.

Con The teacher's greatest impact on students is not and should not be in helping them learn the facts and skills measured by standard achievement tests. Most students can do this for themselves. Researchers will find that teachers exert their greatest influence in shaping self-concept, attitudes toward learning, and cognitive skills that are more complex than those measured by achievement tests.

The following selections highlight different aspects of the influence of teaching quality on learning. N. L. Gage reviews research that attempts to identify the types of teaching skills that have demonstrable positive effects on student achievement. W. James Popham takes a more pessimistic view of the way teachers currently teach. In an experiment that has been widely publicized, he found that untrained persons did just as well as regular teachers in bringing about learning. Ned Flanders and his colleagues ask whether teachers should be judged solely by their students' performance on achievement tests. The purpose of their research project was to determine whether teachers affect students' attitude toward school. Jere Brophy and Thomas Good review the research literature to determine whether teachers affect students through the expectations they form about their learning ability.

Can Science Contribute to the Art of Teaching?

N. L. Gage

N. L. Gage reviews some of the many research studies on the relationship between teacher behavior and student learning outcomes. Some teaching practices, considered desirable by educators, have not been supported by research findings. For example, although many people criticize the lecture method of teaching, research shows that it is neither better nor worse than the discussion method as an influence on college students' scores on final examinations. However, some teacher characteristics, such as warmth and enthusiasm, do appear to facilitate student learning. Do the teaching skills discussed by Gage represent significant aspects of teaching? What skills do the findings suggest that you, as a potential teacher, should try to acquire?

Can science contribute to the art of teaching? To successful teacher behavior? It would be nice if the answer could be a resounding "Yes," based on a long parade of conclusive evidence and examples of richly useful findings. Unfortunately, that happy paper cannot yet be written in any

From N. L. Gage, *Teacher Effectiveness and Teacher Education: The Search for a Scientific Basis.* Palo Alto, Calif.: Pacific Books, 1972. Reprinted with permission of publisher and author.

honest way. Instead, the question must receive a rather more complex response.

First, I shall define the term "successful teacher behavior" and delimit the setting of the kind of teaching to be considered. Second, I shall outline reasons for pessimism as to whether research on teaching has any real likelihood of yielding scientific findings that can be used to improve teaching. Then I shall sketch the nature of the findings that would alleviate the pessimism.

DEFINITION AND DELIMITATION

My definition of "successful teacher behavior" is one based on research on teaching. The findings of such research may or may not accord with common sense. They may or may not accord with the virtues of personality and character, or desirable behaviors, described in writings on ethics, the Boy Scout Handbook, or a Dale Carnegie course. Also, a research-based characterization of successful teacher behavior may not be extremely original, or completely non-obvious. Neither must such a description of behavior be highly systematic, since research findings at any given moment do not necessarily form a coherent scheme. As for validity, it is not inconceivable that in the long run, some non-scientific insight or artistic hunch may turn out to be superior to what can now be cited on the basis of research evidence. The truths propounded in the past by novelists, essayists, or skilled supervisors of teachers may eventually prove more valid than the results of research now available.

Despite these possible limitations, I shall consider here only what the research literature has to offer. This literature takes the form of reports on empirical studies of one kind or another. In these studies, various kinds of teacher behavior have been related to other variables on which some sort of educational valuation can be placed. So, by the present definition, "successful" teacher behaviors or characteristics are those that have been found through empirical research to be related to something desirable about teachers.* The "something desirable" may be improved achievement by students of any of the various cognitive, affective, or psychomotor objectives of education. Or, the "something desirable" may be a favorable evaluation of the teacher by students, a supervisor, a principal, or someone else whose judgment is important. . . .

Now let us specify the kind of setting in which the teacher behavior to be considered takes place. Various innovations now being considered by educators may more frequently in the future make the setting of teaching something other than the conventional classroom. The setting may change in accordance with the needs of the students and the kinds of learning in

* *How could this definition result in a narrow view of teaching?*

which they are engaged. For some kinds of learning, students may be taught in large-group settings, such as motion picture theaters and lecture halls. For other kinds, the setting may be the small-group seminar, or a booth for programmed instruction, "individually prescribed instruction," or independent study. In the future, these settings will, it is said, supplement and perhaps supplant today's conventional classroom.

But these different kinds of settings still lie in the future, for the most part. And my definition of successful teaching requires empirical research demonstrating a relationship between the behaviors of teachers and other desirable things. Most of that research, by far, has been done in classrooms. So this discussion will be restricted to the behavior of teachers in the conventional classroom.*

Reasons for Pessimism

Let us now consider reasons for pessimism on the question, Can science contribute to the art of teaching? To begin, it should be noted that making positive statements about the results of research on successful teacher behavior is not fashionable among educational research workers. Many reviewers of research on teaching have concluded that it has yielded little of value.

This disparaging style in appraising research results has had a great vogue. In 1953, a Committee on the Criteria of Teacher Effectiveness rendered the verdict that "the present condition of research on teacher effectiveness holds little promise of yielding results commensurate with the needs of American education" (American Educational Research Association, 1953, p. 657). In 1958, Orville Brim (1958, p. 32) concluded from his examination of reviews of the literature that there were no consistent relations between teacher characteristics and effectiveness in teaching. In 1963, in the *Handbook of Research on Teaching*, the authors of the chapter on teaching methods reported an impression that "teaching methods do not seem to make much difference" and that "there is hardly any evidence to favor one method over another" (Wallen and Travers, 1963, p. 484). The authors of the chapter on teacher personality and characteristics concluded that "... very little is known for certain ... about the relation between teacher personality and teacher effectiveness" (Getzels and Jackson, 1963, p. 574). And the authors of the chapter on social interaction in the classroom concluded that "until very recently, the approach to the analysis of teacher-pupil and pupil-pupil interaction ... has tended to be unrewarding and sterile" (Withall and Lewis, 1963, p. 708). It would not be hard to find other summary statements to the effect

* *Is the conventional classroom the setting in which teacher influence is most appropriately studied?*

that empirical research on teaching has not yielded much enlightenment about successful teaching.

After a thorough review, Dubin and Taveggia (1968) concluded that college teaching methods make no difference in student achievement as measured by final examinations on course content. Their review was unique in that they examined the data, rather than merely the conclusions, of nearly 100 studies made over a 40-year period. Of 88 independent comparisons of the lecture and discussion methods, reported in 36 experimental studies, 51 per cent favored the lecture method and 49 per cent favored the discussion method! . . .

Some writers hold that all research on school variables, not merely research on teacher behavior, has yielded negative results for the most part. The view that educational research yields negative findings has even been assimilated into a whole theory of the origins and process of schooling. Stephens (1967), after looking at the research reports and summaries, concluded that practically nothing seems to make any difference in the effectiveness of instruction. He considered this "flood of negative results" to be understandable in the light of his theory of spontaneous schooling. This theory postulates spontaneous, automatic forces in the background of the student — his maturational tendencies, various out-of-school agencies such as the home and the general community, and the reputation of the school as a place concerned about academic matters.* The theory also refers to various spontaneous tendencies on the part of humans in the role of the teacher — tendencies to manipulate and communicate. These two kinds of force, the background forces and the automatic teaching forces, account for most of the learning that takes place. Furthermore, these spontaneous and powerful forces operate early in the growth process, when influences on learning have greater effects. Hence, the changes introduced by research variables, administrative factors, and pedagogical refinements of one kind or another are inadequate to produce any major difference.

Stephens documented his position with references to summaries of studies of a host of educational variables, procedures, practices, and orientations — namely, school attendance, instructional television, independent study and correspondence courses, size of class, individual consultation and tutoring, counseling, concentration on specific students, the student's involvement, the amount of time spent in study, distraction by jobs and extracurricular activities, size of school, the qualities of teachers that can be rated by principals and supervisors, non-graded schools, team teaching, ability grouping, progressivism vs. traditionalism, discussion vs. lecture, group-centered vs. teacher-centered approaches, the use of frequent

---

* How is Stephen's theory of spontaneous schooling supported by Bane and Jencks's and by Mayeske's findings (see Sections 3 and 4, respectively)?

quizzes, and programmed instruction. Studies of all these have failed to show that they make a consistent and significant difference. . . .

Apparent support for this view of the effects of educational variables on scholastic achievement can be found in the massive report on *Equality of Educational Opportunity* (Coleman et al., 1966). According to that report, when the social background and attitudes of individual students and their schoolmates are held constant, achievement is only slightly related to school characteristics, such as per-pupil expenditures, books in the library, and a number of other facilities and curricular measures. Conversely, the report found that family background accounted for a relatively high proportion of the variance in student achievement. Stephens seems to be vindicated by these findings.

QUESTIONING THE PESSIMISM

So far we have considered reasons for pessimism about the promise of empirical research on teaching. Now let us raise some questions about these lugubrious views.

In the first place, these dismal generalizations may not do complete justice to the research domains for which they have been made. Here and there, in research on teaching methods, on teacher personality and characteristics, and on social interaction in the classroom, it may be possible to come up with more sanguine judgments about the meaning of the research findings. . . . If so, future conclusions about research on teaching may be less melancholy. Later in this chapter, some preliminary examples of such sifting will be offered.

What about the report on *Equality of Educational Opportunity?* Here also there are reasons to question the pessimism. According to Bowles and Levin (1968a), the research design of that study "was overwhelmingly biased in a direction that would dampen the importance of school characteristics." For example, expenditure-per-pupil was measured in terms of the average expenditure within an entire school district rather than within the given school in which the pupils were located. Hence, the expenditure-per-pupil was overstated for schools attended by lower-class students and understated for schools attended by students of higher social status. . . .

Despite these biases, the report found that measures of teacher quality were significantly related to achievement, probably because teacher characteristics were measured individually and averaged for each school. Indeed, the report stated that teacher characteristics accounted for a ". . . higher proportion of variation in student achievement than did all other aspects of the school combined, excluding the student body characteristics" (Coleman et al., 1966, p. 316). These teacher characteristics were family educational level, years' experience, localism (living in the area most of their lives), teachers' own educational level, score on a vocabulary test, preference for middle-class students, and proportion of teachers in the school who were white.* And such factors make a bigger difference, according to the report, for Negro than for white students, perhaps because their out-of-school environment contributes less of the spontaneous educative forces to which Stephens referred.

Accordingly, the characteristics of teachers who work with culturally disadvantaged pupils become all the more important. In subsequent re-analyses of some of the data of the report, Bowles and Levin (1968b) found that teacher characteristics were very significantly related to the verbal achievement of twelfth-grade Negro students, even when social background factors were held constant. . . .

SOME POSITIVE STATEMENTS

Having emphasized the difficulties of making positive research-based statements about successful teaching behaviors, I wish nonetheless to attempt such statements. My purpose is merely to illustrate the nature of the conclusions that might be drawn from more adequate examination of better research. My procedure will be to present a series of operational definitions of teacher behaviors that seem, more or less, to belong on the same dimension. These definitions will be drawn from various research procedures and measuring instruments. Then I shall cite some of the evidence on which it is possible to base the inference that these behaviors or characteristics are desirable.

WARMTH. One example of this dimension can be seen in the responses of teachers to the Minnesota Teacher Attitude Inventory (MTAI) (Cook, Leeds, and Callis, 1951). Here, the teacher responds on a five-point agree-disagree scale to such statements as "Most children are obedient," "Minor disciplinary situations should sometimes be turned into jokes," "Most pupils lack productive imagination," and "Most pupils are resourceful when left on their own."

As a second example, consider teachers' responses to the California F scale (McGee, 1955), which has been found to correlate substantially . . . with the MTAI (Gage, Leavitt, and Stone, 1957; Sheldon, Coale, and Copple, 1959). Among the F scale's items are "Obedience and respect for authority are the most important virtues children should learn," "People can be divided into two distinct classes: the weak and the strong," and "Most of our social problems would be solved if we could somehow get rid of the immoral, crooked, and feeble-minded people."

A final example can be drawn from the work of Ryans (1960), who

---

* Do these characteristics represent teaching skills? Why would you expect them to be related to student achievement?

developed a Teacher Characteristic Schedule that included such items as the following: "Pupils can behave themselves without constant supervision," "Most pupils are considerate of the teacher's wishes," and "Most teachers are willing to assume their share of the unpleasant tasks associated with teaching."

Now what is the basis for the proposition that certain patterns of responses to attitude statements of this kind are "desirable"? The answer is that these kinds of attitudes and behaviors tend to be correlated positively with favorable assessments of the teachers by students and trained observers, and with students' scores on achievement tests. The Minnesota Teacher Attitude Inventory has fairly consistently been found to correlate positively with favorable mean ratings of the teachers by their pupils (Yee, 1967). The items of Ryans' inventory correlated positively with observers' ratings of elementary school teachers on all three of his teacher behavior patterns — warm, understanding, friendly vs. aloof, egocentric, and restricted; responsible, businesslike, systematic vs. evading, unplanned, and slipshod; and stimulating, imaginative vs. dull, routine (Ryans, 1960). McGee (1955) found that teachers' scores on the California F Scale correlated highly with previous ratings of the teachers by trained observers on dimensions like aloof vs. approachable; unresponsive vs. responsive, dominative vs. integrative, and harsh vs. kindly. Cogan (1958) found that descriptions of teachers by their students on similar items correlated positively with the amount of required and also voluntary school work done by the students.

In short, a substantial body of evidence supports two conclusions: (a) Teachers differ reliably from one another on a series of measuring instruments that seem to have a great deal in common. (b) These reliable individual differences among teachers are fairly consistently related to various desirable things about teachers.

What term can be applied to the desirable end of this dimension of behaviors and attitudes? Teachers at this desirable end tend to behave approvingly, acceptantly, and supportively; they tend to speak well of their own students, students in general, and people in general.* They tend to like and trust rather than fear other people of all kinds. How they get that way is not our concern at the moment. The point is that it is not impossible to find extremely plausible similarities among the teacher behaviors measured and found desirable by a number of independent investigators working with different methods, instruments, and concepts. Although any single term is inadequate, it seems safe to use the term "warmth." Warmth, operationally defined as indicated above, seems — on

---

* *Are these dimensions specific to teaching? Or do they refer to skills that characterize good human relations in general?*

the basis of varied research evidence to be quite defensible as a desirable characteristic of teacher behavior.

INDIRECTNESS. To identify a second dimension of teacher behavior, we begin with two of Flanders's categories.* His Category 3 is "Accepts or uses ideas of student: clarifying, building, or developing ideas suggested by a student," and Category 4 is "Ask questions: asking a question about content or procedure with the intent that a student answer." In the classrooms of teachers that behave in these ways relatively often, one also finds more instances of Category 8: "Student talk-response: talk by students in response to teacher. Teacher initiates the contact or solicits student statement," and Category 9: "Student talk-initiation: talk by students which they initiate. If 'calling on' student is only to indicate who may talk next, observer must decide whether student wanted to talk. If he did, use this category."

A second example of this dimension of teacher behavior may be seen in the research on what is called "learning by discovery." This research deals with the question, "How much and what kind of guidance should the teacher provide? ... the degree of guidance by the teacher varies from time to time along a continuum, with almost complete direction of what the pupil must do at one extreme to practically no direction at the other" (Shulman and Keisler, 1966, pp. 182, 183). This dimension consists of the degree to which the teacher permits pupils to discover underlying concepts and generalizations for themselves, giving them less rather than more direct guidance. The teacher at the higher level of this dimension realizes that it is not always desirable merely to tell the pupil what you want him to know and understand.† Rather, it is sometimes better to ask questions, encourage the pupil to become active, seek for himself, use his own ideas, and engage in some trial and error. This kind of teaching represents a willingness to forbear giving the pupil everything he needs to know; it does not mean abandoning the pupil entirely to his own devices.

Now what is the evidence that this dimension of teacher behavior — exemplified in Flanders's categories, and teaching-by-discovery — has a significant relationship to something educationally desirable? Flanders and Simon (1969) concluded from their examination of a dozen studies that "*the percentage of teacher statements that make use of ideas and opinions previously expressed by pupils is directly related to average class scores on attitude scales of teacher attractiveness, liking the class, etc., as well as to*

---

* Flanders's category system is also discussed in this section.
† Do any teachers you know work in this indirect way? Would you learn better with such a teacher?

average achievement scores adjusted for initial ability" (p. 1426, italics in original). Ausubel (1963, p. 171) reviewed the experiments on learning by discovery and concluded that the furnishing of completely explicit rules is relatively less effective than some degree of arranging for pupils to discover rules for themselves.

It seems safe to say that some use of the guided discovery method, and "indirectness," in teaching is desirable. Teachers not sensitized to its desirability typically exhibit too little indirectness. As Flanders (1965, p. 114) put it, "our theory suggests an indirect approach; most teachers use a direct approach."

COGNITIVE ORGANIZATION. The third dimension of teacher behavior is more difficult to define operationally. And its connection with desirable outcomes is, despite great plausability, not as well established empirically. This is the kind of behavior that reflects the teacher's intellectual grasp, or "cognitive organization" of what he is trying to teach.

In one investigation, teachers were tested as to whether they understood the processes and concepts of arithmetic, such as the reason for moving each sub-product one digit to the left when the multiplier has more than one digit (Orleans, 1952). Other studies have dealt with the degree to which the teacher's verbal behavior reflects an understanding of the logical properties of a good definition, explanation, or conditional inference (Meux and Smith, 1961). Others have studied the degree to which the teacher, or his instructional material, provides a set of subject-matter "organizers" that embody "relevant ideational scaffolding," discriminate new material from previously learned material, and integrate it "at a level of abstraction, generality, and inclusiveness which is much higher than that of the learning material itself" (Ausubel, 1963, p. 214). Similar ideas have been put in such terms as "cognitive structure" (Bruner, 1966), "learning structure" (Gagné, 1965), and "logic tree" (Hickey and Newton, 1964).*

Although the general conception of this aspect of teaching behavior can be identified, operational definitions are hard to come by. Perhaps the best operational definitions of such variables must be inferred from the procedures of those who develop programmed instructional materials. These procedures call for behavioral definitions of objectives and detailed "learning structures" (Gagné, 1965) that analyze the steps involved in achieving a "terminal behavior" into hierarchies of subtasks. Gagné (1965) illustrated such learning structures in mathematics and science; Glaser and Reynolds (1964) worked out a detailed example in the form of the sequence of sub-behaviors involved in programmed instructional materials for teaching children to tell time from a clock.

* *Bruner and Gagné discuss these concepts in Part 1 of the book.*

In some ways, the lessons derived from this kind of technical work on teaching and learning have implications for curriculum development rather than for teaching as such. But the curriculum is inevitably shaped through the teacher's behavior in the classroom as well as by the materials that his pupils read. The implications of such instructional research for the behavior of the live teacher in the classroom seem clear: if curricular material should exhibit a valid cognitive organization, so should the behavior of the teacher.

ENTHUSIASM. Our last example of a sifting of the literature to identify a desirable kind of teacher behavior is one recently provided by Rosenshine (1970). He reviewed the evidence from a variety of sources on the degree to which the teacher's "enthusiasm" was desirable. Some of the studies reviewed were experiments in which "enthusiasm" was manipulated. In other, correlational, studies, enthusiasm as it occurred "naturally" was rated, counted, or measured with an inventory. In some of the studies, the dependent variable was measured achievement; in others, evaluative ratings of the teacher by his students or other independent observers. The varied evidence seemed remarkably consistent in supporting the desirability of teacher enthusiasm. Positive differences between means and positive correlation coefficients appeared far more often than did those indicating a negative relationship between teacher enthusiasm and something desirable about the teacher.*

Two examples of experiments will illustrate these findings. Coats and Smidchens (1966) had two 10-minute lessons presented by two teachers in a static, or unenthusiastic fashion (read from a manuscript, with no gestures, eye contact, or inflections), and also in a dynamic, or enthusiastic fashion (delivered from memory, with much inflection, eye contact, gesturing, and animation). Tests immediately after the lesson indicated much greater learning from the dynamic lecture. Similarly, Mastin (1963) had 20 teachers lecture on two different topics a week apart — presenting one topic in an "indifferent" manner and the other "enthusiastically." In 19 of the 20 classes, the student's mean achievement was higher for the lesson taught enthusiastically.

These four variables — warmth, indirectness, cognitive organization, and enthusiasm — merely illustrate the kinds of contributions that research on teaching, in its present early stages, can support.† In themselves, these findings are far from startling. Any clever student, teacher, or novelist could have told us decades ago about these characteristics of good teaching. But what is important about these tentative conclusions is their

* Correlation coefficients are explained in the glossary.
† Do you agree that using these four teacher variables will result in improved learning?

basis in empirical research.* The ease with which others have told us such truths in the past is matched by their untrustworthiness. Glib insights based on uncontrolled experience can lead us astray. Research on teaching — the effort to apply scientific method to the description and improvement of teaching — is much more laborious and usually makes much less interesting reading than the essay of the shrewd, compassionate, and imaginative observer. The same tortoise-hare comparison would have applied in past centuries to research on psychiatry and the writings of phrenologists, to research on chemistry and the writings of alchemists, and so on. In the long run, as humanity has learned, it is safer in matters of this kind to rely on the scientific method. Applying that method to the phenomena and problems of teaching is our concern.

EXERCISE

1. What is Gage's criterion for labeling as "successful" particular teacher behaviors or characteristics? (p. 209)
2. What was the main finding of the literature review done by Dubin and Taveggia? (p. 211)
3. What is the main premise of Stephens's theory of spontaneous schooling? (pp. 211–212)
4. What were the findings of the Coleman study about the effect of teacher characteristics on student achievement? (pp. 212–213)
5. Describe the four "successful" teaching behaviors identified by Gage through his review of the research. (pp. 213–217)

* Is research evidence more important than common-sense descriptions of "good" teaching? Why or why not?

Teaching Skill under Scrutiny

W. James Popham

W. James Popham conducted an experiment in which he found that teachers are no more effective than untrained persons of comparable intelligence and general education in bringing about student

From *Phi Delta Kappan*, 52, 1971, 599–601. Used by permission of the author, W. James Popham, and the Publisher, *Phi Delta Kappan*, June, 1971.

learning. The measure of learning used in this experiment was the students' scores on specially devised performance tests. These tests measured the extent to which the students had achieved the specific learning objectives given to both the teachers and nonteachers. Popham found that students instructed by untrained staff learned as much as students instructed by trained public school teachers. In many ways, this study tests the usefulness of behavioral objectives and criterion-referenced tests (discussed in Part 4) as much as it tests teacher skill. Although Popham's findings raise serious questions about the quality of teaching being offered to today's students, they also suggest that such a carefully constructed curriculum may help to improve students' learning. Do you feel this was a fair test of the teachers' skill? Also, try to think of learning situations in which trained teachers would be more likely to promote better student learning than their untrained counterparts.

Results of a recently reported series of investigations reveal that experienced teachers may not be significantly more proficient than "people off the street" with respect to accomplishing intended behavior changes in learners. In three separate replications, groups of experienced teachers were unable to outperform nonteachers in bringing about specified changes in learners. This article will (1) summarize those investigations[1] and the rationale underlying them, (2) consider the generalizability of the results, and (3) offer recommendations for altering an unacceptable state of affairs in the teaching profession.

A Measure of Teacher Effectiveness

The research reported here stemmed from an attempt to isolate a readily usable indicator which could be employed to assess a teacher's instructional skill. Anyone who has followed the search for a satisfactory measure of teaching proficiency must conclude that this area of inquiry may well represent one of the most high-investment/low-yield activities of our field. For over 70 years researcher after researcher has tried out such devices as administrator ratings, pupil ratings, systematic observations, and student performance on standardized tests. With few exceptions, the results have been thoroughly disappointing. Briefly, let's see why.

Ratings of teaching skill, whether supplied by administrators, pupils, or a visiting mother-in-law, are notoriously inaccurate. The administrator-rater looks in on Mrs. Jones's class and, if he sees her engaging in those splendid techniques he employed during his own marvelous moments as a classroom teacher, Mrs. Jones gets a good rating. Pupils may rate an instructor positively because he is a lenient grader or because he has a good sense of humor. In other words, ratings of teaching proficiency are based on highly variable conceptions of what constitutes good teaching.* One rater's "dynamic" teacher is another's "unorganized" failure. That these variably derived and often unreliable ratings of teaching skill do not correlate well with most measures of pupil achievement should not surprise us.

Another widely used index of teaching effectiveness involves the use of systematic observations of the teacher's classroom practices. Employing more or less systematized check sheets, someone observes the teacher in action and derives an estimate of the teacher's skill based on the degree to which certain process variables are present (for example, frequency of teacher questions, pupil talk, etc.). The problem with the observation approach is that it is so process-focused that the observer rarely moves to the logical follow-up question: "What happens to pupils as a consequence of the teacher's using these processes?" The chief problem for proponents of observation-derived estimates of teaching skill stems from the clear evidence that widely divergent instructional tactics can be used to promote identical instructional goals. For one teacher a nondirective approach may be ideal, while another teacher might find a highly directive approach preferable.† Yet, because of their idiosyncratic personalities, prior experience and other variables, both teachers' approaches may be equally effective. Thus, while observational techniques may be helpful to a teacher for analyzing his instructional activities, they should not be employed as an index of teacher effectiveness. The correlation between instructional process and results in learners is not strong enough.

The third most widely used measure of teaching skill is pupil performance on standardized tests. But since standardized tests are designed chiefly to discriminate among learners,[2] not necessarily to indicate the degree to which identifiable skills have been mastered, they have not provided us with sufficiently sensitive estimates of how much progress pupils have made with a given teacher. An even more important reason for eschewing standardized tests is the fact that different teachers have markedly different emphases, even in the same course. One geography instructor will emphasize topography, another will stress natural resources. Given the grossness of standardized tests to begin with, such instruments cannot accommodate teachers' differential emphases.

TEACHING PERFORMANCE TESTS

In an effort to provide a more defensible approach to the measurement of teaching skill, a series of investigations initiated at UCLA in 1964 re-

* Are the teacher variables discussed by Gage (in the preceding selection) based upon such subjective judgments?
† How might this statement influence your interpretation of the research data which Gage reports about "indirectness"?

sulted in the development of the *teaching performance test*, a heretofore untried vehicle for assessing instructional proficiency. This approach is predicated on the assumption that the chief reason for a teacher's existence is to promote beneficial changes in learners. While we may expect a teacher to perform other functions, perhaps the most important role of the teacher is to modify learners so that they possess more knowledge, employ it more skillfully, cope more satisfactorily with their environment and, in general, function as more humane members of a perilously threatened world society. One crucial ingredient of the teacher's skill rests on this ability to change learners. A teaching performance test measures such ability.

Briefly, teaching performance tests avoid the measurement problems arising from different teachers' pursuits of different objectives. This is accomplished by asking teachers to achieve the same objectives, yet permitting them to employ their own pedagogical preferences in doing so. By holding instructional goals constant it becomes possible to contrast teachers with respect to their skill in accomplishing identical goals. Procedurally, a teaching performance test is carried out as follows:

1. The teacher is given one or more explicit instructional objectives (and, preferably, a sample of the measurement procedure used to assess each objective), plus any necessary background information related to the objectives.*

2. The teacher is given sufficient time to plan an instructional sequence to accomplish the objective.

3. The teacher then instructs a group of learners in an effort to have the learners achieve the objective.

4. At the conclusion of the instruction the learners are measured with respect to the objectives, their performance providing an estimate of the teacher's instructional skill.

DEVELOPMENT AND VALIDATION

As the chief focus of a four-year investigation at UCLA, three teaching performance tests were developed in the fields of social science, electronics, and auto mechanics.

The social science performance test dealt with the topic of social science research methods and consisted of 13 specific instructional objectives measured by a 68-item posttest. The electronics performance test treated basic power supplies and contained 23 instructional objectives measured by a 47-item posttest. The auto mechanics performance test dealt with carburetion and possessed 29 instructional objectives measured by a 99-

* *Instructional objectives are discussed in Section 14.*

item posttest. In addition, all three performance tests contained a set of resource materials which could be used in planning an instructional sequence to accomplish the objectives. All materials associated with each of the performance tests were reviewed during development by a number of practicing teachers and other subject matter experts. In addition, each test was subjected to several field trials before the final versions were assembled.

In deciding on a reasonable approach to validate this method of assessing teacher effectiveness, a construct validation strategy was selected.* Considering the nature of the requirements of teaching performance tests, it seemed that these tests ought to be able *at least* to distinguish between grossly disparate groups such as credentialed, experienced teachers and those who were neither credentialed nor experienced. In other words, if one were to ask a group of experienced teachers to complete a given performance test, in contrast to a group of people off the street, the experienced teachers ought to markedly outperform their inexperienced counterparts.

To test this validation hypothesis, suitable numbers of teachers and nonteachers were recruited in the Southern California region.[3] After several months of recruiting and establishing administrative arrangements, 13 high school social science teachers, 16 high school and junior college electronics teachers, and 28 high school and junior college auto mechanics teachers were chosen to participate in the research. Identical numbers of nonteachers were also located. For the social science performance test, state college students were selected who were social science majors or minors but who had never taught or completed any professional education course work. For the auto mechanics test, garage mechanics served as the nonteachers. The nonteachers for electronics were television repairmen and electronics industries workers.

All three performance tests were subjected to validation contrasts in school situations involving 2,326 public school students. Although there were slight differences in the three tests, the general procedure required that each participating teacher have at least two sections of an appropriate class. One of these classes was then randomly assigned to the nonteacher, while another was randomly assigned to the regular teacher. Approximately two weeks prior to instruction, both the teacher and the nonteacher received the objectives for the performance test and the resource materials. Each was directed to plan a short unit of instruction to accomplish the objectives. No restrictions regarding instructional tactics were imposed; participants were asked only to achieve as many of the objectives as they could in the time available. Nine instructional hours were

* *Construct validity is explained in the glossary.*

allowed for the electronics and auto mechanics test, four hours for the social science test.

On a prearranged date both the teacher and the nonteacher commenced instruction. At the close of the instructional period a member of the project research staff administered the posttest, previously unseen by teacher and nonteacher participants, to all pupils. In addition, a brief affective questionnaire was administered to students regarding their feelings about the subject matter of the unit.

RESULTS

Contrary to prediction, the experienced teachers did not markedly outperform their inexperienced counterparts on any of the three teaching performance tests. Although there were slight differences in favor of the teachers, none reached statistical significance. Posttest results are presented in Table 1 using average classroom means as the analysis unit.

TABLE 1
Posttest Results for Teacher and Nonteacher Classes.

Test	Subjects	No.	Mean [a]	Percentage correct
Social science	Experienced teachers	13	33.4	66.8
	College students	13	32.3	64.6
Auto mechanics	Experienced teachers	28	48.0	48.5
	Tradesmen	28	46.7	47.2
Electronics	Experienced teachers	16	23.9	51.9
	Tradesmen	16	23.1	50.2

[a] Means of auto mechanics and electronics were adjusted by analysis of covariance for pretest differences.

In addition, analyses of students' responses to the anonymous questionnaires revealed no significant differences between the teacher and nonteacher groups. In short, no reliable differences favoring the experienced teachers were found. Why?

AN INTERPRETATION

Although space limitations preclude an examination of possible methodological defects which might contribute to these results, there appear to be no readily available loopholes by which we can explain away the nonsignificant outcomes.* A more straightforward explanation is available.

* *Might not the careful statement of objectives and the special performance tests be the factors that made it possible for the nonteachers to perform so well?*

Experienced teachers are not particularly skilled at bringing about specified behavior changes in learners.

We should not be surprised that teachers are not skilled goal achievers. Certainly they have not been trained to be; teacher education institutions rarely foster this competence. Nor is any premium placed on such instructional skill after the teacher concludes pre-service training. The general public, most school systems, and professional teachers groups rarely attach special importance to the teacher's attainment of clearly stated instructional objectives.

For further corroboration of this interpretation, one needs only to speculate on the typical intentions of most public school teachers. They wish to cover the content of the course, to maintain classroom order, to expose the student to knowledge, and so on. Rarely does one find a teacher who, prior to teaching, establishes clearly stated instructional objectives in terms of learner behavior and then sets out to achieve those objectives. Only recently, in fact, do we find many teachers who are even familiar with the manner in which instructional objectives are stated in measurable form.

But while it may be true that experienced teachers in general — and there are obviously notable exceptions — are not particularly proficient in promoting learner attainment of specified instructional objectives, this is a *totally unacceptable* state of affairs. Every profession worthy of the name derives its professionalism precisely from the fact that its members possess a special expertise not present in nonmembers of the profession. Lawyers can prepare legal briefs. Surgeons can perform operations. Accountants can balance financial reports. People off the street can't do these things. But do teachers bring anything to bear on an instructional situation other than a general education, native intelligence, reasonable dedication, and borrowed teaching tricks? These attributes will permit a teacher to get through the school day, and a number of pupils will undoubtedly learn something. But contrast our current educational situation with the enormous dividends we might be getting if members of the teaching profession possessed really unique capabilities to promote desirable behavior changes in learners.

CORRECTIVE ACTION

What can be done to improve this situation? How can teachers become more skillful in accomplishing their major classroom mission? One general trend offers the promise of improvement along this line: specifically, the increasingly widespread support of objective-based instruction and, more broadly, the concept of educational accountability.[4] * Rather than attend-

---

* *The pros and cons of instructional objectives and educational accountability are presented in Part 4 of this book.*

ing almost exclusively to instructional *process*, where innovation is applauded for its own sake irrespective of what happens to learners, American educators are beginning to get concerned about *outputs* of the system. More and more we see educators trying to take responsibility for what happens to the learners under their tutelage. Frequently, such accountability strategies are organized around measurable instructional objectives. To illustrate, the Instructional Objectives Exchange,[5] a nonprofit educational corporation, currently receives over 5,000 orders per month for its collections of measurable instructional objectives. Even assuming that many of these objectives collections never leave the educator's bookshelf, their widespread circulation attests to the fact that many educators are becoming far more attentive to results than to process.

A more specific and direct approach can be taken to augment instructional skill. We can provide teachers with what any instructional psychologist would consider a critical ingredient for modifying one's behavior, that is, we can provide teachers with *practice* in doing what we want them to do. First, we must amass a sufficient number of short-term teaching performance tests, perhaps involving instructional periods of no more than 15–30 minutes. At least one commercial firm is now distributing such teaching performance tests[6] and, hopefully, more agencies will soon be developing them.

By employing commercially available performance tests or by constructing their own, both in-service and pre-service teacher educators can arrange for a series of teaching performance test clinics.* To illustrate how such clinics might work, we can consider an in-service example. A departmental faculty — English, for instance — might meet once per week after school for a one-hour session. At the beginning of the hour, as his colleagues observe, one teacher would carry out a previously planned 15-minute lesson with a half dozen randomly selected learners. After the learners had been posttested on their attainment of the objectives, and ideally also on their affective responses to the teaching, they would be dismissed and the staff would clinically analyze the teacher's instruction. The analysis should be *nonpunitive* in nature, for the focus must be on improving the instructional skills not only for the "teacher of the day" but for all those present. Furthermore, analysis of the teaching must be based on results displayed by the learners, not on the observers' personal preferences. If the learners achieved the objectives, what aspects of the instructional plan seemed to contribute? If the objectives were unachieved, what alternative tactics might have been used? The main thrust of the clinic strategy is to make public a teacher's instructional decision making and, obviously, to share demonstrably effective teaching tactics among colleagues. During subsequent weeks, other teachers can take their turns completing the same

* How might these performance tests help you become a skilled teacher?

or different teaching performance tests. As always, the post-lesson clinical analyses would stem from observed results with learners.

Comparable applications, of course, can be designed for pre-service teacher education programs. Indeed, as a vehicle for assessing the adequacy of a teacher education program, such performance tests have considerable utility. If, for example, a pre-service credential program cannot demonstrate that its candidates are far more skilled on such performance tests than they were when they commenced the program, then program modifications are clearly in order.

A CRUCIAL COMPONENT

The ability to bring about specified behavior changes in learners is by no means the only dimension to consider in evaluating a teacher.* One can readily imagine an instructor who was quite skilled in changing specified learner behavior yet grossly deficient in a number of personal and ethical categories. Even so, however, it may not be an overstatement to assert that the skill necessary to bring about intentional changes in learners should be considered a necessary but not sufficient attribute of the high-quality teacher. In view of research results such as those reported here, the teaching profession clearly must initiate schemes without delay whereby its members acquire this essential skill.

EXERCISE

1. What was the main finding of Popham's research project? (p. 219)
2. Popham criticizes ratings, systematic observation, and pupil performance on standardized tests as measures of teacher effectiveness. What is his criticism of each measure? (pp. 219–220)
3. What are the four steps in conducting a teaching performance test? (p. 221)
4. What two strategies does Popham suggest for improving teachers' ability to accomplish specific instructional objectives? (pp. 224–225)

* Should teachers be evaluated on other dimensions besides their ability to help students make gains in achievement test scores? What other dimensions?

Changes in Pupil Attitudes During the School Year

Ned Flanders, Betty M. Morrison, and E. Leland Brode

In two different studies, Ned Flanders and his colleagues found that student attitudes toward their teacher and schoolwork worsened during the school year. The purpose of this study was to examine possible reasons for this phenomenon. Specifically, Flanders, Morrison, and Brode sought to determine whether erosion of student attitudes was related to their IQ, socioeconomic status, and personality characteristics; or to the percentage of A and B grades assigned by the teacher, and his praise and encouragement. Does the study increase your understanding of how teachers influence learning? Does it help you identify any teaching skills you should use or student characteristics you should be aware of if you become a teacher?

Are pupils most optimistic about schoolwork as the school year begins? Does this optimism erode as the school year progresses? Are there particular patterns of teacher behavior which appear when there is less erosion of optimistic pupil attitudes? This article will attempt to answer these questions, not with complete, unequivocal answers, but with some suggestions based on two separate studies.

In a 1960–61 Minnesota study (Flanders, 1963), fairly conclusive evidence was collected indicating that over 3,000 students in two junior high schools scored highest on an attitude inventory assessing positive perceptions of their teachers and their schoolwork in October, only to have a statistically significant decrease in the scores of a January readministration of the same inventory.* A follow-up administration was about the same as January, significantly lower than the October scores.

The 1960 attitude inventory consisted of 59 items roughly divided into four subscales on the basis of content: (a) teacher attractiveness, which included such items as, "I would like to have this same teacher next year," and, "This is the best teacher I ever had," (b) fairness of rewards and

---

From *Journal of Educational Psychology*, 50, 1968, pp. 334–338. Copyright 1968 © by the American Psychological Association, and reproduced by permission of publisher and author.

* *Statistical significance is explained in the glossary.*

punishments, which included such items as, "This teacher punishes me for things I didn't do," and, "This teacher punishes the whole class when he (she) can't find out who did something," (c) teacher competence, which included such items as, "Our teacher is very good at explaining things clearly," and, "It is easy to fool this teacher," and (d) interest in schoolwork, including such items as, "This teacher makes everything seem interesting and important," and, "Most of us get pretty bored in this class." The response to each item was on a 5-point scale from strongly disagree to strongly agree. All items were keyed so that a higher score represented more positive attitudes and perceptions.

The mean score of the October administration of the attitude inventory was 217. The means of the January and May administrations were 204 and 205, respectively — both significantly lower ... than the October administration. These data were collected in so-called academic classes in Grades 7, 8, and 9, excluding such subjects as physical education, music, home economics, and shop.

The results seem quite clear. There is a significant reduction in the average scores of positive pupil perceptions between October and January of the school year.*

THE PRESENT STUDY

During the 1964–65 school year a Michigan Student Questionnaire (MSQ) was administered to 101 sixth-grade classes in 15 school districts near Ann Arbor. Thirty classes were selected for further study from the October distribution to include the top 10, the bottom 10, and 10 near the average of the 101 classes. The test was readministered in January and again in May in these 30 classes, each administration involving more than 800 pupils, and the sample can be considered representative of over 3,000 pupils who were in the larger population.

The MSQ was essentially the same inventory used in 1960–61 except that the items had been simplified in an effort to adjust the vocabulary to the reading skills of sixth-grade pupils. A factor analysis of the MSQ indicated that the most important factor was teacher attractiveness, with additional factors of teacher competence, teacher fairness, and lack of pupil anxiety forming a combination which was less important than the first factor.†

The means for each of the 30 classes are shown in Table 1, arranged in terms of the top, middle, and bottom 10 classes on the October administration.

The 1964–65 results were nearly identical to the 1960–61 results. There was a significant drop in average scores of positive pupil attitudes during

---

* *Why might students' perceptions change like this? What does this say about teacher effectiveness?*
† *Factor analysis is explained in the glossary.*

the first 4 months of the school year. The mean score for the October administration was 178.2 with a standard deviation of 26.52. The January administration had a mean of 172.2 and a standard deviation of 31.13; and the May administration had a mean of 170.6 and a standard deviation of 30.60.*

The rest of this article will discuss the various factors that might be related to the observed change in attitude, one administration compared to the next.

TABLE 1
Means of 30 Classes on the 1964–65 Michigan Student Questionnaire

Class	Administration			Class	Administration			Class	Administration		
	Oct.	Jan.	May		Oct.	Jan.	May		Oct.	Jan.	May
1	204.9	194.7	194.2	11	180.9	163.7	156.3	21	166.4	173.1	175.0
2	201.4	200.0	195.4	12	179.2	180.3	176.2	22	166.2	147.7	150.4
3	200.3	204.9	200.0	13	178.8	173.3	164.5	23	165.1	151.3	143.8
4	199.6	194.7	192.3	14	176.8	171.4	155.7	24	162.7	174.7	173.9
5	197.5	195.2	195.2	15	175.2	151.9	155.7	25	162.7	159.8	160.8
6	197.0	193.5	189.9	16	178.8	178.0	176.1	26	158.1	149.4	147.2
7	193.6	190.6	187.9	17	177.9	185.4	178.2	27	158.1	154.0	161.2
8	192.0	185.7	175.9	18	176.2	166.6	169.3	28	157.2	145.5	139.2
9	191.6	178.9	186.5	19	175.4	169.2	167.0	29	156.6	137.3	147.7
10	190.3	178.3	176.3	20	173.8	170.2	166.5	30	149.9	137.2	142.2

FACTORS NOT ASSOCIATED WITH CHANGE IN ATTITUDE. . . . There is the possibility that change in positive pupil attitudes might be associated with the average class IQ, socioeconomic status, or the percentage of A and B letter grades assigned to the pupils by the teacher. Table 2 shows such data for the nine classes which had high change losses and the seven classes with the least amount of change. The mean IQ for the high-change group was 113.5, while it was 112.3 for the low-change group. Here the IQ scores used were those based on school records and probably involved different published tests. The median socioeconomic rating for the high-change group was 71; a median rating of 70 was obtained for the low-change group. Here a rating on the National Opinion Research Center scale (Reiss, 1961) was made of the wage earner's occupation as reported by the teacher. The mean percentage of A and B letter grades for the high-change group was 56.5 and for the low-change group, 64.5. While this last difference is consistent with a theory that change involving loss of positive attitudes is associated with receiving lower grades, a z test between independent proportions yielded a value of 1.66 which was

* Why would the big change occur between October and January? See the glossary for explanation of standard deviation.

TABLE 2

Comparisons between High- and Low-Attitude Change Classes

High change				Low change			
Class no.	IQ	SES[a] rating	% of A & B grades	Class no.	IQ	SES rating	% of A & B grades
11	121.6	81	75	3	118.1	65	91
23	104.2	67	33	17	114.1	78	55
14	111.7	71	64	25	104.1	69	48
15	118.5	67	52	5	113.1	70	66
28	109.8	74	41	16	120.7	71	81
8	116.8	78	57	12	100.0	63	50
22	110.3	67	63	27	116.1	83	62
13	116.0	83	80				
10	112.7	70	42				

[a] SES = socioeconomic status.

not high enough to reject the null hypothesis at the .05 level of significance.* All of these data suggest that changes in class attitudes are not significantly associated with average IQ, socioeconomic status, or grades given by the teacher.

TWO FACTORS ASSOCIATED WITH CHANGE IN ATTITUDE. In another study, Morrison (1966) has shown that Rotter's notion of "externality" and "internality" (Rotter, Seeman, and Liversant, 1962) can be assessed among sixth-grade pupils. By externality is meant the tendency of a pupil to believe that his successes and failures are caused by forces beyond his control. By internality is meant the tendency to believe that successes and failures are self-determined and products of one's own behavior. External children, according to Morrison's conception, would be more likely to associate the good and bad outcomes of classroom learning activities with the teacher who is a powerful source of influence. Internal children, on the other hand, would see themselves as more closely associated with the good and bad characteristics of learning outcomes.

A test of internality-externality was administered to all the pupils in the 30 classes during the January administration of tests. The test consisted of 26 items, each containing two statements, and the pupils responded by marking the statement in each item which they believed was more often true. Typical items were: (a) "If you study you will do well on a test," or (b) "People who score the highest on a test are lucky." — (a) "Most of the time children get the respect they deserve from

* The z test is explained in the glossary.

others," or (b) "Many times a child can try hard and no one will pay attention to him." — (a) "Usually other people choose me for a friend," or (b) "Usually I choose my own friends." — (a) "Children get into trouble because their parents punish them too much," or (b) "The trouble with most children is that their parents are too easy with them."

Each item was scored 1 if the internal response was chosen and 2 if the external response was selected, giving a possible range from 26 to 52 for the total scores. The actual scores ranged from 26 to 49. Students in the lower third of the distribution (raw scores of 31 and below) were defined as internals and those in the upper third (raw scores of 36 and above) were defined as externals.

In addition to these tests each of the 30 classrooms was visited by an observer trained to code verbal communication into the 10 categories of interaction analysis developed by Flanders (1965).* More than six visits were made to each class and more than 7,000 tallies were recorded by observers. The main results of interaction analysis will be reported elsewhere; the interest for the moment is in the incidence of praise and encouragement expressed by the teachers during these visits. The occurrence of this type of teacher statement varied from a low of .2% to a high of 2.1% of all tallies recorded by the observer. The problems of reliability among observers and the representativeness of the interaction sampled are too complex to be discussed here. It can be said, however, that the relative objectivity of the observation data, or lack of it, would affect the data from all classes equally and cannot account for any of the differences about to be discussed.

It was hypothesized in this study that:

1. External children have a greater negative shift in attitude than do internal children.

2. The classes of low-praise teachers have a greater negative shift in attitude than do the classes of high-praise teachers.

3. The attitudes of external children are more affected by the praise and encouragement of the teacher than are the attitudes of internal children. . . .

Table 3 includes the October means, the May means, and May means adjusted for the initial attitudes, and the change means.† These are arranged in subgroups of internal and external pupils and pupils with high-praise and low-praise teachers. . . .

* Interaction analysis is a well-known method for classifying teacher statements into such categories as "accepting students' feelings," "lecturing," "criticizing," "praising," and "using students' ideas."
† Adjusted means are explained in the glossary.

TABLE 3
Initial, Final, and Adjusted Means
of Attitude Scores ... by Pupil Type and Teacher Style

Teacher style	Pupils		
	Internal	External	All
High-praise			
Initial M	190.6	171.0	183.9
Final M	187.3	159.2	177.7
Adjusted M	163.7	152.1	159.7
Change M	−3.3	−11.8	−6.2
Low-praise			
Initial M	178.7	121.5	143.9
Final M	173.1	111.3	135.5
Adjusted M	159.5	146.0	151.3
Change M	−5.6	−10.2	−8.4
All			
Initial M	185.8	137.8	162.6
Final M	181.6	127.1	155.2
Adjusted M	162.0	148.0	—
Change M	−4.2	−10.7	—

These results indicate that not only did external pupils have less positive attitudes than did internal pupils early in the school year, but when the May scores are adjusted by the October scores, it is apparent that external pupils experienced significantly greater declines in their attitudes than did internal pupils. Also, pupils with low-praise teachers showed greater losses in positive attitudes during the year than did pupils with high-praise teachers. However, there was no evidence that the attitudes of external children were more affected by praise or lack of praise on the part of the teacher than were the attitudes of the internal children.

DISCUSSION AND CONCLUSIONS

In two separate projects the attitude inventory scores indicate that positive perceptions of pupils toward their teacher and their class activities decrease sometime during the first 4 months of the school year. In the second project these changes were shown to be unrelated to IQ, performance grades assigned by the teacher, and the socioeconomic ratings of the father's occupation. Two hypotheses about changes in attitude were supported. First, external pupils experience a greater loss of positive attitudes toward school than do internal pupils. Second, in classrooms of teachers who provide less praise and encouragement there is greater loss of positive attitudes than in classrooms of teachers who provide more praise and encouragement.* The third hypothesis was not supported. . . .

One inference to be drawn is that the type of youngster who is more dependent on external influences seems to be more likely to suffer a loss of positive expectations than is the one who is more dependent on internal influences. In addition, pupil attitudes toward the teacher and the learning activities seem to be related to teacher behavior. Whether this difference in pupil attitudes is the result of the different teacher behaviors, or the different amounts of teacher praise and encouragement are the result of the pupils being more or less deserving of that praise, is not clear from the evidence of the present study. The absence of a significant difference between high-change and low-change classes with respect to the percentage of A and B grades given by the teacher (Table 2) would indicate that the pupils' performance was not the deciding factor. Also, previous studies (Flanders, 1963, 1965) have indicated that teacher behavior is the more dominant factor and that differences in such patterns of teacher influence tend to be greater between different teachers than between different situations for the same teacher.

In this sample, differences among the pupils had a greater effect than the presence or absence of a small amount of teacher praise and encouragement. Future studies of the erosion of positive pupil attitudes may wish to take into account other differences among pupils as well as differences in teacher behavior.

This study did not provide direct evidence concerning two opposite hypotheses about the erosion of positive pupil attitudes. One theory is that the pupils become disenchanted with the teacher during the first few months of the school year. A second theory, based on the assumption that the October scores are inflated or too high, is that as the pupils learn to trust their teacher they do not overestimate their ratings as they felt compelled to do with a strange teacher. Without going into detail, the authors tend toward the first of these two theories, primarily because the teacher's behavior is the predominant influence in the typical classroom; but much more evidence will be required before any conclusions can be reached.†

Meantime, lack of loss of positive attitudes may be the mark of a good match between teaching behavior and particular attributes among pupils. Apparently, in most classrooms such a match does not exist.

---

* Based on these findings, could praise and encouragement be added to Gage's list of effective teacher skills (this section)?
† Which of the two theories do you think is more reasonable?

EXERCISE

1. What changes in student attitudes were found in the 1960–61 Minnesota study and in the 1964–65 Michigan study? (pp. 228–229)

2. What did the investigators find concerning the relationship between change in student attitude and these three factors: student IQ, student socioeconomic status, and grades given by the teacher? (pp. 229–230)

3. What is meant by "internal" and "external" children and what method is used to classify children on these dimensions? (pp. 230–231)

4. What did the investigators find about shifts in attitude among internal and external children? Among high-praise and low-praise teachers? (pp. 231–232)

5. What two theories do the investigators advance to explain negative changes in student attitudes? (p. 233)

Teacher Expectations: Beyond the Pygmalion Controversy

Jere E. Brophy and Thomas L. Good

Pygmalion in the Classroom *created quite a controversy when it first appeared in 1968. Its authors, Robert Rosenthal and Lenore Jacobson, found that if teachers were given made-up information about children's IQ's, the expectations formed by this information affected the children's school achievement. For example, telling a teacher that a child was "slow" or "not intelligent" lowered his school achievement, even though the child's intelligence may have been normal. The results of this study created a great controversy among educators. For example, some argued that intelligence testing in the schools should be abandoned, because teachers would form preconceptions about their students on the basis of IQ scores; these preconceptions would lessen teachers' effectiveness because they*

From *Phi Delta Kappan*, 54, December 1972, pp. 276–278. Reproduced by permission of *Phi Delta Kappan*, and authors.

would "give up" on students with low scores. However, other educators felt that no conclusions could be drawn from the book because the research reported in it was poorly conducted. In the selection that follows, Jere Brophy and Thomas Good review the research that followed Pygmalion. *They conclude that sound evidence now supports the view that teachers' expectations of the students' abilities can affect students' school performance. Could the expectation effect be used to help teachers enhance the learning of all students?*

Rosenthal and Jacobson's 1968 book, *Pygmalion in the Classroom*, has been hotly debated since its publication. This paper attempts to place the debate in the larger context of research on teacher expectation effects. We believe that further debate on the original study is now academic, because much evidence has accumulated to document the reality of teacher expectation effects and identify some of the mechanisms which explain them.

When *Pygmalion* first appeared, it was uncritically accepted by many educators. However, following several critical reviews and replication failures, this initial overly positive reaction was soon replaced by what we consider to be an overly negative reaction. Subsequent research by many investigators using several different approaches has shown that teachers' expectations sometimes do function as self-fulfilling prophecies.

Studies of Induced Expectations

Several studies using the Rosenthal and Jacobson method of *inducing* expectations in teachers have shown mixed, mostly negative results as noted by Elashoff and Snow.[1] However, Meichenbaum, Bowers, and Ross found that teachers gave more positive and less negative attention to students identified as "late bloomers" than to matched controls, and that the "late bloomers" out-performed controls on later tests.[2] Beez found that tutors working with Head Start children they thought to be of high ability taught more than tutors working with children they thought to be of low ability, so that the "high ability" students learned more.[3]

Rothbart, Dalfen, and Barrett studied student teachers working with students described either as "lacking in intellectual potential" or as having "considerably greater academic ability." [4] Teachers were more attentive toward the "brighter" students and rated them as having higher intelligence and potential for future success and less need for approval. Rubovits and Maehr, studying undergraduate volunteer teachers working with students labeled as either gifted or nongifted, found that teachers requested more statements, initiated more interactions, and directed more praise toward the "gifted" students.[5] Medinnus and Unruh observed Head Start teachers working with two of their students, one labeled as "high ability" and one as "low ability." The teachers directed more praise and less criticism to the "high ability" students.[6] *

Why are expectancy effects obtained in some studies and not in others when certain expectations are induced in teachers? One possibility, of course, is controlled and unknown teacher differences. Another is the scope of the study. Replication failures have occurred mostly in studies which spanned the entire school year and used general achievement tests; the studies showing positive results usually involved only brief contacts between teachers and students and used specific, criterion-referenced tests.

An especially crucial factor is the success of the experimental manipulations. Follow-up interviews by Rosenthal and Jacobson showed that some of the teachers in their study did not remember which students had been designated as "bloomers." [7] Fleming and Anttonen tried to raise teacher expectations by inflating certain students' IQs by 16 points. However, students with inflated IQs did not outgain their classmates. Follow-up interviews showed that most teachers rejected the inflated IQs as erroneous and thus did not raise their expectations for these students.[8]

The importance of teachers' acceptance of individual expectations was shown even more clearly in two studies by Schrank.[9] He assigned students to five ability groups randomly instead of by measured ability. The "high" group achieved significantly more than the "low" group, and group achievement means fell into position in the same order as the five "ability" labels. The labels had clearly affected the amount that each group learned. Schrank repeated his study two years later (in 1970), but this time teachers were *told* that students were being assigned randomly rather than by ability. However, they were asked to teach the classes as if they had been ability grouped. Despite this attempt to get teachers to simulate ability group teaching, no expectation effects appeared. The implications here seem clear: Information presented to teachers will not affect their expectations unless it is believed to be accurate. If information given by an experimenter is too discrepant from what teachers see in their everyday interactions with students, it will be rejected.†

This was one reason for the negative results in the Fleming and Anttonen study, and it may also have been a factor in the many failures to replicate Rosenthal and Jacobson's findings. This points up a serious disadvantage in studies using inducement of teacher expectations: When negative results are obtained, we don't know whether the teachers' expectations did not influence their teaching, or, instead, the treatment failed to induce the desired teacher expectations. The success of experiments involving manipulation of teachers' expectations will vary with

---

* *Given the research reported by Gage and Flanders, Morrison, and Brode (this section), would you expect these teacher behaviors to influence learning?*
† *What does this finding suggest concerning teachers' diagnostic skills?*

the type of information presented to teachers, the way it is presented, the status and credibility of the presenter, and the personality and ability of the teacher, among other factors. Studies of this type should routinely include follow-ups to assess whether the desired teacher expectations were actually induced by the treatment.

NATURALISTICALLY FORMED EXPECTATIONS

Rather than attempt to induce expectations, several investigators have questioned teachers to discover their naturalistically formed expectations, then related these to teacher-student interaction or to student achievement.

Brophy and Good [10] had first-grade teachers rank their students according to expected achievement. Three high and three low boys, and three high and three low girls were then observed in each class. Clear teacher expectation effects were found. The teachers were more likely to stay with highs after they failed to answer an initial question (by repeating the question, giving a clue, or asking another question).* In contrast, they tended to end the interaction by giving the answer or calling on someone else in parallel situations with lows. Differences in teacher feedback reactions were also noted. Teachers failed to give feedback to highs in only 3% of their response opportunities, while the figure for lows was 15%. In addition, highs were more likely to be praised when they answered correctly and less likely to be criticized when they answered incorrectly or failed to respond. These differences were observed even though highs made more correct responses and had fewer failures than lows.

A related set of findings was obtained by Rowe.[11] She asked teachers to name the top five and the bottom five students in their classes, then timed the teachers to see how long they waited for a response after questioning a student. Teachers waited significantly longer for a response from the top group. Thus the students least able to respond had to answer more quickly or lose their chance. When Rowe trained teachers to increase their time-wait, students in the bottom groups began to speak up more often, sometimes enough to change the teachers' expectations.

These studies illustrate how differential expectations are communicated through differential treatment of students. Along with some of the results reviewed earlier, they show a tendency for teachers to be rewarding and encouraging toward high-expectation students and to work for good responses from them. In contrast, they tend to be critical toward low-expectation students and to give up on them too easily when they don't respond quickly.

* How would you expect these differences in teaching to influence student learning?

There are also two studies showing how teachers' naturalistically formed expectations influence student achievement. Palardy asked teachers to indicate whether or not they thought boys could learn to read as well as girls in the first grade. From their responses he identified five teachers who did not believe that boys could do as well as girls and paired these teachers with five others who expected no sex difference. Teachers were paired according to sex, race, experience, type of school, and textbook used for teaching reading. The boys and girls in classrooms of teachers who expected no sex difference achieved equally, but in classrooms of teachers who did not expect boys to do as well as girls, the girls outperformed the boys.[12]

Doyle, Hancock, and Kifer asked first-grade teachers to estimate student IQs shortly before an IQ test was administered. The teachers systematically overestimated girls' IQs and underestimated boys'.* Also, reading achievement scores taken at the end of the year showed that students who had been overestimated achieved more than their IQs would predict, while students who had been underestimated achieved less. Thus the teachers produced higher achievement in students for whom they had higher expectations. Furthermore, teachers who generally overestimated their students' IQs produced higher achievement than teachers who generally underestimated them. Thus this study showed both a selective expectation effect operating within each classroom and a more general effect separating high expectation teachers from low expectation teachers.[13]

CONCLUSIONS

In our view the research reviewed leaves little doubt as to the reality of teacher expectation effects. Since *Pygmalion,* much evidence has accumulated to show that teachers' expectations can become self-fulfilling by causing teachers to treat highs appropriately while treating lows in ways that will minimize their learning interests and opportunities. Further proof of the *existence* of teacher expectation effects is not needed; instead, attention should now turn to discovering the causal mechanisms involved and to developing teacher training and intervention strategies that will minimize undesirable expectation effects.[14] †

The available data suggest that although expectation effects are quite real, they are neither ubiquitous nor particularly strong in the usual situation. They are not always found, even when the teacher's naturalistically formed expectations are used.[15] Factors causing a teacher to be influenced either more or less by his expectations have not yet been identified,

---

* See Sadker's article (Section 8) for additional research about sex differences.
† What type of training would help you overcome negative expectations you might have concerning some students?

although we suspect that both cognitive and personality factors are involved. Both teacher training and teacher ability seem important. A master teacher with a rich repertoire of skills for diagnosing and remediating learning problems should achieve greater success and be less prone to rationalizing failures than a teacher who is confused and frustrated in the face of difficulty.

Student differences are also involved. Relaxed and active students who frequently initiate contact with teachers will get more attention and are more likely to correct any misconceptions that teachers may have about them. In contrast, quiet, withdrawn students who avoid teachers and do not say much when questioned leave the teachers much more room for error in judging them. . . .

[Expectation effects] are probably strongest early in the year, before teachers have had much time to observe students. Even across the whole school year, however, teachers' expectations and students' reactions to them are likely to be quite crucial in individual cases, affecting the students' attitudes, self-concepts, and achievement. Thus, we believe this area is well worth further study. In particular, we need data to show *when* and *how* teacher expectations become self-fulfilling. Studies involving naturalistic observation followed by intervention, in which the investigator *helps* rather than simply *manipulates* the teacher, are especially needed.

EXERCISE

1. Why do Brophy and Good feel that further debate about *Pygmalion* is now academic? (p. 235)

2. Considering all the research findings on induced expectations, what were the various ways in which teachers behaved differentially to presumably "high-ability" students compared to "low-ability" students? (pp. 235–236)

3. How do Brophy and Good explain the many failures to replicate the research findings of Rosenthal and Jacobson? (p. 236)

4. Considering all the research findings on naturalistically formed expectations, what were the various ways in which teachers behaved differentially to presumably "high-ability" students compared to "low-ability" students? (pp. 237–238)

5. In the opinion of Brophy and Good, how strong and pervasive are teacher expectation effects? (pp. 238–239)

SCHOOL RESOURCES

Introduction

Many educators feel the surest way to improve student learning is to increase financial expenditures on a per-student basis. More money spent for each student will buy a better physical plant, more multimedia learning materials, more teachers, and smaller classes. Does this increased input (money) lead to increased output (student scholastic achievement)? Two input factors — class size and amount of instruction — will be considered in this section. Does making classes smaller improve student achievement or is there a point beyond which more dollars spent for this purpose have little, if any, payoff in improved learning? Also, does more time in school increase learning enough to justify the increased expenditures involved?

To some extent the arguments for and against the influence of class size and amount of instruction on learning are relative. If class size is already 25 students to 1 teacher, reducing this ratio to 20:1 may not have the same effect as reducing a 50:1 student-teacher ratio to 35:1. Or, if a student spends six hours in school, increasing this to seven or eight hours may not have the same effect as increasing two hours of instruction to four hours. Probably the main argument in favor of small class size is that it increases the teacher's effectiveness. In a smaller class, the teacher has more time to spend with each student, can individualize instruction, and can make greater use of small-group techniques. This reasoning has important implications for the current teacher surplus. If class size were to be reduced appreciably, enough teachers would be required to eliminate this surplus and even create another shortage.

The arguments favoring increased schooling are obvious. With each additional hour of instruction, the student can acquire increased knowledge and skills; or he can practice what he has already learned to improve retention and transfer.

Some critics, though, question whether increased financial expenditures (used to form smaller classes or to offer more instruction) have any effect on student learning. They argue that most learning occurs outside the school and is conditioned primarily by social and familial factors. Therefore, it doesn't much matter what the schools do. (This was the conclusion reached by Bane and Jencks in Section 3.) Another criticism is that class size has no effect on learning because teachers do essentially the same thing in small classes as they do in large classes. In other words, teachers do not know how to take advantage of the opportunity to improve learning provided by a small class.

Three reports in this section contain research data about these issues. Ian Templeton summarizes recent research on the effects of class size on learning. Irving Flinker, a school principal, reports on an experiment he conducted to determine whether reduced class size leads to greater student achievement. Finally, Torsten Husén discusses international studies that investigated whether putting school resources into increased hours of instruction has a significant payoff in student achievement.

After reading these reports, consider whether you agree or disagree with the following views:

Class Size

Pro Teachers with appreciably smaller classes can offer better instruction than teachers with large classes; therefore, their students will learn more.

Con Generally, when class size is reduced, no change occurs in the way the teacher works with students. This may be caused by teachers not knowing how to take advantage of the smaller teacher-student ratio. Or, the teacher may have to continue the same form of instruction because the change in the teacher-student ratio is too small to facilitate new forms of teacher-student interaction. In either case, smaller class size does not lead to improved student learning.

Time in School

Pro Increased time in school, whether measured by hours per day or total years of attendance, will help students acquire more knowledge and skills. This, in turn, will help them be more productive adults.

Con Because schools have little effect on students, students would learn the knowledge and skills required to perform successfully as adults even if educators significantly reduced the amount of required schooling. Students could start school at a later age, graduate earlier, and attend school for fewer hours a day and still achieve the performance level required by society today.

Class Size

Ian Templeton

> *In this selection Ian Templeton reviews ten research studies on the effects of different class sizes on student performance. No one disagrees that decreasing class size adds significantly to the cost of education. But is the additional cost justified by improved student learning? The studies reviewed by Templeton indicate that in some instances students in smaller classes make greater gains than those in larger classes. In others, this does not occur. This disparity in results may be due to several factors. As you read the reports, consider whether the actual reduction in class size was large enough to expect learning to change. Also examine the type of learning outcomes that were measured. Based upon the various learning goals described in Section 2 — "What Should Students Learn in School?", determine whether the outcomes that were measured represent important areas of achievement. Compare the studies to decide whether the type of learning that is measured might have a relationship with improved learning, or a lack of it, in smaller classes. After considering these factors as well as other influences on learning, think about how you would use increased dollars to improve the educational quality of a school or school district. Would you reduce class size?*

It would be wrong to conclude, based solely on the lack of evidence to the contrary, that class size has no effect whatever on student performance. But on the basis of what has been presented to us, we must caution against the use of pupil-teacher ratios as instant measures of anything remotely approaching the quality of education. Additional studies certainly are warranted, particularly those that deal with the attitudes of teachers on class size and the effect of those attitudes, rather than size itself, on the development of children.

Despite diligent searches and widespread opinion to the contrary, the Commission finds no research evidence that demonstrates improved student achievement resulting from decreasing pupil-teacher ratios. — *The President's Commission on School Finance (1972)*

The debate over class size (student-teacher ratio) centers on two important factors — finance and educational quality. The impact of class size

From the *Educational Management Review Series*, August 1972 (No. 8). Eugene, Oregon: ERIC Clearinghouse on Educational Management. Reprinted by permission of the author.

on school finance is obvious: as class size decreases, more teachers must be hired and more classrooms built. Because instructional costs usually constitute about 80 percent of a school district's expenditures, the added costs can be enormous.

Educators concerned primarily with educational quality argue that it increases as class size decreases. According to this viewpoint, class size should be reduced until an optimum learning size is reached.

The pressure for smaller classes comes largely from teachers and concerned parents. Teachers feel that reduced class size provides a more desirable learning environment for students and increases a teacher's effectiveness. On the other hand, many administrators, school board members, and voters deny that class size is as important as teachers maintain and assert that any reduction in class size must be judged against the concomitant cost increases.

This paper reviews current literature on the effect class size has on school finance and educational quality. As will be seen, the literature uniformly emphasizes the tremendous impact of class size on school budgets. It does not, however, uniformly agree on the effect of class size on educational quality, whether quality is measured by student achievement or by other methods. . . .

EFFECT ON FINANCES

Nearly every document on class size mentions the financial impact a reduction in student-teacher ratios would have on a school district's budget. The two examples below indicate the dimensions of this impact as it is described in the literature.

Varner (1968) acknowledges the argument that reducing class size can help optimize learning conditions; he notes, however, that this argument is not as well-defined as that concerning finances. As an example of the potential effect a reduction in class size can have on a school district budget, he offers a hypothetical case:

> The financial consequences of class size can be strikingly illustrated. Let us assume that in a medium-sized school system enrolling 15,000 pupils, the average class size is 30 pupils and the average teacher's salary is $7,000. A reduction in average class size from 30 to 29 pupils would require 17 additional teachers and a budget increase of $119,000 per year. If classes were reduced from 30 to 25 pupils per class, 100 additional teachers would be required. Teachers' salaries alone would add $700,000 to the annual budget requirements of this system.*

* As a teacher, could you function differently if your class was reduced by this number of students?

Earthman (1969) examines the relationship of class size to the use of middle and high school facilities in the planning stage in the Philadelphia school district. Among the factors he considers is the effect of varying student-teacher ratios. For example, one hundred classrooms can serve either 2,500 or 3,500 students, depending on whether the student-teacher ratio is 25 to 1 or 35 to 1.

CLASS SIZE IS NOT IMPORTANT

Drawing from social science research findings on student-teacher ratios, Coleman (1971) reports that minor changes in the ratio are insignificant. Educational policymakers, however, seldom acknowledge these findings, and teachers' spokesmen continue to press for reduction in class size. He concludes his report with a review of recent research findings on student-teacher ratios and suggests some conclusions and implications for policymakers.

The influence of class size on academic attainment and student attitudes toward school was investigated at the Edward W. Clark High School (n.d.). Subjects included 224 male and female students randomly scheduled into average (24–27) and above average (45–52) size classes in business law, introduction to business, and government. Analysis of pretest and posttest scores on teacher-made tests showed no significant difference in achievement for either business law or introduction to business classes, but did indicate a significant difference for the course on government. The document notes that this difference may be attributed to the fact that the students enrolled in the government class were older than the students in the other two classes. Other conditioning factors may have been the subject matter or the instructor's teaching methods. No significant differences in attitudes (satisfaction with the learning environment) were found for any of the three classes, regardless of size.

To produce evidence regarding the influence of class size and class homogeneity on achievement gains in grades 7 and 8, Johnson and Scriven (1967) examined data from 7,500 students in 265 English and mathematics classes. The study measured achievement gains on the reading comprehension and arithmetic test scores from the Iowa Test of Basic Skills.* Results indicated that gain differences attributable to class size and variability were generally very small and inconsistent. Because two-thirds of the classes studied consisted of from 23 to 32 pupils, the largest and smallest classes (larger than 34 and smaller than 24 students) were isolated for separate comparison. Even between these extreme groups, no significant difference in achievement gain was found. Although these tests

---

* With the wide range of learning goals discussed in Section 2, are these the learning outcomes one would expect to be most affected by smaller class size?

do not measure all types of achievement, they do suggest that attention might better be directed toward reducing the number of classes assigned to one teacher than toward reducing the size of the classes.

Class size was among the variables studied by Corey (1967) in his investigation of the outcomes of introductory psychology classes. Pretest and posttest scores for 180 students in four classes and a control group of 50 students measure changes in student self-concept, self-acceptance, concept of ideal self, degree of personal adjustment, and knowledge of psychology.* In general, class size, method of instruction, and difference among instructors did not appear to be important variables in producing affective changes. Neither did academic mastery of psychology appear related to these variables.

Hopper and Keller (1966) report on the relationship between class size and student achievement in junior college writing skills courses. A stratified random sample of 274 students was assigned to three sections of 56 students and four sections of 28 students. Although student preferences varied, pretest and posttest results show that, given the same quality of instructors, program, and students, class size up to 56 does not seem to be a significant variable in the learning of writing skills.

Class Size Is Important

Using statistical comparisons of student achievement tests, Woodson (1968) examines the effects class size has on pupil achievement in 95 school systems. His areas of investigation include whether:

— a measurable relationship can be found between class size and academic achievement of pupils in a given district

— such relationships are the same for pupils of different academic potential

— the size-achievement relationships are the same in various subject areas

— the magnitudes of size-achievement relationships vary when different kinds of class size measures are used

— the size-achievement relationships are the same for districts of different sizes

— the size-achievement relationships are the same from grade to grade

He concludes that there is a small inverse relationship† between academic achievement and class size qualified by the following factors:

— This relationship tends to be smaller for pupils of higher scholastic potential than for pupils of lower scholastic potential.

* Are these better learning outcomes to study in research on class size?
† Inverse relationship is explained in the glossary.

— This relationship tends to be smaller for criteria based upon total achievement test batteries or arithmetic sub-tests than criteria based upon reading sub-tests.

— This relationship tends to be more uncertain of measurement at the sixth grade level than at the fourth grade level.

— This relationship reflects an interplay with school district size. The relationship was essentially obliterated with a group of small, relatively sparsely populated, school districts. However, there was little evidence that district size *per se* reflected itself in the magnitudes of the achievement criteria.

— All of these conclusions are subject to the kinds of class size measures used. The findings from this study raise the possibility that the practice of using "average class size" as the lone measure of class size tends to oversimplify the study of the relationship with pupil achievement.

Vincent (1968b) describes a method for categorizing research on optimum class size in elementary and secondary grades. The Indicators of Quality program observes selected classroom characteristics (individualization of instruction, interpersonal regard, creativity, and group activity) and scores each characteristic positive, zero, or negative. Data from 47 school districts (2,106 elementary and 2,181 secondary classrooms) show a progressively larger difference between positive and negative ratings as class size increases. In the elementary grades a significant break occurs between the 11–15 and 16–20 and the 21–25 and 26–30 class-size intervals. In the secondary grades the only significant break occurs between the 11–15 and 16–20 class-size intervals. Vincent suggests that combining the results of this study with the achievement test criterion will further resolve the class size question.

Olson (1971) reports on a study also using the Indicators of Quality as the criterion of classroom quality.... He found that smaller classes produce significantly higher scores than larger ones and that there are certain breaking points in the student-teacher ratio at which sharp drops in performance scores occur. These breaking points correspond to those Vincent found, except for an additional breakpoint between the 0–5 and 5–10 class size in the elementary classes.

A five-year study (1959–1964) that examined the relationship between class size and pupil achievement in reading and arithmetic is reported by Furno and Collins (1967). Data were taken from the Baltimore public school system records of all 16,449 pupils who were in the third grade in 1959.... The most important finding of the study was that in 61 percent of the class comparisons the smallest class size grouping (1–25) made significantly greater achievement gains, as measured on standardized tests, than the larger classes. The authors include a review of related research and a description of their research design together with extensive comparative tabulations from the study's findings.

Among the basic questions concerning college teaching that McKeachie (1971) attempts to answer is one on class size. His conclusions indicate that small classes are probably more effective than large for attaining the goals of retention, application, problem-solving, attitude change, and motivation for further learning.*

SUMMARY OF THE LITERATURE

After reviewing recent writings on class size, Sitkei (1968) summarized his findings, some of which are as follows:

— Although the research studies of class size are not conclusive, there are twice as many studies in favor of smaller classes over larger classes.

— There is a great deal of variation among school systems and researchers as to what they mean when they speak of a "small" class or a "large" class. . . .

— Small classes tend to have more variety in instructional methods used than do large classes.

— Desirable practices tend to be dropped when class size is increased; desirable practices are added when class size is reduced. . . .

— If the teacher is not informed of changes in class-size policy, the results are poorer than if he is aware of the situation.

CONCLUSION

A review of the literature reveals uniformity of opinion on the cost of reducing class size: it is expensive. Opinion is quite diverse, however, on the educational value of a reduction. A close look at the criteria used to evaluate the effect of class size on educational quality may indicate the reasons for the diversity in judgment.

The literature that assigns little importance to class size tends to be concerned with student achievement on standardized or teacher-made tests. Of the five documents denying importance to class size, four were concerned primarily with student achievement or performance, and the fifth (Corey) included achievement as one criterion.

Of the five documents that consider class size important, only two (Woodson, and Furno and Collins) were primarily concerned with student achievement. Vincent and Olson both used as criteria the Indicators of Quality, which measure processes occurring in the classroom: individu-

* Do these learning outcomes have any relationship to the type of teacher-student interaction that is possible in smaller classes?

alization of instruction, interpersonal regard, creativity, and group activity.* McKeachie's criteria — retention, application, problem-solving, attitude change, and motivation for further learning — are more concerned with the product of education than are the Indicators of Quality, but they measure aspects other than simple achievement.

The studies based on the three largest samples are in agreement that class size is important to educational quality. It is not surprising that Vincent and Olson agree on an optimum class size since they used the same evaluative criteria. Furno and Collins used achievement on standardized tests as their criteria, however, in arriving at the conclusion that the 1–25 pupil group showed the most improvement in their study of elementary students. This is consistent with Vincent's and Olson's findings that in the elementary grades a decline in quality occurs between the 21–25 and the 26–30 class size.

The variations in criteria employed, grade levels studied, and sizes of samples used in the various studies make it nearly impossible to reach any firm conclusions about the relationship between class size and educational quality. It does seem possible, however, to draw several generalizations from the literature:

> — Slight reductions in class size (for instance, from 32 to 30 students) will probably produce little difference in student achievement, but will likely produce an improvement in teacher attitudes and performance.
> — Reductions in class size cannot be considered apart from the accompanying economic implications.
> — The nature of the evaluative criteria may influence conclusions on the effect of reducing class size.†

Teaching methods and scheduling practices are two considerations that complicate a discussion of class size. Olson, for instance, found that teaching style is more important than class size in indicating quality. McKeachie also stresses the importance of the teaching methods used. Varner suggests that new methods of classroom organization and staff utilization, which include team teaching, nongrading, flexible scheduling, and independent study, must be considered in determining optimum class size. He summarizes his study of class size as follows:

> In general, both opinion and research tend to agree that in order to produce optimal results — for both pupils and teachers — the size of class must be appropriate to the intellectual-emotional needs of the pupils, the skills of the teacher, the type of learning desired, and the nature of the subject matter.

How do these criteria relate to Bane and Jencks's conclusion that schools should be made enjoyable places to learn (Section 3)?
†*After reading these generalizations, would you support smaller classes?*

EXERCISE

1. What is the effect of variations in class size on school budgets? (pp. 243–244)

2. What did Vincent and Olson find when they used the Indicators of Quality scale to observe classes which varied in student-teacher ratio? (p. 246)

3. How does Templeton explain the conflicting results obtained in the various studies which investigated the effect of class size on educational quality? (pp. 247–248)

Optimum Class Size: What Is the Magic Number?

Irving Flinker

Irving Flinker, a school principal in Brooklyn, New York, conducted a simple experiment to determine whether reducing class size has an effect on learning. Although the experiment is not rigorous, it will give you an idea of how research can be used to help resolve issues in educational psychology. Flinker's experiment is not rigorous (as he recognizes) for several reasons. First, it is based upon a sample of only three classes. Second, the teacher of the large class had the services of a teaching assistant, but the teachers of the smaller classes did not have this advantage. It is possible that the difference in student achievement between the two groups was caused by the presence of the teaching assistant, not by the factor of class size. Third, because the department chairman took the larger class, the similarity of skill of the three teachers must be considered. As you read the report, think about the teaching situations in the class with 50 students and the classes with 30 students. In which class would you be able to give each student the most help? Which arrangement would you prefer?

NATURE OF THE PROBLEM

Class size has become a key issue in recent collective bargaining negotiations. Teacher unions seek to lower the size to reduce the teaching burden

Reprinted by permission from the April, 1972 issue of *The Clearing House*.

for their members. They claim that children in smaller classes learn more than those in larger classes.

There is no question that there is reduced stress and tension for the teacher of smaller classes because of fewer learning problems, less paper work, fewer behavior problems, easier class control, and less diversion.* The smaller class enables the teacher to become familiar with the individual children. Each child has a better opportunity to participate and express himself orally. . . .

However, there is no conclusive evidence that a class of 30 children obtains better instruction and makes more progress than a class of 40. The money saved in a large school district by increasing class size by a few children may be put to better use by employing more guidance counselors, establishing special classes, and providing after-school enrichment activities. The saving of money results not merely from the reduction of teaching staff but also from the saving of costly space. For example, a school having 1,000 children would need five fewer rooms by changing class size from 30 to 35. Some schools on short double sessions could revert to single regular sessions by increasing class size.

PLAN OF INQUIRY

To obtain more information about the teaching of large classes, we established a large class in the seventh grade numbering 55 children. No attempt was made to measure growth in attitudes, appreciations, habits, and social relationships. The focus of this inquiry was limited to measurable growth in mathematical and language arts skills.†

This larger class was matched with two smaller classes each numbering 34. Care was taken to equate these classes by arranging the 123 children in order of ability as measured by the scores on the Metropolitan Achievement Test in Reading, Form BM. These children were all above average in reading ability. The first, fourth, seventh, tenth, etc. child on the ranked list was placed in the large class of 55. The second, fifth, eighth, etc. child was placed in one smaller class of 34; the remaining children were placed in the other smaller class of 34.

In each of the subject areas the course of study and the quality of instruction were kept as equal as possible. In each area the department chairman took the large class and other teachers were assigned to each of the smaller groups. The three teachers in each area met periodically to assure similarity of content and instructional materials. The calendar

---

Can these results be guaranteed without knowing the students who are to be taught and the approach to learning to be used?

†*How might Banks, Bessell, and Rogers (all in Section 2) respond to this selection of student outcomes?*

of lessons and time of instruction were the same in the three English classes. These factors were also kept constant in the three mathematics classes. The purpose of these meetings was to assure all of the children the same instructional program as far as possible. Naturally, because of the number of teachers involved the element of teaching skill could not be equalized in each area. Another experiment using one teacher for each curricular area would rule out differences in instructional skill. The use of two control groups as a basis of comparison in this study tends to negate marked differences in teaching ability.

In each subject area the teacher of the large group was assisted by an educational assistant. Her duties were mechanical, clerical, and monitorial rather than tutorial. She checked attendance, reported late-comers, corresponded with parents, xerographed, distributed and collected exercises, tests, and assignments. Whenever possible she marked the tests and recorded the scores.

FINDINGS

The study of the effect of large group instruction as compared with average class teaching was accomplished with a minimum of class disruption and special testing. The same class organizations were used for observing the effects of class size in the English and mathematics instruction. The mean reading achievement level of each of the three classes was 8.02, 7.87, and 8.11 respectively in March 1970. There was no significant difference between the reading ability of the large group and that of the two average groups.

In our junior high school we generally use the Metropolitan Achievement Tests in reading and mathematics, and the New York State Junior High School Survey Tests in English. We used the results of these tests to save time, money, and additional testing. The scores resulting from the New York State Survey Tests are expressed in percentiles.... The same forms of the mathematics tests were given in January and June of 1971 to insure maximum reliability and validity of differences in growth. Because of mobility of families in our district, common in urban areas, the register of the large class dropped to 50 and those of the average classes from 34 to 31 and 30 respectively.

In Tables 1 and 2 are recorded the mean scores of the large group and of the two average-size groups combined in each subject area.

Since the classes were not reorganized for mathematics instruction, it was expected that the mean arithmetic ability of the three groups would be disparate. The mean grade level of the large class in mathematics on the November 1970 test was 6.66; the mean grade of group II was 6.21; and the mean grade level of group III was 5.26. The composite mean grade level of groups II and III according to the scores of the November 1970

TABLE 1
English

Group	Mean grade reading level 3/70	Mean grade reading level 6/71	Difference of means	Mean %ile initial achievement test form A, 10/70	Mean %ile initial achievement test form B, 6/71	Difference of means
I	8.02	8.88	+.86	53.4	53.4	−0
II & III	7.99	8.01	+.02	51.8	50.4	−1.4

test was 5.74. It is apparent, therefore, that there was a grade difference of .92 in mathematical ability between the large and small groups, and a significant difference of .75. We should expect that the rate of growth in mathematics would be somewhat better for the larger group.

Inasmuch as the two smaller classes (taken together) were almost a year behind the large group in mathematics at the outset, the measure of comparison could not be the final scores but the difference in improvement between January and June 1971. The mean improvement in this six-month period for the large group was .53, a significant improvement. For the combined small groups the mean improvement was .15, a change which was not statistically significant.*

TABLE 2
Mathematics

Group	Mean grade Jan. 1971	Mean grade June 1971	Difference of means
I	8.45	8.98	+.53
II & III	7.77	7.92	+.15

CONCLUSIONS

The testing results indicate that the large class organization in the seventh grade favors the development of skills and concepts in language arts and mathematics. Such a conclusion runs counter to prevalent opinion regarding the relationship of class size to learning, and calls for possible explanations.†

* With the differences in achievement at the outset, do the gain scores represent the same amount of learning effort for both groups?
† Compare these findings with those reported by Templeton in the preceding selection.

It is noteworthy that the large group had the department chairman in each area. The quality of instruction seems to have helped the large group show slightly superior achievement. Apparently a large seventh grade class having an excellent teacher tends to show better results than an average-size class with an average teacher in English and mathematics.

Although the period of instruction was the same for all classes, the teacher of the large class had more time for actual teaching because of the help of the educational assistant.* It is likely, also, that because of the availability of the paraprofessional worker the large class had better decorum, more quizzes, tests, and written exercises than the regular classes.

Obiter Dictum

Teachers tend to believe that the smaller the class the greater is the probability of individualization of instruction. Unfortunately, the theory does not even approximate the practice. In the departmental program of a junior high school teachers generally do not group children for differentiated instruction. A class of 25 children is treated the same way as a class of 35. It is the rare teacher who plans specifically for grouping, independent study, or individualized instruction.

Teachers tell me that the optimum class size for average children runs between 15 and 20, and for slow children between 10 and 15. School board members, however, who are concerned with budgets, want to see the greatest productivity per dollar of input. More studies such as this one are needed to establish relationships of class size to achieving growth in skills and content of all subjects and in social and personal development. If other research yields findings similar to those obtained in this study, school boards would be well advised to pay higher salaries to master teachers of large classes.

In the meantime we may waggishly answer the question of optimum class size by saying that it is five fewer than the class you now have.

EXERCISE

1. What was the main purpose of Flinker's study? (p. 250)
2. What were the main findings of Flinker's study? (p. 252)
3. According to Flinker, what effect did the paraprofessional worker have in the large class setting? (p. 253)

* Would Torsten Husén's research findings (this section) suggest that increased time for teaching is likely to make a difference?

Does More Time in School Make a Difference?

Torsten Husén

This provocative selection was written by Torsten Husén, a professor at the University of Stockholm. Using available research, he concludes that number of instruction hours does not have much effect on learning. Husén suggests instead that social and familial factors are the main causes of individual differences in student achievement. (Mary Jo Bane and Christopher Jencks reached essentially the same conclusion; see Section 3). Husén emphasizes that resolving this issue (whether more time in school makes a difference) has important policy implications, particularly for developing nations. As you read the selection, consider this question: do you think that important policy decisions about the amount of schooling to provide children, either in developed or in developing nations, should be made using the type of evidence presented by Husén? The research studies reviewed by Husén included measures of learning of knowledge and cognitive skills, but not growth in attitudes, appreciations, interpersonal skills, and other types of learning. Using the views expressed in Section 2, do you think these measures cover an adequate range of desired learning outcomes?

One of the most widely accepted assumptions in education has been that exposure to teaching is highly related to student learning — and in a linear fashion. That is, we have assumed that a 50 per cent increase in full-time schooling would result in a 50 per cent increase in the knowledge retained by students. We have also taken for granted that formal schooling accounts for the major share, if not all, of the knowledge and skills that young people acquire.* Therefore, in order to improve standards, it is necessary to increase the number of years of schooling, or the number of hours a subject is taught per week, or both.

Although the findings of various research studies are still suggestive rather than conclusive, there is enough evidence to call into question this kind of pedagogical folklore. And since staff salaries account for two-thirds

---

* Researchers such as Bane and Jencks (Section 3) and Cohen (Section 5) would strongly question this assumption.

or more of the operating costs of schools, these findings have important policy implications for developed countries and, even more particularly, for developing nations. . . .

In countries with a national curriculum, where the legislature determines the number of hours per week that will be devoted to each subject area, the competition for more time can be fierce. When the upper secondary school curriculum was revised in Sweden, it was contended that a reduction by only one period allotted to mathematics would impair the competitive strength of the nation in the world market and that a similar reduction of teaching time for biology would endanger the quality of medical education. There were even those who claimed that a reduced timetable for Latin would herald the twilight of our culture.

So far only limited empirical evidence has become available to serve those who make decisions about the length of the school year and the time allotted to individual subject areas. Since these matters are, in many cases, decided upon by the national government or state legislature, they tend to be uniform within each country. Therefore, studies of how instruction time in a particular subject is related to achievement would have to be crossnational, or more precisely, multinational. Certain leads can, however, be obtained from national surveys in which students in all subjects have been assigned widely different amounts of instruction time.

In sparsely populated areas in Scandinavia, for instance, it used to be the normal practice, because of either a shortage of teachers or the long traveling distance, to allow children to go to school every other semester or every other day during part or even all of their compulsory school period. In the 1950s a survey was conducted in a rural region of Norway in which two parallel groups of students aged twelve to fourteen were taught full time and half time respectively during the last two grades of compulsory school. The group that received half-time instruction was assigned more homework and proved to be only slightly inferior to the first in mastering the basic skills.* Similar evidence has been collected in Sweden, where since the middle of the 1940s achievement tests in the three R's have been administered to all students at certain grade levels.

During the 1960s the International Association for the Evaluation of Educational Achievement (IEA) launched a series of massive international survey studies of school effectiveness. The first of these studied the mathematics achievement of thirteen-year-olds in a dozen developed countries. The effect of the age at school entry was one of the factors examined by IEA. All countries with some kind of compulsory schooling have regulations that specify the age at which children have to enter school. In countries with well-developed systems of schooling, the age range tends to vary from five to seven. In England and Scotland, for instance, children enter at five, whereas in Sweden and Finland they do not

---

* *What might have occurred if no homework had been assigned?*

start school until seven. In the other eight countries included in the study, the normal age of entry is six.

The main report of the IEA study, published in 1967 under my editorship, stated that "results suggest, but do not establish beyond doubt, that school systems admitting pupils at the age of six produce mathematics scores at the age of fourteen that are superior to those obtained by students in systems admitting children at five or delaying admission to seven." * One cannot, of course, generalize on the basis of observations from so few national school systems. Nevertheless, assuming that it is possible to keep other sources of variation under control, it appears significant that earlier entry alone does not seem to bear any substantial relationship to achievement at the age of fourteen.

The complexity of these matters is suggested by T. N. Postlethwaite, who reanalyzed the mathematics data and concluded that school entry at five did not seem to "be of consequence as far as progress in mathematics is concerned, whereas a loss of a year's schooling between six and seven appears to have a detrimental effect." Furthermore, his findings suggested that earlier entry proved more beneficial to children with a white-collar background than to those from blue-collar families.†

So far the IEA mathematics survey is the only comprehensive multinational attempt to relate the number of hours of instruction to retained skills and knowledge as measured by international achievement tests. From the methodological point of view, the thorny problem is how to relate achievement to the amount of exposure to formal teaching, while accounting for differences in other conditions that also affect achievement, such as parental education, rural-urban residence, and teacher competence. Nevertheless, an attempt was made to find out to what extent differences in achievement among students in the twelve countries were accounted for by home background and by teacher, school, and student variables, respectively. One supposedly important group of school variables included: length of school week, the time given to all homework, the time given to mathematics homework, and the time given to instruction in mathematics. Together these accounted for only about 3 per cent of the total difference in achievement on the mathematics test among the thirteen-year-olds.‡ . . .

Of these four school-related factors, "the time given to all homework" tended to be the important one for the thirteen-year-olds (when 100 per cent of the age group was still in full-time schooling), whereas "the time given to mathematics homework" and "time given to instruction in

---

* How might Rohwer's research on developmental stages of intellectual ability (Section 13) help us to interpret this finding?
† This finding appears to contradict Deutsch's views on compensatory education (Section 4).
‡ These results are similar to those obtained by Mayeske (Section 4).

mathematics" (in that order) were the important ones at the preuniversity level. Thus, at both levels, time devoted to instruction seemed to be close to insignificant in all the twelve countries included in the study.*...

Clearly we all need much more information about those factors that make a difference in the effectiveness of education, but the need is particularly crucial for developing nations. These countries tend to follow institutional patterns developed by the wealthy, industrialized countries at a stage when the social needs were quite different. Universal elementary schooling in western Europe was introduced in a half-industrialized society where parents worked long hours in factories and where the home was progressively less able to serve as a training ground in which members of the family spent the whole day producing and consuming together. In addition to providing children with some basic skills in the three R's and some knowledge of the Scriptures, the school also performed a custodial function. Industry simply needed an institution that could look after the children while it utilized their parents' labor. But there is serious doubt about the value of institutional models evolved in Europe and the United States for developing nations because of the waste involved when children repeat grades or drop out, and because of the high cost of maintaining them.

As Professor John Vaisey of Brunel University in England points out in a recent paper on "The Production Process in Education," economists and others concerned with analysis of the education process have been able to control, in quantitative terms, those factors such as financing, length of the school year, etc., that make up the "inputs" of education. However, very little analysis has been done on the factors affecting student achievement, the "outputs" of education.† ("The way in which the inputs are transmuted into outputs is largely an area of ignorance.") This is one of the primary reasons why, in the present stage of the IEA survey work, the main emphasis will be placed on attempts to discover which factors within the school system — such as teaching, material resources, and staff availability — account for differences in educational attainments among schools as well as among students. The overall aim is to identify those factors that can be controlled or affected by policy decisions, and which seem to play a major role in determining success or failure....

Before the end of 1972 ... we shall be able to provide precise information about the outcomes of the teaching of reading and science in some twenty countries, among them India, Iran, Chile, and Thailand. Representative samples of children at the ages of ten, fourteen, and eighteen have been given identical international tests, both cognitive and noncognitive.

---

* *This result supports Bane and Jencks's conclusions (Section 3).*
† *This is currently a major concern of educational researchers, for example, Bane and Jencks.*

The testing instruments have been carefully pretested, and in each country a special national committee has cooperated with an international committee in the preparation of the instruments.* Precautions have been taken to remove test items that could be suspected of bias against a particular culture or country. Translation problems were given special attention, particularly in the development of tests in reading comprehension.

Recent surveys conducted both at national and international levels suggest that much more of the between-country and between-student variance† than was previously assumed can be attributed to conditions outside the influence of the school, such as socioeconomic structure of the society, local per-pupil allocation, parental education, and type of community (urban, rural or suburban). The Plowden Commission in England, for instance, tried to account for the differences in achievement among eleven-year-old pupils and found that about two-thirds of the variance accounted for could be assigned to background factors, whereas only one-third could be assigned to what happened to the student at school. Similar findings in the United States were reported by Professor James S. Coleman and his associates in their study "Equality of Educational Opportunity." The IEA mathematics survey confirmed the conclusions of these two national studies. The seemingly modest contributions of teaching per se to differences in student performance have quite naturally caused considerable concern among educators.

On the basis of these and other surveys, we can expect widely different levels of attainment between developed and less developed countries, simply because they differ tremendously in their sociocultural structure and therefore in the socioeconomic background of students. The broad occupational sectors in developed countries are the manufacturing and service industries, whereas the developing countries are dominated by an agricultural subsistence economy. Even school resources and teacher competencies equivalent to those in Europe or the United States would not suffice to bring the children anywhere near the level of achievement of those from the wealthier countries. In reading comprehension, for instance, ten-year-olds in the developing countries with about the same number of years of full-time schooling as their coevals in Europe and the United States lag way behind. Since this gap is to a large extent caused by socioeconomic differences, the practical implication is that education cannot serve as a substitute for social and economic reform.

The present IEA survey is not an international horse race, but rather an attempt to take advantage of differences on the input side of educational systems in order to account for differences on the output side. The inter-

---

* How does this testing program compare with our National Assessment? (See Ahmann, Section 15).
† Variance is explained in the glossary.

esting point is how strategic input factors relate to output and how much of the output they account for.

The high price paid for the products of formal schooling in developing countries, in high dropout rates and grade repeating, has in recent years prompted several attempts at alternative strategies that could better utilize the resources available and lead to outcomes more relevant to the social and economic needs of a given country. Importing reform models from the wealthy countries does not help very much, because the developing countries are faced with a shortage of both the skills and the capital required.

As a result of the accumulating evidence, we have recently begun to question the very metaphysics of the European schooling approach. The interest that several international and national technical assistance agencies have begun to show in nonformal or out-of-school education is an important symptom. Programs in which the common denominator is a better integration of education and working life have already been launched in the developing countries, and more will probably follow. It is possible that as these experimental programs progress, the developed countries will find they have as much to learn from the experience of the underdeveloped world, as they have to learn from us.

EXERCISE

1. What did the IEA study find about the relationship between age of school entry and later mathematics achievement? (p. 256)

2. What did the same study find about the relationship between time devoted to mathematics instruction and later mathematics achievement? (pp. 256–257)

3. The Plowden Commission in England, the Coleman study in the United States, and the IEA mathematics survey all reached a similar conclusion. What was it? (p. 258)

4. What implications do these three studies have for education in developing nations? (p. 258)

SEX DIFFERENCES

Introduction

Learning is determined in part by the individual's sex identity, that is, by those physical characteristics which identify one as male or female. Sex identity affects the individual's pattern of abilities, self-concept as a learner, school achievement, and persistence in school. Lois Hoffman illustrates the pervasiveness of these sex-linked differences:

> Little girls want to please; they work for love and approval; if bright, they underestimate their competence. Little boys show more task involvement, more confidence, and are more likely to show IQ increments. Girls have more anxiety than boys and the anxiety they have is more dysfunctional to their performance. There are also differences in the specific skills of each sex: Males excel in spatial perceptions, arithmetical reasoning, general information, and show less set-dependency; girls excel in quick-perception of details, verbal fluency, rote memory, and clerical skills (*Journal of Social Issues*, vol. 28, 1972, p. 130).

These sex differences in learning have been well established through research. Educators and researchers now must ask how the individual's sex identity becomes a basis for determining learning abilities and school achievement. This same issue confronts reseachers who seek to explain the relationships between school achievement and such factors as the individual's race, social class, and intelligence. Are these relationships brought about by genetic factors or by the way society molds the individual?

One of the best known sex differences is that males are superior to females in arithmetical reasoning. Is this superiority inherited? Or does it develop because males are rewarded for achievement in mathematics and the sciences, whereas females are not similarly rewarded and, in fact, may feel that it is "unfeminine" to excel in these subjects? The search for causes of sex differences is an active field of research, as demonstrated in the two papers that follow. In the introduction to *Man & Woman, Boy & Girl*, John Money and Anke A. Ehrhardt summarize the recent evidence about the relative contribution of culture and biology to the behavior of boys and girls. Myra Pollack Sadker examines the various ways in which in-school experiences influence what boys and girls learn and how they behave.

If you become a teacher, you will probably have both boys and girls in your classes. Should you reinforce the sex differences that you see emerging, for example, by encouraging boys when they show interest in science and girls when they show interest in home economics? Or should you minimize sex differences by ignoring the child's sex identity, instead treating him or her as an individual? If you opt for the latter, you would encourage the child's emerging interests whether or not they conflict with stereotypes traditionally associated with sex identity.

Although the following selections do not deal directly with this issue, they have implications for it. If differences in learning abilities associated with one's sex identity are inborn, it might be difficult or even fruitless for the teacher to help some girls to become self-confident in intellectual tasks, interested in arithmetic and other subjects. Similarly, it might be very difficult to change the behavior of some boys so that they develop verbal fluency or affiliative behavior. However, if sex differences are the result of social conditioning, they can be minimized, learned, or unlearned more easily. The question then becomes which goal you wish to accomplish. Do you want the sexes to become more alike? Or do you see social and personal value in maintaining traditional sex roles?

Consider whether you agree or disagree with the following views:

*Environment as a Determinant
of Sex-Linked Behavior Differences*

Pro   Nearly all differences in male-female behavior are the result of social or psychological influences. Thus, by changing the way adults and other children interact with boys and girls, their behavior and attitudes can be changed.

Con   Differences in male and female behavior emerge from differences in anatomy and physiological functioning. Thus, differences in learning between boys and girls will persist despite changes in the way adults and others respond to them.

Changing Sex-Linked Differences in Behavior

Pro   Everyone, whether male or female, should have an opportunity to develop full intellectual potential. Teachers
and others should strive to eliminate traditional sex-role
stereotypes, because these biases influence what is learned
by boys and girls, and thus prevent them from reaching
their full potential.

Con   Many differences in the behavior of boys and girls are
desirable. They should not be eliminated even if it means
some individuals will not achieve their full potential. For
example, achievement of a woman's full intellectual potential may not be desirable if it, in turn, necessitates
the loss of her sensitivity to others.

Man & Woman,
Boy & Girl

John Money and Anke A. Ehrhardt

*One explanation of differences in the behavior of males and females
is that they result from sex-linked differences in physical structure
and hormonal functions. Proponents of this view argue that boys
and girls will develop different patterns of learning abilities and
achievement regardless of the childrearing setting in which they are
placed. In their recent book,* Man & Woman, Boy & Girl, *Money
and Ehrhardt argue against this position by presenting case studies
and other research evidence which suggests that almost all sex differences in behavior are learned. For example, sex-linked physical characteristics provide cues which cause adults to treat males and
females differently even in infancy. At the same time, Money and
Ehrhardt acknowledge evidence which indicates that some forms of
behavior patterns may be influenced by pre- and post-natal differences in hormonal functioning between boys and girls. If environment is as important as Money and Ehrhardt believe, teachers may
be able to influence the sex-linked behaviors that students learn.
Can or should you break down your stereotypes and attempt to*

Abridged from Chapter 1, *Man & Woman, Boy & Girl: Differentiation
and Dimorphism of Gender Identity from Conception to Maturity,* by John
Money and Anke A. Ehrhardt, Baltimore: The Johns Hopkins University
Press, 1972, pp. 1–23. Copyright © 1972 by the Johns Hopkins University
Press. Reprinted by permission of the publisher.

*eliminate sex differences? For example, should you be equally pro-
tective of boys and girls, or equally supportive of their attempts to
act independently?*

INTRODUCTION

In developmental psychosexual theory, it is no longer satisfactory to
utilize only the concept of psychosexual development. Psychosexual (or
gender-identity) differentiation is the preferential concept, for the psycho-
development of sex is a continuation of the embryo-development of sex.
Alone among the divers functional systems of embryonic development,
the reproductive system is sexually dimorphic. So also in subsequent behavioral and psychic development, there is sexual dimorphism.*

In the theory of psychosexual differentiation, it is now outmoded to
juxtapose nature versus nurture, the genetic versus the environmental, the
innate versus the acquired, the biological versus the psychological, or the
instinctive versus the learned. ... The basic proposition should be not a
dichotomization of genetics and environment, but their interaction.† Interactionism as applied to the differentiation of gender identity can be
best expressed by using the concept of a program. There are phyletically
written parts of the program. They exert their determining influence particularly before birth. ... Even at that early time, however, the phyletic
program may be altered by idiosyncrasies of personal history, such as the
loss or gain of a chromosome during cell division, a deficiency or excess
of maternal hormone, viral invasion, intrauterine trauma, nutritional deficiency or toxicity, and so forth. Other idiosyncratic modifications may be
added by the biographical events of birth. All may impose their own im-
primatur on the genetic program of sexual dimorphism that is normally
expected on the basis of XX or XY chromosomal dimorphism.

Postnatally, the programing of psychosexual differentiation is, by phyletic decree, a function of biographical history, especially social biography.
There is a close parallel here with the programing of language development.
The social-biography program is not written independently of the phyletic
program, but in conjunction with it, though on occasions there may be
dysjunction between the two. Once written, the social-biography program
leaves its effect as surely as does the phyletic. The long-term effects of the

---

* Dimorphic *means having two forms or manifestations, though within the
same species. For example, within the human species, there is a juvenile and
adult form, and a male and female form.*
† *What other researchers whose work is included in Part 2 would take a
similar position?*

two are equally fixed and enduring, and their different origins not easily recognizable. Aspects of human psychosexual differentiation attributable to the social-biography program are often mistakenly attributed to the phyletic program.

In the history of the egg from fertilization to birth, the sequence of developmental events can be likened to a relay race. The program of sexual dimorphism is carried first by either the X or the Y sex chromosome, supplied by the male parent to pair with the X chromosome from the female parent. The XX or XY chromosomal combination will pass the program to the undifferentiated gonad, to determine its destiny as testis or ovary. Thereafter, the sex chromosomes will have no known direct influence on subsequent sexual and psychosexual differentiation.

The undifferentiated gonad differentiates and passes the program to the hormonal secretions of its own cells. More accurately, the program is passed to the secretions of the testis. In the total absence of fetal gonadal hormones, the fetus always continues to differentiate the reproductive anatomy of a female. Ovarian hormones are, according to present evidence, irrelevant at this early stage. Testicular hormones are imperative for the continuing differentiation of the reproductive structures of a male.

Testicular secretions, their presence or absence or their intrusion from exogenous sources, account not only for the shape of the external genitals but also for certain patterns of organization in the brain, especially, by inference, in the hypothalamic pathways that will subsequently influence certain aspects of sexual behavior. Thus they pass on the program, dividing it between two carriers, namely, the genital morphology and that part of the central nervous system, peripheral and intracranial, which serves the genital morphology.

Genital morphology completes its program-bearing work by passing the program on, first to those adult individuals who are responsible for sex assignment and rearing the child as a boy or girl, and later to the child in person as he, or she, perceives the genital organs. . . .

The predominant part of gender-identity differentiation receives its program by way of social transmission from those responsible for the reconfirmation of the sex of assignment in the daily practices of rearing.* Once differentiated, gender identity receives further confirmation from the hormonal changes of puberty, or lack of confirmation in instances of incongruous identity.

With the initiation of parenthood, the whole program is set in motion yet once again, as a new generation comes into being.

---

* Here the authors indicate their belief that most differences in male-female behavior are learned.

DEFINITIONS

GENDER IDENTITY. The sameness, unity, and persistence of one's individuality as male, female, or ambivalent, in greater or lesser degree, especially as it is experienced in self-awareness and behavior; gender identity is the private experience of gender role, and gender role is the public expression of gender identity.

GENDER ROLE. Everything that a person says and does, to indicate to others or to the self the degree that one is either male, or female, or ambivalent; it includes but is not restricted to sexual arousal and response; gender role is the public expression of gender identity, and gender identity is the private experience of gender role. . . .

FETAL HORMONAL SEX, THE NERVOUS SYSTEM, AND BEHAVIOR

Normal differentiation of genital morphology entails a dimorphic sex difference in the arrangement of the peripheral nerves of sex which, in turn, entails some degree of dimorphism in the representation of the periphery at the centrum of the central nervous system, that is to say, in the structures and pathways of the brain.

The concept of central nervous system dimorphism of sex was neglected until it was brought into focus by the contemporary surge of research on the influence of prenatal hormones, by way of the brain, on subsequent dimorphism of sexual behavior. This surge of research was initiated by William C. Young, partly in response to early clinical studies on human hermaphroditism showing that individuals of the same hermaphroditic* diagnosis would, if reared oppositely, differentiate a gender identity in agreement with their biography, irrespective of chromosomal, gonadal, or hormonal sex, and even, perhaps, of uncorrected morphologic appearance.[1]

Human hermaphroditic studies have, meanwhile, benefited from the new experimental findings on animals, which suggest that the prenatal hormonal environment does exercise, during a few critical days of brain development, a determining influence on neural pathways that will subsequently mediate sexually dimorphic behavior. In human beings, the pathways have not yet been anatomically identified. The lower an animal in the phyletic scale, the more likely is its prenatally determined behavior

---

* Hermaphroditism *is a condition prenatal in origin in which differentiation of the reproduction system fails to reach completion as entirely female or entirely male.*

to be stereotypic and uninfluenced by later history. The higher primates, and man especially, are more subject to the influence of postnatal biographical history. . . .

Illustrations of the general principle can be found in both male and female hermaphroditism. In the case of female hermaphroditism, one assumes that the excess of male hormone which brings about masculinization of the external genitalia will be present in sufficient quantity, and at the critical developmental period, to influence the brain. To establish a relationship between a prenatal hormonal masculinizing influence and subsequent behavioral traits, the preferred cases are those in which hormonal masculinization ceases at birth. This condition is met in progestin-induced hermaphroditism, since the masculinizing agent was synthetic progestin administered to the mother. It also is met in adrenogenital hermaphroditism, if the excess of adrenocortical androgen is kept suppressed by cortisone therapy from birth onward.

In either syndrome, it is more likely that the baby will have been assigned and reared as a girl than as a boy, though the latter does sometimes occur. Those reared as girls are more instructive for present purposes, as the possible sequelae of prenatal hormonal masculinization on behavior are not masked by social masculinization.

It is a handicap in the study of sexually dimorphic behavior that, for all the millennia in which men and women have existed, no one yet has an exhaustive list of what to look for. Today's information is not, therefore, final or absolute. With the safeguard of this proviso, one may sum up current findings by saying that genetic females masculinized in utero and reared as girls have a high chance of being tomboys in their behavior. The elements of tomboyism are as follows.

1. The ratio of athletic to sedentary energy expenditure is weighted in favor of vigorous activity, especially outdoors. Tomboyish girls like to join with boys in outdoor sports, specifically ball games. Groups of girls do not offer equivalent alternatives, nor do their toys. Tomboyish girls prefer the toys that boys usually play with.

2. Self-assertiveness in competition for position in the dominance hierarchy of childhood is strong enough to permit successful rivalry with boys. Tomboyish girls do not, however, usually compete for top-echelon dominance among boys, possibly because their acceptance among boys is conditional on their not doing so. Rivalry for dominance may require fighting, but aggressiveness is not a primary trait of tomboyism. In fact, aggressiveness per se is probably not a primary trait of boyishness either, except as a shibboleth of shoddy popular psychology and the news media. Tomboyish girls are relatively indifferent to establishing a dominance position in the hierarchy of girlhood, possibly because they are not sufficiently interested in all the activities of other girls. They are more likely to estab-

lish a position of leadership among younger children who follow them as hero worshippers.

3. Self-adornment is spurned in favor of functionalism and utility in clothing, hairstyle, jewelry, and cosmetics. Tomboyish girls generally prefer slacks and shorts to frills and furbelows, though they do not have an aversion to dressing up for special occasions. Their cosmetic of choice is perfume.

4. Rehearsal of maternalism in childhood dollplay is negligible. Dolls get relegated to permanent storage. Later in childhood, there is no great enthusiasm for baby-sitting or any caretaker activities with small children. The prospect of motherhood is not ruled out, but is viewed in a perfunctory way as something to be postponed rather than hastened. The preference, in anticipation, is for one or two children, not a large family.

5. Romance and marriage are given second place to achievement and career. Priority of career over marriage, preferably combining both, is already evident in the fantasies and expectancies of childhood. The tomboyish girl reaches the boyfriend stage in adolescence later than most of her compeers. Priority assigned to career is typically based on high achievement in school and on high IQ. There is some preliminary evidence to suggest that an abnormally elevated prenatal androgen level, whether in genetic males or females, enhances IQ. Once sexual life begins, there is no evidence of lack of erotic response, rather the opposite. There is no special likelihood of lesbianism.

6. In adulthood, according to preliminary evidence, responsiveness to the visual (or narrative) erotic image may resemble that of men rather than women. That is to say, the viewer objectifies the opposite-sexed figure in the picture as a sexual partner, as men typically do. Men objectify the female figure. Tomboyish women objectify the male figure. Ordinary women generally do not objectify. They project themselves into the figure of the stimulus woman and fantasy themselves in a parallel situation, but with the romantic partner of their own desire.

Further evidence is needed to know whether the tomboyish response to erotic imagery is contingent on elevated androgen levels in adulthood, or only on a delayed prenatal androgen effect. . . .

EXTERNAL MORPHOLOGIC SEX AND ASSIGNED SEX

. . . Parents wait for nine months to see whether the mother gives birth to a boy or a girl. They feel themselves so incapable of influencing what nature ordains that it simply never occurs to them that they are also waiting for the first cue as how to behave toward the new baby. Yet, as soon as the shape of the external genitals is perceived, it sets in motion a chain of communication: It's a daughter! It's a son! This communication itself sets in motion a chain of sexually dimorphic responses, beginning with pink and blue, pronominal use, and name choice, that will be transmitted from person to person to encompass all persons the baby ever encounters, day by day, year in and year out, from birth to death. Dimorphism of response on the basis of the shape of the sex organs is one of the most universal and pervasive aspects of human social interaction.* It is so ingrained and habitual in most people, that they lose awareness of themselves as shapers of a child's gender-dimorphic behavior, and take for granted their own behavior as a no-option reaction to the signals of their child's behavior which they assume to have preordained by some external verity to be gender-dimorphic.

There are some parents who are so culturally imbued with parental ideals of juridical fair play that they have a blind spot even for the fact that their behavior toward a daughter is, by certain criteria, different from that toward a son. They insist that they treat all siblings alike, and mean, by implication, that they are impartial in the distribution of rewards and punishments. A videotape would rapidly show, however, that these same parents do indeed have a dimorphism of expectancy built into their interactions with daughters as compared with sons. For other parents, a videotape is not necessary. They are more articulate observers of their own behavior, and can report ways in which they differentially treat sons and daughters.

No parents encounter a more dramatic illustration of the son-daughter dimorphism of their own behavior than do those parents of a hermaphroditic child whose announced sex is reassigned after the period of earliest infancy. Ideally, the clinical evaluation of a hermaphroditic baby should be exhaustive and complete at the time of birth, so that the criteria governing the sex of assignment can be properly weighted and the announcement made unequivocally once and for ever.

The ideal is not always met, because few people are prepared ahead of time to know how to react when a baby is delivered and found to have ambiguous genitalia. All too often, a decision as to the sex of announcement is improvised. Subsequently, after a detailed evaluation, a revision of the announcement may be decided upon. If the revision is made neonatally, one speaks simply of a sex reannouncement. Later, after the baby has begun to absorb the gender dimorphism of the language into the development of his or her sense of gender identity, one speaks more accurately not of a sex reannouncement, but reassignment. A reassignment requires a change in responses from the baby. A reannouncement requires changes in the behavior only of other people. It is ill-advised to impose a sex re-

* Given this state of affairs, do you think the sex biases identified by Sadker (next selection) will ever be eliminated?

assignment on a child in contradiction of a gender identity already well advanced in its differentiation — which means that the age ceiling for an imposed reassignment is, in the majority of cases, around eighteen months.

For a sex reassignment, the age of eighteen months — or the few months preceding it — is quite late enough to make parents overtly cognizant of the gender difference in their behavior when they take a son to the hospital and bring home a daughter, or vice versa. By way of illustration ... one father related a story of his romper-room activities with his two young children, upon arrival home from work in the evenings, after the younger one, a genetic male hermaphrodite with a phallus the size of a clitoris and otherwise ambiguous genitalia, had been reassigned as a girl at age 15 months. The older child, a boy, liked a rather rowdy kind of solo dancing, rock-and-roll type. The younger one liked to follow suit, but the father's impulse was to bring her close to himself, to dance as a couple. Though initially she preferred to copy her big brother, the girl soon learned to enjoy her privileged daughter-role with her father.

This anecdote illustrates very well the principle of complementation in the experiences of rearing which shape the differentiation of gender role and gender identity. Traditionally in psychology, especially social psychology, this principle has passed unrecognized, and attention has been directed exclusively to the principle of identification. The fact is that children differentiate a gender role and identity by way of complementation to members of the opposite sex, and identification with members of the same sex.

It is prerequisite to the effective developmental manifestation of both complementation and identification that the sexes be distinguishable from one another, regardless of how great or small the amount of overlap in appearance and behavior culturally prescribed or permitted in any place or period of history. It is a popular pastime, nowadays, to talk and write about the American male's loss of masculinity, thereby misinterpreting what should more accurately be interpreted simply as an accommodation of certain traditional facets of gender role, male and female, to changing times and circumstances. Nature herself supplies the basic irreducible elements of sex difference which no culture can eradicate, at least not on a large scale: women can menstruate, gestate, and lactate, and men cannot. The secondary sexual characteristics of adulthood are reminders of this dichotomy, but the external sex organs are, of course, the primary visible evidence of the different reproductive role of male and female.

Provided that a child grows up to know that sex differences are primarily defined by the reproductive capacity of the sex organs, and to have a positive feeling of pride in his or her own genitalia and their ultimate reproductive use, then it does not much matter whether various child-care, domestic, and vocational activities are or are not interchangeable between mother and father.* It does not even matter if mother is a bus driver and daddy a cook. It does not even matter if the father (by adoption) is a female-to-male transexual, provided his hormonal and surgical masculinization have given him the outward appearance and voice of a man, and provided he relates to the child's mother as her lover and husband — irrespective of how they actually perform coitally....

Valuable as it is, knowledge of visible sexual anatomy is incomplete. The ideal is for children to be reared to know also the reproductive roles of the sex organs, and to be able to look forward with approval to the proper use of their own, when the time is right. They then are secure in being able to distinguish between the imperative and the optional elements of gender-dimorphic behavior. Their own gender identity then becomes differentiated the more securely....

DIFFERENTIATION OF GENDER IDENTITY

Further testimony to the importance of the early years in gender-identity differentiation may be found in young children of normal genital anatomy who manifest behavior and express desires appropriate to the opposite sex. In some, though not all such cases, one can identify insidious ambiguity in the gender-appropriate signals transmitted from the parents to the child. The diversity of parent-child interaction in such cases, together with the fact that other siblings differ from the index case, requires one to consider the possibility that the boy who becomes an extreme sissy, or the girl who becomes an extreme amazon do, in fact, get born into the family with some degree of prenatally determined disposition that makes them easily vulnerable to postnatal disorders of gender-identity differentiation....

No one knows how many genetic females born with normal female genitalia might, in fact, have been subject to prenatal androgen excess insufficient to influence the external anatomy, though perhaps sufficient to influence the brain. A hitherto unsuspected example of such a prenatal influence was recently reported by Lynwood G. Clemens (personal communication) from Michigan State University. He found that the larger the number of brothers in a litter of rats, the greater the likelihood that the sisters would display masculine mounting behavior when hormonally primed with androgen in adulthood.

The converse of the prenatally androgenized genetic female with normal genital anatomy would be the genetic male with normal genitalia but a prenatal history of androgen deficit. In the male fetus, the influence of

* Are the authors taking this position based on research evidence or based on their own value judgments?

its own testicular androgen can be suppressed by injections of anti-androgen, e.g., cyproterone acetate, into the pregnant mother. There is another recent discovery by Ingeborg Ward that points in the direction of an androgen-deficit effect on the brain of genitally normal males.[2] Pregnant female rats were exposed to the extreme stress of constraint under glaring light, in order to test the effect of the mother's hormonal response to stress on the offspring. The result was that the sons grew up to be deficient in male mating behavior when tested with receptive females. . . .

In human beings, no one yet knows the influence on pregnancy of drugs or foods, or even the mother's own, perhaps anomalous placental hormones, or anomalous hormones or hormone deficiency from another maternal source, on the central nervous system of the fetus and the subsequent gender-dimorphic behavior of the child, boy or girl. This paragraph, therefore, has to be left incomplete, except by way of a warning, namely, that it is premature to attribute all aspects of gender-identity to the postnatal period of gender-identity differentiation.

Nonetheless, the evidence of human hermaphroditism makes it abundantly clear that nature has ordained a major part of human gender-identity differentiation to be accomplished in the postnatal period. It then takes place, as does the development of native language, when a prenatally programed disposition comes in contact with postnatal, socially programed signals. . . .

EXERCISE

1. According to the authors, what basic proposition should guide the study of differences in male and female behavior? (pp. 263, 264)

2. The authors list six characteristics that a girl who receives an excess of male hormone in the prenatal period will be more likely to exhibit than other girls. List the characteristics. (pp. 266–267)

3. Why do some parents fail to recognize that their behavior toward a daughter differs from that toward a son? (p. 268)

4. Why do the authors suggest an age ceiling of eighteen months for sex reassignment of a hermaphroditic child? (pp. 268–269)

5. Although the authors consider gender-identity differentiation to involve both nature and nurture, which do they propose has the major influence? Why? (p. 271)

Elements of Sex Bias in Schools

Myra Pollack Sadker

Numerous differences in the learning behavior of males and females have been documented. In this article, Myra Pollack Sadker, looks at the ways in which the schools encourage the development of these differences, particularly how in-school experiences contribute to women's failure to fully use their intellectual potential to the same extent as men. Sadker's main thesis is that the courses offered, the materials used, and teacher-student interactions combine to make the majority of female students passive, shy and dependent. In contrast, male students are provided with learning experiences which help them become self-assured, competitive, and independent.

In considering Sadker's discussion of sex bias in the schools, you may find it interesting to review your own experiences. Do your elementary and secondary school experiences match those described by Sadker? Also, if you were to become a teacher, how would you use the information contained in this paper? Would you eliminate all differences in learning outcomes between males and females?

In Racine, Wisconsin, a group of teachers attempted to offer a workshop for other teachers on Sexism in Education. They offered to hold the six-week workshop for no remuneration, and sufficient excitement was generated among other teachers so that well over the required number of fifteen had signed up to participate. In a 4 to 4 decision, the Board of Education refused to allow the workshop to be held.

The four board members voting against the workshop charged that the district faced greater problems than sexual discrimination. One of the vetoing members noted:

> Isn't there something more challenging? Why waste time if you've got other problems? I really don't see what this has to do with the teaching of curriculum. It implies we are discriminating, and if we are, aren't we in violation of federal regulations?

Abridged and adapted from Chapters 4 and 5 in *Sexism in School and Society* by Nancy Frazier and Myra Sadker. Copyright © 1973 by Myra Sadker and Nancy Frazier. By permission of Harper and Row, Publishers, Inc.

Another added:

> With the very serious subject matter before us, I don't think a subject of this type has a place.[1]

The workshop on Sexism in Education was the first ever to be vetoed by the Racine Board of Education.

There is a steadily growing body of research documenting loss of academic ability and sense of self-esteem that female students experience as they progress through school. Following is what might be termed a "report card," representative rather than inclusive, that gives some sense of this loss of human dignity and potential.

> Intellectually, girls start off ahead of boys. They begin speaking, reading and counting sooner; in the early grades they are even better in math. However, during the high school years, a different pattern emerges and girls' performance on ability tests begins to decline. Indeed, male students exhibit significantly more IQ gain from adolescence to adulthood than do their female counterparts.[2]

> As boys and girls progress through school their opinions of boys become higher, and correspondingly, their opinions of girls become lower. Children are learning that boys are worth more.[3]

> Grade school boys have positive feelings about being male; they are more confident and assertive. In contrast, girls are not particularly enthusiastic about having been born female. They are less confident about their accomplishments, their popularity and their general adequacy.[4]

> By the time they reach the upper elementary grades, girls' visions of future occupations are essentially limited to four: teacher, nurse, secretary or mother. Boys of the same age do not view their future occupational potential as so limited.[5]

> A more recent study indicates that although more elementary school girls are beginning to consider a variety of careers, they are unable to describe in any specificity what having a career would be like. Boys, in contrast, are able to describe in detail the activities which might comprise their chosen career.[6]

> Although women make better high school grades than do men, they are less likely to believe that they have the ability to do college work.[7]

> Decline in career commitment has been found in girls of high school age. This decline was related to their feelings that male classmates disapproved of a woman's using her intelligence.[8]

> Of the brightest high school graduates who do not go on to college, 75–90% are women.[9]

> The majority of male and female college students feel the characteristics associated with masculinity are more valuable and more socially desirable than those associated with femininity.[10]

> College women respond negatively to women who have achieved high academic or vocational success, and at times display an actual motive to avoid success.[11]

Obviously schools cannot bear full blame for this loss of academic potential and positive sense of self-esteem. However, as perhaps our most organized agent of socialization, it should be most pertinent to analyze how elements of sex bias may be operating in our schools.

SCHOOLING AS A SEXIST ACTIVITY

There are no courses in schools called "How to be a 'Real' Boy" or "Female Role Development." However, through a pervasive network of signals, the school does reinforce and even intensify sex stereotyping. One element of this network involves student interaction with school personnel.

In one study, junior high school teachers were asked to select adjectives that they felt would describe good male and female students: [12]

Adjectives describing good female students*	Adjectives describing good male students
Appreciative	Active
Calm	Adventurous
Conscientious	Aggressive
Considerate	Assertive
Cooperative	Curious
Mannerly	Energetic
Poised	Enterprising
Sensitive	Frank
Dependable	Independent
Efficient	Inventive
Mature	
Obliging	
Thorough	

Such teacher attitudes are stereotypes in miniature of the male and female roles, and as teacher expectation research suggests, they can have a profound effect on student behavior. Sexist attitudes may also confront students within the microcosm of the counseling situation, and it has been demonstrated that counselors respond more positively to female clients who hold traditionally feminine career goals than to those who wish to try out careers in traditionally masculine fields.[13]

Sex stereotyping is also reinforced as differing interaction patterns emerge when teachers talk with male and female students.† It has been found, for example, that teachers express greater approval of girls and greater disap-

---

These adjectives suggest that females are more sensitive to people than males. If the female role is changed, what should be done about these traits?

† Compare these findings with Brophy and Good's research on teacher expectancy and Flander's research on teacher influence. (Both articles are in Section 6.)

proval of boys. In one study, boys received 8 to 10 times as many control messages as did girls.[14] Moreover, when teachers criticize boys, they are more likely to use harsh or angry tones than when talking with girls about a similar misdemeanor.[15] However, teachers not only disapprove more of boys but give them more attention in general, particularly in terms of direct instruction and listening to the child.[16] Although it is difficult to assess the impact of all this attention, including negative attention, one researcher suggests the following result: "One consequence may be a cumulative increase in independent and autonomous behavior by boys as they are disapproved, praised, listened to and taught more actively by the teacher." [17]

In contrast, girls receive approval for exhibiting docile behavior. They are reinforced for silence, neatness, and conformity — and in this dispensation of rewards, the process of learning may become thwarted. Jerome Bruner has commented on the school's probable effect on female students:

> Observant anthropologists have suggested that the basic values of the early grades are a stylized version of the feminine role in society, cautious rather than daring, governed by a lady-like politeness. . . . Girls in the early grades who learn to control their fidgeting earlier are rewarded for excelling in their feminine values. The reward can be almost too successful in that in later years it is difficult to move girls beyond the orderly virtues they learned in their first school encounters. The boys, more fidgety in the first grades get no such reward, and as a consequence may be peer in their approach to learning in the later grades.[18]

The school environment which too often stresses docility operates to maintain the passivity the young female student may bring with her from home. This passive approach to learning is particularly disturbing when one considers Eleanor Maccoby's depiction of the children at age six whose IQ's will be likely to increase by the time they reach ten. They are "competitive, self-assertive, independent, and dominant in interaction with other children. The children who show declining IQ's during the next four years are children who are passive, shy, and dependent." [19]

One study points out the unhappy effect that dependency on rewards may have on intellectual curiosity. Two groups of children, one in nursery school, the other in elementary school, were the subjects. Each child was given two seven-piece wooden puzzles and told that (s)he had 1½ minutes to complete each. The experimenter only pretended to time the children's performances and actually allowed the children to complete only one of the puzzles. After they had attempted to complete both puzzles, the experimenter announced that there was a little extra time to work on one of them again. The children were asked to choose the puzzle they wished to work on a second time.

For the nursery school group, no significant difference was found between the repetition choices of boys and girls. In the grade school group, however, sex differences emerged. Boys more often chose to return to the puzzle they had failed to complete. In contrast, *girls more often repeated the puzzle they had put together successfully*. They avoided the failure situation.[20]

As the young female student becomes programmed into dependency on rewards, she may become more likely to avoid the academically challenging problem wherein lies the possibility of failure and loss of teacher approval — but also the potential for greater academic growth and stimulation.

By the time children enter kindergarten, girls already are identifying with feminine roles and boys with masculine roles. And as young children read the most highly praised picture books, they may be forming negative associations about being female. In Caldecott Medal winners given by the Children's Service Committee for the American Library Association for the most distinguished picture book each year, there is a ratio of eleven pictures of males for every picture of a female. The ratio of pictures of male to female animals was 95 to 1. In the sample of Caldecott winners and runners up in the last five years, only two of the eighteen books were stories about girls. Moreover, *not one* adult woman in the Caldecott sample had a job or profession.[21]

A committee of feminists also studied Newbery Award books. They found that of all forty-nine Newbery Award Winners, books about boys outnumbered books about girls three to one. It is also not too difficult to find quotes in these books that teach humiliating lessons about being born female. The following is from the 1957 winner, *Miracles on Maple Hill:*

> For the millionth time she was glad she wasn't a boy. It was all right for girls to be scared or silly or even ask dumb questions. Everybody just laughed and thought it was funny. But if anybody caught Joe asking a dumb question or even thought he was the littlest bit scared he went red and purple and white.[22]

In another way, fiction written for girls is demeaning, for it often suggests that the only important questions a young woman must deal with concern her relationship to men. Feminists have termed one form of novel the "copout" book. These are books in which high-spirited, daring tomboys achieve popularity or a wedding ring by giving up their independent ways and becoming passive and demure and far less interesting.

School texts have also been examined. The Women on Words and Images studied 134 school readers from sixteen different publishers and found the following ratios: [23]

Boy-centered stories to girl-centered stories   5:2
Adult male main characters to adult female main
     characters   3:1
Male biographies to female biographies   6:1
Male animal stories to female animal stories   2:1
Male folk or fantasy stories to female folk or
     fantasy   4:1

Again, the content conveys some extremely negative messages about females:

> "Women's advice is never worth two pennies. Yours isn't worth even a penny." *Lippincott Basic Reading Series* Book H, 1970.
>
> "Look at her, mother, just look at her. She is just like a girl. She gives up." *Around the Corner*, Harper & Row, 1966.
>
> "We are willing to share our great thoughts with mankind. However, you happen to be a girl." *Ventures*, Book 4, Scott Foresman, 1965.

School reading texts portray boys as able to do so many things. They play baseball games, do magic tricks, get part-time jobs. When girls are present they help with chores around the house, play house or sit and watch their brothers. Moreover, females in these texts are depicted as having less moral strength than males. "Not only are females more often described as lazy and incapable of independent thinking and direct action, but they are also shown as giving up more easily.* They collapse into tears, they betray secrets, they are more likely to act on petty or selfish motives." [24]

History texts may be even more offensive for in these it seems that women are almost systematically selected out. Janice Trecker in her analysis of the twelve history texts most often used in public schools notes that heroic females are not described, nor are areas in which women have made their greatest contributions — theatre, dance, music, day to day life in homes. One text spends five pages discussing the six shooter and barely 5 lines on the life of the frontier woman. In another two volume text, there are only two sentences describing the women's suffrage movement, one in each volume. [25]

In short, a female student desiring to read about another female who is intelligent, creative, powerful, interesting or charismatic will have to wade through many books before meeting one. And it is hard to estimate the impact of this pervasive lack of inspiring models in school reading.

* *What is learned by boys and girls as a result of reading such texts? Do modeling processes occur? (See Brown, Section 1.)*

MALE BOSSES

The elementary school has often been referred to as a feminine environment and indeed, as of 1971, 88 percent of elementary school teachers were female. However, as in so many other fields, female teachers take their orders from a male boss. According to a 1928 National Education Association report, 55 percent of elementary school principals were women. In 1966, men outnumbered women in these principalships by a rate of 3 to 2. In 1971 women were only 22 percent of elementary school principals.[26] In secondary schools only 3 percent of principals are women. In higher levels of administration, women are truly hard to find. Of 13,000 superintendents of schools in 1973, three are women. There are no female state school officers and no U.S. Commissioner of Education has been female.[27]

Although the woman principal is getting harder and harder to find, it is not because the female talent pool in education is inadequate. In 1968, for example, 268 male and 811 female merit scholarship finalists and semifinalists chose secondary education for a career. For elementary education the figures were 146 women and 2 men.[28] Moreover, not only is the female talent pool more than sufficiently rich, but when females do become principals, there is research to suggest that they function very effectively. In a 1955 study, since replicated, it was found that female principals were more democratic and were more concerned with the objectives of teaching, with pupil participation, and with the evaluation of learning.[29]

SEXUAL SEGREGATION

In 1966, a report appeared describing an experiment in sexually segregated classes in which different approaches to learning were used depending on whether the students were male or female. Following are some of the activities that took place in the classes:

1. In working with boys, we employ more science materials and experiments. There is more emphasis on building things and on studies of transportation . . .
2. We have found it well to let the interests of the classes guide the teacher in areas such as science and social studies. . . . From studying the atom, for example, a boy's class moved easily into a study of nuclear fission. It is unlikely that girls would respond this way. Or another example, mold can be studied from a medical standpoint by boys and in terms of cooking by girls.
3. . . . For girls we use quieter games, fairy stories, and games and songs which emphasize activities such as sewing and housekeeping. For boys we use more active physical games

which involve voice and muscle movement and are based on a transportation theme.

4. ... Girls enjoy all stories in readers, even those about boys, but boys do not like stories about girls.[30]

Whenever educational opportunities are segregated on a distinction such as sex or race, superior facilities are awarded to the group to which society accords superior status. Segregation on the basis of sex occurs at all levels of schooling. In the elementary school there is separated lining up — girls on one side of the room, boys on the other. There are contests in which all-girl teams face all-boy teams. And these separations reinforce the notion that the other sex is so totally different as to be considered "opposite."

This informal separation becomes institutionalized when either males or females are excluded from course offerings. Home economics courses for girls only and industrial arts courses for boys only are now being challenged. The following excerpt is public testimony given in the U.S. Courthouse, Brooklyn, New York.

The Witness: I asked Miss Jonas if my daughter could take metal working or mechanics, and she said there was no freedom of choice. ... I didn't ask her anything else because she clearly showed me that it was against the school policy for girls to be in the class. She said it was a Board of Education decision. ...

Question: Now, after this lawsuit was filed, they then permitted you to take the course, is that correct?

Answer: No, we had to fight about it for quite a while.

Question: But eventually they did let you in the second semester?

Answer: They only let me in there.

Question: You are the only girl?

Answer: Yes.

Question: How did you do in the course?

Answer: I got a medal for it from all the boys there.

Question: Will you show the court?

Answer: Yes (indicating).

Question: And what does the medal say?

Answer: Medal 1970 Van Wyck.

Question: And why did they give you that medal?

Answer: Because I was the best out of all the boys.[31]

Policies concerning restricted course policies in the home economics/industrial arts areas are becoming more liberal. However, there has been little change in segregation of athletic facilities, and in no area is biased treatment more evident. Obviously more acclaim is given to male athletes than to female athletes. In use of equipment, field and track, preference is often given to male athletes, and figures on money allotments given to male versus female athletic programs evidence incredible disparities. The Emma Willard Task Force on Education, for example, discloses that in 1970 Minneapolis schools appropriated $197,000 for boys' athletics and only $9,000 for girls' athletics.[32]

When vocational-technical courses are segregated by sex, the effects are more pernicious. Courses offered for boys — drafting, engineering, etc., hold potential for higher economic returns than vocational technical courses for girls which are clustered in clerical skills and cosmetology. Thus in school course offerings we see the beginnings of later economic discrimination against women.

DIRECTIONS FOR CHANGE

There have been many changes in sexist policies and attitudes. Sometimes change occurs through the actions of a concerned teacher, parent, or community member. For example, a member of the Committee to Eliminate Sexual Discrimination in the Public Schools of Ann Arbor, Michigan wrote a letter questioning a publisher about sex bias prevalent in a new text. She received an encouraging reply.

> I'm afraid I will have to agree with your general remarks about the illustrations on the pages you cite. . . . I am sure this happened quite unintentionally and unconsciously, though that may merely tend to confirm how deep and instinctive such stereotypes go. . . . I would also agree that textbook companies have a particularly great responsibility to avoid stereotyping of any kind, just as we now attempt to do in depicting members of minority groups, and that we should also endeavor to provide all children with the most positive self-image that we can. In line with your suggestions, I will ask our authors and editors to see if the pages you list can be changed in the next printing of the book.[33] *

Others have not met with such understanding of the operation of sex stereotypes — and now there is legal support to aid in these more difficult cases. Title IX of the Higher Education Act of 1972 states, "No person in the United States shall on the basis of sex be excluded from participation in, be denied the benefits of, or be subjected to discrimination under any education program or activity receiving federal financial assistance."

Action by dedicated, courageous individuals — although providing models for others — will be too fragmented to achieve substantive changes. It must be the role of schools of education to educate prospective teachers

---

* Given the findings of Bane and Jencks (Section 3), Mayeske (Section 4), and Husén (Section 7), should we expect these textbook changes to influence the attitudes acquired by students?

— and re-educate experienced teachers — in nonsexist teaching practices. Teachers must be taught to analyze curricular material, and their own attitudes as well. . . .

In October of 1972, the National Education Association held a Conference on Sex Roles and Sex Role Stereotypes. The research, the development of new curricular materials, the ideas for new approaches to teacher preparation that emerged during this conference were exciting — and even a bit overwhelming. When schools of education reflect similar concern for sexism in education and translate this concern into how teachers are prepared, then some revolutionary and most positive changes will take place in the classrooms of our public schools.*

EXERCISE

1. List the 10 ways in which women lose academic ability and self-esteem while in school as reported by Sadker. (p. 273)

2. According to Sadker, what types of behavior do the sex role stereotypes in the schools encourage in female students? (p. 275)

3. In what ways do schools promote sexual segregation? (pp. 279–280)

4. Name the three types of action Sadker suggests be taken to alleviate sex bias in schools. (pp. 280–281)

* What would you do, if anything, to eliminate sex bias from your classroom?

Ways To Help Students
Learn Better

Section Nine

INTRODUCTION

Many of you may be planning careers in teaching, administration, or research out of a desire to improve the conditions that exist in schools. Part of this desire to innovate and reform education may have grown from your dissatisfaction with some school experiences. Deciding specific ways to improve the schools is the subject of the readings that follow. They may help you form reasoned opinions about promising directions for change in education. However, the basic goal of education is to help the student to learn. In evaluating proposed innovations, ask yourself, "Will these instructional materials or procedures provide a better learning experience for students than they receive under present conditions of schooling?"

One way to start thinking about educational reform is to consider what you have learned in Parts 1 and 2 of this book. In Part 1 you read about different theories of the learning process. Can these theories be used to improve learning? For example, B. F. Skinner's principles of learning already have been applied extensively in guiding the development of teaching machines, programmed instruction, and computer-assisted instruction. (Of course, you can ask whether these developments are improvements over existing practices.) Jerome Bruner and Jean Piaget have developed cognitive theories of developmental stages in learning; these theories have many implications for school instruction, particularly instruction of young children. Consider, too, Robert Gagné's speculations about different types of learning, each of which requires a different type of instructional process. Are schools and teachers doing a poor job because they rely on a few instructional techniques to teach many different kinds of skills?

The readings in Section 2, "What Should Students Learn in School?", offer a perspective that must be considered in evaluating proposals for educational reform. Even if such techniques as programmed instruction or the discovery method are successful in bringing about learning, we must ask if this learning is worthwhile. The major disagreement in formulating learning goals occurs between such educators as Robert Ebel, who stresses the value of learning facts and basic skills, and Carl Rogers, who emphasizes the humanistic goal of maximizing each student's personal development. Programmed instruction and computer-assisted instruction are consistent with Ebel's objectives, whereas the open classroom and the discovery method are more often associated with the humanistic ideals espoused by Rogers.

In Part 2 various factors were explored that may determine why some students learn more than others in school. The overall trend of these selections can be summarized by Bane and Jencks's statement, based on their own research, that "the character of a school's output depends largely on a single input, the characteristics of the entering children. Everything else — the school budget, its policies, the characteristics of the teachers — is either secondary or completely irrelevant. . . ." In other words, the schools have some effect, but not nearly as much as we might suppose, on how well students learn. More important are the students' out-of-school learning experiences, which are largely a function of their social class status, sex, and ethnic group identification. If this is true, we must consider educational reform from a wider perspective. To improve student learning, we may need to change what happens to the student outside of school as well as within it. The heredity-environment issue is also relevant to this problem. If learning ability is mostly inherited, educators can do little to enhance it, either in or out of school. However, if learning ability is shaped primarily by one's environment, educators can do a great deal to increase it. The heredity-environment issue is by no means settled. Arthur Jensen's review of research indicates that genetic factors play a strong role in learning ability, but George Mayeske and Martin Deutsch present other data that suggest the importance of the child's home environment in determining school success.

The selections that you will read in Part 3 directly reflect these issues in educational psychology. The contrast between educational technology and discovery learning in Section 10 is related to the controversy between Skinner's and Bruner's theories of learning. Sections 11 and 12 — "Radical Change" and "Training Better Teachers" — show the current controversy over the relative influence of in- and out-of-school learning experiences. Section 13, "Coping with Group Differences," includes different views on how schools might adapt to the range of learning abilities and styles which exist among students.

We introduce Part 3 with two selections that deal with broader questions concerning educational reform: What direction is education likely to take in the next five or ten years? With limited resources, where should we concentrate our reform efforts? Can the theories and research findings of educational psychology provide a sound basis for reform? If reform is so badly needed, as many educators have argued, why have the schools been so slow to change? The selections, by Harold Shane and Owen Nelson, and by John Goodlad, consider these questions. As you review the data provided in each, decide whether you agree with any of the following views:

Change in Education

Pro   Despite predictions by some educators to the contrary, the basic structure of the schools will not change in the foreseeable future. The structure hasn't changed much in the last fifty years; there is no reason why it will change now.

Con   The present school structure is out of date. Educators will be forced to reform radically to catch up with other changes taking place in our society.

The Value of Educational Psychology

Pro   Educational psychology is not an ivory-tower subject. Its theories and research findings can be used to help students learn better. This has been true in the past, and will be true in the future.

Con   Educational psychology is an ivory-tower subject. It is a science, and therefore not able to cope with the human problems of education.

What Will the Schools Become?

Harold G. Shane and Owen N. Nelson

Harold Shane and Owen Nelson report the results of a survey in which teachers, school administrators, curriculum specialists, and other educators predicted coming changes in our educational system. Some changes — for example, multimedia instruction — are widely accepted in principle, if not yet in practice. Other changes — using drugs to increase intelligence and mandatory foster homes — are much more controversial. Many changes mentioned here are the subjects of individual readings further on in this book. As they are discussed here, though, you may be impressed by the complexity of our educational system and by the sheer number of changes that are being suggested. You might ask yourself how many of these proposed reforms could be implemented in the next two decades, assuming that all or most are desirable. Instead of seeking changes on many fronts, should educators concentrate their efforts on a few major reforms until they become firmly established? If you think this approach is desirable, which two or three of the following predicted changes would you recommend for concerted effort? Also,

From *Phi Delta Kappan*, 1971, 52, 596–598. Reprinted by permission of the authors and Phi Delta Kappa.

could you defend your choices from what you know about how learning occurs and the factors that influence it?

Man has always had a keen interest in his future. In the present climate of speculation, how does the U.S. educator perceive our changing schools in the interval between 1975 and 2000? *What* does he believe may happen, *when* it is likely, and does he *like* what he anticipates? What changes seem likely to come about easily, and where will the schools resist change most vigorously?

In an effort to obtain thoughtful conjectures about developments just over the horizon, the authors invited 570 persons[1] to react to 41 possible educational futures, all of them discussed in more than 400 books and articles dealing with alternatives for the next 30 years. Of the respondents, 58% answered 205 queries which dealt with (1) curriculum and instruction, (2) new organizational patterns and pupil policies, (3) economic and political influences, (4) teacher preparation and status, (5) the school's relationships to society, and (6) biological intervention and mediation tactics such as the use of drugs to increase children's teachability.

The responses reveal the status and direction of educators' thinking. They merit added consideration because of the "self-fulfilling prophecy" phenomenon, which suggests that the beliefs of our sample, if widely held, could perceptibly influence future developments in education. A few of the questions in all six areas have been selected for discussion here.

CURRICULUM AND INSTRUCTION

MULTIMEDIA. Almost all of the educators (93%) anticipate that a mix of learning resources will replace the traditional monopoly that the textbook has enjoyed as a mainstay of instruction. Virtually everyone (96%) agrees that a multimedia approach is desirable, that such approaches would be fairly easy to bring about, and that they will become prevalent between 1975 and 1985.

STUDENT TUTORS. The use of student tutors (for example, 11-year-olds working with six-years-olds in reading) will be commonplace if not a standard procedure by the early 1980's, in the opinion of almost three-quarters of the survey participants.* Four out of five feel the idea is excellent, and two-thirds think it woud be easy to start such programs.

A NEW ENGLISH ALPHABET. The predictions and enthusiasm of a few linguists notwithstanding, most respondents are pessimistic about the pros-

* *Student tutoring is discussed by Herbert Thelen in Section 12.*

pects for a phonetic alphabet of approximately 45 letters, which more nearly coincides with the number of phonemes (significant speech sound units) in English. While three out of four concede the virtue of such a change, over half think it is unlikely to be adopted and assign a low priority to the task.

INCREASED TIME FOR THE EXPRESSIVE ARTS. Teachers of drama, art, and music will be cheered to know that over half of their fellow educators participating in the survey are convinced that work in the expressive arts will double its present time allotment in the curriculum within 10 to 15 years. Seventy-five percent also believe the 100% increase is desirable.

CONTROVERSIAL ISSUES. An overwhelming 91% of the educators feel that, before 1980, instruction in the social studies will come to grips with controversial topics (activist movements, discrimination, and so on), and over 90% think that it is high time to give top priority to the forthright study of these social issues. Opinion is split as to how much public resistance there might be to controversial content and issues on which the schools took a stand.

With reference to sex education, and despite the fact that 60% feel it would be difficult, 89% of the educators believe that comprehensive study of human sexuality in all its aspects should begin in the primary years. Four-fifths urge that the introduction of sex education programs receive high priority.

ORGANIZATION AND PUPIL POLICIES

A 12-MONTH-YEAR AND PERSONALIZED PROGRAMS. The organization of U.S. education and many of its long-familiar policies are due to change sharply and rapidly if the views of professors, teachers, and administrators are accurate. No later than the mid-Eighties, 84% believe, our schools will be open for 12 months and students' programs will be so personalized that the individual can leave school for three months each year, choosing both the time and the length of vacations. Educators concede, however, that the public will be reluctant to accept such flexibility. Noncompetitive "personalized progress records" are endorsed,* but a strong minority (38%) foresee that grades will be used to report pupil achievement for another 10 to 15 years.

EARLY CHILDHOOD EDUCATION. Respondents were optimistic when asked whether school services would extend downward to enroll three-year-olds and to provide health services for babies no later than at age 2. Three-

---

* *Issues about grading are discussed in Section 16.*

quarters of the replies favor such early childhood programs. Some 73% further urge that high priority be assigned to early childhood education and estimate that programs for the youngest will be a universal reality by around 1985. A large majority of the sample is convinced that the British infant schools will influence practice, and they believe this is a good thing.*

REVISION OF COMPULSORY ATTENDANCE LAWS. Opinions of the survey population are almost evenly divided on whether compulsory attendance laws will be relaxed, although 63% favor the idea if exit from and reentry into school can be made more socially acceptable, personal, and flexible. Attendance policies will be hard to change, 60% said, although most feel that they ought to be eased to permit students to leave school sooner to enter the world of work.

FUNDING AND FINANCIAL POLICIES

GOVERNMENTAL AGENCIES. The respondents forecast (62%) and endorsed (88%) rapid consolidation of federal education programs. Strong and united professional action is required to accomplish this goal, and 82 out of 100 urge a high priority for coordinated action by school officials. Even so, 10% of the respondents conjecture that it will be the year 2000 before cooperation among governmental agencies replaces duplication and competition. One extreme cynic cast a write-in vote for 2500 A.D. as the probable year of consolidation for overlapping agencies.

DIFFERENTIATED STAFFING. Despite heated opinions on differentiated staffing, 74% of the educators favor differentiation with teacher-pupil ratios, but with paraprofessionals and educational technology utilized to decrease teacher-pupil *contact hours*. This is viewed as a means of increasing productivity, efficiency, and wages. Another large group, 66%, indicate that differentiated staffing probably will be accepted, though not without a struggle. If the respondents' hunches prove accurate, a substantial degree of differentiation will be attained within the decade.

PERFORMANCE CONTRACTING. The average respondent is opposed to the idea of corporation management of school systems, but feels there is an even chance it will be more widely adopted.† Estimates on when business may engage in increased school management responsibilities vary somewhat, but four out of five educators feel it could occur quickly. Ten percent believe that the purchase of instruction from corporations will be far more widespread as soon as four years from now.

* *The British infant schools led to the open classroom movement, described in Section 10.*
† *Performance contracting is discussed in Section 15.*

VOUCHERS FOR TUITION PAYMENTS. Little enthusiasm is indicated for a voucher system. Seventy-one percent of the sample feel that such a plan will not get off the ground, and 67% condemn the idea. If vouchers ever are distributed, fewer than 15% see them coming into general use before 1985.

SALARY AND TEACHER PERFORMANCE. The antipathy toward merit rating which teachers have expressed for many years apparently has transferred to salary schedules based on teaching performance. Nearly 54% feel that performance-based wages and increments are not likely in the future. However, two-thirds of the replies acknowledged the desirability of basing salaries on competence.[2]

Teacher Preparation and Status

TEACHER EDUCATION AND CERTIFICATION. Major changes in the preparation and licensing of teachers are widely accepted by those polled. For example, 92% feel that teacher education will be drastically modified to prepare pre-service students to work in teams or partnerships, to individualize instruction, to make use of educational technology, and to encourage greater pupil participation in the process of education. Routine use of sensitivity training in teacher education is foreseen by 64% of the respondents. Virtually all respondents (98%) favor major changes. There is also a pronounced feeling (82%) that alternatives to state-controlled teacher licensing are desirable, that they will be instituted (73%), and that they will be widely accepted by 1980 or 1985.

A strong current of opinion suggests that ways of obtaining teaching certificates should be liberalized (67% said "yes") and that few if any of the new avenues should involve merely adding courses in professional education. Major changes are presumably to be inaugurated in the immediate future and, for the most part, completed in 10 to 15 years.

THE SELF-CONTAINED CLASSROOM. "One teacher–one group" instruction is on the way out, according to 69% of the respondents predicting the shape of the future. Another larger group (75%) apparently say "good riddance" to this venerable institution.

In place of the self-contained classroom, 67% of the educators see (and 79% cheerfully accept) some form of "flexible teaching partnerships." Presumably, such partnerships would be an extension of the team concept, but would involve greater "horizontal" and "vertical" deployment of a differentiated staff; that is, a given teacher would work "vertically with more children of different ages and "horizontally" in more varied capacities.*

* More radical proposals are offered by Allen Graubard and by Ivan Illich in Section 11.

THE SCHOOL AND SOCIETY

SOCIETAL SERVICES. The school is viewed as an agency responsive to social change by most of the participants. Judging by majority opinions of social engineering, we can anticipate (1) psychiatric treatment without cost to students (76% said "yes," 87% "desirable");[3] (2) massive adult education and vocational retraining programs (92% said "yes," 95% "desirable"); and (3) school programs designed to help adults adjust to increased leisure and longer periods of retirement (85% said "yes," 94% "desirable").

MANDATORY FOSTER HOMES. Respondents were asked whether they thought that children, before age three, might be placed in foster homes or kibbutz-type boarding schools to protect them from a damaging home environment. Opinions are about evenly divided on whether this is a good or bad policy, but the likelihood of such a development in the U.S. is rejected by over 70%.

INTERVENTION AND MEDIATION

One of the more controversial items among the 41 in the educational futures instrument is whether or not, in the years ahead, schools should and will use chemical compounds to improve the mood, memory, power of concentration, and possibly the general intelligence of the learner.* Most of the respondents feel that what is measured as intelligence can be increased substantially. Ninety percent of the survey participants consider it appropriate to try to increase the IQ through such mediation tactics as enriched environment in early childhood, and 82% also express confidence that measurable intelligence will be increased by or before 1990.

However, the use of drugs to increase "teachability" was labeled as both unlikely (57% say it will not occur on a widespread scale) and a bad practice to boot. Fifty-six percent rejected the idea of using stimulants, tranquilizers, or antidepressants.

"INTERVENTION" IN EARLY CHILDHOOD. The presumed importance of education under school auspices in the learner's early years is supported by survey respondents. Over 70% feel that "preventive and corrective intervention" before age six might, within the next 25 years, make the annual per-pupil expenditures for the early-childhood group even higher than per-student costs at the university level.

CONCLUSION

Our small sample — directly or by implication — expresses great confidence in the influence of and financial support for education between 1975

---

* Edward Sullivan discusses this possibility (Section 11).

and 2000. The respondents expect and desire substantial educational changes; their dissatisfaction with the status quo comes through clearly.* If the 333 respondents who struggled patiently through the survey instrument represent U.S. educators as a whole, then the coming decade should attain levels of humaneness and educational zest and venturesomeness reminiscent of the 1930's, the heyday of the progressive education movement.

EXERCISE

1. Who were the subjects of Shane and Nelson's survey, and how did they select the educational futures to which the subjects reacted? (p. 288)

2. According to the survey, what four changes in curriculum and instruction are most likely to occur in the coming decades? (pp. 288–289)

3. According to the survey, how difficult will it be to institute personalized instructional programs and to revise compulsory attendance laws? (pp. 289–290)

4. How did the educators who were surveyed feel about basing teacher salaries on evaluations of their teaching performance? (p. 291)

5. According to the survey, what are the major anticipated changes in the role of the teacher? (p. 291)

6. How did the surveyed educators react to the ideas of free psychiatric care for students, mandatory foster homes, and using drugs to enhance learning? (p. 292)

* If the respondents desire change greatly, why has there been so little of it?

The Schools versus Education

John I. Goodlad

In the preceding selection Harold Shane and Owen Nelson predicted exciting new developments in store for education in the next two decades. However, John Goodlad has some sobering reflections about the possibilities for school reform. He reports on a series of visits which his colleagues and he made to kindergartens and primary schools to determine the prevalence of such educational innovations as individualized instruction, the inquiry method, multimedia learning tools, and team teaching. Unfortunately, his observations indicate that these innovations have not worked their way into the schools. Instead, Goodlad found that the schools were "mired in tradition, insensitive to pressing social problems, and inadequate to the demands of learning." Goodlad suggests several reasons for this resistance to change: lack of systematic updating of teacher skills, lack of support from school administrators and the community, and lack of exemplary models of innovation. After reading Goodlad's paper, you might consider whether educators should concern themselves more about the process of bringing educational change and less with the specific changes that might be introduced? (If you reread the selection by Shane and Nelson, for example, you will find that they mostly ignore the problem of how educational change can be brought about.)

The years from 1957 to 1967 constituted the Education Decade for the United States. It began with Sputnik and the charge to education to win the cold war; it ended with a hot war and the growing realization that education is a long-term answer to mankind's problems and must not be confused with short-term social engineering. The danger now is that we are becoming disillusioned with education, without realizing that we are only beginning to try it.

During the Education Decade, the school years were extended upward and downward, the school curriculum was revised from top to bottom, the Elementary and Secondary Education Act of 1965 brought the federal government into education as never before, the schools became both a focal point for social protest and a vehicle for social reform, and schooling joined politics and world affairs as leading topics of social discourse. "Innovation" and "revolution" were used interchangeably in discussing the changes taking place in the schools.*

But the education scene today remains confusing. Put on one pair of glasses and the schools appear to be moving posthaste toward becoming centers of intense, exciting learning, marked by concern for the individual. Put on another, and they appear to be mired in tradition, insensitive to pressing social problems, and inadequate to the demands of learning.

Where are the schools today? How widespread have been the changes during the decade since Sputnik? What kind of changes are needed in the 1970's, and what lies ahead for the balance of the century?

* *This act provided funds to train educational researchers, sponsor local innovation in the schools, purchase teaching aids, and to perform other activities designed to upgrade education.*

While conducting studies of new approaches to school curricula during the early 1960's, I visited many schools and classrooms. Although the Education Decade was well underway, the reforms it espoused were not conspicuously present. Was the sample of schools visited inadequate, or were proposed changes losing their momentum before reaching their target? Several colleagues joined me in an effort to probe more deeply as we visited some 260 kindergarten through third-grade classrooms in 100 schools clustered in or around the major cities of thirteen states.

If the most frequently discussed and recommended educational practices of the Education Decade were already implemented, what would constitute a checklist of expectations? The following would seem reasonable. First, teaching would be characterized by efforts to determine where the student is at the *outset* of instruction, to diagnose his attainments and problems, and to base subsequent instruction on the results of this diagnosis. Second, learning would be directed toward "learning how to learn," toward self-sustaining inquiry rather than the memorization and regurgitation of facts. Third, this inquiry would carry the student out of confining classrooms and into direct observation of physical and human phenomena. Fourth, classrooms would be characterized by a wide variety of learning materials — records, tapes, models, programed materials, film strips, pamphlets, and television — and would not be dominated by textbooks. Fifth, attention to and concern for the individual and individual differences would show through clearly in assignments, class discussions, use of materials, grouping practices, and evaluation. Sixth, teachers would understand and use such learning principles as reinforcement, motivation, and transfer of training. Seventh, visitors would see vigorous, often heated, small and large group discussions, with the teacher in the background rather than the forefront. Eighth, one would find rather flexible school environments — marked by little attention to grade levels — and extensive use of team teaching activities involving groups of teachers, older pupils, parents, and other persons in the teaching-learning process. And, certainly, it would be reasonable to expect to find innovative ways of dealing with special educational problems such as those presented by environmentally handicapped children.*

Although these expectations seemed reasonable at the outset of our visits to schools, they did not constitute an accurate description of what we found. We were unable to discern much attention to pupil needs, attainments, or problems as a basis for beginning instruction, nor widespread provision for individual opportunities to learn. Most classes were taught as a group, covering essentially the same ground for all students at approximately the same rate of speed. Teaching was predominantly telling and questioning by the teacher, with children responding one by one or occasionally in chorus. In all of this, the textbook was the most highly

* *Do you concur with Goodlad's list of recommended educational practices?*

visible instrument of learning and teaching. If records, tapes, films, film strips, supplementary materials, and other aids to learning were in the schools we visited, we rarely saw them. When small groups of students worked together, the activities engaged in by each group member were similar, and bore the mark of the teacher's assignment and expectations. Rarely did we find small groups intensely in pursuit of knowledge; rarely did we find individual pupils at work in self-sustaining inquiry. Popular innovations of the decade — non-grading, team teaching, "discovery" learning, and programed instruction — were talked about by teachers and principals alike but were rarely in evidence.

On a more general and impressionistic level, teachers and students did not appear to be intensely involved in their work. Only occasionally did we encounter a classroom aura of excitement, anticipation, and spontaneity; when we did, it was almost invariably a kindergarten class. This is not to say that classroom inhabitants were uninvolved but rather to suggest that it may be erroneous to assume that teaching and learning in the schools, more than other human enterprises, are characterized by excitement and enthusiasm. On the positive side, however, the teachers we observed were warm and supportive, and not sadistic as some polemicists have pictured them to be.

From the data, we were unable to differentiate practices in schools enrolling a high proportion of disadvantaged or minority group children from practices in other schools. Our descriptions of classrooms enrolling predominantly Mexican-American children, for example, were not distinguishable from our descriptions in general. Nor were there marked differences in our respective descriptions of classrooms in the inner city, on the fringe of the urban environment, and in suburbia.*

It is dangerous to generalize about something as large, complex, and presumably diverse as schooling in the United States, or even about the first four years of it. As far as our sample of schools is concerned, however, we are forced to conclude that much of the so-called educational reform movement has been blunted on the classroom door.

Yet, the responsibility for this situation does not rest entirely with schoolteachers and principals. The elementary schools were anything but the "palaces" of an affluent society. In fact, they looked more like the artifacts of a society that did not really care about its schools, a society that expressed its disregard by creating schools less suited to human habitation than its prisons. These artifacts effect the strange notion that learning proceeds best in groups of thirty, that teachers are not to converse with each other, that learning should be conducted under rather uncomfortable

---

* *It is a popular belief, though, that inner-city children receive markedly different and inferior instruction compared to suburban children.*

circumstances, and that schools proceed best with their tasks when there is little or no traffic with the outside world.

We had hoped to conduct sustained interviews with the teachers we observed, but there were rarely quiet, attractive places to confer. We held our interviews on the run, or, more favorably, when we were able to have breakfast or dinner together. These teachers wanted to talk about education: what "good" things we had observed elsewhere; what we thought about current innovations; whether we had any suggestions for improving the teaching we had just observed; and on and on. Interestingly, those with whom we talked had a rather favorable image of what they were doing in the classroom; they thought they were individualizing instruction, teaching inductively, and encouraging self-propelled learning. Neither principals nor teachers were able to articulate clearly just what they thought to be most important for their schools to accomplish. And neither group was very clear on changes that should be effected in the near future.

Both our observations alone and those with teachers lead to several disquieting conclusions. Public schooling probably is the only large-scale enterprise in this country that does not provide for systematic updating of the skills and abilities of its employees and for payment of the costs involved. Teachers are on their own as far as their in-service education is concerned, in an environment designed for "telling" others, yet one that is grossly ill-suited to intellectual pursuits with peers. Teachers, we presume, will readily cast aside their old, inappropriate ways and acquire markedly different ones through some processes of osmosis.

Sixteen or more years of schooling should educate teachers and others for self-renewal and this frequently is the case. But general failure to do so for large numbers of people constitutes the greatest failure of our educational system. In the colleges as well as in the lower schools, the processes and fruits of human experience are so cut up in the curriculum and so obfuscated by detail that cohesiveness, relationships, and relevance are obscured.

Another aspect of our educational malaise is that an enormous amount of energy goes into merely maintaining the system. Studies have shown that administrators favor teachers who maintain orderly classrooms, keep accurate records, and maintain stable relations with parents and the community. Other studies reveal that most managers in the educational system, such as principals and supervisors, tend to be recruited from among teachers who demonstrate these orderly qualities. Because they are rewarded for maintaining the system, administrators are not likely either to challenge it or to reward subordinates who do.

Just as teachers and principals appear to be uncertain as to what their schools are for, the communities they serve provide no clear sense of direction or guidelines. There is evidence to suggest that parents are somewhat more favorably disposed toward educational change than are teachers or school administrators, but legions of educators who push at the forefront of innovative practice stand ready to show their community-inflicted scars. Many parents are more interested in changes in the abstract or for someone else than in changes involving their own children. Social change is a formidable enterprise under the best of circumstances; schooling too often presents only the worst of circumstances, with resistance being built into both the setting and the internal structure.

It should come as no surprise, then, that comprehensive experiments in schooling are the rarest of all educational phenomena. Small wonder that teachers practice so little individualizing instruction, inductive teaching, non-grading, team teaching, or other recently recommended practices. They have not seen them. If teachers are to change, they must see models of what they are to change to; they must practice under guidance the new behaviors called for in the exemplary models.* If teachers are to change, the occupation itself must have built into it the necessary provisions for self-renewal. The creation of these conditions is an important agenda item for the decade ahead.

Seers of bygone decades occasionally asked whether our schools had outlived their usefulness — and we laughed. The question is no longer funny. The schools are conspicuously ill-suited to the needs of at least 30 per cent of their present clientele: the large numbers of children from minority groups who live in harsh environments; the tens of thousands who suffer from crippling mental, physical, and emotional handicaps; and a few whose rare gifts separate them sharply from their peers. But the lack of "fit" between school and client extends into other realms until one is forced to ask whether our educational system serves even 50 per cent of its clientele in reasonably satisfying ways. Learning disabilities evidenced in the primary grades often go undiagnosed, persisting throughout life and seriously limiting human relations participation. Talents in music, art, and creative writing lie largely outside the school's scope and are usually brought to fruition in the home where parents can afford to, or not at all where parents cannot. The human models in these fields, so necessary to refinement of childhood talent, are inaccessible to the school because of teacher certification restrictions or sheer failure to recognize their powerful role in educating the young.

It is also questionable whether those students who appear to be adjusting well are acquiring desirable traits and repressing undesirable ones. Success in school seems to assure further success in school; good grades predict good grades. But academic success neither assures nor predicts good work

* For a discussion of the role of modeling in learning, read the selection by Roger Brown in Section 1.

habits, good citizenship, happiness, compassion, or other human virtues.*
The incidences of drop-outs, non-promotion, alienation, and minimal
learning reinforce our apprehension that schools have become or are fast
becoming obsolete. They appear to have been designed for a different
culture, a different conception of learning and teaching, and a different
clientele.

The task of rehabilitating the schools, then, is indeed formidable. We
dare not ask whether we *should* rehabilitate our schools, although this is a
good question. Impotent and irrelevant though much schooling may be,
the schools are at present the only educational institution deliberately
created and maintained for inculcating something of man's heritage, for
developing the basic tools of literacy, and for instilling some powers of
rational thought and criticism. Although our civilization abounds in educational institutions and media, from scuba-diving school to television, none
is centrally committed to this basic, cultural role. By seeking to rehabilitate
the *educational* role of the school, rather than its various ancillary functions (baby-sitting, social stratification, economic investment, etc.), perhaps we will keep the meaning of education before us, experiment with
improved means, and ultimately transfer the process to new and better
institutions should the schools fail us and we them.† ...

EXERCISE

1. Why does Goodlad describe the educational scene today as
   "confusing"? (p. 294)

2. What were the eight recommended educational practices of
   Goodlad's checklist? (p. 295)

3. According to Goodlad, how do classroom practices vary from
   one type of school to another, inner-city versus suburb or
   minority-dominated versus white? (p. 296)

4. What are three reasons Goodlad feels schools have failed to
   adopt educational innovations? (pp. 297–298)

5. Why does Goodlad believe the schools are worth saving by rehabilitation? (p. 299)

* How does David Cohen (Section 5) support this statement?
† Goodlad appears to think that schools are worth "rehabilitating." Do you agree?
Compare with Illich (Section 11), who believes that schools are an outmoded
institution.

Section Ten

IMPROVING
CLASSROOM INSTRUCTION

Introduction

One way to try to improve learning is to maintain the traditional school structure, but change what happens within the classroom. (In the next section, we will consider how learning can be improved by changing the school structure.) For example, the information and skills to be learned in the classroom can be changed and updated, which often happens as new technology, new scientific discoveries, and new social situations make existing information and skills obsolete. The materials used to teach can also change. At one time, a slate and pencil were the major tools of learning. Then books became the primary learning tool. Now teaching machines and computers are being introduced into some classrooms. Also, the way time is spent in the classroom can be the source of innovation. Fewer lectures and more small group discussions and independent study sessions are part of the current revisions in using learning time.

The major goals of all these changes in the school classroom are to increase the amount learned by the student and to make his learning experiences more pleasant and rewarding for him. The innovations described in this section represent two views about how these goals are best accomplished.

On one hand, some educators advocate a highly structured curriculum in which the learning objectives and materials have been predetermined by the curriculum developer or teacher. Skills and knowledge are broken down into small, precise units of learning. These units are formed into a sequence of learning steps that lead the student from easy to complex ideas and skills. This type of learning analysis has been recommended by Robert Gagné (Section 1), among others. Also, reinforcement theories developed by Skinner and other behaviorists (see Skinner, Section 1; Bushell, this section) have been used to direct and motivate the student in this type of classroom teaching structure. Some innovations described in this section — programmed instruction, computer-assisted instruction, and token economies — are examples of highly structured systems built on these teaching principles.

In contrast to these carefully programmed forms of instruction is improving classroom learning by stressing freedom of individual choice and participation within a free-moving group process. Commonly referred to as the "open classroom," this approach tries to be exactly that. The learning setting, what is learned, the order in which it is learned, and what is used to learn are "open," that is, not predetermined by the teacher or curriculum developer. The student plays a strong role in determining how and what he will learn. This is a very recent innovation in American schools, although it harks back to the progressive education movement of the 1930's and reflects the influence of the British infant schools which have become popular in England during the last decade. Rathbone discusses the basic features of an open classroom program, emphasizing its purported advantages and disadvantages.

Actually, improving learning for students may not be an either-or situation. The selections included in Section 2 show that the schools can pursue *many* learning goals. Some types of learning may occur best by using programmed instruction; other types can only be accomplished within an open classroom. Also, some students may perform better in a programmed learning environment, others in an open program. In his discussion of Skinnerian theory and open education, Madden suggests that some aspects of each approach may be needed to improve education.

As you read the following articles which describe the basic characteristics of programmed and open education, and their respective pros and cons, decide where you stand.

Programmed Instruction

Pro   The student is too naive to know what he should learn or how he should learn it. These decisions must be made by experts in the fields of psychology and curriculum, who develop programmed sequences of instruction.

Con   Even the youngest student will learn better if he helps to decide what and how he will learn, which is why the open classroom is more effective than programmed instruction.

Programmed Instruction in the Schools: An Application of Programming Principles in Individually Prescribed Instruction

C. M. Lindvall and J. O. Bolvin

A major attempt to introduce the principles of programmed instruction into a regular school program is the system of Individually Prescribed Instruction (IPI). This program was developed jointly by the University of Pittsburgh Learning Research and Development Center and by Research for Better Schools, an educational laboratory. Both these agencies were created by special national legislation. Their goal is to reduce the gap between the findings of educational research and their application in the schools. The learning materials in the IPI program are arranged so that an individual student goes through a sequence of worksheet exercises that increase progressively in the difficulty of the knowledge to be learned and the tasks to be performed. Little or no outside assistance is needed to complete the exercises. Learning prescriptions are prepared that tell the student what exercises he is to study. Tests are given before, after, and during the learning sequence to determine what the student needs to learn and whether he is learning it. Information about how well he did on a particular test is given to the student almost immediately. He does not move ahead until a particular skill is mastered. He works at his own rate. He generally meets with the teacher only when he needs special help. Lindvall and Bolvin present the principles of educational psychology on which IPI was built. The basic characteristics of the program remain the same even after nine years of adaptation and testing. As you read the description of IPI, decide whether an entire education program could and should be based upon IPI.

Adapted from C. M. Lindvall and J. O. Bolvin, "Programed Instruction in the Schools: An Application of Programing Principles in Individually Prescribed Instruction" in H. G. Richey (ed.), *Programed Instruction*. Sixty-sixth Yearbook of the National Society for the Study of Education, Part II, Chicago: University of Chicago Press, 1967, pp. 217–254. Adapted with permission of the National Society for the Study of Education.

An Overview of Individually Prescribed Instruction: Theoretical Bases and Operational Procedures

One of the basic assumptions underlying the development of Individually Prescribed Instruction is the idea that learning is something that is ultimately personal and individual. Learning may take place within a social context, and many types of instruction are traditionally carried out with groups of students. But it is the individual who learns, not the group. This, in turn, dictates that instructional plans should be prepared for the individual, not for the group. Instruction is conventionally planned as though the classroom group were an organic unit and as though this unit were doing the learning. Obviously, if learning is individual, this type of planning cannot be of maximum effectiveness. Furthermore, ability grouping or other attempts to make sub-groups within the classroom which are more homogeneous than the total group will not really solve the problem. Learning takes place only on an individual basis; consequently instruction must be individualized.

Teaching machines and programed textbooks have exemplified a useful approach to the individualization of instruction. They have shown that if conditions are arranged so that a pupil can work through a sequence of learning experiences that are carefully graded in terms of increasing difficulty, each pupil can progress at his own individual pace and with little or no outside assistance to acquire relatively complex skills and types of knowledge. A second assumption of the IPI project is that the same type of planning and "programing" that is employed with a programed textbook can be used to develop a more extensive program extending over grade lines and covering, at least, all of the elementary school years and involving a much greater variety in types of learning experiences than can be presented in a textbook. . . .

The application of some of the basic ideas of programed instruction to the development of a total school program results in a new concept of what a school is. Under this concept a school is not a place where pupils "attend classes." Instead, it is a place where a pupil works through a sequence of learning experiences at a pace and in a way suited to his interests and abilities. The function of the school is to provide him with this type of opportunity, to identify meaningful and effective sequences and to arrange for materials and experiences that permit each pupil to progress through such sequences.* Such a plan will not involve artificial barriers which force the pupil to keep pace with a class or a group or to confine

* Albert Taylor criticizes programed instruction later in this section. What concerns would he have about this function of the school?

his study to what is typically covered at a given grade level. Conditions should be such that, for example, an extremely bright first-grade pupil might master all of the skills and content that are traditionally taught during the first three or four years of school. On the other hand, a slow student might take two or three years to acquire the abilities that the "average" child masters in one year.

Still another assumption basic to the planning of the IPI procedure was the idea that if principles of programing were applied, the desired flexibility in rates of pupil progress would not involve any plan for special promotions, for "retentions," or for any type of complex grouping or regrouping. If pupils are progressing individually, how they are grouped, classified, or housed is not of major concern....

The Individually Prescribed Instruction (IPI) program was first put into operation in September 1964 in the Oakleaf Elementary School in the Baldwin-Whitehall School District. This school has one class or section at each grade level, K through 6, and the IPI procedure has been used with instruction in reading, arithmetic, and science. In the other elementary school subjects, instruction is carried out under rather traditional methods.

Largely for purposes of administrative convenience, when pupils are studying one of the subjects with which IPI is used, there is some grouping of classes. The kindergarten and grades one and two work together in one study area, grades three and four constitute another group, and five and six still another. This grouping procedure is followed at Oakleaf in order to best utilize available space, the teaching staff, and clerical assistance. During the first year in which the program was in operation, only two groups were used, kindergarten through three, and four through six. It is felt, however, that the procedure could also be carried out with equal effectiveness under almost any type of grouping arrangement.

While studying under IPI, students work mainly in a large study area seating 50 to 80 pupils, formed by opening a folding door between two standard size classrooms. Student study is largely independent. The visitor to a study area will see pupils working at desks or other student stations writing on exercise sheets, reading, working problems, listening to recordings, or carrying out simple science experiments under directions provided through a tape playback device. Teachers will be moving about the room to provide help as it may be needed. This help may be given to the pupil right at his desk, or he may be taken to a side room for more extensive individual instruction. Also present in the study area will be one to three teacher aides who are helping to score papers and distribute materials. When a student completes a given exercise, it will be scored either by one of these aides or by the pupil himself so that he will know how well he is doing. At frequent intervals the material with which he is working will include a "curriculum-embedded test," a brief quiz covering the material taught by a limited number of exercises. Scores on these tests are essential aids to the monitoring of pupil progress. As the pupil moves along through the curriculum, his progress is guided by a series of "prescriptions," each of which indicates what materials he is to study next. These prescriptions are developed regularly either outside the classroom or in pupil-teacher conferences. In prescription writing account is taken of where the student is in the sequence, how well he has done on the lesson exercises, his scores on the curriculum-embedded tests, and any other information that the teacher may have available. Guided by the prescription, the pupil works then on lesson materials primarily of a self-study type, demanding only occasional help from the teacher. He is thus able to proceed through the instructional sequence largely independently, at a pace suited to his abilities, and using materials and modes of instruction selected to meet his needs.

How is this type of instructional situation achieved? What are the essential elements in this type of "programing" for individualized instruction? Having discussed in general terms the nature and operations of Individually Prescribed Instruction, let us examine in some detail the specific elements involved in developing such a program. . . .

Steps in the Development of Individually Prescribed Instruction

1. *The objectives to be achieved must be spelled out in terms of desired pupil behaviors.* In typical classroom situations, the details of what is to be taught are frequently covered by what is included in the textbook, workbook, or similar materials. The teacher merely has to know that "these are the materials that are to be covered this week." Many of the specifics regarding what is to be covered are kept in the mind of the teacher and are presented only as the lesson is actually being taught. This system may be somewhat effective where the method of instruction employed is that of teacher presentation to some total classroom group. However, it is not sufficient if individualized instruction is to be achieved. Such instruction requires the extensive use of self-teaching materials — materials with which the student may work quite independently of teacher help. The first prerequisite to the development or identification of materials of this type is to know exactly what it is desired that the pupil should learn.* It is not enough that the specifics of what is to be learned are clearly formulated in the mind of the teacher. If IPI is to function effectively, it must be possible to determine whether or not the instructional materials and procedures do, in themselves, enable the pupil to achieve the desired mastery. To determine this it is necessary to know exactly what the pupil is ex-

---

* Should the student participate in this decision? If yes, how?

pected to be able to do after he has had this learning experience. It requires the definition of instructional objectives in terms of specific pupil behaviors. . . .

Some examples of specific objectives together with associated evaluation procedures are the following, which are taken from units in counting or numeration and in place value.*

> Objective: Supplies the number which is one more, one less, or in between two given numbers (to 200).
> Suggested evaluation: "Circle the number which is one less than 97."   99   94   96   98
> Objective: Completes patterns for skip counting by 3's and 4's from any starting point.
> Suggested Evaluation: "Complete the Pattern."
> 360, 363, _____, _____, _____, 375, _____.
> Objective: Identifies the place value of the units, tens, hundreds, and thousands digit in numbers to 1000.
> Suggested Evaluation: "4625 means _____ thousands, _____ hundreds, _____ tens, and _____ ones." . . .

2. *To the extent possible, instructional objectives should be ordered in a sequence which makes for effective pupil progression with a minimum number of gaps or difficult steps and with little overlap or unnecessary repetition.* An essential characteristic of an effective instructional program is that it permits pupils to make progress in achieving mastery of the desired skills and content. This progress probably will take place in the most desirable manner if the steps represented by the specific objectives are arranged so that each step helps the pupil to approach the subsequent step.† In programed instruction this has frequently been described as the principle of "small steps." . . .

In developing an instructional sequence an ideal condition would be achieved if, for example, all of the objectives in elementary school arithmetic could be ordered in one long chain of prerequisite abilities running from the very first grade up to the most complex ability that could conceivably be mastered by the brightest sixth-year pupil. In planning the IPI program this was quickly recognized as an impossibility. Several types of mathematical abilities were perceived, each of which can be organized in the form of a linear hierarchy of objectives, each of which, however, is somewhat independent of the other. For example, it appears necessary that skills in addition be learned in some sequential order leading from the simple to the complex. Rather arbitrary decisions, however, may be made as to when the teaching of subtraction skills should be permitted

---

* *Compare with the objectives of open education (Rathbone, this section).*
† *Gagné's analysis of the learning process (Section 1) would support this procedure.*

to interrupt the pupil's progress in addition. For this reason the sequencing of objectives in arithmetic was done separately within each such area as numeration, place value, addition, subtraction, multiplication, division, combination of processes, measurement, etc. Furthermore, to provide break-points in each of these sequences, at which points a student could move from one area to another, each sequence was divided into units, each unit being made up of a limited number of objectives. These levels were labeled with letters A, B, C, and so on, and each can be thought of as somewhat comparable to a grade level.... When a pupil begins study in a unit he typically works in that unit until he can exhibit mastery of all of the objectives contained within it. However, the exact order in which he moves from one unit to another can be varied somewhat from pupil to pupil, depending upon a diagnosis of each pupil's needs and the capabilities which he can demonstrate after completing a unit....

3. *If pupils are to work through a curriculum on an individual basis, it is essential that instructional materials be such that pupils can learn from them without constant help from a teacher and can make steady progress in the mastery of the defined objectives.* In conventional teacher-directed instruction it is possible to use textbook and workbook materials with which it is necessary for the teacher to explain procedures and operations before the pupil is prepared to profit from his own reading or study. However, under individualized instruction, where each pupil may be at a different point in the lesson materials, this necessity for extensive teacher help would require the employment of many additional teachers.* For this reason, it is essential that lesson materials be largely self-instructional. The identification and production of materials of this type was the next step in the development of the IPI project, following the defining and sequencing of objectives....

A major disappointment in the identification of materials for the IPI project has been the inability to locate published programed textbooks which can be utilized to teach the defined objectives. In most cases those that are available do not present topics in the desired sequence nor teach exactly what is desired....

In view of the present lack of availability of program texts for use in the IPI project, except with a limited number of units, a need has developed for making other types of materials as self-instructional as possible. This has meant that much effort has been devoted to developing instruction in printed form or perhaps on a sound recording which will be sufficient to enable the student to work on his own with lesson sheets or other types of instructional activities. The attempt to do this has been very revealing in showing the inadequacies of the instructions which accompany many workbook exercises. Such instructions are typically of some help if they are supplemented with a rather complete explanation by a

* *Why not use pupils as teachers? See Thelen's article, Section 12.*

teacher; they are, however, entirely insufficient if they represent the only information available to a pupil. Of course, the development of instructions which are of the needed clarity and completeness is a task involving frequent and continuing revisions on the basis of what is learned from pupil performance. . . .

4. *In individualized instruction care must be taken to find out what skills and knowledge each pupil possesses and to see that each one starts in the learning sequence at the point which is most appropriate for him.* From what has been described so far, the program for Individually Prescribed Instruction can be seen to consist of sequences of behavioral objectives together with the materials and activities which enable pupils to achieve these objectives. After these had been developed, the next step in planning the program was to devise procedures for determining where each pupil is to start his study within each sequence. When a student comes to any new instructional situation, whether it is beginning the first day of his first year in school or merely moving on to some new unit of study from the prerequisite unit, he brings to that situation certain knowledge and certain abilities that are not the same as those of his fellow pupils. If instruction is to be efficient and challenging, it must take into account these individual differences in entering behaviors, it must place the pupil at the point in the learning sequence which is appropriate for him, and it must accommodate his program to his needs. For this reason, essential tools in the IPI procedure are the batteries of placement tests that are used in each subject. . . .

The result of the placement testing is that it is possible to say of each pupil, "He should start at level D-Numeration, level D-Addition, level C-Subtraction . . ." and so on. That is, this process places the pupil at his proper level in the curriculum sequence in every subarea of reading, of arithmetic, and of science.

However, placing a pupil in the proper unit does not provide a complete answer as to the exact lesson materials with which he should start working. Within each unit there are a number of objectives, and although he is placed in a given unit, it may still be true that the student already has command of one or some limited number of these. To provide exact information concerning this, each pupil is given a pretest over the materials of a unit before he starts work in it. The pretest contains items covering every objective in the unit and hence provides information concerning the pupil's command of *each* objective. This information permits the teacher to determine what a student needs to study and where he should start work. On the basis of this information the teacher then develops a "prescription" which lists a certain limited number of instructional exercises on which the pupil is to start work.* . . .

---

* *Compare this procedure to the selection of learning materials in an open classroom (see Rathbone, this section).*

5. *For individualized instruction, conditions must be provided which permit each pupil to progress through a learning sequence at a pace determined by his own work habits and by his ability to master the designated instructional objectives.* Under Individually Prescribed Instruction, when a pupil has been given his own prescription and has secured the materials with which he is to work, he takes his place at his own desk or some other type of study station (language lab booth, science lab area, chair in the library, etc.) and begins his independent study. With the types of materials that are used, most students can proceed quite readily with little or no assistance from a teacher....

A typical student prescription contains enough lesson material for a day's work or to teach one objective, whichever would take the shorter period of time. It involves, as a final exercise for each objective, a "curriculum-embedded test." This test, which the pupil may look upon as only another worksheet, is somewhat of a "final examination" on that one objective and is used as the principal basis for determining whether or not the pupil has mastered the objective.*... If the student has done satisfactory work, his next prescription will probably call for him to go on to study the next objective in the unit. If he displays some weakness, the teacher will probably prescribe additional work on this particular objective....

When a pupil has covered all of the objectives within a given unit, he is given a unit posttest to determine the extent to which he has mastered and retained all of the content of the unit. If he does not show the prescribed mastery on this test, he will be given further work which will help him to make up his deficiencies. When he successfully completes the posttest, he is moved on to some new unit....

Through this procedure of carefully monitoring a pupil's progress through the use of a variety of evaluation devices and then developing prescriptions tailored to the individual, the IPI procedure attempts to keep each pupil working with materials that are a continual challenge to him but that are not too difficult to prevent him from making steady progress....

6. *If instruction is to be effective, it must make provisions for having the student actually carry out and practice the behavior which he is to learn.* This principle, whether expressed in the rather classic phrase that "we learn by doing" or in the programer's emphasis on "active responding," is of basic importance in identifying instructional activities for use in IPI. It alerts one to the fact that if pupils are to acquire some skill or ability, they must not merely read about it or be told about it. Rather, they must be provided with an activity that gives them actual practice in what they are to learn. The emphasis is not on "How can I tell him about this?" or "How can I explain this to him?" but rather on "How can I get the pupil

* *What criticism might Taylor (this section) make of this approach to testing?*

to do something that will give him actual experience and practice in this desired behavior?" ...

Identifying and developing curriculum materials in this way poses a real challenge to persons responsible for this. ...

7. *Learning is enhanced if students receive rather immediate feedback concerning the correctness of their efforts in attempting to approximate a desired behavior.* A basic principle in most types of programed instruction has been that of "immediate confirmation," letting the student see the correct response to a frame almost immediately after he has made his own response or, in some way, informing him concerning his success. This may be thought of as a major feature of programed instruction as contrasted with conventional classroom procedures. Too frequently under typical procedures a pupil works problems, answers questions, or takes a test and then must wait for a day or more to learn whether or not what he has done is correct. This can result in a lack of reinforcement for correct performances or conversely, in some tendency for the student to learn incorrect responses because of the delay in informing him of his error. In any case, this delay in feedback to the student probably makes for inefficient learning.

In the IPI procedure the attempt is made to keep the student rather continuously informed regarding his performance. His worksheets are scored, either by himself or by a teacher aide, almost immediately after completion. In this sense each worksheet is comparable to a "frame" or a short series of frames in a program to which a student makes an "active response" which in turn is given "immediate confirmation" when the paper is scored. ...

8. *The final criterion for judging any instructional sequence must be its effectiveness in producing changes in pupils, and feedback concerning pupil performance should be used in the continuing modification and improvement of materials and procedures.* Certainly another major contribution of the programed instruction movement to the improvement of educational curricula has been its emphases on the need for repeated trials of a program with students and the revision of the program on the basis of results from these trials. Most other procedures for curriculum development have called attention to the need for this type of trial, but programed instruction has outlined procedures for doing this as an essential step in the program development process.

With rather conventional teaching procedures, weaknesses in materials and techniques may be overlooked if these affect the performance of only a minority of students in a class, or compensations for such weaknesses may be made through supplementary explanations by the teacher. However, procedures involving individualization and self-instruction make such weaknesses glaringly apparent. If an individual pupil is halted in his progress through the curriculum because he cannot work a given exercise or because he repeatedly fails a particular test, something must be done about this situation. The curriculum developer is essentially forced to revise materials on the basis of this feedback from pupils.

The revision of materials and procedures on the basis of pupil performance has been an important feature of the IPI project. All instructional materials have been looked upon as being on trial until they have been tried out with some limited number of pupils. The person developing a lesson has asked himself the question, "Can pupils learn from this?" and then has used the lesson with some small sample of children to obtain an answer. After materials have been made an integral part of the program, they are still subjected to this type of scrutiny. In many cases the feedback on pupil performance has been rather informal in nature. Teachers have merely reported that "Pupils are having difficulty with this exercise." Frequently, such appraisals have been accompanied by suggestions as to what changes should be made, and it has been relatively simple to make rather immediate revisions. In other cases the necessary revision has been much more extensive. At certain points it has involved a rather wholesale reordering and revision of the sequence of objectives as well as of the lesson materials. For example, at the end of the first year of trial of the IPI program at the Oakleaf School the mathematics sequence was given a careful examination, certain objectives were changed, new ones were added, and the needed teaching materials were developed. This type of broad-scale examination of the curriculum is an essential feature of the IPI project and should probably be a part of any curriculum development effort.

Steps have also been taken to develop a rather formal procedure for using test results to locate needed revisions.

INDIVIDUALLY PRESCRIBED INSTRUCTION AS AN APPLICATION OF THESE PRINCIPLES

Individually Prescribed Instruction may be considered as the application of the foregoing principles to develop and carry out a program for the individualization of instruction. It will be noted that these principles contain no mention of the subject matter content that is to be taught or of the source of the objectives stressed. The IPI procedure is not limited to any particular type of content objectives, nor is it a curriculum project developed for the purpose of teaching some new and different subject matter. Rather, it is a procedure for planning and carrying out instruction that can be applied to any content for which objectives can be defined in specific behavioral terms and organized in some meaningful sequences.* ...

Basically, IPI represents an instructional technology that it should be possible to apply to an almost unlimited variety of educational goals. ...

* Can you think of learning objectives for which IPI procedures would be inappropriate?

EXERCISE

1. List the three basic assumptions underlying the development of IPI. (pp. 303, 304)

2. What aspects of the conventional classroom are removed when IPI is installed? (pp. 303–304)

3. What does a learning prescription indicate for the student in an IPI program? (p. 305)

4. Who decides what the student will learn in an IPI program? (pp. 305–306)

5. According to Lindvall and Bolvin, what is an essential characteristic of an effective instructional program? (p. 306)

6. Why must lesson materials in individualized instruction be mostly self-instructional? (p. 307)

7. Why are placement tests used in IPI? (p. 308)

8. For what purposes do IPI students most frequently interact with a teacher? (p. 308)

9. What eight principles of programmed instruction are applied in IPI? (pp. 305–310)

Computer-Assisted Instruction: Problems and Performance

Keith A. Hall

> *Because scoring students' work sheets and recording test scores are major tasks in programmed instruction, some educational developers have considered using a computer to perform these clerical operations. The use of the computer has been tested at all levels of education, kindergarten through advanced medical training. Keith Hall reports on some of these uses and discusses the reasons why many educators think computers can improve instruction. There are many similarities between the rationale for computer-assisted instruction (CAI) and Individually Prescribed Instruction (IPI). Both systems build upon the same basic principles of learning, developed by B. F. Skinner, Robert Gagné (both Section 1),*

Reprinted by permission of the author and *Phi Delta Kappan*, June 1971.

*and others. However, the role of the teacher in a CAI program is
modified even more than in an IPI setting. Do you think the computer threatens to replace teachers, or is it likely to free them for
more important instructional tasks?*

INDIVIDUALIZED INSTRUCTION

Many devices and machines have promised in the past to provide improved instruction in the schools. Among these are motion pictures, television, language laboratories, programmed instruction, and teaching machines. None of these techniques has lived up to its early promise in
contributing to the instructional program of the schools. This is the result
of a lack of learning theory to undergird the use of most of these devices.*
For the first time in education a new technology — computer-assisted instruction — promises to provide some of the quantum jumps in instruction
that have been hoped for in the past. Computer-assisted instruction has
the flexibility and capacity for individualizing instruction which seems to
be necessary for achieving adaptive education.

There are three fundamental characteristics of computer applications in
instruction which suggest that significant steps in improving instruction
can be achieved through the utilization of computers. The first of these
characteristics is the ability of a pre-stored program in a computer system
to evaluate a student's responses and provide information regarding the
correctness of these responses. In a typical classroom of 30 students, only
the very bright, aggressive students will be able to respond to and receive
feedback from the teacher as many as five times each period. The poorer
and more reticent students may receive feedback two or three times each
week during the school year. Results to date show that students receiving
instruction from computers respond anywhere from once every four seconds to once every 30 seconds. This means that each student whose instruction is being provided through computers is responding and receiving
feedback from 40 to 600 times during a 40-minute session at a computer
terminal.

A second characteristic of computer-assisted instruction (CAI) is active
responding by the student. Generally, high-ability or advanced students
are able to sit down with a textbook or a reference book and learn through
reading and other study skills. However, this is often the very problem
that a slow student encounters — he simply cannot learn by reading alone.

A third characteristic of computers for instruction is their ability to
individualize instruction not only at the level of achievement but in reference to the specific interests and abilities of the student taking the course.

---

* *Is this the real reason why these devices have not had more of an impact on
schools? See Goodlad (Section 9) for alternative views.*

The computer can keep a record of the student's performance and progress through a course and alter that course based upon the immediate past history of the individual student with that subject matter. This dynamic characteristic of CAI makes it possible to begin considering not the passage of time nor the covering of a specific text nor doing a given number of problems as criteria for progressing through the curriculum, but the mastery of predetermined criterion levels.

History of CAI

Sidney Pressey in the early 1900's and B. F. Skinner in 1954 provided the earliest attempts to "automate" instruction. Both Pressey and Skinner developed techniques of administering instructional materials to students by means of teaching machines or programmed texts. Much of Skinner's work was based on his experimental studies in training pigeons to perform certain tasks — some very simple and some very complex.* It was soon discovered, however, that programmed texts and teaching machines were extremely limited in the extent to which they could adapt to individual differences among students or provide a stimulating responsive environment for students. The obvious limitations of these devices prompted investigation of applying computers to instructional tasks.

In 1959, researchers at IBM developed a course to teach stenotyping and binary arithmetic by computers. At the same time, refinements were being made in computer systems, terminal configurations, and the number of terminals that a given computer could support. . . .

Systems developed in the late 50's and early 60's used either an electric typewriter or a teletype terminal as an interface device by which the student received information from the computer and through which he transmitted information to the computer. The system designed specifically for instructional purposes and others designed since 1967 have utilized a small television screen as the major display device for the student. The television set has a typewriter keyboard and often a light-pen through which the student can feed responses to the program.† More complete systems include random-access audio, playback/record capability, and random-access image projectors, all under program control.

Types of CAI

In considering the concept of computer-assisted instruction, it is important to recognize the different applications of computers in instruction

---

Skinner discusses this work in Section 1.
† *How does this arrangement limit the types of learning experience which the student can have?*

which are referred to collectively as computer-assisted instruction.* The first of these applications is the use of a computer as a *laboratory computing device*, which is perhaps the most common use of computers in public education. A single terminal (generally an electric typewriter or teletype) is placed in a classroom and provides direct access to a computer at some remote location. The students are allowed to develop programs related to the course work which they are taking. This use most often occurs in a mathematics, physics, or chemistry class. There are an estimated 500 high schools in the United States with this capability.

A second definition of computer-assisted instruction involves the use of the computer as a *record keeper and retriever* which is primarily used by faculty members or administrators for batch processing of data regarding students or instruction in the school. This category quite often includes the scheduling of classes, printing of report cards, and storage and retrieval of test results which are utilized by guidance counselors and other staff.

A third form of CAI can be defined as *simulation*, with the computer responding adaptively to learner input. A great deal of work in this application of computers to instruction has been done in the field of medicine. Sim One[1] is a lifelike device with a plastic skin which resembles that of a human being in color and texture. It has the configuration of a patient lying on an operating table, the left arm extended and ready for intravenous injection, right arm fitted with blood pressure cuff, and chest wall with a stethoscope taped over the approximate location of the heart. Sim One breathes; has a heart beat, pulse, and blood pressure (all synchronized); opens and closes his mouth; blinks his eyes; and responds to four intravenously administered drugs and two gases administered through a mask or tube. The physiological responses occur automatically as part of a computer program.

At Bolt, Beranek, and Newman, Inc.,[2] a computer has been programmed to simulate the conditions of a patient brought into a hospital emergency room. A physician in training sits down at a teletype terminal and by requesting information, tests, and symptoms from the computer regarding his "patient" is able eventually to provide a diagnosis of the specific injuries that the "patient" has received. An even more elaborate diagnostic simulation program is under development at the University of Illinois Medical School in Chicago.[3]

The fourth definition of CAI involves the computer in the role of a *tutor*.† There are various forms which this definition might assume, the most common being that of providing drill and practice problems to students at a terminal and the most complex being that of sequential exposi-

---

Which of these applications of CAI has the best chance of improving learning?
†*Brown describes how new behaviors may be learned through modeling. What types of learning-through-modeling might occur in this form of CAI?*

tion which provides the primary source of instruction for the student. In this latter form, a relatively complete course is presented to a student by means of a computer.

RESEARCH FINDINGS

Studies have shown the superior, or at least equal, progress of students learning through computer-assisted instruction when it is compared to conventional instruction. Suppes reports that for experimental classes in McComb, Mississippi, which were provided 10 to 15 minutes each day for drill and practice at a computer terminal, the range of the average mathematics advancement of the pupils was from 1.10 to 2.03 years among the experimental classes as compared to 0.26 to 1.26 years in the control classes.[4] Butler reports similar results in New York City in 1968 and 1969 in the fourth and fifth grades of the classes which were studied.[5] It is important to emphasize that this record achievement is the result of only 10 to 15 minutes each day at a computer teletype terminal for drill and practice of mathematics materials.* It is difficult to predict what the results would be if students were utilizing a computer terminal which could provide more sophisticated applications of computer-assisted instruction for a longer time period each day.

One of the difficulties in evaluating CAI today is the choice of an adequate criterion. When instruction is individualized and is adapted to the specific weaknesses and strengths of the pupils, it is inappropriate to use a norm-referenced measure for evaluating student progress. A more appropriate approach is to utilize a criterion-referenced measure to determine when the students have reached the desired level of achievement.† The difference in objectives and evaluative devices makes it difficult to compare progress in CAI with progress in the conventional classroom. Even with these problems of evaluation, a consistent result in the use of computer-assisted instruction has been that the same amount of material has been learned in a CAI environment as in a conventional classroom, although with a considerable saving of time in favor of CAI.

The attitude of students has often been questioned with respect to computer-assisted instruction. Quite frequently it is asked whether or not CAI makes the student just another number in a group of students, or whether the student feels that this is an impersonal means of instruction. Although preliminary findings suggest that students in CAI do not feel depersonalized, adequate empirical data will not be available until students

---

* *Given these results, are computers a useful tool for promoting learning?*
† *The distinction between norm-referenced and criterion-referenced measurement is described by Jason Millman (Section 16).*

have been exposed to CAI over a number of years in varying subject matter areas. . . .

COST OF CAI

Four contingencies seem to be operating which may affect the probability of public schools accepting CAI. The first contingency is the relative cost of CAI and other modes of instruction. Three dollars per student hour may seem high, but it is not as high as the cost of some specialized instruction such as remedial education, vocational education, or homebound education. Nor is it high if the social costs of allowing individuals to remain uneducated are considered. Another contingency is the fact that technology costs are decreasing. On some of the earlier modified business machines which were utilized for computer-assisted instruction, the cost per pupil hour was as high as $35 to $40. With the development of a computer system designed specifically for instructional purposes, this cost dropped drastically to $5 per hour or slightly less. A third contingency is the rising personnel costs in the public schools. To some extent, public schools and the U.S. Post Office have had similar problems; and to some extent, they have responded to the problems in a similar way. There is an ever-increasing amount of work which needs to be done in both instances, and in both instances the solution to this increasing workload has been increasing the number of personnel to do that work. The increasing number of personnel and the increasing cost of this staff suggest that schools should very seriously consider modern educational technology as an alternate approach for meeting some of these goals. One of the goals of CAI development should be to establish a differentiated staffing program in the instructional environment so that much of the routine clerical and administrative work which teachers quite frequently do can be done with paraprofessional help, thus releasing the experienced teachers' time for the specific task of attending to the individual needs of students.

The fourth operational contingency which may increase the acceptance of CAI in the public schools is the fact that a computer system which is installed primarily for computer-assisted instruction may serve well for administrative functions of that school district. Much of the cost of a CAI system could be justified on this basis. . . .

SUMMARY

Computer-assisted instruction has the flexibility and capacity for individualizing instruction necessary for achieving adaptive education. Three characteristics of computer applications in instruction make this possible: (1) active responding by the student; (2) continual evaluation of the student's responses; and (3) adaptation of the instruction to individual responses, levels of achievement, and the specific interests of the student taking the course.

Early uses of computers for instruction date back to 1959. These systems used typewriters or teletypes for the student stations and would support only one station at a time. Later systems have been developed which use more sophisticated cathode ray tubes as student stations and will support as many as 32 stations simultaneously. Other systems using teletypes or typewriters can support up to 200 terminals concurrently. These various systems are being used for laboratory computing devices, record keeping and retrieval, simulation, and tutorial instruction.

Differences in objectives and evaluation techniques make it difficult to compare student progress in CAI with student progress in the conventional classroom. When instruction is individualized, it is adapted to the specific weaknesses and strengths of the pupils, and it is therefore inappropriate to use a norm-referenced measure (which is quite acceptable for conventional classes) for evaluating student progress. In the same vein, a criterion-referenced measure which is appropriate for use in measuring student progress in CAI is inappropriate for evaluating student progress in traditional classes. Even with these problems of evaluation, investigations have consistently shown that the same amount of material has been learned in a CAI environment as in a conventional classroom, although with a considerable saving of time in favor of CAI.

Operational use of a CAI system requires quantities of curriculum material suitable for full daytime use by students in the school, appropriate curriculum for adult education or in-service education for teachers during the after-school and evening hours, and administrative applications which would utilize the midnight to 8:00 a.m. time period. The combination of these various applications makes it economically feasible to install systems in many school districts. . . .

EXERCISE

1. What three characteristics of computer-assisted instruction suggest that computers can improve student learning? (pp. 313–314)

2. List the four types of CAI described by Hall. (pp. 315–316)

3. What do studies of CAI show regarding student progress? (p. 316)

4. Why is it difficult to compare student progress in CAI with student progress in conventional programs? (p. 316)

5. What contingencies may affect the probability of schools accepting CAI? (p. 317)

Those Magnificent Men and Their Teaching Machines

Albert J. Taylor

> *The two preceding selections presented several advantages for such highly programmed learning approaches as Individually Prescribed Instruction and computer-assisted instruction. Specifically, the authors argue that such programs increase the efficiency with which students learn a given amount of information, increase motivation for learning by providing frequent feedback to the student about his progress, and individualize instruction by allowing students to move at their own rate of learning. (If you have ever been in a class where you were far ahead or behind most of the other students, you can appreciate the potential value of these programs.) However, this and any other new approach to education warrant careful critique before being considered an improvement over existing practice. Albert Taylor criticizes the various adaptations of programmed instruction, mainly because they provide a very limited type of learning experience for the student, and involve a very limited conception of the goals of education. Compare Taylor's views to those of Carl Rogers and Harold Bessell (both, Section 2). Would Rogers and Bessell, who favor a humanistic approach to education, ever accept the views of the behaviorists who developed programmed instruction? Also, how would the developers of IPI and CAI respond to Taylor's criticisms?*

If the promised land in education is not immediately at hand, it is at least close enough that we may be led there in a few simple steps. This seems to be the assurance that we are being given by those ingenious devils who've left their learning laboratories long enough to devise programs for instruction and to develop a variety of engaging machines for presenting such programs.

How far the machine may take us is not quite resolved. Estimates appear to range from our having acquired a device on the order of a textbook or training film to an ultimate order in which the student simply inserts his charge-a-plate type card into the machine and spends his days as a student pushing various keys or buttons.

From *The Educational Forum*, vol. 36, no. 2 (January 1972), 239–246. Used by permission of Kappa Delta Pi, An Honor Society in Education, owners of the copyright.

Aside from the declaration of the permanence of the machine as an educational fixture, about the only other point of agreement among the theorists is that the machine will *not* replace the teacher. Everyone gives us this assurance. But notice! The machine is not called a teacher-assisting machine; the program is not referred to as a programmed instructional aid. Their names are, respectively: teaching machine and programmed (programed) instruction. Descriptions of them inevitably portray for us the ways in which these devices do the job better than the teacher. We are consistently warned that in our automated world, there is no excuse for the gross inefficiency that exists in the conventional classroom.

That we must automate education is considered unquestionable. This process involves essentially four parts. First, the student reads a small unit of information. He makes a response by filling in a blank or pressing a key or button. He checks his response against the correct response which is immediately provided. Finally, he advances to the next step in the program, provided his response has been correct.

In linear programming, one of the two alternatives available, the steps or units of information are so small that the single response allowed the student is almost certain to be the correct response. In branching, the other approach, the student selects an answer from among multiple choice offerings. The latter allows enough latitude for the student to make errors and when this occurs he is directed through a series of steps designed to correct his error. Branching allows the student to take larger steps than he takes in linear programming.

Although teaching machines of several types are available, they are not essential. The units of information might also be presented on an ordered series of index cards. Specially prepared textbooks or workbooks with questions and answers presented on separate pages are also on the market.*

Among the claims made for this approach are that: such programs teach much more efficiently than can the classroom teacher in a conventional setting or, put another way, they expedite learning; students participate actively in the instructional process; the program allows for individualization of instruction; the student is motivated because of his active participation; knowledge can be disseminated much more quickly. These claims aren't made in splendid isolation. Accompanying each set of claims is the rationale based on principles of learning established in the laboratories of experimental psychologists.

In the face of all this, it seems that there is little that the teacher and the public can do beyond make way for the machine. . . .

There is, however, a basis for assessing the situation. . . . Suppose we take a look at the claim that the teaching machine expedites learning. What is the state-of-affairs that this describes? In the case of reading, this

---

* *This is basically what was done with Individually Prescribed Instruction.*

means that the student is able, in most instances, to depress the key, push the button, fill in the blank, or in some such fashion produce a response that corresponds to the correct answer. With the use of a machine he comes to make this response in less time than with a conventional teacher. The state-of-affairs described by "learning" in programming language is exactly this type of responding and nothing more.

We need to take this a step farther, however. What constitutes correctness in the programmer's vocabulary? The state-of-affairs described by the term "correct" is simply and solely the answer provided by the programmer. This seems appropriate and harmless. And it may be when we are considering the single item in beginning reading. But the term "correct" also means "whatever answer the programmer has provided" when we are talking about correctness in history, or government, or whatever content we decide to program.

What philosophic judgments may we render then? The first is that when the programmer claims that machines expedite learning, he does not mean by "learning" what we usually mean. The state-of-affairs which is generally represented by those who are not teaching machine experts may include something like the simple response described by the programmer, but it also involves much more than this.

The state-of-affairs generally represented by "learning" includes a host of responses in the area which we usually designate as attitudes. If we were to examine the whole situation described by "learning to read" we would see that the student responds in more ways than merely pushing a button or filling a blank. He acquires feelings and develops general ways of approaching the items at hand.* ...

The point to remember is that when the programmer talks about learning, he is not talking about what generally goes under the heading of learning. He does not mean what we mean. In the case of a student in a programmed learning situation, the student may be "learning" to hate reading, or he may develop the notion that "learning" means agreeing with unquestionable answers, but all of this is ignored by the programmer. When the programmer claims that machines expedite learning, there is no question about the truth of his statement. Of course it is true. But it is "true" only insofar as we are using "learning" in the same precise, narrow fashion of the programmer. Unless we remember that he is saying nothing about learning as it is generally conceived we can be grossly misled by the claim of the programmer.

The other claims may be examined in the same fashion. The state-of-affairs referred to by the claim that the student participates actively in the learning process is not the state-of-affairs usually referred to by statements

* How might a behaviorist like Skinner (Section 1) respond to this view of learning?

concerning active participation in learning. What is generally meant is that when, for example, the student is learning history through active participation he is not merely memorizing the conclusions of a particular historian. Rather, it means that he is involved, at some level, in historical analysis. He is "doing" history as the historian does history. This is not what is meant by the programmer. "Active participation" to the advocate of programming means pushing a key or button, or filling a blank, and it means nothing more than this. . . .

We might also note that when the advocate of automated education refers to individualization of instruction, he is not conforming to standard usage. In the presence of the machine, individualization of instruction means merely that the machine will not allow the student to go on to the next frame until he has given a correct response. (Remember "correct"?) This may take longer for some individuals than for others.

In standard use, the term "individualization" means much more than this. It generally denotes not only allowing more time to "master" the same content; it may also mean altering the content, allowing for different responses, employing different types of approaches, having different feelings, drawing different conclusions, valuing different things, etc.

In programmed instruction, the only permissible variant is time. Ultimately, every student must use the same procedure for arriving at the same answers as everyone else. This is a very strange, unusual, and limited use of the term "individualization." * . . .

The proponent of the teaching machine also has a specialized usage for the common term "motivation." He grants the importance of motivation. He acknowledges that without motivation there is no learning. To this recognition of the importance of motivation he adds the assurance that the machine motivates learning. . . .

Analysis reveals that because of his peculiar use of the term "learning," what the programmer means by "motivated to learn" is that the student generally does not hesitate to approach the machine and to push the button or fill in the blank. There is no other content to his claim. . . .

In the case of the claim of rapid dissemination of knowledge we similarly find a need for clarification. "Knowledge" in the language of programming is not the whole realm of meanings assigned to the term generally. As the term is generally used, "knowledge" denotes our whole intellectual heritage, reflecting not simply inert conclusions nor mere familiarity with things, places, and persons.† "Knowledge" also encompasses our standards, tastes, habits, conceptions of truth and evidence, ways of getting and securing beliefs, etc. But this broad sweep of meaning is not what the programmer means.

* *Compare with Lindvall and Bolvin's view of individualization (this section).*
† *In Bereiter's view (Section 2), can teachers teach such "knowledge"?*

The programmer's meaning is limited by his usage to just that material which is capable of being rendered into a logical series of verbalisms. "Knowledge," in other words, is exactly those inert ideas which most thinkers have deplored our regarding as knowledge. The knowledge which we designate as "history," for example, becomes just those conclusions established by some chosen historian, arranged in a particular logical or chronological fashion. Similarly, "science" becomes the conclusions of particular scientists at a particular point in time.

"Learning science" or "learning history" then means making some type of series of responses that corresponds with a series of "correct answers" in a program. If we wished to talk about the "methods" of history or science, we could be talking only about making verbalizations about method. The procedure that the student would be involved in when dealing with the methods of history or science would be identical with that when he is dealing with the inert ideas of these areas of knowledge. Also, the procedures involved in "learning history" are identical with those involved in "learning science" or "learning" anything. In either case, what the student experiences is a far cry from what is generally meant by "history" or science. Comparably, what is meant by "knowledge" in the language of teaching machines is far removed from what is meant by "knowledge" in the standard use of that term. We need not doubt that *something* can be disseminated rapidly. But we must not make the error of thinking that it is "knowledge" in the popular sense of that term.

Beyond examining the claims of the teaching machine advocate in order to understand what he is really claiming, we might also extend our analysis to his explanations. . . .

Explanations offered by learning theorists of the automated instruction variety go back to the experiments conducted with animals in their laboratories. In other words, the particular kinds of theories offered are based on the use of models.* The models in this case are usually pigeons or monkeys. The assumption is that a bar-pressing response by a pigeon in a specially prepared box is identical to the key- or button-pressing response, or the writing in of a verbal response, by a student. . . .

What does this mean when we translate such an [assumption] into actual practices? In the case of reading, it means that we identify "learning to read" with the bar-pressing behavior of the pigeon. In this context, "learning" becomes a conditioned motor response. "Learning to read" becomes a matter of invariably pushing the "correct" key or button, moving the muscles in such a fashion as to produce a particular written pattern, or vocalizing a particular sound. Either "learning to read" means this rather simplistic overt motor response, or the model is not an adequate explana-

---

* *Does Taylor identify the theories actually applied in programmed instruction?*

tion of what goes on in reading.* The programmer cannot have it both ways. There are those who believe that there is more to human learning, than the single, or two or three, discrete responses in a highly controlled stimulus situation.

All of this is not to say that teaching machines, or programmed instruction do not produce results. Indeed they do. But we need to consider what results we are talking about. What is called for is the two-fold process of (1) analyzing the statements or claims of the programmer, and the relationships between his theories and what they purport to explain; and, (2) carefully studying *all* the consequences or outcomes of using the machine rather than focusing solely on particular outcomes and proceeding as though they were the only outcomes. What we must judge is not simply whether or not the machine has results but whether or not the results are those that we want....

The charge that contemporary education is "inefficient" may be entirely true. The question remains, however, as to whether or not this constitutes a problem. Aside from considering what we want to regard as "efficiency," a fact that is overlooked by those who wish to automate education is that automation is not limited to education. We must therefore educate for an automated age. The effect of automation in other areas is to so increase man's productivity that he is left with much more time on his hands. In fact, man has come to enjoy twice the time for leisure that he had at the turn of the century. In effect, he has been given an additional lifetime of leisure. What is to fill this leisure time? Perhaps one of the luxuries that he can afford now, more than ever before in his history, is the luxury of a leisurely, fully humanized education....

Before we allow those magnificent men and their teaching machines to rush us into automation, we ought to consider not only what the machine is capable of, but what we would like to do for ourselves.

EXERCISE

1. According to Taylor, what is the advantage of a programmed learning unit that uses branching over one that uses linear programming? (p. 320)

2. What important features of learning does Taylor suggest are ignored by programmed instruction? (pp. 321–322)

3. What aspect of learning can be individualized by using programmed instruction? What aspects cannot be according to Taylor? (p. 322)

---

* *Which of Gagné's types of learning (Section 1) are involved in learning to read via a teaching machine?*

4. How does Taylor define "knowledge"? What meaning does the programmer give knowledge? (pp. 322–323)

5. What animal behavior does Taylor compare button-pressing in programmed instruction to? (p. 323)

6. What important judgment about using teaching machines does Taylor think we should make? (p. 324)

7. In Taylor's opinion, how should automation affect our decision about using teaching machines? (p. 324)

A Token Manual for Behavior Analysis Classrooms

Don Bushell, Jr.

The basic principles of Individually Prescribed Instruction (Lindvall and Bolvin, this section) and computer-assisted instruction also have been applied to classroom management. This approach, sometimes called "behavior modification" or "contingency management," emphasizes rewards. By selective use of rewards, the teacher systematically helps the student modify or change his behavior. A first step in developing this type of learning program is a careful analysis of the student's current level of performance. This analysis is followed by a plan for changing the student's behavior so that he will perform better, that is, so that he will acquire more knowledge, behave in a more socially acceptable way, or perform a skill more proficiently. Deciding what constitutes "acceptable" behavior and effective rewards is important. Don Bushell has developed a brief manual to help a teacher operate a classroom based on the principles of behavior modification. This particular type of classroom uses tokens as rewards for successful performance. Tokens are given to students for performing small pieces of school work successfully. These tokens, in turn, are used to buy time for recess, painting, or some other activity the student wants to do. In effect, this "token economy" has many of the characteristics of the adult economic world. Would you be willing to apply such a system in your classroom, if you become a teacher?

The material quoted here is part of a token manual that is used in the training program for teaching parents (parents of the children) who serve as instructional aides in Behavior Analysis Follow Through classrooms. Used with permission of the author.

INTRODUCTION

This manual is to help you teach in a Behavior Analysis classroom. The Behavior Analysis program emphasizes the use of positive reinforcement, or rewards, in teaching children; and it also makes it possible for the child, the learner, to be responsible for the consequences of his own behavior. These two things, positive reinforcement and responsibility, come together in a set of procedures called The Token System.

We now know that children do better work and learn more if their good behavior is praised and rewarded *immediately*. Consequently, a major objective in creating an effective classroom learning situation is to give immediate praise and reinforcement to the children's good behaviors. There are many things in the classroom which can be used as incentives or reinforcers. Some examples include: the attention and approval of the teachers, the chance to play with a favorite toy, being with other children on the playground, listening to a story, and reading a favorite book.*

These incentives will improve or strengthen a particular good behavior if they are presented *immediately* after that behavior occurs. This presents a problem. No classroom could operate with a system which sent a child out to play immediately after each correct answer or cooperative act. The solution is the token system. A token can be delivered quickly (immediately after a good behavior); it does not interrupt what the child is doing; and it can be exchanged later for any and all of the enjoyable things listed above.

A token can be any object, but during the early grades it is best if the token is an object which the child can hold and put in his pocket. It might be a match stick, a marble, a cardboard disc, or a plastic poker chip. No matter what it looks like, giving a child a token always says "You're doing good work. Thank you." The following pages describe how you can use the token system to improve the learning of the children in your classroom.

The token system is a teaching tool which is used in all Behavior Analysis classrooms because it:

1. *Motivates* — gives the children an incentive and keeps them interested in their work.
2. *Reinforces* — helps the children learn by increasing the amount of positive attention they get immediately, and
3. *Teaches independence* — gives the children the freedom to earn for themselves the opportunity to engage in their favorite activities.

* *Is using such incentives a form of bribery? Shouldn't learning be for the sake of learning?*

EXCHANGE PROCEDURES

The token system is an exchange system. You give the children tokens for the answers which you like (paying attention, working on an assignment, correct answers, helping, etc.) and the children give you tokens for things which they like (stories, games, recess, play materials, etc.).* To keep the exchange going, Behavior Analysis classrooms have "earning" periods, followed by "spending" periods, followed by "earning," etc., throughout each day.

GIVING TOKENS

A good teacher pays high wages. Most of your time will be spent praising and rewarding the children for the good things they are doing.

You must know what each child is able to do, so you can praise his individual improvements. You may give one child tokens for getting right answers to math problems while another child might earn tokens just for getting out his math book and opening it to the right page. What you give the tokens for depends on what you are trying to teach a particular child.

The children are never in competition with one another for tokens. Each child earns tokens for doing things which are good for *him* regardless of what other children may be doing.

Praise what the child has just done, each time you give a token. "That's good writing, Timmy. Now do the next row just as well." There is no need to mention the token at all. Just present it as you tell the child that he is doing what you like. "Thank you for listening so carefully, Sallie." "I like the way you put your book away when you were through with it, Dan." "That's right, Charles, good work." Try to use the child's name when you praise his good work.

Give tokens and praise immediately. Giving a token and praising a child *immediately* after he has put his materials away will help him much more than, "I like the way you put your things away last period." Last period is too long ago, even if it is only 15 minutes ago.†

Each child should earn tokens every period. The tokens cannot work unless the children receive them and have the opportunity to exchange them. If you are working with a group of six children during a handwriting lesson, you may give tokens to some of them for getting a whole row

---

* *This exchange system can be criticized as being too teacher-centered. What are some positive features?*
† *Skinner makes a similar point about the need for immediate positive reinforcement (Section 1).*

correct and you may give tokens to another because he got just one letter. Even though different children will earn for different things, all of them must have the opportunity to earn similar amounts. This means you will have to give each child enough of your help and attention to permit him to earn what he is capable of earning.

EXCHANGING TOKENS

Every child should be able to exchange his tokens for something during every spending period under most circumstances. There need to be several different items or activities available, at different prices, during each spending period. Children with a larger number of tokens will be able to exchange them for more expensive items, but there will also be less expensive items available for children with fewer tokens. Sometimes different amounts of a single activity can be exchanged for different amounts of tokens. For example, each minute of free play may cost one token. Some children will want to exchange ten of their tokens for ten minutes of free play, and others will only have enough for, or want, five minutes.

Setting prices is easier if you decide in advance how many responses you want a child to make during the earning period just before the exchange. If you want each child you are working with to complete at least six arithmetic problems during the earning period, you will probably set the prices of exchange activities between 4 and 8 tokens. These prices should allow children who complete an average amount of work to exchange for moderately attractive items and those who do better work will be able to exchange for more expensive activities. You will want to be careful that some children are not always limited to exchanging for the lowest priced items. If you see this happening you will want to spend extra time helping that child so he will progress faster and have the opportunity to exchange for more valuable events.*

The price of an item or event should reflect how important it is to the children. Prices will vary from time to time, but during one exchange period, blocks may cost 5 tokens, listening to a story may cost 10, and painting a picture to take home may cost 15. To decide how much any given activity is worth to the children you will need to watch the children very closely and listen to what they say about things they want to do. The teacher's job during the spending period is to make sure that the things which the children want are available. If you are not sure whether one item is more valuable to the children than another, try them both out. During one spending period, for example, you may make blocks and a story each worth 5 tokens. If, when both have the same price, most of

---

* *Can all learning objectives be analyzed this way?*

the children choose the story, you may want to raise the price of the story to 7 and lower the price of the blocks to 4.

Vary the prices and the activities. Changing the prices and the kinds of activities which the children can earn adds interest to the entire exchange process and prevents the system from becoming a dull routine. If recess is always at 10:30 and always costs 10 tokens, the children will soon develop a pattern of working only until they have earned their 10 tokens and then they will quit (even if it is only 10:00). To avoid this, and to make the whole system more exciting, arrange for recess to cost 8 on some days, and 10 or 11 on others. Sometimes it will be at 10:30, sometimes at 10:15, and sometimes at 10:35. With this kind of changing system the only way the children can be sure they will be able to exchange for recess no matter when it comes or how much it costs is to work steadily throughout the earning period. . . .

There are some occasions where a very special event requires several earning periods. A trip to the zoo might be a case where you will want to set a single, and rather high price. This is an exception to the rule of not announcing the price of an event in advance. It is very unusual and should be saved for special activities, but you and the other teachers may decide that a zoo ticket will cost 20 tokens and can be purchased anytime before noon on Friday. At the end of each day during the week before the trip, the children can turn in their tokens in exchange for check marks on a chart. Twenty check marks can be exchanged for the zoo ticket on Friday, which is then collected just as everybody is ready to leave.

Start each day fresh. Your schedule will need to be arranged so that all the tokens a child earns during each day are spent during that same day. If there are tokens left at the end of a day, remove them after the children have left so they will be ready to start with a clean slate the next day. If you find that several children have large numbers of tokens left at the end of the day, it may mean that you need more good spending activities for these children, or your prices are too low. If the children are allowed to save tokens from day to day, they may accumulate enough to spend an entire day without doing any of their lessons but participating in all the activities.* . . .

Summary

As you can now see, the token system is a way of emphasizing the good things which the children are doing for you, and it provides tangible evidence of your approval. It sets up a system where children do not have to be coaxed and urged to "Get busy!", "Hurry up!", and "Pay atten-

* Bushell implies that this is an undesirable situation. Do you agree?

tion!" They will work actively at their assignments because it is in their own best interest. In other words, you have set it up so they are working for themselves rather than just taking orders. Most of us prefer that kind of arrangement, and the children are certainly no different.*

Tokens are always associated with positive events. When they are received they are accompanied with your praise and encouragement, and when they are spent it is in exchange for things the children value. The tokens are never associated in any way with negative or unpleasant events. You will never take tokens away from a child for misbehavior.... There are no fines, no taxes, and no dues in a token system. Neither are they associated with any kind of pressure. You won't for example, say anything like, "Hurry up or you won't earn enough tokens for recess." However gentle you may be, that still is a threat, and tokens must never be associated with threats.

It is worth repeating that the whole concept of the token system is the concept of *positive reinforcement for good learning behavior.* If you have good items for trade, and vary the prices, times, and quality of these items, you can develop an exciting token system that will guarantee consistent high motivation for all of the children. For the child, your classroom can be the most fun place he knows because here he can earn the opportunity to do the things he likes best. If you can start a child off in school by teaching him that the classroom is a lively, interesting place where there is seldom any punishment and always a lot of excitement, then that child is going to get a much better education.

Suggestions to Remember

1. Give lots of tokens and praise.

2. Give a token for good behavior *immediately.*

3. Never talk about tokens except to announce exchange prices. If a child asks for tokens or tries to bargain with you, pretend you didn't hear him and give your attention to another child who is working.

4. Ignore behavior you don't like.

5. Start each day fresh. Empty the tokens from all pockets at the end of each day so everyone starts each new day with a clean slate.

6. Never take tokens away....

7. Vary the prices, times, and content of spending activities.

8. Provide as many activities for the children to choose among as possible.

9. Keep it fun. Make it exciting — for you and for the children.

* *Key point, but do you agree that children have the same motivational system as adults?*

EXERCISE

1. Why is it important that the student be rewarded *immediately* under a behavior analysis system? (p. 326)
2. Why are tokens used as incentives rather than immediate chances to play with toys? (p. 326)
3. What are the advantages of a token system? (p. 326)
4. Why is exchanging tokens an important part of the system? (pp. 328, 329, 330)

Examining the Open Education Classroom

Charles H. Rathbone

Such forms of instruction as IPI, CAI, and behavior modification stress the importance of making learning more efficient. Specifying learning goals is considered to be a complex task that requires the work of highly trained experts. The student has little or nothing to say about what he will learn or how he will learn it. In contrast, proponents of open education consider student involvement to be the key to successful learning. The student is expected to learn better if he is studying something that interests him and is attempting to reach learning goals that he has helped to define. Proponents of the open classroom contend that programmed forms of education merely compound the existing problems of in-school learning. Open educationists believe that students need to learn to feel, to respond to other people, and to function as autonomous individuals, rather than to learn teacher-selected facts more efficiently. The major features of the open classroom as it is implemented in the United States are described by Charles Rathbone in the following article. In addition to reporting the positive features of an "open" instructional program, he asks several pertinent questions about the capability of all students to perform well in it. Because Rathbone directs an open education school (New City School, St. Louis, Missouri), his comments are based upon actual experience as well as a review of the literature. How would you function in such a class-

From *School Review*, vol. 80, Aug. 1972, no. 4, 521–549. Reprinted with permission of University of Chicago Press and author. © 1972 by the University of Chicago.

room as a student or as a teacher? Do you think that programmed and open classroom instruction can possibly be combined?

Interest grows in the *open education* or *integrated day* methodology, as practiced in British primary schools and elsewhere. It is hoped that this interest will lead to a closer and more precise description of what actually occurs within these informal classrooms. This paper offers, first, a preliminary specification of four key organizational features of the open education environment: (1) the organization of space, (2) the organization of time, (3) the way in which children are grouped together, and (4) the organization of instruction.[1] . . .

SPATIAL ORGANIZATION

As Philip Jackson has vividly demonstrated in *Life in Classrooms*,[2] schools are indeed crowded places; aside from elevators, subways and the very smallest eat-on-the-run restaurants, one rarely encounters such tight quarters, such sheer density of humanity. Of course, one very efficient way of dealing with intensely crowded conditions is to exercise tight organizational control over the division and distribution of the space involved, describing the exact perimeter of each subdivision and assigning each individual his carefully bounded place. This solution is often adopted in traditional schools: each child has his own chair and desk and all are arrayed in rows, aligned as on a grid, each equidistant from the other. In many cases, this organization is permanently imposed, the desks being literally bolted to the floor. Each separate territory, then, is (1) marked by a particular piece of furniture located in a specific, fixed place; (2) made as equal to all other territories as possible in terms of square feet covered and furniture provided (desk design, inkwells, etc.); (3) assigned to a particular child and expected to serve the total range of activities he engages in during the school day.

The open education school rejects this solution to the problem of overcrowded quarters. Instead of tightening up the spatial organization and making more precise assignments and prohibitions, it has loosened them. The typical classroom consists of a number of not very sharply divided areas where children work individually or in groups at designated activities associated with that particular area. . . .

The organizing principle governing spatial differentiation within the open education classroom . . . reflects a concern not so much for an individual's territorial rights or for maintaining fixed limits on a child's mobility and "range," but rather for the function to which the various areas are devoted. Teachers regard each as an area for learning *something* and, as such, each is equipped especially for a particular purpose ("equipped" in this sense meaning not only furnished with the necessary tools and curriculum materials but "equipped" with the proper amount of space and light).

Functional differentiation of space implies a number of subsidiary considerations:

Although most work areas can be arranged for in advance, because of the inherent flexibility of this system, ad hoc preparation of space to perform new and unanticipated functions is relatively easy to accomplish.

Unless one assumes a rigid schedule with fixed times for changing activities, this method of spatial organization implies a certain freedom for the individual child to move from area to area as he finishes one project and begins another.

With provisions for so many different activity areas within the classroom, no single teacher can possibly supervise each area each minute: this implies either a higher teacher-pupil ratio or a situation in which some children may not even be able to see the teacher, much less be supervised on an individual basis.

This system of organization eliminates the need for large quantities of identical furniture. It also makes multiple sets of identical curriculum material unnecessary, as only a limited number of children can work within a certain area at the same time.

To this point, discussion has been confined to flexibility within the classroom's four walls. Equally significant, however, is the flexibility of its assumed perimeter. Corridors (especially in English schools where they are particularly wide and well lighted) often appear crammed with carts (and other rolling stock such as tricycles, wagons, dollies, etc.), theatrical apparatus (costume wardrobes, risers, etc.), Wendy (play) houses, easels, and so forth. Often multiple exits to the outside are available, and children are allowed and expected to take advantage of them as they will. Rabbit hutches and chicken coops are kept outside, as are playground toys of various sorts: the extended environment is not only acknowledged, it is capitalized on and made deliberately inviting. . . .

Further means of extending boundaries and generally moving away from the self-contained classroom are provided when two "extended" classrooms coexist in the same school. This situation allows opportunities for a number of interchanges to occur and is considered beneficial in several respects. If one classroom contains a radio set or a small group interested in ornithology, the child from a neighboring "classroom" may temporarily take advantage of this special resource and the ensuing intellectual experience which would not otherwise be available to him.* The situation is similar for social and psychological learnings — just as this fluidity permits the child some selection of which teacher to work with and model himself after, so it gives him a chance to belong to and participate in a larger community than the one defined by his immediate class. This enables him not only to observe another instructional group at work (which in itself is often valuable), but to have, as well, the experience of temporary membership in that group's unique human relationships, its special value systems, etc....

ORGANIZATION OF TIME

In England, open education is often known as "Integrated Day Programme," a reference which underscores its flexible temporal element. For, within the designated school day, there are remarkably few fixed time periods of any sort, especially those during which all children are obliged to give their collective attention to a single event or task. Instead, schedules are loose. Children take on or conclude their work in a given area on an individual basis and at no fixed time. Hence, at any given moment, one is likely to find some children just starting, some just ending, and others very much in the middle of a variety of tasks.

This is not to imply that no organization or instructional time exists; it does; but, again, it is likely to be an organic, functional sort of organization, not one published in advance or governed by a solely extrinsic purpose. Moreover, this organization is flexible throughout; unlike modular scheduling, it makes no attempt to define more and more closely how smaller and smaller units of time shall be spent. Instead, it delegates responsibility for deciding these matters to individual teachers and their children. Whenever possible, temporal arrangements coordinate with instructional exigencies, which themselves are individually determined....

Flexibility within the school day is often paralleled by a flexibility in the very definition of "school day." Often these schools extend the school day by making school buildings and grounds accessible to children outside "official" hours — a further acknowledgment that school time is but a portion of a child's total educational experience.

The presumed advantages† of this flexible time system are many; in addition to those already mentioned, proponents would advance the following:

For the child who is eager to pursue a complicated task, who wants to

* *Do these boundaries differ from those set in an IPI program (Lindvall and Bolvin, this section)?*
† *Which of these advantages also apply to programmed instruction?*

exert sustained effort and get the job done, this system reduces the chance of his losing interest or losing heart due to constant interruption.

To force a child who is already bored or uninterested in the matter before him to remain with it until some formal time period is over is to teach him that his own judgment is inconsequential in matters to which the teacher ascribes importance. Moreover, it is likely to make the task less attractive for him next time he faces it (for he will remember the boredom and frustration, not what preceded them).

Time to listen to oneself, to reflect, and to meditate is important, especially for young children in school; yet it can never be satisfactorily scheduled. A fluid time schedule increases a child's opportunity to seize these moments as they occur.

Satisfactory consideration of individual rates of learning is likelier when child A's instruction is not made dependent on the speed of child B's learning.

Children's interests fluctuate incredibly — both between children and, with a given child, between one day and the next. Children do exhibit natural "rhythms of learning," spurts of interest, periods of intense and profitable concentration. To attempt to predict and account in advance for the amount of time any particular child will need (or wish to take) painting a picture or writing a story or learning a concept regarding multiplication is hopelessly impossible; a flexible schedule, however, allows the child an opportunity to make those determinations himself, on the spot and (presumably) with accuracy.

Learning the value of long, sustained application is more likely when a child has an opportunity to choose such involvement on his own, tries it, and is suitably rewarded by the ensuing experience.

A school experience which provides opportunity for continuous learning prepares children for a unified life of continuous living, not one mechanically disjointed and filled with disparate activities.

The Organization of Groups of Children

. . . Open education schools do operate on a classroom system where specific teachers are responsible for specific groups of children (often numbering forty or more in England), but typically this aggregation is organized along the lines of what is known as "vertical" grouping. Traditional classrooms allow for a relatively narrow age spread (a typical fourth grade in the United States, for example, will contain few youngsters who will not, at some time during the nine-month school year, be ten years old), but the opposite is true of classes which are vertically grouped. Vertical grouping, sometimes known as "multiage," "mixed," or "family" grouping, means the deliberate inclusion of children of different ages within a single educational environment; in England this often means placing five-, six-, and seven-year-olds within the same "infant" class or, at the "junior" level, placing eights, nines, tens, and elevens together to learn.

Within this broad mix of ages and abilities, then, short-term, functional grouping occurs constantly. Often self-selected, sometimes teacher-assigned, these subgroups congregate within a particular area for the purpose of working at a particular task. For example, a seven-year-old might read a story to four fives; two sixes might construct a castle out of X-blocks together; eight beginning readers might work together for twenty minutes with the teacher, then work at painting and nature study individually. Constant realignment is a characteristic of these functional groups: it is as though the children were continuously coming together as small work crews; and when the work is done, they disperse momentarily, only to re-form into new and different groups....

Implicit in the concept of vertical grouping — or certainly coexisting with it — is the notion of ungradedness. For in a mixed-age class of forty juniors, there are no boundaries of "grade" or "class"; each child does the tasks he can, and if socially he mixes best with the eights but intellectually he's capable of doing math with the best of the elevens, there are no pressures inhibiting him from dividing his energies in exactly those ways. Nor is the teacher under obligation to split the total group — as he often is in a traditional setting — into mutually exclusive, subject-oriented subgroups of equal size, and then to proceed from one to the next, from "slow" to "average" to "advanced" math, for example. Here the decision that six children need special work with computation places no imperatives on the remainder of the class....

As a consequence of this general attitude, the class lesson, the characteristic *modus operandi* of the traditional classroom, comes under heavy attack by proponents of open education. It is seen as something prepared in advance and pitched at some "imaginary mean," reflecting an adult-dominated environment which assumes that children have neither the competence for nor the right to make meaningful decisions concerning their own learning, and predicated simply upon an efficient transmission of knowledge from someone who has it to a group of those who do not. Because the class-lesson format tends to produce boredom, a sense of being manipulated, and, ultimately, a kind of despair, the strongest objections against it are raised in the context of its psychological and emotional impact upon the children themselves....

The Organization of Instruction

Under ordinary circumstances, consideration of a classroom's "organization of instruction" includes asking a number of questions concerning the subjects that are studied, the order in which they are presented, the number of hours allocated for the study of each one, and how those hours are broken into lecture or group presentation, large- or small-group discussion, individualized independent study, etc. In the open education classroom, however, where so many of these are neither fixed nor formalized, "organization of instruction" becomes "organization of learning materials" — that is, investigation of the selection, arrangement, and assignment of specific items of instructional equipment within the classroom.

It is the teacher who exerts principal control over the original stocking of equipment: he is responsible for requesting, ordering, finding (or scrounging) whatever he determines is appropriate, and it is he who decides which materials shall be made accessible to the children, and when. Specific determination of these matters differs, of course, from teacher to teacher and from school to school; nonetheless, there do seem to be certain special considerations — or at least emphases — which pertain to open education classrooms in general:

Selection of materials is made principally according to the teacher's perception of children's needs.* In general terms, he will know their ages and abilities; more specifically, he will assess each child's particular requirements. Thus the teacher will be able to stock the classroom on the basis of his general knowledge and professional experience, yet suggest specific material following a diagnosis of the needs of each individual child. The teacher's job is to assist the child, who is already working on a problem of some sort, to extend his understanding of the matter at hand; that is, if he is in the midst of learning something about buoyancy in the water play area, the teacher might wish to introduce some additional material so that the child might learn to differentiate between a metal boat that sinks and one that floats. Thus most material available reflects a day-to-day response to the *current* and *particular* needs of a given group of children. Standardization in the selection of learning materials is therefore rare; no two classrooms are likely to be identically equipped on any given day.

With thirty children and only thirty pieces of equipment, any one child could only change activities by disrupting or coordinating his switch with some other child. The open education classroom seeks, therefore, to maintain a high density of materials, with few duplicates. When possible, multipurposed material is preferred over single-functioned objects; "raw" material that can be employed in a variety of ways is favored over ready-made "prepared" equipment that has but one lesson to teach. Teachers are suspicious of "unitized" or "purpose-specific" packaging by commercial publishers. Instead, they encourage children to introduce their own mate-

---

* *Would a proponent of Skinner's approach to learning select materials in this way?*

rials into the classroom and often seem to prefer scrounged or "junk" materials. Similarly, in selecting what to include in his classroom, the teacher does not hesitate to take his own interests and skills into account. A teacher with a particular interest in gemology, for instance, might well include in his classroom a number of books and rocks and display cases pertaining to his hobby. This would be done, naturally, to *enrich* the environment; he would not seek to force all students to follow him in this specialty, for to do so would be thought to have an *impoverishing* effect in the long run.

With regard to the *quality* of materials, there seems to be a general avoidance of nonfunctioning "toy" materials; that is, when children are permitted access to tools, they are given real tools, sharp enough to work properly; if a school decides to purchase microscopes, it is more likely to buy one good one than six inferior ones. Similarly, there is considerable emphasis on materials which incorporate or demand *overt activity* on the part of the child. Items that can be lifted, counted, weighed, measured, etc. are favored over those demanding mere passive observation. . . .

Although open education places great emphasis on the quality of learning material made available to children, it also recognizes that in and of itself this material is relatively useless. Without the involved, intellectual participation of teachers' and children's *minds*, acting upon and interacting with these materials, they are of little educational value. Although the teacher is principally responsible for stocking and equipping the classroom — both on a year-to-year and a day-to-day basis — the child in the open education classroom must, at another level, also be responsible for selecting and utilizing this learning equipment.* In other words, he is considered very much an "organizer" of instructional materials himself, responsible for writing his own agenda and designing his own ongoing curriculum. It is taken for granted that, while the teacher is organizing for instruction, the child is organizing for learning. . . .

Some Problems and the Need for Critical Analysis

Although descriptive analysis of the observable features of an educational environment is useful, it is also limited. For, insofar as classroom practice derives from pedagogical or philosophical belief, any attempt to separate its practical reality from the teacher's idealistic intent tends to distort the observer's perspective on both. The difficult task is to distinguish fact (what *actually* occurs or exists) from expectation (what someone *thinks* will occur or exist) from intent (what someone *wants* to have happen). To this point, the present description has set forth, uncritically,

* *This is a basic difference between open education and programmed instruction.*

many expectations and hopes of open education's proponents as they have related to the four organizational elements. To redress this imbalance, the final section will take a more critical position; in particular it will consider the issues of *definition, appropriateness,* and *evaluation.*

DEFINITION. Much discussion of open education — published and otherwise — has been characterized by a general vagueness of definition. Proponents speak of teaching "this way," or make reference to a nebulous "it" which "got started" in certain primary schools in England sometime after the war.... Particularly troublesome has been the definition of its educational objectives. In conversation with practitioners, one gets the feeling that at heart they honor some important but invisible affective curriculum — a host of unspecified, implicit educational objectives concerning the affective, psychological and attitudinal expectations of the open classroom. Were these objectives to be set down as "desired outcomes," * they might include:

The child will take responsibility for his own decisions and actions.

The child will be autonomous, acting and making decisions independently.

The child will have the ability and desire to set his own goals.

The child will possess self-discipline and will not need externally applied discipline.

The child will learn self-direction as a basis for organizing his life; he will be self-actualizing.

The child will have a capacity for long-term involvement at learning tasks of his own choosing.

The child will possess a willingness to experiment; he will demonstrate an ability to seek new solutions and new problems.

The child will have self-confidence.

The child will exhibit trust in himself and others.

The child will feel free; he will be socially and intellectually adaptable.

The child will feel comfortable with and confident of his own learning processes.

The child will be in touch with his own inner impulses; he will not fear fantasy or feeling.

The child will value the ethic of open education.

Yet rarely is any of these advanced as a clearly specified, intentional goal. As a result there is a promise, a hint, an intimation — but rarely a hard-and-fast commitment to a stated objective.... There is ambiguity, as well, about the intellectual content of these classrooms: discussion of

* *Compare the specificity of these "desired outcomes" with the examples given by Lindvall and Bolvin (this section). Are Rathbone's objectives measurable?*

the standards established for intellectual rigor is especially vague. Clearly, children in open education classrooms are expected to learn — and they do learn — such things as mathematics and music and geography. Yet all too rarely is there discussion of *which* mathematics, *which* music, *which* geography — or of the criteria employed in answering these questions.

From field observation one intuitively feels that children are in fact learning to think and to perform important skills, but certain doubts linger. Is this intellectual climate so permissive that "anything goes?" Are consistent standards maintained in ways recognizable to the children? Although multi-age grouping may reinforce the common humanity and essential equality of all students, might not it be taking place at the cost of mediocre levels of achievement? Could it be argued, for instance, that in a vertically-grouped situation a real leveling occurs, one that invites contentment with one's present position and discourages competitive striving for excellence? . . .

APPROPRIATENESS. Issues of appropriateness, although discussed among practitioners, are seldom raised in the literature on open education: the assumption seems to be that if it is good for one group of children, it must be good for all, and that if it is good for one child at five, it must be good for him when he is eight or fifteen. Clearly empirical research is needed; while waiting for its findings, however, it is permissible, even important, to speculate about the possible inappropriateness, or at least the *qualified* appropriateness, of the open education classroom:

Contending that a child's socioeconomic home background in large part determines not only his view of the world but his ability to cope with its manifold structures, it might be argued that for some "disadvantaged" lower SES children the flexibility of open education's organizational features would prove dysfunctional. Perhaps these children have a special need for clear and consistent — even inflexible — time schedules, rules for behavior, subject-matter distinctions, etc.* Perhaps, too, there are stages when even the average, normal child needs discipline from without to shore up his developing discipline from within.

To what extent may open education overemphasize the importance of the experiential, especially the "messing about," aspect of learning? Aren't some ideas best learned through direct observation or vicariously or by abstract reasoning, rather than through direct experience? Aren't there times (and subjects) when the quickest, most efficient, and most thorough way to learn something is simply to be told? Moreover, mightn't

---

* *Jensen makes specific recommendations for teaching lower SES and ethnic minority children (Section 4). Would he view open education as dysfunctional for them?*

it be true that all children are not equally comfortable with "things?" Aren't there some children who, naturally verbal and basically people-oriented, tend to become frustrated when faced with a constant barrage of strictly manual, manipulative tasks? *

Open education often appears to assume that all children will make profitable decisions, even when these decisions concern, not present desires, but what will be best for them in the long run. By allowing children such a wide range of choice, mightn't schools be risking the possibility that children will grow "lop-sided," becoming specialists prematurely?

A difficult question also arises concerning the appropriateness of open education in the higher grades. Some might well argue that, although multiple entry points permit easy access to the disciplines in their simpler, less complex lower orders, the higher one goes in disciplined knowledge, the more single-pathed the trail. There is also at stake here the question of goals: Are the goals of secondary schools essentially different from those of the lower grades? If so, open education might well prove appropriate for the one but inappropriate for the other.

Finally, there is the question of manipulation. Given its fundamental beliefs about freedom and choice, can open education ever be appropriate if it is presented as the *exclusive* mode for educating children? Or must it always exist as an alternative, an elective?

EVALUATION. Unresolved issues of appropriateness, combined with considerable definitional vagueness on the part of practitioners, conspire to make the evaluation of open education particularly troublesome.... Clearly, the most crucial question to be researched concerns the nature and quality of children's learning in the open education classroom. What do children really learn in this environment, and do they learn it better than in other kinds of classrooms? What elements within its general environment make it more (or less) conducive to which kinds of learning? And, assuming that the open education classroom is as susceptible to "unintended teaching" as any other, one needs to inquire into the precise nature of the unintended teaching and unintended learning that occur here....

There is a clear need, also, for the development of new, sophisticated instruments of assessment....For, when proponents of open education do manage to set down the questions they would most like answered, the list does not readily lend itself to any simple or established system of measurement. For example, Hull asks: [3]

> Do the students talk with each other about their work? Do they challenge ideas and interpretations with the purpose of reaching deeper

* *The basic question here is: can we designate instructional techniques without taking into account characteristics of the learner?*

understanding? Do they initiate activities which are new to the classroom? Do they continue to explore things which are not assigned — outside school as well as within? Do they persist over a period of days, weeks or months on things which capture their interest? Are they able to say, "I don't know," with the expectation that they are going to do something about finding out? Are they willing to attempt to express ideas about which they have only a vague and intuitive awareness? Do they recognize their own potential in growing towards competence? Can they deal with differences of opinion or differences in results on a reasonably objective basis, without being completely swayed by considerations of social status? Are they charitable and open in dealing with ideas with which they do not agree? Can they deal with distractions, avoid being at the mercy of the environment? Are they able to make connections between things which seem superficially unrelated? Do they have a sense of humor which can find expression in relation to things which are important to them?

Those of us concerned with the spread of open education in this country need, and await, instruments for measuring "autonomy," "creativity," and "responsibility." Meanwhile, if the movement is to develop and strengthen, we must gather all the "informal" evidence we can on how children learn in the open education setting, and on how teachers and schools change as they move toward less formal ways of dealing with children and curriculum in classrooms. . . .

EXERCISE

1. According to Rathbone, what are the advantages of the flexible boundaries of the open school? (pp. 333–334)

2. Why are time schedules kept flexible in an open classroom? (pp. 334–335)

3. What is vertical grouping? (pp. 335–336)

4. What type of learning materials are emphasized in open education programs? (pp. 337–338)

5. Why is it difficult to evaluate open education programs? (p. 341)

6. Can open education be considered to be an appropriate learning program for all students? What types of questions might be asked about its universal application? (pp. 340–341)

Skinner and the Open Classroom

Peter C. Madden

In 1971 the well-known behaviorist B. F. Skinner wrote Beyond Freedom and Dignity, *in which he states that although modern man turns to science and technology as a means for solving major problems, almost all these problems involve human behavior. He suggests that a technology of behavior is needed to resolve these problems. Operant conditioning — using reinforcers to encourage individuals to behave in particular ways — is the basis for the technology. A reinforcer is something that makes it more likely that a person will perform a particular behavior again. For example, as explained by Skinner, food is a reinforcer for a hungry organism; anything the organism does that is followed by the receipt of food is more likely to be done again whenever the organism is hungry. In this instance, food is a positive reinforcer. Donald Bushell's token manual (this section) is an example of how operant conditioning has been applied to a structured learning experience for students. However, proponents of open education (see Rathbone, previous selection) reject operant conditioning as a means for improving learning. In the following article, Peter Madden attempts to reconcile the principles of operant conditioning and the principles that underlie the open classroom. Specifically, he proposes that systematic use of reinforcers can improve open education programs. Do you agree?*

Now that the furor over the publication of B. F. Skinner's new book, *Beyond Freedom and Dignity,* is dying down, it may be possible to examine the implications of this major work from some different perspectives. It appears that the detailed points of the behaviorist position were largely overlooked in the critical shock created by Skinner's sweeping conclusions and proposals. No doubt the tendency of some ardent behaviorists like Skinner to pontificate rather than persuade has contributed to the hostility his observations received.

That is unfortunate, for it is details that behavioral research has always

From *School Review*, vol. 81, no. 1 (November 1972), pp. 100–107. Reprinted with permission of the University of Chicago Press and author. © 1972 by the University of Chicago.

handled most successfully.... I discovered in the early chapters many ideas of great relevance to the attempt by the University of North Dakota's New School for Behavioral Studies in Education to find ways to make classrooms less rigid and more humane.

From this point of view, *Beyond Freedom and Dignity* offered these suggestions about our cultural system:

1. The study of behavior has demonstrated by now that techniques like positive reinforcement offer a more effective way of changing and controlling behavior than such traditional means as punishment or requests for cooperation.*

2. There is no real freedom for the individual from the controlling pressures of either the natural or social environment. However, it is possible for the controls to become less visible in a free society since most of its members conform out of a sense of loyalty, peer-group pressure (real or perceived), or simply out of habit and convenience.

3. Advocates of human dignity object to large-scale adoption of behavioral theories by insisting that people continue to get credit for voluntary "good" acts. But in order to deal with those who refuse to be good voluntarily, a society is forced to maintain numerous punitive and disciplinary institutions.

4. While there is general acceptance of a belief that a poor environment can often explain failures of both individuals and groups, there is less willingness to accept the other side of that coin. Individual and group successes may be equally attributable to environmental forces and not actually the personal triumphs often envisioned.

5. Various types of positive reinforcements are available which could largely replace the aversive conditions and punishments which now operate in our society. The most effective reinforcers are those which simultaneously serve the need of the individual for gratification and the need of his society for cultural survival.

It seems to me these are Skinner's major observations in relation to the operation of societies in general and schools in particular. When taken in smaller doses, Skinner's ideas are neither as novel nor as provocative as the early criticism indicated. It has been almost a cliché for years that a greater investment in (positive) education, for example, should eventually lead to a lesser need for (negative) prisons. As to the effects of the environment, there is also consensus that the slums are surroundings which make solutions to educational and social problems difficult if not impossible.†

There is also widespread recognition that punishment is a rather ineffec-

---

* *Bushell's training manual (this section) is based on this premise.*
† *Is Madden saying that schools cannot influence the learner to the extent that the out-of-school environment can?*

tive means of changing behavior. Despite centuries of using punitive methods to control classroom behavior, student conduct (as traditionally defined by teachers and parents) remains a major problem in today's schools and consumes an enormous investment in time and effort. Massive expenditures on law enforcement and "rehabilitation" notwithstanding, the recidivism rate of most prisons remains at 80 percent or more.

As a psychologist who practices in schools, I often find it useful to view a school as a minisociety with a well-defined cultural system. Looking at schools and classrooms from Skinner's point of view, it is obvious that there is *always* control of conduct in the school. In an open classroom the teacher may have made a conscious decision to abandon some of the more traditional procedures, goals, and controls in order to substitute those of his own choosing. Among the ideals often selected by teachers in open classrooms are independent study, self-selection of curricular materials, creative expression by students, and development of a free, humane classroom atmosphere.

Many prominent writers concerned with open classrooms seem to suggest that these independent, creative activities will develop naturally if the child is just released from teacher-directed pressure and left free to choose what he wants to do in the classroom. This point of view is often reinforced by educators and students in colleges which are trying to develop teachers for open classrooms.

My experience tells me that the system just does not work that way, and I think a close examination of Skinner's ideas will reveal why. For one thing, a child is not — in fact — free simply because the teacher chooses not to exert obvious control over his behavior. Children enter a classroom filled with expectations derived from the conditioning of their previous experiences in schools. Graduates of the New School sometimes report strong initial pressure to reproduce the system to which the child has become accustomed. Both parents and students often ask for the workbooks to be brought back and complain that they do not know what to do under the new classroom system. . . .

Second, each child comes equipped with behavior norms which have been internalized through several years of interaction with and reinforcement by teachers, parents, and peers. Most children will go along with whatever new scheme the adults in authority come up with, especially in middle-class schools. Their conceptions of what constitutes acceptable behavior conform so closely to those of the adults that few conflicts arise in any classroom situation. These children move easily, if passively, through a variety of classroom environments ranging from the permissiveness of kindergarten to the rigidity of military training.

With these children, the major task of the teacher is simply to reinforce the efforts the children make to conform to the new system. Our North Dakota elementary students and New School undergraduates find that their anxiety in open educational situations is dispelled over a period of time, largely because they have been reinforced by their teachers for adopting such desired new behaviors as independent action in choosing and attempting to complete their own school experiences.

Some new teachers in open classrooms attempt a more passive role in which they offer a variety of attractive and interesting activities without giving children any sense of direction from above. These teachers refuse to use reinforcement because they view it as an imposition upon the students' freedom to pursue activities for their own intrinsic satisfaction. Unfortunately, the result is often chaotic classroom behavior. The children may respond to this situation by turning elsewhere in the environment for gratification, often to peers who tend to reward playing or similar behavior which provides instant and continuous reinforcement.

A common reaction of such teachers, who as students were often the most strenuous advocates of the right of children to be free and self-directed in the classroom, is despair and anger at what they come to regard as ingratitude on the part of the children to respond positively to the experience offered them. . . .

What these teachers apparently failed to understand was that control is not a process to be avoided but a tool which must be exercised in either a positive or a negative way. Having refused to systematically help children adapt to change through supportive means of control like positive reinforcement, they eventually had to regress to the traditional forms of structure and punishment, or negative reinforcement.*

As Skinner noted, a major problem for any society, whether nation or classroom, is dealing with individuals who do not behave in accordance with the society's need for cooperative, or at least nondestructive, behavior. . . .

Advocates of freedom, says Skinner, have traditionally dealt with uncooperative individuals by stating that they have the right to behave in any manner they wish *if* they are willing to abide by the consequences of their actions. Proponents of dignity add that to take away an individual's option to behave as he wishes if he will be held accountable infers that he loses the right to be "good" of his own accord. However, almost no one feels that freedom and dignity can or should be allowed to operate without accountability. For this reason, all the traditional aversive rituals and punishments are maintained despite their lack of effectiveness in dealing with individuals who abuse others in society while exercising their own freedom.

Thus, the test of any educational approach comes when teachers have to deal with the small number of countercontrol students in their classrooms. The rest of the students tend to have internalized enough conforming behavior standards and identify with the teacher to a degree that they will

* *Madden is assuming that learning is extrinsically motivated. What type of teacher control is necessary if we assume that learning is intrinsically motivated?*

go along with whatever the school seems to demand of them this year....

Traditional classroom teachers have generally relied on punishments and aversive techniques to maintain control of this dissident minority. Open classroom teachers who attempt to avoid using control or reinforcement tend to find themselves forced eventually to adopt similar methods as the result of pressure exerted by students, parents, administrators, or their own anxiety. The only viable alternative I can see is to recognize that every society requires some form of control. There seems to be no escape.

By examining the propositions that true freedom may be much more illusion than fact, while dignity may require punishment and degradation as an alternative, Skinner may have done educators a valuable service. Once we recognize the futility of completely discarding controls and creating absolute freedom, we can begin to maximize freedom and make controls less aversive and more humane. Skinner suggests that a greatly increased, well-organized use of positive reinforcement techniques may be the only way to reconcile any society's need for control with the individual's desire for freedom from aversive or punishing contingencies.

In the schools, this means a virtual abandonment of the kinds of threats and punishments so familiar to every teacher and student. Teachers must develop new powers of observation and learn to note, record, and reward the good things children do rather than swoop down with vengeance upon their errors. The classroom atmosphere must become positive and loving, drawing out desired behavior with encouragement and rewards rather than stressing and punishing failure. While this sounds idyllic, it is a mere technical skill, part of Skinner's "technology of behavior." After learning how to operate this way, teachers often respond, "Why, that is nothing more than common sense." Positive reinforcement may be merely common sense but in few classrooms today is it common practice! *...

If teachers view freedom of choice and self-direction as skills to be learned in small, sequential, reinforced steps rather than as the natural condition of American schoolchildren today, they find the path to creating and maintaining an open classroom much easier....

As Skinner notes, the power of positive reinforcement is both vast and neutral. While we may not be able to avoid control, we can and must consistently examine the values and goals of the controllers. Teacher education programs which offer this skill must also provide students with a grounding in humanities and philosophy that will give them a sense of values....

The effect is circular in operation. Positive reinforcement techniques will make possible the creation of an open classroom while the operation of

---

* As a student yourself, how often do you receive any type of positive reinforcement in your classes?

the open classroom will, in itself, minimize the negative effects of control.* The result can and should be the development of a humane classroom culture in which each child can learn not only to be free and independent but how to reconcile the demands of social living upon freedom.

EXERCISE

1. When is positive reinforcement (praise and reward) more desirable than negative reinforcement (punishment)? (pp. 344–345)

2. Madden suggests students express anxiety when they first enter an open education program. Why is this anxiety dispelled over time? (pp. 345–346)

3. According to Skinner, what rights do advocates of freedom and dignity think an uncooperative individual should have? (p. 346)

4. In Madden's opinion, can controls be completely discarded in the classroom? What reasons does he give for his answer? (pp. 346–347)

---

* *Will positive reinforcement work this way if the teacher rewards conforming, noncreative behavior in his students?*

Section Eleven

RADICAL CHANGE

Introduction

Frustration with the limited success of attempts to change schools (see Goodlad, Section 9) and the continuing low achievement of significant numbers of students within schools (Mayeske, Section 4) have led some educators to consider radically different approaches to improving learning.

Some of these approaches involve developing new schools outside the existing school system. Because these schools are not restricted by the regulations and organizational structure of the conventional school, the developers contend that students, parents, and other community members can have a greater voice in planning the learning program. New teaching methods, new instructional materials, and new ways of organizing for learning can be designed, implemented quickly, and tested. This approach has become known as the "free school movement" (or "alternative schools") because these schools are "free" of the controls that are usually placed upon the public schools. In this section Allen Graubard discusses the types of school emerging from this movement. Related to the free school, but more radical in design, are learning systems that eliminate even the physical structure of a school. All, or part, of the educational experience takes place in the social setting of the community, as Ivan Illich discusses in "Education without School: How It Can Be Done."

Will both free schools and the more radical educational systems provide opportunities to learn the skills and knowledge considered important by the authors presented in Part I? Will the range of skills presented by Robert Ebel, Carl Rogers, Harold Bessell, and James Banks be taught in these new programs? Also, will any of these skills be taught better than in the traditional school structure? In a provocative paper, Philip Jackson raises some questions about "deschooling" education that should be considered in evaluating the proposals of Graubard and Illich.

Free schools, alternative schools, and similar innovations involve changing the traditional school structure in some way. Another radical approach is to change the learner himself. For example, advancements in medicine, biology, and chemistry suggest that learning can be improved by using such techniques as electrical stimulation of the brain, drugs, and even hypnosis. These techniques are a fundamentally new approach to increasing learning, particularly when compared to the traditional approaches of attempting to increase learning by improving the curriculum or the teaching process (for example, programmed instruction and the open classroom). Edward Sullivan and Martin Astor each discuss these new techniques. Although some educators believe that changing the learner by psychochemical or hypnotic methods has merit, it does raise many questions about the human rights of the learner. To determine where you stand, as an individual or as a teacher, you may find it helpful to decide whether you agree or disagree with the following views.

The Free School Movement

Pro   The traditional school structure cannot be expected to change. The only alternative is to develop entirely new schools that are free of the old rules and regulations. The new schools will be more sensitive to today's student and therefore will help him learn better.

Con   Innovations being introduced into the traditional school structure, such as the open classroom or individualized instruction, will do as much, or more, to improve learning as the free school movement. Free schools have a negative effect because they draw effort away from improving traditional schools.

Changing the Learner

Pro   The learner, not the learning environment, should be changed. Educators should use medical, biological, and chemical methods to improve the learning capability of the student.

Con   The many faults in the educational system must be removed before we can consider changing the learner. Chemicals cannot make up for bad schools.

The Free School Movement

Allen Graubard

Since the 1960's, many people have moved outside the public school system to establish new schools that are free of traditional academic and political restrictions. Allen Graubard, author of Free the Children: Radical Reform and the Free School Movement *(Pantheon Books), reports on a survey of these alternative schools made between March and August 1971. A major finding is that the number of "free" schools has increased sharply since 1970, which is consistent with the spread of open education (see Rathbone, Section 10) and the growing emphasis on the human aspects of education. The rapid growth of free schools suggests that people are dissatisfied with traditional education. Decide whether the various free schools described by Graubard could exist within a public elementary school or high school. How would your teaching role differ in a free school as compared with a public school? One survey shows that the average life of a free school is only nine months. Why might this occur?*

About nine of every ten American school children attend the public schools. The great majority of the remaining ten per cent satisfy the compulsory school attendance laws in parochial schools, although this number has declined sharply over the past few years. A small number of children are educated in private "prep" schools, which are often small, expensive, and elite. The economic troubles of the past few years have been an important factor in the decline in both the number and enrollments of these non-public schools.

Yet, while the customary American private school education has begun to decline, a very special kind of private school has appeared and grown astonishingly in numbers. These schools have received increasing attention from the media and from people interested in educational reform. They are most frequently called "free schools," though they are also known as "new schools" or "alternative schools." In five years the number of these free schools has grown from around 25 to perhaps 600; around 200 have been founded in the past year alone. These schools are usually very small: in absolute numbers of participants — students, parents, and staff — the phenomenon is very limited, but their public impact and symbolic significance are relatively great.

From *Harvard Educational Review*, vol. 42, no. 3 (August 1972), pp. 351–373. Reprinted with permission of publisher and author. Copyright © 1972 by the President and Fellows of Harvard College.

This essay presents some objective data about free schools along with a discussion of the various educational and social change concepts which underlie them. Particular emphasis is given to the extent to which differences of social class, ethnicity, and political perspective contribute to the variation of styles within the broad free school movement. My purpose is to give an overview of the movement, to analyze its significance, and to speculate about its future, especially in relation to reform within the public school system.

The basic theoretical concept is, naturally, freedom. The literature of radical school reform associated with free schools vehemently opposes the compulsory and authoritarian aspects of traditional public and private schools. This literature attacks the emotional and intellectual effects of conventional pedagogy and projects a radical theory in which freedom is the central virtue.... The general notion is that children are naturally curious and motivated to learn by their own interests and desires.* The most important condition for nurturing this natural interest is freedom supported by adults who enrich the environment and offer help. In contrast, coercion and regimentation only inhibit emotional and intellectual development. It follows that almost all of the major characteristics of public school organization and method are opposed — the large classes, the teacher with absolute power to administer a state-directed curriculum to rigidly defined age groups, the emphasis on discipline and obedience, the constant invidious evaluation and the motivation by competition, the ability tracking, and so forth.

We can see in this central concept of freedom two distinct ideological sources for an alternative school movement, one political and one pedagogical (or more broadly, cultural). These sources are in real tension, sometimes even contradiction. By the *political* source, I mean the spirit behind the first "freedom" schools — those in Mississippi, in 1964 — when groups of people sought control of the oppressive educational processes to which they and their children were being subjected. This spirit is seen in the movement for community control. It views the public schools and most professional educators with great hostility, and it articulately opposes indoctrination in the content and method of the public schools. This spirit has been most extensively expressed in black communities' struggle for control of public schools. But over the past few years some minority community groups have turned their anger and energy toward starting their own alternative schools, despairing of the possibilities of working inside the system.†

---

* *Advocates of free schools believe in intrinsic motivation for learning. Skinnerians (e.g., Bushell, Section 10) believe in extrinsic motivation. Can either side be proven right or wrong?*
† *Does the community know enough about learning to design new schools?*

These schools emphasize control by the local community, black (or brown or red) consciousness in the curriculum, and the schools' participation in the political and social struggle for equality; the pedagogical idea of allowing each child the freedom to unfold his or her individuality is not given so dominant a position as in most middle-class free schools. So, in many of the black community schools, there is a good deal of structure and organization, including, sometimes, required classes, well-organized compulsory activities run by the teacher, intensive drilling in basic skills — items which contradict in varying degrees the more strictly pedagogical concept of freedom.

If one looks back about six or seven years, one can see the two strands in the earliest days of the free school wave — there were a few Summerhillian schools (e.g., Lewis-Wadhams in New York State, founded in 1963) and a few black community schools starting in the ghettos (e.g., Roxbury Community School, 1966).

Each kind of school is an alternative, articulating a profound opposition to the methods and results of the public schools (this is not true of most private schools); each is a "free" school. But one trend emphasizes the role of the school in the community's struggle for freedom and equality (the freedom of the "Freedom now!" cry of the civil rights movement), while the other represents the strongest possible claim for the individual child's freedom from coercive approaches to learning and social development as expressed by the organization and techniques of most public schools.

The complex differences and possible tensions between these two sources of freedom make it difficult to specify clearly what is a free school and what is not....

Free Schools: Some Data and a Typology

The complicated problem of definition should be kept in mind in approaching the data that follows. How "free" must a school be for it to count as a "free school" pedagogically? And if a black school is militant and community-controlled, but has rather traditional pedagogy and methods, is it a "free school"? For most of the schools, identification is not a problem. But there are fairly significant grey areas which have occasioned some subjective judgments in gathering the data. Consequently, the data, though it looks precise, being numbers and percentages, should be taken softly, and it is offered in this spirit. It was gathered between March and August, 1971, by the New Schools Directory Project,[1] a group of free school people who wanted to compile an accurate and detailed directory of existing alternative schools....

The Project proceeded as follows: a small central group went over every existing listing of "free schools" to contact free school people in different areas of the country, including regional free school switchboard people. These contacts gathered some rough "objective" information by checking the local lists and visiting other free schools in their area. All leads were checked in an effort to find previously unlisted schools. Rough as the methods were, I think we missed only a few of the free schools then in existence. (Some 200 schools opened in September 1971, and most of these were not included in the survey.) My own check of the data indicates that the range of accuracy was 80–90%.

The survey limited itself to "outside-the-system" schools. Free school-type programs within the public school system have proliferated rapidly, with important implications for the free school movement. But the concern of the survey was with the grass roots movement that had begun outside of the state-controlled system.

The number of free schools has increased dramatically during the past five years. . . . A few very progressive or Summerhillian schools (less than five) were founded every year during the early 1960's. Then, in 1966 and 1967, the real rise of free schools began, simultaneous with the growth of a widespread movement for social change and an increasingly radical critique of American institutions. Around 20 free schools were founded in 1967 and 1968. Over 60 were founded in 1969. By 1970, the number was around 150, and, as mentioned before, the number of new free schools begun during 1971–72 is substantially greater. . . .

Given the difficulties of starting schools, this dramatic rise in the number of parents, students, and teachers who are willing to make the enormous commitment needed to start their own school is significant far beyond the actual numbers. It is obvious that if there were a free-choice tuition voucher plan or the widespread possibility of alternatives inside the public school system, the number of new free schools and participants would be much greater than at present. . . .

The following figures are based on the survey of 346 schools. . . .

DISTRIBUTION BY STATE. . . . Thirty-nine states have at least one free school. It should be noted that four states — California, New York, Massachusetts, and Illinois — have fifty-two per cent of the total surveyed. California alone has twenty-seven per cent. There appear to be several particular areas of free school concentration — the San Francisco Bay area, the Chicago area, the Boston area, Madison-Milwaukee, and Minneapolis-St. Paul. There is good reason to think that cosmopolitan urban areas, especially those with high concentrations of university and college-associated people, generate the critical masses of people who share the philosophy of free schools and have the willingness and capability to commit the necessary time, energy, and resources to such efforts.* . . .

* Could it be that free schools reflect adult biases about the learning process, rather than what is best for children?

STAFF CHARACTERISTICS.... In most free schools there are part-time and volunteer teachers, as well as parents, who participate in teaching and other staff activities. In many schools some of the volunteers and part-time teachers share community governance and policy-making with full-time staff. It is impossible to ascertain precisely either the number of volunteers or the time that part-time and volunteer staff put in. What can be said is that free schools generally emphasize the importance of individual attention and small intimate groups, and the staff-student ratios bear this out. A rough estimate which included all volunteers and part-time staff would be about 1:3, while a figure which involved only full-time staff would be 1:7.*

Black teachers are concentrated almost completely in the relatively small number of black community schools and street academies. It is obvious that free school teachers are a considerably younger group than teachers in general. As compared to the national mean age for teachers of thirty-seven years, almost seventy per cent of free school teachers are below thirty, and it is safe to say that at least eighty-five per cent are below the national mean age.

This age distribution suggests some fairly obvious speculations. First, a significant part of the free school movement is related to the youth and student movement of the 1960's, both political and cultural. Second, many schools are started by young parents of very young children, and some of them become the teachers. Finally, the financial situation of most free schools makes it difficult for older people with families to participate, given their need for job security and dependable income. Young people, mobile and without encumbering family responsibilities, constitute the most obvious pool for very low paid and volunteer staff.

SCHOOL SIZE AND FINANCES. The data on school size and finances are especially interesting and revealing. A discussion of these figures will serve as a basis for a detailed typology of the free schools.

Most urban Americans think of schools as institutions housed in large expensive buildings, containing anywhere from a few hundred students (elementary) to two, three, or four thousand students (high schools). In contrast, the average size for the free schools in this survey is approximately thirty-three students. Approximately two-thirds of the schools have an enrollment of less than forty.... This fact can be explained mainly as a conscious commitment to a special kind of intimate community. Many free school people value the idea that everyone in the school knows everyone else fairly well; that staff people can truly relate to each other and to all the children, thus avoiding the impersonality associated with

* *Wouldn't this teacher-student ratio significantly improve learning even in a conventional classroom (see Templeton, Section 7)?*

mass education institutions. Many free schools refuse to expand beyond thirty or forty, fearing that some of the essential qualities of the free school atmosphere would be lost. Some schools have actually decided to reduce enrollment from around thirty down to twenty because the people involved felt that even thirty was too large a group. . . .

The main source of income, as one would expect for non-public schools, is tuition. Eighty-one per cent of the schools charge tuition, with almost all of them stating that they give scholarships. Since the great majority of these schools use a sliding scale for tuition, the concept of "scholarship" is quite hazy. Most schools ask people to pay what they feel they can afford, hoping there will be enough high tuition payers to balance the people who can afford little. This is important since most free schools do not want to see themselves as "elite" private schools providing a special form of education for those who can afford it. Tuition for most traditional private schools ranges from $1500 to $4000 per year, while a sampling of schools in the survey shows that the normal range for free schools would be $0 to about $1200 per year. It is impossible to determine the average paid tuition, as we were unable to get accurate data concerning how many paid what.

Almost all the schools which do not charge tuition are true community schools and street academies serving poor and minority groups. There is no tuition because the people starting the schools intended to involve groups who can not afford it. The founders wanted to provide true alternatives to the public system rather than private schools that are alternatives only for those who can afford them (and a few scholarship cases). A good example of the tuition-free school is the Children's Community Workshop School in Manhattan. An elementary school with around 125 students, it is completely integrated racially and by class, and is parent controlled, with many poor black and Puerto-Rican parents involved. The school has been supported (with a large, well-paid staff) by contributions from foundations, but financial hardships during the past year have threatened its survival. However, the local school board has voted to grant the Workshop School "public" status, and stability may be achieved with public money. . . .

TYPES OF FREE SCHOOLS. Within the summary data presented above it is important to distinguish among several different types of free schools: The "classical" free school, the parent-teacher cooperative elementary school, the free high school, and the community elementary school.

The *"classical" free school* is the Summerhillian-influenced community, usually quite small and enrolling students of all ages. Many of these are boarding schools that aim to be truly self-sufficient, intimate, even therapeutic whole communities. As the Summerhill Ranch School in Mendocino, California, wrote in its brochure:

Educationally, this school can be described as 24-hour life tutorial, where students and staff learn in accordance with their own interests ... our emotional developments remain primary. Self-awareness, individuality and personal responsibility to oneself and to others here are most important. We have not the rewards and punishments nor the competitiveness of public schools. Many of us regain self-confidence and awareness here, both of which aid us in dealing with the impersonal real world.*

These schools are almost exclusively white and middle-class in their constituency, and, when boarding schools, they are naturally quite expensive. They emphasize the emotional and expressive aspects of the personality rather than the formal academic curriculum or job preparation. Development replaces achievement as the primary purpose. Collective decision-making often plays a central role in school activities.

A second type, which overlaps the first, is the *parent-teacher cooperative elementary school*. These schools are formed by parents, especially young, white, liberal, middle-class parents who do not want their children subjected to the regimentation of the normal public schools. They read John Holt's books and Joseph Featherstone's articles on the open classroom as it has developed in the British Infant Schools.† Some parents call others; they organize a meeting and decide to start a free elementary school. They find sympathetic teachers who are willing to sacrifice financial reward for the satisfaction of the job. Often one or more of the parents will be full-time teachers in the school. A parent board officially controls the school and participates regularly in school activities, though the staff handles much of the day-to-day operation. Tuition is paid on a sliding scale and usually some minority students are admitted free or almost free; but in general, these schools do not really appeal to poor-minority parents, and in any case, they are not intended to confront the problems of ghetto families and their children. . . .

Another type, the *free high school*, includes several variants, again determined by the social class constituency and the way the political and the pedagogical aspects of the "freedom" idea interact. They are high school counterparts to the Summerhillian schools, oriented toward the white middle class and hip youth counterculture. In contrast with the types mentioned above, prospective students usually provide the initial impetus, along with some committed adults who are potential staff. Deeply disenchanted with the public schools, these young people want to be involved honestly in the planning and governance of their own school. Several of these middle-class high schools project a politically radi-

---

* Can this type of emotional development also be encouraged in a conventional classroom? Harold Bessell (Section 2) claims that it is possible.
† Holt's ideas about teaching and learning are presented in Sections 1 and 13.

cal perspective in their rhetoric, curriculum, and other activities. This does not mean that all the young people in such schools are activists, but that some of the originators and staff are, and that activism is in the atmosphere. These schools often participate in anti-war and civil rights activities, and the classes often focus on the Vietnam War, draft resistance, women's liberation, and the legal rights and difficulties of youth.

In the past couple of years, several white working-class high schools have formed, a development with no parallel in the earlier progressive education movement. These schools involve mainly drop-outs and potential drop-outs who feel very hostile to their public high schools....

These working-class schools differ from their middle-class counterparts by directing a much greater focus on vocational help and remedial work and by exhibiting a real concern with thinking through what it means to be of the working class....

The working-class schools — with their constituency of public school "drop-outs" and "push-outs" — thus directly confront the tracking function of the public schools which "prepare" these students for the lower rungs of the social and job hierarchy.* In contrast, students in middle-class free schools have been slated for college and high career achievement. For them, the free high school is a way to get off, for a while at least, the beaten path to college and beyond.

Another variant of the high schools for drop-outs, more established and larger than the white working class schools, are the street academies for poor minority youth. The most famous of these is Harlem Prep, with over 400 students, but there are such places in most large cities. They are organized by adults, often with the support of community groups (e.g., the local Urban League). They seek to reawaken motivation in young people who have been completely turned off by school. While there is an atmosphere of discipline, the students do not perceive it as the same sort of discipline they experienced in the public schools. Instead, street academy discipline comes from having staff who can relate well with the students, and from the idea of black people "getting it together."

The street academies have a sense of participation, though far from the Summerhillian image of community, participatory democracy, and almost unlimited individual choice. The pedagogy with its emphasis on skills is more conventional, and the strong commitment to getting the young people into colleges differs from the mood of the dominant free high school culture.

The *community elementary schools*, as noted above, tend to be much larger and more highly organized than the average free school. More than the middle-class groups, the people who start community schools see the

---

* According to Bane and Jencks (Section 3), do schools influence an individual's eventual level of employment?

struggle for community control of the public schools as a vital goal; for them the politics of control are more important than the pedagogical emphasis of middle-class reform groups. These community schools put great stress on skills and on cultural consciousness and pride. Low-income parents, wary of romantic "freedom and spontaneity" rhetoric, often seem to support the more traditional classroom approaches, including strict discipline. Nevertheless, there is still a good deal of pedagogical innovation and libertarian atmosphere in these community schools. The implication here is that when the parents and community people feel they are in control, they are more open to "experimentation" than when it — like all the other school stuff they know — is imposed by the system which has been failing their children for years. . . .

Free Schools and Social Change

The classification above describes ideal types. Many of the schools, of course, combine aspects of different types. For example, the New Community School, a high school in Oakland, has a large white middle-class group, but provides a strong Black Studies program for its large minority of poor black students. Behind the different schools stand a variety of conceptions, not only of education but also of social change and how educational reform relates to more general political and social issues.

Within the Summerhillian tradition there is a definite "apolitical" quality. The school-community deliberately looks inward, sometimes consciously disengaging itself from the larger community and its affairs; the public schools are simply ignored. This perspective makes a minimal political demand on the larger society: to be left alone by the authorities — for instance, health and fire officials who don't like "hippie schools" — so that those who share the philosophy can "do their own thing."

A more social change-oriented expression of this apolitical perspective conceives of the free schools as exemplars and models of what good schools could be like, moving others, even in the public schools, to change. Another more radical rationale conceives of the growth of these free schools as a kind of strategy to attack and weaken the public school system as more and more people withdraw from it to start their own free schools. Throughout, one underlying view of social change is that the libertarian pedagogy and the schools based upon it will develop children who are joyful, cooperative, and peaceful, neither racist nor sexist nor repressed — and the more people like this, the greater the progress toward solving social ills and building a humane, just society.* . . .

The political strand in the education reform movement insists on the

---

* Should schools be used to bring about social change, or should they reflect the prevailing culture?

essentially political nature of the educational system. In particular, it stresses the way the groups in control of the major institutions of society use the school system and other institutions to help maintain the status quo. (This assertion need not evoke a plot; it is true about institutions in any social order.) From this point of view, the very concept of educational reform presents ambiguities. Black and other minority communities either start their own community schools outside the system or try to exert enough political power to get control of the public schools in their communities. They want to make schools major instruments in the struggle for freedom and equality. But many of the problems of the schools are not the product of the schools alone. The value of liberal education, the chance for getting jobs which are intrinsically satisfying and financially rewarding, the sense of growing up in a stable, sustaining social community — these conditions are not readily available to poor and minority youth. Neither community control of schools, nor a really effective alternative school like Harlem Prep, nor the new white working-class high schools can change the basic discouraging social reality that most "lower class" or "disadvantaged" young people encounter. From the political perspective, although these community free schools can often do good things for some young people who were "failed" and unhappy in the public schools, they have only been able to work with a very small number — and they have not been able to "save" all of these.

So, from this perspective, truly liberating educational reform that works for all children can only come with major social, political, economic, and cultural transformations that eliminate not only bad educational conditions but also the roots of those conditions in other institutions....

LOOKING AHEAD. Alternatives inside the public sector supported by local, state, or federal aid, are sure to spread in the very near future. (A recent column by Albert Shanker in the weekly propaganda slot the teachers' union buys in *The New York Sunday Times* confirmed this assertion. Shanker attacks the claims of success for alternative schools — in a misleading and dishonest manner. But his tone is very defensive, as if against a growing trend he opposes.) Many parent groups are organizing to ask the school authorities for alternative public schools committed to libertarian methods.... The number of teachers, parents, and students who want such schools is growing, even though most Americans would still say that they basically approve the traditional style of the average public school. As noted, the number of free schools continues to increase rapidly. But contrary to the predictions of some free education activists, this development will not mushroom into thousands of schools and hundreds of thousands of students. As the difficulties of running free schools and scrounging even for meager resources become more widely known, enthusiasm will diminish. And as pressure for reform builds up on the public school system, it will seem more realistic as a strategy to get an alternative public school established, even at the cost of some compromise with the system, than to establish another small and fragile free school that might easily fail after a couple of years. Even now, some schools that started outside the system are trying to figure out ways of being accepted as public schools in some form, without giving up their essential spirit or autonomy.... For many free school people with a political perspective, the possibility of free schools being alternative public schools will be very attractive, despite the constant danger of being coopted and controlled.* As part of public systems, reformers will be able to gain more visibility and influence for their innovations. Also, public financial support will enable schools serving poorer communities to achieve the stability needed to attract parents to what might at first seem a dubious experiment.

Some free schools will prefer to maintain their independence so as to ensure freedom from the pressures and compromises inevitably imposed by involvement in the public system. This stance includes both politically and pedagogically oriented school reformers, since it is obvious that there are free schools expressing both strands that would be too "far out" for any state system to tolerate.

Within a few years the free school movement has emerged as a significant phenomenon, if not for its actual numbers, then for its symbolic significance as representative of the spreading popularity of radical reform ideas. There have been other movements of radical progressive reform; movements that do not seem to have accomplished the serious changes of the sort they initially envisioned. We can hope that the new wave of radical school reform will find ways to avoid repeating this melancholy history.

EXERCISE

1. What is the basic concept of a free school? What characteristics of the public school are opposed? (p. 352)

2. What are the two ideological sources for an alternative school movement? How do these movements differ in the things emphasized in the "free" schools? (pp. 352–353)

3. How do free schools compare with public schools in enrollment and type of staff? (pp. 355–356)

4. Describe the four major types of free schools. (pp. 357–359)

5. Why does Graubard think the public school system will absorb the free school movement? (pp. 360–361)

---

* *Shouldn't schools be left outside the political arena? Or is the learning process social-political in its very nature and consequences?*

Education without School: How It Can Be Done

Ivan Illich

> *In the preceding article, Allen Graubard described schools being established outside the regular public school system. A different and more radical approach is to consider an educational program that does not need a "school" — a program which eliminates the conventional elements of buildings, textbooks, teachers, and administrators that currently make up an educational system. Ivan Illich describes one such program, called an "inverse" of school. He looks at what is needed to learn, where these resources might be, and how they could be made available to learners of all ages. The research of the authors presented in this book — Popham's findings regarding trained and untrained teachers, Brown's discussion of modeling, Marland's plan for career education, Husén's review of time spent in school, Hall's discussion of computer-assisted instruction — are all considered in Illich's system. Do you believe children and adults could acquire all the skills needed in a modern, technological society by using the four learning networks which Illich proposes?*

A NEW STYLE OF EDUCATIONAL RELATIONSHIP

A common complaint about schools — one that is reflected, for example, in the recent report of the Carnegie Commission is that in school registered students submit to certified teachers in order to obtain certificates of their own; both are frustrated and both blame insufficient resources — money, time, or buildings — for their mutual frustration.

Such criticism leads many people to ask whether it is possible to conceive of a different style of learning. The same people, paradoxically, when pressed to specify how they acquired what they know and value, will readily admit that they learned it more often outside than inside

Abridgment and adaptation of "Learning Webs," from *Deschooling Society* by Ivan Illich, Copyright © 1971 by Ivan Illich. Originally appeared in *The New York Review of Books*, under the title "Education Without School: How It Can Be Done." Reprinted by permission of Harper and Row, Publishers, Inc., and the author.

school.* Their knowledge of facts, their understanding of life and work came to them from friendship or love, while viewing TV or while reading, from examples of peers or the challenge of a street encounter. Or they may have learned what they know through the apprenticeship ritual for admission to a street gang or the initiation to a hospital, newspaper city room, plumber's shop, or insurance office. The alternative to dependence on schools is not the use of public resources for some new device which *makes* people learn, rather it is the creation of a new style of educational relationship between man and his environment. To foster this style, attitudes toward growing up, the tools available for learning, and the quality and structure of daily life will have to change concurrently.

Attitudes are already changing. The proud dependence on school is gone. Consumer resistance is increasing in the knowledge industry. Many teachers and pupils, taxpayers and employers, economists and policemen would prefer not to depend any longer on schools. What prevents their frustration from shaping new institutions is a lack not only of imagination but frequently also one of appropriate language and of enlightened self-interest. They cannot visualize either a deschooled society or educational institutions in a society which disestablishes school.

In this essay, I intend to show that the *inverse of school* is possible: that we can depend on self-motivated learning instead of employing teachers to bribe or compel the student to find time and the will to learn; that we can provide the learner with new links to the world instead of continuing to funnel all educational programs through the teacher.† I shall discuss some of the general characteristics which distinguish *schooling* from *learning* and outline four major categories of educational institutions which should appeal not only to many individuals but also to many existing interest groups.

AN OBJECTION: WHO CAN BE SERVED BY BRIDGES TO NOWHERE?

We are used to considering schools as a variable, dependent on the political and economic structure. If we can change the style of political leadership, or promote the interests of one class or another, or switch from private to public ownership of the means of production, we assume the school system will change as well. The educational institutions I will propose, however, are meant to serve a society which does not now exist, although the current frustration with schools is itself potentially a major

* *Many educational psychologists take this position, e.g., Bane and Jencks (Section 3).*
† *Notice the emphasis on intrinsic motivation for learning. Compare with Skinner's principles of extrinsic reinforcement (Section 1).*

force to set in motion change toward new social arrangements. An obvious objection has been raised to this approach: Why channel energy to build bridges to nowhere, instead of marshaling it first to change not the schools but the political and economic system?

This objection, however, underestimates the repressive political and economic nature of the school system itself, as well as the political potential inherent in a new educational style. In a basic sense, schools have ceased to be dependent on the ideology professed by a government or the organization of its market. Even the Chinese feel they must adopt the basic international structure of schooling in order to become a world power and a nation state. Control of society is reserved everywhere to those who have consumed at least four units of four years, each unit consisting of 500 to 1000 hours in the classroom.

School . . . is the major component of the system of consumer production which is becoming more complex and specialized and bureaucratized. Schooling is necessary to produce the habits and expectations of the managed consumer society. Inevitably it produces institutional dependence and ranking in spite of any effort by the teacher to teach the contrary. It is an illusion that schools are only a dependent variable — an illusion which, moreover, provides them, the reproductive organs of a consumer society, with their immunity.

Even the piecemeal creation of new educational agencies which are the inverse of a school would therefore be an attack on the most sensitive link of a pervasive phenomenon, which is organized by the state in all countries. A political program which does not explicitly recognize the need for deschooling is not revolutionary; it is demagoguery calling for more of the same. Any major political program of the seventies should be evaluated by this measure: How clearly does it state the need for deschooling, and how clearly does it provide guidelines for the educational quality of the society for which it aims?

The struggle against domination by the world market and big power politics might be beyond some poor communities or countries, but this weakness is an added reason for emphasizing the importance of liberating each society through a reversal of its educational structure, a change which is not beyond any society's means.

GENERAL CHARACTERISTICS OF NEW FORMAL EDUCATIONAL INSTITUTIONS

A good educational system should have three purposes: it should provide all who want to learn with access to available resources at any time in their lives; empower all who want to share what they know to find those who want to learn it from them, and finally, furnish all who want to present an issue to the public with the opportunity to make their challenge known. Such a system would require the application of constitutional guarantees to education. Learners should not be enforced to submit to an obligatory curriculum or to discrimination based on whether they possess a certificate or a diploma. Nor should the public be forced to support — through a regressive taxation — a huge professional apparatus of educators and buildings which in fact restricts the public's chances for learning to the services the profession is willing to put on the market. It should use modern technology to make free speech, free assembly, and a free press truly universal and, therefore, fully educational.

Schools are designed on the assumption that there is a secret to everything in life, that the quality of life depends on knowing that secret, that secrets can be known only in orderly successions, and that only teachers can properly reveal these secrets. An individual with a schooled mind conceives of the world as a pyramid of classified packages accessible only to those who carry the proper tags. New educational institutions would break apart this pyramid. Their purpose must be to facilitate access for the learner: to allow him to look into the windows of the control room or the parliament, if he cannot get in the door. Moreover, such new institutions should be channels to which the learner would have access without credentials or pedigree — public spaces in which peers and elders outside his immediate horizon now become available.

I believe that no more than four — possibly even three — distinct "channels" or learning exchanges could contain all the resources needed for real learning. The child grows up in a world of things, surrounded by people who serve as models for skills and values. He finds peers who challenge him to argue, to compete, to cooperate, and to understand; and if the child is lucky, he is exposed to confrontation or criticism by an experienced elder who really cares. Things, models, peers, and elders are four resources — each of which requires a different type of arrangement to ensure that everybody has ample access to them.

I will use the word "network" to designate specific ways to provide access to each of four sets of resources.... What are needed are new networks, readily available to the public and designed to spread equal opportunity for learning and teaching.

To give an example: The same level of technology is used in TV and in tape recorders. All Latin American countries now have introduced TV; in Bolivia the government has financed a TV station, which was built six years ago, and there are no more than 7,000 TV sets for four million citizens. The money now tied up in TV installations throughout Latin America could have provided every fifth adult with a tape recorder. In addition, the money would have sufficed to provide an almost unlimited library of prerecorded tapes, with outlets even in remote villages, as well as an ample supply of empty tapes.

This network of tape recorders, of course, would be radically different from the present network of TV. It would provide opportunity for free expression: literate and illiterate alike could record, preserve, disseminate, and repeat their opinions. The present investment in TV instead provides bureaucrats, whether politicians or educators, with the power to sprinkle the continent with institutionally produced programs which they — or their sponsors — decide are good for or in demand by the people. Technology is available to develop either independence and learning or bureaucracy and preaching.

FOUR NETWORKS

The planning of new educational institutions ought not to begin with the administrative goals of a principal or president, or with the teaching goals of a professional educator, or with the learning goals of any hypothetical class of people. It must not start with the question, "What should someone learn?" but with the question, "What kinds of things and people might learners want to be in contact with in order to learn?"

Someone who wants to learn knows that he needs both information and critical response to its use from somebody else. Information can be stored in things and in persons. In a good educational system, access to things ought to be available at the sole bidding of the learner, while access to informants requires, in addition, others' consent. Criticism can also come from two directions: from peers or from elders, that is, from fellow learners whose immediate interests match his own or from those who will grant him a share in their superior experience. Peers can be colleagues with whom to raise a question, companions for playful and enjoyable (or arduous) reading or walking, challengers at any type of game. Elders can be consultants on which skill to learn, which method to use, what company to seek at a given moment. They can be guides to the right questions to be raised among peers and to the deficiency of answers they arrive at.

Educational resources are usually labeled according to educators' curricular goals. I propose to do the contrary, to label four different approaches which enable the student to gain access to any educational resource which may help him to define and achieve his own goals:

1. Reference Services to Educational Objects — which facilitate access to things or processes used for formal learning. Some of these things can be reserved for this purpose, stored in libraries, rental agencies, laboratories, and showrooms like museums and theaters; others can be in daily use in factories, in airports, or on farms but made available to students as apprentices or on off-hours.

2. Skill Exchanges — which permit persons to list their skills, the conditions under which they are willing to serve as models for others who want to learn these skills, and the addresses at which they can be reached.

3. Peer Matching — a communication network which permits persons

to describe the learning activity in which they wish to engage in the hope of finding a partner for the inquiry.

4. Reference Services to Educators-at-large — who can be listed in a directory giving the addresses and self-descriptions of professionals, paraprofessionals, and free-lancers, along with conditions of access to their services. Such educators, as we will see, could be chosen by polling or consulting their former clients.

REFERENCE SERVICES TO EDUCATIONAL OBJECTS. Things are basic resources for learning. The quality of the environment and the relationship of a person to it will determine how much he learns incidentally.* Formal learning requires special access to ordinary things, on the one hand, or, on the other, easy and dependable access to special things made for educational purposes. An example of the former is the special right to operate or dismantle a machine in a garage. An example of the latter is the general right to use an abacus, a computer, a book, a botanical garden, or a machine withdrawn from production and placed at the full disposal of students.

At present, attention is focused on the disparity between rich and poor children in their access to things and in the manner in which they can learn from them. OEO and other agencies, following this approach, concentrate on equalizing chances by trying to provide more educational equipment for the poor. A more radical point of departure would be to recognize that in the city rich and poor alike are artificially kept away from most of the things that surround them. Children born into the age of plastics and efficiency experts must penetrate two barriers which obstruct their understanding: one built into things and the other around institutions. Industrial design creates a world of things that resist insight into their nature, and schools shut the learner out of the world of things in their meaningful setting. . . .

Industry has surrounded people with artifacts whose inner workings only specialists are allowed to understand. The nonspecialist is discouraged from figuring out what makes a watch tick, or a telephone ring, or an electric typewriter work by being warned that it will break if he tries. He can be told what makes a transistor radio work but he cannot find out for himself. This type of design tends to reinforce a noninventive society in which the experts find it progressively easier to hide behind their expertise and beyond evaluation.

The man-made environment has become as inscrutable as nature is for the primitive. At the same time, educational materials have been monopolized by school. Simple educational objects have been expensively packaged by the knowledge industry. They have become specialized tools for

* Advocates of open education share a similar view about the use of resource materials to facilitate learning (Rathbone, Section 10).

professional educators, and their cost has been inflated by forcing them to stimulate either environments or teachers.

The teacher is jealous of the textbook he defines as his professional implement. The student may come to hate the lab because he associates it with school work. The administrator rationalizes his protective attitude toward the library as a defense of costly public equipment against those who would play with it rather than learn. In this atmosphere, the student too often uses the map, the lab, the encyclopedia, or the microscope at the rare moments when the curriculum tells him to do so. Even the great classics become part of "sophomore year" instead of marking a new turn in a person's life. School removes things from everyday use by labeling them educational tools.

If we are to deschool, both tendencies must be reversed. The general physical environment must be made accessible, and those physical learning resources which have been reduced to teaching instruments must become generally available for self-directed learning....

The control of school over educational equipment... increases enormously the cost of... materials. Once their use is restricted to scheduled hours, professionals are paid to supervise their acquisition, storage, and use. Then students vent their anger against the school on the equipment, which must be purchased once again.

Paralleling the untouchability of teaching tools is the impenetrability of modern junk. In the thirties, any self-respecting boy knew how to repair an automobile, but now car makers multiply wires and withhold manuals from everyone except specialized mechanics. In a former era, an old radio contained enough coils and condensers to build a transmitter that would make all the neighborhood radios scream in feedback. Transistor radios are more portable, but nobody dares to take them apart. To change this in the highly industrialized countries will be immensely difficult; but at least in the Third World, we must insist on built-in educational qualities.

To illustrate my point, let me present a model: By spending $10 million it would be possible to connect 40,000 hamlets in a country like Peru with a spiderweb of six-foot-wide trails and maintain these, and, in addition, provide the country with 200,000 three-wheeled mechanical donkeys — five on the average for each hamlet. Few poor countries of this size spend less than this yearly on cars and roads, both of which are now mainly restricted to the rich and their employees while poor people remain trapped in their villages. Each of these simple but durable little vehicles would cost $125 — half of which would pay for transmission and a six horse-power motor. A "donkey" could make 20 mph, and it can carry loads of 850 pounds (that is, most things besides trunks and steel beams, which are ordinarily moved).

The political appeal of such a transportation system to a peasantry is obvious. Equally obvious is the reason why those who hold power — and thereby automatically have a car — are not interested in spending money on trails and in clogging roads with engine-driven donkeys. The universal donkey could work only if a country's leaders were willing to impose a national speed limit of, say, 25 mph and adapt its public institutions to this. The model could not work if conceived only as a stopgap.

This is not the place to elaborate on the political, social, economic, financial, and technical feasibility of this model.[1] I only wish to indicate that educational considerations may be of prime importance when choosing such an alternative to capital-intensive transport. By raising the unit cost per donkey by some 20 percent, it would become possible to plan the production of all its parts in such a manner that, as far as possible, each future owner would spend a month or two making and understanding his machine and would be able to repair it. With this additional cost it would also be possible to decentralize production into dispersed plants. The added benefits would result not only from including educational costs in the construction process. Even more significantly, a durable motor which practically anyone could learn to repair and which could be used as a plough and pump by somebody who understood it would provide much higher educational benefits than the inscrutable engines of the advanced countries.

Not only the junk but also the supposedly public places of the modern city have become impenetrable. In American society, children are excluded from most things and places on the grounds that they are private. But even in societies which have declared an end to private property, children are kept away from the same places because they are considered the special domain of professionals and dangerous to the uninitiated. Since the last generation the railroad yard has become as inaccessible as the fire station. Yet with a little ingenuity, it should not be difficult to provide for safety in such places. To deschool the artifacts of education will require making the artifacts and processes available — and recognizing their educational value. Certainly, some workers would find it inconvenient to be accessible to learners, but this inconvenience must be balanced against the educational gains. . . .

If the goals of learning were no longer dominated by schools and schoolteachers, the market for learners would be much more various and the definition of "educational artifacts" would be less restrictive. There could be tool shops, libraries, laboratories, and gaming rooms. Photolabs and offset presses would allow neighborhood newspapers to flourish. Some storefront learning centers could contain viewing booths for closed-circuit television; others could feature office equipment for use and for repair. The jukebox or the record player would be commonplace, with some specializing in classical music, others in international folk tunes, others in jazz. Film clubs would compete with each other and with commercial television. Museum outlets could be networks for circulating exhibits of works of art, both old and new, originals and reproductions, perhaps administered by the various metropolitan museums.

The professional personnel needed for this network would be much more like custodians, museum guides, or reference librarians than like teachers. From the corner biology store, they could refer their clients to the shell collection in the museum or indicate the next showing of biology videotapes in a certain viewing booth. They could furnish guides for pest control, diet, and other kinds of preventive medicine. They could refer those who needed advice to "elders" who could provide it.

Two distinct approaches can be taken to financing a network of "learning objects." A community could determine a maximum budget for this purpose and arrange for all parts of the network to be open to all visitors at reasonable hours. Or the community could decide to provide citizens with limited entitlements, according to their age group, which would give them special access to certain materials which are both costly and scarce, while leaving other, simpler materials available to everyone.

Finding resources for material made specifically for education is only one — and perhaps the least costly — aspect in building an educational world. The money now spent on the sacred paraphernalia of the school ritual can be freed to provide all citizens with greater access to the real life of the city. Special tax incentives could be granted to those who employed children between the ages of eight and fourteen for a couple of hours each day if the conditions of employment were humane ones. . . .

Until recently the dangers of school were easily underestimated in comparison with the dangers of an apprenticeship in the police force, the fire department, or the entertainment industry. It was easy to justify schools at least as a means to protect youth. Often this argument no longer holds. I recently visited a Methodist church in Harlem occupied by a group of armed Young Lords in protest against the death of Julio Rodan, a Puerto Rican youth found hanged in his prison cell. I knew the leaders of the group who had spent a semester in Cuernavaca. When I wondered why one of them, Juan, was not among them, I was told that he had "gone back on heroin and to the state university."

Planning, incentives, and legislation can be used to unlock the educational potential within our society's huge investment in plants and equipment. Full access to educational objects will not exist so long as business firms are allowed to combine the legal protections which the Bill of Rights reserves to the privacy of individuals with the economic power conferred upon them by their millions of customers and thousands of employees, stockholders, and suppliers. Much of the world's know-how and most of its productive processes and equipment are locked within the walls of business firms, away from their customers, employees, and stockholders, as well as from the general public, whose laws and facilities allow them to function. Money now spent on advertising in capitalist countries could be redirected toward education in and by General Electric, NBC-TV, or the Budweiser beer company. That is, the plants and offices should be reorganized so that their daily operations can be more accessible to the public in ways that will make learning possible; and indeed ways might be found to pay the companies for the learning people acquire from them.*

An even more valuable body of scientific objects and data may be withheld from general access — and even from qualified scientists — under the guise of national security. Until recently science was the one forum which functioned like an anarchist's dream. Each man capable of doing research had more or less the same opportunity of access to its tools and to a hearing of the community of peers. Now bureaucratization and organization have placed much of science beyond public reach. Indeed, what used to be an international network of scientific information has been splintered into an arena of competing teams. . . .

In a world which is controlled and owned by nations and corporations, only limited access to educational objects will ever be possible. But increased access to those objects which can be shared for educational purposes may enlighten us enough to help us to break through these ultimate political barriers. Public schools transfer control over the educational uses of objects from private to professional hands. The institutional inversion of schools could empower the individual to reclaim the right to use them for education. A truly public kind of ownership might begin to emerge if private or corporate control over the educational aspect of "things" was brought to the vanishing point.

Skill Exchanges. A guitar teacher, unlike a guitar, can be neither classified in a museum nor owned by the public nor rented from an educational warehouse. Teachers of skills belong to a different class of resources from objects needed to learn a skill. This is not to say that they are indispensable in every case. I can not only rent a guitar but also taped guitar lessons and illustrated chord charts, and with these things I can teach myself to play the guitar. Indeed, this arrangement might have advantages — if the available tapes are better than the available teachers. Or if the only time I have for learning the guitar is late at night or if the tunes I wish to play are unknown in my country. Or I might be shy and prefer to fumble along in privacy.

Skill teachers must be listed and contacted through a different kind of channel from that of things. A thing is available at the bidding of the user — or could be — whereas a person formally becomes a skill resource only when he consents to do so, and he can also restrict time, place, and method as he chooses.

Skill teachers must also be distinguished from peers from whom one would learn. Peers who wish to pursue a common inquiry must start

* *Couldn't information about plants and offices be taught more efficiently through well-written books? Are "field trips" necessary?*

from common interests and abilities; they get together to exercise or improve a skill they share: basketball, dancing, constructing a campsite, or discussing the next election. The first transmission of a skill, on the other hand, involves bringing together someone who has the skill and someone who does not have it and wants to acquire it.

A "skill model" is a person who possesses a skill and is willing to demonstrate its practice. A demonstration of this kind is frequently a necessary resource for a potential learner. Modern inventions permit us to incorporate demonstration into tape, film, or chart; yet one would hope personal demonstration will remain in wide demand, especially in communication skills. Some 10,000 adults have learned Spanish at our center at Cuernavaca — mostly highly motivated persons who wanted to acquire near-native fluency in a second language.* When they are faced with a choice between carefully programmed instruction in a lab or drill sessions with two other students and a native speaker following a rigid routine, most choose the second.†

For most widely shared skills, a person who demonstrates the skill is the only human resource we ever need or get. Whether in speaking or driving, in cooking or in the use of communication equipment, we are often barely conscious of formal instruction and learning, especially after our first experience of the materials in question. I see no reason why other complex skills, such as the mechanical aspects of surgery and playing the fiddle, of reading or the use of directories and catalogues, could not be learned in the same way.

A well-motivated student who does not labor under a specific handicap often needs no further human assistance than can be provided by someone who can demonstrate on demand how to do what the learner wants to learn to do. The demand made of skilled people that before demonstrating their skill they be certified as pedagogues is a result of the insistence that people learn either what they do not want to know or that all people — even those with a special handicap — learn certain things at a given moment in their lives, and preferably under specified circumstances.

What makes skills scarce on the present educational market is the institutional requirement that those who can demonstrate them may not do so unless they are given public trust through a certificate. We insist that those who help others acquire a skill should also know how to diagnose learning difficulties and be able to motivate people to aspire to learn skills. In short, we demand that they be pedagogues. People who can demonstrate

---

* Illich and his colleagues operate a language training center for Latin American studies in Cuernavaca, Mexico.
† Modeling another person's behavior appears to be a basic learning process (see Brown, Section 1).

skills will be plentiful as soon as we learn to recognize them outside the teaching profession. . . .

Converging self-interests now conspire to stop a man from sharing his skill. The man who has the skill profits from its scarcity and not from its reproduction. The teacher who specializes in transmitting the skill profits from the artisan's unwillingness to launch his own apprentice into the field. The public is indoctrinated to believe that skills are valuable and reliable only if they are the result of formal schooling. The job market depends on making skills scarce and on keeping them scarce, either by proscribing their unauthorized use and transmission or by making things which can be operated and repaired only by those who have access to tools or information which are kept scarce.

Schools thus produce shortages of skilled persons. A good example is the diminishing number of nurses in the United States, owing to the rapid increase of four-year B.S. programs in nursing. Women from poorer families, who would formerly have enrolled in a two- or three-year program, now stay out of the nursing profession altogether.

Insisting on the certification of teachers is another way of keeping skills scarce. If nurses were encouraged to train nurses, and if nurses were employed on the basis of their proven skill at giving injections, filling out charts, and giving medicine, there would soon be no lack of trained nurses. Certification now tends to abridge the freedom of education by converting the civil right to share one's knowledge into the privilege of academic freedom, now conferred only on the employees of a school. To guarantee access to an effective exchange of skills, we need legislation which generalizes academic freedom. The right to teach any skill should come under the protection of freedom of speech. Once restrictions on teaching are removed, they will quickly be removed from learning as well.

The teacher of skills needs some inducement to grant his services to a pupil. There are at least two simple ways to begin to channel public funds to noncertified teachers. One way would be to institutionalize the skill exchange by creating free skill centers open to the public. Such centers could and should be established in industrialized areas, at least for those skills which are fundamental prerequisites for entering certain apprenticeships — such skills as reading, typing, keeping accounts, foreign languages, computer programming and number manipulation, reading special languages such as that of electrical circuits, manipulation of certain machinery, etc. Another approach would be to give certain groups within the population educational currency good for attendance at skill centers where other clients would have to pay commercial rates.

A much more radical approach would be to create a "bank" for skill exchange. Each citizen would be given a basic credit with which to acquire fundamental skills. Beyond that minimum, further credits would go to those who earn them by teaching, whether they serve as models in organized skill centers or do so privately at home or on the playground.* Only those who have taught others for an equivalent amount of time would have a claim on the time of more advanced teachers. An entirely new elite would be promoted, an elite of those who earn their education by sharing it.

Should parents have the right to earn skill-credit for their children? Since such an arrangement would give further advantage to the privileged classes, it might be offset by granting a larger credit to the underprivileged. The operation of a skill exchange would depend on the existence of agencies which would facilitate the development of directory information and assure its free and inexpensive use. Such an agency might also provide supplementary services of testing and certification and might help to enforce the legislation required to break up and prevent monopolistic practices.

Fundamentally, the freedom of a universal skill exchange must be guaranteed by laws which prevent discrimination only on the basis of tested skills and not on the basis of educational pedigree. Such a guarantee inevitably requires public control over tests which may be used to qualify persons for the job market. Otherwise, it would be possible to surreptitiously reintroduce complex batteries of tests at the work place itself which would serve for social selection. Much could be done to make skill testing objective, e.g., allowing only the operation of specific machines or systems to be tested. Tests of typing (measured according to speed, number of errors, and whether or not the typist can work from dictation), operation of an accounting system or of a hydraulic crane, driving, coding into COBOL, etc., can easily be made objective.

In fact, many of the true skills which are of practical importance can be so tested. And for the purposes of manpower-management, a test of a current skill level is much more useful than the information that a person — twenty years ago — satisfied his teacher in a curriculum where typing, stenography, and accounting were taught. The very need for official skill testing can, of course, be questioned: I personally believe that freedom from undue hurt to a man's reputation through labeling is better guaranteed by restricting than by forbidding tests of competence.

PEER MATCHING. At their worst, schools gather classmates into the same room and subject them to the same sequence of treatment in math, citizenship, and spelling. At their best, they permit each student to choose one of a limited number of courses. In any case, groups of peers form

---

* Assuming that people have varying degrees of teaching ability, what happens to the educational opportunity of those who cannot teach well?

around the goals of teachers. A desirable educational system would let each person specify the activity for which he seeks a peer.

School does offer children an opportunity to escape their homes and meet new friends. But, at the same time, this process indoctrinates children with the idea that they should select their friends from among those with whom they are put together. Providing the young from their earliest age with invitations to meet, evaluate, and seek out others would prepare them for a lifelong interest in seeking new partners for new endeavors. . . . Good schools try to bring out the common interests of their students registered in the same program. The inverse of school would be an institution which increases the chances that persons who at a given moment share the same specific interest could meet — no matter what else they have in common.

Skill teaching does not provide equal benefits for both parties as does the matching of peers. The teacher of skills, as I have pointed out, must usually be offered some incentive beyond the rewards of teaching. Skill teaching is a matter of repeating drills over and over and is, in fact, all the more dreary for those pupils who need it most. A skill exchange needs currency or credits or other tangible incentives in order to operate, even if the exchange itself were to generate a currency of its own. A peer-matching system requires no such incentives, but only a communications network.

Tapes, retrieval-systems, programmed instruction, and reproduction of shapes and sounds tend to reduce the need for recourse to human teachers of many skills; they increase the efficiency of teachers and the number of skills one can pick up in a lifetime. Parallel to this runs an increased need to meet people interested in enjoying the newly acquired skill. A student who has picked up Greek before her vacation would like to discuss — in Greek — Cretan politics when she returns. A Mexican in New York wants to find other readers of the paper *Siempre* — or of "Los Asachados," the most popular political cartoons. Somebody else wants to meet peers who — like himself — would like to increase interest in the work of James Baldwin or of Simón Bolívar.

The operation of a peer-matching network would be simple. The user would identify himself by name and address and describe the activity for which he seeks a peer. A computer would send him back the names and addresses of all those who have inserted the same description. It is amazing that such a simple utility has never been used on a broad scale for publicly valued activity.

In its most rudimentary form, communication between client and computer could be done by return mail. In big cities, typewriter terminals could provide instantaneous responses. The only way to retrieve a name and address from the computer would be to list an activity for which a peer is sought. People using the system would become known only to their potential peers.

A complement to the computer could be a network of bulletin boards and classified newspaper ads, listing the activities for which the computer could not produce a match. No names would have to be given. Interested readers would then introduce their names into the system. A publicly supported peer-match network might be the only way to guarantee the right of free assembly and to train people in the exercise of this most fundamental civic activity. . . .

To deschool means to abolish the power of one person to oblige another person to attend a meeting. It also means recognizing the right of any person, of any age or sex, to call a meeting. This right has been drastically diminished by the institutionalization of meetings. "Meeting" originally referred to the result of an individual's act of gathering. Now it refers to the institutional produce of some agency.

The ability of service institutions to acquire clients has far outgrown the ability of individuals to be heard independently of institutional media, which respond to individuals only if they are salable news. Peer-matching facilities should be available for individuals who want to bring people together as easily as the village bell called the villagers to council. School buildings — of doubtful value for conversion to other uses — could often serve this purpose. . . . One way to provide for schools' continued use would be to give over the space to people from the neighborhood. Each could state what he would do in the classroom and when, and a bulletin board would bring the available programs to the attention of the inquirers. Access to "class" would be free or purchased with educational vouchers. The "teacher" could even be paid according to the number of pupils whom he could attract for any full two-hour period. I can imagine that very young leaders and great educators would be the two types most prominent in such a system. The same approach could be taken toward higher education. Students could be furnished with educational vouchers which entitle them for ten hours yearly private consultation with the teacher of their choice and, for the rest of their learning, depend on the library, the peer-matching network, and apprenticeships. . . .

Some who share my concern for free speech and assembly will argue that peer matching is an artificial means of bringing people together and would not be used by the poor — who most need it. Some people get genuinely agitated when mention is made of creating ad hoc encounters which are not rooted in the life of a local community. Others react when mention is made of using a computer to sort and match client-identified interests. People cannot be drawn together in such an impersonal manner, they say. Common inquiry must be rooted in a history of shared experience at many levels and must grow out of this experience — or in the development of neighborhood institutions, for example.

I sympathize with these objections, but I think they miss my point as well as their own. In the first place, the return to neighborhood life as the primary center of creative expression might actually work against the reestablishment of neighborhoods as political units. Centering demands on the neighborhood may, in fact, neglect an important liberating aspect of urban life — the ability of a person to participate simultaneously in several peer groups. Also, there is an important sense in which people who have never lived together in a physical community may have occasionally far more experiences to share than those who have known each other from childhood. . . . Peer matching could significantly help in making explicit the many potential but suppressed communities of the city.

. . . Far from artificially removing men from their local contexts to join abstract groupings, peer matching should encourage the restoration of local life to cities from which it is now disappearing. A man who recovers his initiative to call his fellows into meaningful conversation may cease to settle for being separated from them by office protocol or suburban etiquette. Having once seen that doing things together depends on deciding to do so, men may even insist that their local communities become more open to creative political exchange. . . .

PROFESSIONAL EDUCATORS. As citizens have new choices — new chances for learning — their willingness to seek leadership should increase. We may expect that they will experience more deeply both their own independence and their need for guidance. As they are liberated from manipulation by others, they learn to profit from the discipline others have acquired in a lifetime. Deschooling education should increase — rather than stifle — the search for men with practical wisdom who are willing to sustain the newcomer on his educational adventure. As teachers abandon their claim to be superior informants or skill models, their claim to superior wisdom will begin to ring true.

With an increasing demand for teachers, the supply should also increase. As the schoolmaster vanishes, the conditions arise which should bring forth the vocation of the independent educator. This may seem almost a contradiction in terms, so thoroughly have schools and teachers become complementary. Yet this is exactly what the development of the first three educational exchanges would tend to produce — and what would be required to permit their full exploitation — for parents and other "natural educators" need guidance, individual learners need assistance, and the networks need people to operate them.

Parents need guidance in guiding their children on the road that leads to responsible educational independence. Learners need experienced leadership when they encounter rough terrain. These two needs are quite distinct: the first is a need for pedagogy; the second, for intellectual leadership in all other fields of knowledge. The first calls for knowledge of human learning and of educational resources; the second, for wisdom based on experience in any kind of exploration. Both kinds of experience are indispensable for effective educational endeavor. Schools package these functions into one role and render the independent exercise of any of them if not disreputable at least suspect.

Three types of special educational competence should in fact be distinguished: one to create and operate the kinds of educational exchanges or networks outlined here; another to guide students and parents in the use of these networks; and a third to act as *primus inter pares* in undertaking difficult intellectual exploratory journeys. Only the former two can be conceived of as branches of an independent profession: educational administrators or pedagogical counselors. To design and operate the networks I have been describing would not require many people, but it would require people with the most profound understanding of education and administration, in a perspective quite different from, and even opposed to, that of schools.

While an independent educational profession of this kind would welcome many people whom the schools exclude, it would also exclude many whom the schools qualify. The establishment and operation of educational networks would require some designers and administrators, but not in the numbers or of the type required by the administration of schools. Student discipline, public relations, hiring, supervising, and firing teachers would have neither place nor counterpart in the networks I have been describing. Neither would curriculum making, textbook purchasing, the maintenance of grounds and facilities, or the supervision of interscholastic athletic competition. Nor would child custody, lesson planning, and record keeping, which now take up so much of the time of teachers, figure in the operation of educational networks. Instead the operation of networks would require some of the skills and attitudes now expected from the staff of a museum, a library, an executive employment agency, or a maitre d'hotel. . . .

If the networks I have described can emerge, the educational path of each student would be his own to follow and, only in retrospect, would it take on the features of a recognizable program. The wise student would periodically seek professional advice: assistance to set a new goal, insight into difficulties encountered, choice between possible methods. Even now, most persons would admit that the important services their teachers have rendered them are such advice or counsel, given at a chance meeting or in a tutorial.

While network administrators would concentrate primarily on the building and maintenance of roads providing access to resources, the pedagogue would help the student to find the path which for him could lead fastest to his goal. If a student wants to learn spoken Cantonese from a Chinese neighbor, the pedagogue would be available to judge their proficiency and to help them select the textbook and methods most suitable to their talents, character, and the time available for study. He can counsel the would-be airplane mechanic on finding the best places for apprenticeship. He can recommend books to somebody who wants to find challenging peers to discuss African history. Like the network administrator, the pedagogical counselor conceives of himself as a professional educator. Access to either could be gained by individuals through the use of educational vouchers.

The role of the educational initiator or leader, the master or "true" leader, is somewhat more elusive than that of the professional administrator or pedagogue. This is so because leadership is itself hard to define. In practice, an individual is a leader if people follow his initiative and become apprentices in his progressive discoveries. . . .

To rely for true intellectual leadership on the desire of gifted people to provide it is obviously necessary even in our society, but it could not be made into a policy now. We must first construct a society in which personal acts themselves reacquire a value higher than that of making things and manipulating people.[2] In such a society exploratory, inventive, creative teaching would logically be counted among the most desirable forms of leisurely "unemployment." But we do not have to wait until the advent of Utopia. Even now one of the most important consequences of deschooling and the establishment of peer-matching facilities would be the initiative which "masters" could take to assemble congenial disciples. It would also — as we have seen — provide ample opportunity for potential disciples to share information or to select a master. . . .

The disestablishment of schools will inevitably happen — and it will happen surprisingly fast. It cannot be retarded very much longer and it is hardly necessary to vigorously promote it, for this is being done now. What is worthwhile is to try to orient it in a hopeful direction for it could take place in two diametrically opposed ways.

The first would be the expansion of the mandate of the pedagogue and his increasing control over society, even outside school. With the best of intentions and simply by expanding the rhetoric now used in school, the present crisis in the schools could provide educators with an excuse to use all the networks of contemporary society to funnel their messages to us — for our own good. Deschooling, which we cannot stop, could mean the advent of a "brave new world" dominated by well-intentioned administrators of programmed instruction.*

On the other hand, the growing awareness on the part of governments, as well as of employers, taxpayers, enlightened pedagogues, and school administrators that graded curricular teaching for certification has become harmful could offer large masses of people an extraordinary opportunity:

* *Is Illich being fair to programmed instruction in this statement?*

that of preserving the right of equal access to the tools both of learning and of sharing with others what they know or believe. But this would require that the educational revolution be guided by certain goals:

1. To liberate access to things by abolishing the control which persons and institutions now exercise over their educational values

2. To liberate the sharing of skills by guaranteeing freedom to teach or exercise them on request

3. To liberate the critical and creative resources of people by returning to individual persons the ability to call and hold meetings: an ability now increasingly monopolized by institutions which claim to speak for the people

4. To liberate the individual from the obligation to shape his expectations to the services offered by an established profession by providing him with the opportunity to draw on the experience of his peers and to entrust himself to the teacher, guide, adviser, or healer of his choice

Inevitably deschooling of society blurs the distinction between economics, education, and politics on which the stability of the present world order and the stability of nations now rests.

In addition to the tentative conclusions of the Carnegie Commission reports, the last year has brought forth a series of important documents which show that responsible people are becoming aware of the fact that schooling for certification cannot continue to be counted upon as the central educational device of a modern society. Julius Nyere of Tanzania has announced plans to integrate education with the life of the village. In Canada, the Wright Commission on postsecondary education has reported that no known system of formal education could provide equal opportunities for the citizens of Ontario. The president of Peru has accepted the recommendation of his commission on education, which proposes to abolish free schools in favor of free educational opportunities provided throughout life. In fact he is reported to have insisted that this program proceed slowly at first in order to keep teachers in school and out of the way of true educators. . . .

The alternative to social control through the schools is the voluntary participation in society through networks which provide access to all its resources for learning. In fact, these networks now exist but they are rarely used for educational purposes. The crisis of schooling, if it is to have any positive consequence, will inevitably lead to their incorporation into the educational process.

EXERCISE

1. How does Illich propose political programs of the 1970's be evaluated? (p. 364)

2. What four resources does Illich propose to use in setting up a new learning exchange (p. 365)

3. What question does Illich think should guide the planning of a new educational institution? Why does he use this question? (p. 366)

4. Describe the four ways in which Illich plans to make resources available to the student. (pp. 366–378)

5. What is a "skill model," according to Illich's definition? (p. 372)

6. Describe the two ways Illich proposes for making the "teachers of skills" available to the student. (pp. 373–374)

7. Illich lists three types of educational competence. Describe the roles assumed by individuals at each competence level. Which present educational roles are eliminated from this list? (pp. 378–379)

8. List four goals of educational revolution proposed by Illich. (p. 380)

Deschooling? No!

Philip W. Jackson

Allen Graubard and Ivan Illich have discussed various shortcomings of the public schools and recommend new educational institutions. Philip Jackson, director of an elementary school located at the University of Chicago, recognizes many problems that Graubard and Illich identified. He does not agree with their solutions, though. He argues that such innovative ideas can best be implemented within the existing educational framework. Thus, a controversy exists. Educators, parents, students, and others agree that the school system has inadequacies, but they disagree about how to alleviate these weaknesses. Must entirely new institutions be created? Or can meaningful change occur within existing educational institutions? Where do you stand?

The criticism of schools is a profitable pastime, as a visit to our local bookstore or a glance at a current issue of almost any of our most widely

From *Today's Education*, vol. 61, no. 8 (November 1972), pp. 18–22. Reprinted with permission of publisher and author.

circulated magazines will quickly show. There, in volume after volume and article after article, some of our most well-schooled and well-read journalists, novelists, academicians, ex-teachers, and just plain critics describe the evils of our educational system and discuss what should be done about them. The quality of the writing and the sharpness of the criticism vary from one author to the next, but the overall tone is one of uniform dissatisfaction with things as they are.

Despite the up-to-the-minute freshness of much of this writing, the fact that many people seem to be unhappy with current educational practices is not exactly new. Our schools have long been the target of critics from all walks of life. Moreover, it would be surprising if this were not so, given the centrality of schooling in the lives of our citizens and the complexity of the institution designed to perform this important service.

What *is* new in the current situation is a marked increase in the amount of criticism, reflecting a corresponding growth in the size of the critics' audience. What is also new and even more important in the current scene is a marked radicalization of the critics' proposals for change.

Until quite recently, the desirability of schools and of compulsory attendance by the young were more or less taken for granted by friend and foe alike. The aim of both, even of those who were most unhappy with the status quo, was not to do away with schools as we now know them, but somehow to improve their operation.

Now from a growing number of writers — including such prominent critics as Ivan Illich, Everett Reimer, John Holt, and the late Paul Goodman* — the message is that improving what we presently have is not enough. Today's schools, so the argument goes, have outlived or outgrown their usefulness. They are institutional dinosaurs that should either be hunted down or allowed to sink of their own dead weight into the swamps of academia.

The aggressive brashness of such a charge, with its not-so-subtle promise of a good old-fashioned free-for-all between defenders of our schools and their attackers, is bound to generate excitement and to bring out crowds of onlookers. And, clearly, the school-is-dead argument has done just that. Its proponents appear on talk shows, testify before Congressional committees, are given front-page space in Sunday magazine sections, and are even in demand as speakers at educational conventions!

For those of us who work in these allegedly dead or dying institutions, living, as it were, like parasites ecologically tied to the fate of our dinosaur hosts, there is the serious question of what to do in the face of such allegations. Should we simply ignore them and get on with our work? Should

* *Illich's views are presented in this section; Holt's are presented in Sections 1 and 16.*

we pause to reply? Might we, in a more hopeful vein, actually learn something from those who would have us go out of business and, armed with that new learning, return with even greater strength and deepened conviction to the task at hand? In my judgment, there is something to be said on behalf of each of these alternatives. . . .

The answer, in part, depends on how serious we judge the threat to be, a judgment that requires a detailed examination of the critics' charges. . . .

Even if the threat is real, the fact remains that we do have schools that have to be run as best we know how. No matter what the future holds, millions of students and the public at large are counting on us to perform those duties for which we are being paid. Teaching, if it is done well, and school administration, if it is done at all, are full-time jobs, requiring almost all the available time and energy of those who engage in them. . . .

The truth is that most of us who work in schools are (or should be!) too busy to be more than casually engaged in listening to the school-is-dead critics or in responding to what they say. Teaching is a serious undertaking, as is the job of administering a school. . . .

Fortunately for those of us who are interested in preserving our school system, the writings of most critics reveal weaknesses that seriously damage the force of their argument. The most blatant of these is surely to be found in the demagogic style that characterizes so much of the school-is-dead literature. The tone throughout is strident and at times borders on hysteria.*

We are told that our present schools are little more than prisons or concentration camps for the young. Teachers (*all* teachers, presumably) are depicted as mindless and inhumane, and administrators are described as pigheaded and petty tyrants whose main purpose in life seems to be to keep the halls clean and the cafeteria running smoothly. Students, poor things, are crushed by their exposure to these horrible conditions and leave school much worse off than when they entered — with psyches destroyed, spirits sagging, and minds devoid of any true knowledge. . . .

It does not require much analytic power to discern the emotionalism and propagandistic aims of such prose. Hopefully, even the casual reader will take these qualities into account as he judges the critics' case. What does require closer analysis is the detection of flaws in the critics' logic or the scantiness of the evidence they present. Also, more than a casual reading is required to reveal deficiencies in the historical perspective of those who criticize today's schools and in the reasonableness of the alternative proposals they put forth.

---

* Does this criticism apply to the preceding article by Illich?

Let us consider one or two quick examples of what such an analysis might yield.

Take, for instance, the following statement by John Holt that appeared in a recent issue of *Harper's Magazine* in an article entitled, significantly enough, "The Little Red Prison."

"Thus, as more people learn in school to dislike reading, fewer buy books from bookstores and borrow them from libraries. The bookstores close and the libraries cut back their services, and so we have fewer places in which people outside of school can have ready access to books. This is just one of the ways in which too much school works against education."

. . . But we must ask: It is true? *Are* more people learning to dislike reading in school? Is the sale of books *really* declining? Are libraries across the nation cutting back their services because of a shortage of interest in their wares? The answer, as all the statistics on publishing and library usage clearly indicate, is emphatically "No!"

Or take another instance, this one chosen almost at random from Ivan Illich's book, *Deschooling Society*. In attempting to analyze what he calls "the phenomenology of school," Illich offers his readers the following gem of syllogistic reasoning:

"School groups people according to age. This grouping rests on three unquestioned premises. Children belong in school. Children learn in school. Children can be taught only in school. I think these unexamined premises deserve serious questioning."

Indeed they do, Mr. Illich. But so does the logic by which the premises are said to lead to the conclusion: "School groups people according to age." We can begin with the assumption that Illich was referring not to the system of grades by which students customarily are grouped *within* school, but rather to the fact that children go to school and adults, for the most part, do not. School, in other words, segregates children from adults. Fair enough, but how does that fact "rest" on the premises? And, further, are the premises themselves seriously held by a significant segment of our population, including, incidentally, our professional educators? Who among us seriously believes that children can be taught only in school? *

. . . The chief danger in focusing on flaws in the deschoolers' argument is that such a strategy may blind us to the strengths that are also there. In our zest to prove them wrong, in other words, we may overlook the extent to which the critics are right. And, let's face it: There *is* basis for concern about what our schools are doing and how their operation might be improved. Perhaps, contrary to what John Holt contends, more and more students are not being taught to dislike reading by their school ex-

* *Can you think of an educational psychologist who believes that most or all learning occurs in school?*

perience, but a goodly number *are*, and we should be worried about that.

Obviously our high schools are *not* the concentration camps that some critics would have us believe, but many students within them do feel constrained and bridled by their experience, and that fact should trouble us.

Certainly the vast majority of our teachers and school administrators are *not* the mindless and unfeeling creatures depicted by some of the less responsible attackers of our schools, but too many of them *are* halfheartedly engaged in what they are about, more concerned with the benefits of their position than with the services they perform.* We cannot rest easy so long as this is true.

The list could be extended, but the point is already obvious: There is serious work to be done within our schools.

This brings us to the third and last of the alternative responses educators might presumably take in the face of the deschooling argument. The first was to ignore the critics and get on with our work. The second was to expose weaknesses in the critics' argument, to counterattack, so to speak. The third is to learn from the critics, not simply by having them reinforce our awareness of our schools' shortcomings, but by seeing where their efforts fall short of perfection and by trying to avoid similar pitfalls as we go about trying to improve our schools. Two such shortcomings are worthy of mention and serve well as examples of lessons to be learned from those who would bring lessons, as such, to an end.

As I study the contemporary critics of our schools, it becomes increasingly evident to me that most of them are animated more by a sense of what is *wrong* with our present system than by a conception of what education is all about and how it might proceed. They lack, in other words, a vision of the good in educational terms. What they are *against* is more evident than what they are *for*.

This same tendency, incidentally, is also apparent within the ranks of professional educators as they impatiently work to reduce the abrasiveness of schooling without pausing to give sufficient thought to the educational purpose of the institution. I plead as guilty as the rest in yielding to the natural appeal of such a tactic. After all, it is easier to put oil on squeaky wheels than to ask about where the vehicle is headed in the first place and to ponder the necessity of a change in direction. The danger, of course, is that by so doing we may create a smoothly running machine that is moving in the wrong direction or not at all. . . .

Our goal, in other words, cannot simply be to eliminate the discomfort of schooling, though certainly there is much that should be eliminated. Nor can it even be simply to provide environments in which students are

---

* How can these teachers be identified? How can they be helped? (See articles in Section 12.)

learning things they *want* to learn — a favorite image of many of the romantic critics. It must be to create environments — institutions, if you like — in which students are being educated, a different matter entirely.

This last point deserves elaboration, for it contrasts nicely with one of the major premises in the deschooling argument. Many of the more radical critics are fond of reminding their readers that education involves more than schooling — that it can occur in the absence of teachers and courses and classrooms and all of the paraphernalia that we have come to associate with formal schooling. The same argument, incidentally, has recently been adopted as the slogan of several not-so-radical researchers and professors of education who use it to justify turning their attention away from schools and toward other institutions and agencies within our society that perform an educative function.

Now no one can dispute the truism that reminds us of differences between the concepts of education and schooling. Perhaps such a reminder needs to be presented more frequently and more forcefully today than in the past. But there is another truism that needs to be stated with equal force, for it often seems to be overlooked by friend and foe alike. It is that education, in addition to being more than schooling, is also more than learning.

John Dewey, more than any other educator with whom I am familiar, understood supremely both of the cautions to which I have now made reference: that the foundations on which to build a new and constructive view of schooling cannot simply be a reaction to the ailments of our present system and that education involves much more than letting students "do their thing" even when the latter results in significant learning.

Disturbed by the excesses of the reform movement carried out in his name, Dewey pointed out:

"There is always the danger in a new movement that in rejecting the aims and methods of that which it would supplant, it may develop its principles negatively rather than positively and constructively. Then it takes its clue in practice from that which is rejected instead of from the constructive development of its own philosophy."

And, in my judgment, this seems to be precisely what today's would-be reformers are doing. They are saying, in effect, "Here are the features of schooling that are unpleasant. Let us, therefore, make the absence of those features our goal in the design of alternate forms of schooling." * The missing element, of course, is a conception of what the process of education leads *toward,* and this can only be supplied by an ethic and a psychology which are conjured in a coherent philosophy or *theory* of education....

* *Do you think open classrooms and the free schools are being developed from a positive or negative analysis of educational goals?*

It is no easy task to keep our educational purpose in mind while carrying out our day-to-day responsibilities in classrooms and administrative offices; in short, to blend theory and practice. To achieve that end requires nothing less than that each of us, again in Dewey's words, be "possessed by the spirit of an abiding student of education."

Such is the challenge that lies before us if we are to learn from our critics. . . . Moreover, if we are to avoid a tone of defensiveness and apology, our conviction must be voiced in the language of educational purpose. This means more than empty slogans cloaking an absence of thought, but, rather, a lively and tough-minded discourse that means what it says, that changes as schools change, and that mirrors the reality within them.

Our schools are neither dead nor dying, but neither, unfortunately, are they marked by a degree of vitality and energy that befits the grandeur of their mission. Paradoxically, and even ironically, the writings of those who would bury us may well stimulate such an infusion of new life.

EXERCISE

1. According to Jackson, what is new about the critics' recent comments about the schools? (p. 382)

2. What is the most blatant weakness in the critics' writings about schools? (p. 383)

3. If educators emphasize the flaws in the critics' arguments, what important information may be overlooked? (pp. 384–385)

4. List the three alternative responses educators might make to the deschooling argument. (p. 385)

5. What mistake do the designers of new approaches to education often make? (pp. 385, 386)

Medical, Biological, and Chemical Methods of Shaping the Mind

Edward A. Sullivan

> *Most educators attempt to increase school achievement by improving the curriculum or the training given to teachers. In the following article, Edward Sullivan, assistant professor of education at*

Reprinted by permission of the author and *Phi Delta Kappan*, April, 1972.

Providence College in Rhode Island, takes a more radical view. He suggests that recent developments in medicine, biology, and chemistry make it possible to change the student so that he can learn better. He reviews seven specific biochemical techniques that might be applied in education. Although these techniques are still in the early stages of testing and development, at least one — using amphetamines to treat hyperkinetic (overactive) children — has been used for many years. As a teacher, would you be willing to have your students participate in these new "learning" programs? In the near future? After a great deal more testing?

Much research has been done recently to find out what can be done medically, biologically, and chemically to aid the learning process. Some of this research is examined here.

Dr. José M. R. Delgado[1] of the Yale University School of Medicine has pioneered in the field of electrical stimulation of the brain (ESB). He has been able to establish direct nonsensory communication between a computer and the brain of a chimpanzee and demonstrate that behavior can be influenced by remote radio command. He has also pioneered in the use of electrode implantation for the diagnosis and treatment of epilepsy, schizophrenia, and excessive anxiety. Delgado has predicted that within a few years we will be able to construct a model of our own mental functions through a knowledge of genetics and the cerebral mechanisms which underlie our behavior. He has also predicted that at some time in the near future we will be able to use cerebral pacemakers to treat Parkinson's disease, fear, and violent behavior by direct stimulation of the brain.

To demonstrate his ability to use ESB to control violent behavior, Delgado entered a bull ring in Spain in which the bull had electrodes implanted in its brain. As the bull charged, Delgado activated a radio transmitter. The signal affected an inhibitory area of the brain, causing the bull to halt its charge at Delgado.* By pushing another button on the transmitter, he caused the bull to turn and walk away. Although this demonstration of ESB raised questions about the possibility of remote-controlled behavior, Delgado stated that ESB merely sets off a train of programmed events: biochemical, thermal, enzymatic, and electrical. He further stated, "Nothing which is not already in the brain can be put there by ESB."

Because of the possibilities of ESB, Delgado sees the need to

develop an educational system that is based on the knowledge of our biological realities, an education that would attempt to: First, establish good "automatisms" in the child and, second, as he matures, permit his thinking capability to evolve without being sub-

* *Picture a similar situation in the classroom with a misbehaving child.*

jected to unknown forces and impulses which may overpower his rational intelligence.[2]

Other research is being done in the area of biofeedback, the process which occurs when the activities of an organism are modified continuously by the interaction between its signals or output and the environment. Every human task depends upon biofeedback. As you read this sentence or turn the page, sensory data, fed back to your brain, indicate the next step to be taken (in this case, the reading of the next word) in a largely unconscious process.

Until a few years ago physiologists believed that we were regulated by two distinct nervous systems, one giving us voluntary control of muscles and the other, the autonomic nervous system, controlling such "involuntary" acts as heart rate and blood pressure. New advances in the study of biofeedback have shown that these "involuntary" acts can be regulated by an individual.[3] This is possible through the use of electronic instruments (e.g., the electromyograph) which inform the individual of changes in heart rate, blood pressure, or muscle contractions by amplifying the signals given off as these changes occur. The individual, then, can listen to the changes taking place within his system. By being instantly aware of these changes as they occur, it is possible for the individual to recognize cues which indicate that a change is taking place and, as a result, develop control over the autonomic nervous system. It has been shown that it is possible, using biofeedback, for a person to conquer the symptoms of hypertension by means of mental processes without the use of drugs. The treatment consists primarily of education in blood pressure control. Even patients with serious cardiac problems can learn to control their heart rate and blood pressure. Psychologists have also been able to relieve people of a number of fears through biofeedback. Ailments such as headaches and insomnia have also been overcome through this process.[4]

Can life be changed for the better if we are able to teach children in their first years of school how to develop autonomic control? It might lessen the tensions that eventually evolve into disease. If so, teaching autonomic control can become just as important as teaching children to read.

Biofeedback has also been used as an educational tool to free slow readers of their main difficulty, the silent mouthing of words. Slow readers are placed individually in a laboratory with an electrode over their Adam's apple and are given a book to read for an hour. Whenever the reader mouths a word silently his larynx tenses and a noise is switched on. Because the noise is so unpleasant, slow readers, both children and adults, learn to abandon silent mouthing of words in 45 minutes.[5] *

* *What principles of learning are being applied here? Are they ethical?*

Another area of research is the study of the biology of human violence. Dr. Vernon Mark, a neurosurgeon at Boston City Hospital, and Dr. Frank Ervin, a research psychiatrist at Massachusetts General Hospital, have been working to refute the theory that an individual misbehaves because something is wrong in his environment. The theory postulates that if the environment can be changed, then the behavior can be changed. Drs. Mark and Ervin feel that, while environment and upbringing are important factors, the arrangement and functioning of the brain cells are a coequal factor in producing behavior. Their experience has convinced them that a large percentage of repeatedly violent people suffer from certain types of epilepsy or other brain defects that make them behave the way they do. Dr. Ervin hopes that at some time in the near future it will be possible to teach victims of brain damage, through biofeedback, to use the proper nerve circuits to prevent the seizures which lead to violence.[6]

Dr. Ervin is also developing a 30-minute screening test for violence-prone individuals. Screening devices of a slightly different nature have been developed already. Examples are the Glueck Scale developed by Sheldon and Eleanor Glueck to determine the probability of young children becoming juvenile delinquents and the profile which has been developed for airline clerks and security men to spot prospective airplane hijackers. It is Ervin's hope that the test he develops will be administered to all who are brought before the courts accused of violent crime, those involved in repeated assaults against others, and habitual traffic offenders. However, when a similar proposal to screen all children between the ages of 6 to 8 for potential antisocial behavior was made to the White House in 1970 there was a great deal of opposition to it.

At present the violent are punished by being sent to prisons or to custodial care institutions, where they are generally neglected.[7] It is Dr. Ervin's belief than many of these people may have treatable brain disorders with definite physiological causes. If this is so, then it should be possible to develop a method to diagnose, to treat, and even to prevent the problem of violent behavior.

Doctors who treat people with brain disorders have noted that many people who commit violent crimes are repeat offenders. It has also been noted that many of the conditions which go with poverty and deprivation can lead to brain damage. Such damage may occur in childbirth if good medical care is lacking. Malnutrition, often present in poverty areas either prior to or after birth, can also result in brain damage. At the Johns Hopkins University Hospital doctors have noted that brain injuries to children are more common in the slums than in the rest of the community. A probable factor is the greater incidence of fights and accidents among slum children.

The conditions of poverty seem to contribute more than pressure and frustration to produce violence. If it is true that the conditions of poverty — lead poisoning, malnutrition, poor pre- and post-natal medical care, beatings, fights, high accident rates, etc., all of which can cause brain damage — do lead to violent behavior, then there is no real point to attempt rehabilitation of the violent unless such rehabilitation cures the brain damage.

Preventive rehabilitation is also necessary. This would involve as one phase the removal of the conditions which cause brain damage. One such condition is lead poisoning. . . .

[A]nother cause of brain damage is malnutrition. Studies have shown that among the poor a disproportionate number of children are mentally retarded. The poor also have a higher infant mortality rate, a higher incidence of infectious and chronic diseases, and a great number of premature and low birthweight infants. The common denominator of all these ills seems to be malnutrition. Studies in nutrition have shown that the earlier in life that the malnutrition occurs the more severe is its effect and the less likely is recovery.[8] . . .

There is good evidence of the relation between an expectant mother's nutrition and intelligence of her offspring. When the mother-to-be receives a proper diet as well as vitamin supplements, the I.Q. of her children as measured at the ages of 3 and 4 surpasses that of children whose mothers do not receive an adequate diet or vitamin supplements.[9]

In a study conducted by Harmeling and Jones[10] it was found that school dropouts had an average birth weight lower than that of slow learners. The slow learners, in turn, had an average birth weight lower than that of "normal" learners. The reason for the finding appears to be that infants who are malnourished in utero weigh the least at time of birth. Malnutrition before birth, as noted previously, can lead to brain damage. It can also lead to premature birth.*. . .

Programs to prevent malnutrition are difficult for school officials to devise and implement, for a variety of political and economic reasons. However, schools should find it relatively easy to educate teen-age girls about the importance of a proper diet, especially if and when they become pregnant. . . .

A whole new field of research is opening up in the area of chemical influence on brain processes and learning. Kenneth Clark, in his presidential address to the American Psychological Association in Washington (September 1971), stated that recent studies of electrical and chemical control of the brain

> . . . suggest that we might be on the threshold of that type of scientific, biochemical intervention which could stabilize and make

---

* This study attributed slow learning to malnutrition. Contrast with Deutsch (Section 4), who attributes school learning problems to the child's out-of-school environment.

dominant the moral and ethical propensities of man and subordinate, if not eliminate, his negative and primitive behavioral tendencies.

Clark has proposed the development of "psychotechnology," the study of ways in which new drugs may be used to subdue hostility and aggression and allow more humane and intelligent behavior to emerge. . . .

As would be expected, there has been a great deal of opposition to Clark's proposal, the main theme being that the type of control possible through drugs and psychotechnological techniques can never be the solution to the problems that beset humanity. . . .

Linus Pauling[11] has stated that normal mental functioning depends on the presence of molecules of many substances — the B vitamins, vitamin C, uric acid, and other substances normally present in the brain. According to Pauling, the average person gets enough of these substances in his daily diet or produces enough of them through his own body chemistry, while the mentally ill person either does not produce enough of them or uses them up too quickly. Mental patients may thus be suffering from a type of deficiency disease, according to Pauling. The cure, obviously, is proper chemical balance.

Bernard Agranoff [12] has demonstrated that there is a connection between the consolidation of memory and the manufacture of protein in the brain. His studies have led him to "view learning as a form of biological development." According to Agranoff,

> One may think of the brain of an animal as being completely "wired" by heredity; all pathways are present, but not all are "soldered." It may be that in short-term memory, pathways are selected rapidly but impermanently. In that case protein synthesis would not be required. . . . If the consolidation of memory calls for more permanent connections among pathways, it seems reasonable that protein synthesis would be involved.[13]

It has also been theorized that the learning process depends upon a permanent alternation of RNA (ribonucleic acid) inside the nerve cell. Experiments have shown that learning produces an increase of RNA in brain cells.[14] Dr. Ewen Cameron, director of the Veteran Administration's Psychiatry and Aging Research Laboratories at Albany, New York, has fed yeast RNA to patients with poor memories. He and his patients were certain that the RNA did help their remembering processes.

James McConnell has demonstrated the chemical transference of learning in the experiments he performed with planaria and rats. Rats were trained to push levers in a cage and then run to another location for a reward. When the brains were removed from these rats and ground up and injected into other rats, this learning was transferred to the untrained rats.

From experiments such as those mentioned above the following conclusions can be drawn in regard to the chemical basis of learning: (1) Memory is a chemical process and drugs can limit or improve memory. (2) Chemicals can either speed up the learning process or prevent the learning process from taking place, (3) Learning of a basic nature can be transferred from one animal to another by using chemical means only.*

If it is true that knowledge is obtained by changing the RNA molecule inside the cell, it should be possible to identify the particular chemical changes that produce particular behavioral changes in human beings. Once this occurs it should be possible to synthesize the chemicals needed to produce the change and inject them directly or give them in pill form. This could be the so-called "smart pill" for which many generations of students have longed.

Dr. Sidney Cohen of the UCLA Medical School has indicated that, in functional terms, human intelligence involves three different skills. These are: (1) the ability to pay attention or concentrate; (2) the ability to form a permanent memory trace — in the form of changed RNA molecules or in the form of protein manufactured under the direction of RNA; and (3) the ability to develop a retrieval system by which the memory is scanned and focused.†

Cohen believes that all three processes can be improved chemically, leading to the improvement of thinking abilities. The "smart pill" envisioned by Dr. Cohen may be several pills influencing the various processes involved in learning. It is also likely that such pills would work best with improved psychological methods of training the mind, according to Cohen.

Dr. Georges Ungar[15] of the Baylor University College of Medicine has isolated, identified, and possibly synthesized the first component of what may be a system of molecular coding by which information is processed in the brain. Ungar has begun experimenting to duplicate for man chemicals which tell mice what to do when they are injected into their brains. He hopes by doing this to improve the brain functions of the mentally retarded and senile.

An area of concern currently being examined is the use of amphetamines to control hyperkinesis in school children. Amphetamines — the so-called pep pills — have been used for many years to treat the hyperkinetic child.[16] Such children cannot sit still, have a very short attention span, and are generally behavior problems in school. Amphetamines, which are stim-

*Given that these conclusions are true, should we launch large-scale programs to search for ways to apply them to human learning?
†Shouldn't Cohen have included skills of higher cognitive thinking? (See Guszek, Section 2).

ulants, seem to act like sedatives for these children, allowing them to control their behavior. The amphetamine actually does not act as a sedative; it acts in an unknown way to enable the hyperkinetic to focus his attention and control his muscles. The amphetamines result in learning improvements for from one-half to two-thirds of the pupil hyperkinetics taking them.

Dr. Maurice Laufer believes that hyperkinesis is a physically based problem that has something to do with chemical transmissions in the brain but is not necessarily the result of brain damage. The brain is just not functioning as it should.[17]

There has been some fear that children taking the amphetamines would become addicted to them. But recent evidence indicates that amphetamine addiction, if there is any, is primarily psychological rather than physical. Children taking amphetamines under medical supervision perceive the drugs as medicine which will eventually be given up. It would seem that the dangers of addiction are minimal for the hyperkinetic child receiving skillful medical treatment.

The fear has been expressed by many critics of the use of amphetamines that they are being used to control and suppress behavioral problems which result not from hyperkinesis but from a poor home life or from boredom with school. This is a valid fear. Nevertheless, it should not prevent the use of amphetamines. Rather, it should lead to greater care in seeing to it that these drugs are prescribed only for those students who are hyperkinetic.

There is still another area of research with overtones of *1984* and *Brave New World*. Embryos are now being fertilized in vitro and grown to the multicelled stage.[18] One hope of biochemists involved in this research is that, since a number of genetic defects originate in the improper splitting of the chromosomes at early stages, observation of cell division will lead to discovery of the cause of the improper splitting.

Joshua Lederberg, a Nobel Prize-winning geneticist at Stanford University, has predicted that within 10 or 15 years a human being will be produced by "cloning" — a process in which a cell from a single human being could be made to give an exact infant duplicate of the adult who donates the cell.[19] Cloning would allow for human mass production; science would be able to order up carbon copies of individuals now alive.

The ramifications of such a development, if Lederberg is right, are truly incalculable. The whole society might be transformed if genetic deficiencies could be eliminated by in vitro reproduction or by cloning.

Much research has been done in medical, biological, and chemical methods of shaping the mind. More is coming. Educators are just beginning to notice this research. It is the area of development which seems to offer greatest hope for the future of education. It is also an area of great danger, for all powerful discoveries are dangerous if misused. We are indeed on the verge of a brave new world.*

EXERCISE

1. What is ESB? How does it affect learning? (p. 388)
2. What sorts of involuntary acts can biofeedback help to control? (p. 389)
3. According to Drs. Mark and Ervin, what causes violent behavior? (p. 390)
4. What evidence suggests that malnutrition causes brain damage? (p. 391)
5. How did Cameron improve the memory of his patients? (p. 392)
6. What conclusions can be drawn in regard to the chemical basis of learning? (pp. 392–393)
7. Describe the three major features of intelligence identified by Sidney Cohen. (p. 393)
8. What is hyperkinesis? How are drugs used with hyperkinetic children? (pp. 393–394)
9. What are the ramifications of "cloning"? (p. 395)

Part III of this book presents some of the newest methods for improving learning. Do you agree with Sullivan that the biochemical approach is the most promising of them?

Learning through Hypnosis

Martin Astor

The influence that a person's emotional state has on learning is recognized by psychologists and teachers. A learning environment that maintains a low level of anxiety and a supportive emotional tone is considered essential for good teaching. However, a teacher who has difficulty building such an environment often has few alternatives to which he can turn. In this article, Astor proposes

From *The Educational Forum*, vol. 35, no. 4 (May 1971), pp. 447–455. Used by permission of Kappa Delta Pi, An Honor Society in Education, owners of the copyright.

using hypnosis to help reduce anxiety and to build a student's self-image. This is a radically new alternative for improving learning. Decide whether, as Astor contends, hypnosis parallels operant conditioning as a learning tool. (See Skinner, Section 1, and Bushell, Section 10, for explanations of operant conditioning.) After the proper training, would you be willing to use hypnosis in your classroom?

Inclusion of hypnosis in schools as an educational technique does not as yet exist on a controlled, deliberate, and systematic basis. But hypnosis is being used in and out of schools in different ways under different rubrics. Consider a large group of children in a hot, stuffy classroom with a very insipid teacher who insists they all sit still, hands clasped, feet together on the floor for hours on end, and do nothing but fixate their eyes and ears upon her dullness. This is the worst example of a form of educational hypnosis that occurs in the educational lives of many children. Is it not time that we disallow this type of insidious, purposeless, mind-blowing education and replace it with something constructive, socially useful, and creative? . . .

It is the purpose of this article to invite thought about possible use of hypnosis in education. Although we know that there are many cautions, limitations, and drawbacks with regard to hypnosis as a learning methodology, the focus of the article is on the positive.

This article was prompted when similarities were noted in the physical behaviors of hypnotic subjects during induction and in the behavior of children who were working with programmed instruction on "teaching machines." Both the hypnotic subject and the programmed child fixate their eyes, maintain body immobility, concentrate so they may fully invest their psychic energies into the suggested imagery, and are highly motivated to allow their minds and bodies to go deeper and deeper into the simulated experience. It was further noted that there were very marked parallels between hypnotic induction procedures and Skinnerian operant conditioning procedures which are used for the development of software as input into automated learning systems. If we break down the operant conditioning model, we get five basic learning activities.[1]

1. Small steps — The material is graded on such a gradual basis that the student almost always gets the correct answer. This constitutes assurance of continuous positive reinforcement.

2. Active responding — The student is actively involved in cranking the machine, pushing the buttons, writing his answers, checking his work, reviewing material, etc. He is "learning by doing."

3. Immediate confirmation — As soon as the student completes his answer to a question, he can check his answer immediately.

4. Self-pacing — Each student proceeds at his own pace or rate of speed, depending on his abilities, interest, motivation, etc.

5. Program testing — "Revision of Programmed Course on Basis of Student Performance." Upon completion of programmed material the student has a record of his achievements. He can evaluate his strengths and weaknesses and if necessary, he can take part in a remedial program of some kind.

Note how these learning activities arc paralleled by hypnotic induction procedures listed below.

1. Grading suggestions (Small steps) — The operator (hypnotist) begins induction by making very subtle permissive suggestions that don't appear to be suggestions at all. He makes easy progress from suggestion to suggestion.

2. Cooperation and motivation (Active responding) — The more highly motivated and cooperative the subject, the more involved he gets in the hypnotic process, the more it is likely that he will be successfully hypnotized. The subject is actively involved in responding and in noting his own feelings, actions, and reactions.

3. Immediate praise (Immediate confirmation) — Whether the subject resists or complies with anything suggested, the operator always praises the subject and reassures him all is going well. The subject is constantly lulled and reassured so that all positive behavior is immediately reinforced so as to effect continued compliant responses.

4. Timing and individualization of material (Self-pacing) — The rate of speed, methods, and kinds of materials used depend largely on the subject's idiosyncratic needs, actions, and reactions. There is no such thing as a standardized induction; each client has his own unique pace and requirements. The subject chooses his own speed of progress.

5. Record keeping (Program testing) — The operator is always noting actions, reactions, and comments of the subject and is always changing and shaping his material to fit the needs, expectations, and requirements of the subject.

The parallels between the operant conditioning learning model and basic procedures for hypnotic induction are very clear.* The goal of programmed learning is to get someone to learn without consciously seeking to memorize and organize; to make learning as easy, pleasant, and efficient as possible; it suggests a certain kind of automaticity in the learning process. In hypnotic induction we have similar emphases; to cooperate, to relax, to let

* Does this parallelism speak well for operant conditioning as a learning technique?

oneself become open and easy so that behaviors and experiences occur by themselves with a kind of "letting-go" or non-interfering naturalness on the part of the subject. The subject is always praised and is left with a good feeling.

Erickson[2] and Estabrooks[3] argue for the use of hypnosis in education. Erickson likens hypnosis to readiness to use one's learnings, and Hull[4] presents experimental evidence that hypnosis facilitates recall of early childhood memories. Bowers claims that hypnosis improves performance on creativity tests.[5] Estabrooks points to the fact that children are easily hypnotizable, and he feels that hypnosis at an early age can strengthen direction, stability, and educational motivation of children.[6] Erickson sees a parallel between the teacher and the hypnotist as they both seek to alter the "perception and conceptions" of their subjects.* There is a report from Japan that 60 children five to thirteen years of age were involved in two hypnotic sessions per week after school hours.[7] Parents and teachers testified that the children did their homework "immune from temptations of outside distractions"; there was no anxiety or blanking out on exams; that "lazy" children improved their performance, and that the "average" child sharply improved in his work. Hypnosis helped the children to produce what they already knew at the right moment.† . . .

At the present time Dr. Joseph Illovsky, a psychiatrist and Director of Health and Learning, Inc. in New York City, is experimenting with a form of educational hypnosis in three different schools. He is working with immature, emotionally upset children, who have a short attention span and who are all nonreaders. The 48 children involved range from six to eight years of age, and they are treated in groups daily for 20 minutes during school hours. By use of tape recorder the children are relaxed, sleep is induced, and then various post-hypnotic suggestions are made to them. For example, they are told to relax the moment they enter the reading room, or the moment they hear their reading teacher say, "Let's read." They are given specific suggestions to remember sounds of letters and words and to concentrate and remember everything that occurs during their regular reading lesson. The children are also trained to relax whenever they feel emotionally upset. The specially trained reading teachers generally feel that the children are quieter and more relaxed during the reading period than before these treatments. Dr. Illovsky is optimistic that these children will be helped to improve in their reading skills. He has already had success with an earlier group of older children with a similar program at the Central Islip State Hospital. In this latter study, after six months ". . . The hypnotized group . . . had gained an average of two years and three months

* Do you think teachers and hypnotists have the same objectives in mind when they work with children?
† Do these benefits outweigh any negative features which hypnosis might have?

in their reading. . . . The control group during the same period had gained an average of nine months. The hypnotized group showed greater readiness to attack new work, very little lasting discouragement and more ability to study together with other boys than the non-hypnotized control group." [8] . . .

Teachers could benefit enormously from learning to become hypno-educators. A well-trained hypnotic operator is an excellent teacher; he recognizes the importance of individual differences and he adapts his material to the subject's intellectual ability and previous educational experiences. He works with the whole child in the developmental sense and in relation to his emotional state of being. He is an expert on motivation for enlisting the cooperation of his subject. . . .

The induction of hypnosis is only a small part of the total educational hypnosis process. If hypnosis were to be used in education, a whole new branch of teacher training would be needed. Teachers would need to learn a lot more than they do at present about the intricacies of developmental learning processes and they would require much more training in the methods for helping children to learn. This kind of teacher is much less concerned with subject matter than he is with an understanding of the learning processes, as well as the character, potential, and personality of each individual child in his classroom.*

If learning can be defined as change in behavior as a result of experience, we need to find ways of providing opportunities for children to experience life as fully and as richly as possible. They should be deeply involved in their learning experiences from the tops of their heads to the tips of their toes, inside and outside of their bodies — and not just from the neck up. When we allow stimuli to enter into us anatomically the learning gets lodged into the gut and has excellent retrieval potential. Cognitive learnings and memorization of facts are only part learnings of a very limited form. Deeper learnings that lead to significant changes in persons in the functionally adaptive and socially constructive sense are much more wholistic educational goals than mere emphasis on rote memorization.† Educational hypnosis offers promise for more permanent behavioral change in children than most of the other modalities used in the classroom. . . .

Consider the educational and mental health implications of the case below. The child described was treated by the author once a week over a period of six months during which time hypnosis was used extensively.

---

* However, many educators feel that teachers (particularly elementary school teachers) would do a better job in the classroom if they were given more training in subject matter and less training in teaching methods.

† These learnings are also a goal of free schools (see Graubard, this section), but how likely is it that hypnotic techniques would be used by free school teachers?

THE CASE OF MARY J.

M.J., age 15, referred to therapist by school counselor with complaint that child was acting out. Initial interview revealed that child was nervous, anxious, disassociated, and fearful that she would lose control over her behavior. She accepted the assumption of her parents and school counselor that she was "bad" and needed "correction." She suffered from a very poor self-concept and low sense of self-esteem. She believed herself to be helpless and hopeless — that no one could help her. In school she was failing her major subjects and was frequently reported for misbehavior. She had few close friends, was psychologically dependent on pot, and had some promiscuous involvements.

During initial stages of treatment Mary was trained in self-relaxation and in the ability to use her own imagery for inducing insight dreams. The therapist induced a series of ego integrative suggestions stressing feelings of wholeness, togetherness, and control. These suggestions were frequently repeated over a period of two months. At a later period sensory awareness exercises were introduced in both waking and hypnotic states. This served to sensitize the patient to her own body feelings. While the ego integrative exercise served to enhance her feelings of self-esteem, the direct, supportive educational suggestions assured her of her ability to perform well when properly self-motivated and in control of her own mind, body, and emotions.

After six months of treatment the patient's condition and situation was dramatically improved. Her school grades went up from failures to passing. She was no longer considered a behavior problem at home or at school. There was a marked reduction of tension and anxiety and as a result she became more physically intact and verbally articulate and she no longer feared losing behavioral controls. Her "smoking" habit became something she could take or leave and instead of one night stands with numerous men, she settled for enjoying a healthy sexual attachment to a young man a few years her senior.

In Mary's case, hypnosis had an emotionally maturing effect.* It had been used to help her to become more realistic, much less anxious, and more in control. With her improved self-concept she no longer needed to handle her anger through self-denigration and thus improved her relationships with people sexually and socially. Having gained a feeling of inner self-control she was able to give up her external dependencies. A happier,

* Astor attributes the beneficial effects to hypnosis. Are there other factors that could explain the effects equally well, e.g., Mary's relationship with a therapist who cared about her?

relaxed, together person with a good sense of self-esteem, she was able to actualize her potential in and out of school by improving in her work and her behavior.

Having opened our minds to the potential creative and positive uses of hypnosis in education, what about the drawbacks, dangers, and limitations? Won't parents object to allowing their children to be hypnotized? Does it not give teachers too much power and control over children? How do we know there aren't any physical dangers involved? Is it not too manipulative and mechanistic to be used as an educational resource in a society that seeks to further humanistic ideals? Doesn't it weaken the ego and open the person to possible psychological damage? Isn't it unethical and immoral to use hypnotic suggestion in such an extreme form on a captive audience of helpless children? These are legitimate questions.

The author believes that some parents will object to educational hypnosis and others will be delighted to have it made available to their children. The question of teacher-power breaks down to the question of basic trust. The teacher still remains a teacher, not a hypnotist. He is using hypnosis as he would any other educational tool, aid, or resource. More than anything else, his technical competence as a teacher will determine the quality of his work as a hypno-educator. To the author's knowledge there is no danger of physical harm to the child in using hypnosis as an educational tool. The only dangers that exist would stem from poor educational practices rather than poor hypnosis. Suggestion of any kind is dangerous when misused or abused out of ignorance or malice. Hypnotic suggestion used by a skilled practitioner for constructive purposes to enhance the human organism is a desirable practice. . . .

Hypnosis is not being advised for all children at all times. Not all people are hypnotizable, and not everyone who is hypnotizable can go into it in depth. Nor are we advising that hypnosis should interpenetrate all aspects and functions of education. All we are saying is that the power of suggestion is a potential resource ready to be channeled, harnessed, and utilized as an aid in facilitating certain kinds of learning for some children.* Strange as it may sound, educational hypnosis can be used to free children to do their own things through greater self-discipline, self-control, and deeper learnings. The inclusion of this new technology in education would require the better training of teachers in areas of learning theory and learning processes. Educational hypnosis can potentially become a catalytic agent in changing the whole structure and strategy of education in our society.

* Would educators be more responsive to this technique if it were called "suggestion" rather than "hypnosis"?

EXERCISE

1. What features of programmed instruction does Astor compare with the experiences of a child undergoing hypnosis? (p. 396)

2. List the five steps that are similar in operant conditioning and hypnotic suggestion. (pp. 396–397)

3. What types of hypnotic suggestion were used by Illovsky to improve students' reading? (p. 398)

4. As an educational tool, what, if any, are the dangers and limitations of hypnosis? (p. 401)

5. Can hypnosis be used with all students? What are its possible limitations? (p. 401)

Section Twelve

TRAINING BETTER TEACHERS

Introduction

In some more progressive schools of education teacher trainees are designing individual study programs and participating in joint faculty-student committees for revising the teacher education curriculum. (This might be a good model for elementary and high schools to follow, too.) But what constitutes an effective teacher education program? Several of the readings in this section are attempts to answer this question.

Ideally, teacher education programs, both for the student teacher and the practicing teacher, should incorporate the best of what we know about teaching and learning. Unfortunately, at least some educators have concluded that these programs are generally ineffective. For example, John Goodlad, a distinguished educator, thinks that a major barrier to improving education has been our failure to upgrade continually the skills of practicing teachers (Section 9). In a following selection, Walter Borg and his colleagues criticize teacher preparation programs for relying heavily on lecture and discussion. They suggest these techniques are not appropriate for training teachers in the skills that constitute teaching. Borg and his colleagues use an analogy to make this point. They observe that one does not train surgeons by telling them how to do it; guided practice and feedback are essential. Yet guided practice and feedback occur infrequently in traditional teacher training.

A major development in teacher training in the last few years has been a movement called competency-based teacher education (CBTE). The basic idea is that teachers should be trained in specific skills of teaching, and they should be held accountable for acquiring these skills. For example, they should learn how to ask good questions, explain concepts clearly, respond to students' ideas,

403

and conduct role-playing. Some advocates of CBTE have proposed that teachers should be certified to teach only when they can demonstrate that they are competent to bring about gains in student learning. In part CBTE is a reaction to the implicit assumption behind many teacher-education programs — that a teacher is somehow qualified to teach once he has earned enough credits in education courses and has completed a student teaching program. CBTE programs also have been influenced heavily by new developments in educational psychology, particularly by accountability, behavioral objectives, and criterion-referenced measurement. These concepts are discussed in Part 4 of this book.

The article by Barbara Dunning and Meredith Gall in this section describes a recently developed teacher-education package that uses the learning principles of modeling, practice, and feedback to develop specific teaching skills in mathematics tutoring. These training materials, and others like them, are currently being used in several CBTE programs. These materials, and CBTE programs generally, have not been without critics. The critics fear that CBTE could be used to train a generation of teacher-technologists who have demonstrated competence in specific areas of instruction, but who lack humanism and the desire to transform education. They point out that CBTE programs tend to formulate learning objectives for teachers that emphasize trivial, quantitative aspects of teaching. (The same criticism has been applied to the use of behavioral objectives to define learning goals for students; see Guth, Section 14.) These criticisms and others are expressed in the paper by Robert Nash and Russell Agne. Stuart Cohen and Richard Hersh respond to these criticisms in their selection.

Although CBTE reflects newer trends in education, it is mainly based on the traditional assumption that the teacher is the key agent in bringing about learning. It still assumes the need for university programs in teacher education and practicing teachers who work in the schools. However, as we pointed out in Part 2, a major thesis of contemporary educational theorists and researchers is that much learning occurs outside the school. Perhaps we should be concentrating more on increasing the effectiveness of such out-of-school agents as parents, community workers, and employers to function as teachers. For example, Glen Nimnicht and Edna Brown describe their development of materials to train parents to tutor their young children. Another approach, described by Herbert Thelen, is to enlist students themselves as teachers. A main argument favoring this approach is that the student being tutored learns at the same time the student tutor benefits in improved self-esteem, motivation, and academic achievement.

Almost all educators agree that we need to train better teachers, but they differ about how best to accomplish this goal. You may find it helpful to decide whether you agree or disagree with the following views.

Competency-Based Teacher Education

Pro Competency-based teacher education is a welcome development because it ensures that teachers acquire specific skills that will make them effective in the classroom. In previous programs student teachers had only to earn course credits, not demonstrate competency.

Con Competency-based teacher education is not what is needed at all. It diverts our attention from what is really needed — to train teachers who have personal maturity, a commitment to reform education, and belief in humanistic ideals.

Training Classroom Teachers

Pro The traditional teacher will still be the key person in a reformed educational system. Therefore, most of our attention should be given to developing innovative teacher training programs in education schools and to upgrading the skills of practicing teachers.

Con Working with student teachers and practicing teachers only preserves the status quo. They have had their day. To truly reform education, we should concentrate our efforts on training other groups which have a teaching role, such people as parents, employers, and students themselves.

Why Do Conventional Teacher Education Programs Fail?

Walter R. Borg, Marjorie L. Kelley, Philip Langer, and Meredith D. Gall

The authors of this selection worked together in the late 1960's at the Far West Laboratory for Educational Research and Development, now located in San Francisco, California. The purpose of the Laboratory, part of a national network funded by the U.S. Office of Education, is to develop innovative educational products of

An excerpt from the book, *The Minicourse: A Microteaching Approach to Teacher Education*. New York: Macmillan Educational Services, 1970. Reprinted with permission of the publisher. Copyright © 1970 Macmillan Publishing Co.

*demonstrated effectiveness. To develop materials for teacher educa-
tion, the authors first reviewed current programs. The result of their
review was strong criticism of these programs, particularly poor
teaching methods to train teachers. This finding is ironical, because we would expect to find that teacher-training programs provide exemplary models of good teaching practices. Also, the authors
decry the fact that traditional programs do not train teachers adequately in specific classroom skills. Before accepting the authors'
findings, however, consider the possibility that they evaluated existing programs against inappropriate criteria. Some educators would
be more interested in how well teacher-education programs help
student and practicing teachers to advance in their personal development and to acquire a commitment to reform education. Robert
Nash and Russell Agne (this section) are two educators who take
this view.*

CONVENTIONAL TEACHER EDUCATION PROGRAMS

PRESERVICE PROGRAMS. An examination of the preservice teacher education programs offered at most colleges and universities reveal that such
programs fall into three major categories:

The first category emphasizes *curriculum content,* mastery of the knowledge and concepts that make up the content of the instructional program.
This category consists primarily of the subject matter or curriculum that
the teacher is expected to transmit to the pupil. The great mass of content
in this aspect of teacher education is transmitted to the teacher in the form
of verbal abstractions. The teacher subsequently transmits a similar body
of information to his pupils, again predominantly in the form of abstract
concepts. Although subject-matter instruction is sometimes supervised by
the college of education, it usually comes under the control of specialists
in other colleges.

The second category emphasizes *professional knowledge,* which teachers
need as functioning members of their profession and which includes such
areas as educational psychology, child and adolescent development, and
educational evaluation. Again, most information in this category is presented in the form of abstractions. The teacher must apply these abstractions to concrete educational situations, and this leap from abstract to
concrete may be difficult to make. As a result, teachers frequently find
themselves unable to apply knowledge they have gained, and are often extremely critical of this aspect of their training when they recognize that the
needed information is not given in usable form.

The third category emphasizes *classroom skills and behavior,* the teaching act itself. This category includes both teaching and human interaction
skills as well as behavior patterns that the teacher needs to function
efficiently in the classroom. Student-teaching is the major training com-

ponent in this phase of teacher education, although teaching methods courses are also important. It is in these courses that the greatest discrepancy usually occurs between the form in which the teacher-to-be receives information — chiefly in verbal abstractions — and the form in which he must subsequently use the information — by developing patterns of effective classroom behavior.*

Regarding this third category, Willis (1968), in a survey of teaching-methods courses in four-year teacher education institutions in Wisconsin, found that lecturing and group discussion were the instructional techniques most frequently used. He concluded that teaching was being considered mostly in the abstract and that systematic analysis of teaching behavior was almost entirely lacking. Student-teaching programs do present information in a form reasonably convertible to the classroom situation, although the vast majority of such programs do not focus on the development of specific behavior patterns nor do they provide the trainee with the kind of effective feedback required for efficient development of skills. In addition, a series of studies by Joyce (1969) at Columbia University raised serious doubts about the effectiveness of conventional student-teaching programs. He observed student-teacher behavior near both the beginning and the end of student-teaching, using a simplified system of interaction analysis. His major finding was that student-teachers became more authoritarian and punitive as a result of their training.† Such findings suggested that student-teaching, which in the past has been regarded as the most effective aspect of preservice teacher education, may be, in fact, of little value.

It seems fair to conclude that current teacher education programs are probably most effective in preparing the teacher in specific subject matter. Such programs are generally less effective in providing teachers with a sound professional foundation, i.e., with the knowledge and insight needed to understand the learner and the teaching-learning process. It is suggested that most current programs are seriously deficient with regard to building the specific skills and behavior patterns the teacher needs to structure efficiently a variety of classroom teaching-learning situations.

IN-SERVICE PROGRAMS. Although one can find a few promising programs and innovations in teacher-training institutions, the great majority of preservice programs offer similar courses and conduct student-teaching in about the same way. Therefore, in preservice education, a fairly uniform "conventional" program, which can be examined and questioned, does exist, and has been subjected to research such as that cited above.

No such uniform conventional program can be described, however, for

* Do you think the authors should have included personal development as a fourth category of preservice programs?
† How and why might student teachers have learned these behavior patterns?

in-service education. If any such generalization is possible, it is that schools do very little in-service training, and what they do is poor.* Most school districts budget little or no money for such training, and limit themselves to a program consisting of faculty meetings and one-day teacher institutes. College extension courses are also used widely. As a rule these courses are even less well taught than regular courses since they are often turned over to the inexperienced professor or the part-time faculty member who is willing, but not especially able. For the most part, these courses aim at increasing teachers' professional knowledge or competence in new curriculum content.

Local workshops are also part of many in-service programs. These often focus on specific new curricular materials, such as a new science or mathematics program, and are useful in updating the teacher's knowledge, but they rarely provide any effective training in the new methods needed to use the curriculum to its best advantage. In fact, perhaps the most remarkable thing about in-service education as a whole is that so little of it focuses on these teaching methods. Actually, the reverse should be true. The in-service setting is particularly well suited to instruction in classroom skills, since the teacher has ample opportunity to practice new skills in his own classroom. Furthermore, most in-service teachers, especially those just starting their careers, intensely want to develop better teaching skills.

WHY DO CONVENTIONAL TEACHER EDUCATION PROGRAMS FAIL? Let us consider further the skills required for effective classroom teaching, and explore the reasons for the failure of most conventional teacher education programs to equip teachers-in-training with these skills. Many of the skills involved in teaching, such as effective questioning, have been known for decades. Yet research shows virtually no difference in the questioning patterns of today's teacher and those teachers of fifty years ago. This suggests that although we may know many things that would make the teacher more effective, on the whole we have not transmitted this knowledge in a usable form. The attempts of teacher education institutions to equip their students with classroom skills have generally suffered from four serious deficiencies:

1. *Emphasis is on telling, rather than doing.* Instruction is largely divorced from actual classroom behavior. Attempts to structure behavior by telling the teacher-in-training how to behave are generally not effective for developing the complex skills needed in teaching. The Willis (1968) survey of educational methods courses in four-year teacher education institutions in Wisconsin showed that lecturing and discussion were by far the

* *Compare with John Goodlad's criticisms of in-service teacher training (Section 9).*

most widely used instructional techniques. Yet experience from educational, military, and industrial settings indicates that interaction skills are more effectively learned through guided experience in the behavior itself. How much confidence, for example, would you have in a surgeon if you knew that he had never perfected his techniques with animals, never worked with cadavers, and never practiced under the guidance of an expert the specific skills needed in a given operation — if, in fact, he had learned surgery by listening to lectures given by someone who had not performed an operation in ten years, and had been graduated from medical school largely on the basis of his ability to pass multiple-choice tests? * We leave it to the teachers among our reading audience to judge how relevant this analogy is to the training they were given in specific classroom skills.

2. *Instruction is general, rather than specific.* Development of a skill requires that the learner have specific behavioral goals clearly in mind. Most teacher-training programs deal with vague generalities, such as "Individualize your instruction to meet each pupil's needs," rather than systematic definition and development of specific teaching skills. The teacher is usually unable to translate the generalities given by textbook, professor, and student-teaching supervisor into the specific techniques he needs for the classroom.

3. *Effective models are not provided.* One useful aid in learning specific skills is the study of a model. However, even in programs in which the trainee has a model available, such as the supervising teacher in practice-teaching, the student teacher is rarely told what to look for, and often works with a model who is weak in essential skills. Many methods courses rely heavily on such trainee observations of model teachers in action. Unfortunately, these courses produce even poorer results than student teaching does, because they provide no opportunity for the trainee to practice the teaching skills he has observed.

4. *Effective feedback is not provided.* In practicing a newly acquired skill, the learner can progress much more rapidly if he receives information about his performance.† This feedback is usually more effective if it is both *specific* and *immediate*. It is still more effective if the learner can then immediately apply what he has learned. It is in this area of providing effective feedback that the typical student-teaching experience fails most dismally. Evidence is accumulating that supervisory feedback contributes little or nothing to teaching improvement. Acheson's study (1964) of supervisory feedback in the Stanford Intern Program compared the effects on teaching behavior of various combinations of television feedback (i.e., viewing one's own teaching on videotape) and supervisory feedback. He found

---

* *Do you think the analogy with surgery training is appropriate?*
† *What educational theorists in Part I of this book talk about the use of models and feedback in learning?*

that a supervisory conference combined with television feedback was no more effective than television feedback alone. Furthermore, a supervisory conference without television produced no more change than occurred in a control group that received no feedback. In an in-service setting, Tuckman and Oliver (1968) showed that, while pupil feedback led to positive teacher change, supervisor feedback led to negative change — in the direction away from the supervisor's recommendations. Supervisory feedback seems to suffer from two major deficiencies: first, it is too general; second, it is threatening and produces anxiety in many teachers and student teachers. . . .

EXERCISE

1. According to the authors, what are the three major objectives of most preservice teacher education programs? (pp. 406–407)

2. What was the main finding of Joyce's study? (p. 407)

3. What is the authors' primary criticism of in-service workshops? (p. 408)

4. According to the authors, what are four ways in which conventional teacher education programs fail? (pp. 408–410)

5. What was the main finding of Willis's study? (pp. 408–409)

A Very Legitimate Pride

Barbara B. Dunning and Meredith D. Gall

> *The authors work at the Far West Laboratory for Educational Research and Development, described in the introduction to the preceding selection. In this article, Dunning and Gall describe a set of teacher-training materials (a "Minicourse") which is being used in some competency-based teacher education programs (CBTE), a major new development in teacher education. These materials incorporate some of the main characteristics of CBTE programs: emphasis on specific classroom skills; behavioral objectives, which teachers are to achieve; and such learning principles as observation of models, practice, and feedback. However, they do not prescribe specific levels of competence teachers should achieve. For example, one goal of this minicourse is to increase teachers' use of diagnostic*

From the *Arithmetic Teacher*, 1971, pp. 339–345. Reprinted with permission of publisher and authors.

*questions. In some CBTE programs, teachers would have to dem-
onstrate ability to ask a specific number of such questions during a
tutoring session. If they could demonstrate this competence, they
would not need to undergo training. If they could not demonstrate
this competence, they would receive training of the type provided
by the minicourse until they achieved competence. Later in this section, arguments in favor of CBTE are presented by Stuart Cohen
and Richard Hersh, and criticisms are given by Robert Nash and
Russell Agne. Does the minicourse overcome the deficiencies of
traditional training programs identified by Walter Borg and his
colleagues in the preceding selection? Would you like to take a
minicourse?*

In a lecture in the 1920s, Alfred North Whitehead said:

> In ... the reform of mathematics instruction, the present gen-
> eration of teachers may take a very legitimate pride in its achieve-
> ments. It has shown immense energy in reform, and has accom-
> plished more than would have been thought possible in so short a
> time.

Today's mathematics teachers continue to be leaders in reform. Yet even
though curriculum *content* has been revolutionized for post-Sputnik generations, the nation's schools and colleges have not yet experienced a comparable revolution in teaching techniques.

At the Far West Laboratory for Educational Research and Development,
the Teacher Education Program ... has concentrated its efforts on creating, field testing, and evaluating a series of inservice and preservice Minicourses that enable teachers to learn essential skills during regular school
hours, without leaving their own buildings.

The newest of these self-contained, self-evaluative Minicourses is "Individualizing Instruction in Mathematics." It helps teachers learn to work
effectively one-to-one with their students and to deal successfully with their
students' mathematics problems. Use of this Minicourse multiplies teacher
effectiveness and adds new classroom skills to the teacher's repertoire.

Teachers today are steadily moving away from their "traditional" roles
as lecturers, organizers of content, and testers. Now — using "modern"
mathematics and armed with new knowledge about how youngsters learn
— the best teachers are becoming facilitators, tutors, and stimulators of
small-group or individual activities.* And now that rigorous field testing has
validated the Laboratory's newest Minicourse for national installation, *any*
elementary teacher can easily master the skills necessary for tutoring and
individualizing in mathematics.

---

* *Are these in fact the characteristics of the "best" teachers?*

The Laboratory's development team began the research and development cycle for this Minicourse in 1968. A review of previous research focused on the work of Bernstein (1959), Tilton (1947), Ross (1963), and Roberts (1968). This research highlighted the very real benefits that students derive from individualized tutoring. . . .

If there is one point on which all writers about mathematics tutoring agree, it is the importance of *diagnosis.** Brueckner and Bond (1955), for example, state that, "the continuous application of diagnostic methods to ferret out the difficulties pupils may be having with arithmetic is vital." Five categories of diagnostic questions evolved from the literature search:

1. *General diagnostic questions.* For example, "How did you get your answer?" or "What part don't you understand?"

2. *Diagnostic questions about number concepts.* For example, "What is the value of 4 in the numeral 46?" or "What is another name for 12?"

3. *Diagnostic questions about reading difficulties.* A student's inability to read a verbal problem obviously interferes with his ability to solve it. When a student has difficulty with a verbal reasoning problem, the teacher asks the student to read it aloud.

4. *Diagnostic questions about word definitions.* Even when a student can read a verbal problem he may not understand the meaning of all the words. During one field test, a teacher worked with a student for the number of stamps found on a page of a stamp album. A diagnostic question revealed that the student was familiar with record albums but couldn't visualize a stamp album with pages.

5. *Diagnostic questions about the selection of a number operation for solving a verbal problem.* For example, "What number operation do you use to solve this problem?" These types of questions enable a teacher to identify common student difficulties.

After the teacher diagnoses the nature of the student's difficulty, he is ready to move into the second phase of the tutoring sequence, *demonstration.* At this point, tutoring involves demonstrating to the student the solution of the problem. The following six demonstration techniques are particularly useful with students who have difficulty with number operations and verbal problems.

1. *Estimation.* This technique can be used prior to developing an understanding of the exact procedures. For example, a student must solve this problem: $42 - 29 = \boxed{}$. If he figures that 42 is almost 40 and 29 is almost 30, he can estimate that his answer will be about 10.

---

* *Diagnostic testing is a major emphasis of new developments in evaluation (see Section 16).*

2. *Expanded notation*. Expanded notation is helpful in explaining such concepts as place value and regrouping.

3. *Number line*. Through the use of the number line a teacher can supplement his verbal explantion of new mathematics concepts with pictorial demonstrations.

4. *Manipulative materials*. Although seldom used beyond the primary grades, manipulative materials such as Cuisenaire rods, pieboards, and place-value charts are highly recommended for use with all students who have a weak understanding of number concepts.*

5. *Picture or diagram*. This method is excellent for demonstrating verbal problems. Words and numbers become more comprehensible to a student when depicted in a picture.

6. *Number sentences*. The number sentence is a useful technique because it helps the student see the relationship between the quantities given in a verbal problem and because it develops his understanding of mathematics as a quantitative language.

The step that logically follows the demonstration phase of the tutoring sequence is *evaluation*. At this point the teacher evaluates the student's learning by assigning an example for him to solve. This example should be similar to one that originally gave the student difficulty. If the student is unable to solve it, the teacher must recycle the tutoring sequence through further diagnostic questioning and demonstration. But if the student can correctly solve the evaluation example, the teacher should conclude the tutoring session by assigning additional examples for practice. However, the teacher should assign examples only after the student demonstrates his understanding by solving an evaluation example correctly. Otherwise, practice simply strengthens incorrect habits (Glennon and Callahan 1968, p. 81; Brownell and Chazal 1935).

The basic Minicourse tutoring sequence, then, consists of four easy sequential stages: diagnosis, demonstration, evaluation, and practice.†

Two other skills have proved effective in tutoring: *verbal praise*, particularly *specific verbal praise*, a commendation tied closely to the student's performance (for example, "Good, you know how to regroup!"); and *prompting questions*, that is, questions asking the student to do or tell something (for example, "Will you please draw a picture of the problem?"), rather than the teacher doing or telling.

Athough the main objective of this Minicourse is to increase teacher skills in mathematics tutoring, the course also aims to increase the *amount* of time spent in individualized mathematics instruction. Therefore, the Teacher Handbook includes a final lesson that shows how the teacher can

* *Why do you think manipulatives are seldom used beyond the primary grades?*
† *Would you use the tutoring techniques described above in your own teaching?*

reorganize the classroom to provide increased time for tutoring. Suggested techniques include providing partial scoring keys for students' seatwork, tutoring at a worktable rather than by walking about the room, and using student tutors for routine tutoring tasks.

The Minicourse, as developed and field tested, met virtually all the objectives listed in Table 1. The teacher learns these specific skills during the regular school day by practicing them, on released time, with his own students. "Individualizing Instruction in Mathematics" — like all other Minicourses produced to date — follows a carefully planned instructional sequence.

TABLE 1
Minicourse 5 Objectives and Skills

Instructional Sequence 1	
Objective	To improve teacher skill in rewarding pupils' correct responses and encouraging their active participation in the tutoring process.
Skills covered	Using verbal praise to reward correct responses. Asking prompting questions to increase pupils' active involvement in the tutoring process.
Instructional Sequence 2	
Objective	To increase teacher skill in diagnosing pupils' deficiencies in understanding of mathematical concepts and computational procedures.
Skills covered	Asking general diagnostic questions (e.g., "How did you get your answer?"). Number operations: asking questions to test pupils' understanding of place value, regrouping, and other number concepts. Verbal problems: asking questions that test pupils' ability to read the problem and to decide on an appropriate number operation.
Instructional Sequence 3	
Objective	To increase teacher use of techniques that help to develop pupils' understanding of mathematical concepts and computational procedures.
Skills covered	Estimating an answer prior to using a computational algorithm. Number operations: depending on the situation, using expanded notation, the number line, or manipulative materials. Verbal problems: having the pupil draw a picture of the problem and having him write a number sentence to express the problem's requirements.

Instructional Sequence 4

Objective	To increase teacher skill in evaluating student progress and assigning practice examples.
Skills covered	Assigning an evaluation example. Assigning practice examples.

Instructional Sequence 5

Objective	To improve teacher skill in organizing the mathematics class period for individual tutoring.
Skills covered	Having pupils correct their own work. Having pupils tutor each other (peer tutoring).

First, the teacher reads a handbook lesson describing the skills to be practiced. Next he views a short instructional film that illustrates each skill, with appropriate cues and verbal reinforcement. Then he views a brief model film that lets him check his understanding and discrimination of what he has seen demonstrated.

The following day, the teacher selects two students who need tutoring and practices (about ten minutes with each student) the same skills in a microteaching situation. The teacher videotapes these microteaching sessions so that he can replay them later and evaluate them by using checklists in his handbook.* Thus, he gets immediate feedback in a nonthreatening and comfortable atmosphere.

Moreover, a day or two later the teacher has a second chance to practice the same skills during a "reteach" session with different students in front of the videotape recorder.

No supervisor is needed, but the teacher can play back his tapes with another teacher who is taking the course at the same time. One videotape recorder lets four to eight teachers in the same building take the course at one time. An administrator acts as local "coordinator" — to be sure that the videotape equipment is scheduled as needed and that teachers get an hour a day, three days a week, for their microteaching practice sessions.

The Minicourse *works* because teachers spend 70 percent of their time practicing classroom skills rather than just reading or hearing about them. If, during the rigorous development, evaluation, and revision stages, any Minicourse fails to accomplish its objectives satisfactorily, it is further revised and retested until the performance goals are reached.

The mathematics Minicourse was first tested with 47 teachers (grades 3 to 6) in three San Francisco Bay Area school districts. Their mean age was 34.6, and their mean years of teaching experience was 9.1. The effectiveness of the Minicourse was determined by videotaping two tutoring sessions for each teacher, *before* and *after* the course. Tables 2 and 3 show the key

---

* *What do you think is the learning value of self-videotaping?*

TABLE 2
Teachers' Use of Specific Tutoring Skills
Before and After the Minicourse

	Pretape average	Posttape average	Percentage of teachers improving
Verbal praise[a]	7 occurrences	11 occurrences	70%
Diagnostic questions[b]	10 occurrences	15 occurrences	79%
Demonstration techniques[a] (tutoring on number operations)	18 seconds	168 seconds	65%
Demonstration techniques[a] (tutoring on verbal problems)	48 seconds	165 seconds	80%
Evaluation[b]	27 teachers	30 teachers	(no change)
Practice[b]	1 teacher	11 teachers	18%

[a] Based on about ten minutes of tutoring.
[b] Based on about twenty minutes of tutoring.

TABLE 3
Number of Teachers Using Each Demonstration Technique
Before and After Minicourse 5

	Number of teachers	
	Precourse	Postcourse
Estimation	6	21
Expanded notation	11	19
Number line	2	11
Manipulative materials	8	19
Picture or diagram	18	35
Number sentence	14	24

results of this analysis, with the most impressive gains being achieved in the amount of time spent using demonstration techniques during tutoring. . . .

These findings seem impressive in view of the fact that nearly all the teachers who participated in the field testing had many years of experience and had previous inservice training in modern mathematics instruction. Another 150 teachers across the nation participated in operational field tests that proved the Minicourse to be fully ready for general use, without any Laboratory supervision.[1]

The Minicourse has also been tested with student teachers. Kenneth Nelson and Douglas Rector at the State University of New York (Fredonia) have offered this Minicourse to several hundred undergraduates as part of a mathematics methods course. Since it is difficult logistically to obtain real pupils with whom to practice, some student teachers play the role of pupils while others practice tutoring them. Roles are then reversed so that everyone has the opportunity to evaluate his performance in both roles on videotape playback. As one might expect, their research data reveal that student teachers make substantially larger gains in tutoring skills than do inservice teachers.

Teachers enjoy taking the Minicourse. Everything needed comes in one self-contained package — an introductory film, eight instructional and model films, a coordinator's handbook, and teacher's handbook (including self-evaluation forms and follow-up lessons). By following the daily course schedule (for twelve days, one hour per day) and the step-by-step instructions, teachers acquire the skills through repeated practice and — by videotape feedback — "see themselves as others see them." Yet their tapes are always "confidential" — no supervisor or colleague is allowed to view a teacher's videotape without his permission. . . .

Minicourses have proved to be an extremely valuable alternative in the professional development of inservice and preservice teachers. Moreover, they provide an excellent mode of training for paraprofessionals, student teachers, interns, or inexperienced personnel who can tutor students under the guidance of experienced teachers.* . . .

EXERCISE

1. How do the authors describe the mathematics teacher's traditional role, and what are his new roles? (p. 411)

2. What are the four steps of the basic tutoring sequence? (pp. 412–413)

3. What are the basic features of the instructional strategy used in the minicourse? (p. 415)

Is this a good use of paraprofessionals?

Competency in Teacher Education: A Prop for the Status Quo?

Robert J. Nash and Russell M. Agne

>   *Robert Nash and Russell Agne strongly criticize competency-based teacher education, including the type of skill-training materials described by Barbara Dunning and Meredith Gall in the preceding selection. Their basic criticism is that competency-based teacher education is neither adequate for training the type of teacher needed in education today nor does it meet the needs of students now entering the teaching profession. As the title of their article suggests, Nash and Agne view this movement as conservative and reactionary rather than as a step forward in teacher education. Do you agree? Before you form your opinion, we suggest you read their article and the rejoinder that follows by Stuart Cohen and Richard Hersh. Also, because both articles discuss competency-based teacher education in general terms, you might read the preceding selection, "A Very Legitimate Pride," to understand what CBTE means.*

For a multiplicity of complex reasons, colleges of education around the country are adopting a competency-based mode for professional training.[1] Teacher educators are growing impatient with the piecemeal and obsolete curricula innovations that have characterized so many of their programs in the past. Amidst the inchoate but rising public demand that teachers in the cities and suburbs become professional skill strategists who can successfully prepare children to read, write, and compute, teacher educators are beginning to reassess their training mission. And as more public schools turn to performance contracting* with business and industry to insure that their students learn the basic skills necessary for technological survival, colleges of education are reevaluating their own preparation programs in order to reaffirm their central position in the education of this country's teachers. As a result, curriculum reforms in teacher education are based on

From *The Journal of Teacher Education*, 22, 1971, pp. 147–156. Reprinted with permission of the publisher.

* *For a discussion of performance contracting, see the selections by Mecklenburger and Wilson and by Farrell in Section 15.*

the premise that the teacher's primary professional responsibility is to master those performative skills that will insure that students in schools everywhere (by virtue of their own skill proficiencies) can compete equitably and successfully for diminishing job openings and prestigious college admissions.

Four general assumptions underlie a competency-based teacher preparation program:

1. The primary purpose of professional teacher training is to produce teachers who possess those specialized techniques, skills, and dispositions that will facilitate learning in any educational environment. The operative belief here is that good teaching occurs when the trainee has mastered a welter of carefully specified training protocols that foster these basic skills.[2]

2. Through a series of managerial and instructional units, the teacher trainee is able to achieve the objectives of the teacher preparation program. Basic to these units are modular experiences that will allow the trainee to proceed at a pace consistent with his own interests and abilities. Microteaching, simulation, behavioral objective exercises, and differentiated staffing techniques are meant to increase the skill proficiencies necessary for good teaching.[3] *

3. The measurable outcome of a competency-based program is the trainee's proficiency in demonstrating his mastery of the requisite teaching skills. By successfully meeting designated, preestablished performance criteria, the trainee is able to demonstrate his ability to step into the classroom as a highly qualified, master teacher.

4. All of the above are meant to make teachers more accountable to a client public, because evaluation of teachers is shifted from student input to professional output. If a child fails, it is because the educational system has failed to produce sophisticated equipment and superior performance specialists who can diagnose and remediate learning deficiencies in children.[4] †

In spite of the above rationale for competency-based teacher preparation programs, it is our belief that the competency thrust in colleges of education, as now practiced, is failing to respond to the *cri de coeur* of many education students for substantial personal, educational, and social reform. Stated more sharply, our contention is that for some of our students the whole competency leitmotif is but another self-authenticating prop for the status quo.

Because of our overzealous preoccupation with quantifiable and incre-

* *Microteaching and behavioral objectives are discussed by Borg et al. (this section) and in Section 14.*
† *Block expounds the same point of view in his discussion of the mastery learning model (Section 15).*

mental competency procedures, we are becoming deafened to the cries of students for competencies in areas that do not lend themselves to precise assessment. We look for immediately observable, cut-and-dried evidences of behavior modification (as exemplified by such assessment procedures as Flanders' interaction analysis), while our students scream for help in developing competencies to rectify personal, educational, and social dislocations.* Most of us want our students to become reconstructive agents for personal and social change (reasons that may have attracted us to teacher education), but our competency compulsiveness fails to convey this to them. Instead of preparing them to operationalize their desires to create open classrooms, stimulate reform dialogue and activity within the school community, and comprehend the harshest political realities of the larger socioeducational setting, we are exclusively stressing the necessity for component skill development along acceptable professional norms. The disastrous consequence of this is that our students perceive our efforts to prepare them to be learning specialists as nothing more than a systematic attempt to fit them into a lifetime of quiescent professional conformity....

We believe that a competency model for teacher education can ultimately prove to be both a practical and a humane response to those students who want to change the status quo through their teaching commitment.† But before this is possible, we realize that the competency curriculum is but one methodological approach to the preparation of teachers. Competency must never become an all-embracing, sacralized idea-system that treats as heretical any critique of or departure from its tenets. We must also realize that teacher preparation can be made to serve the reform needs of students only when its performance proclivities are subordinated to the collaborative student-instructor quest for a larger sense of purpose in the educational-social venture. Charles Silberman has stated:

> This means developing teachers' ability and their desire to think seriously, deeply, and continuously about the purposes and consequences of what they do — about the ways in which their curriculum and teaching methods, classroom and social organization, testing and grading procedures, affect purpose and are affected by it.[5]

We maintain that at least two kinds of understandings are necessary if ever we are to use our competency models realistically and humanely. First, we must reacquaint ourselves with the new idealism that our students are bringing to teacher education. Generally, they are rejecting business, scientific, and technological career preparation in favor of teaching because they desire a lifetime of human service in a profession potentially capable

* *Flanders' interaction analysis system is described in Section 6.*
† *Then why are Nash and Agne so critical of competency-based teacher education?*

of effecting widespread personal and social reform. And second, we must understand the alarming nature of the student charge that a professional training exclusively rooted in competency techniques subverts larger reform notions by reinforcing three kinds of status quo: personal, educational, and social. The remainder of this paper will deal with these two understandings.

It is axiomatic that colleges of education tended, in the past to attract students from middle-class backgrounds who were less interested in helping their fellow man toward personal self-fulfillment and a more humane social order than they were in pursuing employment security, materialistic well-being, acceptable social status, and a perpetuation of a conservative value system.[6] In the last few years, for putative reasons that have ranged from the increasing depersonalization of man in an excessively organizational technocracy to the severe personal and cultural dislocations brought on by an adventurist war in Southeast Asia, young people have had different expectations for their college education. One educational psychologist has stated that in the future all undergraduates wil become much less interested in acquiring a vocation and going up in the world than they will be in finding themselves and in reexamining their society's basic purposes. He also predicts that as our society becomes more affluent we can expect growing numbers of students to be activistic (not necessarily militant or violent) and to use their college training for personal and social reform.[7] A Harris poll, taken May 20–28, 1970, supports these propositions:

1. Seventy percent of the 800 undergraduates interviewed said that if America continues its "arrogant, imperialistic policies" it will be in trouble.
2. Sixty-five percent agreed that "our troubles stem from making economic competition the basis of our way of life."
3. Eighty-one percent said that "until the older generation comes to understand the new priorities and life-style of the young, serious conflict is going to continue."
4. Seventy-six percent stated that most young Americans are dissatisfied with the direction in which America is heading.[8] *

. . . If the above analysis is accurate, then it is fair to say that at least some of our students are fundamentally different from the type that was attracted to teacher education even one decade ago. Although it is difficult to assess a precise level of social consciousness by utilizing polling techniques that may or may not be conclusive for education students, it is still a fair presumption that today professional education students are motivated by more personalistic, communitarian, and socially activistic purposes than their predecessors. If this is true, then these students are going to be decisively critical of a professional preparation that threatens to trivialize or ignore their nonprofessional concerns.

Many of our students are skeptical about the competency model because

* Do these descriptions of college students apply to you?

they believe it to be unresponsive to their personal-social ideals and because it serves to buttress at least three kinds of interrelated status quo:

1. A professional curriculum that emphasizes professional skills only and is oblivious to the feelings, values, and attitudes of the trainee serves to underscore the larger society's devaluation of the person in favor of the functionary-expert. Many young prospective teachers (like their youth counterparts everywhere) are disdaining the injunction to sharpen their skills and become proficient professionals because they sense that the pursuit of self-understanding and personal meaning is infinitely more fundamental to their future lives. One of the reasons that competency is implicitly repugnant to some of the young is because it suggests that, at best, their lives have worth only if they are trained and qualified to perform a given, professional function. As they enter a college of education, the most idealistic among these students strive to achieve a coherent awareness of themselves as integrated persons; for them, a grasp of their own personhood and a keener understanding of their personal value and goal systems are prior to any kind of professional commitment.*

What they meet is a competency program which assumes that from the very beginning prospective teachers ought to be honing their skills as learning strategists. Students are locked into a systematic, sequential, and continuing program that exposes them to a series of managerial and instructional units whose ultimate objective is to achieve the purposes of the program. The self-validating circularity of the competency curriculum effectively militates against the student's personal search for meaning and self-integration, because it assumes a priori that students who want to become teachers have resolved value and identity conflicts before they enter the program. Such naïveté would be humorous if it were not so widespread in teacher education today.

Actually, the inability of competency-based professional programs, as now structured, to accommodate the student's search for value and selfhood is understandable. At this time, we have been unable to formulate experiences that would objectively enable a student to resolve those questions relating to such personal issues as loneliness, meaninglessness, anxiety, sexual and drug conflicts, authority problems, hostility, hopelessness, and the discrepancies between reality and idealism.[9] One of the most glaring inadequacies of the competency-based model is that it excludes from its program structured opportunities for students to explore, express, and comprehend their feelings.† This conflict is sharpened as they move closer to the time when they have to take their professional places in a social system

* *We agree. That is why we included the value-oriented section, "What Should Students Learn?" in this book.*
† *How would Cohen and Hersh (next selection) respond to this criticism of competency-based teacher education?*

that ignores or exploits their personal feelings and values them primarily because of the expertise they have to offer. . . .

2. A professional curriculum that is content merely to prepare students to take their places as skilled professionals in the conventional public school classroom is serving to perpetuate an educational status quo tragically in need of renewal. We believe that competency programs should help students to understand and to respond to the proliferating and ubiquitous critique of American education. Also, we should be encouraging students to dream the impossible dreams of educational reform, and to experiment boldly and imaginatively in their own personal and professional lives. They have been attending school for at least a dozen years before they enter teacher education programs, and through direct contact, have formulated their own criticisms of compulsory education at all levels. What they ask in their professional courses is that their critiques be rendered articulable and then resolved, if possible. Similarly, they implore us to confront openly the indictments of our harshest judges in the media and in the local community. If we are preponderantly occupied with staffing classrooms and administrative offices with functionaries who have been cautioned never to be doctrinal deviationists or who have been effectively deterred from making a systematic examination of a variety of educational criticisms, we are succeeding only in providing schools with a plethora of talented robots. Neither our students nor our schools will be long satisfied if our training mission is restricted to the production of somnambulant conformists.[10]

Furthermore, a competency-based program runs the danger of subtly inculcating a philosophy of education that accentuates the established educational values of a technocratic age. This philosophy is in direct contradiction to a student's expressed desires for educational reform. A program that stresses performance criteria, measurable outcomes, specifically planned objectives, a systems-analysis approach and pre- and postassessment techniques risks including in its curriculum only those learnings that are capable of being objectively measured. Consequently, other types of learning that defy precise assessment will be underplayed or ignored.*

In contrast, many of our students are exploring the value of learnings that are not exclusively verbal or mathematical. They are developing qualities of individual achievement that are artistic, musical, political, emotive, mechanical, theatrical, religious, graphic, and communal. They are asking that curricula be more flexible; that classrooms be open and, if necessary, abandoned in favor of experiences in the home and community; that grades be abolished and that major and minor study areas be dissolved and replaced with interdisciplinary, relational studies. Students are beginning to perceive that teachers are most effective when they are facilitative and

---

* Hans Guth makes a similar criticism of behavioral objectives.

enabling, and they look to competency programs for help in establishing predisposing climates for learning in the classroom. The failure of most current competency programs is that the teacher is always projected as an authoritative superordinate in the classroom while the child is kept in a suspended state of dependency, anxiously awaiting the cues of his teacher or the latest learning device. For many students, educational reform can occur only when the roles are equalized — if not reversed.* ...

3. A professional curriculum that stresses the virtues of accountability and professionalism and emphasizes the acquisition of skills as the exclusive professional objective of teachers is incapable of responding to many young people's desire to improve society. Many of our students are insistent that the school assume its long overdue role as a dynamic agent for social reform. If the school is ever to become an instrument for personal and cultural renewal, then each teacher must aspire to something more than a supinely deferential professional role. Traditionally, a sense of professionalism has caused teachers to resist external changes. (Witness the teachers' unions in our large cities when community control begins to threaten their positions.) Appeals to professionalism in education have fostered conformity to the internal profession rather than encouraging external service to society. What many students are beginning to understand, however, is that much of the competency-motivated talk about professionalism has been induced not because of a commitment to personal and social reform through service but because of the internal pressures for personal and political conformity. Simply stated, our demands for professional conduct have become demands for a conservative politics and life-style.[11]

Robert Dreeben has commented that the dilemma of professionalism is rooted in its loyalty to the middle-class value orientation; its sycophantic deference to administration; its studied silence about the deficiencies of public school education; and its gospel of dedication, which is usually constructed as a kind of occupational subservience.[12] In addition, appeals to professionalism have often been used to stifle dreams of social and political reform by converting radical young teachers into competent technicians who are accountable to the public only on the basis of how well they teach children to read, write, and compute.

In contrast, our students are interpreting professional accountability in different ways.† They do not believe that a teacher is accountable only when he has performed classroom management tasks or when he has modified individual behavior. Neither is a professor of education accountable merely because he has performed — for a stiff fee — consultancy ser-

---

* *Is competency-based teacher education inherently opposed to such role equalization or reversal?*
† *Accountability in education is also discussed in Section 15.*

vices that have resulted in computerized and modular classroom schedules, differentiated staffing, a new multimedia building, or an individualized reading program. And neither are teachers' unions and associations accountable simply because they have applied sanctions in situations where conditions are inimical to the competent performance of teaching activities. The advocacy of accountability and professionalism, in spite of its basic validity, is becoming nothing more than a way for teachers and administrators to latch on to fashionably respectable catchwords in order to justify their adherence to the educational and social status quo.

Instead, our students are demanding that the spurious distinction between political and professional conduct be obliterated. They rarely use the term "professional" because of its suggestion of internal service conformity. They see the vocation of teaching as the promotion of the teacher's own visionary truth in the service of others. They are asking that the schools and universities initiate a community dialogue that will result in substantive social changes. These students believe that the more critical the social crisis the more intense is the teacher's responsibility to question all received dogma and to act against injustice and repression in order to defend the creative mind. If their professional training is limited only to a series of managerial and instructional units meant to increase skill proficienices, then many will find themselves incapable of initiating and participating in that reform dialogue with the community. . . .

In summary, it is believed that the competency movement in teacher education has been but one response to the preparation of teachers. Insofar as it has helped students gain the assurance that they can function in an instructional setting because they have mastered a variety of teaching skills, its effect has been benign. But when it has underplayed or ignored the personal, educational, and social reform desires of its training constituency, it has done nothing more than perpetuate the status quo. Colleges of education should be capable of much more.

EXERCISE

1. According to Nash and Agne, what four assumptions underlie competency-based teacher education programs? (p. 419)

2. What is the authors' major criticism of competency-based teacher education? (p. 419)

3. According to Nash and Agne, how do the motives of today's undergraduates differ from those of their predecessors? (pp. 420–421)

4. Why do Nash and Agne claim that current competency-based programs are unable to accommodate the student's "search for value and selfhood"? (p. 422)

5. What is the authors' main criticism of performance criteria, measurable outcomes, and specifically planned objectives? (p. 423)

6. According to Nash and Agne, what is the difference between traditional views of professional accountability in education and the views held by today's students? (pp. 424–425)

Mirror, Mirror on the Wall, Am I the Best Teacher of Them All? There Is No Substitute for Competence

Stuart Cohen and Richard Hersh

Stuart Cohen and Richard Hersh wrote the following paper in response to the preceding selection by Robert Nash and Russell Agne. Cohen and Hersh argue that the principles of competency-based teacher education can be used to help student teachers accomplish all the goals which Nash and Agne claim are not being accomplished in current competency-based programs. For example, Cohen and Hersh point out that teachers can be trained to have "competency" in clarifying their own values and in teaching values to students. Cohen and Hersh also defend using behavioral objectives in teacher education. They attempt to demonstrate that behavioral objectives do not necessarily emphasize trivial forms of learning, as Nash and Agne claim. Further, they argue that using behavioral objectives can actually help teachers become agents of educational and social reform by ensuring that they acquire the specific competencies required to carry out reform. Have Cohen and Hersh effectively refuted Nash and Agne's criticisms of competency-based teacher education?

Past and present education programs have emphasized evaluating what a teacher does (input), without examining the consequences of that behavior on student learning (output). This narrowness of perspective may be due to inadequate evaluation devices. One also could argue that the singular concern with input has negated attempts to wrestle with output and stunted the development of efficacious assessment techniques. Regardless

From *The Journal of Teacher Education*, 23, 1972, pp. 5–10. Reprinted with permission of publisher and authors.

of the cause, teachers are presently being trained to carry on this mirror-mirror-on-the-wall evaluation of their effectiveness in the classroom. The status quo in teacher-training institutions is represented by input factors, such as number of courses taken, number of state requirements fulfilled, and number of hours in a certain subject matter area, and by quasi-output, such as grading systems based on hidden and often capricious criteria of the individual professor, the normal curve with a built-in competition and failure component, and a plethora of paper-and-pencil exams.*

Clearly, Robert Nash and Russell Agne are justified in their concern for changing the status quo.[1] Their concern, however, that competency-based teacher education serves as support of the status quo, is unjustified. The major reason for the establishment of competency-based teacher education programs is to focus attention, not on inputs but on educational outcomes. Nash and Agne cite four general assumptions that underlie such a program:

1. The primary purpose of professional teacher training is to produce teachers who possess those specialized techniques, skills, and dispositions that will facilitate learning in any educational environment.[2]
2. Through a series of managerial and instructional units, the teacher trainee is able to achieve the objectives. . . . Basic to these units are modular experiences that will allow the trainee to proceed at a pace consistent with his own interests and abilities.[3]
3. The measurable outcome of a competency-based program is the trainee's proficiency in demonstrating his mastery of the requisite teaching skills.[4]
4. If a child fails it is because the educational system has failed to produce . . . superior performance specialists who can diagnose and remediate learning deficiencies in children.[5]

The above assumptions are correct. The implications Nash and Agne attribute to such assumptions, however, reflect a restricted conceptualization of a competency-based program. Occasionally in their vacillation, they even made statements supporting a competency model:

> We believe that a competency model for teacher education can ultimately prove to be both a practical and humane response to those students who want to change the status quo through their teaching commitment.[6]
> Competency curricula can help students realize their dreams of educational reform by equipping them with the skills they will need to effect change.[7]

---

* *If you are currently in a teacher-education program, is this true of your training?*

Paradoxically, Nash and Agne's major assertion is that "training exclusively rooted in competency techniques subverts larger social reform notions by reinforcing three kinds of status quo: personal, educational, and social." [8] According to them, competency models maintain the "personal status quo" by ignoring the changing idealism of current undergraduates enrolled in teacher education programs. They state that "professional education students are motivated by more personalistic, communitarian, and socially activistic purposes than their predecessors." [9] They further assert that "many young prospective teachers ... are disdaining the injunction to sharpen their skills and become proficient professionals because they sense that the pursuit of self-understanding and personal meaning is infinitely more fundamental to their future lives." [10] The assumption here is that the development of skills for becoming an effective teacher is incompatible with the development of skills for value clarification, which, along with learning facilitation, is learnable and therefore teachable. A competency-based program can teach prospective teachers to assess their own value indicators: attitudes, purposes, and activities. [11] It can also teach them to use value indicators in sampling their own students' behavior. Only then can they have an affective index on the impact of their own instruction. A clarinet teacher who teaches children to perform scales brilliantly but whose students discontinue playing the clarinet would hardly be considered a competent facilitator of learning. Contrary to Nash and Agne's assertion, a competency model does not ignore affective objectives but instead requires that prospective teachers become proficient in utilizing them.

In their assertion that a competency model will maintain the educational status quo, they inveigh against the dangers of measurement and objectification. Their fear is that a competency-based program will "limit ... professional training to the mastery of a series of routinized and uninspiring tasks." [12] They also critize a competency-based program as having "effectively ignored or underplayed those learnings that may be emotional, experience-based, inductive, and spontaneous." [13]

These are serious charges that warrant a discussion of the nature of behavioral objectives and criterion-referenced measurement.* A behavioral objective is a clarifying vehicle used to define the sample of behavior to be examined as a basis for making inferences. Each objective has a criterion, either quantitative, qualitative, or both. We all make judgments about people based on their behavior; that is, based on what they say and do. The inferences are based on both the quality and the quantity of behavior sampled.

Traditional education, based on norm-referenced measurement, forces

---

* *Compare Cohen and Hersh's discussion of behavioral objectives and criterion-referenced measurement with those by Guth and Popham (Section 14) and by Millman (Section 16).*

competition among students. Only the top percentage can receive high grades and, of necessity, a certain number are doomed to failure. In fact, education is one of the few professions that boasts of its failures. ("It must have been a good test: 40 percent of my students received D's and F's.") The criteria used to obtain results prior to applying the curve to grades are usually determined by the individual teacher, often on an ad hoc basis. The job of the student becomes one of developing strategies for guessing these private criteria.[14] A competency-based program necessitates behavioral objectives. When objectives are clearly and publicly stated, the pupil no longer has to develop strategies for determining the teacher's goals. They are also subject to the scrutiny of public inquiry, thus minimizing the possibility that capricious and ad hoc criteria will be applied to the evaluation of any student. Trivia made public are more susceptible to change than trivia that are part of the private domain of the individual instructor.

Measurement based on criteria rather than on norms means that a student is assessed relative to the criterion and not against his peers. The goal of instruction is to maximize each student's attainment of the objectives; any student failure is considered the consequences of faulty instruction. Diagnosis of instructional weakness is demanded to provide new learning activities that are geared to help the individual student attain the objectives. Contrast this competency-based approach with traditional practice that not only promotes failure but also labels failure as something wrong with the student and not with the instructional system.* Count the vast number of normative tests and labels existing in our current educational system, e.g., "grade equivalent," "underachiever," "minimal brain-damaged," "level-three child," "percentile rank," "culturally deprived," and a host of other invidious labels guaranteed to preserve the status quo of the school system. In a noncompetency program, one attempts to improve it by getting better students; in a competency program, one produces better results by improving the instructional system.

Specifying outcomes in terms of student performance in no way restricts the kinds of learnings sought. A taxonomic analysis of objectives will allow an analysis of the goals of an educational program. Not only can the objectives be classified with respect to the cognitive, affective, or psychomotor demands upon the learner but also with respect to the level of demand within each classification.[15] If objectives are never specified and no attempts made to assess outcomes, an analysis of a teacher education program is impossible. Thus, inferences made about an individual's ability to facilitate the learning of others and to produce changes in the school

---

* Bloom's model of mastery learning also counters this traditional practice (see Block, Section 15).

system will more than likely be based upon inadequate and spurious samples of behavior.

One further note. Competency-based programs identify goals, not teaching means. Nash and Agne misconstrue the nature of behavior objectives if they believe that these goal statements necessitate "routinized and uninspiring tasks." If they desire that students become effective social change agents, then they might ask themselves what samples of behavior, both on the job and during preservice, will provide the best data upon which to base their inferences. If they wish to estimate how their prospective teachers would perform in a faculty meeting containing a number of conservatives demanding dress codes, they could have their students role play such a meeting. Such an activity tends to be rather spontaneous and emotional; yet, it allows one to assess a student's competency in handling a situation of this kind.

The least cogent reason offered by Nash and Agne for a competency model's supporting the educational status quo appears in two different but related assertions: first, "the failure of most current competency programs is that the teacher is always projected as an authoritative superordinate in the classroom while the child is kept in a suspended state of dependency . . .";[16] second, "the whole operant architectonic . . . is content mainly to conserve the status quo in classrooms." [17]

Nash and Agne do not seem to recognize that dependence and independence are learned. If independence is to be an educational as well as a personal and social goal, teachers must be taught to facilitate independence on the part of the children. Wishing that they become independent is a goal statement with possible implications for teaching methodology, but the statement of the goal alone is no guarantee of success. Silberman, among many others, laments the de facto dependency developed in children by present methods of teaching. The word "prison" seems to serve as a more accurate description of many schools, and we know prisons do not purposefully foster independence. Nor is the open classroom concept a guaranteed methodological approach to teaching independence.* Teachers unskilled in dealing with freedom in the classroom often produce anarchy, with learning occurring by chance alone. A behavior modification approach that maximizes success experiences and strives for the attainment of critical thinking skills (as evidenced by the attainment of objectives at and above the application level of Bloom's cognitive taxonomy) can produce independence.† This will be so for a number of reasons. Behavior modification principles are based on the uniqueness of each individual. The child or teacher trainee is not forced into a large-lecture, lock-step

---

* The open classroom is discussed by Rathbone and Madden (Section 10).
† An example of the behavior modification approach appears in Bushell's token manual (Section 10).

instructional system. Failure is minimized. The person has a history of success upon which to base future risk taking. In essence, neither dependence nor independence is a necessary by-product of a competency-based system. Yet a competency program allows for independence as a goal of instruction when behaviors indicative of independence (challenging an instructor, volunteering to explore a new topic, defending one's position despite a majority of peer opinions to the contrary, and many others) are specified.

To suggest that present competency-based programs are inadequate does not explain that inadequacy. Nash and Agne want "students to become reconstructive agents for personal and social change" and suggest that the quest for competency fails to convey this objective.[18] Given this laudable objective, how will the authors know if they have helped students become reconstructive agents? Surely they will base their assessment on more than a sample of their students' opinions.

To suggest that we should prepare teachers to operationalize their desires to create open classrooms is fine, but to operationalize anything necessarily implies specific skills and observable behaviors. How does one know when he has achieved an open classroom? What teacher and student behaviors might we expect to observe in an open classroom that are different from those in a traditional classroom? If these questions cannot be answered, then the concept of "operational" is meaningless.

To say that present competency-based programs are not perfect is certainly accurate, but this should not negate inroads already made nor the potential paths still open. That the affective and philosophical areas have been neglected is not to imply that they must of necessity continue to be ignored. Certainly we want prospective teachers to ask questions of social consequence and philosophical import. Can we not expect specific competence in these areas, or do the authors offer opinioning as the equivalent to philosophical competence? If we are sincere about changing schools and the social environment within which schools exist, we must specify goals in such a way as to be able to determine whether or not they have been achieved. Saying that we cannot at present measure certain competencies is different from saying that we should not.

Competency models do not confuse feeling competent with performing competently. Many teachers trained under noncompetency programs may view themselves as being very competent, at least in facilitating the learning of individuals. Yet, Popham has shown that teacher effectiveness based upon certification credentials is more myth than reality.* In his study,[19] he contrasted the performance of noncertified, nonexperienced individuals with that of certified and experienced teachers and found that the latter did not significantly outperform nonteachers.

* See Popham, Section 6.

To insure that the welcome idealism of many of today's prospective teachers does not turn to rancor as a result of encounters with the school systems, a competency model is more than ever necessary. It takes a multitude of skills to become an effective change agent. Unless our teacher education programs teach these skills, we will turn out ineffective idealists combating the educational system with the strategy of catharsis alone. Not only is it the responsibility of teacher-training institutions to infuse their prospective teachers with the desire to produce both individual and social change but also to maximize the probability that they will be educated to produce change. Such competence will not occur by chance alone, nor even by a collection of well-intentioned professors. The exigency of today's world demands competence, and the demand for competence necessitates a broadly conceived, systematized, competency-based model for teacher preparation.

EXERCISE

1. How do Cohen and Hersh describe the status quo of teacher-training institutions? (p. 427)

2. How do the authors counter Nash and Agne's criticism that competency-based programs maintain the "personal status quo"? (pp. 427, 428)

3. According to Cohen and Hersh, what is the advantage of criterion-referenced measurement over norm-referenced measurement? (p. 429)

4. How do the authors counter Nash and Agne's criticism that competency-based programs project the teacher as "an authoritative superordinate in the classroom"? (pp. 430–431)

5. Why do Cohen and Hersh believe that it is important to distinguish between "feeling" competent and "performing" competently? (pp. 431–432)

Tutoring by Students

Herbert A. Thelen

> *Many educators believe that any school reform is bound to fail*
> *unless it is supported by well-trained, competent teachers. How-*
> *ever, others think that teachers themselves are part of the status quo;*
> *to bring about real change, it will be necessary to recruit other*
> *groups to perform a major teaching role. In the following selection*
> *Herbert Thelen describes the use of students as teachers in various*
> *student-tutoring projects around the country. Two features of these*
> *projects are particularly noteworthy. First, in many projects older*
> *students tutor younger students. That is, there appears to be more*
> *between-grade tutoring than within-grade tutoring. Second, as*
> *might be expected, the student being tutored often improves in his*
> *academic achievement; what has surprised some educators, however,*
> *is the accumulating evidence that the tutor himself shows improve-*
> *ment in learning and self-esteem as a result of playing the role of*
> *teacher. Why does student tutoring appear to be so successful in*
> *bringing about learning, both for the tutor and the tutee? Also, as a*
> *teacher, what use might you make of this technique?*

During the last several years, a few dozen schools in the United States
have experimented with students teaching each other. The purpose seems
to be to help the tutor, the tutee, or both.[1] Compared to the tutee, the
tutor may or may not be older, brighter, or more maladjusted; of a different
socioeconomic class; or attend the same school. The tutor may drag the
tutee over teacher-prescribed remedial materials or he may teach a lesson
he himself has planned for his pupil; he may serve as drillmaster, friend,
consultant, guide, big brother, or teacher. Participants in tutoring programs may be volunteers or they may be selected by authorities; individual,
classes, or special clubs set up for the purpose may be involved. Tutoring
programs have so far been conceived, planned, and supervised by teachers,
but there is no reason why students could not shoulder much of this
responsibility.

The practice of students helping each other is not new. Friends have
always done some homework together — on their own time, outside of
school. The "little red school house," in which six to twenty students of all

Excerpted from "Tutoring by Students," a longer article in *School Review*,
77, 1969, pp. 229–244. Reprinted with permission of the author and University of Chicago Press. © 1969 by the University of Chicago.

ages studied in one room presided over by a single teacher, relied heavily on students learning from each other — if only by eavesdropping on each other's recitations. Under the Lancastrian Monitorial System of the 1820s, the teacher instructed a group of older students who would in turn drill younger ones on the lesson. Under the project method, teachers may assign tasks to small groups of children partly in the expectation that they will learn from each other.

These practices were developed to instruct the learners. Today's new element is the anticipation of benefits to the tutor. It is hoped that he will develop his own academic skills or understanding further, as he employs them to teach another; that he will form a better character (e.g., attitudes), become better adjusted or more adequate as a person, discover new interests or commitments for his life. At the University of Chicago we became interested in tutoring first graders (six-year-olds) as a way to help fifth grade problem pupils in slum schools. We felt that discussion among the tutors about their own teaching experiences would be as valuable as the experience of tutoring.*

Three facts prompted this paper: first, that the various tutorial schemes have arisen independently of each other in all parts of a large country; second, that the arrangements for tutoring take a great number of different forms; and third, that the educators (almost to a man) feel that tutoring works. (I can think of no other innovation which has been so consistently perceived as successful.) These three conditions, taken together, are intriguing. They seem to suggest that there is some widespread societal need, goal, or attitude which may be attained or realized through almost any arrangement of students helping each other. The benefits do not seem to depend on such particulars as subject matter, academic status or competence, or the nature of the lesson plan; what does seem salient is the helping relationship between students which is newly created and formally legitimized by the school authorities.

In the remainder of this paper I shall describe briefly some tutoring activities in different school systems across the nation; speculate on these school activities as responses to certain conditions in modern society; and finally project some further ideas about how the helping relationship might revitalize our school and invite the reader to both visualize the various phenomena of "tutoring" and appreciate their germinal value for school reform.

THE VARIETIES OF STUDENT TUTORING

In New York City, each of thirty students enrolled in the teacher preparation program at Hunter College tutors one fifth or sixth grader in Public

* Compare with Bessell's magic circle technique (Section 2).

School 158.* Each of these children then tutors a third grader on the lesson just taught by the college students. The college students spend six hours a week during one semester in the project: They hold their own seminar for four hours and they tutor and supervise tutors for two hours. The fifth-grade tutor and the third-grade tutee may be selected as having similar learning problems, and the college tutor plans a lesson that will benefit both children. Many benefits are claimed: the regular classroom teacher has assistance in dealing with learning problems of individual pupils; the older pupil gains new respect for himself and the teacher; the college students, invited to experiment with a microcosmic learning situation, are challenged to create learning activities and pedagogical principles.[2]

Also in New York City, Dr. Albert Deering reports that a program called Homework Helper was developed five years ago by Mobilization for Youth, the Lower East Side antipoverty agency, and has been operating in two school districts. It is now being expanded and offered to twenty-nine school districts and within six months it is hoped that 5,000 elementary school tutees and 2,000 high school tutors will be busily at work within about 100 centers set up in neighborhood schools. The cost of the program will be about $1.2 million. According to the New York Times,

> The tutors work with the pupils on a one-to-one basis two days each week. They help them with their homework and then give them instruction in reading. High school and elementary teachers are assigned to the centers to supervise the tutors. The tutors are paid up to $2 an hour for their work. . . . A study of the program released last year by Columbia University School of Social Work found that the tutors from slum areas not only helped their pupils but also made great improvements in reading themselves . . . [thus the tutees in the program] showed a 6.2 month gain in their reading levels after 5 months. A control group that had had no tutoring showed the usual slum school rate, a 3.5 month gain in the same period. The tutors improved even more than their pupils. In a seven month period their mean gain in reading level over their control group was a year and seven months.[3] †

One of the antipoverty organizations, the National Commission of Resources for Youth, is currently developing plans to pay poor boys to tutor youngsters. This organization sees tutoring as a new kind of job that can be created for fourteen- and fifteen-year-old boys as a way to induct them

* Is this an effective technique for training preservice teachers? Does it overcome the failings of preservice programs noted by Borg and his colleagues (this section)?
† Would any of the learning theories you've read about explain the improved learning of tutors?

into the world of work and also to get some money into their pockets.

In University City, Missouri, students of Brittany Junior High School spent five hours a week tutoring youngsters at Blackberry Land and Delmar-Harvard elementary schools. The tutors

> began by sitting in small groups and discussing what it means to learn to learn, how they are most comfortable when they learn, what difficulties they had and might expect primary one pupils to have. Then, individually and in groups, they set to work at tables and desks to prepare lessons and materials. Two boys cut paper and print flashcards, carefully lettering first year vocabulary. A girl looks at filmstrips through a viewer to decide which she could use and what kind of lesson she might build around it. Three girls sit at a tape recorder and read a young child's story aloud; then listen to and evaluate the playback. Later they will make worksheets for the stories. A boy works with a pegboard, planning a lesson around patterns and colors and numbers. . . . Each child is building an abacus; he will design it and select his own materials and perhaps later create a mathematical teaching lesson around it.[4]

From the typewritten reports of the teachers, we find that:

> The tutoring program served definite functions within the general program. Primarily, the tutoring program was a motivational device used to encourage students to learn basic skills. Students thought that they "knew" how to do most of the skills taught in the primary and middle grades. They hesitated about learning primary-level reading and math skills for their own benefit, but they were willing to "relearn" such skills so that they might become tutors. In addition, the tutoring program provided a means for building the self-images of these disabled [underachieving] learners. The students were very enthusiastic about obtaining the status of teacher.* This prestige was accentuated by the freedom required for the tutoring schedule; students left the building daily either by bus or by walking across the street to the elementary school. In the eyes of their non-project peers, these activities were highly privileged. Furthermore, the attitudes of the elementary students increased the self-images of the tutors. For the elementary pupils, the tutors were very special. The young children appreciated the academic help, but they also valued the personal attention lavished on them by their tutors. . . . Many of these elementary students did not receive the necessary positive attention of parents or peers, and the junior high students were able to provide this much needed social developmental influence. Moreover, the project students gained social skills as they developed positive relationships with the younger children. . . . Finally, the feeling of being needed further developed a positive self-image for the tutors.[5]

* How would you account for this enthusiasm?

The activities among the tutors are probably as important as the tutoring experience itself. The teachers report that

> prior to the tutoring assignment tutors observed elementary class-rooms and made reports of their observations. An observation sheet helped the students look at the classroom objectively, and served as the basis for oral reports to the group [of tutors]. . . . Students also practiced being tutors by role playing and critiquing one another's teaching techniques. Students wrote "lesson plans" and presented their lessons for peer criticism. They also learned to listen and sometimes to accept peer criticism. . . . They discussed teaching techniques and considered how they learned specific tasks.[6]

An interesting but unforeseen development was that of dependence of the primary grade child on the junior high school tutor; it is reported that certain of the youngsters refused to work except when their tutor was with them. Weaning procedures are to be devised! * . . .

. . . [T]o complete our sample of student-helping activities, in Beth-page, Long Island, is a different pattern of students helping each other within interage classes. All the students in the John H. West Elementary School are in classes which have "a two- or three-year-age spread. For example, one class might have 6- 7- 8-year-olds, 7- 8- 9-years-olds, or 9- 10-11-year-olds, etc." Thus a child might be put into a class in which he is among the youngest or the oldest students, depending on his needs, or a brother and sister might be in the same class.† Moreover, subgrouping within the class is extremely flexible. Grade levels are constantly disregarded. A child who needs to review some basic skills moves to the group that is learning the skill he needs, whether it be phonics, spelling, punctuation, number work, or something else. The interage class is intended to capitalize on maximum *heterogeneity*, in sharp contrast to the increasing tendency to group students *homogeneously* (by I.Q. or achievement). Because of this heterogeneity, there are always some students who know enough more than others to be helpful to them. There is also considerable "osmosis" as in the little old red school house, where children overheard each other's lessons. Both fast and slow learners form part of the classroom society; each has a place, and the fast one is not exploited nor the slow one stigmatized. Clearly the interage class is an imaginative application of recent knowledge of the operation of small groups. Also arrangements such as this expand the "helping relationship" in the entire school day, rather than into just a few hours of specially arranged tutoring.[7]

The innovations I have described arose spontaneously and simultaneously in many parts of the country. They were not stimulated by a central

---

* *Why do you think this dependence develops? Is it healthy?*
† *Might it not harm a child's self-esteem to be placed in a class of students much younger than he?*

directive from Washington, a dramatic book, or an authoritative bit of research. What accounts for this emergence? Did the innovators sense some new promise, some spirit of the age waiting to be born? Are these practices in some sense prophetic, the harbingers of a new understanding, condition, or period in education? These questions are practical, not poetical; if we can identify whatever it is that makes these practices so exciting and somehow appropriate to our times, then we can build on that knowledge to bring about much more effectively the reconstruction needed in education. Let us then identify some of the novel elements which seem most significant and inquire into their meanings in and for the larger society.

MEETING INDIVIDUAL NEEDS. . . . The highest priority of the schools is to get each student to stay in school, to learn to read, and to earn a high school diploma. This will call for a great amount of attention to individuals; for a great deal more teaching than now exists. Yet there is no insurmountable problem of means: there are suitable reading materials, teaching programs, and audiovisual aids in unprecedented variety and quality. The shortage is of teachers, not materials or know-how.* Student tutoring seems to be a promising answer, especially if it were built into the school day on a regularly scheduled basis.

COMBATING PREJUDICE. . . . Discrimination in school takes several forms: first, the methods of teaching were designed for middle-class children and are simply unsuitable for children of poverty; second, schools which are attended by Negroes tend to be poorer in resources and teaching skills than those attended by whites; third, when both races attend the same schools they tend to be divided into "homogeneous ability groups" which quite effectively segregate the races. . . .

Against this background, student tutoring looks promising as a way to eliminate two of the three forms of discrimination. With respect to suitable methods of teaching, the tutor can be an older child from the same socioeconomic background or culture as the tutee, thus eliminating the culture barrier. With respect to the lower-level teaching skill in predominantly Negro schools, student tutors could help beef up the teaching, but the only real cure for bad teaching is good teaching. With regard to the lower economic support of Negro schools, no method of instruction would directly ameliorate the situation, but the values and attitudes behind tutoring could, over time, develop strong school-community relationships and through this, more community support. Third, as the report on interage grouping shows, student tutoring built into the regular classroom learning process actually capitalizes on heterogeneity and therefore is a method

* Do you agree with Thelen's analysis of what schools need most?

through which racial and class integration can be achieved. It is especially intriguing to think of the possibilities of Negroes helping whites, of younger children helping older ones, and of ethnic minority members helping the majority.

Cooperation versus competition — Our country was built on the notion that individuals compete, on the basis of merit or ability, for power, money, and other goods, and, conversely, that family position, titles, precedence, etc., are irrelevant to the rights and privileges one may enjoy. . . .

Now this entire system is breaking down. It is breaking down because one of the major assumptions on which the meritocratic system is based is no longer tenable: the assumption that goods and services are "scarce"; that there is not enough to go around. The fact is that after eight years of continuous relentless prosperity, we *do* have enough to go around; enough food, television sets, cars, books — everything. Competition is no longer required as the basis for distributing goods.

To return to tutoring, students learning through *helping* each other is a very promising alternative to learning through *competing with* each other.* And it also makes the acquisition of knowledge and skills valuable, not in the service of competition for grades but as the means for personally significant interaction with others.

Creative adaptation — The survival of any institution, whether it be a club, factory, or nation, depends on its responsiveness to changing conditions in itself and its environment. Our society has become stalemated, and there is a sense of drift and despair. The reasons are not hard to find. First, there has been a great increase in size and complexity of all operations, whether they be educational, religious, industrial, military, etc. The complexity reflects a fantastically expanded range of publicly recognized goals and concerns. Every decision has vast and unknowable consequences. To cite one, in the most oversimplified terms possible: Shall we spend a billion dollars in Vietnam or in thirty large cities at home? At the local level, shall we bring ten Negro students by bus to attend an all white school? For each person or goal favored by a decision, several other persons or goals are bound to be disfavored. For every goal there are interested parties or "vested interests," and the trick is to satisfy each sufficiently to keep its support — but not to the extent of antagonizing others. And when a decision *is* made, it has to be implemented by very large cumbersome machinery in which many parts must act semi-independently and yet in concert. It is no wonder that the problem of getting action and change is formidable. . . .

The description of stalemate and institutional unresponsiveness that I have just given fits the school very well. It is true that many changes are

* *Thelen seems to be saying that it is no longer adaptive for students to learn how to compete with each other. Do you agree?*

made in procedures and techniques — including the introduction of student tutoring — but it is very rarely the case that anything of the innovation remains after the innovator leaves. But student tutoring seems to me to be especially promising as a focal point for change, for new ideas and inspiration within the school. It depends on an entirely new kind of interaction among students under conditions such that revealing feedback can be obtained by the teacher. It calls for teachers to cooperate across grade lines in an enterprise that is to the advantage of both. It invites recognition of all sorts of individual characteristics of pupils that are usually ignored; and it makes creative thinking about lesson plans and activities the norm rather than the exception. It is also likely to interest and involve the parent group, thus creating a reference group or "imaginal audience" whose expectations will help maintain action.*

There are many more connections that could be suggested between events emerging in the large society and the helping arrangements emerging in schools. Interesting as it would be to develop the analogy or identity further, our real point is rather different: to develop some basis for forecasting the educative possibilities of the helping experiences. To the extent that these experiences in school are archetypal representations of significant encounters the student will have in the larger society their educational potential is worth trying to realize. Our little analysis convinces us that participation and understanding of oneself in the school helping situations may be helpful, if not actually required, for one to become educated for the modern world; that it will be worthwhile, as we experiment with the helping relationships among students, to recognize and demand that the student recognize those qualities and principles which are also viable in the large society and which may be its best hope. . . .

EXERCISE

1. What does Thelen see as "today's new element" in the use of student tutors? (p. 434)

2. Using Thelen's description of various student tutoring programs, list at least three benefits which have been attributed to the tutor and three benefits attributed to the tutee as a result of participating in the tutoring process. (pp. 434–437)

3. According to Thelen, what are two ways in which student tutoring could help to eliminate discrimination against minority groups in the schools? (pp. 438–439)

4. Why does Thelen see student tutoring as "a focal point for change, for new ideas and inspiration within the school"? (p. 440)

Do you think Thelen is making too many claims here for student tutoring?

The Parent-Child
Toy Library Programme

Glen P. Nimnicht and Edna Brown

> *Glen Nimnicht, a leading figure in the field of early childhood education, heads a group which is developing innovative materials and procedures for use in Headstart and similar programs. In the following article, he and his colleague, Edna Brown, describe a set of materials which places parents in the role of teacher. Their approach reflects a major finding of the educational research reported in Part II of this book — that much of a child's learning occurs outside of school, and that this out-of-school learning has a strong effect on his school achievement. A significant feature of the authors' toy library program is that the materials were empirically tested before they were put into practice. Of course, this program represents just one way in which educators can improve the quality of a child's out-of-school learning environment. Can you think of other programs that could be developed? Also, suppose you are planning to become a teacher. From what you have just read, do you think that you would have more beneficial impact on children by training their parents or by teaching the children yourself directly?*

The specific intent of the Parent-Child Programme is to develop an education programme for *parents* of young children, coupled with a toy-lending library that the parents can use to aid the intellectual development of their children. This programme would become the basis upon which a more complex system of education for three- and four-year-old children could be built, but it would stand independently as a means of helping a large number of parents and stimulating their children's development. Previous and current research make this approach appear highly promising.

Rolcik (1965) found a significant relationship between school achievement and parental interest in the child and his education. Shaw and White (1965) found a relationship between child-parent identification and school performance. Norman (1966) found that parent value systems influenced academic achievement. Hess and Shipman (1965) concluded that cogni-

Reprinted with permission from the *British Journal of Educational Technology*, 3, 1972, pp. 75–81.

tive growth is dependent on cognitive meaning in parent-child communication.

Wattenberg and Clifford (1964) reported that a measure of self-concept in kindergarten is as good a predictor of reading ability in the third grade as an intelligence test administered at the same time. Bowman (1958) pointed out that pupil self-concept is the mechanism that mediates parent influence on the school. He also concluded that parental influence on self-view is more important than school influence and that the most effective method now known to change a child's self-concept is to train parents to do it.

McCandless (1961) reported a study by Irwin that children whose mothers read to them 10 minutes a day between the ages of 12 and 20 months improved in "all phases of speech." This finding is consistent with Gray and with Cazden, who concluded that the sheer number of well-formed sentences a child is exposed to is a significant predictor of language skill.* In his survey of gifted children, Fowler (1962) stated that these children were usually exposed to parental instruction, many learning to read at three and going on to notable academic success. This same review found that early stimulation by oral, written, and pictorial materials, as well as general experiences in observation and discrimination, contribute favorably to verbal memory and language improvement.

On the assumption that parents can provide significant educational experiences for their pre-school children, we have initiated a Parent-Child course in conjunction with our Toy Library[1] at the Far West Laboratory for Educational Research and Development. Parents whose incomes are too high for their children to be eligible for Head Start programmes but too low to provide tuition to private nursery schools may enrol, without charge, in an eight-week course taught by a member of our staff or by a teacher-librarian trained by us. Parents are instructed in the educational use of the toys, which they borrow from the Library, as well as in a few basic educational concepts and facts of child development.

The toys have been designed by personnel of the Programme for Education Beginning at Age Three[2] to teach specific fundamental concepts and skills, to promote verbal fluency and to develop problem-solving techniques. One or more learning episodes, sets of procedures to teach basic skills or concepts, have been devised for each toy. Parents are shown how to present the toys to their children, how to use the episodes, how to talk about the toys, and how to encourage and accept the autonomy of their children in the learning situation.

A parent-training class begins with coffee and a short period for book browsing. Then the toy demonstrated the previous week is discussed and evaluated before the new toy is introduced and the parents role-play the

Can you explain Gray's finding in learning theory terms?

game for it. A general objective for children, such as healthy self-concept or use of specific language, is explained and discussed. Usually a film concerning child development or ways in which parents can work with children is shown. Materials for teaching the course include a booklet for parents and another for the teacher-librarian, a slide set, filmstrips and audio tapes. Parents may borrow toys from the Library more than once. In fact, it often takes more than one week for a parent and child to use all the episodes with a single toy. Parents are encouraged to continue to use the Library after they complete the course and to take home any of the toys that are available but that are not used in the course.

Our emphasis is not on education *per se* but on the child. Parents are helped to see their youngsters as independent, self-motivating beings and not as objects of an educational effort or foci for parental expectations. We believe that a positive feeling about himself is of the utmost importance for a child's success in school and out.* Thus the first of our aims of the Parent-Child course is to aid parents to facilitate the development of a healthy self-concept in their children. One of the ways of doing this is to make the environment responsive to the child; that is, he is free to explore, manipulate, accept or reject the objects — and the people — around him as he wishes.

The parent makes the learning environment responsive to her child in several ways. Each day she invites him to play with the toy; but, if he refuses, she does not insist and does not ask him to play again that day. If he initiates the play, she works with him as long and as often as he likes. She stops the game when he loses interest or becomes tired. (The mother, of course, will end the game when she has other demands on her time.) The child's introduction to the toy is an exploratory one in which, without instruction from his mother, he begins to discover how the toy works and what he can do with it.† Some toys have several games (learning episodes), with rules, planned for sequential training; but the child always may play the games out of sequence or change the rules.

Permitting the child to control his learning environment is only one way in which the parent can help him to develop a healthy self-concept. Another is to express approval of both his person and his performance. Mothers are urged to tell their chidren that they are pleased with their appearance, their manner, their knowledge. Parents often increase their own regard for their children. In the class discussion sessions, mothers and fathers learn that the capabilities and accomplishments of their children are very much like those of other children who are the same age. Occa-

---

* *However, does a healthy self-concept lead to success in school, or does success in school lead to a healthy self-concept?*
† *Don't some children need more guidance than is provided by the authors' responsive model?*

sionally a mother reports that her child knew more than she thought he did.

Development of a healthy self-concept is the first of four objectives of the Parent-Child course. The other three are:

1. To help parents promote their children's intellectual development, using toys and learning episodes that are designed to teach specific skills, concepts, or problem-solving abilities;

2. To help parents stimulate their children's intellectual abilities by improving interaction between parents and child; and

3. To help parents participate in the decision-making process that affects the education of their children.

According to data gathered from parents and from test scores, we have been successful in achieving the first three objectives of the course. We have no information that indicates that parents are influencing the politics or procedures of their school.

The first objective is to help facilitate the development of a healthy self-concept in their children. Therefore, we measured not the child's attitude toward himself but the parents' attitude toward the child.* Parents answered three questions about their interest in the course; and our analysis of their responses shows that parents do make a more positive assessment of their children's competence and that they are responding to their youngsters in a more positive manner. We assume that, if the parents' new behaviour persists, it will help to improve self-concepts of the children.

We use our Responsive Environment Test, containing 13 sub-tests which include colour matching, colour naming, colour identification, shape matching, shape naming, shape identification, letter recognition, numerical concepts, relational concepts, sensory concepts, problem-solving, verbal communication and verbal comprehension, to discover if the children's intellectual development had been increased. Nineteen children of parents in two programmes in Utah were tested both before and after the course. Scores were significantly higher after the course than before in all areas but colour matching, shape matching, letter recognition and sensory concepts.† We believe there were no gains in letter recognition or sensory concepts because we had no specific toys or learning episodes to teach those things. Scores for shape and colour matching were very high at the beginning of the course, so there was little room for gain. Although none of the toys themselves was specifically designed to increase verbal communication

---

Do you agree with this procedure? Wouldn't it have been better to measure the child's attitude directly?

†*How do we know the favorable results were not due to maturational processes or to another learning experience which the children may have had at the same time as the authors' course?*

and verbal comprehension, the course as a whole was directed toward these goals. Thus we account for the significant improvement in the use of language. Further evidence that the course was successful comes from the positive statements made by parents about their children's development.

Concentrating, as we were, on educating the children with the toys in a one-to-one play relationship at home, we overlooked the value of adult discussion groups. Several parents remarked that the most interesting part of the course, for them, was interaction with other parents. They were introduced to one another at the first class meeting, and their roles as parent-teachers were reinforced by a film and a discussion. At the beginning of each of the following classes, parents talked about their experiences with the toy they had used the previous week. After the new toy had been introduced and explained, parents role-played the learning episodes with one another. The informality of the classes and the exchange of experiences no doubt made it easier for parents to support and to learn from one another.

As information about the course spreads through communities, more parents become interested in it and request that it be taught to them. Comments by parents who have taken the course help us to refine it so that we, in turn, are more helpful to other parents; but the parents in the first two courses made an important contribution when they tested our toys and their accompanying learning episodes with their children and supplied data that indicated to us which toys were appropriate for use in the Parent-Child context and which were not.

We first selected toys and learning episodes that met our criteria for clarity of purpose and procedure, for accommodating sequences of learning activities leading to manipulative problem-solving and abstract thinking, for useful content, and for strengthening the child's self-concept in an independent learning situation. Then parents used selected toys with their children and supplied us with data to measure the interest value of those toys. . . .

We set up two criteria to measure interest and analysed data supplied to us by parents. We judged that a toy held the interest of the children if (1) 80 per cent of them were still interested in the activity at the end of a week or lost interest only because they mastered the activity and if (2) the average child played with the toy more than five times or played with it at least once without being asked. Only six of the nine toys tested initially met the interest criteria and were selected to be used in the Parent-Child course. They are: sound cans, colour lotto, graduated wooden table blocks, stacking squares, Number-ite, and a flannel board with 36 felt shapes. Other toys and learning episodes were redesigned and added to the course; they are the feely bag and the alphabet board.

Each of the toys — the stacking squares, for example — is designed to allow the child to make discoveries about it and to progress from simple perceptual and conceptual development, such as colour, size and identity, to the ability to solve such problems as identifying the object that does not belong in a group or completing a pattern.

The stacking square toy is made of sixteen wooden squares of four different sizes and four different colours (red, yellow, green, blue), that fit on a spindle in a graduated stack from the largest to the smallest. Projections on the spindle prevent the smaller squares from sliding to the bottom; thus there is only one way in which the squares can be stacked by size.

This toy has five learning episodes, but the parent can make up more. She introduces the squares to the child by taking them off the spindle and permitting him to play with them in an unstructured way. The purpose of this introduction is to allow the child to explore the game and to teach the parent to observe the child. She watches to see if he discovers that the squares will go on the spindle in a certain order, if he arranges the squares by colour, or if he groups them by size. Then she picks up one square and asks the child to point to another that is the same size. She is helping him to learn the concept "the same as" and "not the same as" and to look for differences in the sizes of the squares.

The purpose of the second episode is to teach or strengthen the learning of "the same colour" and "not the same colour" and the colours, red, yellow, green, and blue. The parent asks the child to show her a square that is the same colour as the one she is holding.

The third, fourth and fifth episodes deal with problem solving. For the third episode, the parent lays out four squares of the same colour or size and a fifth square of a different colour or size, then asks: "Which one doesn't belong in this group?" The last two games are pattern extensions. For episode four, the parent makes a graduated stack of four squares of the same colour, places the largest square on another colour next to the stack, and asks the child: "What goes there?" In the fifth game, the squares are laid out in different patterns; and the child is asked: "What comes next?" The child can also make patterns for the parent to complete.

Evidences of success of the Parent-Child course and the instructional toys range from test scores to the expressed interest of parents. The purpose of the course is not only to teach the mother to teach her child but also to help her have a good personal relationship with him. Before a mother can promote a healthy self-concept in her child, she must see him positively. By playing with him, by comparing notes with other parents, and by learning about child development, she recognizes that her child is growing, intellectually, in a normal way.* Parents do seem to have better feelings about their children; they do want to promote their educational development, and we think that the children do learn certain behaviours,

* The authors appear to view the mother as the primary teacher. What role, if any, should the father play?

such as a precise and positive use of language, which are very useful to them.

EXERCISE

1. Based on the research reviewed by Nimnicht and Brown, what are at least three parental factors that are related to a child's school success? (pp. 441–442)

2. What is the major objective of the toy library program? (p. 443)

3. What do Nimnicht and Brown mean by a "responsive" learning environment? (p. 443)

4. What purpose did Nimnicht and Brown have for administering the Responsive Environment Test? (p. 444)

5. From the parents' view, what is the most interesting feature of the program? (p. 445)

COPING
WITH GROUP
DIFFERENCES

Introduction

Students differ in such areas as learning style, rate of learning, academic interests, and level of intellectual attainment. Because these differences exist, many educators believe the best way to improve learning is to tailor an instructional program for each student. However, to make this goal a reality would demand financial and personnel resources which are simply unavailable in American education. Computer-assisted instruction and programmed instruction, discussed in Section 10, are attempts to individualize the rate at which students proceed through curriculum materials. Another approach has been to form students into groups which share a learning-relevant characteristic and then provide each group with appropriate instruction. Issues and problems involved in forming these groups are the subject of this section.

The most prevalent form of grouping, of course, is the grade system. Assigning students to kindergarten, first grade, second grade, etc., is done on the assumption that teachers can offer better instruction if they work with a group that is fairly homogeneous in age and amount of previous schooling. However, most schools still contain students with a wide range of individual differences. Teachers sometimes deal with this problem by forming groups within a classroom; for example, a teacher might form several reading groups to reflect different levels of reading proficiency.

Another approach to creating homogeneous groups of students is the practice of "ability grouping" used in many school districts. Students are assigned to different groups (sometimes called "tracks" or "streams") at each grade level depending upon their previous school achievement, IQ, or other criterion. The rationale is that teachers can provide better instruction for low, average, and high ability students if they are taught separately rather than together. However, this rationale has been questioned by many educators.

The basic question is whether ability grouping helps students learn better than grade level assignment only. A literature review by Glen Heathers is included in this section to help you determine what is known about the effects of ability grouping on student achievement. The two articles that follow it reflect the current controversy that surrounds ability grouping. Zak Bayuk claims that a particular form of ability grouping can help solve some problems that beset education, whereas Stanley Urevick argues that ability grouping has detrimental consequences for students and for society.

In recent years minority-group and low socioeconomic status students have become a great problem to American educators, as evidence increasingly shows that many do not succeed within the regular school system. To meet the special needs of this group, many compensatory education programs have been established that operate outside the regular school structure. (Headstart and Follow Through are the best known.) In effect, compensatory education is a form of ability grouping because the children share a common pattern of intellectual strengths and weaknesses. Again, the basic question is whether compensatory programs are effective. Do they bring about improved learning in the children who participate in them? The review of evaluation studies of summer compensatory programs by Gilbert Austin and his colleagues suggests that they are not very effective; similar findings have been obtained in early evaluations of Headstart and Follow Through. Why? In a provocative essay, William Rohwer suggests that early childhood programs, including those emphasizing compensatory education, generally are not effective because they come at the wrong stage of the child's intellectual development. As an alternative, he proposes that differences in intellectual skills between racial and socioeconomic groups can best be reduced or eliminated when students reach adolescence. The rationale used by Rohwer is that the capacity to learn certain intellectual skills develops by a process of maturation. This capacity is not present in childhood for at least some students, but does appear in adolescence.

Ability grouping and compensatory education both reflect attempts to adapt instruction to group differences in ability. A different basis for grouping was tested by George Domino. In his research study, reported here, he compared two methods of instruction and found that method 1 was better than method 2 for learners who achieve independently; however, method 2 was better than method 1 for learners who achieve by conforming to the expectations of others. This finding suggests that these two types of learners should not be instructed together. Instead, they should be formed into homogeneous groups and be taught by the method of instruction that is effective for them.

Do grouping procedures represent an effective approach for helping students to learn better? To determine where you stand, decide whether you agree with these views:

Grouping Students for Instruction

Pro Some form of grouping should be used because students differ in learning style and rate.

Con Assigning students to groups on any basis is a makeshift solution to the problem of individual differences. We must strive to tailor an instructional program for each student.

Ability Grouping

Pro Ability grouping is more effective than heterogeneous grouping (low, average, and high ability groups taught together) as a method of instructing students.

Con Heterogeneous grouping is more effective than ability grouping as a method of instructing students.

Ability Grouping

Glen Heathers

Glen Heathers reviews research on the effectiveness of ability grouping. These studies ask whether grouping students into ability groups produces superior learning compared to the method of heterogeneous grouping. The traditional classroom of one teacher and twenty or more students is an example of heterogeneous grouping because students with different aptitudes, interests, and achievement levels are instructed together. Heathers found that ability grouping produces detrimental effects on slow learners. Of course, this generalization only applies to the type of ability grouping used in the studies reviewed by Heathers. It does not tell us whether other forms of ability grouping could be devised that would be effective for slow learners. If you become a teacher, you might be asked to teach within an ability grouping system — sometimes called a "tracking" system. Would you be effective working entirely with slow learners or entirely with fast learners? Would you prefer to teach a heterogeneous group?

... For over a century, group teaching of grade-level classes has dominated instruction in elementary and secondary schools. Both grade place-

Reprinted with permission of Macmillan Publishing Co., Inc. from "Ability Grouping" a section of the article "Grouping" by Glen Heathers, in Robert Ebel (ed.) *Encyclopedia of Educational Research*, 4th ed. New York: Macmillan, 1969. Copyright © 1969 by Macmillan Publishing Co., Inc.

ment and group teaching tend to ignore differences among students. The grade system calls for presenting the same basic grade-level curriculum to all students having the same number of years of schooling. Group teaching has been mainly whole-class teaching in which the methods and pacing of instruction, as well as the lessons taught, are largely the same for all members of the class.

The large differences in intellectual abilities and educational attainments among students of any age level have forced a continuing examination of grouping practices and of instructional methods. A result has been the invention and tryout of many ways of setting up instructional groups as well as various methods of instruction that are intended to take account of differences among the students in a group. These two approaches to dealing with individual differences usually have developed independently of each other. Innovators either have tried changing the composition or size of the group or have tried new methods for differentiating the instruction given group members, not both.

... The great bulk of research on grouping has dealt with attempts to measure the effects of dividing students of a given grade level in a school into classes of restricted range in ability or achievement. Ability grouping, as that term is conventionally used, includes achievement-level grouping of members of a grade level. Achievement-level grouping that brings together students from different grade levels is variously called nongraded, ungraded, multigrade, multiage, and interage grouping.

The term "ability grouping" covers a great array of methods for setting up instructional groups. In the elementary school a frequent practice has been to assign the students of a grade level to groups made relatively homogeneous in IQ, reading achievement, or the two criteria combined. In secondary schools, a frequent practice has been to assign students to one of three tracks representing high, medium, and low levels of intellectual performance. The criteria for assigning students to tracks may be IQ, general grade average, achievement-test scores in such subjects as reading and mathematics, and teachers' ratings.* Because of the variety of methods included under the rubric of ability grouping, it is vital to specify the students, curricular areas, and criteria involved in any instance of ability grouping.

Ability grouping became common in the United States around 1920, closely following developments in testing that provided standardized group measures of intellectual performance. The rapidity of adoption of ability grouping is indicated by Otto and Sanders (1932), who report that, as of 1926, elementary pupils in at least some grades were grouped by ability in 36 out of 40 American cities with populations over 100,000. In the late 1930's and the 1940's there was a decline in ability grouping, related

---

* Do you think any one of these criteria is better than the others?

in good part to objections raised by proponents of progressive education who felt that the practice stigmatized slow learners and made snobs out of the ablest students.

Since 1955 there has been a marked resurgence of interest in ability grouping, stimulated by the increased concern about academic attainment, especially on the part of gifted students. In a survey by the National Education Association (1962) it was found that 52 percent of a national sample of principals of large elementary schools saw an increase in ability grouping in their schools between 1956 and 1961, while only 7 percent saw a decrease during that period. However, heterogeneous grouping through grade 8 remained the commonest practice in America's schools, according to a study by Dean (1960): In 1960 a national sample of school leaders reported ability grouping in grades 1–6 at only 17 percent of schools and in grades 7 and 8 at 34 percent of schools....

The basic assumptions underlying ability grouping are that it materially reduces the range of learning-related differences within a group as compared with random grouping and that this reduction of range facilitates teaching and learning. There is no doubt that one can achieve the intended reduction of range in terms of any one grouping criterion or in terms of a set of closely correlated criterion variables. Thus, if 75 students are divided into three classes of 25 in terms of rank-order scores on an intelligence test, the mean range for the three classes will be one-third that of the total group. However, students' characteristics as learners are not adequately represented by their scores on a general intelligence test.* A student's ease and rate of learning vary greatly from one learning task to another. Also, his level of achievement varies considerably from one curriculum area to another and from topic to topic or task to task within each area.

It is generally recognized that scores on intelligence tests and standardized tests of achievement are substantially correlated. However, when pupils are grouped on the basis of IQ alone it has been found that the range of scores on achievement tests is still great. Goodlad (1960) cites evidence to indicate that dividing students of a grade level into groups on the basis of a measure of general intellectual performance reduces variability in school achievement only about 7 percent for a two-group division and 17 percent for a three-group division. With larger numbers of groups, the reduction of range becomes greater. The most effective way to reduce the range of a class in achievement is to group differentially, subject by subject, and to base this grouping on separate measures of achievement for each area. However, within such groups there would remain large differences in ability and in many other variables that influence learning.

* *Why administer intelligence tests, then?*

The theoretical bases for ability grouping ordinarily have been implied rather than stated in research reports. A common assumption is that a teacher can more readily adapt instruction to differences among students when the range of differences within a class is reduced. Why should this be so? The answer, seldom stated in reports of studies, is that group teaching becomes more manageable when the members of a group have more characteristics in common. In short, the chief working assumption underlying ability grouping is that it facilitates teaching the members of a group as though they did not differ from one another.

Usually, reports of studies of ability grouping are vague about the ways in which teachers are expected to differentiate the instruction they offer classes representing different ability levels. Most often, the reports infer that teachers will vary one or more of the following: learning tasks, including the use of enrichment activities or advanced materials with gifted students; instructional methods — drill with slow groups, projects with abler groups, etc.; and the pace of advancement, with slow groups normally being allowed more time for each unit of work.

Some assumptions about the effects of ability grouping concern students' reactions to their group assignments. It has been claimed often that the rapid learner should benefit from ability grouping through being freed from instruction geared to less-capable learners and through being challenged to keep up with his intellectual peers. The slow learner, it is claimed, should benefit from instruction geared to his capabilities and from experiencing success more often in the absence of the ablest students. Opponents of ability grouping have claimed that slow learners are stigmatized by being placed in low groups and that they are apt, as a result, to lose interest in studying.*

A limitation in research on ability grouping is that virtually all of the studies, including the large-scale researches conducted most recently, have failed to measure ways in which the instruction given to ability group compared with that given to the relatively heterogeneous groups making up the control populations. . . . The explanation is not hard to find. Obtaining specific data on instructional practices in the classroom is enormously difficult and time-consuming. Valid and efficient ways to measure classroom practices are virtually lacking. Teachers are unprepared to provide reliable data on how they teach. Staffs of research projects are never large enough to gather the needed data from a large number of classrooms over a lengthy period of time.

What effects has ability grouping been found to have on students' achievements? No consistent effects have been found when mean scores of experimental and control populations representing the full range of

* *Who makes the stronger case — the advocates or opponents of ability grouping?*

abilities were compared. Thus, Eckstrom (1959) identified 13 studies with findings favoring ability grouping, 15 where no significant effects were found or where results with heterogeneous groups were superior, and 5 where results were partially favorable and partially unfavorable to ability grouping.

Major studies conducted since 1959 have found no clear and consistent effects of ability grouping on students' achievements when total student populations were used. This finding has been obtained in the studies by Goldberg and others (1966) and by Wilcox (1961), where no efforts were made to differentiate the instruction given to groups of different ability levels, and in the studies by Borg (1966) and Drews (1963), where such efforts were made. In some studies the results varied significantly with the learning tasks under consideration. Thus, Borg found that achievement in subject matter tended to be greater with ability grouping, while study methods tended to be superior with heterogeneous grouping. . . .

There is mounting evidence that ability grouping is apt to have significant, and significantly different, effects on the achievement of students of high and low ability even when it does not significantly influence the achievement means of total student populations. The studies reported up to about 1955, as summarized by Goodlad (1960), tended to favor ability grouping for both rapid and slow learners, with the latter benefiting more from the practice. Recent studies have cast serious doubt on this conclusion from earlier studies. Daniels (1961) found ability grouping to produce losses with both high-ability and low-ability students, though the latter suffered the greater losses. Some investigators, notably Borg (1966) and Heathers (1967), have found ability grouping to be associated with gains for rapid learners that were offset by losses for slower learners.* This is a case of the rich getting richer and the poor getting poorer. The fact that Daniels (1961) and Heathers (1967) have found ability grouping to be associated with an increase in the dispersion of students' scores on standardized tests of academic achievement is readily understood when one considers that the practice tends to widen the gap in attainments between educationally advantaged and disadvantaged students.

Recent studies have in some cases found ability grouping to be associated with increased attainments by high-ability students and in other cases with decreased attainment. The former relationship was found in studies by Borg (1966), Douglas (1964), and Heathers (1967), while the latter was found by Abrahamson (1959) and Goldberg and others (1966). Probably these opposite findings reflect differences in the adaptation of instruction to meet the capabilities of superior students.

Major studies reported in the 1960's lend strong support to the view

* Would you consider this finding to be an argument for or against ability grouping?

that ability grouping is associated with detrimental effects on slow learners. Such learners have been found to receive lower scores on achievement tests when placed in low-ability groups than comparable students received when taught in heterogeneous groups. This finding has been reported by Borg (1966), Dockrell (1964), Douglas (1964), and Heathers (1967). Several explanations can be offered to account for this. One is that slow learners, in the absence of superior students, have fewer opportunities to learn vicariously through paying attention during classroom discussions. Other explanations fall under the heading of "self-fulfilling prophecies," namely, that teachers expect less from students who are assigned to low groups and teach them correspondingly less.* Also, students who are assigned to such groups expect less of themselves and behave accordingly. . . .

There is evidence from some studies that the quality of instruction offered low groups tends to be inferior to that offered groups made up of abler students. In the study reported by Heathers (1967), teachers indicated that they stressed basic skills and facts with slow learners and used drill a great deal with these students. On the other hand, they stressed conceptual learning with high-ability groups and encouraged students in these groups to conduct independent projects. Squire (1966) reports that a national study of the teaching of English in high school revealed that teachers tended to employ dull, unimaginative instructional approaches with slow-learning groups.

Ability grouping has been criticized as a form of segregation that has unfavorable emotional-social effects on children who are assigned to low groups. Such groups tend to be used as dumping grounds for students who, for a variety of reasons, perform poorly in their academic work. Low achievement in school subjects results sometimes from limited intellectual endowments, but it may result also from low motivation to study, from emotional difficulties, from poor health, and from environmental handicaps. It is commonly recognized that low-ability groups in elementary school have a disproportionate number of boys, of children from lower-class origins, and of children from minority groups. Ability grouping may thus be, in effect, an agency for maintaining and enhancing caste and class stratification in a society.†

Studies have shown that children from the middle and upper classes are found mainly in the high-ability groups, while children from the lower classes are found in the low-ability groups. This finding appears in reports by Douglas (1964), Husén and Svensson (1960), and Willig (1963).

---

* For a discussion of self-fulfilling prophecies, see the article by Brophy and Good (Section 6).
† Urevick makes the same argument (this section).

Deutsch (1963) presents a strong case for heterogeneous grouping in integrated schools.

Daniels (1961) found that once a child is assigned to an ability level he is very likely to remain there. In his study, although teachers thought that about 17 percent of students were shifted from one level to another each year, actually only about 2 percent were shifted.

Research on the effects of ability grouping on noncognitive variables has been summarized by Borg (1966). In Borg's own study, high-ability students were found to lose sociometric status with ability grouping, while low-ability students gained. However, both categories of students showed a loss in self-esteem with ability grouping. In studies by Drews (1963), Goldberg and others (1966), and Wilcox (1961), slow learners had higher self-concept ratings with ability grouping. Evidence that students prefer membership in high-ability groups comes from the study by Luchins and Luchins (1948), in which bright students indicated they would not want to be transferred from the topmost ability group to the next lower group even though the teacher in the latter group was "better and kinder."

A pair of studies by Atkinson and O'Connor (1963) tested the prediction that the effects of ability grouping would vary according to the strength of the student's motivation to succeed compared to the strength of his anxiety about failing. A study with sixth graders found that ability grouping had positive effects on achievement for those students who had high motivation to succeed compared to the strength of their anxiety about failing. A study with ninth graders did not support this finding. These studies have added an important dimension to research on ability grouping by seeking to test whether students' personality characteristics are determinants of the effects of such grouping. . . .

CRITIQUE

. . . Even today it appears that grouping as a central theme of organization for instruction has nearly run its course and is in the process of being replaced by a familiar theme — individualized instruction — that became a focus of educational reform in the mid-1960's.*

The concept of individualization has acquired such potency that it is reducing to subordinate status even those grouping arrangements being promoted under the banners of nongrading and team teaching. A major factor in the increasing attention being given to individualization is the development of technological devices and learning programs suitable for independent study. Also, recent research has made important contributions to the growing disenchantment with grouping as a theme in organization for instruction. . . .

* Individualized instruction is discussed in Section 10.

EXERCISE

1. What is ability grouping and what are the two basic assumptions that underlie it? (pp. 451, 452, 453)
2. What procedure does Heathers recommend to reduce the range of a class in achievement? (p. 452)
3. What is the usual finding when the achievement of all students in an ability grouping program is compared with the achievement of all students in a heterogeneous grouping program? (pp. 452, 453–454)
4. What have major studies of the 1960's found about the effect of ability grouping on slow learners? (pp. 454–455)
5. In Heathers' study, how did instruction differ for low-ability groups compared to high-ability groups? (p. 455)
6. What does research have to say about the effect of ability grouping on self-concept? (p. 456)
7. According to Heathers, what new method of organizing instruction is replacing grouping of students? (p. 456)

The Case for Elitism

Zak Bayuk

In this brief article Zak Bayuk recommends a form of ability grouping already practiced in various forms in American schools. According to Bayuk's plan, students would be formed into two groups on the basis of their test scores. One group would take a college-oriented curriculum; the other would be instructed in a vocation-oriented curriculum. Bayuk contends that his grouping system would make education more meaningful for all students and would help to eliminate disciplinary problems in the classroom. Do you agree? In the next selection, Stanley Urevick argues against ability grouping because of the negative results he believes it will produce. Who do you think makes a stronger case — Bayuk or Urevick?

Reprinted by permission from the April, 1972, issue of *The Clearing House*, pp. 506–507.

Surely American educators are the world's greatest optimists. They are imbued with democratic ideals and in a sense have created their own traditionalism by contending that each child will choose his pathway and secure a meaningful education. Moreover, they have modeled their schools to accommodate students who virtually all conceive their futures contingent on later success in college. The college oriented curriculum has brought about massive failure and dropping out in high school, coupled with a rising disciplinary problem, yet many students will not be diswayed from their goals — being brainwashed that they must go to college — and manage to defer their failure till a later date. But the fact remains; they do fail.

Frequently there arise with small success radical experiments to implement democracy in our schools. Curriculum is made even more anarchic, transposed to allow the student yet more freedom to seek his way. Sometimes, when well structured, the results are gratifying, especially in the experimental school composed of bright youngsters selected for the ensuing changes. The experiment is, however, rendered invalid when we consider that success is predictable when dealing with a handpicked group. Separating the gifted on simply the experimental basis is doing little to change the existing order nationwide.

Today's reality is captured when one is apt to hear in the teachers' lounge of any high school operating under not so ideal conditions that "if only I were rid of Johnny So-and-So or Billy So-and-So, I'd have a good class." The complaints are voiced because the teacher faces the onerous task of trying to teach Johnny and Billy something they probably cannot hope to master at this time, while the so-called "good kids" just glide along succeeding in what is required — which is often watered down in content.

More often experiments in democracy in schools fail for the very reason that most underdeveloped countries fail in employing it. Though Americans idealize democracy, they practice it in a very queer way, most evident in the illogical yet liberal practice of allowing the students to select their courses of study. It is not hard to determine that despite lofty ideals, students, especially on the lower end of the success continuum, develop little or no democratic tradition, and similar to the underdeveloped nation will have a difficult time when thrust into a democratic environment. Going from our tightly structured schools to loosely structured experimental schools, many students are inclined to misbehave more.*

Partially valid is the old expression that "you cannot make a silk purse out of a sow's ear," and totally true is that you cannot send every child to college and expect him to succeed. However, with the proposed reforms

* *Do you think Bayuk's description of American education is accurate up to this point?*

presented herein, it is my opinion that we can make many more silk purses than anyone ever dreamed, and we can also take a huge step in the advancement of American education.

The answer is "elitism," a word that traditionally has had a "nasty" connotation with American educational theorists. Theorists maintain that the slower child is appreciably aided by being in contact with a more heterogeneous group, especially during the formative years.* Moreover, they indicate that the critical age of learning in the biological and psychological development of the human being comes between the third and fifth years of life. Sociologists, on the other hand, point out that there is an inexorable trend for our society to be dominated by a "gifted elite."

Taking this evidence into account, justification can be seen for retaining the heterogeneous grouping through the formative years. In fact, theory would dictate that in view of the critical age of development, our schools might best begin, as many European schools do, when children have reached age three.† However, when children reach grade eight, they have pretty well established performance patterns; a high correlation exists between achievement scores in ninth and twelfth grades. Thus the proposed dual system would commence in grade nine with the administration of a nationally standardized examination of verbal and quantitative skills. Standards for passing and failing would be established according to criteria reflecting regional performance. A student would be guaranteed the option of taking the examination as many times as he wished and at any time during his tenure in the system in an attempt to pass the test.

Subsequent to the examination, the two groups will be dispersed within two systems, one operating under a college-oriented curriculum, the other a vocationally-oriented curriculum. The vocationally oriented system will not be lacking in the traditional 3 R's nor in the humanities, but the central focus will be on job training. In both systems the choices of students to pursue their pathways will be less subject to whimsy and hence should be more valid.

Elitism does not mean we will be regressing to a smaller, less comprehensive educational system. On the contrary, it is envisioned that more money, teachers, and equipment will be made available than ever before in creating two great systems of public education with ample mobility between them.‡

No longer would the slower student be a prisoner of the system, facing tasks he cannot possibly perform. Frustration would ease for those who cannot read and who, according to their grade level, must read Shakespeare. The high school would not be detaining children who might be

---

Does Heathers' research review (the preceding selection) support this statement?
†*Rohwer takes a different position later in this section.*
‡*How much mobility do you think would occur in practice?*

out helping to feed their families instead of wasting their time in exchange for a meaningless education. Elitism would make education more meaningful, and in doing so would alleviate disciplinary problems. Schools would eventually attain the reverence that was heretofore only relegated to the college.

Until the day comes, and it will come, when chemical means are devised to transmit learning, or when child conception becomes more discriminantly and selectively controlled, the two-system educational ideal would seem logical, especially in view of our ever-burgeoning population.*

EXERCISE

1. According to Bayuk, what has been the effect of the college-oriented curriculum? (p. 458)

2. Why does Bayuk recommend heterogeneous grouping until the eighth grade? (p. 459)

3. What are the objectives of the two curricula recommended by Bayuk? (p. 459)

4. How would the changes recommended by Bayuk purportedly help the slower student? (pp. 459–460)

* See Sullivan on the use of biochemical techniques to facilitate learning (Section 11).

Ability Grouping:
Why Is It Undemocratic?

Stanley J. Urevick

> In the preceding section Zak Bayuk argued for a particular type of ability grouping because of its presumed good effects: a more meaningful education for all students and a reduction in classroom discipline problems. However, Stanley Urevick is opposed to ability grouping because of its presumed detrimental effects. He believes that ability grouping aggravates discipline problems rather than reduces them; more important, ability grouping develops undemocratic attitudes in students. On the other hand, Urevick sees several ad-

Reprinted by permission of publisher and author from the May, 1965 issue of *The Clearing House*, pp. 530–532.

vantages to an educational system based on heterogeneous grouping; for example, it creates many opportunities for students to learn from each other, and it ensures that every student receives a quality education. Urevick and Bayuk obviously differ about the merits of ability grouping. Are their disagreements resolvable? Could research of the type reviewed by Glen Heathers earlier in this section be done which would test their claims about ability grouping?

Ability grouping is bunk. At least that's what many teachers are inclined to believe, and not without reason. Practical experience bears it out and common sense substantiates it. When we examine ability grouping as it is applied today, we will see that it is not only unfair but obviously detrimental to our democratic ideals.

On the surface, ability grouping is the ideal way to arrange students in a school. After extensive testing, the categorized student is neatly placed in a group with students of very much his level of ability. Since the teacher knows exactly what he has at hand, he can tailor his teaching methods to the needs of the group and, consequently, teach more effectively. The group learns more because the teacher is more efficient. The class functions smoothly because its homogeneous. Everything is ideal except democracy. Democracy has been grouped outside the school.

Ability grouping is fine in theory. Anyone who has worked with it knows it certainly saves teaching time and money.* But can the future of our country be measured in time and money? Of course not. Our nation's future will always be measured by the caliber of citizens we produce: by the way they act, feel, cooperate, and contribute to each other's well-being. Ability grouping cannot satisfy these ends. It goes astray for many reasons.

First, it goes against the grain of American ideals and democratic principles. Teachers know this better than anyone else. All of us want to be the best teachers we possibly can; and all of us know that our efforts will not be rewarded at the end of one year. The results of our teaching will not be measured by the test scores our students make on a standardized ... test, but by the impact our students make on our society. The main purpose of secondary education is to develop well-rounded citizens with good character and a deep belief in our democratic way of life.† This cannot be achieved by ability grouping.

Ability grouping by its very nature, is undemocratic. It sets certain students not only apart from each other but either above or below each other. This artificial stratification, based on questionable test score results, classifies students as either fast or slow, with a few falling in between. It

* *Why would ability grouping necessarily save teaching time and money?*
† *Is this the main goal of secondary education? Compare with Ebel (Section 2), who argues that the main goal is learning of useful knowledge and skills.*

fills the student in the fast section with a false sense of knowledge. A superiority complex is created. Another student, in a slow section, observes this and soon begins to feel that he isn't as good. This feeling of inferiority leads to a defeatist attitude. He's stuck where he is, so he orients his philosophy around the acceptance of a secondary role in the school. Eventually the second-class student openly rebels. This rebellion shows itself as an overt discipline problem. Statistics showing the close correlation between discipline problems and the ability group bear this out. The higher the group, the fewer problems. The lower the group, the more problems. The teacher in the lower group always gets the higher percentage of discipline problems.

Grouping isn't fair, because the slower students keep getting the slower education. After five years in slow sections, how can they help but be slow? This is made very evident when they take standardized tests and constantly get low test scores. On the other hand, fast learners keep getting the fast teaching that keeps them in the upper 25 percentile. One cannot help but conclude that ability grouping perpetuates its own undemocratic system. But that isn't the worst of it. The fast learners continue to move ahead — fast. The slow learners continue to stay behind — slow. And each group reinforces its own shortcomings. Democracy is not at work in these classrooms, but a class system is.

In the fast sections, the students' objective is to see how well they can do, not because they want to do well but because home pressures demand it. Grades become all-important and motivation is strictly to excel (many times at any cost — even cheating). * The slow sections also have their standards. Get by if you can. If you can't, don't worry; you're a dummy anyway. This outlook always breeds discipline problems — problems that will have side effects on our society for years to come.

The real damage to democracy is done not after the system takes hold in our schools but after it takes hold in our society. Students graduating from high school who were the products of slow sections retain many of the undemocratic attitudes they learned in school. And they're going to instill *their* children with these same attitudes. "I don't want you to be a dummy like me, son. I want you to study hard and get into those fast sections. I want you to be able to hold your head up high." While the graduate of a fast section will tell his daughter, "You belong in the super-fast section where you'll learn the things that will give *you* the keys to the future. I know what kind of people are in those retarded sections."

This is no exaggeration. It is happening right now, when it shouldn't be and needn't be. We cannot afford to discriminate anywhere in our society.

* *Are you willing to accept the author's analysis without empirical research to support it? What other motives might the fast learner have, besides the desire to excel?*

We have to give *all* of our children quality education. This doesn't mean we should change our teachers — we have the finest in the world. But it does mean we must change our system. We must return to a heterogeneous or democratic system. If we already have it, we must make sure that it isn't changed.

Students learn from each other. No matter how slow a student is, he can still teach a fast student something, even if it's no more than a feeling of compassion and understanding for someone who just can't seem to make the grade.* In addition, a slow student might be motivated by the very presence of a fast student. Some of the enthusiasm that a fast student generates might rub off on him; or he might decide to compete with the fast student and give him a run for the money. He might even be embarrassed into doing his best. Whatever happens, he is much better off in a heterogeneous group than in a homogeneous one. In the former, he would be in a mixed class and, as in a mixed society, all members would have something to contribute. In the latter, he would be surrounded by equally slow students, all of whom would have little if any interest in excelling.

Our society cannot afford to let its youth be stratified in the schools. Everyone deserves the same opportunity, and everyone needs it. True, the years after high school may show that some students are more able than others to satisfy certain tasks; but let us help them get that far rather than tell them in the junior and senior high schools that they just don't have what it takes. Students mature at different rates. Talents are sometimes slow in developing. Interests, emotions, and attitudes constantly fluctuate. We cannot risk our nation's future on an ability system. Every student must have exposure to quality education. Democratic living and functioning begins in our schools. If our youths do not see it in action there, how can we expect them to apply it when they are on their own?

Many schools tried ability grouping in its early days, only to return to heterogeneous grouping when both educators and parents realized that they could not continue to sacrifice the supposedly below average and average for the geniuses. But crowded schools, a shortage of teachers, and national pressures have revived the trend. If it continues, our educational system may create a regimented cell-like commune instead of a meaningful and spiritually elevating democracy.

Is ability grouping bunk? Those who use it know it has shortcomings but maintain it is convenient and is the best system now at hand. But is that a good reason for using a system that is obviously detrimental to democracy? When we search our consciences we can only conclude that ability grouping stands on very shaky ground. Are we willing to risk its

* Thelen also extols the positive benefits of peer and cross-age tutoring (Thelen, Section 12).

far-reaching side effects on the future of our nation? Most of us would rather not. In the meantime, where the system moves on, the slow stay slow and the fast would be fast anyway. Ability grouping may be bunk, but democracy is not.*

EXERCISE

1. Why does Urevick believe that ability grouping is undemocratic? (pp. 461–463)

2. What two advantages does Urevick see in ability grouping? (p. 461)

3. According to Urevick, what three factors led educators back to ability grouping? (p. 463)

* Has this article convinced you that ability grouping is detrimental to democracy?

Interactive Effects of Achievement Orientation and Teaching Style on Academic Achievement

George Domino

Most educators would agree that because students have different learning styles and aptitudes no single instructional method is best for all students. Ability grouping, discussed in the preceding three selections, is one method of adapting instruction to learner characteristics. However, the authors of these selections are not very specific in describing how instruction would vary for above-average, average, and below-average learners. In the following selection, George Domino provides an explicit method for matching a particular type of learner with a particular type of instruction. He distinguishes between students who achieve by conforming to the expectations of others and students who achieve by acting independently. In the experiment reported here, Domino found that college students who score high on a measure of achievement-via-independence learned best when the instructor emphasized ideas rather than

From the *Journal of Educational Psychology*, 62, 1971, pp. 427–431. Copyright 1971 by the American Psychological Association, and reproduced by permission of publisher and author.

facts and actively involved them in the learning process. In contrast, college students who score high on achievement-via-conformance learned best when the instructor emphasized factual knowledge, used the lecture method exclusively, made classroom attendance mandatory, and tied lecture content closely to textbook assignments. Do these findings make sense to you? Do you see how they can be applied to the teaching of students at all grade levels?

Although both educators and researchers are concerned with maximizing academic achievement, little empirical work has been reported that attempts to systematically alter selected aspects of the college environment in an effort to directly influence academic achievement.

Domino (1968) studied the academic performance of high and low scorers on the Achievement-via-Conformance (Ac) and Achievement-via-Independence (Ai) scales of the California Psychological Inventory (Gough, 1957) to test the hypothesis that conforming and independent achievement orientations are differentially related to academic achievement. The results not only supported this notion, but indicated that for students high on one achievement dimension and low on the other, there was a distinct interaction between the student's achievement orientation and the demands of the college environment. Students high on Ac obtained higher grades in courses rewarding conforming behavior whereas students high on Ai obtained higher grades in independence rewarding courses.

The present study is concerned with the general hypothesis that there is an interaction between a student's achievement orientation and the teaching style he is exposed to, and that this interaction will differentially affect both the amount of learning that takes place and the student's expressed satisfaction with his scholastic environment. Specifically, it is hypothesized that students high on Ac or Ai who are taught in a manner consonant with their achievement orientation will perform better academically and report greater satisfaction than their peers who are taught in a manner dissonant with their achievement orientation.

Method

SAMPLE. In September 1968, the entering class (N = approximately 900) of a large university was administered the CPI as part of a freshman testing program. In September 1969, from a frequency distribution of scores on the Ac and Ai scales, the top 50 high Ac-low Ai and the top 50 low Ac-high Ai students were identified, eliminating those whose SAT scores fell below 550 or above 650.* These 100 students were assigned to four introductory psychology sections, with the same instructor, in such

---

* SAT *is an acronym for Scholastic Aptitude Tests, which are usually administered to high school seniors applying to college.*

a manner that each section contained 25 students, with equal sex composition, comparable mean SAT scores, but homogeneous with respect to their Ac or Ai scores. Table 1 presents a demographic description of the four sections.

TABLE 1
Summary Statistics for Four Sections

	Sections			
Variables	High Ai	High Ai	High Ac	High Ac
CPI Ac				
range	15–25	16–25	28–32	28–32
M*	20.7	21.2	29.4	29.2
SD*	2.9	2.2	1.6	1.5
CPI Ai				
range	22–26	21–26	12–19	14–19
M	23.7	23.5	17.4	17.3
SD	1.4	1.4	1.5	1.2
Sex composition				
Male	11	9	12	12
Female	13	12	13	11
Total	24	21	25	23
SAT Verbal				
M	612.5	612.2	595.4	604.6
SD	32.2	26.8	26.2	32.5
SAT Math				
M	602.3	594.5	588.1	584.6
SD	35.8	26.5	34.6	32.7

Note. — Twelve males and 13 females were assigned to each section. Withdrawals reduced the registration to the numbers shown under sex composition. All values are for the participating students.

PROCEDURE. Neither the instructor nor the students were aware that class assignments had been made on other than routine scheduling by the registrar's office. The instructor, however, cooperated with the author in a study of the effectiveness of teaching styles, by teaching Sections 2 and 3 in a "conforming" manner, and Sections 1 and 4 in an "independent" manner, using the criteria indicated by Domino (1968). Thus for one group of high Ai students and one group of high Ac students, instructional material was presented solely through lectures, great emphasis was placed upon factual knowledge, classroom attendance was required, and course content closely paralleled textbook assignments. For the high Ai and high Ac sections taught in an independent manner, emphasis was

* M and SD are abbreviations for mean and standard deviation, respectively. These terms are explained in the glossary.

placed upon ideas rather than facts and upon the active participation of students in the learning process. All four sections were assigned identical textbook readings and examinations, but for the independent sections the examinations served as a guide for the student rather than a grading device.

INSTRUMENTS. At the termination of the semester all students were administered a final examination consisting of 200 multiple-choice items tapping mostly factual content, as well as six essay questions which demanded both convergent and divergent thinking (Guilford, 1959).* Both the multiple-choice items and the essay questions were formulated prior to the beginning of the course and independently of the course instructor.

Essay answers for each student were independently rated by three psychologists using two 9-point scales, one scale rating amount of factual knowledge present and the other degree of original thinking present. All judges rated all essay answers on both dimensions, with order of ratings randomized for both dimensions.

Students evaluated both the course and the instructor using 7-point rating scales; although code numbers were used to provide anonymity and to obtain honest responses, it was possible to compare these ratings with other variables. Finally, for each student, his introductory psychology grade (assigned without reference to the final examination) and his cumulative GPA for the first 2 years (not considering his introductory psychology grade) were available.† . . .

RESULTS

. . . A preliminary question needs to be asked regarding the interrater reliability of the factual knowledge and original thinking ratings of essay answers. . . . Analysis of the data revealed that interrater reliability . . . was acceptable, . . . although not exceptionally high. . . .

A second concern is in relation to the independence of both the factual knowledge-original thinking ratings and the teacher effectiveness-course evaluation ratings. Factual knowledge and original thinking ratings did not correlate significantly with each other.‡ . . .

Student ratings of teacher effectiveness and course evaluation do correlate significantly with one another, but in a rather moderate manner. . . .

The relevancy of the multiple-choice items can also be questioned. It would be impossible, and basically not relevant, to argue that the items represent the basic knowledge a student ought to acquire in an introduc-

* *These concepts are explained in the selection by Guilford (Section 5).*
† *GPA is an abbreviation for gradepoint average.*
‡ *Correlation is explained in the glossary.*

tory psychology course. What can be argued is that the items are in fact tapping cognitive processes of relevance to traditional academic achievement; scores on the multiple-choice items did indeed correlate significantly with both psychology grades and with GPA.

Table 2 presents the results of the analyses ... performed on each of the seven dependent variables.* ... For the multiple-choice items, factual knowledge ratings, teacher effectiveness ratings, course evaluation ratings, and introductory psychology grades, there are significant interaction effects between achievement orientation and teaching style.† For the original thinking ratings, teacher effectiveness ratings, introductory psychology grades, and GPA, there are significant achievement orientation effects.‡ No significant teaching style main effects were obtained.§

DISCUSSION

The major concern of this study was with the hypothesized interaction between student achievement orientation and teaching style. Despite the artificiality of having the same instructor role play both independent and conforming teaching styles, the results quite clearly indicate a very definite interaction between student achievement orientation and teaching style. If it can be argued that educational aims should include both the imparting of factual knowledge and some degree of satisfaction on the part of students, then one method of achieving these aims is to match student achievement orientation with teaching style. On the other hand, the results indicate that teaching style has no effect on original thinking; to elicit original thinking from students one must begin with students whose achievement orientation is conducive to independent, original thinking. These results can be seen as either disconcerting or reassuring depending upon what one believes are the effects of college courses on students' original thinking abilities.

The obtained significant interactions have implications for educational practices which can be perceived in rather different ways. One may argue, for example, that homogeneous grouping of students on the basis of their achievement orientation is a desirable practice, since it maximizes both their factual learning and their reported satisfaction. Yet, homogeneous grouping may deny both the independent and the conforming student the

* *Dependent variables are explained in the glossary.*
† *An interaction effect means that the effectiveness of independent and conforming teaching styles depended upon the particular group of students assigned to them.*
‡ *An achievement orientation effect means that one group of students had higher scores than the other group on the original thinking ratings, etc.*
§ *The fact that no teaching style main effects were significant means that there were no stable differences between independent and conforming teaching styles in affecting achievement.*

TABLE 2
Summary Statistics and Analyses
of Variance Results on Dependent Variables*

Variable	Group[a]	M	SD	Results of ANOVA	
				Source	F
Multiple choice	1	98.2	21.6	Achievement orientation	0.00
	2	89.6	25.1	Teaching style	1.08
	3	103.5	29.6	Interaction	6.50[b]
	4	84.7	23.7		
Factual knowledge ratings	1	6.7	1.7	Achievement orientation	.75
	2	5.7	2.0	Teaching style	.83
	3	6.7	1.7	Interaction	10.68[c]
	4	5.0	2.2		
Original thinking ratings	1	7.0	1.3	Achievement orientation	66.73[c]
	2	7.1	1.2	Teaching style	.19
	3	4.2	1.5	Interaction	.33
	4	4.6	2.1		
Teacher effect	1	6.8	.5	Achievement orientation	7.66[c]
	2	6.3	1.1	Teaching style	2.31
	3	6.5	.8	Interaction	14.42[c]
	4	5.5	1.1		
Course evaluation	1	6.7	.6	Achievement orientation	.54
	2	5.5	1.7	Teaching style	.47
	3	6.3	1.2	Interaction	12.07[c]
	4	5.6	1.4		
Psychology grade	1	3.5	.5	Achievement orientation	8.66[c]
	2	2.9	.8	Teaching style	.68
	3	3.1	.8	Interaction	20.54
	4	2.3	.8		
GPA	1	2.8	.5	Achievement orientation	6.31[b]
	2	2.7	.5	Teaching style	.24
	3	2.5	.4	Interaction	.02
	4	2.6	.4		

[a] Group 1 = high Ai with independent teaching style; Group 2 = high Ai with conforming teaching style; Group 3 = high Ac with conforming teaching style; Group 4 = high Ac with independent teaching style.
[b] $p < .05$.†
[c] $p < .01$.†

valuable insights that result from exposure to heterogeneity.‡ It is quite clear, however, that the interaction of achievement orientation with teaching style is an important dimension which has been seriously neglected

* Analysis of variance is explained in the glossary.
† The symbol p stands for probability level, which is explained in the glossary.
‡ Which of these two arguments do you think is stronger?

by both educators and researchers. It is possible to provide students with the type of educational setting that would most effectively utilize their potential, and also to expose students to diversity of opinions and achievement orientations. Only by first recognizing these dimensions, however, can their relevancy to self-actualization be utilized in a positive manner. . . .

EXERCISE

1. In Domino's 1968 study, in what kind of course did high Ac students do better? In what kind of course did high Ai students do better? (p. 465)

2. In the study reported here, what is the difference between a conforming and an independent teaching style? (pp. 466–467)

3. Table 2 presents statistical results for seven variables. Which variables were affected by a significant interaction between student achievement orientation and teaching style? (p. 469)

The Effectiveness of Summer Compensatory Education: A Review of the Research

Gilbert R. Austin, Bruce G. Rogers, and Henry H. Walbesser, Jr.

The most publicized compensatory programs are Headstart and Follow Through. However, many other compensatory programs have been established in the schools, including those reviewed here by Gilbert Austin and his colleagues. They examine evaluation studies which investigated how effectively summer compensatory programs promote student learning. These programs help elementary school students make "modest" gains in mathematics, reading, and language communication. However, the available research does not reveal how long these gains persist or whether these students, deprived of compensatory education, would have made the same gains, perhaps from maturation during a summer. Austin and his colleagues indicate that the evaluation studies were generally not well designed

From *Review of Educational Research*, 42, 1972, pp. 171–181. Reprinted with permission of publisher and authors. Copyright by the American Educational Research Association, Washington, D.C.

or executed. As a result, it is often difficult to interpret the research data, which lowers the value of evaluation research for many educators. However, it would be unfortunate if educators abandoned research assessing the effectiveness of their programs. Do you agree?

This review is concerned with the Summer Compensatory Education Program component of the Title I of the Elementary and Secondary Education Act of 1965. It is important at the outset to recognize the multiplicity of goals of the Title I Programs. The Law represents a federal effort to meet the problems of poverty, delinquency, unemployment, illiteracy, and school dropouts. Its stated purpose is "to provide financial assistance . . . to local educational agencies serving areas with concentration of children from low-income families to expand and improve their educational programs . . . [to meet] the special educational needs of educationally deprived children (USOE, 1969, pp. 1, 2)."

It would seem from these broad purposes that the intent of Congress was not to implement a new method of teaching reading, mathematics, or some other specific subject matter, but rather, to implement a program of sufficient breadth and impact to bring about a major rise in the intellectual, social, and political attainments of the disadvantaged.

Since schools are commonly perceived as major social vehicles for these types of goals, it seemed appropriate to work through them. Programs covering both the regular school year and the summer session were supported, but this review restricts itself to the latter. . . .

The sections of the review will present, in turn, some historical notes on summer school programs, objective data on cognitive growth, subjective data on program effectiveness . . . and conclusions.

HISTORICAL NOTES ON SUMMER SCHOOL

The early part of the twentieth century saw the initiation of the concept of summer school. According to the literature, students enrolled in summer programs for a variety of purposes, including recreation, removal of academic deficiencies, enrichment or supplementary courses, and the acceleration of programs (NEA, 1968; Roncour, 1963). However, until the decade of the 1950s, summer programs with an emphasis on compensatory education appeared only occasionally as an incidental component of the recreational aspect of summer school.*

A significant step forward in compensatory education programs was marked by the "Demonstration Guidance Project" in the New York City

* *Deutsch was one of the original proponents of compensatory education (see Section 4).*

public schools in 1956. This program attempted to upgrade students from limited cultural experiences by including remedial, academic, and counseling functions and parental involvement. Blended with the curriculum were cultural enrichments such as visits to plays, concerts, and other activities available in a large urban center. At the time, the program was considered successful enough to be incorporated into the New York City public schools under the title "Higher Horizons" (Shaw, 1963).

Rapid increases in the frequency of summer schools were observed throughout the decade of the 1960s. A report by the National Education Association Research Division (NEA, 1964) pointed to a particular increase for programs with enrichment objectives and with more attempts to recognize and deal with the special problems of the culturally deprived. Much greater diversity was also introduced into the summer school during this decade. Although most of the summer school programs directed at remedial education focused on the secondary level, programs for the elementary level also received attention (Hanson, 1964). . . .

GROWTH IN COGNITIVE AREAS

Generally, compensatory education implies a lack in the attainment of some educational goal. In its current usage, it usually implies retardation in the cognitive areas of reading and arithmetic skills. Congress has appropriated considerable amounts of money with the hope that disadvantaged pupils can "catch up" in these areas. Let us then consider this question: Does the published literature indicate that summer compensatory education helps disadvantaged children in the achievement of these important skills?

An example of one of the more comprehensive evaluations of a summer program is shown by the work of Fox and Weinberg (1967) in the New York City Public Schools. A target population, consisting of those who had failed to show satisfactory progress in reading, received a basic skills program emphasizing reading and arithmetic. For the data analysis, a judgmental sample (selected to be representative of the range of schools) was selected and the results of the program were evaluated with pre- and post-test administration of subtests of the Metropolitan Achievement Test. The median reading grade level score increased from 5.1 to 5.5. However, of the 664 students in the sample, 282 showed gains with a median of 0.94 months, while 193 showed losses with a median of 0.69 months.* Since it is not likely that a student's reading ability would actually decline during an instructional program, it can only be assumed that the losers and also about as many of the gainers were the result of chance errors in

* *Regression effect, median, and tests of statistical significance are explained in the glossary.*

the test. It was further noted that the program "produced the largest gains in children who were the most severely retarded (p. 29)." This is what may be expected by chance from the so-called "regression effect." Without a randomly formed control group, it is difficult to determine if these larger gains were beyond chance expectation. Somewhat similar results and conclusions were reported for the mathematics program.

In a study with the Milwaukee Public Schools (1968a), the investigators obtained pre- and post-measures of reading and mathematical achievement and separately examined gain scores in both areas for lower, middle, and upper grades. The authors did not consider it appropriate to run statistical tests of significance on these six sets of gain scores, but all six differences were positive. Since the probability of such an event occurring by chance is only about .016, it is not unreasonable to assume that some actual changes in achievement did occur.

Wasik and Sibley (1969) studied 20 culturally deprived kindergarten children during an eight-week summer program incorporating systematic classroom management. Measures of language, intelligence and pre-reading showed statistically significant gains, but no data from a control group were available.

EXPECTED SUMMER GAINS WITHOUT INSTRUCTION. Would the students in these studies have shown about the same gains during the summer without any instruction? The Iowa Tests of Basic Skills are normed on the assumption of one month of growth during the summer (Beggs and Hieronymus, 1968, p. 91). Yet, many writers assume that students lose in achievement over the summer. Soar and Soar (1969) attempted to study this problem by comparing elementary school students in the fall and spring of the fifth grade and in the fall and spring of the sixth grade. They found summer gains of between three and five months in grade norms. However, as they point out, the spring scores were taken about a month before school let out, and the fall scores a month after school began, after the teachers had reviewed for a month. Further, the grade placement norms for fifth graders are determined from a set of items that overlaps, but is not identical, to the set of items used for sixth grade norms. Nonetheless, Soar and Soar interpreted their data as showing evidence that many students do, indeed, exhibit gains over the summer. Thus, it would seem desirable, in evaluating the effectiveness of summer programs, to show evidence that any summer gains exceeded those which might be expected without supplementary programs. . . .

Did the students continue to show their increased ability when they enrolled in school in the fall, or had they regressed back to their pre-summer levels? This question remains unanswered since none of the studies reviewed reported any follow-up measures with regard to long-term retention.

RATING SCALES. While the goals of a mathematics program can usually be evaluated with objective paper and pencil tests, the goals of other programs not infrequently must be evaluated by directly observing and evaluating the student as he performs a given task. To evaluate a summer clinic for speech handicapped children, Fox and others (1967) collected pre- and post-tapes for each subject. Two speech experts later rated these tapes on a five-point scale without knowledge of the temporal order. The judges agreed on 54 percent of their judgments. In half of the cases in which the judges agreed, the students were perceived as improving, while in the remaining half, no changes were seen. These results are difficult to interpret, inasmuch as they can be accounted for by a random model. The low reliability of ratings continues to characterize studies using the rankings of judges. . . .

PROGRAM OBJECTIVES. It might be expected that the usual program would state its cognitive goals in terms of observable student behavior. This was not the case, however, since most programs listed goals written in terms of what the program would present. For example,

"Make available remedial instruction at no cost to the participant."

"To do remedial and experimental work in composition [Medford Public Schools, 1969, pp. 5, 40]." . . .

The lack of objectives stated in terms of measurable student achievement appears to be common to many programs which fail to show concrete evidence of cognitive growth.* A group of migrant children in Iowa (Iowa, 1969) were administered pre- and posttests in a program to improve English skills. The results showed positive gains on some tests, negative on others; but, perhaps due to a lack of behavioral objectives, the authors did not attempt to interpret the results.

Hayes and Kerr (1970) found no significant gains for tenth graders studying a science program. They attributed the findings to poorly stated objectives (p. 135). . . .

PROBLEMS OF IMPLEMENTATION OF EVALUATION PROGRAMS. Several authors have indicated that funds were made available too late to implement the desired evaluation model. For example, Williams and Tannenbaum (1967, p. 19) reported that funding was delayed until a few weeks before the project began. No definite plans could be made until that time, thus necessitating much last-minute preparation. The Milwaukee Public Schools (1968b) desired to conduct a seminar on racial prejudice involving 300 pupils, but the funding was not made available until shortly before the registration deadline. As a consequence, only 49 students completed

---

* The pros and cons of writing measurable objectives are discussed by Guth and Popham in Section 14.

the program. Many directors claimed that when funds were withheld until shortly before the onset of a project they did not have adequate time to make definite arrangements for testing programs and other evaluation methods.

NONCOGNITIVE DATA

In a number of projects, academic achievement was chosen as a dependent variable.* . . . However, many educators have argued against this choice. Cohen (1970) maintains that "achievement scores are not an adequate summary of the legislation's diverse aims [p. 217]," mainly because "higher school achievement [is] simply a proxy for one of the program's main aims — improving adults' social and economic status [p. 218]." Since Cohen believes that there is very little evidence to warrant inferring a causal connection between the two, he argues that "it is, therefore, difficult to conclude that improving schools' production of poor children's achievement was the legislation's major purpose [p. 220]." In this section we will examine some of the data reported on noncognitive variables.

Data on attitudes are commonly collected via questionnaires, but the difficulty is frequently encountered of making inferences from a group of returns representing a relatively small proportion of the potential respondents. In a typical study, Williams and Tannenbaum (1967) reported a "generally positive attitude" on the part of the teachers (p. 48), but out of 108 teachers, only 32 percent responded to the questionnaire. There was apparently no offer to mail the results to the teachers, or to elicit free-response suggestions for improvements.

AFFECTIVE . . . VARIABLES. One of the most frequently espoused goals of Title I programs is to improve student attitudes toward school. Because this affective objective is so commonplace, it might be anticipated that much empirical data would be collected and reported. But, alas, as with the cognitive goals, data on the affective goals and their acquisition were rare.

Morris and Wheater (1966), anticipating that readers would look for objective data, defended the virtues of subjective statements. The stated goals of their project included the development of leadership, art appreciation, awareness of the technological age, self-improvement, and so on.† Children were asked to write an essay on why they liked their favorite teacher, both at the beginning and end of the program. They also indicated their likes and dislikes on a checklist of activities (for example, playing

---

* *Dependent variables are explained in the glossary.*
† *Are these worthwhile goals for a compensatory education program? Should the programs instead have focused on basic academic skills?*

games). These were subjectively evaluated (no data were reported), and the project was judged a success.

In a seminar on racial prejudice (Milwaukee Public Schools, 1968b), the program evaluation consisted of requesting students and teachers to make comments concerning the program. Both groups tended to make favorable comments. As evidence for the effectiveness of another program, it was noted that the students expressed a desire to stay at the school longer (Costa, 1967). In a program designed to foster interest in minority group music, 20 high school minority group musicians were paid to develop and present assembly programs. To obtain data, the researchers interviewed teachers and principals to inquire how well they thought the programs held student interest. No actual data were presented, but the evaluators concluded that the program was successful (Fox and Ward, 1967).

The above studies are typical of those reviewed in that most projects relied on student and teacher questionnaires as the only evaluation devices. Almost without exception, the results were favorable to the program. Fox and others (1969) have suggested that the contradiction between these positive perceptions of progress and the results of objective measures of gain has a dual interpretation: (1) the perceptions of teachers and pupils are more sensitive than the available measuring instruments, and (2) the desire of teachers and pupils to see the program succeed affects their evaluation. Although it was often reported that a summer program was a success in improving pupil competencies, attitudes, and attendance, not one study was found by these reviewers to indicate whether or not the new attitudes, achievements, and habits were observable during the subsequent school year. . . .

CONCLUSIONS . . .

In the opinion of the reviewers, the following conclusions* can be inferred:

1. Summer Compensatory Education programs in elementary mathematics, reading and language-communication have generally shown modest achievement gains. However, since no randomly formed control groups were used, "maturation" (Campbell and Stanley, 1963) remains a threat to the validity of the studies. Further, no data were found to demonstrate whether these gains persist over time.

2. Students reported an increased desire to attend school and learn the cognitive skills. However, no data were reported to indicate if those behavior changes were observable during the school year.

* *Compare with Rohwer's analysis of the effectiveness of compensatory education (Rohwer, this section).*

3. Relatively few of the programs had behaviorally stated objectives at the outset of the programs to provide direction for evaluation activities.

4. Many of the projects claimed to have been funded too late to allow the implementation of their proposed evaluation procedures. . . .

EXERCISE

1. What are four purposes for which summer programs have been used? (p. 471)

2. What did Soar and Soar conclude about student achievement gains during the summer without any instruction? (p. 473)

3. According to the authors, are behavioral objectives important in evaluating the effectiveness of compensatory programs? (p. 474)

4. According to the authors, what are two shortcomings in data collected on changes in student attitudes as a result of participation in a summer compensatory program? (pp. 475, 476)

5. What is the authors' main conclusion about the effect of summer compensatory education on growth in student cognitive skills? (p. 476)

Prime Time for Education:
Early Childhood or Adolescence?

William D. Rohwer, Jr.

William Rohwer presents several challenging ideas and research findings about educational reform. He provides insights about the failures and prospects of compensatory education. Evaluations of early childhood compensatory programs such as Headstart, Follow Through, or special summer projects (reviewed in the preceding selection) typically show that they produce modest gains, if at all, and that these gains do not last once the children enter regular school programs. The research reported by Rohwer suggests that these special programs are not effective because they come at too early a stage in the child's intellectual development. In fact, re-

From *Harvard Educational Review*, 41, 1971, pp. 316–341. Reprinted with permission of the publisher and author. Copyright © 1971 by the President and Fellows of Harvard College.

*searchers have obtained some evidence that early childhood educa-
tion can do more harm than good. As an alternative, Rohwer makes
a case for waiting until adolescence to provide compensatory education, which would reduce racial and socioeconomic group differences in intellectual skills. Has Rohwer's presentation changed your
views about the value of early childhood education? Has he made a
convincing case for adolescence as a critical learning period?*

Research and development efforts in early childhood education have
achieved notable success. We have learned much concerning the course
and determinants of intellectual development during the infant, preschool,
and primary years. In addition, it is now demonstrable that the intellectual development of children from low-income families can be effectively
fostered during these years. A satisfactory level of momentum has been
established with respect to both the interest and the effort devoted to
the early childhood years; barring fiscal betrayal, this momentum should
eventually increase markedly the quality and outcomes of preschool and
primary schooling.

However, until some fundamental assumptions of early childhood educators are seriously questioned, increased investment in current preschool
and primary school programs may be unwise; in particular it has not been
established that early childhood is the optimal age range for imposing the
academic content traditionally required.* In addition, early childhood or
early elementary school programs may have a slight, or even negative, effect
on the attainment of educational goals. Thus, research and policy in early
childhood education should be evaluated in light of two larger educational
issues: (1) developmental changes in children's mental capacity and (2)
the relationship of educational objectives to the demands of society....

Evaluation of Early Childhood Programs

A case in point is supplied by the controversies surrounding the effectiveness of programs of early childhood education. In a widely noted recent
article, Jensen (1969) reviewed studies evaluating the results of early
education programs designed for children from low-income families. In
summary, Jensen concluded that "Compensatory education has been tried
and it apparently has failed." † It is remarkable that the opposite conclusion can be justified just as well: early childhood education programs have
been tried and they apparently have succeeded.

---

*Compare with Bruner's views about the importance of learning in early
childhood in Section 1.*
†*Compare with Austin's conclusions about summer compensatory programs
(this section).*

The simultaneous assertion of these ostensibly contradictory conclusions deserves explication. . . . For the moment, assume that the criteria for evaluating programs designed to promote educational advancement in early childhood principally include successful performance on standardized tests of scholastic achievement and of intelligence, that is, IQ tests. Judged in this way, the evidence is compelling that *large-scale* programs, such as Headstart, have apparently failed (Evans, 1969). But the evidence is equally compelling that a number of small-scale efforts have succeeded (much of this evidence is also reviewed by Jensen, 1969, pp. 104–107). . . . Thus . . . it is a relatively straightforward matter to rationalize the contradiction between judgments of both success and failure: the research and development phases of early childhood programs have succeeded, but large-scale implementation has, for the most part, failed.

Unfortunately, the question of "success" is even more complicated than the discussion thus far indicates. Jensen (1969), for example, argues that even the demonstrable benefits produced by some small-scale programs often disappear over time; gains observed in treatment groups relative to control groups at the end of preschool programs diminish by the end of the first or second grades of formal schooling. Although empirical support of this point is equivocal, the problem of diminishing benefit warrants serious examination if we want to improve present programs. . . .

The Objectives of Formal Schooling

The effectiveness of schooling practices should be judged by the degree to which they assist the student to be adaptive with respect to *extra-school* tasks. The only school tasks that should be regarded as indices of academic success must either be isomorphic with, or must entail the use of, skills that are prerequisite for effective performance on extra-school tasks.* . . . In the present discussion, the active assumption is that, for both children and adults, extra-school tasks come in an extraordinary variety: the tasks of seeking, finding, acquiring, and remembering information; the tasks of extending, transferring, and creating new information; the tasks of communicating information, thoughts, and feelings to oneself and to others as well as of comprehending such communications from others; the tasks of understanding and accurately predicting future events; and the tasks of acquiring tactics and strategies for reaching chosen goals and for enjoying the journey, either alone or in concert with others. Clearly these tasks vary widely in character; some appear practical, some intellectual, others emotional. They all share, however, a major demand that the individual develop well-honed cognitive skills and coordinate them with his actions.

It may be useful to highlight the preceding prescriptions by contrasting

---

* *What do you think the author means by "extra-school tasks"?*

them with methods presently in use for legitimizing instructional practices. Doing so, however, is fraught with difficulty since schooling practices vary so widely at all levels of public education in the United States. With this caution in mind, it can be said that instructional practices and evaluation of student progress almost never have validity in a concurrent sense. It is difficult, for example, to propose a concrete illustration of the manner in which third-grade curricula, instruction, and evaluation relate to the tasks faced by a third grader in the home, peer, and community domains of his life.

Ostensibly, it is predictive validity rather than concurrent validity that seems to provide legitimacy for current school practices.* It is argued broadly that successful learning in college is necessary for post-college success, that successful performance in secondary school is necessary for success in college, that successful performance in elementary school is necessary for success in secondary school, and so on back to the learning presumably fostered by preschool education programs. Thus, for example, it might be asserted with considerable apparent justification that the acquisition of reading skills in the primary grades is the *sine qua non* for eventual extra-school competence.

This way of legitimizing present school practice is vulnerable in two aspects. One of these concerns the timing of demands made on students for learning particular contents and skills during specified periods of schooling. These demands are justified by the notion of critical periods, as in the case of reading or language acquisition, or in terms of the presumption that the skill or content is prerequisite for some subsequent learning. Either means of justification is defensible provided that it is demonstrably valid; the problem is that for many kinds of school learning, neither a critical period (Kohlberg, 1968) nor prerequisite status has been demonstrated empirically. . . .

In a cross-national study of mathematics achievement (Husén, 1967), stratified samples were drawn from the total population of all students enrolled in the modal grade for thirteen-year-olds in twelve different nations: Finland, Germany, Japan, Sweden, Belgium, France, Israel, Netherlands, Australia, England, Scotland and the United States.† Among other observations a score was obtained for each student on a standardized test of mathematics achievement and, in an attitude inventory, on a scale designed to reflect the degree of positive attitude toward school. For each national sample, information was also obtained yielding the median age of school entry. Thus it is possible to rank the samples in terms of age of school entry and to obtain rank correlation coefficients between this variable and those of ranked mean mathematics test scores and ranked mean attitude-toward-

* *Predictive validity and concurrent validity are defined in the glossary.*
† *Husén's research is discussed also in Section 7.*

school scores. The results reveal a negligible negative correlation between age of school entry and mathematics achievement and a strong negative correlation* between entry age and attitude toward school. The average performance of students on the mathematics test did not improve significantly as a function of additional years of schooling despite the fact that the extremes of the nations sampled were separated by nearly two years of formal academic work. More alarming is the suggestion inherent in the high negative correlation between entry age and attitudes toward school that the longer the student was enrolled prior to testing the more negative his attitudes toward school itself. Clearly, there is no indication in these results that revising the mandatory age of school entry to younger levels would improve the student's chances of subsequent school success. . . .

A second source of vulnerability in the legitimizing rationale is even more serious than the first: The evidence that academic success determines, or even relates to, the level of post-school achievement is beset with a pervasive artifact and, therefore, provides little justification for the validity of school criteria of student progress. There is massive evidence that a substantial correlation exists between a variety of indices of occupational attainment, prestige, status, salary, and level of educational attainment (Duncan, Featherman, and Duncan, 1968). The artifact is that a specified level of educational attainment is usually required for entry into an occupational category. An alternative way of attempting to demonstrate the predictive validity of school criteria of student progress is to examine the relationship between school performance within occupational categories so as to escape the artifact of educational level as an entry credential.

Hoyt (1965), confining himself to studies using this alternative methodology, has reviewed a large amount of data bearing on the relationship between college grades and adult accomplishment. The results are impressive. For the most part, there is no detectable relationship between grade point average (GPA) in college and several criteria of later achievement. . . . When significant correlations have been observed in these studies, they hold only for the initial three or four years after the end of formal schooling. . . . On the whole, then, available evidence is most discouraging to the view that instructional practices and within-school criteria of student progress can be legitimized in terms of their predictive validity for later-life success.

THE FAILURE OF PRESENT SCHOOLING PRACTICES. The fact that neither concurrent nor predictive validity can be demonstrated for schooling practices would be interesting but less unsettling if (a) schooling were a benign experience and (b) the degree of within-school success did not have critical post-schooling consequences. Were both of these statements

---

* *Correlation is explained in the glossary.*

true, schooling might be legitimized in terms of its intrinsic worth as an autonomous activity. Unfortunately, schooling is not an altogether benign experience for substantial numbers of children. If schooling were a valued experience, if it did not evoke hurt, pain, and anger, it would not result in high drop-out rates, vandalism or physical aggression toward peers, teachers and administrators, nor in quiet but widespread negative attitudes toward education among those less inclined to act visibly in accord with their feelings. Furthermore, the degree of school success attained, as indexed by grades at all levels, critically affects the range of opportunity for post-school accomplishment because it is a major determinant of acceptability for entrance into occupational, social, and civic roles. . . .

SKILL PROFICIENCY VS. CONTENT PROFICIENCY. To the extent that the present analysis is valid, it calls for a reconsideration of the goals of education and revision of the practices instituted to promote and evaluate the attainment of those goals. It is appropriate to begin a discussion of such a revision with a brief restatement of the goals of education assumed here. The goal of education is to assist the student to be adaptive with respect to extra-school tasks. It is plausible to presume that the components of this goal prominently include the following three: (1) to promote the student's acquisition of a repertory of skills for accurately locating and efficiently learning new information and new skills; (2) to promote the student's acquisition of a repertory of skills for extending information, creating information, and for solving problems; (3) to promote the student's acquisition and maintenance of motivational systems that will incline him to engage in learning and problem-solving.* It is important to note that these components are content-free, that is, the kinds of information and problems and learning referred to encompass social, emotional, personal, and practical, as well as intellectual domains. . . .

The contrast between the recommendations advanced here and prevailing educational practices is best illuminated by a consideration of comparative assumptions and relative emphases. In an ironic way, American public education is still organized in accord with some of the basic assumptions of a classical philosophy of education. Principal among these is the assumption that mastery of the contents of a particular set of academic disciplines results not only in intellectually literate students, but in students amply equipped with intellectual skills as well. To be sure, the particular disciplines have changed considerably from those characterizing a traditional classical education. Proficiency in classical languages and literature, for example, is no longer expected, but this has been replaced by proficiency in modern languages and literature. Arithmetic and geometry

* *Are these component goals too broadly stated to be meaningful? Can we train students in intellectual skills apart from specific content?*

have been replaced by modern mathematics and the expectation of proficiency in some of the social and natural sciences has been added.

There is obviously nothing inherently wrong with any of these school disciplines. Nevertheless, the meaning of *proficiency* in them is open to dispute. The manner in which proficiency is judged suggests strongly that it refers to behavior demonstrating that the student has learned and can accurately recall the contents, that is, the information (both factual and theoretical) of the various disciplines.* ...

With some striking exceptions to be mentioned shortly, another possible meaning of the term proficiency receives substantially less emphasis. In this second sense, the term refers to competence in the skills that produce information and theory in the various disciplines. Some of these skills are discipline-specific, others are more general, but in most cases they can be characterized accurately as methods for acquiring, retaining, and extending or producing trustworthy or heuristic information. The contrast between these two meanings of the term proficiency may be clarified by examples. At the preschool level, content proficiency is illustrated by uttering the names of the months of the year in correct order; skill proficiency is illustrated by the subvocal rehearsing of the order of months before reciting them. At the elementary level, an example of content proficiency is listing the capitol cities of the states, given the state names as cues; skill proficiency might be constructing a mnemonic link between each of the state names and the capitol names in order to memorize them. Content proficiency at the secondary level is exemplified by stating Ohm's law; skill proficiency, by conducting experiments to test the law. At the college level, content proficiency might be expressed by answering questions drawn from a text on modern English history whereas skill proficiency might consist of writing a brief text on a subtopic of modern English history, including the prerequisite document research. At the graduate level, content proficiency is exemplified by the ordered recall of experimental results in support of a psychological hypothesis about interference as a cause of forgetting; skill proficiency might consist of formulating such a hypothesis and of subjecting it to experimental test. ...

One justification for emphasizing content over skill proficiency during formal schooling is that the acquisition of a large volume of content is prerequisite for effective skill acquisition. Similarly, a justification for teaching in terms of abstract school tasks rather than in terms of concrete extra-school tasks is that real phenomena are so complex that they retard learning. A second justification for the abstracted character of education is the assumption that the abstract mode is conceptually more powerful than the concrete. None of these justifications is compelling. With regard to the first, it has not been demonstrated that the mastery of large

---

* *This statement is supported by Guszak's research (Section 2).*

amounts of content is necessary for skill acquisition. Even if content mastery were necessary, we know that appropriate methods for presenting content can increase learning rates so as to provide ample time for skill learning in the context of immediate relevant experiences (Rohwer, 1970). The issue raised by the second justification is also in dispute. Abstract conceptual skills, as in the capacity to manipulate symbols effectively, are surely powerful, but the evidence is not at all clear that even abstract thinkers par excellence, such as mathematicians, ever abandon their penchant for manipulating ideas in terms of relatively concrete exemplars.

Thus it is possible to provide a rationale for suggesting that it might be salutary for the prevailing neo-classical philosophy of education to yield to a form of education in which objectives are explicitly defined in terms of skills.

From Objectives to Practice: The Promise of Research

Before a change in educational objectives can effect profound revisions in schooling practice, a number of questions must be answered. What kinds of skills can be taught effectively? What are the components of such skills? How does the timing and sequence of instruction in intellectual skills relate to characteristics of the child such as age, IQ, SES, and ethnicity? The fact that these questions remain unresolved is not because they are unanswerable; it is because researchers have not addressed them. Accordingly, a case will be presented here for undertaking research concerned with these issues and an illustration will be provided to prompt speculation about what such inquiry might reveal.

Virtually any intellectual skill can be taught if it can be specified in behavioral terms. This assertion can be supported by empirical research that has already been conducted (e.g., Olton and Crutchfield, 1969) or by the simple observation that, by the time they reach adulthood, many persons have acquired a modest but relatively effective repertory of such skills despite the fact that they have rarely received explicit instruction in them. To be more specific, it is plausible to believe that a variety of intellectual skills are teachable and that an enumeration of them would include virtually all of the skills that have been studied by experimental psychologists working in the areas of learning (acquisition, retention, transfer) and thinking (classification, concept attainment, problem-solving, creativity).

One strategy for achieving behavioral specification of the subprocesses that comprise learning and thinking skills ... may be illustrated in terms of the program of research we have pursued during the last several years. A recounting of this case study will also provide occasions for commenting on problems particularly in need of research and for making recommendations about promising routes to their solution.

When we began, our intent was to identify processes and conditions that promote markedly efficient learning. At this stage, we were not so much concerned with the relevance of our chosen criterion of learning for either educational or extra-school tasks as we were with selecting a tool that would permit incisive analyses of research questions. Accordingly, in most of our work, we have used the method of paired associates. Typically, this task involves presenting a list of word pairs to the learner for study and assessing his acquisition of the list by testing his ability to recall correctly one word from each pair when the other word from the pair is given as a cue. This task is not an intrinsically important one nor is its validity obvious as judged by the standard of extra-school demands. Its use, however, is justifiable in terms of the fact that a great deal is known about the method as a tool of basic research. Nevertheless, we made an important assumption in deciding on the method of paired associates, namely, that it would engage the same kinds of learning processes as are activated by other more complicated and naturally-occurring tasks. This assumption, of course, is subject to empirical verification and recently we have begun to subject it to test (Matz and Rohwer, 1971).*

At the outset, it was necessary to discover how presumably proficient learners seek to master paired-associate (PA) tasks; samples of college students were assumed to qualify as proficient. For present purposes, think in terms of PA tasks where the subject is to learn pairs of nouns in such a way that when one member of such a pair is presented, he can recall and designate correctly the other member of the pair as originally presented to him. When college students are interviewed after performing a task like this, the results indicate that those students who learn best *elaborate* the PAs (Runquist and Farley, 1964; Bugelski, 1962; Martin, Cox, and Boersma, 1965). These self-reports provide two meanings for the term *elaboration* as a method for improving learning: one verbal, the other pictorial. In the case of verbal elaboration, subjects report forming a sentence containing the two members of each pair. On the pictorial side, they report forming a mental image of the two objects or events named by the members of a pair, usually a scene in which the two objects are somehow joined, either spatially or by virtue of their joint participation in a brief episodic narrative of some kind. . . .

For one of these hypotheses, that sentence elaboration facilitates noun-pair learning, a cross-sectional developmental study (Jensen and Rohwer, 1965) provided qualified support. Samples of students were drawn from seven grade levels: kindergarten, second, fourth, sixth, eighth, tenth, and twelfth. All were assigned the task of learning the same list of noun pairs (presented pictorially) but only half of those in each sample were

* As you read more about paired associates, consider whether you think Rohwer's assumption is correct.

instructed to elaborate — to formulate and utter a sentence containing the two members of each pair when they were first presented. For second, fourth, and sixth graders, the sentence instruction had the effect of producing performance that was six to eight times as good as that usually observed for such children; in fact, these instructions increased their performance to a level equivalent with that of the older, presumably more proficient, samples. The general result for the older samples was that performance in the instructed groups was not detectably better than that in the control groups. These findings suggested that sentence elaboration is substantially responsible for the ability of more proficient (older) learners to exceed the performance of less proficient (younger) learners. Results similar to these, where learning is markedly facilitated, have now been obtained numerous times under a variety of conditions. . . .

TESTING OTHER POPULATIONS. Our next obligation was to appraise the generality of our findings for populations other than that sampled in the initial studies. In order to test the limits of our generalizations, we decided to select populations reputed to be widely disparate in performance on learning tasks: children from high-SES white residential areas and children from low-SES Black residential areas. . . .

In one respect the results of the experiments were very encouraging — our conclusions did have generality. We regularly failed to detect differences between the two populations sampled when elaboration conditions were manipulated by varying the manner in which the learning materials were presented (Rohwer, 1967, Experiment XIII; Rohwer and Lynch, 1968; Rohwer, Lynch, Levin, and Suzuki, 1968). However, when population differences in PA performance were detected, they emerged in the elaborated conditions more often than in the non-elaborated conditions (Rohwer, Ammon, Suzuki, and Levin, 1971). That is to say, high-SES white children profited more from elaborated conditions than did low-SES Black children. We next undertook to measure the effects of *training* on performing a transfer task (Rohwer and Ammon, in press). We instructed samples of high-SES white and low-SES Black second-grade children how to create connecting sentences and visual images (verbal and pictorial elaborative techniques) during five daily training sessions of fifteen minutes duration each. While this training yielded positive benefits relative to control group performance, the magnitude of benefit was rather small compared to that produced by simply presenting learning materials in an elaborated form; more improvement in performance was produced by elaborated presentation than by one and one-quarter hours of direct instruction in elaborative techniques. The population difference was more markedly in favor of the high-SES white children after training than before.

In a final attempt to test the limits of our hypothesis, we conducted another training study. . . . [T]he results revealed no detectable effects of elaboration training, despite the fact that six days of fifteen-minute instructional sessions had been given in the manner of individual tutorials.

The question posed by the failure of these two studies to improve substantially the learning efficiency of either high-SES white or low-SES Black children is the following: Why does presented elaboration facilitate learning whereas elaboration training does not? The question is challenging and the task of answering it is not an easy one. Arrayed against all of the instances of positive effects produced by presented elaboration and brief elaboration instructions is the failure of the two studies of elaboration training to produce transferable facilitation of learning.

RELATED RESEARCH FINDINGS. This account of efforts to train children in the use of elaborative skills is reminiscent of two other lines of research in experimental child psychology: research on production and mediation deficiencies (cf. Flavell, 1970), and research on facilitating the acquisition of skills characteristic of the stage of concrete operations, for example, conservation skills, as described by Piaget (cf. Kohlberg, 1968). Borrowing these two sets of constructs, it might be said that with respect to sentence elaboration skills, children of the ages sampled suffer from a production deficiency, not a mediation deficiency — when it is provided, the child can use sentence elaboration but he does not autonomously produce it himself; and, children of these ages appear not to have reached a transitional stage with respect to the use of elaboration skills, that is, they cannot be easily trained to use them on transfer tasks.

The curious aspect of these analogies is that both in the case of work on mediation and production deficiencies and in the case of developmental substages transitional to concrete operations, the chronological age range involved is typically five to seven years. In contrast, little, if any, developmental changes have been unearthed for this age range in phenomena attendant to the skills of sentence elaboration. This curiosity suggests an interesting hypothesis: *the capacity for autonomous sentence elaboration becomes visible (i.e., the production deficiency disappears) in the age range identified with the emergence of formal operations rather than during that identified with the emergence of concrete operations.*[*]

Data relevant to this hypothesis have recently been secured in an experiment designed to indicate the developmental level at which autonomous elaborative activities begin to characterize PA learning processes in children. Equal numbers of subjects were sampled from the first, third, sixth, eighth, and eleventh grades in two school districts — one serving a high-SES white population and another serving a lower-SES white population.[1] All subjects were asked to learn the same list of 36 orally presented

---

[*] *The Piagetian concepts of concrete operations and formal operations are explained by Bruner in Section 1.*

noun pairs. Within each subsample, children were randomly assigned to four treatment conditions: control, rehearsal, presented sentence, generated sentence. Instructions for the control condition directed the subject to listen to each noun pair and to learn it in such a way that he could reproduce the second member of the pair when presented with the first. In the rehearsal condition, subjects were asked to repeat aloud each noun pair immediately after it was presented until the onset of the next pair. The distinctive feature of the presented sentence condition was that every noun pair was presented in the context of a declarative sentence and subjects were instructed to repeat the sentence aloud during the inter-pair intervals. Finally, those in the generated sentence condition were asked to construct and repeat a sentence for each of the noun pairs presented. The results are displayed in Figure 1 as a function of conditions, grades, and populations.

The results for the low-SES white samples are relatively simple to describe: differences between the two sentence conditions were detectable only in the sixth-grade sample where generated sentences produced better performance than presented sentences; differences between the control and rehearsal conditions were detectable only in the eleventh grade sample where rehearsal instructions were associated with better performance than control instructions; and, at all grade levels, the combination of the two sentence conditions was associated with better performance — two to three times better than the combination of the rehearsal and control conditions. The control condition was the only one which permitted autonomous elaboration to occur; in the other conditions, the inter-item study trial interval was filled by the learner's own overt verbal activity. Thus, at some point in the age range sampled, performance in the control condition was expected to show a positive shift, relative to the other conditions, because of increased autonomous elaborative activity. As the results in Figure 1 indicate, however, such a shift did not occur for the low-SES white population at any of the grade levels.

In marked contrast, the results for the high-SES white samples show a dramatic shift of precisely the kind expected across the sixth to eleventh grade range. For grades one, three, and six, the pattern of results in the high-SES samples is similar to that of the low-SES samples: the control condition does not differ significantly from the rehearsal condition; the two sentence conditions do not differ significantly; and performance associated with the sentence conditions is markedly superior to that in the control and rehearsal conditions. In the eighth-grade samples, however, the pattern changes such that the control condition is significantly superior to the rehearsal condition although still inferior to that in the two sentence conditions. And, by the eleventh grade, the shift appears to be complete: the control condition is better than any of the others, including

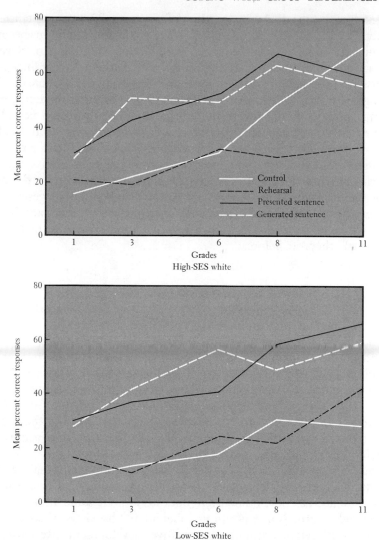

FIGURE 1.
Mean Per Cent Responses Correct
as a Function of Conditions and Grades
(upper panel: high-SES white; lower panel: low-SES white).

both sentence conditions even though the sentence conditions are still superior to the rehearsal condition. Apparently, autonomous elaborative activity, at least on this PA task, begins to emerge in high-SES white samples in the age range 11 to 14 years but does not emerge in low-SES samples even by age 17.* Finally, the deficiency in PA learning efficiency between high- and low-SES samples in the control condition becomes pronounced only in the age range spanned by the sixth to eleventh grade samples, not in the first- and third-grade samples. Accordingly, the conclusion is compelling that attempts to assist students to increase their learning skills through training in autonomous elaborative activity are more appropriate in the adolescent than in the early childhood period.

We extended the generality of these conclusions through a replication of the four-condition design which included low-SES Black sixth and eighth graders. Even more pronounced contrasts emerged relative to high-SES white performance, with the larger differences occurring in the older group. Comparison with the data of the previous study suggests, then, that population differences attributable to enhanced autonomous elaborative activity emerge more forcefully after the chronological age of (about) eleven than they do before....

IMPLEMENTATION AND POLICY IMPLICATIONS

The view of intellectual development advanced here suggests that attempts to increase the autonomous cognitive competence of students are more likely to succeed if they are delayed, for many children, until near the end of the elementary school years. The view also suggests that the probability that such efforts will succeed can be further increased by (a) designing explicit instruction to promote the acquisition of autonomous intellectual skills, and (b) by evaluating student progress and instructional effectiveness directly in terms of performances that display those skills rather than in terms of performances that demonstrate the acquisition and retention of prescribed, discipline-oriented content.

It should be made explicit that the present view of intellectual development has no necessary dependence on either a maturational or a learning view of intellectual development. It does accord, in some respects, with the relatively maturational positions inherent in the views of some exponents of a Piagetian account of cognitive development. Recently, for example, Elkind (1969) has written, "Not only is there no clear-cut longitudinal data to support the claims of the lastingness of preschool instruction, there is evidence in the opposite direction. The work cited by Jones (1954) and by Piaget (1967b) in the quotations given earlier in this paper are cases in point. This evidence, together with more recent data reported in Jensen's paper, suggest a negative correlation between early physical maturation and later intellectual attainments.... This (sic) data suggests the hypothesis that *the longer we delay formal instruction, up to certain limits, the greater the period of plasticity and the higher*

* *This is a key finding of Rohwer's research.*

the ultimate level of achievement. There is at least as much evidence and theory in support of this hypothesis as there is in favor of the early-instruction proposition (p. 332)."

The position described in this way by Elkind is also consistent with the data reviewed earlier in this paper from the study by Husén (1967) regarding the relationship between age of school entrance and mathematics achievement at age 13. Additional evidence is easy to come by. Kohlberg (1968), like Elkind, writing from a Piagetian perspective, has reviewed a number of studies designed to assess the effects of formal schooling on the age of achieving the various component structures and skills referred to as concrete operations. When the criterion used is performance on tasks of the Piaget variety, the results typically reveal no beneficial effects of schooling. . . .

Similarly, the view advanced here disavows optimism about the long-term advantages that can accrue from intensive programs of preschool education.* Skepticism on this issue arises from two convictions: that the character of learning and thinking processes in adulthood is discontinuous, in a practical sense, with the character of such processes in early childhood; and that the character of the demands made by intellectual tasks in adulthood is discontinuous with the character of task demands in early childhood. Furthermore, the present view asserts that the character of school learning tasks at virtually all levels, as education is currently conducted, is discontinuous with the character of task demands outside of school.

Despite enormous skepticism about the durability of effects achieved through intensive early childhood education, the present view of intellectual development arises from and is rooted in experimental analyses of learning phenomena. This aspect of the present view is revealed not only in the kinds of data that form its base but also in its implication that training in the use and acquisition of autonomous learning and thinking skills should be quite beneficial, *provided that such training is properly timed and sequenced.* For example, I am currently persuaded that low-SES white and Black children in the adolescent age range can be effectively assisted to engage in the kinds of mental activity that appear to make high-SES white children so proficient on PA learning tasks without explicit and systematic instruction. Such optimism about the possible salutary effects of later educational intervention is not entirely speculative. As Elkind (1969) notes, "While children all over the world and across wide ranges of cultural and socioeconomic conditions appear to attain concrete operations at about the age of 6 or 7 (Goodnow, 1969),

---

* *Has Rohwer changed your mind about the value of early childhood education? Compare his arguments and evidence with those of Deutsch (Section 4), who strongly favors early childhood education.*

the attainment and use of formal operations in adolescence, in contrast, appear to be much more subject to socioculturally determined factors such as sex roles and symbolic proficiency ... (p. 333)." And he might have added the factor of the content and procedures of schooling.

If the views advanced here were adopted, what are their implications for the content and practice of schooling for children aged eleven or twelve and under? A strong implication might be that formal schooling prior to these ages should be abandoned on the grounds that it does more harm than good. If the hypothesis proposed by Elkind (1969) is correct, this conclusion is compelling. That is to say, if formal schooling that seeks to accelerate intellectual development prior to the adolescence transition results in less plasticity and a lower final level of intellectual capacity, then it should surely be discarded.

Another line of reasoning that might be used to recommend the dissolution of early formal schooling is motivational in character. As illustrated by the results of the Husén (1967) study described previously, the effects of early school entrance on attitudes toward school are even more deleterious than its effects on mathematics achievement. This evidence is in accord with Elkind's view that current schooling practices often result in "intellectually burned" students, that is, children who, by the time they complete elementary school, have experienced frustration and failure so repetitiously that they view themselves as incapable of intellectual competence and see learning as incapable of affording them any satisfaction, much less real joy.

My own inference from all of these considerations is not that formal schooling prior to adolescence should be abandoned, but that it should be radically changed. I have already suggested the direction of changes that seem promising to me but a reiteration at this point might be in order. The guiding principle of early education (preschool and elementary) should be to provide the child with repeated experiences of gratification resulting from intellectual activity.* Lest this recommendation be grossly misread, it must be emphasized that it refers to satisfying work and play, not to training in techniques of self-indulgence and mediocrity. Accordingly, children might learn skills of auditory and visual discrimination, of counting and classifying, of feeling and satisfying curiosity, of communicating with and understanding others, even of reading and writing during the elementary years. But mastery would not be required at a particular early age, rather at the time the child can acquire the skills (and the prerequisite subskills) readily and successfully. Furthermore, those skills selected for instruction in the pre-adolescent years would be legitimized by their validity for the accomplishment of extra-school tasks either concur-

* Bane and Jencks make similar recommendations (Section 3), but for somewhat different reasons.

rently or in the future. Finally, the evaluation of student progress and of the efficacy of instruction would be in terms of the performance of skills rather than in terms of the retention of content.

This sort of revision of elementary schooling is certain to evoke considerable opposition despite argument and evidence that can be marshalled in its support. If the source of this opposition is a fear, as I suspect it is, that a system of education of the kind envisioned here will result in generations of students who, intellectually and socially, are self-indulgent know-nothings, then somehow that fear must be allayed. One strategy for accomplishing this constitutes the chief recommendations of this paper. The strategy requires a set of tactics for demonstrating the practicality of promoting the development of autonomously competent persons through instruction in intellectual skills, skills of learning and thinking, beginning at the transition to adolescence. In order to achieve such a demonstration, research and development focused on the target age range must be fostered in a massive way, for, at present, we know almost nothing about intellectual development during adolescence. It is particularly important that such programs of research should be comparative in nature, including populations of students from low-income families since it is precisely these populations that suffer the most practical damage and who are the most "intellectually burned" by current schooling practices. Fortunately, the yield of the proposed programs of research and development will be salutary as well for more affluent populations in which the damaging effects of schooling are better hidden but no less personally painful.

EXERCISE

1. How does Rohwer evaluate the success of early childhood programs designed for children from low-income families? (pp. 478–479)

2. What conclusions does Rohwer draw from Husén's research? (pp. 480–481)

3. What was the major finding of Hoyt's review of research on the relationship between college grades and adult achievement? (p. 481)

4. In Rohwer's view, what are the proper goals of education? (p. 482)

5. What methods of learning are used by students who are skillful in recalling paired associates? (pp. 485, 486)

6. What was the major finding of the study done by Rohwer and Ammon? (pp. 486–487)

7. What is the major policy implication that Rohwer draws from the research presented in his essay? (pp. 490, 492, 493)

PART FOUR

Ways To
Evaluate
Student Learning

Section Fourteen

BEHAVIORAL OBJECTIVES

Introduction

Behavioral objectives are precisely stated learning goals. They tell the educator exactly what skills the learner should acquire as a result of instruction; the skills are described in observable and measurable terms. Many educators are interested in behavioral objectives as an alternative to the statements of learning goals that usually guide instruction; for example, "the purpose of instruction is to help students become effective citizens in a Democratic society" or "the purpose is to have students acquire knowledge about the basic principles of physics." According to proponents of behavioral objectives, these statements are too vague. Two teachers both might say that their goal is to train students to become effective citizens, yet in fact they could be conducting quite different forms of instruction. Also, if learning goals are vaguely stated, they will be difficult to measure and therefore difficult to use in evaluating instruction. For example, it would be difficult to construct a test to measure whether students "know" basic principles of physics as a result of instruction. Does "knowing" mean the ability to recite the principles, to explain them in the student's own words, or to apply them in solving physics problems?

Behavioral objectives provide a more precise way of stating learning goals so that measurement is facilitated. For example, as a result of instruction, the pupil is to pronounce correctly eight out of ten "new" words by applying his knowledge of the blends *bl*, *st*, and *pr*. The precision of this goal facilitates precise measurement of what students are learning in school. The need for precise measurement has been made clear by several recent trends in education. Increasingly, parents and other members of the community want to know what students are learning or not learning in school. Also, the accountability movement in education (see Section 15) is placing more responsibility on school districts to demonstrate their effectiveness. This requires that they measure what they teach, which in turn requires precisely stated learning objectives. Another force in education that has brought behavioral objectives into prominence is the movement toward individualized instruction (see Section 10) and mastery learning (see Block, Section 15). Evaluation has a major role in these instructional models. Usually the student takes a pretest to diagnose his present performance level on a set of learning objectives; then, if necessary, he receives instruction until he can demonstrate mastery. The emphasis is on continuous evaluation of the student to guide instruction. Good evaluation requires precise measurement, which in turn requires precise statements of learning objectives.

Though behavioral objectives have had a major impact on American education, they are still considered controversial. Some critics reject behavioral objectives because they believe that certain important learning goals cannot be stated behaviorially. If you read Section 12, on competency-based teacher education, you will recall that Robert J. Nash and Russell M. Agne rejected this approach to teacher training because it was based on the use of behavioral objectives. The controversy that surrounds behavioral objectives reflects other issues in educational psychology, too, such as the conflict between behavioral and cognitive theories of learning. The formulation of behavioral objectives is consistent with the view of learning held by such behavior theorists as B. F. Skinner. They view learning as a process of shaping behavior to a predetermined goal (in effect, a behavioral objective). Cognitive learning theorists find it difficult to state behavioral objectives because they tend to focus on nonobservable learning outcomes, such as the mental processing of several ideas concurrently or the development of new cognitive capabilities. Also, they are more interested in discovery learning in which the learner generates his own knowledge. Stating behavioral objectives for this type of learning is difficult because the outcomes generally are not known in advance. Educators who view learning as a process of training students in specific knowledge and skills, such as Carl Bereiter (Section 2), tend to be more supportive of behavioral objectives than humanistic educators, such as Carl Rogers (Section 2), who believe the goals of learning are to generate self-awareness and understanding of others.

A recent review of research (P. C. Duchastel and P. F. Merrill, "The Effects of Behavioral Objectives on Learning: A Review of Empirical Studies," *Review of Educational Research*, 1973, vol. 43, no. 1, 53–69) on effects of behavioral objectives on learning provides some empirical evidence to assist in evaluating the logical arguments for and against them. According to this review, when a significant effect on learning has been found, it favors using behavioral objectives. However, studies which report no significant differences between students whose learning is based on behavioral objectives and those whose learning is not are as numerous as those which report a difference.

Given this variation of empirical evidence, what do you think about the following views?

> *Behavioral Objectives*
>
> Pro   Behavioral objectives greatly clarify the goals of education. They help both teacher and student. They contribute to improved learning for students and help the teacher better evaluate exactly what learning has occurred.
>
> Con   Behavioral objectives do more harm than good. They focus the teacher's attention on trivial learning goals. The most important goals of education cannot be stated in behavioral terms. Students' learning, therefore, is restricted rather than improved when behavioral objectives are used to guide or to evaluate learning.

The following articles include a variety of arguments about behavioral objectives. Thorwald Esbensen describes how to write objectives in the first selection. The other articles show different positions on the usefulness of objectives in education. Hans Guth argues that behavioral objectives cannot be used in teaching English. James Popham attempts to defend behavioral objectives by responding to criticisms raised by Guth and others.

Writing Instructional Objectives

Thorwald Esbensen

Thorwald Esbensen's brief article on how to write behavioral objectives (he calls them "instructional" objectives) is a good introduction to their purpose and construction. As Esbensen indicates, the purpose of an instructional objective is to specify clearly what students are supposed to be learning in a unit of instruction. One way to achieve clarity is by specifying observable skills which the student should be able to perform as a result of his learning experience. Further clarity is achieved by specifying the conditions and level of skills which can be observed if learning has been successful. As you consider the type of objectives Esbensen indicates should be written, it is important to remember that learning and performance may differ. Performance is observable. It may or may not have a one-to-one relationship with learning. For example, moving a switch to turn on an electric light is performance. But does this performance represent all that the individual has learned about

Reprinted by permission of the author and *Phi Delta Kappan*, January 1967.

what must happen before the light will illuminate; or should other types of performance also be measured to obtain a complete record of what has been learned? Also, as we noted in the introduction to this section, such learning as the development of new cognitive capabilities may not be measurable by observing performance. Esbensen's assumption that learning brings about observable changes in student behavior, therefore, warrants thoughtful examination throughout his discussion of how to construct instructional objectives. Would you use such objectives to guide your teaching?

For many years, educators have talked about the importance of instructional objectives. The purpose of an instructional objective is to make clear to teachers, students, and other interested persons *what it is that needs to be taught* — or what it is that *has been taught.**

A well-written instructional objective should say three things: (1) what it is that a student who has mastered the objective will be able to *do*, (2) under what *conditions* he will be able to do it, and (3) to what *extent* he will be able to do it. To put the matter in a single sentence, a well-written instructional objective should specify under what conditions and to what extent a certain kind of student performance can be expected to take place.

Performance — conditions — extent. Let us consider first the word *performance*. Performing means doing. A student who performs something does something.

Here are two statements. Which one is expressed in terms of student performance?

A. *The student will have a good understanding of the letters of the alphabet, A through Z.*

B. *The student will be able to pronounce the name of the letters of the alphabet, A through Z.*

Statement B tells what it is that the student will be able to *do*. He will be able to *pronounce* the names of the letters of the alphabet, A through Z.

Statement A tells us that the student will have a good *understanding* of the letters of the alphabet. But this is not very clear. We cannot tell what it is that the student is supposed to be able to *do* as a result of this understanding.

Let's try another pair of statements. Which one is expressed in terms of student performance? †

---

* *If the objective states what is to be taught, will the learner, in turn, know what he is to learn?*

† *Which of these objectives, A or B, would you prefer to have used to evaluate your learning?*

A. *The student will have an adequate comprehension of the mechanics of punctuation.*

B. *Given a sentence containing an error in punctuation, the student will correct the mistake.*

Statement B tells what it is that the student will *do*. Statement A, which says that the student will have an adequate *comprehension* of the mechanics of punctuation, is pretty vague. We cannot tell what it is that the student is supposed to be able to *do* as a result of his comprehension.

At this point, an objection may be raised. Isn't the person who is comprehending something doing something? Isn't intellectual performance an acceptable kind of student performance?

Certainly. The difficulty is that mental activity, as such, is not directly observable. We cannot literally open up a person's head and see the thinking that is going on inside. If it is to be of use to us, a statement of performance must specify some sort of behavior that can be observed.

This does not mean that we are not concerned about intellectual performance. It does mean that since mental activity, as such, is not directly observable, some sort of behavior that is observable will have to stand for or represent the intellectual performance we have in mind.*

For example, suppose that we are interested in having students know something about the writing style of Ernest Hemingway. Whatever may be intellectually involved in the attainment of this goal, it should be apparent that the language of our aim as stated leaves much to be desired.

What is the student who *knows* able to do that the student who does *not know* is not able to do? This is the important question, because we cannot measure the accomplishment of our instructional purpose until we have worked out a clear answer to it. Although there is no single answer (our objective of "knowing something" is too vague for that), here is a possible statement of desired performance: Given 10 pairs of short prose passages — each pair having one selection by Ernest Hemingway and one by a different author — the student is able, with at least 90 percent accuracy, to choose the 10 selections written by Hemingway.

Performance — conditions — extent. We have been talking about *performance*. Let us now consider *conditions*.

Here is one of our earlier statements concerning the alphabet: *The student will be able to pronounce the names of the letters of the alphabet, A through Z.* We have said that this statement is expressed in terms of student performance. Does this statement also set forth the *conditions* under which the performance is to take place?

It does not. For one thing, we cannot tell from our statement whether the student is to pronounce the names of the letters *at sight* or *from*

* *Do all types of mental activity have observable outcomes?*

memory. If the letters are to be shown, we do not know whether the student is to work with capital letters, small letters, or both.* Nor do we know whether the student is to work with these letters in regular sequence or in random order. Obviously, each set of conditions is substantially different from the rest, and will make its own special demands upon the student who attempts to accomplish the objective.

Let's examine two more statements. Which one sets forth the *conditions* under which a certain kind of performance is to take place?

A. *Given the Dolch list of the 95 most common nouns, the student will be able to pronounce correctly all the words on this list.*

B. *The student will be able to pronounce correctly at least 90 percent of all words found in most beginning reading books.*

Statement A, which tells us that the Dolch list will be used, sets the conditions for the demonstration of student mastery. We are told that these particular words, and no others, are the ones at issue for this objective.

Statement B, offering us only the dubious clue of "words found in most beginning reading books," does not tell us enough. Our conditions need to be defined more precisely than this.

We come now to the matter of the *extent* and *level* of performance. A well-written instructional objective will establish an acceptable minimum standard of achievement.

Look at this objective: *Given 20 sentences containing both common and proper nouns, the student will be able to identify with very few mistakes both kinds of nouns.* Does this objective establish a minimum standard of achievement?

It does not. It leaves open the question, How many mistakes are "a very few"?

Here is the Hemingway objective we looked at earlier: *Given 10 pairs of short prose passages — each pair having one selection by Ernest Hemingway and one by a different author — the student is able, with at least 90 percent accuracy, to choose the 10 selections written by Hemingway.* Does this objective establish a minimum standard of achievement?

It does. The student is expected to be able to make at least nine correct choices out of the 10. This constitutes a minimum standard of achievement.

Let's try one more objective: *The student should be able to pronounce from memory, and in sequence, the names of the letters of the alphabet, A through Z.* Does this objective establish a minimum standard of achievement?

It does. The objective implies that we are looking for 100 percent mas-

* *How would this information aid in evaluating students' learning?*

tcry. However, we could, if we wanted to be explicit, restate our objective in this way: *The student should be able to pronounce from memory, in sequence, and with 100 percent accuracy, the names of the letters of the alphabet, A through Z.*

An instructional objective should not ordinarily be limited to specific *means* (particular materials or methods), but should be stated in terms that permit the use of various procedures.* Look at this statement of an objective: *Given the California Test Bureau's E-F level programmed booklet on capitalization, the student is able to work through the exercises in this booklet with at least 90 percent accuracy.* Is this objective limited to the use of a particular instructional item or procedure?

It is. The objective is expressed exclusively in terms of performance with a specific booklet. Although the particular kind of skill development that is promoted by this booklet is presumably also fostered by other instructional materials and methods, no such options are available under the terms of our objective as it is now written.

Look at this statement of an objective: *Given 20 sentences containing a variety of mistakes in capitalization, the student is able, with at least 90 percent accuracy, to identify and rewrite correctly each word that has a mistake in capitalization.* Is this objective limited to the use of a particular instructional item or procedure?

It is not. The objective as expressly stated permits us to use a number of instructional items that show promise of being able to help students attain the desired performance. Among these items are not only the California Test Bureau's E-F level material but the somewhat simpler C-D level presentation, a programmed booklet by D. C. Heath, Unit 11 of English 2200, Unit 9 of English 2600, Lessons 87 and 88 of English 3200, several filmstrips on capital letters, and so on.

Finally, a well-written instructional objective will suggest how its accomplishment can be measured. This follows from our view that a well-written objective specifies under what *conditions* and to what *extent* a certain kind of student *performance* can be expected to take place.

Look at this objective: *The student should know the alphabet.* Does this objective suggest how its accomplishment can be measured?

It does not. The reason for this judgment is that *knowing the alphabet* can mean different things to different people. Therefore, depending upon what is meant, the measuring of this knowing will take different forms.

Suppose we elaborate upon our objective so that it reads: *Shown the letters of the alphabet in random order (in both upper and lower case form), the student is able to say the name of each letter with 100 percent*

---

* *Block (Section 15) supports using various methods to achieve a learning goal. Why is this desirable?*

accuracy. Does our objective now suggest how its accomplishment can be measured?

It does. The objective as stated makes plain how its accomplishment can be measured.

If teachers at all levels of schooling would be this explicit in writing instructional objectives, they might reasonably hope to eliminate almost immediately one major cause of learning failure among students: the traditional fuzziness of classroom assignments.*

EXERCISE

1. What are the three characteristics of a well-written instructional objective? (p. 500)
2. According to Esbensen, why can instructional objectives not be stated in terms of the student's intellectual performance? (p. 501)
3. Should an instructional objective specify the materials or methods that are to be used? (p. 503)
4. What is the relationship between a well-written instructional objective and the measurement of learning? (pp. 503–504)

* *As a prospective teacher, would you want to be this explicit in stating your objectives?*

The Monkey on the Bicycle: Behavioral Objectives and the Teaching of English

Hans P. Guth

> In the following paper, Hans P. Guth strongly criticizes the use of behavioral objectives in teaching English. Guth, who is an English teacher, believes that the view of instruction implied by behavioral

From *The English Journal*, September 1970, pp. 785–792. Reprinted with permission of publisher and author. Copyright © September 1970 by the National Council of Teachers of English.

The poem, "The Opening" by Jon Swan is reprinted by permission; © 1960 The New Yorker Magazine, Inc.

objectives is incompatible with the goals he tries to accomplish in his own teaching. For example, one of his goals is "making the student branch out emotionally and intellectually and opening something up through imaginative experience." Guth argues that this goal is incompatible with the behavioral objectives approach because it deals with internal experience, not overt behavior. In other words, Guth believes that the important goal in teaching English is to help the student have certain perceptions and awareness, not to teach him specific skills that can be demonstrated through behavior. Guth has a cognitive view of learning, whereas proponents of behavioral objectives subscribe to a behavioral view. One way to read this article is to assume, at least temporarily, that the three major goals of teaching English identified by Guth cannot be stated in behavioral terms. Does this mean that behavioral objectives have no place in English instruction, as Guth implies? Assuming that the three major goals cannot be stated in behavioral terms, how can we ever know if Guth, or any other English teacher, is successful?

Author's Note: Many are the movements — or "trends" — that sweep over the teaching of English. Some, like courses in rock lyrics, add a touch of color to the passing scene. Some, like semantics or transformational grammar, survive after the original disciples have discovered new prophets and add something lasting to our efforts to help students understand and master language. Some, like the liberal or "permissive" movement in usage, or our growing recognition of America's cultural and linguistic pluralism, in slow but profound ways change our conception of who we are and what we do.

All of these movements have a common element: They gained momentum because they speak to English teachers as people with a common commitment — to our language and its role in our culture. But English teachers also have to reckon with movements of a different kind: these come to us, for better or for worse, from the outside. They import into our subject assumptions not our own. They are part of more general developments that we are often powerless to resist. Such was "progressive education," now remembered mainly in the anti-liberal polemics of education's rear guard mythologists. Such was the subject-matter panic of the post-Sputnik age. And such, finally, is the current movement toward behavioral objectives, which asks English teachers to identify specific behavioral goals, to design steps leading efficiently toward these goals, and to demonstrate results by measuring observable differences in student performance after teaching has taken place. This movement has powerful support from cost-conscious public officials, business-oriented administrators, and a market-wise communications industry.

No one who knows English teachers will be surprised to find that many of them regard the behavioral objectives movement with open hostility. It asks them for "data" at a time when many of them are in search of "soul." It asks them to make their students "perform" when many of them are concerned with "reaching" the student. It asks them to administer tailor-made "learning sequences" at a time when many are concerned with liberating the student's locked-in creative and human potential. The cynic, in this situation, will feel that nothing is less likely to result from the familiar triangle of conservative administrator, liberal teacher, and radical student than increased "efficiency." No doubt, in the long run, the pent-up frustrations of the teacher and the sheer rebelliousness of today's students will defeat the manufacturers of learning modules and performance tests.

In the meantime, however, teachers want to teach. They want to teach English. To make this possible, they will have to define more articulately and more forcefully than in the past what it is that English teachers do. They will have to explain why the goal of English is something larger and more obscure than a skill that can be measured at so many words typed a minute, or so many pages read with "comprehension" in a quarter of an hour. The following talk, first delivered at the NCTE convention in Washington, D.C., November 1969 was an attempt to help towards such a definition and explanation.

...I'd like to start out with a broad generalization on this matter of defining the objectives of English. It seems to me that there are two large groups in the profession who have a position on this subject. First, there are those that I'm going to call the "vocal minority," and I mean "vocal" in the sense that they do verbalize freely about the matter of objectives. When they do a unit on place names, it is preceded by seven stated goals. They publish forty-eight approved objectives for the teaching of literature and things of this sort. On the other hand, there are the people that I am going to call the "inarticulate majority," the group to which I belong, because when I am asked to define the objectives of English, I always feel somewhat uneasy. All I really want to do is take my ditto sheet with the sample sentences from Stephen Crane, or the poem by Robert Frost. I want to go into the classroom, close the door softly behind me, and do my thing.*

For instance, I take a ditto sheet into the classroom that has some sentences in pidgin English that I collected in Hawaii last summer. I present those sentences that I collected, and we talk about them. In class, I don't particularly theorize or argue. I simply take these along and read a few of them. They go like this:

* Does this guarantee that students will learn?

My car went broke down. You can give me ride?

Yesterday she like go leech one ride from Dennis, but Dennis no like give her one.

Hurry up! We going home. You no like go or what?

He been work too hard.

Ugly dat one!

"Daddy, where you?" "I stay here."

Now suppose the assistant principal sitting in the back of the room came up to me afterward and said, "What are you doing this for? What's the point of taking this kind of thing in?" I suppose if backed into a corner, I would try to get at some of the things that I've tried to do with this ditto sheet. For example, one thing this exercise does is to help make students aware of language as language.* Everyone uses language all the time, never really thinking about it or becoming aware of it. To the student, language is much the way water is to the fish in the sea. And contrast is a great educating agent. When we see something done differently, when it doesn't fit the mode, when we look at some of these pidgin sentences and they sound like English but not quite, we say, "Now what's the difference between this and the way we say it?" And then all of a sudden we become aware of some of the things that make our language work.

Let us look at some of these expressions, such as "My car *went* broke down" and "I'm going to tell mommy you *went* do that." If we get enough of those, we realize that *went* here doesn't have anything to do with *go*. It simply expresses past tense. "You went do that" means "You did that." The *went* is a past signal. It's an "auxiliary" to help form the past tense. And as we're going through, we soon find a future signal in this pidgin dialect. The word *going* is used as a future signal. And in a statement like "I *been* go shopping," *been* is used as the "perfect" auxiliary. If we do this for awhile, the student soon says, "Well, this thing has a system. In fact, it has a grammar. It's not mistakes; it's not as though the persons who speak it make it up as they go along. They follow certain rules." † And, after the students have studied the sentences, they have learned something very essential about language: it has a system; it can be investigated; even something as unstable as this pidgin dialect has certain built-in rules.

Another thing I'm trying to get at is that the students using this kind of dialect are people, not just with parents from Korea and China, but from the Philippines, Samoa, mainland USA, and what not. Yet these people are living together in the islands, and they have to communicate in

---

* *Could this goal be stated as a behavioral objective using Esbensen's criteria?*
† *What kind of learning is involved here?*

English. I want my students to realize one important fact that stares us in the face once we think about it: Many Americans — not just in Hawaii, but all over the country — are bilingual.* And even if they aren't bilingual, somewhere in their background they have some contact with some kind of language other than English. They have some aunt, or grandmother, or friend, or somebody who, in fact, probably speaks a sort of working pidgin still, after twenty years or fifteen years or thirty years in this country. And this puts quite a different perspective on American English as a *common medium*, as something that people from many different backgrounds had to adopt or are still adopting as a means of communication. And we realize then that American English is one of the things that hold our country together. In our diversity of backgrounds and interests it provides the common medium.

Another thing I am trying to get at through these sentences is that language is basically intended to be responded to positively, to be fascinating. We don't go through these pidgin sentences in order to say, "Look at these ignorant people out there in the Pacific who can't even speak their own language properly." That's not the point of the assignment. The point of the assignment is to say, "Look at this use of language. Marvel at it. Be fascinated by it. Be entertained." This is something where we say, "Look at this kind of thing. Study it. Learn something from it."

Now, the trouble with trying to list these worthy objectives, the trouble with trying to formalize these worthy goals, is two or threefold. First of all, it's a lot to ask of these eight little sentences. It's a lot to ask to get all of these things out of this one sheet. In fact, even as I state these goals, we realize that these are not the objectives for this particular assignment. These are the *long-range goals* that we English teachers always work toward. These are the kinds of things that are implied in everything we do. For instance, fostering a positive interest in language, and showing that we approach language as a marvelous, flexible instrument, and that we are interested in what language can do — we do that all the time, even when we are off duty....

The second problem that we have with these so-called objectives is that we write all of them down in our lesson plans — this is what we want to do — and then half of it comes off in class, and the other half doesn't.† In other words, these things that I described are *opportunities*. If we have a

* *Try to state this learning goal as a behavioral objective.*
† *James Popham's response to the second reason for opposing behavioral objectives applies here. Does this open-ended approach to instruction leave too much learning to chance?*

good class hour, some of these things will come out, we hope. Some of this will come through. But we wouldn't want to be judged by results that say, "You've done Items 1 and 3, but did you slip up on Item 2!"

Finally, and most importantly, the whole thing is too *verbal*. It's so easy to state these goals that make us feel good and make us sound good, but it's so easy for these words just to be words. We are confronted in this country now with a whole generation that is suspicious of big words, brave words uttered by people over thirty. In fact, the assistant vice-principal, if he is still listening to me, by now is saying, "Hans, you are quite a talker, aren't you? In fact, now I realize why on campus they call you 'Talk-talk Guth.' "

If we talk about objectives at all in the teaching of English, we must be careful to make sure that these aims — these objectives — are not just words, that we talk not just about what people *say*, but especially what they are going to *do* in their classrooms — that we don't just talk about what people *think* about English, but also very much about what they *feel*; that we don't talk just in terms of official aims, but that we very much talk in terms of hidden premises, tacit assumptions, habits, customs, preferences, likes and dislikes. And in the short time I have left, I would like to verbalize perhaps the two or three most basic long-range goals of English, asking not just: "What is the goal officially?" but: "What kind of ditto sheet did *you* take into the classroom? And what short story did *you* assign for Monday morning? And what piece of student writing are you carrying around so that you can pin it up on the bulletin board?"

My first ditto sheet today has on it a poem, because my basic definition of an English teacher is a person who takes a poem to class or assigns a short story, or a play — in other words, someone who exposes students to imaginative literature.* And I don't mean by literature necessarily a classic. I don't mean anything élitist; I don't mean anything college-level. My little girl is in the first grade, and she comes home these days humming little tunes, reciting little verses. And I say, "There's a language arts teacher at work somewhere! Someone is doing the job that she is being paid for." So literature here is a very broad area that includes all the creative, imaginative dimension of language — from the nursery rhyme to the play by Shakespeare. The following poem from the *New Yorker* (April 2, 1960) is a dialog between the seed and the flower. I hope it will illustrate for us the first basic long-range goal of English instruction.

---

* *How would this definition of an English teacher need to be changed to meet the requirements for accountability in education? (See Section 15.)*

The Opening

by Jon Swan

Seed said to Flower:
You are too rich and wide.
You spend too soon and loosely
That grave and spacious beauty
I keep secret, inside.
You will die of your pride.

Flower said to Seed: Each opens, gladly
Or in defeat. Clenched close,
You hold a hidden rose
That will break you to be
Free of your dark modesty.

And if you say, "What's your objective in reading that poem?" I say, "I want to hear the silence deepen in the room as I read. I want to see the eyes glisten in the room. I want someone to say in the back row, 'That was nice.' " And you'll say, "Aren't you going to analyze it? Aren't you going to ask seven questions about this poem?" I say, "Yes, of course. For one thing, we want it to sink in. We want to be able to go back over it again, and we want to talk about it, and make sure the experience comes through." One intriguing thing about the poem is that the pattern is like a pendulum swinging, "Seed said to flower . . . flower said to seed." And we want to talk a little about the symbolism, because another intriguing thing about the poem is that the symbolism is so basic, that so many things in life are like the seed. Something is there that could grow, if it could only develop. In fact this whole matter of teaching English can be reduced to the metaphor of the student's potential: If we're lucky, we'll make it unfold; we'll make it broaden out. And if we're not so lucky, we will help stunt it; we will help repress it.

The first long-range goal in the teaching of English is making the student branch out emotionally and intellectually and opening something up through imaginative experience. And the important point about that is that this is not behavior in the overt sense. This deals with *internal experience.** And even though there are these external symptoms of the glistening eyes and of going to the bookshop afterwards and saying, "Do you have that collection of poems by Dylan Thomas?", those are just the symptoms. We don't teach literature just to produce the symptoms. I don't teach literature to teach the students how to make purring noises when I read Thomas to them.

. . . I have already hinted at the fact that in California we are again in

---

* *If it's an internal experience, how could Guth know when he's achieved his long-range goal?*

one of these censorship quarrels, where the textbook authors are busy going through their books changing all the *damns* to *darns*, and changing all the *My Gods*, to *My Gosh*, and changing all the *Hell no's* to *Hell yes*. In fact, one of the authors now concludes his letters "Gosh Bless." And it's a futile and degrading thing. We encounter a four-letter word, and we try to explain that this word in context is not really obscene. And we don't really know how to handle this matter successfully. Ultimately, this is a matter of how well we ourselves use language. Here you stand: you are an English teacher. You are supposed to make language work for you and be persuasive and eloquent and have the public accept your version of the thing. But we realize that this is very difficult. We seem ourselves defeated in what is actually our second major assignment as teachers: to work in this area of using language for a purpose, as an instrument in human relations, in organizations, in politics. This is our second goal — one that we English teachers often neglect, because our first love often is literature, and we don't always get around to this realization that language is around us everyday and in everyday prosaic situations. One thing we should try to do for the student is to say, "Well, here is language. You can make it work *for* you, rather than *against* you." ...

... I'm going to say just one or two words about the third long-range objective of the teaching of English. I mentioned the fact that sooner or later we ditto a little piece of student writing, or we pin something up on the board, or some of us even tape a little exchange that happened in the classroom, because, again, part of the definition of the teacher of English is that he is the person who says to the student, "Speak it to me," or "Write it to me." As one teacher said in the *English Journal*, "Dearly Beloved, say something to me. Would you please say something to me?" And when we look at these oral and written compositions that we get from our students, what do we look for?

I brought as Exhibit C a little exchange that someone recorded in a fourth-grade class, from an article called "Poetry in an Elementary Classroom." Apparently the person had taken in a Robert Frost poem, the one about the horse and the man in the woods on a winter evening, the dark lonely woods, covered with snow, the man lingering there and the horse wanting to go home to the stable. So at the end of this the teacher turned to the group and said, "Now what is the basic difference between the horse in this poem and the man?" And one student says, "Well, the horse has four legs, and the man has two." And the teacher says, "Good." And then someone else says, "One of them is happy and the other one is sad." And the teacher says, "Fine." And then another student says, "The man knows he's going to die and the horse doesn't." And the teacher doesn't say anything. He lets it sink in. And the point about that response by the student is that it is *true*. It is significant. It's worth taking in. It's worth pondering. And when composition ceases to be a skill that's taught, and becomes expression — communication — in the true sense, then we read it not as an exercise, but then we read because we want to see what the student has to say.

This perception of relations is what we aim at when we say that we want our students to think.* Thinking establishes relations within the content of the student's experience. That content builds up slowly, and from a hundred sources, many of them not funded by the school board. A good teacher tries to broaden the student's experience. But he is not so foolish as to take a bow when the student's experience quotient goes up from 68 to 92.

Summing up these three goals of English, I think we can label them roughly: first, *imagination*, the area of extending feeling and thinking on the part of the student; second, *power*, the ability to use language, for a purpose — the power of words, the power of language as a medium; third, *understanding*, the ability to relate a piece of poetry to your own experience, to relate one piece of poetry to another and talk about a common theme or something of that sort.† I call these humanistic goals, because they all have to do with the basic goals of humanistic education, which are to develop more fully and to bring out more fully whatever human potential there is in the student.

Where does this leave then people with the tests and the measurement items, the learning modules, the clearly defined, limited objectives? They come to us, and they say, "Here, you do six units of this or that, and in the statistics the performance rate goes up 25 per cent, and that is so much per dollar per pupil." All this kind of talk reminds me of the monkey we see on the Ed Sullivan show. Ed Sullivan once in a while has three trained chimpanzees who ride the bicycle. They do three laps and the audience goes wild, because the Ed Sullivan audience just loves to see a monkey do his three laps on the bicycle. In terms of overt behavior and of measurable results, and of something we can demonstrate to the taxpayer, those monkeys are a tremendous success. When they started out being educated, they knew nothing about riding a bicycle. And now that they've been trained, they ride that bicycle and they do the three laps. But when you watch the monkey a little more closely, you realize that the monkey's heart is not really in it. And all the while that he's on that bicycle, his mind is somewhere else. His attention wanders. And you realize there's more to this monkey than Ed Sullivan will ever understand. There is a great unused potential for monkey business, and for monkeyshines. So my suggestion is — and I try to word it as rationally and calmly

* *Compare with Guszak's ideas on thinking as a goal of education (Section 2).*
† *Using Esbensen's criteria in the preceding selection, try to state several conditions under which these goals might be demonstrated.*

as I can — when the measurement people come to us with their instruments, my answer is: "Don't make a monkey out of me. I refuse to get on your bicycle." *

EXERCISE

1. According to Guth, what are three problems involved in stating specific objectives for his lesson on pidgin English? (pp. 508–509)

2. According to Guth, what are the three basic long-range goals of teaching English? (p. 512)

3. What does Guth mean by, "We don't teach literature just to produce the symptoms?" (p. 510)

4. What point is Guth trying to make by his analogy of the monkey on the bicycle? (pp. 512–513)

* Has Guth made a convincing case against behavioral objectives?

Probing the Validity of Arguments Against Behavioral Goals

W. James Popham

This paper was delivered by W. James Popham to a national convention of educational researchers. Although written in the late 1960's, it is still pertinent to the current controversy surrounding behavioral objectives. Popham refutes such critics of behavioral objectives as Hans Guth (see the preceding selection) who believe that behavioral objectives do not reflect the most important goals of education. As you read Popham's comments, you will find that he deals with many arguments Guth raises. Does Popham provide an effective response to the criticism that some important instructional goals involving changing the learner's perceptions and feelings cannot be stated (or measured) behaviorially?

A symposium presentation at the annual American Educational Research Association Meeting, Chicago, February 1968. Reprinted with permission of the author.

Within the last few years a rather intense debate has developed in the field of curriculum and instruction regarding the merits of stating instructional objectives in terms of measurable learner behaviors. Because I am thoroughly committed, both rationally and viscerally, to the proposition that instructional goals should be stated behaviorally, I view this debate with some ambivalence. On the one hand, it is probably desirable to have a dialogue of this sort among specialists in our field. We get to know each other better — between attacks. We test the respective worth of opposing positions.... Yet, as a partisan in the controversy, I would prefer unanimous support of the position to which I subscribe. You see, the other people are wrong. Adhering to a philosophic tenet that error is evil, I hate to see my friends wallowing in sin.

Moreover, their particular form of sin is more dangerous than some of the time-honored perversions of civilized societies. For example, it will probably harm more people than the most exotic forms of pornography. I believe that those who discourage educators from precisely explicating their instructional objectives are often permitting if not promoting, the same kind of unclear thinking that has led in part to the generally abysmal quality of instruction in this country.

In the remainder of this paper I shall examine eleven reasons given by my colleagues in opposition to objectives stated in terms of measurable learner behaviors. I believe each of these reasons is, for the most part, invalid. There may be minor elements of truth in some; after all, the most vile pornographer must occasionally use a few clean words. In essence, however, none of these reasons should be considered strong enough to deter educators from specifying all of their instructional goals in the precise form advocated by the "good guys" in this argument....

Reason one: Trivial learner behaviors are the easiest to operationalize, hence the really important outcomes of education will be underemphasized.

This particular objection to the use of precise goals is frequently voiced by educators who have recently become acquainted with the procedures for stating explicit, behavioral objectives. Since even behavioral objectives enthusiasts admit that the easiest kinds of pupil behaviors to operationalize are usually the most pedestrian, it is not surprising to find so many examples of behavioral objectives which deal with the picayune. In spite of its overall beneficial influence, the programmed booklet by Robert Mager (1962) dealing with the preparation of instructional objectives has probably suggested to many that precise objectives are usually trivial. Almost all of Mager's examples deal with cognitive behaviors which, according to Bloom's taxonomy, would be identified at the very lowest level.

Contrary to the objection raised in reason one, however, the truth is that explicit objectives make it far *easier* for educators to attend to *important* instructional outcomes. To illustrate, if you were to ask a social science teacher what his objectives were for his government class and he responded as follows: "I want to make my students better citizens so that they can function effectively in our nation's dynamic democracy," you would probably find little reason to fault him. His objective sounds so profound and eminently worthwhile that few could criticize it. Yet, beneath such facades of profundity, many teachers really are aiming at extremely trivial kinds of pupil behavior changes.* How often, for example, do we find "good citizenship" measured by a trifling true-false test. Now if we'd asked for the teacher's objectives in operational terms and had discovered that, indeed, all the teacher was attempting to do was promote the learner's achievement on a true-false test, we might have rejected the aim as being unimportant. But this is possible *only* with the precision of explicitly stated goals.

In other words, there is the danger that because of their ready translation to operational statements, teachers will tend to identify too many trivial behaviors as goals. But the very fact that we can make these behaviors explicit permits the teacher and his colleagues to scrutinize them carefully and thus eliminate them as unworthy of our educational efforts. Instead of encouraging unimportant outcomes in education, the use of explicit instructional objectives makes it possible to identify and reject those objectives which are unimportant.

Reason two: Prespecification of explicit goals prevents the teacher from taking advantage of instructional opportunities unexpectedly occurring in the classroom.

When one specifies explicit *ends* for an instructional program there is no necessary implication that the *means* to achieve those ends are also specified.† Serendipity in the classroom is always welcome but, and here is the important point, *it should always be justified in terms of its contribution to the learner's attainment of worthwhile objectives.* Too often teachers may believe they are capitalizing on unexpected instructional opportunities in the classroom, whereas measurement of pupil growth toward any defensible criterion would demonstrate that what has happened is merely ephemeral entertainment for the pupils, temporary diversion, or some other irrelevant classroom event.

Prespecification of explicit goals does not prevent the teacher from taking advantage of unexpectedly occurring instructional opportunities in the classroom, it only tends to make the teacher justify these spontaneous learning activities in terms of worthwhile instructional ends. There are undoubtedly gifted teachers who can capitalize magnificently on the most

* *Might this happen with the three learning goals identified by Guth in the preceding selection?*
† *Esbensen also recommends that objectives allow for multiple ways to acquire a particular skill. Would he include this type of spontaneous event?*

unexpected classroom events. These teachers should not be restricted from doing so. But the teacher who prefers to probe instructional periphery, just for the sake of its spontaneity, should be deterred by the prespecification of explicit goals.

Reason three: Besides pupil behavior changes, there are other types of educational outcomes which are important, such as changes in parental attitudes, the professional staff, community values, etc.

There are undoubtedly some fairly strong philosophic considerations associated with this particular reason. It seems reasonable that there are desirable changes to be made in our society which might be undertaken by the schools. Certainly, we would like to bring about desirable modifications in such realms as the attitudes of parents. But as a number of educational philosophers have reminded us, the schools cannot be all things to all segments of society. It seems that the primary responsibility of the schools should be to educate effectively the youth of the society. And to the extent that this is so, all modifications of parental attitudes, professional staff attitudes, etc., should be weighed in terms of a later measurable impact on the learner himself. For example, the school administrator who tells us that he wishes to bring about new kinds of attitudes on the part of his teachers should ultimately have to demonstrate that these modified attitudes result in some kind of desirable learner changes. To stop at merely modifying the behavior of teachers, without demonstrating further effects upon the learner, would be insufficient.

So while we can see that there are other types of important social outcomes to bring about, it seems that the school's primary responsibility is to its pupils. Hence, all modifications in personnel or external agencies should be justified in terms of their contribution toward the promotion of desired pupil behavior changes.

Reason four: Measurability implies behavior which can be objectively, mechanistically measured, hence there must be something dehumanizing about the approach.

This fourth reason is drawn from a long history of resistance to measurement on the grounds that it must, of necessity, reduce human learners to quantifiable bits of data. This resistance probably is most strong regarding earlier forms of measurement which were almost exclusively examination-based, and were frequently multiple-choice test measures at that. But a broadened conception of evaluation suggests that there are diverse and extremely sophisticated ways of securing qualitative as well as quantitative indices of learner performance.*

One is constantly amazed to note the incredible agreement among a group of judges assigned to evaluate the complicated gyrations of skilled

---

* *Holt (Section 16) opposes all forms of testing and grading. How would he react to the idea of qualitative measures of performance?*

springboard divers in the televised reports of national aquatic champion-
ships. One of these athletes will perform an exotic, twisting dive and a
few seconds after he has hit the water five or more judges raise cards reflecting their independent evaluations which can range from 0 to 10.
The five ratings very frequently run as follows: 7.8, 7.6, 7.7, 7.8, and 7.5.
The possibility of reliably judging something as qualitatively complicated
as a springboard dive does suggest that our measurement procedures do
not have to be based on a theory of reductionism. It is currently possible
to assess many complicated human behaviors in a refined fashion. Developmental work is underway in those areas where we now must rely on
primitive measures.

*Reason five: It is somehow undemocratic to plan in advance precisely
how the learner should behave after instruction.*

This particular reason was raised a few years ago in a professional journal
(Arnstine, 1964) suggesting that the programmed instruction movement
was basically undemocratic because it spelled out in advance how the
learner was supposed to behave after instruction. A brilliant refutation
(Komisar and McClellan, 1965) appeared several months later in which
the rebutting authors responded that instruction is by its very nature undemocratic and to imply that freewheeling democracy is always present
in the classroom would be untruthful. Teachers generally have an idea
of how they wish learners to behave, and they promote these goals with
more or less efficiency. Society knows what it wants its young to become,
perhaps not with the precision that we would desire, but certainly in general. And if the schools were allowing students to "democratically" deviate
from societally mandated goals, one can be sure that the institutions
would cease to receive society's approbation and support.

*Reason six: That isn't really the way teaching is; teachers rarely specify
their goals in terms of measurable learner behaviors; so let's set realistic
expectations of teachers.*

Jackson (1966) recently offered this argument. He observed that teachers just don't specify their objectives in terms of measurable learner behavior and implied that, since this is the way the real world is, we ought
to recognize it and live with it. Perhaps.

There is obviously a difference between identifying the status quo and
applauding it. Most of us would readily concede that few teachers specify
their instructional aims in terms of measurable learner behaviors; *but they
ought to.* What we have to do is to mount a widespread campaign to
modify this aspect of teacher behavior. Instructors must begin to identify
their instructional intentions in terms of measurable learner behaviors.
The way teaching really is at the moment just isn't good enough.

*Reason seven: In certain subject areas, e.g., fine arts and the humanities,
it is more difficult to identify measurable pupil behaviors.*

Sure it's tough. Yet, because it is difficult in certain subject fields to identify measurable pupil behaviors, those subject specialists should not be allowed to escape this responsibility. Teachers in the fields of art and music often claim that it is next to impossible to identify acceptable works of art in precise terms but they do it all the time. In instance after instance the art teacher does make a judgment regarding the acceptability of pupil-produced artwork. What the art teacher is reluctant to do is put his evaluative criteria on the line. He has such criteria. He must have to make his judgments. But he is loath to describe them in terms that anyone can see.

Any English teacher, for example, will tell you how difficult it is to make a valid judgment of a pupil's essay response. Yet criteria lurk whenever this teacher does make a judgment, and these criteria must be made explicit.* No one who really understands education has ever argued that instruction is a simple task. It is even more difficult in such areas as the arts and humanities. As a noted art educator observed several years ago, art educators must quickly get to the business of specifying "tentative, but clearly defined criteria" by which they can judge their learners' artistic efforts (Munro, 1960).

Reason eight: While loose general statements of objectives may appear worthwhile to an outsider, if most educational goals were stated precisely, they would be revealed as generally innocuous.

This eighth reason contains a great deal of potential threat for school people. The unfortunate truth is that much of what is going on in the schools today is indefensible. Merely to reveal the nature of some behavior changes we are bringing about in our schools would be embarrassing. As long as general objectives are the rule, our goals may appear worthwhile to external observers. But once we start to describe precisely what kinds of changes we are bringing about in the learner, there is the danger that the public will reject our intentions as unworthy. Yet, if what we are doing is trivial, educators would know it and those who support the educational institution should also know it. To the extent that we are achieving innocuous behavior changes in learners, we are guilty. We must abandon the ploy of "obfuscation by generality" and make clear exactly what we are doing. Then we are obliged to defend our choices.

Reason nine: Measurability implies accountability; teachers might be judged on their ability to produce results in learners rather than on the many bases now used as indices of competence.

This is a particularly threatening reason and serves to produce much teacher resistance to precisely stated objectives. It doesn't take too much insight on the part of the teacher to realize that if objectives are specified in terms of measurable learner behavior, there exists the possibility that

---

* *Would explicit evaluative criteria given at the beginning of instruction help you as a student learn more?*

the instructor will have to become *accountable* for securing such behavior changes.* Teachers might actually be judged on their ability to bring about desirable changes in learners. They should be.

But a teacher should not be judged on the particular instructional *means* he uses to bring about desirable *ends*. At present many teachers are judged adversely simply because the instructional procedures they use do not coincide with those once used by an evaluator when "he was a teacher." In other words, if I'm a supervisor who has had considerable success with open-ended discussion, I may tend to view with disfavor any teachers who cleave to more directive methods. Yet, if the teacher using the more direct methods can secure learner behavior changes which are desirable, I have no right to judge that teacher as inadequate. The possibility of assessing instructional competence in terms of the teacher's ability to bring about specified behavior changes in learners brings with it far more assets than liabilities to the teacher. He will no longer be judged on the idiosyncratic whims of a visiting supervisor. Rather, he can amass evidence that, in terms of his pupils' actual attainments, he is able to teach efficiently.

Even though this is a striking departure from the current state of affairs, and a departure that may be threatening to the less competent, the educator must promote this kind of accountability rather than the maze of folklore and mysticism which exists at the moment regarding teacher evaluation.

Reason ten: It is far more difficult to generate such precise objectives than to talk about objectives in our customarily vague terms.

Here is a very significant objection to the development of precise goals. Teachers are, for the most part, far too busy to spend the necessary hours in stating their objectives and measurement procedures with the kind of precision implied by this discussion. It is said that we are soon nearing a time when we will have more teachers than jobs. This is the time to reduce the teacher's load to the point where he can become a professional decision-maker rather than a custodian. We must reduce public school teaching loads to those of college professors. This is the time when we must give the teacher immense help in specifying his objectives. Perhaps we should *give* him objectives from which to choose, rather than force him to generate his own.† Many of the federal dollars currently being used to support education would be better spent on agencies which would produce alternative behavioral objectives for all fields at all grade levels. At any rate, the difficulty of the task should not preclude its accom-

* *This type of reasoning is the basis for the move to accountability and performance contracting (see Section 15).*
† *If Guth (in the preceding selection) were given objectives, would he use them?*

plishment. We can recognize how hard the job is and still allocate the necessary resources to do it.

Reason eleven: In evaluating the worth of instructional schemes it is often the unanticipated results which are really important, but prespecified goals may make the evaluator inattentive to the unforeseen.

Some fear that if we cleave to behaviorally stated objectives which must be specified prior to designing an instructional program, we will overlook certain outcomes of the program which were not anticipated yet which may be extremely important. They point out that some of the relatively recent "new curricula" in the sciences have had the unanticipated effect of sharply reducing pupil enrollments in those fields. In view of the possibility of such outcomes, both unexpectedly good and bad, it is suggested that we really ought not spell out objectives in advance, but should evaluate the adequacy of the instructional program after it has been implemented.

Such reasoning, while compelling at first glance, weakens under close scrutiny. In the first place, really dramatic unanticipated outcomes cannot be overlooked by curriculum evaluators. They certainly should not be. We should judge an instructional sequence not only by whether it attains its prespecified objectives, but also by any unforeseen consequences it produces. But what can you tell the would-be curriculum evaluator regarding this problem? "Keep your eyes open" doesn't seem to pack the desired punch. Yet, it's about all you can say. For if there is reason to believe that a particular outcome may result from an instructional sequence, it should be built into the set of objectives for the sequence. To illustrate, if the curriculum designers fear that certain negative attitudes will be acquired by the learner as he interacts with an instructional sequence, then behavioral objectives can be devised which reveal whether the instructional sequence has effectively counteracted this affective outcome. It is probably always a good idea, for example, to identify behavioral indices of the pupil's "subject-approaching tendencies." We don't want to teach youngsters how to perform mathematical exercises, for example, but to learn to hate math in the process.*

Yet, it is indefensible to let an awareness of the importance of unanticipated outcomes in evaluating instructional programs lead one to the rejection of rigorous preplanning of instructional objectives. Such objectives should be the primary, but not exclusive, focus in evaluating instruction.

While these eleven reasons are not exhaustive, they represent most of the arguments used to resist the implementation of precise instructional objectives. In spite of the very favorable overall reaction to explicit objectives during the past five to ten years, a small collection of dissident edu-

---

* *How might you measure quantitatively whether a student likes or hates math?*

cators has arisen to oppose the quest for goal specificity. The trouble with criticisms of precise objectives isn't that they are completely without foundation. As conceded earlier, there are probably elements of truth in all of them. Yet, when we are attempting to promote the wide-scale adoption of precision in the classroom, there is the danger that many instructors will use the comments and objections of these few critics as an excuse from thinking clearly about their goals. Any risks we run by moving to behavioral goals are miniscule in contrast with our current state of confusion regarding instructional intentions. The objections against behaviorally stated goals are not strong enough. To secure a dramatic increase in instructional effectiveness we must abandon our customary practices of goal-stating and turn to a framework of precision.*

EXERCISE

1. What is Popham's rationale for saying that explicit objectives make it easier for educators to attend to important instructional outcomes? (pp. 514–515)

2. How does Popham counter the criticism that objective measurement of human learning or performance is dehumanizing? (pp. 516–517)

3. According to Popham, what steps might be taken to develop objective measures of learning in the arts and humanities? (p. 518)

4. According to Popham, why should teachers not be held accountable for the instructional procedures that they use in class? (p. 519)

5. How does Popham counter the criticism that prespecified goals will make the curriculum evaluator overlook important, unforeseen consequences of a new curriculum? (p. 520)

* *Will increased precision improve learning outcomes?*

Section Fifteen

THE ACCOUNTABILITY MOVEMENT

Introduction

Who should be held accountable for whether students learn in school? Should it be teachers and school administrators, parents, or perhaps the students themselves? These questions have become important to American educators in recent years. Out of these questions has grown the accountability movement, whose followers seek to make teachers and administrators accountable, that is, responsible for whether students achieve or fail in school. Although the literature does not always make it clear to whom they are accountable, generally in an accountability program teachers are accountable to administrators, and the administrators are accountable to the school board, parents, citizens, and various funding agencies.

The accountability movement has been supported and influenced by several other recent developments in education. First, educators' conceptions of the causes of individual differences in learning have gradually shifted. In the past intelligence and aptitude were the main explanations for why some students do well in school, whereas others fail. A related belief is that intelligence and aptitude are inherited characteristics (see Jensen, Section 3), and therefore the schools cannot be held accountable for student failure to learn. However, the predominant contemporary view is that intelligence and aptitude are highly influenced by the environment. It follows then that most students are capable of success in learning, given appropriate instruction. If students fail to learn, the schools are to blame for providing ineffective instruction. The accountability movement adheres strongly to this contemporary view of the cause of learning failure.

A related trend is the growing interest which many people (particularly those who pay the costs of education) have in educational "outputs." In the past, educators have attempted to improve education primarily by increasing the quantity and quality of "inputs." Inputs are the many factors which are introduced to influence the learning behavior of students, for example, teachers, textbooks, instructional techniques, and inservice teacher training. As the costs of these inputs increased dramatically in the last decade, many have asked, "Are these inputs effective?" That is, do increases in input, such as hiring more teachers to reduce class size, result in increased output? Output usually means student learning in the form of acquisition of knowledge, skill, and understanding and development of such affective attributes as self-concept, attitudes, and values — the main outcomes of the educational process. Outputs can be measured quantitatively by students' scores on tests, number of students who graduate from high school, and other ways.

Input and output have become part of the language of the accountability movement. Increasingly, educators are being asked to demonstrate that a certain amount of input will result in a certain amount of output. In the past a school district might have applied for federal funds, perhaps to purchase audiovisual equipment, which would be justified by presenting a rationale based on principles of educational psychology. Now it is likely that the district also will have to evaluate this input to determine whether it results in improved learning (the output) among students who use it. In short, educators are being held accountable for their expenditures.

As this discussion suggests, the accountability movement is compelling educators to take a renewed interest in measuring learning. Because they are being held accountable for student achievement, teachers want to be sure that the tests accurately reflect what they have taught and what their students have learned. Educators also are taking a renewed interest in behavioral objectives because they must know precisely what their objectives are to determine whether the tests accurately measure them. It should be no surprise, then, to find that behavioral objectives are an integral component of most accountability programs. Also, when we say that educators are accountable, it means that they are accountable to various groups which usually do not have professional training in education. Therefore, information about what a student has learned must be communicated in terms that are clear and easily interpreted. This is one of the purported advantages of behavioral objectives.

Another feature of accountability programs related to evaluation is that student progress in learning is monitored more frequently than in traditional programs. Because accountability makes teachers responsible for student learning, they are likely to test students more often for diagnostic purposes. For example, the teacher may wish to determine whether further practice or change in instructional strategy is needed so that the student will eventually master a particular learning objective.

Advocates of the accountability movement claim that it will improve education in several ways. First, it places the burden of responsibility on educators to bring about student learning. They cannot ignore students. They must show results, as evidenced by students' scores on objective tests. Some people believe that the accountability movement will be of particular benefit to minority-group students, whom they claim have been ignored and allowed to fail unnecessarily under the traditional system. A second claim is that accountability takes the burden of failure off the student. In an accountability program, the student cannot be made to feel that he lacks intelligence if he has difficulty in learning. Rather, he will be motivated by the teacher's imposed responsibility for having him succeed in school. A third advantage claimed for the accountability movement is that it will facilitate educational reform. As educators become accountable for producing results, that is, improved test scores, we should expect them to abandon ineffective instructional techniques and to adopt new ones that succeed. Fourth, as educators become more accountable to the public which supports them, communication should be improved between them, which may increase public support of education and involvement in the educational process.

As with almost any new movement in education, accountability is controversial. Some critics see serious disadvantages in the accountability approach:

1. Accountability programs often rely on behavioral objectives, which provide too narrow a focus for instruction. (For other criticisms of behavioral objectives, see Nash and Agne, Section 12; Guth, Section 14.)

2. Accountability programs place too much emphasis on students' test performance, which presents a danger that teachers will teach-to-the-test, and will ignore important learning objectives not covered by the test. A related criticism is that students will become preoccupied with earning good scores on tests, and thus will not emphasize the real purpose of education, which is to learn.

3. The accountability movement places responsibility where it may not belong. In an accountability program the teachers and administrators are usually held responsible for student learning. However, ample evidence (see Part II) indicates that parents and the out-of-school environment have a major influence on student learning. Should educators be held accountable for students' success in school if they do not have control of students' out-of-school learning experiences?

4. Accountability tends to pervert the educational process, because its educators view instruction as a process of inputs and outputs, rather than as a process which involves people who have individual needs and feelings.

5. Some critics believe that educational tests can accurately measure individual differences in school achievement, but they are not capable of measuring gains in student learning. Because accountability programs require measurement of learning gains, they cannot function properly without valid tests designed for this purpose. (Mecklenburger and Wilson in this section discuss this point.)

The critics of accountability might agree with its advocates that reform in education is urgently needed. However, they do not agree that the accountability movement will bring about the type of reform which is best for students.

The articles in this section provide background information about the accountability movement in education, and some of the arguments supporting or criticizing it. James H. Block describes a model of mastery learning, the principles of which underlie most accountability programs now in use. Performance contracting (also called "educational engineering") is a type of accountability program in which a private educational firm is hired by a school district to raise the achievement level of some or all of the district's students. The firm is held accountable in that payment for their services by the school district is tied to students' learning gains during a specified time. In their article, James Mecklenburger and John A. Wilson discuss the strengths and weaknesses of performance contracting. The article that follows by Edmund Farrell is strongly critical of performance contracting. The next three selections are discussions of the National Assessment program, a major effort to measure what students are learning in the schools throughout the United States. Ralph Tyler discusses how National Assessment can be used in accountability programs. J. Stanley Ahmann presents some of the findings that resulted from the first year's assessment activities. Zoe Von Ende provides perspective on National Assessment by presenting her firsthand observations of its current strengths and weaknesses in carrying out its mission.

The following views reflect some major issues involved in the accountability movement. Where do you stand?

Accountability of Teachers

Pro   All or nearly all students can be expected to master the skills and knowledge needed to function successfully in a sophisticated, technological society. Teachers, therefore, should be expected to have at least 90 per cent of the students in their classes master the learning objectives assigned to them. Teachers whose students do not perform this well should be required to receive new training or leave teaching.

Con   Even if all students can master the skills and knowledge required in modern society, many things can influence when a particular student will be ready to learn them and how and where he will learn them. The teacher is only one of many persons and agencies who can affect his learning. Teachers, therefore, cannot be held accountable for the learning outcomes of their students.

Accountability Programs

Pro   It is important to know what is being achieved by students for the dollars spent. National Assessment and performance contracting are making a valuable contribution by providing us with this information.

Con   National Assessment and performance contracting encourage teachers to teach-to-the-test. Also they emphasize a limited range of learning objectives so the information they provide about student learning is of limited value.

Teachers, Teaching, and Mastery Learning

James H. Block

Learning for mastery is a new approach to instruction and evaluation of students. According to James H. Block, mastery learning should enable at least 90 per cent of students to succeed, that is, to receive the equivalent of A grades. The essential feature of mastery learning is that students are given all the time they need to achieve a given level of performance in a school subject. Also, as students work through a unit of instruction, they are tested frequently to determine their progress and the need for alternative instructional procedures and materials. In contrast, traditional schooling usually provides the same instruction to all students in the same amount of time. Traditional grading makes the assumption that only a small percentage of students will succeed; typically, only ten or fifteen percent of students receive A grades in a course. Because Block believes that most students can succeed with good instruction, he holds schools accountable for providing that instruction. He does not believe that teachers and administrators can blame students' failure to learn on their lack of aptitude. According to Block and others, aptitude is not inborn; rather, it is a function of how much time the student needs and is allowed to master a subject. As you read this selection, you might compare the principles of mastery learning with the curriculum program called Individually Prescribed Instruction, described in the Lindvall and Bolvin article (Section 10). Would mastery learning work for any or all school subjects?

From *Today's Education*, November 1973. Reprinted with permission of *Today's Education*, NEA Journal, and the author.

For example, do you think it is possible and desirable to design instruction so that 90 per cent of a random sample of students achieve mastery of calculus?

In recent years, it has become fashionable among critics of American education to blame our teachers' lack of ability, dedication and/or motivation for the many problems consuming our schools. While these critics may be right in a few cases, evidence continues to mount that they are wrong in the vast majority (see for example, Peterfreund, 1970). For the most part, our teachers lack neither the abilities nor the intentions to be good teachers. What they often do lack are the instructional *tools* required to translate their abilities and intentions into action.

Over the last few years, therefore, educational researchers have begun to develop fledgling theories of instruction from which these tools might be identified, developed where missing, and made available to teachers. One of the best known of these theories is mastery learning. While not all scholars accept this theory, mastery learning is one of the few approaches to instruction that has consistently yielded improved student learning under a wide variety of conditions both here and abroad (Block, 1971, 1973a; Peterson, 1972). Accordingly, the purpose of this paper is to introduce the reader to the theory and practice of mastery learning.

A Brief History of Mastery Learning

Mastery learning is both a philosophy about schooling and an associated set of instructional strategies whereby this philosophy can be implemented in the classroom. This philosophy asserts that under appropriate instructional conditions virtually *all* students can and will learn well most of what they are taught.*

Actually, the roots of this philosophy go back several hundred years. For example, they can be found in the writings of the Jesuits, Comenius, Pestalozzi and Herbart (Bloom, 1973). But it was only in the latter part of the 19th century and in the early years of the 20th that the mastery learning idea was applied to U.S. education by figures such as Washburne and Morrison (Block, 1971). And it was not until the late 1950's and early 60's that the technology required to sustain an efficient and effective mastery learning strategy became available. Only in roughly the last decade, therefore, have feasible mastery learning procedures become available to the American classroom teacher.

There are two major types of mastery learning strategies presently in use (Block, 1971, 1973a and b). Both types attempt to better individualize instruction by (a) helping students when and where they have learning

* *This is a basic premise of accountability in education.*

difficulties, (b) giving them sufficient time to learn, and (c) clearly defining what they will be expected to learn and to what level. But one type uses primarily an *individually-based* instructional format where each student learns independently of his classmates [see for example, Computer Assisted Instruction (Atkinson, 1968; Suppes, 1966); Individually Prescribed Instruction (Glaser, 1968); Personalized System of Instruction (Keller, 1968); and Audio-Tutorial Instruction (Postlethwait, Novak, and Murray, 1969)].* The other employs a *group-based* approach where each student learns cooperatively with his classmates [see, for example, Bloom (1968), Kim (1971)]. Since few schools may possess the resources required to implement an individually-based approach to mastery learning, let us focus here on only one example of the group-based approaches, *viz.*, Bloom's (1968) "Learning for Mastery" strategy.[1]

BLOOM'S "LEARNING FOR MASTERY" STRATEGY

The genesis for Bloom's mastery learning ideas was a conceptual model of *school learning* suggested by Carroll (1963). This model rested on the observation that a student's aptitude for a particular subject predicted either the level to which he could learn the subject in a given time or the time he would require to learn it to a given level. Hence, rather than defining aptitude as an index of the level to which a student could learn, Carroll defined *aptitude as a measure of learning rate*.† A student with high aptitude for a subject would learn it quickly, while one with a low aptitude would learn it more slowly.

In its simplest form, Carroll's model suggested that if each student was allowed the time he needed to learn some subject to some mastery criterion and he spent the necessary time, then he would be likely to attain mastery. The time spent was determined by either the student's *perseverance*, i.e., the amount of time he was willing to spend actively engaged in learning, or the *time* he was *allowed* to learn. The *time needed*, on the other hand, was determined by the student's *aptitude* for the topic, the *quality* of his instruction and the instructional materials and the student's *ability to understand* the instruction and the materials. If the quality of instruction and the instructional materials was high, then the student would readily understand the instruction and would need little time to learn the topic beyond that required by his aptitude. If the quality of the instruction and the materials was low, however, then the student would need much additional time.

Bloom transformed this conceptual model into a working model for mastery learning by the following logic. If aptitude was predictive of the

---

* Some of these instructional approaches are described in Section 10.
† Which view of aptitude would help you be most effective as a teacher?

rate, but not necessarily the *level*, to which a student could learn, it should be possible to fix the degree of learning expected of each student at some mastery performance level. Then, by attending to the time allowed and the quality of instruction — the variables under teacher control in Carroll's model — the teacher should be able to ensure that each student attain this level.

Elaborating on this logic, Bloom argued that if students were normally distributed with respect to aptitude for some subject and they were provided with *uniform* instruction in terms of time allowed and the quality of their instruction, then few students would attain mastery and the relationship between aptitude and achievement would be high. But if each student received *differential* instruction, in terms of the time allowed and the quality of his instruction, then a majority of students, perhaps 95 per cent, could be expected to attain mastery and there should be little or no relationship between aptitude and achievement.

The mastery learning strategy developed in accordance with this reasoning is designed for use in the group-based instructional situation where the calendar time allowed for learning is relatively fixed. As noted above, Carroll's (1963) model of school learning proposed that each student can master a given topic if he is provided the time he needs to learn. Consequently, Bloom's mastery learning strategy attempts to minimize the time a student needs to learn so that it is within the fixed amount of calendar time available. This is accomplished through two distinct sets of steps. One set occurs prior to the actual classroom instruction. The second takes place in the classroom. In discussing both sets of steps, I will first describe what should occur in theory and then what does occur in practice.

PRE-CONDITIONS FOR MASTERY LEARNING

The teacher who wishes to achieve mastery learning begins by adopting the assumption that most of his students can learn well and that he can teach so that most *will* learn well. Practically, this means that the teacher shifts from the belief that only a small percentage of his students can really earn A's to the belief that almost all of them can earn A's.* It also means that the teacher decides to base each student's grade on his actual performance rather than on the student's rank in class.

The teacher, then, turns to the problem of formulating what he means by mastery of his course.† Ideally, the teacher would first define what material all students will be expected to learn. This entails the formulation

---

* How does this view of student performance fit with Holt's views regarding testing and grading (see Section 16)?
† Compare this process with the way IPI materials are developed (see Lindvall and Bolvin, Section 10).

of a set of course objectives. He would then determine to what level or mastery performance standard they would be expected to achieve these objectives. Finally, the teacher would prepare a final or summative examination (Bloom, Hastings, and Madaus, 1971) over all these objectives for administration at the course's close. Each student's score on this test could then be compared against the pre-set mastery standard to test for mastery or non-mastery of the course's objectives.

In actual practice, though, teachers have found it useful to use their old course achievement tests as their working definition of the material that each student will be expected to master. They have also found it convenient to administer one or more of these tests throughout the course for grading purposes. Finally, rather than grading the student's performance on a mastery/non-mastery basis, the teachers have found it useful to fix an absolute grading scale wherein mastery corresponds to a grade of A or B and non-mastery corresponds to a grade of C, D, or F. This scale is formed by determining the level of performance that students traditionally had to exhibit on the course examinations in order to earn an A, B, C, D, or F. All students who achieve to a particular level using mastery learning methods then receive the grade that corresponds to this level.*

Next, the teacher breaks his course into a sequence of smaller learning units where each unit typically covers about two weeks' worth of material. In practice, these units will correspond roughly to chapters in the course textbook or to a set of topics. Then, for each unit he develops perhaps the single most important component of the Bloom-type mastery learning strategy, the unit *feedback/correction* procedures. The purpose of these procedures is to monitor the effectiveness of the group-based instruction so that it can be supplemented and/or appropriately modified to better suit the learning requirements of each student.

First, the teacher constructs a brief, ungraded, diagnostic-progress test or *formative* evaluation instrument for each unit (see Airasian, 1971 or Bloom, Hastings and Madaus, 1971). The quizzes and homework that most teachers now use to determine how students are progressing ordinarily do not describe student learning in great enough detail so that the teacher is able to prescribe what each student might do to overcome his particular learning problems. Mastery learning requires *prescriptive* evaluation instruments such as these formative tests.

These tests are explicitly designed to be an integral part of each unit's instruction and to provide specific information or feedback to both the teacher and the student about how the student *is changing* as a result of the group-based instruction. Typically, a score of less than 80 to 85 per

---

* *Is this grading procedure consistent with the views of aptitude described earlier in this article?*

cent correct on these tests indicates that the student is having learning problems.

Then the teacher develops a set of alternative instructional materials or correctives keyed to each item on each unit formative test. All students cannot learn for mastery unless some students are provided with alternative ways of learning certain material in addition to the group-based instruction. To date, cross-age and same-age peer tutoring and especially small group study sessions in which each student is given a chance to teach and to be taught have proven to be highly effective. Alternative textbooks, workbooks, programmed instruction materials, academic games and puzzles, and selected "affective" educational exercises (Brown, 1971) have also been tried.*

These correctives teach the material tested by each item, but they do so in ways that differ from the group-based instruction. Typically the correctives will attempt to present the material in a different sensory mode or modes or in a different form of the same mode than will the group-based instruction and/or to involve the student in a different fashion and/or to provide not only different types of encouragements for learning but also different amounts of each type. Should a student encounter difficulty in learning certain material in the unit from the group-based instruction, he can then use these correctives to explore alternative ways of learning the unmastered material, select those correctives best suited to his particular learning requirements, and overcome his learning problems before they impair subsequent learning.

The construction of these feedback/correction procedures is time-consuming for the *individual* teacher. However, if small *groups* of teachers in the same subject matter area work together, we find that both the formative tests and the accompanying correctives for an entire year's work can be developed in just a few weeks working two to three hours a day. The first formative test and the relevant correctives are much harder to come by than the remaining tests and correctives.

OPERATING PROCEDURES

The teacher is now ready to teach. Since students are not accustomed to learning for mastery or the notion that they all might earn A's, usually the teacher must spend some time at the course's outset orienting the student to the procedures to be used. During this period the following points have been stressed.†

* This approach is consistent with Esbensen's view that students should be able to achieve a learning objective in a variety of ways.
† Have you ever been in a learning situation where these principles were operating? Did the experience in fact differ from your other learning experiences? How? What does it make the teacher accountable for?

1. The student will be graded solely on the basis of his summative examination performance.

2. The student will be graded against predetermined performance standards and not relative to the performance of his peers.

3. All students who attain a particular level of performance will receive the corresponding grade (hopefully an A) and there will be no fixed number of A's, B's, C's, D's, or F's.

4. Throughout the course, the student will be given a series of ungraded, diagnostic-progress tests to promote and pace his learning.

5. Each student will be given all the help he needs to learn.

This orientation period, combined with continual encouragement, support and positive evidence of learning success, should develop in most students the belief that they can learn and the motivation to learn.

Following this period, the teacher teaches the course's first unit using his customary group-based instructional methods. When this instruction is completed, the teacher administers the unit formative test to determine how each student is achieving rather than moving on to the next unit. The students score their own tests. Then the teacher certifies the progress of those students who have achieved mastery on the unit, i.e., scored at or above about 80–85 per cent correct on the test, and he encourages those students who have not to use the unit's correctives to complete their learning of unmastered material. These students are then given the responsibility to use the correctives to complete their learning of the unit as soon as possible and preferably before the group-based instruction on the next unit begins. Typically, the students will use the correctives on their own time, except that at the beginning of the course, class time is often set aside to get students into the habit of using the correctives.

This cycle of group-based instruction, formative testing, and certification or correction is repeated on each learning unit until the course has been completed. Summative tests are administered as required throughout the course although ideally the teacher need give only one final examination per quarter, term or semester. All students who score above a certain performance level over these tests earn A's. All students who perform at lower levels earn appropriately lower grades, though we typically find that when students learn by mastery methods the number of B's and C's is small and there are virtually no D's and F's.

MASTERY LEARNING IN THE CLASSROOM: SOME STUDENT LEARNING OUTCOMES

In the years since the publication of Bloom's "Learning for Mastery" strategy, extensive school-based mastery learning research has been carried out around the world, at all levels of education, in all types of schools, in an increasingly wide variety of basic and more specialized subjects, and in the physical and social sciences, the humanities, and the professions, especially medicine and dentistry. Bloom-type mastery learning strategies have been successfully used for small samples of students in classrooms where the student-teacher ratios have ranged from 20 to 30 to 1 and for large samples up to 500,000 students where the student-teacher ratios approach and surpass 70 to 1. They have even been used effectively to teach the rudiments of such advanced topics as matrix algebra, probability theory, statistics, and mathematical proof to elementary school students (Block, 1972; Romberg, Shepler and King, 1970).

There are some problems in interpreting the results of most of this research (Block, 1973a). First, most of the research comes from more structured subjects such as mathematics and the sciences, from introductory and intermediate rather than advanced courses, and from schools in the middle range of the socio-economic status spectrum. Second, the research tends to be done in the classroom rather than the laboratory and by teachers rather than experimenters. Third, it tends to paint perhaps an overly rosy picture of impact that mastery learning approaches can have on student learning. This is because the research is usually published and published research tends not to report negative results. Fourth, the research sometimes comes from projects wherein it is difficult to determine whether mastery learning ideas have actually been applied. And finally, the research is so voluminous that one runs the risk of over-interpretation or under-interpretation simply because important studies might not have been unearthed. Taking all these problems into account, however, the following statements still seem fair (Block, 1973a).*

COGNITIVE OUTCOMES

ACHIEVEMENT. In general, two to three times as many students who have learned a particular subject by mastery methods have achieved A's, B's, or their equivalent as have students who have learned the same subject by more conventional, group-based instructional methods. Thus, if 25 per cent of a group of students earned A's and B's when learning by an ordinary, group-based, non-mastery instructional method, then typically 50–75 per cent of a similar group earned A's and B's when learning by group-based, mastery methods. The data also indicate that mastery approaches to instruction can drastically cut the number of students who receive C's, D's, and F's.

Do these findings support the theory upon which mastery learning is built? Are they what you would expect to find? Why?

RETENTION. There is also a small but growing body of evidence that mastery learning approaches to the instruction of selected topics can yield better retention of the material learned than do the ordinary non-mastery approaches. And related experimental research suggests that not only *can* these approaches yield greater retention for most students, they *must* yield it.

TRANSFER OF TRAINING. Finally, there are a few classroom and experimental studies whose findings hint that mastery approaches to the instruction of selected topics can yield greater transfer of training than the ordinary non-mastery approaches. These highly tentative findings seem to hold whether transfer is defined as the ability to apply past learning to the solution of new problems or to the facilitation of new learning.

AFFECTIVE OUTCOMES

So far, we have considered the effects of mastery learning strategies on the cognitive or intellectual aspects of student learning. There is also a growing body of evidence on the impact of these strategies on the affective or emotional aspects of student learning.

INTEREST, ATTITUDES, AND CONFIDENCE. At least in the short run, mastery approaches to learning can yield greater student interest in and more positive attitudes toward the topics learned than non-mastery approaches. Block (1972) has shown, however, that if students are asked to master a subject too well, they may eventually "turn off" to it. Further, mastery approaches can generate increased confidence among students regarding their ability to learn. Finally, students really enjoy learning by mastery approaches.

ACADEMIC SELF-CONCEPT AND MENTAL HEALTH.* There have been no studies of the effects of mastery learning approaches on affective traits that develop over long periods of time, such as self-concept and mental health. Related research suggests, however, that the provision of repeated successful short-term learning experiences might help shape positive long-term interest in and attitudes toward school, school-related and later learning and might help develop a positive academic self-concept (Bloom, 1971; Kifer, 1973; Purkey, 1971; Torshen, 1970). More speculative research suggests that the provision of a long history of positive school learning experiences may even help to partially immunize students against school-induced mental and emotional disorders (Stringer and Glidewell, 1967).

* *Developing affective outputs such as these can be an important area of teacher accountability.*

Learning to Learn

Last, but not least, mastery approaches to learning have yielded some evidence that they are helping students learn how to learn. This evidence is primarily anecdotal and impressionistic and is of at least three different types. First, students who have learned for mastery using a wide variety of correctives have been observed to become more accustomed to the notion that there are many ways to learn besides lectures and textbooks. I have been especially intrigued with the extent to which students have turned to other students for aid and assistance and how they have come to exhibit increased cooperation and decreased competition in their learning. Second, students who have learned for mastery have been observed to become more careful and selective in their learning. On the one hand, they do more informal formative evaluation and, thereby, gain some measure of quality control over their learning and their study habits. On the other, they also spend more time actively engaged with the material to be learned rather than with extraneous material or non-learning activities. Finally, the students who have learned for mastery have been observed to acquire some facility in providing self-reinforcement for their learning. That is, they exhibit the capacity to generate their own learning rewards (e.g., the chance to tutor a peer) rather than relying only on those rewards the teacher might provide. Work is presently under way to study each of these phenomena in more detail. It may well be the case that this research will provide a far more compelling case for the classroom use of mastery learning than even the past research.

Mastery Learning and the Teacher

What, then, are the implications of mastery learning for the role of the classroom teacher?

By adopting the view that all can learn and by defining mastery, the teacher is essentially determining what ought to be or to occur in his classroom. Similarly, by adopting the view that all will learn and then using feedback/correction procedures to reach mastery, the teacher is translating these "oughts" into concrete materials, plans, and actions. Since we call such conceptions of what ought to be values, the first implication of mastery learning for the teacher is that he must become accustomed to *explicit valuing*. That is, the teacher must not only determine what ought to be the case in his classroom, but he must also get used to making these oughts explicit in how and what he teaches.

To value something in the abstract or in private may be relatively easy; to make one's values concrete and public is much more difficult because this opens one up to possible criticism by those who disagree with one's values. This is especially the case where, as in mastery learning, many of the values (e.g., all can and will learn) to which the teacher explicitly ascribes may be at loggerheads with the values held by his colleagues and superiors. Besides valuing, therefore, the mastery learning teacher must stand ready to *justify* the values represented in his instruction.* The mastery learning teacher, for example, can expect to be required to defend his grading standards when perhaps 80 per cent of his students earn A's.

A third implication of mastery learning is that the teacher needs to exercise a measure of quality control in his teaching. We have already discussed the need for the teacher to construct feedback/correction procedures. One dimension of the teacher's quality control responsibilities is to see that these feedback/correction procedures are actually used to pinpoint and to overcome student learning problems. Time after time we find that when a mastery learning strategy fails, it fails not because the teacher has not prepared appropriate feedback/correction procedures, but because he failed to implement them. In particular, we often find that the teacher has a tendency to fail to induce his students to correct the learning difficulties revealed by formative testing.

The second dimension of the teacher's quality control responsibilities is the monitoring of the effectiveness of his instruction from one cycle of his course to the next. Not even the best mastery learning strategies will help all students earn A's the first cycle. It is only through the cycle by cycle exercise of some quality control procedures that the teacher will eventually be able to ensure that as many students as possible earn A's.

Often we find that the teacher can improve the quality of his instruction during one cycle of his course by using the formative test results and other information from the previous cycle as his bench marks. By using one year's results as a quality control check on the next, therefore, the teacher can have a greater impact on more and more students' learning over the years. For example, by noting which items on each unit formative test most students answered correctly and incorrectly, the teacher can determine the material for which the group-based instruction was generally effective and for which it was not. The teacher could then tally the types of correctives to which the students turned for supplementary instruction over this material. By studying how these correctives present the material and/or involve the students and/or encourage their learning, the teacher could then revise his original instruction accordingly to better teach this material in the future.

The final implication of mastery learning for the role of the classroom teacher is that the teacher must do more *communicating* and *cooperating* with his colleagues and students. In terms of colleagues, this increased cooperation and communication will yield at least two benefits. First, it can allay some of their misgivings and guard against the possibility that

* *This is an important aspect of accountability in education.*

what one is doing will be misperceived. Second, as was noted previously, it can cut the work load required to construct feedback/correction procedures.*

In terms of the students, increased cooperation and communication can have several salutary effects. First, it can smooth the introduction of mastery learning ideas into the classroom. Students can provide invaluable feedback to the teacher about what they like and do not like about a particular mastery strategy and about how the strategy might be changed. Second, it can help to implement a successful strategy. There is no reason why students in a mastery learning situation cannot be trusted to perform many activities that the teacher would ordinarily perform. Students might correct their own formative tests, construct their own correctives, and tutor each other. Third, and finally, increased cooperation and communication can create a learning environment in which students see themselves as having a stake. I would hazard the guess that no learning environment, not even a mastery learning environment, can have a dramatic impact on students' learning unless students perceive themselves as belonging.†

I hope that these implications do not convey the impression that mastery learning is difficult to realize in the classroom. It is not. My point in broaching them is simply to suggest that mastery learning is not a painless panacea. There are certain costs associated with teaching by mastery learning methods as well as manifold benefits for your students and most of all, you. You will have to decide whether the chance to have a clear and consistent positive impact on most of your students' learning is worth the effort and energy that teaching for mastery requires.

EXERCISE

1. How does Block explain teachers' inability to teach all children well? (p. 527)

2. How does Block explain the relationship between aptitude and mastery? (p. 528)

3. According to Block, what are the preconditions for mastery learning? (pp. 529–531)

4. How are evaluation instruments (tests) used in mastery learning? What is the purpose of a formative test? (p. 532)

5. What results have been obtained when mastery learning is used in the schools? What explanations can be given for the findings? (pp. 533–535)

6. How does mastery learning change the communication patterns in a school? In a classroom? (pp. 536–537)

* This is also a goal of open education (see Section 10).
† This is a key point. Do you agree? Why?

Learning C.O.D.
Can the School
Buy Success?

James A. Mecklenburger and John A. Wilson

> *James A. Mecklenburger and John A. Wilson began investigating performance contracting as part of their doctoral study at Indiana University. They describe the methods of performance contracting and review the assets and problems of the approach. Performance contracting makes an agency outside the school district accountable for raising the achievement of the district's students to a predetermined level. The agency-contractors are often private profit-making industries. Thus, performance contracting has created a new liaison between industry and education.*
>
> *Note the similarities between performance learning and the learning for mastery model described by James Block in the preceding selection. Also, note the differences. Which approach do you think is superior? In further response to this article, you may wish to read the selection that follows by Edmund Farrell, who is quite critical of the performance contracting movement. Also, Robert Stake (Section 16) describes problems in testing for learning gains — an essential feature of performance contracting.*

One of the newest, most controversial, and, perhaps, least understood phrases in the contemporary lexicon of education is "performance contracting." A performance contract, strictly speaking, is a variety of legal contract. The contractor is rewarded according to his measured performance at a specified task. Evelyn Wood Reading Dynamics, for example, has offered such a contract for years: Triple your reading rate, or your money back. Aircraft corporations frequently sign performance contracts. But performance contracting for instructional programs — *paying according to how much children learn* — is new to public schools. There have been fifty performance contracts in education since they began in 1969; there may be fifty again this year.

Performance contracting has a Pandora's Box quality; applying business-military-government procedures to education unlocks debate over a whole series of educational issues.

"Hucksters in the schools!" is the cry of the American Federation of Teachers (AFT). Many educators concur. In contrast, two polls by the National School Board Association during 1970–71 show two-thirds of its members sympathetic to or favoring performance contracting. "Performance contracting does what [teachers] won't do — it rises or falls on *results*, not on schedules and seniority and protected mediocrity," said one school board member. Some performance contract advocates hail the dawning of new school-government-business cooperation; some critics denounce the beginning of an "educational-industrial complex."

The sharpest controversy emerges from the tense alliance that performance contracts create between school people and industry-government people. For example, such tensions nearly wrecked a project in Gary, Indiana, during its first semester in 1970. Don Kendrick, "center manager" of the project, arrived in Gary with experience as a systems analyst in the Air Force and at Lockheed. He considered schooling comparable to aircraft production — each was a system producing a product, whether airplanes or learning — and made no secret of the comparison.

"I'm a systems analyst," he told one visitor. "I view things analytically. Keep out emotions.... Industry says we want a job done. This is the difference [between industry and schools]. You don't have to love the guy next to you on the assembly line to make the product. He puts in the nuts, you put in the bolts, and the product comes out. Teachers can hate me and still get children to learn." As one Gary teacher remarked, "There's no way a man with that attitude can succeed in a school. No way."

The fault was not Kendrick's but was inherent in the situation. Because business and school allies are people with vastly different experience, ideas, expectations, and jargon, merely talking together is sometimes difficult. People who talk of management, cost-effectiveness, needs assessment, and *product* emphasis rouse hostility in people who talk of the whole child, individual differences, *my* classroom, or the learning *process*. Much of the public debate over performance contracting (and over accountability, which is frequently associated with it) has foundered on this rocky language dilemma.

Performance contracts have taken a number of different forms, and the variety is likely to increase in the future. The first such contract between the schools of the twin cities of Texarkana, on the Arkansas-Texas border, and Dorsett Educational Systems stipulated that Dorsett would be paid a certain amount for each child in grades six to eight whose performance in English and mathematics was raised by at least one grade level.* In

* Stake discusses the inadequacy of grade level scores as a measure of learning (Section 16).

1970, under a more daring agreement, the Behavioral Research Laboratories (BRL) of Palo Alto, California, contracted to take over completely the organization and administration of one elementary school in Gary, Indiana, for four years — with payment to be based on student achievement. And the most ambitious program, funded by the Office of Economic Opportunity at $6.5-million, resulted in contracts similar to that in Texarkana being negotiated between the schools in eighteen cities and six different performance contractors, involving more than 27,000 children.

Companies with performance contracts in schools presume that schools ought to be "learning systems." The systems idea is not new; it has been applied with varied sophistication and success to military, engineering, city planning, and other enterprises. The most prominent example is the space effort, and one hears the argument *"If we get men to the moon, why can't we teach kids to read?"* Or, *"If industry had forty per cent rejects in its system, it would revise the system; therefore schools too should revise their system."* Some apostles suggest that schools, like the Apollo missions, should try to be "zero-defect systems."

The jargon surrounding systems ideas is nearly impenetrable. In effect, a system is a goal-oriented enterprise. It is characterized by formal procedures for defining goals, for identifying the tasks necessary to the achievement of these goals, for organizing to accomplish the tasks, for measuring one's success, and for revising the process as experience (data) dictates.*

Applied to schools, the goal or product of a system is usually said to be student learning — measurable, observable student learning.

This demand for observable outcomes, for specificity of goals, coincides with pressures within education (associated with B. F. Skinner's behavioral psychology) to define teaching-learning in terms of "behavioral objectives" — that is, precise and observable student behavior. Some contractors now call these "performance objectives." One product of the behavioral objectives movement has been programed instruction in which a student proceeds step by step through a preordained learning sequence until he achieves an objective, as demonstrated on a test. Because such instruction is inexpensive, individual, and above all produces measurable results, programed instruction is integral to virtually all performance contractors' learning systems.†

Since materials provide the instruction, teachers' roles change; adults now coordinate the learning system, making certain that each child has the right materials at the right time. Teachers "teach" only when a child

* *Notice how "a system" incorporates features of behavioral objectives, Individually Prescribed Instruction (IPI), and mastery learning.*
† *Taylor expresses concern about the use of programmed instruction in Section 10.*

needs assistance.* Appropriately, in many projects, teachers are now "learning directors" or "instructional managers" and classrooms have become "learning centers."

Several learning systems employ only a few certified teachers, replacing them with paraprofessionals or "assistant learning directors" who are usually local parents. A few systems have replaced teachers entirely — a fact not lost on teacher unions and associations.

The result of these innovations is often praised as "individualized instruction." Advocates of such learning systems assert that children learn at different rates so that group instruction is neither efficient nor effective. Confusion surrounds the term "individualized," however, because many educators use it synonymously with "personalized" or "humanized" — thinking that "individualized" implies regard for each student as a unique human being, capable of freedom of choice in the learning process. A few learning systems foster a personal touch; others pay little heed; most are highly structured, individualizing only the *rate* of instruction.

Neither the systems approach nor individualized instruction is the unique province of performance contractors, however. Other educational technology companies, university and government research laboratories, publishers, and teachers also have experimented with systems approaches. As a Michigan Education Association position paper summarized the situation, "What the performance contractor sells is not new ideas per se, but the way in which new ideas are put together to produce a result. The primary reason for [his] success lies in the fact that he brings to the school a *well thought-out system* and operates the system free and *unencumbered by the school administration of the district*." (Emphasis theirs.) . . .

Within a learning center, terminology is pseudomedical: Learning managers "diagnose" what the student needs to learn and then "prescribe" the learning sequence each student will follow.

Testing has been the sticky wicket for learning systems, but particularly for performance contractors, whose payment is usually based upon test scores. Most contracts employ individual student scores on standardized achievement tests as the basis for paying the contractor. A number of the nation's leading testing experts have heaped scorn on this procedure, calling performance contracting a gimmick, highly questionable and invalid.†

The culprit is the so-called grade-equivalent score. This score implies that a student is above or below grade level. The assumption is that tests provide precise yardsticks of student progress, and educators have allowed

* *Compare this definition of teaching to the one described by Rathbone in his discussion of open education (see Section 10).*
† *Robert E. Stake is one of these experts. See Section 16 for his views.*

parents and school boards to believe in these scores. But these tests are not precise. As measuring devices for individual learning, they have the accuracy more of a fist than a micrometer. Henry Dyer, vice president of Educational Testing Service, called grade-equivalent scores "statistical monstrosities." The tests yield scores that can be treated as precise data, but these numbers are actually very imprecise. So many factors can influence these scores that they become virtually meaningless. Maturation, testing conditions, the timing of tests, student attitude, and pure chance can create statistical increases that would fulfill a performance contract without the student's learning anything.

In recent months, some performance contracts have moved in more defensible directions — either using different kinds of tests, or employing more statistically reliable applications of standardized tests (which more adequately measure group performance than individual performance), or setting goals not requiring testing.

Nevertheless, scratch almost any performance contract and a defensive scream emerges over testing. Said one superintendent, "For better or worse or right or wrong, that's the way we do it! We let kids into college based on the SAT, and we let them into graduate school based on the Miller Analogy, and we let them into industry based on all kinds of standardized tests." No doubt, the testing and measurement of performance are the Achilles' heel of performance contracting.

How a student should be motivated to proceed through a learning system — especially a student who habitually performs poorly in school — is a question about which contractors differ. Some assert that learning is its own reward. Some presume a bribe — by any other name — at the right moment helps; they use dolls, radios, Green Stamps, hamburgers, and trinkets as rewards or incentives. Some contractors emphasize praise and motivation. Others presume comfortable surroundings will motivate students, so they create colorful, carpeted, air-conditioned learning centers.

Some contractors have adopted the practice of "contingency management," which assumes that if the classroom environment contains appropriate rewards for desirable behavior, undesirable behavior will disappear.* A few contractors take this theory seriously and train their staffs to use varied techniques of positive reinforcement.

The most intricate incentive system we witnessed was in Grand Rapids. It was conducted by Alpha Learning Systems, and teachers reinforced both good behavior and good academic work by distributing tokens (rubber washers in elementary school, paper money called "skins" in junior high). For a portion of the school day, youngsters go to a Reinforcing Events Room where they use tokens to purchase goods and activities they enjoy — for example, jump ropes, puzzles, soft drinks, candy, and toys

* Bushell explains contingency management in his article in Section 10.

for elementary children; pinball, billiards, soft drinks, candy, and dance music for adolescents....

Implicit in the learning systems we have discussed is a mechanical conception of learning: Learning (of certain kinds) can be divided into discrete units; units can be labeled (with objectives) and tested. Students must acquire learnings — as many as possible. The system succeeds when the child tests 100 per cent. Learnings are things; since contractors are paid for student learning, learning, by implication, is a commodity to be bought and sold. Most performance contracting so far has tied simple, perhaps ill-conceived, goals to crudely designed monetary rewards for the successful contractor. Perhaps most performance contracts exemplify what Ivan Illich characterized...as the school mentality: "Knowledge can be defined as a commodity" since "it is viewed as the result of institutional enterprise [and] the fulfillment of institutional objectives."

However, not all performance contracts have displayed this mentality; and they need not do so. "Performance" can be far more widely construed than it has been. Teaching methods can differ entirely from today's practices. And the use of incentives can be applied to others than private corporations.

We are encouraged by an extraordinary performance-contracted project in Cherry Creek, Colorado, in which teachers, not a corporation, contracted with the school district to try a new idea.* "I-team" was a dedicated effort to create within the public school a very personalized program to provide potential dropouts with a meaningful, responsive educational program tailored to them — virtually a "free school" within the public schools. The contract calls for a salary bonus to the teachers if the program succeeds in achieving its original objectives. There are ten objectives ranging from changes in attendance patterns to change in academic work, from changes in attitude to change in social behavior.

Outside evaluators, using several different tests, unobtrusive measures, and personal observation, ruled on the program's success (and expressed their own amazement at how successful I-team had been). In the judgment of the evaluators, the performance contract provided a useful incentive for excellent teachers to perform at their best.

Performance contracts, then, need not necessarily purchase rigid learning systems for teaching reading or mathematics. They are one device for making changes in schools, and many kinds of programs could develop under them....

Change is the keynote in talk of performance contracting, and with some justification. In at least some cases, parents see clear proof that kids

* *How might you expect teacher expectancy to affect the outcomes of this contract?*

learn; school boards find a new way to share responsibility and to seek federal funds; superintendents gain prestige as innovators; testing experts acquire some long-awaited attention; work and salary patterns for teachers begin to change; new professions in education begin to emerge; an opening has been made for entrepreneurs; and whole school systems seriously address fundamental educational issues.

There are modest changes, such as better ways to teach reading, to squeeze the tax dollar, or to sell more textbooks; and major changes, such as paying children to learn, ending the autonomy of the classroom teacher, shifting power away from old vested interests, even redefining what school is and what learning is.

It is also claimed that performance contracting stimulates change in the schools generally through the innovative example it gives, through the possibility it provides for school boards to experiment without high risk — they can claim credit for successes and blame the contractor for failures — through the provision of system design and management skills not usually available to the schools, and through simply shaking up the system so that it is easier to get change started and keep it going.

The most elaborate and most formal answer to the question of how performance contracting changes schools has been advanced by Charles Blaschke and Leon Lessinger. Blaschke, drawing upon defense industry procurement procedures, planned the Texarkana project. Lessinger, then an Associate U.S. Commissioner of Education, funded it. Lessinger now invokes Texarkana as the best example of what he calls "educational engineering." This formal and complex process systematically links planning, teaching, and evaluation. Planning is in two parts. All interested parties are consulted until an entire educational project is outlined, based on specified needs — a process called "needs assessments." Then a Request For Proposals (RFP) is issued to competing companies, asking them to bid on the project.

After a contract is agreed upon, an outside evaluator to do the testing and final report and an "educational auditor" to superintend and attest to everyone's honesty (similar to a certified public accountant) are hired. Presumably, everything is the focus of community attention, open, and scrupulously honest. At the end of the year, a project will have had every opportunity to prove itself.

Blaschke has adapted the term "turnkey" from the building trades, where a contractor may accept full responsibility for construction of a building, then turn the keys over to the new owner. Similarly, an educational contractor may run a project for a year or more, then turn it over to the school system. This has occurred in some cities, including Texarkana, where in the third year, beginning this fall, the school system will run the program begun by the contractor.

Some contracts have followed the Lessinger-Blaschke model, from needs assessment to turnkey; but in many contracts, such as the one set up in Gary, the contractor was selected without competitive bidding. Most companies prefer to negotiate performance contracts without competitive bidding. Some contracts dispense with the evaluator, with the school board assuming responsibility for evaluation. Some contracts dispense with the auditor. Similarly, at the end of a project the school may accept the entire program, adopt part of it, or drop the whole thing. . . .

The Gary contract, calling for the turning over of an entire elementary school, Banneker School, to BRL, was the boldest challenge to date, not only to tradition but also to the education establishment. George Stern, then president of BRL, rejoiced that through the contract BRL had "gained the clout to implement all our ideas." But the reality wasn't as simple as merely signing a contract. Nowhere has the power struggle inherent in performance contracts been more explosive.

In the first skirmish, a summer ago, Indiana Attorney General Theodore Sendak, at the request of the state Department of Public Instruction, expressed his informal opinion that contracting for the operation of a public school by a private corporation would be illegal. School City of Gary (which is the name given to the city's public schools) and BRL felt compelled to modify their contract to reduce somewhat the school board's delegation of authority to the company. In late summer, state Superintendent of Public Instruction Richard D. Wells asked School City to consider planning for one year before beginning the project or, failing that, to hire BRL as consultant only; he offered Gary $20,000 to pay for BRL's consultant services. Not to be co-opted, School City chose to continue in its own direction.

When it became clear that neither Sendak's opinion nor Wells's advice had deterred the contract, the Gary Teacher's Union voted to strike over involuntary teacher transfers and other contract violations. School City countered by seeking a judicial restraining order, after which the union felt constrained to use its own grievance procedures. The results are still being argued.

After extensive investigation, the state Department of Public Instruction in January challenged the legality and quality of the project: Classes were too large; state-adopted textbooks were being ignored; some staff were uncertified; only reading and mathematics had been taught.* Some community elements in Gary and some school administrators joined with the state in insisting that subjects other than reading and mathematics be

* Based on the discussions in Part II of this book, which of these factors might influence student outcomes?

taught. BRL is paid only for reading and math test score gains, although the company contracted to operate the entire school; BRL argued that it had planned from the beginning to phase in a broader curriculum. It was phased in quickly.

"There is nothing uniquely innovative about the Banneker program," asserted a state investigatory report in February, "except the abdication of professional responsibility on the part of School City of Gary and the placement of primary emphasis upon building and maintaining a systems model instead of upon the children and their needs and interests." The State Board of Education decommissioned Banneker School in February, a move which threatened to cost Gary $200,000 in state aid and resulted in adverse national publicity.

Some changes in the program resulted quickly; a change also occurred in the political climate — Governor Edgar D. Whitcomb visited Banneker School just before the March state Board of Education meeting, calling the school a "worthy experiment." The board recommissioned Banneker School.

Finally, under School City's prodding BRL consented to run a 1971 summer program, using Banneker's teachers under BRL guidance, to produce an expanded curriculum that would be suitable for the wide range of academic ability found among the children in the school. Perhaps coincidentally, several BRL and Gary administrators connected with the project will not return this second year.

Similarly, performance contracting upset the national power structure in education. After a series of blistering resolutions at their August convention, the AFT established "listening posts" East, Central, and West to monitor performance contracting; its publications were filled with accusations, many of them embarrassingly accurate. And its *Non-coloring Book on Performance Contracting* is a vicious piece of political cartooning that has been reprinted widely.

The National Education Association (NEA) seemed to want, at first, to respond in the same manner as the AFT, but two of its locals signed contracts with the Office of Economic Opportunity (OEO), forcing the national organization to bite its tongue. The NEA was hardly solid on the issue, in any case. Its Michigan affiliate wrote and spoke very highly of the benefits caused by performance contracts in Michigan, and NEA locals elsewhere were at least respectful of projects in their jurisdiction.

Clearly, the final verdict on performance contracting is far from in. Some contracts have shattered complacency, inspired creativity, improved learning, and turned the spotlight of public attention on the quality of classroom instruction. But others have inspired greed and chicanery, created poor environments for children, and fomented unhealthy dissension.

Performance contracting has as its kernel a powerful idea: Someone other than children must bear the responsibility for whether children learn successfully.* Who bears that responsibility, and to what measure, are questions loaded with dynamite. Surround these questions with money, risk, publicity, new teaching strategies, new people, new rhetoric, systems analysis, contingency management, and more, and it is no wonder that this recent, and thus far miniscule, phenomenon has raised such a ruckus in public education.

To date, most performance contracts have been primitive in design, method, and evaluation, their high-flown rhetoric notwithstanding. Results are beginning to be reported. Some projects undoubtedly will appear to do very well; others will be instructive as failures. All should be regarded with the kind of hopeful skepticism that greets the first trial of any new invention.

However, there are signs of emerging sophistication. Here and there, creative and knowledgeable people are questioning the narrow definitions of performance that have bred mostly mechanical teaching of basic skills; they are questioning the evaluation that places wholesale reliance on inappropriate tests; and they are sharpening their contracting skills so that projects of more than publicity value emerge.†

If this sophistication grows and triumphs over the hucksters and panacea hounds who also flock to inventions, the performance contracts of the early 1970s could well be the first ripple of a new wave in education.

EXERCISE

1. According to the authors, what feature of performance contracting causes the greatest controversy? (p. 539)

2. List three types of performance contracts described by the authors. (pp. 539–540)

3. Why is the use of "individualized instruction" to describe the learning systems installed under performance contracts questionable? (p. 541)

4. How are performance contracts attempting to resolve the problem of inadequate tests? (p. 542)

5. What is meant by a "mechanical conception" of learning? (p. 543)

6. Why is "change" central to performance contracting? (pp. 543–544)

7. What was the main cause of the controversy related to the Gary, Indiana, performance contract? (p. 546)

8. According to the authors, what is the most powerful idea associated with performance contracting? (pp. 546–547)

* A key point of any move toward accountability in education.
† If performance contracts improve, will they be a good way to go about reforming education?

Performance Contracting:
Some Reservations

Edmund J. Farrell

> *What happens when performance contracts are let? Can the,*
> *result in desirable educational outcomes, as Mecklenburger and*
> *Wilson suggested in the preceding selection? Edmund Farrell,*
> *assistant executive secretary of the National Council of Teachers of*
> *English, believes that performance contracting has at least five*
> *flaws, and thus it is not an effective method of improving education.*
> *You might wish to compare Farrell's reservations about performance*
> *contracting with Hans Guth's criticisms of behavioral objectives*
> *(Section 14). Both Farrell and Guth are English teachers, and both*
> *have a similar view of education. Does teaching English have some*
> *special feature that leads one to oppose precise statement of learn-*
> *ing goals? To a great extent, their disagreement with advocates of*
> *behavioral objectives and performance contracting reflects the con-*
> *flict in educational goals between the humanists (for example, Carl*
> *Rogers) and the technologists (for example, Carl Bereiter), repre-*
> *sented in Part 1 of this book. After reading Farrell's article, do you*
> *think performance contracting does more harm than good? Or do*
> *you agree that this approach is helping to bring about much needed*
> *reform in education? Do you think that it is possible and even de-*
> *sirable to combine humanistic goals with performance contracting?*

. . . [In this paper] I speak as one who has followed in journal articles, news releases, and the speeches of others the [performance contracting] movement from its inception, who has read the words of Leon Lessinger, heard Charles Blaschke in person, monitored from afar the flow of monies from the Office of Educational Opportunity.* I know about the scandal in Texarkana, where Dorsett Educational Systems was accused of contaminating results by teaching to the tests, and about the disputed success of the Behavioral Research Laboratories in the Banneker Elementary School in Gary, Indiana, a school in which the state education code was

From the *English Journal*, vol. 61, no. 4 (April 1972), pp. 560–564. Copyright © 1972 by the National Council of Teachers of English. Reprinted by permission of the publisher and the author.

* *These projects are discussed in the previous selection.*

violated for the first four months of the contract, during which time BRL taught reading and mathematics to the exclusion of other subjects.

But beyond suggesting I have done my homework, I do not want... to discuss specific contracts, school districts, or learning corporations associated with performance contracting. Instead, I would like to share with you some of the deeply felt reservations I have about the language and the practices associated with the present movement, whether participated in by teachers who incorporate themselves, or by industries which exist outside the schools. Some of these reservations are more personal and less analytical than are others.

First, *on the matter of accountability:* Contrary to the oft-repeated rationale for performance contracting, I do not hear the public loudly demanding that teachers or schools be held fiscally responsible for the success of their methods. I believe that the term *accountability* when used in reference to the schools is an invention of government and industry, neither of which, incidentally, holds itself sufficiently accountable for the present condition of our society.

I first heard the word *accountability* applied to the schools in 1968 in New Orleans at a conference sponsored by the United States Office of Education. The theme of the conference was "Educational Systems for the '70s," and as befitted such a theme, those of us in attendance were entertained with charts of the Polaris Missile Program and heady talk about Program Planning Budgeting Systems (PPBS) and the "missions" of the schools.* We were also introduced to the rhetoric of accountability by being served warning that taxpayers and parents — those androgynous and conveniently polymorphic groups from whose ranks teachers themselves seem forever exempt — would not tolerate for much longer the failure of the schools to achieve their missions, among which appeared to be that of making sure that every student scored average or better on all standardized examinations.

I find it curious that despite all the talk of accountability, the Gallup Poll last year found citizens strongly supportive of the Senate and House override of President Nixon's veto of the education budget. This year, in a survey of the public's attitude toward the schools, the Gallup Poll reported that only 8 per cent of the parents held the teachers principally responsible for students' failure, and only 6 per cent held the schools responsible. On the other hand, 54 per cent thought students' home life to be the principal cause of failure. When juniors and seniors in high schools were polled on this same issue, 51 per cent believed the students themselves to be primarily responsible for their failure; 25 per cent cited

---

* *What similarity, if any, does an educational mission such as teaching children to read have with developing a missile?*

home life as the main cause; 11 per cent, the teachers; and 5 per cent, the schools (*Phi Delta Kappan*, September 1971). In short, parents and students appear to be more intuitively sophisticated about educational accountability than are performance contractors.*

To determine adequately who or what is responsible for which aspects of student performance requires the most judicious uses of multiple-regression analysis, as Henry S. Dyer, vice-president, Educational Testing Service, and Stephen M. Barro, an economist with Rand Corporation, pointed out in the December 1970 *Phi Delta Kappan*. It requires, suggests Barro, analysis of such variables as the student's ethnicity, socioeconomic status, home, family, and neighborhood characteristics, age, intelligence, prior performance, etc. It requires analysis of classroom characteristics — class size, amount of instructional support, amount of materials, condition of physical facilities, etc. It requires careful analysis of the characteristics of the teacher and of the staff, as well as of the group characteristics of the pupils, i.e., the "peer-group influence" that may affect individual performance.† Such analysis, which is time-consuming, expensive, and complex, exposes the simplism inherent in much of the current rhetoric of educational accountability and performance contracting. . . .

Second, *on the matter of individualized teaching:* Those who have maintained that performance contracting has promoted greater individualization of instruction have, on the whole, spoken nonsense. Too often they have confused instruction which permits students to learn identical materials at different rates of speed with authentic individualized instruction, whereby each student has a curriculum tailored to his unique interests and abilities.‡ Forcing all students, for example, through a set of programmed reading materials, regardless of the varied rates at which they proceed, is more akin to brainwashing tactics than it is to the fostering of democratic pluralism in the classroom.

Third, *on the matter of extrinsic rewards:* When students involved in performance contracting are presented with such extrinsic rewards for learning as S&H Green Stamps, transistor radios, television sets, and pseudo-money with which to buy goods, they are being taught that education is not an enterprise sufficiently rewarding unto itself but rather a means to materialistic ends.§ I am well acquainted, as you are, with the

---

* *Do Block's comments (this section) about the way we are conditioned to fit students' achievement to a normal curve support or refute this statement?*
† *Using the views of persons such as Bane and Jencks, Mayeske, Popham, Templeton, and Husén (see Part 2), which of these variables would you say are most accountable for student performance?*
‡ *Do you take this statement as a criticism for programs such as Individually Prescribed Instruction? (See Section 10.)*
§ *Is this a matter of values or empirical research? If values, could research make any contribution to the discussion?*

arguments in favor of extrinsic rewards, including the largely-unproved claim that eventually students will become less interested in the rewards as they internalize the joys of learning. I am not persuaded by the arguments, however, for they are too clearly Machiavellian or too blind to the present consequences of American capitalism and consumption. At a time when we need to be teaching students how to create a world in which they can cope adequately with far fewer goods, we should not be reinforcing a societal system which has led less than 6 per cent of the world's population to consume 40 to 60 per cent of the annual production of the earth's natural resources.

Fourth, *on the matter of testing:* When I review the literature (the word *literature* is used in strange and various ways) of performance contracting, I cannot find a reputable psychometrician or other specialist in educational measurement who will support at present the use either of pre-post standardized normative tests or of criterion-referenced tests to establish the success or failure of contractors in meeting their guarantees.*

In an address to the American Educational Research Association, delivered in New York City on February 5, 1971, Roger T. Lennon, senior vice president, Harcourt Brace Jovanovich, Inc. and president, The Psychological Corporation, voiced serious doubts about both the validity and the reliability of present measuring instruments as used by performance contractors. After surveying the inherent weaknesses of gain-score achievement tests in determining an individual student's short-term progress in subjects such as mathematics and reading, Lennon concluded,

> . . . maybe the cumulative impact of all the problems enumerated . . . is sufficient to lead us finally to speak the unspeakable: to declare that the grade equivalent, at whatever level, is an inappropriate unit for the measurement of gain of an individual pupil over relatively brief periods — say as much as a year of ordinary growth.

. . . After conceding that reasonably dependable estimates of average gains, as opposed to individual student gains, can be obtained at least in reading and arithmetic in present learning situations established through performance contracts, Lennon then proceeded to question the logic that would "permit a school system to ascribe even average gains unerringly to the contractor's performance or his special type of intervention." . . .

Fifth, *on the corruption of both language and the process of education:* I am one of those who came to teaching after having had as a youth considerable experience in the world of business. Beyond having performed a number of menial tasks, such as picking prunes, bell-hopping, stocking shelves in a grocery store, and setting pins in a bowling alley, I

* *Why are these tests questioned as measures of successful teaching? See Mecklenburger and Wilson (this section).*

also had sold clothing in the men's department at Montgomery Ward, had been the publicity director of a country fair, and had sold electrical supplies for my father, who managed an electrical wholesale company.

In good part, I entered teaching because I believed it to be one of the last refuges in the society where open communication might take place without either party — student or teacher — feeling a need to hold his hand on his wallet. True, I was paid by taxpayers, many of them parents of my students, for my endeavors. And while one might say I was trying to "sell" ideas and skills, not all of which, I might add, were "bought," the metaphors are quite loose: money just was not a factor influencing day-to-day relationships in the classroom. I could trust the students, and they could trust me, since neither of us was trying to mulct the other of cash.

I would like to believe that teachers have resisted as long as they have the awarding of merit pay, not because they are incapable of citing superior teachers, but because they have intuitively recognized that the process of education is contaminated when student performance is too closely tied to a teacher's income: even the most competent and humane teacher will view his students as means to his ends if his salary is contingent solely upon their short-term performance and attitudes. If the universe of possible modes of assessing the teacher's competency is reduced to the single criterion of student performance on standardized posttests, the teacher is unfairly tempted to preserve both his ego and his job by teaching to those examinations.*

As teachers of English, we should appreciate better than do most persons the capacity of metaphor for influencing human behavior, its capability of shaping the way we perceive our world and its concomitant influence on our attitudes toward what we perceive....

What I am leading to, of course, is what I regard as the present misuse in education of language that dehumanizes students and corrupts the processes by which they learn, metaphorical language that would lead teachers to perceive knowledge or experience as "inputs," performance on tests as "outputs," and graduates as "products" of school "plants." Once such metaphors, most of them from industry, become fully operative in education, the ethics of the marketplace become tenable in the classroom: students are seen as objects not meant to serve their own ends but those of the manipulator — the teacher or the contractor — and the open processes of communication, which must exist for schools to be truly educative, are dead-ended.† If that unhappy time comes to all classrooms, my initial (and still valid) reason for entering teaching will no longer

* *What other measures of teacher competence might be considered?*
† *What type of study would verify or refute this statement?*

hold, and I will have no choice but to leave the profession.

But I do not really anticipate the arrival of that day, for I have found that humanists will not go gentle into such good nights. Rather, I foresee the time when American education and the society in which it exists will be held accountable for matters that really count. If by the year 2000 this nation is still racist; if it is still unmindful of its poor; if it is still waging unpopular and undeclared wars in developing areas of the world; if it is still engaged in an armaments race, despite there now being in storage the equivalent of two hundred pounds of TNT for every pound of human flesh on earth; if it is still wantonly consuming the globe's resources and irresponsibly polluting land, water, and sky, then it, and education, and we shall surely have failed. And I promise you, history will hold us accountable.*

EXERCISE

1. What data are used by Farrell to support his thesis that the public does not want teachers to be held accountable for the success of their students? (pp. 549–550)

2. What variables does Barro suggest should be considered before one can determine who or what is responsible for student performance? (p. 550)

3. Why does Farrell think performance contracting has failed to promote individualization of instruction? (p. 550)

4. Why is Farrell opposed to using extrinsic rewards for learning? (pp. 550–551)

5. What types of testing problems occur in performance contracts? (p. 551)

6. Why may payment of teachers based upon student performance be a dangerous system? (p. 552)

7. What movement in the schools do humanists need to counteract in Farrell's opinion? (p. 552)

* What reply could an advocate of performance contracting make to Farrell's plea for humanism in education?

Why Evaluate Education?

Ralph W. Tyler

> *During the early 1960's, those responsible for education at the national level acknowledged that the charter of the U.S. Office of Education requires the commissioner to determine periodically the progress of education. With the encouragement of Francis Keppel, then U.S. Commissioner of Education, a distinguished group of educators formed the Exploratory Committee on Assessing the Progress of Education. The committee chairman was Ralph Tyler, author of the following selection and a former professor at the University of Chicago and director of the Center for Advanced Study in the Behavioral Sciences. The result of the committee's efforts is the evaluation program called National Assessment. According to Tyler, the National Assessment is "designed to sample the things which children and youth are expected to learn in school, and to find out what proportion of our people are learning these things." Tyler explains how the findings of National Assessment can be used in educational accountability programs. He believes that the type of evaluation data provided by National Assessment will help to improve education. Do you agree?*

The need for a continuing assessment of the progress of education in this country arises from the great demands which are now being made upon education. Most of the goals we seek as a people require education as a means of reaching them. To meet these demands, the American people are furnishing far greater resources for our educational institutions than have ever been available before. Yet much more is being requested. It is clear that the resources required cannot be provided except by using the greatest care in their allocation and use. The public needs to understand more adequately what educational progress is being made and where the critical problems lie on which much greater attention and effort must be focused.* The public needs this kind of information in order to give intelligent backing for the decisions that must be made to use resources wisely to produce maximum results.

From *Compact*, vol. 6, no. 1 (February 1972), pp. 3–4. Reprinted with permission of the publisher.

* Farrell in the preceding selection suggests that the public does not want this information. How could you determine where it actually stands?

We have data of this kind about other matters of public concern, such as our population growth, its rate of increase, the extent and direction of migration; about the income levels of our people and the incidence of disease. Need for this information was recognized a generation ago and, over the years, means for obtaining the information were worked out and are continually being refined. We now have useful, comprehensive and comparable data regarding types of morbidity and mortality for various ages, occupations, regions and the like. We know the diseases that are currently the chief causes of death in different age groups, and in different occupations and income categories. We have helpful estimates of production, prices and unemployment ratios. These kinds of data enable the public to understand progress and problems in these fields, and they furnish perspectives from which to make decisions.

But before the advent of the National Assessment, we had no comprehensive and dependable data about the educational attainments of our people. The data available at the state and national level have been reports on numbers of schools, buildings, teachers and pupils, and about the monies expended, but we have not had sound and trustworthy information on educational results. Because dependable data were not available, personal views, distorted reports and journalistic impressions have been the sources of public opinion, and the schools have been attacked by some and defended by others without having necessary evidence to support either claim.*

Teaching Johnny to Read

For example, some years ago, a book entitled "Why Johnny Can't Read" had a great influence on public opinion, without any evidence being presented as to how many Johnnies can't read, and in what population groups is there a considerable fraction of non-readers. It turned out that the effect of this arousal of public opinion was to redesign programs for teaching reading largely in schools in which most children were learning to read, rather than focusing the added effort and expenditure on schools where there were serious problems in learning to read. Had data been available at that time on the reading achievements of American children, the public would have had information about the incidence of inadequate reading abilities and could have supported efforts to attack the problems where they were rather than to have stimulated programs that did not reach the schools where they were needed.

Some persons question the statement that the public has not had comprehensive and dependable information about what American children and youth have learned. They know that educational achievement tests

* *Can you think of an instance where this has happened?*

have been on the market for 50 years and that they are used widely. Would not the compilation of the scores on standard achievement tests furnish the data the public needs?

The standard achievement tests in common use do not give a dependable measure of what children have learned.* They are not constructed to do so. A typical achievement test is explicitly designed to furnish scores that will arrange the pupils on a line from those most proficient in the subject to those least proficient. The final test questions are selected from a much larger initial number on the basis of tryouts and are the ones which most sharply distinguished pupils in the tryouts who made high scores on the total test from those who made low scores. Test questions are eliminated if most pupils can answer them or if few pupils can answer them, since these do not give much discrimination.

As a result, a large part of the questions retained for the final form of a standard test are those that 40 to 60 percent of the children are able to answer. There are very few questions that represent the things being learned either by the slower learner or the more advanced ones. If a less advanced student is actually making progress in his learning, the typical standard test furnishes so few questions that represent what he has been learning that it will not afford a dependable measure for him. The same holds true for advanced learners.

The Score's Not the Answer

This is not a weakness in the test in serving the purpose for which it was designed. The children who made lower scores had generally learned fewer things in this subject than those who made higher scores and could, therefore, be dependably identified as less proficient. Furthermore, a good standard test has been administered to one or more carefully selected samples, usually national, regional or urban samples, of children in the grade for which the test was designed. The scores obtained from these samples provide norms for the test against which a child's score can be related. These tests thus provide dependable information about where the child stands in his total test performance in relation to the norm group. But when one seeks to find out whether a student who made a low score has learned certain things during the year, the test does not include enough questions covering the material on which he was working to furnish a dependable answer to that question.

The National Assessment has been designed to sample the things which children and youth are expected to learn in school, and to find out what

* *These are the reasons achievement tests are questioned as measures in performance contracts.*

proportion of our people are learning these things.* The instruments used in the assessment are not tests which give each person a score or a grade. They are exercises that children, youth and young adults are given. Instead of a score, the results are reported in terms of the percent of each population group that was able to perform the exercise. These exercises show the public both what our children are learning and how many are learning each thing. The public is thus able to make judgments about each exercise. How important is this for children to learn? And, in what regions, and other circumstances, are most children learning this, and in what circumstances are only part of the children learning?

SCHOOLS MUST TEACH STUDENTS, NOT MERELY "SORT" THEM

The purpose of the National Assessment is closely related to the current call for accountability in education. In contrast to earlier years when schools were expected to give major emphasis to sorting pupils so that only a fraction of those who entered school at six years of age would graduate from high school, the discussion of accountability today emphasizes the purpose of the school as learning rather than sorting.† It seeks to hold the school accountable for educating all the children, not simply furnishing opportunities for the elite. In meeting the demand that all children learn what the school is expected to teach, data are needed about what is being learned by all parts of the population. Schools are discovering that the commonly used standard tests do not show what pupils have learned nor what proportion of the children has learned each of the things the school is teaching. An increasing number of schools is asking for exercises like those developed in the National Assessment so that they can use them as part of their programs for accountability.

Such instruments could furnish information about the progress and problems of the school in providing the kind and quality of service that the public is now expecting. A constructive dialogue can then be maintained with the community regarding the educational objectives, the efforts the school is making to reach these objectives, the progress pupils are making in their learning, the difficulties being encountered and the steps being taken to overcome these difficulties.‡ Ample information on these matters can make the dialogue a constructive one and can reassure the

---

Because many educational psychologists do not agree on what should be learned (see Part I), how would you decide what to sample?

†*How does this change in purpose affect the role of the teacher?*

‡*Can noneducators understand these details of instruction? How could the information be presented to the community?*

general public about the integrity of the school in meeting its responsibilities.

In this program for accountability carried on in the local school district, the National Assessment not only furnishes an example of the kinds of instruments to be used to appraise the results of the school's efforts, but the reports of the National Assessment also give a helpful background for the dialogues with the public. The clientele of the local school sometimes places the blame for difficulties in pupil learning upon the teachers and principals without knowing that certain problems are characteristic of the entire nation or region. Because the National Assessment provides background data, the public can gain a broader perspective from which to view the local problems. There will be less tendency to attack the local schools groundlessly because the public will see that most difficult educational problems are not localized and cannot be blamed upon a particular administrator or set of teachers.

In summary, the National Assessment provides a means of helping the public understand the results being achieved by our educational system and the problems encountered. It furnishes a basis for intelligent examination of the situation and helps to identify the places on which to focus more effective efforts.

EXERCISE

1. How is the National Assessment like the national census? (p. 555)

2. Tyler indicates that *Why Johnny Can't Read* caused some schools to change their reading programs when this change was not necessary. Could National Assessment data prevent such problems? How? (p. 555)

3. According to Tyler, what is the purpose of a standardized achievement test? (p. 556)

4. Why do standardized tests do a poor job of measuring the progress of less advanced students? (p. 556)

5. How do the instruments used in the National Assessment differ from a standardized test? (pp. 556–557)

6. How can the information obtained in the Assessment be used by educators? (pp. 557–558)

The First Results

J. Stanley Ahmann

J. Stanley Ahmann, staff director of the National Assessment of Educational Progress, presents some findings from the first year's assessment program. Approximately 80,000 students and young adults were tested to determine what they knew in science, citizenship, and writing. From the findings reported here, do you think that the National Assessment is generating useful knowledge about education? Will this knowledge help the schools meet the challenge of accountability? As a prospective teacher, is it helpful to you to have such knowledge, or would you prefer to have available other kinds of information about students' achievement?

Data representing the output of the American educational system was gathered for the first time by the National Assessment of Educational Progress in 1969–70. During this year hundreds of exercises were administered to a national sample of approximately 80,000 young Americans in order to discover what they know and can do in the areas of Science, Citizenship, and Writing. The sample was subdivided into four age groups, namely 9-year-olds, 13-year-olds, 17-year-olds, and young adults (ages 26 through 35).

The three learning areas in the assessment are quite different, one from another. Science is a highly organized learning area that is readily found at many of the grade levels in the typical school program. It is likely that the students in the typical school have been exposed to various aspects of science throughout most of their elementary and junior high school years — and possibly some of their senior high school years. In contrast, Citizenship is much less well defined and is not typically taught as a formal subject-matter area. As some have said, citizenship is "everybody's business and nobody's business." At the same time that it is acknowledged as a highly significant area in the school curriculum, it is difficult to find the intensity of instruction as is so often present in science, with the possible exception of certain cognitive aspects such as knowledge of structure and function of government. Finally, Writing is one of the basic skills which has an important role in the early years of the typical school pro-

From *Compact*, vol. 6, no. 1 (February 1972), pp. 13–17. Reprinted with permission of the publisher.

gram, and presumably permeates many aspects of content areas in the later school years.

What then has been learned about the output of the American educational system as a result of the assessment in the areas of Science, Citizenship, and Writing? . . .

Following are some of the highlights for the three learning areas involved in the first assessment year.

ACHIEVEMENT IN SCIENCE

Consistent with the principles of good achievement testing, the development of each learning area began with the establishment of the objectives of that area.* In the case of science the objectives are classified into three levels in a hierarchical fashion. Four major objectives were used, namely:

Objective I: Knowledge of fundamental facts and principles of science.
Objective II: Abilities and skills needed to engage in the processes of science.
Objective III: Understanding of the investigative nature of science.
Objective IV: Attitudes and appreciations of science and scientists.

Approximately 500 exercises were developed on the basis of these objectives and their subobjectives. They vary greatly in their nature, many of them being of the traditional paper-and-pencil type, while others required the manipulation of apparatus.

The analysis of the Science data has proceeded farther than the analysis of data from any other learning area. In general, it is found that the knowledge of science increases with age, with the exception that the retention of information about science tends to diminish somewhat between ages 17 and young adult when that knowledge concerns aspects of science normally learned in the classroom.†

An interesting sex difference appears in the achievement of science. There is a definite tendency of the boys to surpass the girls in this regard. The male advantage is comparatively modest at age 9, increases somewhat at age 13, and becomes even more pronounced at ages 17 and young adult. A study of the Science exercises reveals that the boys do better on physical science exercises than on exercises with biological science content. Furthermore the best performance of the girls was often found in the case of exercises having biological science content.‡ These kinds of findings

---

* Guth (Section 14) would be concerned that beginning by stating behavioral objectives would omit important aspects of learning in the three areas. What might be omitted under this plan?
† What explanations might be given for this finding?
‡ According to Sadker (Section 8) what features of the school might help to create this outcome?

certainly give rise to speculation with regard to the sex role question, that is, the expectations of society for boys and girls. Are these differences culturally determined in large measure?

Striking differences in achievement in Science were also found in the case of Black respondents. By and large they performed between 12 percent and 16 percent below the national average at the four age levels. On the other hand, Blacks performed best on those science exercises largely dependent upon daily experience and common knowledge. Their poorest performance occurred in the case of those exercises which involved a detached research attitude toward the objects and phenomena of Science....

Relative achievement in science was also reported for respondents living in communities of various size and type. For example, it was found that respondents living in highly affluent suburbs performed 5 to 11 percent better than the country as a whole. In contrast, respondents living in highly rural areas performed from 4 to 6 percent below the nation, whereas respondents living in the core areas of large cities showed a 7 to 15 percent deficit.

In view of the fact that the home environment no doubt influences achievement in science, an effort was made to obtain a measure of this variable, at least crudely, by determining the educational level of the parent of the respondent. When the respondents were classified according to the educational level of their parents, remarkable variations in achievement were observed. At the four age levels, performance of respondents reporting neither parent educated beyond eighth grade was from 7 to 12 percent *below* the national average.* Respondents with at least one parent who attended high school fell from 2 to 8 percent *below* the nation. On the other hand, respondents with at least one parent who graduated from high school achieved between 1 to 3 percent *above* the national average, whereas those of one parent educated beyond high school performed from 5 to 9 percent *above* the national average. Thus we see that a direct relationship exists between the level of performance in Science and the level of education of the parents of the respondent. As the level of education of the parents rose, so did the achievement level in Science of the respondent.

Achievement in Citizenship

Achievement in Citizenship is most difficult to define. In an operational sense it can be considered to be the achievement of eight major objectives as determined by various specialists and teachers in this area, as well as concerned laymen. These objectives include such vital goals as: concern for the welfare and dignity of others, support for the rights and freedoms

* *This finding parallels the data reported by Bane and Jencks (Section 3).*

of all individuals, seeking of community improvement through active and democratic participation, helping to maintain law and order, etc.* As one might suspect, there is less emphasis on cognitive achievement in this learning area than in Science. At the same time, a greater emphasis on attitudes and appreciation exists in Citizenship assessment than in Science. The Citizenship exercises included both paper-and-pencil materials as well as group discussions.

Again, it was found that there was improvement in achievement between ages 9 and 13, and between ages 13 and 17. A slight decline was found between ages 17 and young adults. This decline did not occur consistently enough to indicate a definite pattern. The instances of lower success for adults can possibly be explained by such factors as loss of skill from lack of practice, or improvements in school programs since the adults received their formal education.

The difference in achievement in Citizenship between male and female respondents was much less pronounced than that which was found in the case of Science. In general, the differences at each age level were slight with perhaps a slight advantage in the case of young male respondents.

Illustrative of the kind of information which can be gained from the analysis of an individual exercise exists in the instance in which stated attitudes of young people towards the acceptance of other races was solicited. The following exercise was presented to the 13-year-old, 17-year-old and young adult respondents:†

> *People feel differently toward people of other races. How willing would you be to have a person of a different race doing these things?*
> A. Be your dentist or doctor?
> B. Live next door to you?
> C. Represent you in some elected office?
> D. Sit at a table next to yours in a crowded restaurant?
> E. Stay in the same hotel or motel as you?

(For each situation, the respondent had to decide whether he was willing to or preferred not to have this contact with a person of a different race.)

In Table 1 are the data expressed in terms of percent "willling" for 13-year-olds, 17-year-olds, and young adults. Although there is general acceptance of other races in most public situations and relationships, the pattern is somewhat uneven. It should be noted that the acceptance of other races dropped off noticeably when the question is raised of "living

* *Using Esbensen's criteria (Section 14), how would you measure these objectives?*
† *Would this item provide a good measure of your attitude?*

next door." For example, about 90 percent of the young adults in big cities were willing to eat together in a crowded restaurant but only about 65 percent were willing to live next door to persons of another race.

TABLE 1
Stated Acceptance of Other Races in Public Situations
and Relationships (percent "willing")

[Ages]			
13	17	Adult	Situation
80	70	74	A. Be your dentist or doctor?
82	71	67	B. Live next door to you?
80	77	82	C. Represent you in some elected office?
82	83	88	D. Sit at a table next to yours in a crowded restaurant?
88	85	89	E. Stay in the same hotel or motel as you?
90	89	87	Willing to associate with a person of a different race in three or more of the above situations
77	79	77	Four or more
57	57	57	All five

Exercises such as the foregoing reveal only the stated attitude of the respondent. It is quite possible of course that the actual attitude of these individuals is somewhat different. Nevertheless, it is gratifying to many that comparatively high percentages of the members of the sample were willing to at least state that they wish to associate with people of other races in a wide variety of public situations.

ACHIEVEMENT IN WRITING

As in the case of Science, the Writing assessment was also based upon four major objectives. Three of these are writing to communicate adequately in a social situation, in a business situation, and in a scholastic situation. The fourth is appreciation of the value of writing.*

Basically, three types of exercises were used: (1) short answer or short essay exercises, where the responses were scored according to whether certain pieces of information were included; (2) multiple-choice questions; and (3) essays requiring writing on a given topic. The essay results

* Guth (Section 14) contends that such learning as appreciation cannot be measured in observable ways. Do the measures used here appear to sample such affective outcomes?

were scored for general writing ability, including grammar, word choice, originality, and depth of thought. Later, some of these exercises were also scored in terms of mechanical aspects of writing, such as punctuation, capitalization, agreement, and paragraphing.

A sharp difference in performance in Writing existed between male and female respondents. When consideration was given to all of the Writing exercises, the female advantage was pronounced and increased with age. The performance of girls was much better than that of boys on non-essay exercises that require completion of specific writing tasks such as filling out the parts of an envelope or writing an invitation to a class play. Surprising to some is the fact that the results show that the two sexes succeed to about the same degree when writing essays. There is essentially no sex difference in essay performance.

Certain regional patterns were also revealed by the analysis of the data in Writing. For instance, there is a tendency for the southeast to perform below the nation as a whole and lower than any other region compared to the nation. Also, the southeast success decreases as age increases, with typical performance ranging from about 3 percent below the national average at age 9, to about 8 percent below at the adult level. On the other hand, the northeast achievement is highest at ages 9 and 13, but the lead moves to the west at the age of 17, and the central region is highest in Writing at the adult level. . . .

The foregoing is but a tiny sample of the mass of data which was generated by the first assessment year. The full magnitude of the data being produced is difficult to comprehend even when one recognizes that the three learning areas mentioned will be joined by seven others before the first cycle of assessment is complete. Furthermore, steps are already underway for reassessment in the case of the areas mentioned as well as others. In the typical reassessment the objectives will be re-examined and at least 50 percent of the exercises to be used will be new. The remainder will be exercises used in the first assessment but not released to the general public.

Reassessment of Science is scheduled for 1972–73, of Citizenship for 1974–75 and of Writing for 1973–74. Comparisons will then be made with respect to the level of achievement for those exercises which were not released. For the first time it will be possible to determine whether changes have occurred in level of performance in these learning areas. Is the achievement of young Americans in Science, Citizenship and Writing increasing or decreasing? * A definitive answer to this question will be of inestimable value to decision makers concerned with education.

If you were given this information, how would you use it as a teacher?

EXERCISE

1. Describe the sample population included in the 1969–70 data for the National Assessment. (p. 559)

2. What approach to test construction was used in the Assessment? (p. 560)

3. List three major National Assessment findings in science. (pp. 560–561)

4. How did parents' education levels relate to achievement in science? (p. 561)

5. How would you summarize the sample's attitudes toward acceptance of other races? (pp. 562–563)

6. In what ways did the sexes differ in their writing skills? (p. 564)

7. Achievement in science was scheduled for reassessment in 1972–73. What comparisons will this make possible? (p. 564)

Layman's View

Zoe Von Ende

Most selections in this book were written by professional educators. The following article was written by Zoe Von Ende, a newspaper writer. Her firsthand observations have resulted in some positive perceptions of National Assessment, but she has negative reactions as well. Von Ende is concerned that National Assessment will not bring about any fundamental change in teaching methods used in the schools. Do you think that she may be asking National Assessment to accomplish a goal which it was not designed to accomplish? How do you think Ralph Tyler, one of the original developers of the National Assessment program, would respond to her criticisms (Tyler, this section)?

My experience with National Assessment has been limited to only two encounters: participating in a writing review conference, headed by former U.S. Senator Wayne Morse, and through a feature story I wrote dealing

From *Compact*, vol. 6, 1972, pp. 6, 23. Reprinted with permission of the publisher.

with sexual differences in learning as revealed in NAEP data on science, writing and citizenship. Presumably, my role as parent helped qualify me for both assignments.

Consequently, my feelings and impressions about National Assessment are ambiguous. I find much that I like; but there are some aspects I question, such as:

1. I am most favorably impressed with the people associated with National Assessment. Everyone I have met, mostly staff members in Denver, are thoroughly professional in their approach to their jobs, highly motivated, flexible and objective.

2. I am equally impressed with the thoroughness that has gone into the selection of exercises. Other technical aspects of the program, sample-taking and administering, for instance, appear to be well done, too.

3. The broad base of participation from citizens evidently is good, also. It may slow the program, but I think it's basic to the success, particularly when it comes to eventual presentation of materials to those most political people, local school board members.

4. Great effort is being made to take into account socioeconomic differences in individuals being tested. The criticisms registered by my panel often, maybe usually, dealt with our finding middle-class bias in the exercises. We were most emphatic every time we came upon this, stating our opinions and reasons for them.

By Whose Standard?

At this point, though, I come to the point of my negative reactions to National Assessment. They include:

1. Removing that middle-class bias is so difficult, maybe impossible. My greatest concern here is that cultural values inferred from the exercises seem to me to be on an absolute, not relative, basis. By your or my standards, a 13-year-old, for instance, writes poorly, yet she definitely conveys a message. The message might be that she is totally unable to articulate her feelings or observations, yet it is a message. Children in the group we looked at did not react in the expected manner to Cannonball Adderley's version of "Mercy, Mercy." However, they told me one important thing: they didn't relate to *that* particular music.

2. Like so many others, I am concerned with eventual utilization of National Assessment results. My biggest concern is that teaching methods will be largely unchanged; that change, if any, will be on emphasis of subject matter. It seems to me that many learning difficulties lie mostly in the realm of attitude, motivation and methods of schools rather than in subject matter per se. Questions I ask myself about National Assessment

are: Will it, or can it, stimulate teachers and school generally to innovate, to stimulate learning, to develop the stamina so necessary to establish individualized goals, to accommodate the system to the student rather than vice versa? Can National Assessment help schools get rid of the right-answer syndrome and replace it with learning how to learn?

3. The National Assessment questions that we reviewed, like practically every other test I've ever had anything to do with, did seem to test ability to answer questions more than ability in a given area. Is this a built-in weakness?

Publicizing National Assessment seems to me to be an important and difficult job. News from National Assessment isn't startling and headline-grabbing. It's more likely to be quiet and significant, not loud and significant. And, as I said before, acquainting local people, political leaders especially, with the whole project is essential to its basic purposes.* It therefore must compete with hundreds of stories for space in the local paper or time on local television programs, assuming National Assessment wants its message spread to those overworked, nebulous grass roots.

EXERCISE

1. What are the four characteristics of National Assessment best liked by Von Ende? (p. 566)

2. According to Von Ende, what aspect of education is National Assessment likely to change, and what aspect is it not likely to change? (pp. 566–567)

* How will these individuals use the information from National Assessment?

TESTING
AND
GRADING

Introduction

Tests and grades have a major role in the American educational system. Most educators believe they have a particularly strong influence on students. The complaint is often heard that, under the current system, many students work toward the objective of getting a good grade rather than learning for the sake of learning. Tests are also important to students because they are often the basis on which grades are assigned, and they are used to make such important decisions about the student as acceptance into college.

Although most educators would agree on the importance of tests and grades in current educational practice, they disagree with each other concerning their value and needed changes. Should tests and grades be abolished? Are they effective in their present form? Should new testing and grading practices be developed? These are the issues which are dealt with in the following four selections.

Some background information may be useful in understanding the controversy that surrounds tests and grades. A major function of test scores and grades is to provide quantitative evaluations of how well a student has learned. This function can be performed in two basic ways. One method is to evaluate a student's learning achievement by comparing his test performance with the test performance of other students. For example, if one student receives a test score of 90 or an A grade and another receives a score of 65 or C grade, we are supposed to infer that the first student knows more than the other. This widely used method is sometimes called "norm-referenced" testing or grading.

The other basic method of evaluating a student's learning is by comparing it with a fixed criterion. Pass-fail grades are an example of "criterion-referenced" grading because a "pass" is determined by whether the student achieves an acceptable performance level, not by whether he outperforms another student. Mastery learning is

568

built around this form of evaluation. In criterion-referenced measurement there is no restriction on how many students can succeed in a curriculum subject. In norm-referenced testing and grading, on the other hand, the distribution of scores is usually fixed. In a typical school setting, no more than 15 per cent of students will receive A's, about 30 per cent will receive B's, etc.

Whether a norm-referenced or criterion-referenced approach is used, tests and grades can have several uses. First, they provide quantitative evaluation of how well a student has learned. Second, they give the student feedback on his learning achievement. Tests and grades tell a student how well he did compared with other students, or whether he has achieved competence by meeting a criterion level of performance. A third use of tests and grades is to make decisions. For example, a college admissions officer might decide to admit a student on the basis of his Scholastic Aptitude Test scores and his high school grade-point average. Also, the student, perhaps with the assistance of a counselor, might review his grades and test scores to help him decide on a future course of study or career direction.

Fourth, tests and grades can be used to evaluate the educational system. For example, they are used this way in accountability programs (see Section 15). This use of tests and grades is distinctive in that the student is not being evaluated. If test scores indicate that a student has not mastered a particular subject, instruction is continued and modified until he does achieve mastery. This method usually involves multiple administration of similar tests. Typically, though, comparable tests are administered at the beginning and at the end of instruction to measure each student's learning gain. Fifth, tests and grades are frequently used in research investigations, for example, to identify factors that influence students' test scores and grades. Other investigations evaluate new instructional techniques by determining whether they increase learning gain from pre-instruction testing to post-instruction testing. Several examples of both types of research are included in Parts 2 and 3 of this book.

Three of the following selections consider grading practices. John Holt and Robert Feldmesser take conflicting positions on the value of norm-referenced grading. Holt believes that all grades should be abolished because they have detrimental effects on learning. He feels they foster unhealthy competitive attitudes in students, hurt self-esteem, and create misleading expectancies about the student's future school performance. Feldmesser, however, claims that grades have positive functions: they satisfy the student's curiosity about how he is doing in a course; they help the student decide his future course of study; and they are an effective motivational device. Jason Millman takes a somewhat different tack by recommending a new approach based on criterion-referenced grading. He believes that his approach is free of the criticisms typically made of norm-referenced grading practices.

You may find it difficult to decide whether you agree with Holt, Feldmesser, or Millman because their positions are based on opinion and personal observation rather than on research evidence. What kind of evidence could you collect to evaluate the merit of each position?

Tests are an important factor in assigning grades. Often teacher-made tests are used to evaluate students, and the resulting test scores are translated into grades. Sometimes such test scores are used directly as is the case with the Scholastic Aptitude Test, tests used in accountability programs, and tests administered as part of a district-wide or state-wide testing program. Many educators and students accept test scores uncritically, but Robert Stake discusses several problems associated with them in this section.

The following views reflect controversies that surround current testing and grading practices. Where do you stand?

Tests and Grades

Pro   Tests and grades have been misused by some, but this should not cause us to overlook their positive functions when used effectively; for example, to provide the student with feedback on his performance, and to help him make important school and career decisions.

Con   Whatever the potential benefits of tests and grades, most often they are misused in practice. They hinder learning and can have harmful effects on a student's self-concept. Therefore, they should be abolished.

Norm-Referenced Evaluation of Students

Pro   Norm-referenced tests and grades should be used instead of a criterion-referenced approach. Students need to know their strengths and weaknesses compared to each other, because eventually they will have to compete against each other in the world of work.

Con   Criterion-referenced tests and grades are preferable because they tell the student exactly what he has mastered and they eliminate unhealthy competitive attitudes in students.

Marking and Grading

John Holt

John Holt is a distinguished teacher and writer on problems of American education. (Another selection from his writing appears in Section 1.) In this article he argues that teachers should eliminate all testing and grading because these practices impede the learning process. However, he acknowledges that in most schools teachers must test and grade; they have no choice. Because of this reality, Holt offers several guidelines that teachers can use to reduce the negative effect of tests and grades. Specifically, he recommends that teachers grade as seldom as possible, as leniently as possible, and as privately as possible. Do you agree with Holt's position that tests and grades should be abolished? If you do, would you extend his position to contexts other than school? For example, would you oppose "grading" an individual by making a merit rating of his job performance?

In the kind of learning I have been talking about there is no place and no need for conventional testing and grading. In a class where children are doing things, and not getting ready to do them sometime in the distant future, what they do tells us what they have learned. Unfortunately, and probably for some time, most schools demand grades. How can we make this business, always harmful to children, somewhat less harmful?

In recent classes, at the Harvard Graduate School of Education and at the University of California at Berkeley, as a short-time visitor I was able to give a Pass (in the first case) or an A (in the second) to all students who signed up, regardless of what else they did or did not do — though I would rather have given no grades at all. But in all my previous teaching I had to give regular grades. That is, I had to say that some students were better than others. At first I thought this a good thing, believing, as many teachers do today, that grades, particularly bad grades, spurred students on to work harder. Later I came to feel that it was bad, but it was grade or don't teach, and for many reasons which seemed to me good at the time, I wanted to teach. In time I arrived at a rule that seemed to work — if you must grade, grade as seldom as possible, as privately as possible, and as easily as possible.

Specifically, if we have to submit a grade or report card once a term, or quarter, or semester, that should be the *only* mark we give the child in that period. How then do we get the grade? To my students in ninth-, tenth-, and eleventh-grade English, in a very grade-conscious school, I said that I would get their grade from a cross-section of what I felt to be their best work. What sense does an average grade make in a course like English? Do we average a serious writer's best work against his worst? If I assigned a paper, and a student did badly on it, this only showed that this was the wrong paper for him, where he could not show what ability he had. The remedy was to try to give a wide enough variety of choices and opportunities for writing, reading, and talking so that everyone would have a fairly good chance of showing his best talents.

It is not just in English that it makes no sense to figure students' grades by taking an average of all their daily or weekly work. It makes no sense in any subject. Take the case of arithmetic. Here are two children, trying to learn, say, long division. One child gets it at the first crack. All his homework and class papers in long division are excellent. At the end of the marking period he gets an A. The other child has a hard struggle. His first papers are very bad. Only after many failures does he finally catch on. But he does, and at the end of the marking period he too does a perfect paper. In a class where daily grades are averaged in, his perfect final paper will be averaged against all the failures he made while he was learning, and he will be given a low or perhaps even a failing mark. This is idiotic, unfair, outrageous. The aim of the class is to learn long division, not to have a contest to see who can learn it in the fewest number of tries. Anyone who learns it, however long it takes, however many times he fails along the way, should get a perfect mark for that part of the course.* ...

We should also mark as *privately* as we can. Only the teacher and the student, not the other children, should know what marks anyone is getting. It is no one else's business. No big 100's or 60's or A's or E's on individual papers, no gold stars on the walls. If for official records we have to make a kind of pecking order of the children, we should at least make it as invisible as possible. If the children feel they are all in some kind of race, and if everyone knows who are winners and who are losers, the losers are going to try to protect what little is left of their pride and dignity by getting out of the race, by refusing to run. Not only that, but a lot of them are going to try to put a stop to the whole race — which is what much of our school troubles today are about.

We can at least make clear to the children how little grades mean to us.

---

* *Holt is describing a mastery learning situation (see Block, Section 15) based upon criterion-referenced testing (see Millman, this section).*

In my last fifth-grade class, I told the children that I did not believe in grades, that learning could not be measured and labeled with a number or letter or word, that I only gave them grades because if I didn't the school wouldn't let me teach them at all, and that the grades had nothing to do with what I thought about them as people. This was lame and feeble enough, I admit. It might have been better for the children in the long run if I had fought the school on this issue (though it didn't seem as important then as it does now), even at the risk of getting fired for it. But what I did say was better than nothing. It did something to make them feel that the class was not just one more place where they raced against each other to get points from me. I then said that any grades I gave were for themselves and their parents and were nobody else's business, and that I didn't want people saying, I got so and so, what did you get? At least in my presence, the children seemed to obey this request. Later my ninth-, tenth-, and eleventh-grade students did not.

We should grade, if we have to, as easily as possible. Particularly at the low end. Put a safety net under everybody. To my ninth-, tenth-, and eleventh-graders I made it clear that nobody in class would get lower than a C −, whatever they might do or not do. This at least freed them from the burden of failure. Free of it, they went on to do good work, very often better work than they had done before. The only student who perhaps did not "deserve" the C − I gave him told me years later that although he did very little work in my class, he found there an interest in both reading and writing that continued to grow even after he left the school.

There is absolutely no excuse for a teacher or a school failing a student. We are there for them, not they for us. We have the age, the experience, the knowledge, the money, the power. If a student spends a year in my class and learns *something*, then I have no right to fail him. I must find a way to give him *some* positive and legitimate credit for whatever he has learned. If at the end of a year he has truly learned *nothing*, if the experience has brought nothing new at all into his life, has not in any way helped him to grow out into the world, then *I* am the one who should be failed, not him.*

People say angrily, what good does it do to promote a child from one grade to the next if he doesn't know what he is supposed to know? One answer is, as I showed in *How Children Fail*, that most of the children who fool their teachers and testers into thinking that they know what they are supposed to know, don't really know it, and have to be "taught" it or most of it all over again. A more important reason is that the child who is kept back against his will is hardly ever helped, and is almost always

* *This is the basic premise of teacher accountability. How would Farrell (Section 15) respond to this charge?*

badly hurt, by the experience. Sometimes children who feel themselves unready to go ahead may ask or even agree freely to repeat a year. Sometimes — not always — this helps them to get more confidence, and to do better in their later schooling. But children who are kept back against their will are humiliated, made to feel stupid, labeled as stupid, and thus are even less able to learn the following year whatever it was that caused them trouble the year before.* I have known a number of children who at one time or another had been kept back a year or more. All were poor students and afraid of school. Almost all of them *still* did not know the things they had been kept back to learn.

We hear all the time how terrible it is that thirteen- or fourteen-year-old children in the seventh or eighth grade do not know how to read. It is terrible, and all the more so because the fault is not theirs but the school's, for reasons made very clear in Dennison's *The Lives of Children*. But would these children be more likely to learn to read if they were surrounded by six-year-olds? It is worth noting — and this experience has been duplicated by many others — that the only way in which Dennison could get twelve-year-old José to have reading lessons at all was to have them *alone, behind a locked door*, so that none of the other children, whose own insecurities would surely have caused them to make fun of him, could see his struggles and failures. I have often said to teachers working with older children who were unable or barely able to read that if they wanted to help, not only would the help probably have to be given in secret, but even the offer to help. The problem lies almost wholly in the anxiety, shame, and self-contempt and self-hatred of such children, and putting them in classes with much younger children can only make this much worse. The remedy is to get away from all grading and labeling, and make school a place where each child and every child is helped, in the way most helpful to him, to find what is the best way for him to learn what he needs and wants to know.

In any case, we are simply not honest when we say or claim to believe that in keeping a child back we are doing it to help him. We do it to punish. Being kept back is a severe and long-lasting punishment, and schools use it so that the threat of it will "make" children do the work. If we think otherwise we are just fooling ourselves. The children are not fooled.

Teachers quite often ask me something like this, "If I give Jimmy a better grade than he deserves, say an A or a B, won't it make it harder for him when he gets into his next class and can't live up to that standard?"

There are two worries here. The first might be put something like this: "If I give Jimmy a good mark this year, and next year he doesn't do nearly

* *In an open education classroom this situation should not occur. Why? (Refer to Section 10 for discussion of open education.)*

as well, won't everyone think I am running an easy class or am a poor teacher?" When I say this to groups of teachers, I hear enough nervous laughter to tell me that this is exactly what many of them are thinking. Indeed, most teachers, and with good reason, are afraid of what may be said about them if they give Jimmy a better mark than he got *last* year. Even in the small and relatively humane and kindly schools where I have taught, I have often been challenged for giving A's or B's to children whom everyone had come to think of as only worth C's or D's. Even in these schools, it was hardly ever taken as likely or even possible that the child might really have been doing better work. Many other teachers have told me similar stories. Many have even told me that they have been specifically *forbidden* to give A's to children in a low track, the reason being, "If they *could* get A's, they wouldn't be in the low track." This is really terrible. We say that we want to help children who are doing badly in school to do better, but we all too often assume that they are incapable of improving. In such circumstances teachers are only being realistic in thinking that giving bad marks to children is a way of protecting themselves. . . .

Teachers also fear what may happen to Jimmy next year if they grade him easily this year. To this I say, "Make no mistake about it, if you have to send children on to their next class with labels around their necks, the better labels you can give them, the better off they will be." * Robert Rosenthal and Lenore Jacobson in *Pygmalion in the Classroom* (Holt, Rinehart & Winston), have shown . . . that when we expect children to do well in school they are more likely to do well than when we expect them to do badly. Here, as in so many other areas of human life, the behavior we get from other people is much closer to what we *expect* to get than what we think we want to get. If Jimmy comes into that next teacher's class with an A stuck on him, the teacher will be pleased. We all like A students; they give us no trouble. He will think, "Good, another A student; won't have to worry about him, anyway; why don't they send me more like that?" He will welcome Jimmy to his class, make him feel at home, give him every encouragement. It is certain that, given this kind of treatment, Jimmy will in fact do much better work than he was used to doing. But suppose that it still is not as good as this teacher would like. He will think, "Perhaps he is having a little trouble getting adjusted, perhaps something happened to him over the summer, I must be patient and encouraging." After all, A students are valuable resources, and must be treated carefully. If on the other hand Jimmy comes to this teacher with a D hanging around his neck, the teacher will think, "Oh hell, another

* Brophy and Good (Section 6) suggest teachers sort out performance labels that are reasonable and unreasonable for students. If that is so, is this assumption sound?

dummy, why do I always get so many of them, I wonder what's wrong with this one, what kind of trouble he will give me, we'll probably have to spend most of our time hashing over that old stuff," etc. These feelings will not be lost on Jimmy. He will catch them in the first day, in the first hour he is in that class. No, all labels are libels, but good labels are much less bad than bad labels.

There is a side advantage to be gained, a fringe benefit, from grading as seldom as possible. It will free us from the dull, useless, and time-wasting drudgery of correcting papers. Teachers, particularly those with big classes, spend an enormous amount of time on this donkey work. If papers have to be corrected . . . we should let the children correct their own. Give them an answer book or answer sheet. Most publishers of textbooks that have problems in them supply the answers. We can get copies, or make copies for the children. If the class is in arithmetic, we can get a calculating machine — electric ones now cost as little as sixty dollars — and teach them to run it. We should anyway; these machines are what the children will be using in the larger world — nobody out there is figuring with pencil and paper.

Or we might have the children make up, as a class project, their own answer sheets. This will force them to confront and think about the vital question, "How can we tell whether an answer is right?" They think you find out by asking the teacher. But who tells the teacher? Someone, somewhere, has to have some other ways of deciding whether an answer is right. What are these ways? If you use a machine, how can you tell whether the machine is running properly, or when it breaks down, or has made a mistake? How do people in the larger world tell? How does the supermarket know that its cash registers are working properly? Perhaps some children could save some supermarket slips and check up on the machines. Machines *do* make mistakes. How do we check them? How does the bank check its computers? Such questions might lead a class into looking at double-entry bookkeeping, which is a subject so important and interesting, and so connected with the larger world outside, that it ought not to be saved for a few students studying accounting. . . .

Elsewhere, in "Making Children Hate Reading" in *The Underachieving School*, I have said why I think spelling tests, and indeed most of what we do about spelling, is foolish and harmful — as they say in Washington, counter-productive. Meanwhile, if we must give spelling tests, let the children correct them by looking up each word, as they spelled it, in the dictionary. If they can't find it, either they are using the dictionary wrongly or they can't spell the word. Let them find, first of all, whether they *are* looking in the right place in the dictionary. Obviously, if they can't do that, the dictionary isn't going to be of much help to them in spelling. If they are using the dictionary properly, and still can't find the word, that means they have spelled it wrong. What then? For most children, I would tell them the correct spelling. To a certain kind of child, I might say, "How many other ways can you think of to spell it that would sound right, that I could read and know what the word was saying? Write a few of them, pick the one that looks most likely, and see if you can find it." Or I might tell him to ask one of his friends. This would confront him with the interesting problem — how do I tell which of my friends are good spellers when I don't spell well myself?

I deeply believe that all this messing with spelling is foolish. If children read for pleasure, and to find out things they want to find out, and write in order to say what they want to say, they will before long spell better than most people do now. . . .

One year a student came into one of my English classes — very bright, quiet, a bit shy. At the beginning of the year I told the class that spelling was not going to be part of our year's work, that I would not fuss about their spelling, and indeed that I would only indicate or correct misspelled words on their papers if they put S's in the corner of their papers. Only the good spellers ever put S's in the corner of their papers. By the time I had read a couple of this student's papers, I realized that I had a problem. . . . His frequency of error, as they say, was about twenty-five words per page. Sometimes, in one paragraph, he spelled a word two or three different ways. I began to get cold feet. I could hear a voice from the future asking me, "But why didn't you *do* something?" So, like all of us in these situations, I began to think about covering my tracks a bit. Also, I really wanted to help.

So, one day, in private, I said to this student, "I really meant what I said about not bugging you about spelling. But I can see you have something of a problem. As it happened, I have worked with kids who spelled badly, and I think I know some tricks that may work. I don't want you to feel that I am indifferent. So if you would like some help, don't hesitate to ask — I'll be glad to give it." He looked at me a while, then heaved a great sigh up from his shoes and said slowly, "I've been getting help for years." I said, "Say no more. I won't raise the subject again, if you don't." He didn't, and I didn't. He was in my class for two years, wrote a number of interesting papers, and was in other areas a brilliant student. By the end of the second year in my class his misspelled words per page were down to five or less. By now they may well be down to none.

On this matter of corrections. We have our ends and means confused, our cart in front of the horse. We often talk and act as if children learned something in school — say, fractions — so that they could do papers about it. On the contrary, they do the papers *only* to learn about fractions.*

* *Here Holt seems to be opposing all forms of testing.*

There is *no other reason* for the papers. So why not say, here is the chapter on adding fractions, read it, ask about anything in it you don't understand, work out some of the examples in the text and then compare them with the text, and when you think you understand the chapter, do a few of the problems at the end. Then check them with your answer sheet. If you got them right, you are ready for the next chapter. If not, try them again, see if you can catch your own mistake. If you can't, ask a friend, or come and ask me — that's what I'm for — and I'll try to help you find where you got off the trail.

Many people say, "But won't the children cheat?" This shows how much we, like the children, have slipped into the habit of thinking of school as a contest, a battle of wits between teachers and children, waged according to certain rules. There is no contest — or there shouldn't be. If the children know that we are not trying to judge or catch or trap or humiliate or defeat them, they will quickly stop trying to think of ways to escape or outwit us. Then we can begin — many of us for the first time — to do our real job, which is not proving that children are not learning, but helping them learn.* ...

To sum up, whatever concessions we may have to make to testing, marking, and grading in the short run, in the long run our duty is to oppose them. To some groups of teachers, after they had shown by raised hands that on the whole they thought grades did more harm than good, I used to ask two more questions. First, "How many of you give grades?" Almost all did. Second, "How many of you have said publicly, or even to the parents of the children you teach, or to the school you work in, that you think on the whole grades hurt more than they help?" Almost no hands were raised. Now we can hardly call ourselves professional while we act like this. ...

In the article, "Why We Need a New Schooling," which I wrote for *Look* magazine (January 13, 1970), I said that any tests that were not a personal matter between the learner and someone helping him learn, but were given instead to grade and label students for someone else's purposes (employers, colleges, evaluators of schools, administrators, anxious parents, etc.), were illegitimate and harmful. I then said that students should organize to refuse to take such tests, and that *teachers should organize to refuse to give them*. The students will probably lead the way in this. We may not have long to wait before they begin. When they do, we should give them all the support and cooperation we can. They are not trying to destroy our authority, but to restore it. Only when we stop being judges, graders, labelers, can we begin to be true teachers, educators, helpers of growth and learning. ...

* *In what ways, if any, can tests help students learn?*

EXERCISE

1. Why did Holt grade his students by taking a cross-section of their best work rather than by averaging all their work? (p. 572)

2. According to Holt, what is the likely effect of making public knowledge of students' marks and grades? (p. 572)

3. Why does Holt believe that a teacher has absolutely no excuse for failing a student? (p. 573)

4. What is Holt's recommended procedure for giving spelling tests? (pp. 576–577)

5. How does Holt respond to the criticism that students will cheat if they have an answer sheet available for their class assignments? (p. 578)

The Positive Functions of Grades

Robert A. Feldmesser

Robert Feldmesser, a sociologist, defends the use of grades as strongly as John Holt criticized them in the preceding selection. He believes that the traditional grading system (A–F letter grades or 0 to 4 scale) benefits college students in several ways. For example, a course grade satisfies a student's natural curiosity about how well he is doing. Also, course grades help the student decide where he should concentrate his efforts — what field of study to pursue, or whether he should continue college. Grades also provide a motivational device to help the professor induce students to learn material whose importance they may not appreciate when they are studying it. Feldmesser acknowledges that grades can be used in ways that hinder student learning. However, he contends that misuses are preventable if grades are administered fairly and in proper perspective. Do you agree with Feldmesser's position? You might note that Holt discusses grading of elementary school children, whereas Feldmesser addresses the problem of grading college students. Could this difference explain their conflicting positions on the merit of grading and evaluating students?

From the *Educational Record*, Winter 1972, pp. 66–72. Reprinted with permission of the publisher.

The custom of giving grades in college courses, recording them in permanent form, and calculating a grade point average is clearly under attack. A survey conducted by the American Council on Education in fall 1970 found that 44 percent of entering freshmen favored abolishing grades.[1] Many faculty members find merit in the objections of students, and many institutions are, indeed, modifying their grading practices.

Yet there is general agreement that it is educationally beneficial for a college student to receive some evaluation of his work, that is, some judgment about the quality of his academic performance which he can use to guide his future academic behavior. A grade is essentially one form of evaluation: specifically, a form so highly condensed or abstracted that it can be expressed as a number, or as a letter that can be converted into a number, and entered on a permanent record. Admittedly, all forms of evaluation may not be equally beneficial, and some may not be beneficial at all. The controversy about grades, therefore, resolves into the issue of the worth of this particular kind of evaluation.

Do grades serve any evaluative function that cannot be served, or served better, by some other form of evaluation? It is the contention here that they do. Grades have the first-order function of providing unique and useful information to the student, and second-order functions of generating other kinds of evaluation and enhancing their effectiveness. Grades *can* be justified on the basis of their contributions to student learning, apart from their putative usefulness to administrators, graduate schools, employers, or society in general. To support the benefits of grades *for the student* is to meet the opponents of grades on their most defensible ground.*

Grades here mean the familiar A–F or 4–0 systems and their variants, as distinguished from both total abolition of grades and pass-fail and similar arrangements that allow no differentiations among students who meet minimum course requirements and which are advocated as a way to relieve the pressure of conventional grades. Although a position supporting grades bucks a strong tide, one may hope that, in the long run, rationality can be made to prevail over the whims of fashion.

The kind of evaluation most widely favored is one highly detailed and specific, giving the student a maximum of information about his performance along each of the relevant dimensions of a course. This sort of feedback, it is said, helps him identify his strengths and weaknesses so he can most wisely allocate his time and energy in his future academic

---

* *What information can a grade provide that a mastery profile of skills will not provide?*

work. There is no quarrel here with the argument that this type of evaluation is indeed useful.*

SUPPLEMENTARY ROLE

There is, nevertheless, an important role to be played by the summative
evaluation called a grade. This role does not preclude a multidimensional
evaluation but supplements it. A grade should be considered an effort to
put back together, to synthesize, the separate judgments about a student's
work. It gives the student some sense of the quality of his performance
on the whole. To a student in a biology course, for example, it is not
enough to know that his lab work was weak while his grasp of abstract
concepts was strong, and that he was high on understanding of cell structure but low on understanding of ecological relationships and middling
on understanding of reproductive systems. He will also want to know what
it all adds up to: whether, all things considered, he did well or poorly or
something in between. The grade thus satisfies a natural curiosity, but,
while that seems like a virtue in itself,[2] the grade does more. It helps a
student decide whether, taking one thing with another, biology is a field
in which further inputs of his resources are likely to be productive for
him, or whether he should switch to another field.† In other words, if it
is useful to him to have judgments about one aspect of his course
work as distinguished from other aspects, it is also useful to him to have
judgments about one course, holistically considered, as distinguished from
other courses.

This same logic can and should be applied to the infamous grade point
average. It helps a student to know how well he is doing in higher education generally, all *courses* considered, so that he can make a more informed decision about whether further study is the right thing for him
and, if it is, what sorts of institutions would be most suitable. In the absence of this information, he may waste his time by pursuing his studies
or waste his talents by not pursuing his studies. Calculation of a grade
point average obviously requires grades, as they have been defined above....

SECOND-ORDER FUNCTIONS

The second-order functions of grades derive from another need: the
need to report evaluations to a central agency of authority within the

* *This is the criterion-referenced evaluation supported by Holt (previous article) and Millman (next article).*
† *Do you think a grade provides the information necessary for making this kind
of decision?*

educational institution. If a central agency is to receive evaluations of all students in all courses during the entire time they are in college, the evaluations must be highly condensed — preferably to a single symbol — so the central agency does not have to devote an inordinate amount of resources to record keeping — which is to say that if evaluations are to be reported, they must take the form of grades.* Thus, to establish the functional necessity of reporting is to establish by implication the need for grades.

Why, then, is reporting a functional necessity? In particular, why is it important to the student's learning, since that is the criterion here? There are two basic arguments. . . .

REPORTING REQUIREMENT

The reporting requirement exercises a coercive force on the instructor in behalf of his students. At the very least, it compels him to make some minimal evaluation — the minimal represented by the grade itself.

But in most cases, the reporting requirement probably prods the instructor to make more than a minimal evaluation. If he has to submit a grade, he will probably feel an obligation to develop some reasonable basis for it, if only so he can defend it if questioned. Hence, he will set up more or less detailed evaluative procedures; and if he is going to do that anyway, it takes little extra effort to inform his students of the results as his course progresses. This step also helps avoid a situation in which students could claim that their grade was unfair because it took them by surprise or that they could have taken corrective action if they had been informed earlier. Moreover, the reporting requirement has a quality-control function, analogous to that of the requirement for public trials: it restrains the instructor from making evaluations that merely reflect his ideological or punitive inclinations, lest he be called upon to justify his grade. In the absence of this requirement, some instructors would probably be quite ruthless about "maintaining academic standards." [3]

BASIS FOR DECISIONS

. . . [M]any students — and their number is, if anything, increasing — deliberately decide, on what seem to them sufficient grounds, that the content of a particular course, or particular parts of a course, is irrelevant to their needs and, therefore, should *not* be learned. It can be said that that is their business; if they choose not to learn, they will and should bear the consequences of their decision. But this attitude amounts to a shirking of the faculty's educational duty, if not to a denial of its educational pretensions.

* *Are computers a way to resolve this problem? (See Hall, Section 10.)*

The student, after all, is young, and his very presence in a course indicates that he knows relatively little about the field. Consequently, he does not necessarily know what parts of a course will be relevant to his needs over the long run. His teachers claim more foresight in such matters; if they are unwilling to make that claim, they should not be his teachers. Thus, instructors are entitled — and obliged — to exert some pressure on the student to induce him to learn material whose importance he is not yet in a position to perceive. One effective and appropriate way to apply this pressure is to make it in the student's immediate interest to take his instructors' evaluations seriously. This step can be accomplished, in turn, by using those evaluations as the basis for important short-run decisions about the student, for example, decisions about further study or employment.* Finally, if evaluations are to be the basis for such decisions, the evaluations must be reported to some central agency with the authority to make those decisions or to transmit the information to others who can. The knowledge that important decisions will be based on a student's grade is another force compelling instructors, too, to take more care with grades than they otherwise might.

REINFORCING EFFECT

Something more is involved here than the familiar motivational function of grades (though it may be noted that students do have difficulty generating their own motivation in the absence of grades).[4] Students, like other people, interpret the significance of communications in part by the significance attributed to them by others. If no one else cared what evaluations had been made of his work, why should the student care? If no one else based any important decisions on those evaluations, wouldn't the message to the student be that the evaluations were, in fact, not important? Why, then, should he allow them to influence his academic behavior? It is apparent, then, that grades reinforce the feedback function of other evaluations. . . .

Whatever the merits of the preceding arguments, a great many criticisms of grades continue to be made.[5] It may be a plausible hypothesis that the dysfunctional outweigh the functional consequences of grades. However, some criticisms of grades are totally unwarranted, suffering from defects in logic. Others are more properly directed at the *misuse* of grades rather than at grades per se, or at evaluation generally rather than at grades specifically. A few do refer to the technical deficiencies of grades themselves. Most valid criticism can be met by institutional changes.

Is this a potentially punitive use of grades? Compare with Holt's position (this section) about reporting grades to other agencies.

REWARDS FOR LEARNING

One common objection to grades is that they are extrinsic rather than intrinsic rewards. In the minds of many people, a moral stigma is attached to the pursuit of learning for the sake of external rewards. But, why is it so heinous to learn as a means toward an end? How well would college faculty fare on this test of academic purity: how much of a faculty member's time is spent acquiring new knowledge for the sheer delight of it, and how much to be a better teacher, or to contribute to the solution of a social or technological problem, or to dazzle students, or to have something to publish? This is not simply an ad hominem thrust; the model offered by the faculty is probably more powerful than the grading system in influencing attitudes toward learning. . . .

GRADES VS. SUCCESS

It is also said that there must be something wrong with grades because they are not good predictors of "success" in later life. But, as Donald P. Hoyt has suggested, that is not necessarily a condemnation. Grades should measure learnings; success is in large part a result of what has been done with the learning.[6] Moreover, it is not completely clear that knowledge and understanding are ingredients necessary to success in society.* . . .

PROMOTING COMPETITION

A third unwarranted criticism is that grades foster competitive attitudes. This criticism applies to grades only insofar as it applies to evaluations of human performance generally, because a comparison with the performance of other humans is usually the most meaningful frame of reference, if not the only one, for such evaluations.†

Furthermore, a certain kind of competitive perspective is actually quite desirable. In considering his future, a student should take into account his comparative advantages vis-à-vis others in his field so he can better determine where he can make his most satisfying contribution. Thus, he might want to choose a field in which other people would work less effectively than he. At the very least, a student deserves the information about

---

Is this a useful rebuttal to Bane and Jencks' statement regarding the limited influence of the school?

†*How might an advocate of criterion-referenced testing (say, Millman) react to this assumption?*

which fields those are, and grades provide a convenient way to tell him. This aspect of grades has nothing to do with inducing men to cut each other's throats, or even with preparing them to live in a competitive world — the implications and justifications of grades which students are increasingly resisting. In the perspective suggested here, grades foster a competitive attitude only by spurring students to realize that their own talents and energies compete with each other in the sense that resources put to one use cannot be put to another.

Another unwarranted criticism is that a low grade discourages a student from further study of a subject. Isn't that exactly what a low grade should do? If, despite efforts to learn, a student is performing poorly in, say, math, he *should* be discouraged from taking further math courses; this action is an aid to his education, not a detriment, for he might learn more in art history or economic theory.* Letting a student know that he is performing poorly is preferable to permitting him to entertain an illusion about himself.

A student can be given a negative evaluation in a course, however, without having it broadcast to the world, that is, without having it entered on his transcript and incorporated into his GPA. This permanent record, it is complained, does the damage. Since the GPA is important to students, even a slight decline is said to arouse inordinate anxiety, and students will go to great lengths to avoid it, for example, confining themselves to courses in which they are confident they can earn high grades.[7] That undesirable by-product implies a misuse of grades. . . .

FUNCTION OF ANXIETY

The anxiety aroused by fear of a low grade is but the obverse side of the motivational coin. If a grade is to motivate, then a high grade must be a never-guaranteed but ever-possible outcome; a low grade, therefore, must be an avoidable but also ever-possible outcome. If the possibility of a low grade creates anxiety in the student, he should be able to reduce that feeling by studying to avoid the low grade. That is one way in which the motivational function is served, and evidence indicates that it works, when the anxiety is *moderate*.[8]

Anxiety interferes with learning only when it becomes excessive, and — neurotic personalities aside — that happens when too much importance is attributed to a single grade. There are several ways to prevent excessive anxiety.

* *If you were an advocate of mastery learning, how might you respond to this statement?*

DIMINISHING PRESSURES

First, a student should be allowed to weight his grades differentially, so he can give low weight to grades in those courses that arouse the most anxiety in him. Second, he should be helped to understand that a grade is not a judgment of his moral worth, but merely an information statement, and a tentative and fallible one at that. Third, there should be strict limitations on the use of a student's grade record. While it must be available to college authorities, for reasons stated above, these officials should adopt explicit restrictions on its use. It should not be a basis for determining financial aid or participating in extracurricular activities. Certainly it should never have been given to draft boards without the student's permission. Indeed, beyond its use by the college itself, in admitting students to honor sections or in dismissing them for unsatisfactory academic work, the grade record should be regarded as the property of the student alone, so he can prevent its use as a threat. This rule would not defeat the reporting function. If graduate schools or employers wanted to see a student's grade record, they should be required to obtain it through the student, and he should have the right of refusal. He would be quite aware of the significance that would be attached to his exercise of that right. If he gave permission for his record to be sent outside the institution, the "authority" of the college would become simply the capacity to certify that the grade record was accurate.* . . .

ACCURATE EVALUATION

In the end, it is their lack of validity that emerges as the most legitimate criticism of grades. Whatever valuable functions they could perform in the abstract will not be performed if grades are not valid measures of learning; and all too often, they are not.† . . .

This, however, is a remediable defect. Valid educational evaluations are difficult but not impossible to arrive at; certainly they can be far more closely approached than at present. If they are rare in the experience of most college students, the main reason is that the overwhelming majority of college faculty have had no training whatsoever in making them. . . . As McGeorge Bundy said years ago:

> The ordinary college teacher, giving out grades in the ordinary way on the basis of a few special papers or tests and a single final examination, is a fountain of error, and everyone knows it except the man himself.[9]

Do these requirements, in any way, conflict with the author's earlier assumptions?

†*How could you test the validity of the grades you receive?*

Ultimately, training in evaluation should be the responsibility of the graduate schools that produce college teachers. Meanwhile, each college could well undertake to fill the gap itself. It could, for one thing, publish a clear statement about grading policies and practices;[10] faculty and students should naturally participate in drawing it up — an instructive experience in itself. For another thing, a college could conduct a seminar on evaluation at the opening of each academic year, with all faculty members expected to attend in their first year and perhaps every third or fourth year thereafter to keep up to date on theories and technologies. It would be highly desirable for students to attend this seminar, too. Exposure to the mundane procedures involved in evaluation would help students appreciate the fallibility of evaluative instruments, would tend to divest grades of their moral overtones, and might thereby lead to a more relaxed attitude. Furthermore, knowledge on the part of faculty that their students were moderately sophisticated in the matter of grades would be an efficacious way to enforce good practices. These steps would help overcome the evil that grades can do, allowing everyone to take full advantage of their positive functions.

EXERCISE

1. According to Feldmesser, in what two ways do grades help the student? (p. 580)

2. According to Feldmesser, what are two second-order functions performed by grades? (pp. 582–583)

3. How does Feldmesser respond to the criticism that grades are extrinsic rather than intrinsic rewards? (p. 584)

4. How does Feldmesser respond to the criticism that grades foster competitive attitudes? (pp. 584–585)

5. How does Feldmesser respond to the criticism that a low grade discourages a student from further study of a subject? (p. 585)

6. According to Feldmesser, under what conditions does anxiety facilitate or hinder learning? (p. 585)

7. According to Feldmesser, what are three ways in which the anxiety-provoking characteristic of grades can be reduced? (p. 586)

8. What explanation does Feldmesser give for the low validity of many educational evaluations? (p. 586)

Reporting Student Progress: A Case For a Criterion-Referenced Marking System

Jason Millman

>   In the preceding selections, John Holt and Robert Feldmesser took opposing positions on the value of assigning grades. Feldmesser, in particular, discussed traditional grading systems based on norm-referenced testing in which students are compared with each other. Jason Millman suggests a new approach to grading based on criterion-referenced testing. In this type of testing, a student's performance on a test is evaluated against a predetermined criterion score, not against the performance of other students. Criterion-referenced testing is becoming increasingly popular, particularly in accountability and mastery-learning programs based upon behaviorally stated learning objectives. (See articles by Esbensen, Block, and Mecklenburger and Wilson.) Millman claims several advantages for criterion-referenced report card grading: the report card communicates clearly to parents what their children are learning; it helps to improve students' attitudes toward themselves; and it eliminates competition between students for grades. Do you think that Millman's method is better than letter grades (A–F) and other norm-referenced grading systems? Do you think his method is better than assigning no grades at all, as Holt recommends?

Two major trends in the sixties in education have been increased implementation of individualized instruction and greater emphasis by test specialists on criterion-referenced measurements. My primary purpose in this paper is to indicate how these trends invite a completely different format than that presently used for the reporting of school progress to students and to their parents.

INDIVIDUALIZING INSTRUCTION

Instruction can be individualized in two ways: pacing and branching.* Linear programming is an example of individualizing instruction by per-

---

Reprinted by permission of the author and the publisher, *Phi Delta Kappan*, December 1970.

* *Lindvall and Bolvin (Section 10) and Block (Section 15) discuss these approaches to individualization in more detail.*

mitting each student to go through a set of instructional materials at his own rate. Use of self-teaching materials effects differential progress. When individuals are permitted to learn at their own rate, the more able students will complete the instruction and demonstrate competence *many* times more quickly than the less able students.[1]

Providing alternative instructional materials is a second way to individualize instruction. This method may be implemented on a macro level (e.g., students study different elective courses) or on a more micro level (e.g., the particular way a student is taught a unit of instruction depends on his interests and learning style). Of course, individual pacing and providing alternative instructional materials can be combined.

Regardless of how the instruction is individualized, the usual procedures of assessing student progress seem inappropriate. When students in a class are proceeding at their own rate or "doing their own thing" or both, the practice of assigning grades on the basis of the administration of a common achievement test is inapplicable.[2] More appropriate would be a report of an individual's own progress. These points will be elaborated in this article.

CRITERION-REFERENCED MEASUREMENT

Since the writings of Ebel and Glaser on the subject [3] there has been increased attention to criterion-referenced measurement, which relates test performance to absolute standards rather than to the performance of others.*

> Criterion-referenced measures are those which are used to ascertain an individual's status with respect to some criterion, i.e., performance standard. It is because the individual is compared with some established criterion, rather than other individuals, that these measures are described as criterion-referenced. The meaningfulness of an individual score is not dependent on comparison to others.
> ... Norm-referenced measures are those which are used to ascertain an individual's performance in relationship to the performance of other individuals on the same measuring device. The meaningfulness of the individual score emerges from the comparison. It is because the individual is compared with some normative group that such measures are described as norm-referenced. Most standardized tests of achievement or intellectual ability can be classified as norm-referenced measures.[4] †

---

* *This is the key difference between Millman's form of grading and that supported by Feldmesser.*
† *A test is "standardized" by creating standard conditions of test administration and by collecting norms.*

OBJECTIVE: Given a set of objects, the student will be able to identify the longest and/or shortest (Words to be read aloud to the student).

FIGURE 1.
Example of Criterion-Referenced Measurement

An example of a criterion-referenced test is presented in Figure 1. These items were chosen because they constitute a representative set of situations which a student should deal with correctly if he is to demonstrate proficiency in the desired skill. Regardless of how his classmates perform, the student passes the test only if he answers all (or, possibly, nearly all) of the questions correctly. These same items could be part of a norm-referenced test. In such a case, they would have been selected because of their usefulness in discriminating among the students. How well a student does on such a norm-referenced test would be determined by comparing his score with those of his classmates.

A, B, C Grading is Norm-Referenced

The grading systems which use number or letter scales, as found in the vast majority of schools,[5] are indicators of the comparative performance of students and are devices for *ranking*. Thus, this system is not useful for indicating an individual's progress against performance criteria. Some teachers may object, arguing that their grades *rate* their students' command of course content or degree of fulfillment of predetermined course objectives. Consider these four arguments against such a position:

1. Teachers who say, "The test scores speak," and "I do *not* grade on a curve," find themselves using adjustments to make the grade distributions more reasonable. These adjustments take such forms as giving another test, raising marks by some mysterious formula, making the next test easier, and altering grading standards. Naturally, a teacher's increased experience with what students in his school and in his course can do on his examinations reduces the extent of the adjustments necessary to insure that a reasonable curve will result.

2. There is a marked similarity between grade distributions found in high schools and those found in colleges having a different quality of students. If grades were assigned according to standards so that an A, in introductory physics for example, meant a certain proficiency, then the percentage of students earning an A should be substantially different at the different schools. This is not the case.

3. Perhaps the most convincing evidence to support the claim that A, B, C grading or one, two, three grading is norm-referenced is that as the quality of students entering any given college goes up over the years, as attested to by objective test data, the grade distributions of that college remain essentially unchanged.

4. Regardless of what the teacher feels the grade signifies, the students feel they are competing with each other, that is, that the grade is a measure of comparative achievement.

Instructional Goals and Management

A key task of our schools is to maximize the amount of a subject each student has "mastered." [6] * Indeed, a reason for having individualized instruction is to maximize achievement by appropriate pacing and provision of instructional materials. The rational management of such an individualized instructional system requires knowing whether each student can perform at some criterion level on measures of the component objectives

* Note the reference to mastery. (See Block, Section 15.)

of the system. Such criterion-referenced measurement characterizes the management of the well-known University of Pittsburgh Individually Prescribed Instruction system.[7] *

REPORT CARDS

If criterion-referenced measurement is to serve guidance and monitoring functions for the instructional program, it is a logical next step that such measurement become the basis for communication regarding student progress. Not only could student records contain a listing of skills to be checked as proficiency is demonstrated, but so too could the reports going to the students and their parents.

The essential features of such a report card are: a listing of objectives (most likely abbreviated descriptions of tasks), space to indicate if proficiency has been demonstrated, and a checking system which identifies objectives achieved since the previous report.† Since parents, quite reasonably, desire norm-referenced information, some grade designation *might* be included at the lower grades. For high school or junior college courses, skills for which proficiency is usually demonstrated may be differentiated from optional or supplementary skills. A sketch of the kind of report card being suggested is shown in Figure 2.

The number of skills shown on the report card will probably be less than the number used in the school record. For example, before the teacher would check "Understands dollar value of money," he may require identification of coins, converting dollars to equivalent amounts of other coin values, counting dollar value of coin sets, and making change.

The report card should probably use objectives stated narrowly enough so that all students will have a chance during a marking period to demonstrate proficiency on tests relative to at least one objective. . . .

IS THE PLAN FEASIBLE?

It is not reasonable to expect the typical school to itemize, from scratch, a comprehensive set of objectives and to construct related criterion-referenced measures. In the elementary school, students often use workbooks containing exercises which could serve as criterion-referenced tests. The tasks these students are expected to perform are isomorphic to the objectives.

Further, the objectives of many new curricula have already been identified and test items covering these objectives have been provided. More

---

* *Individually Prescribed Instruction is discussed in Section 10.*
† *This reporting system reflects some of the criteria for well-stated behavioral objectives proposed by Esbensen (Section 14).*

FIGURE 2
Report Card Based on a System of Criterion-
Referenced Measurement.

MATHEMATICS
Grade Two

Skill	Date
Concepts	
Understands commutative property of addition (e.g., $4 + 3 = 3 + 4$)	*9/27*
Understands place value (e.g., $27 = 2$ tens $+ 7$ ones)	*10/3*
Addition	
Supplies missing addend under 10 (e.g., $3 + ? = 5$)	*10/8*
Adds three single-digit numbers	————
Knows combinations 10 through 19	————
ªAdds two 2-digit numbers without carrying	————
ªAdds two 2-digit numbers with carrying	————
Subtraction	
Knows combinations through 9	*10/4*
ªSupplies missing subtrahend — under 10 (e.g., $6 - ? = 1$)	————
ªSupplies missing minuend — under 10 (e.g., $? - 3 = 4$)	————
ªKnows combinations 10 through 19	————
ªSubtracts two 2-digit numbers without borrowing	————
Measurement	
Reads and draws clocks (up to quarter hour)	
Understands dollar value of money (coins up to $1.00 total)	————
Geometry	
Understands symmetry	————
Recognizes congruent plan figures — that is, figures which are identical except for orientation	————
Graph Reading	
ªKnows how to construct simple graphs	————
ªKnows how to read simple graphs	————

ª In Jefferson Elementary School, these skills are usually learned toward
the end of grade two. Some children who need more than average time to
learn mathematics may not show proficiency on tests of these skills until they
are in grade three.

frequently the staff in individual school systems is constructing "behaviorally stated" objectives in conjunction with learning packages covering
these objectives. Commercial firms are now including tests in their learning packages....

When instruction is individualized, students must assume an increased
responsibility for their own activities. It is reasonable to expect that at

least the older students can assume responsibility for self-administering the criterion-referenced tests and, in some cases, scoring them.* The teacher need only place a single checkmark (or date) to record the fact that proficiency has been demonstrated. At reporting periods, the teacher merely transfers these checks to the cards.

When considering feasibility, it should be remembered that a school system need not convert to the criterion-referenced reporting system in all subject areas at once. A school system, or an individual school or teacher, may choose to utilize the criterion-referenced reporting system first in subject areas where the defining and measuring of objectives is easiest. These areas would include mathematics and those vocationally oriented courses in which a large segment of the objectives involves performance skills.

ADVANTAGES

The emphasis on proficiency forces the school staff to focus on both instructional process and outcomes rather than on process alone and to view formal education "as an enterprise which is designed to *change* human beings so that they are better, wiser, more efficient." [8] The instructional means are judged by the ends achieved. In these days when decentralization brings parents closer to the schools, when parents demand more information, when school bond issues are being rejected because of ignorance about the school's benefit as well as for financial reasons, and when accountability is in fashion, the staffs of our schools would be well advised to demonstrate that the modifications they wish to promote do occur.†

The report card format suggested in this paper permits a degree of communication and accountability to the parent not possible with other systems of reporting. Every student will be shown to be learning, and both the parent and student will know better what has been learned and what can now be done.

Besides change of focus, other advantages of a criterion-referenced system have been listed elsewhere.[9] These include improved student attitudes where the less wholesome competition for grades gives way to competition (frequently within oneself) to acquire proficiencies in much the same way that a scout earns his badges.

LIMITATIONS

Objections have been raised against requiring that objectives be stated in behavioral terms and also against criterion-referenced measurement.

---

* *Will this provide an accurate record of what the student has learned?*
† *For a different view of accountability read Farrell's article.*

There is the danger that objectives involving hard-to-measure qualities like appreciations and attitudes may be slighted. If such objectives are taken seriously by the school staff, then it has a responsibility to provide experiences for developing the desired qualities.* It is then possible to list on a criterion-referenced report card "expressive objectives" [10] meaning that certain tasks or encounters are to be experienced. To take an example, *to visit a slum area* may be an objective (more appropriately, a learning activity) which is satisfied when the visit is actually made. Nevertheless, school staff should give thought both to the intended changes in appreciation, understanding, and so forth, in the learners which lie behind the selection of the activity and to the criteria for determining whether these changes did take place. . . .

In terms of sheer number of words written, criterion-referenced tests have not received as much criticism as has the requirement that objectives be stated in behavioral terms.[11] There are however, at least two very difficult problems associated with criterion-referenced testing: specifying the universe of tasks and determining proficiency standards.† Both of these difficulties remind us that the wording of the objective is perhaps less important than the selection of tasks and criteria.[12]

As Loevinger has pointed out in another context,[13] one cannot define a universe of possible test items (tasks) and sample randomly from them except in some unusually restrictive situations. The second difficulty arises from the fact that the choice of a proficiency standard is, to a large extent, arbitrary. Whether a student's performance is good enough to permit him to commence instruction in new skills is, in the final analysis, a matter of judgment.

These very real difficulties are not limited to criterion-referenced tests. To insure that norm-referenced tests have content validity, the universe of relevant content must be defined. Further, in determining who gets a satisfactory score (for example, on an achievement test used to assign grades), one cannot escape the fact that these decisions also involve judgment and are often quite arbitrary.

Some things can be done to deal partially with these problems. Criterion tasks should be constructed which sample a great range of situations and methods covered by the objective. For example, in Figure 1, note that the longest object is not always the largest, nor does it span the most distance horizontally. It was a conscious decision to include in the item universe only comparisons among pictures of objects of the same class and to exclude items which required reading and fine perceptual discriminations.

---

* *Millman seems optimistic about describing affective learning in behavioral terms. Would Guth have this same opinion? (See Section 14.)*
† *These are similar to Esbensen's requirements for behavioral objectives, (Section 14).*

The question of what proportion of correct responses is needed to demonstrate proficiency is not an easy one to answer.* Perfect or near-perfect performance should be required if (a) the objective is worded such that near mastery is expected, (b) the skills are deemed important for future learning, (c) items are the objective type (thus increasing the likelihood of successful guessing), and (d) the test is short and thus likely to be unreliable. Less stringent cutoffs might be employed if any of the above four conditions are relaxed. Certainly, there is no good reason why the same cutoff score should be used on every test.

Many, but by no means all, of the problems involved in using a system of criterion-referenced testing will be minimized with increased experience with this mode of assessing school progress.† The more refractory of these problems are inherent in any measurement system. But when a school staff is committed to changing students, to helping them grow and learn and feel, and to focusing on outcomes, then reporting school progress using a criterion-referenced measurement system not only follows logically, but there is, in fact, no viable alternative.‡

EXERCISE

1. Why does Millman believe that individualized instruction requires criterion-referenced grading rather than norm-referenced grading? (p. 589)

2. What is the major difference between criterion-referenced tests and norm-referenced tests? (p. 589)

3. What evidence supports the statement that norm-referenced grading exists in most colleges? (p. 591)

4. What are the three basic features of Millman's report card system? (p. 592)

5. What three advantages does Millman see in criterion-referenced grading? (p. 594)

6. What are three problems with criterion-referenced tests according to critics? (pp. 594–595)

* *Is there a way to answer this question through research? (See Stake, next selection.)*
† *Millman presents additional information on setting standards for criterion-referenced testing in the Spring 1973 issue of* Review of Educational Research.
‡ *Would a reporting system based on Millman's criteria be acceptable to Holt? (See first article, this section.)*

Measuring What Learners Learn (With a Special Look at Performance Contracting)

Robert E. Stake

Standardized tests (tests with norms and standard conditions of administration) have an influential role in American education. Many educators feel they are the authoritative method for evaluating students' abilities and scholastic achievement. However, in the following article Robert Stake, a well-known research methodologist, points out several weaknesses in standardized tests. He specifically criticizes their use in performance contracting (see Farrell, Section 15), as well as other types of educational tests and other testing situations, for example, using standardized tests in research studies or teacher-made tests to assign grades. Can the weaknesses in testing which Stake identifies be eliminated if educators adopt the criterion-referenced testing approach recommended by Jason Millman in the preceding article? Or do you think that Stake's article could serve as a mandate to reject all formal testing, as recommended by John Holt (first article, this section)?

"Can there be teaching if there is no learning?" Hear again one of the lines from the educator's catechism. The question is not to be taken literally. Good teaching, elegant teaching, without student benefit, of course is possible — though doubly wasteful. The question is rhetorical. Professionals and laymen alike sanctify that teaching-learning contract that results in better student performance.

Measuring the learning is no small problem. Teachers, as a matter of course, usually are able to observe that individual students are or are not learning. Sometimes they cannot. And increasingly, outsiders are reluctant to take the teacher's word for it. Gathering "hard-data" evidence of student learning is a new and ominous challenge. Of course, we have tests. But the results of our testing have seldom been adequate grounds for the continuing faith we have in education.

Reprinted with permission of the author from a paper approximately 15 per cent greater in length. A shorter version was printed in *Phi Delta Kappan*, June 1971.

PRESENT DEMANDS

Expectations of testing are on the rise because schools have been told to be accountable — to demonstrate publicly what they are accomplishing (Lieberman, 1970; Bhaerman, 1970). Increasing educational costs and increasing frustration with social and political problems have brought higher demands for answers to an important question: What are we getting for our education dollar?

Educators have been challenged to become more explicit and more functional in lesson plans and school budgets; to identify the gains and losses children make in reading, singing, and the many human talents; and to realize that the events of the classroom are not unrelated to the events of the street, the marketplace, and City Hall (Cohen, 1970). Educators have been told to learn about systems analysis, operations research, cost-benefit analysis, program planning and budgeting, and other models for orderly and dispassionate treatment of institutional affairs (Lessinger, 1970).

Some critics of contemporary education are bothered greatly by the fact that educational practice is so intuitive, impulsive, inefficient, and resistant to change. Others continue to be bothered more by passionate but naive efforts to substitute technical procedures for personal attention....

TESTS FOR PERFORMANCE CONTRACTS

The performance contract is an agreement between a group offering instruction and a school needing services (Lennon, 1971).* Reimbursement is to be made in some proportion to measured student achievement. Especially for children having special needs, such as nonreading, handicapped, or gifted children, a new way of getting special instruction is appealing. A "hard-data" basis for evaluating the quality of instruction is appealing. In performance contracting student gains are the criterion of successful teaching.

In the first federally sponsored example of performance contracting for the public schools, Dorsett Educational Systems of Norman, Oklahoma, contracted to teach reading, mathematics, and study skills to over 200 poor-performance juniors and senior high school students in Texarkana, Texas. Commercially available, standardized tests were used to measure performance gains.

Are such tests suitable for measuring specific learnings? To the person not intimately acquainted with educational testing it appears that per-

* Performance contracting is discussed in detail in Section 15.

formance testing is what educational tests are for. The testing specialist knows that this is not so.. . .

Most tests are indirect measures of educational gains, correlates of learning rather than direct evidence of achievement.* Correlation with important general learning is often high, but correlation of test scores with performance on many specific educational tasks is seldom high. Tests can be built for specific competence, but there is relatively little demand for them and many of them do a poor job of predicting later performance of either a specific or general nature. General achievement tests "predict" better. The test developer's basis for improving tests has been to work toward better predictions of later performance rather than better measurement of present performance. Assessment of what a student is now capable of doing is not the purpose of most standardized tests. Especially when indirect-measurement tests are used for performance contracting, but even with direct-assessment tests, errors and hazards abound.

In this paper I will identify the major obstacles to direct measurement of the specific things that learners learn.

The Errors of Testing

Answering a *National School Board Journal* (November 1970) questionnaire on performance contracting, a New Jersey board member said, "Objectives must be stated in simple, understandable terms. No jargon will do and no subjective goals can be tolerated. Neither can the nonsense about there being some mystique that prohibits objective measurement of the educational endeavor." † Would that our problems would wither before stern resolve. But neither wishing nor blustering rids educational testing of its errors. They exist.

Just as the population census and the bathroom scales have their errors, educational tests have theirs. . . . Looking into the psychometrist's meaning of "A Theory of Testing," one finds a consideration of ways to analyze and label the inaccuracies in test scores (Lord, 1952). There is mystique, but there is also simple fact: No one can eliminate test errors. Unfortunately, some errors in testing are large enough to cause wrong decisions about individual children or about school-district policy. . . .

Some technical errors in test scores are small and tolerable. But some testing errors are intolerably large. Today's tests can, for example, measure vocabulary word-recognition skills sufficiently accurately. Today's tests

---

* In other words, most tests probably do not measure the specific skill or skills listed in a given behavioral objective.
† Esbensen and Popham (Section 14) would agree with this statement. How would Guth (Section 14) and Farrell (Section 15) respond?

cannot adequately measure listening comprehension or the ability to analyze the opposing sides to an argument.

Today's test technology is not refined enough to meet all the demands put on it. The tests are best when the performance is highly specific — when, for example, calling for the student to add two numbers, recognize a misspelled word, or identify the parts of a hydraulic lift.* When a teacher wants to measure performances calling for the higher mental processes (Bloom et al., 1956), such as generating a writing principle or synthesizing a political argument, our tests give us scores that are less dependable.[1]...

UNREACHED POTENTIALS

Many educators feel that the most human of human gifts — e.g., the emotions, the higher thought processes, interpersonal sensitivity, moral sense — are beyond the reach of psychometric testing. Most testing specialists disagree. While recognizing an ever-present error component, they believe that anything can be measured. The credo was sounded by E. L. Thorndike (1918):

> Whatever exists at all exists in some amount. To know it thoroughly involves knowing its quantity as well as its quality. Education is concerned with changes in human beings; a change is a difference between two conditions; each of these conditions is known to us only by the products produced by it — things made, words spoken, acts performed, and the like. To measure any of these products means to define its amount in some way so that competent persons will know how large it is, better than they would without measurement. To measure a product well means so to define its amount that competent persons will know how large it is, with some precision, and that this knowledge may be conveniently recorded and used. This is the general *Credo* of those who, in the last decade, have been busy trying to extend and improve measurements of educational products.
>
> We have faith that whatever people now measure crudely by mere descriptive words, helped out by the comparative and superlative forms, can be measured more precisely and conveniently if ingenuity and labor are set at the task. We have faith also that the objective products produced, rather than the inner condition of the person whence they spring, are the proper point of attack for the measurer, at least in our day and generation.
>
> This is obviously the same general creed as that of the physicist or chemist or physiologist engaged in quantitative thinking — the same, indeed, as that of modern science in general. And, in general, the nature of educational measurements is the same as that of all scientific measurements.

* See Millman (preceding selection) for further discussion.

Testing men believe it still. They are not so naive as to think that any human gift will manifest itself in a 45-minute paper-and-pencil test. They believe that, if given ample opportunity to activate and observe the examinee, any trait or talent or learning that manifests itself in behavior can be measured with reasonable accuracy. The total "cost" of measuring may be a hundred times that of administering the usual tests, but they believe it can be done. The final observations may rely on professional judgment, but it would be a reliable and validated judgment. The question for most test specialists then is not "Can complex educational outcomes be measured?" but "Can complex educational outcomes be measured with the time and personnel and facilities available?" *

If we really want to know whether or not a child is reading at age-level, we have a reading specialist listen to him read. She observes his reading habits. She might test him with word recognition, syntactic decoding, and paragraph-comprehension exercises. She would retest where evidence was inconclusive. She would talk to his teachers and his parents. She would arrive at a clinical description which might be reducible to such a statement as "Yes, Johnny is reading at or above age-level."

The scores we get from group reading tests can be considered estimates of such a clinical judgment. These test scores correlate positively with the more-valid clinical judgments. Though more objective, such estimates are not direct measurements of what teachers or laymen mean by "ability to read." Achievement gains for a sizable number of students will be poorly estimated by them. It is possible that the errors in group testing are so extensive that — when fully known — businessmen and educators will refuse to accept them as bases for contract reimbursement.†

PROFESSIONAL AWARENESS

Classroom teachers and school principals have tolerated standardized test errors (as much as they have) because they have not been obligated to make important decisions on the basis of test scores alone. Actually, it is seldom in day-to-day practice that they use test scores (Hastings, Runkel, and Damrin, 1961); but, when they do, they use them, in combination with other knowledge, to estimate a child's progress in school and to guide him into an appropriate learning experience. They do not use tests as a basis for assessing the quality of their own teaching.‡

---

* *Key point; here Stake has identified a major problem in education research as well as in ongoing measurement of student learning.*
† *Does this suggest that increased expenditures for measuring student learning are necessary if learning outcomes are to improve?*
‡ *Are tests, in their present form, an acceptable measure of teacher accountability?*

In performance contracting the situation is supposed to be drastically changed. Tests are indicated as the sole basis for contract reimbursement. The parties must decide how much to pay the contractor for instructing each child. An error in testing means money misspent. Graduation and reimbursement decisions are to be made without reliance on the knowledge and judgment of a professional observer, without asking persons who are closest to the learning (i.e., the teacher, the contractor, the student) whether or not they see evidence of learning. They are to be made entirely by objective and independent testing. The resulting human errors and technical misrepresentations will be numerous. On the following pages I will discuss four major hazards: (1) attending to the wrong objectives, (2) selecting the wrong tests, (3) misrepresenting the test scores, and (4) adding to the depersonalization of contemporary life.

CHOICE OF OBJECTIVES

I am addressing this paper to the measurement of objectives already specified. It is important to recognize that at no time — in any real educational practice — are instructional objectives completely and finally specified.

No statement of objectives is final. Changes in aim, as well as changes in priority, occur throughout training even in the more highly structured instructional programs. Some people feel that this is what is wrong with much classroom instruction: It cannot pick a target and stay fixed on it. But other people are convinced that classroom instruction is too fixated, too inflexible, that teachers are too unwilling to adapt to the changing goals of students and society....

SPECIFICATION BENEFITS. Identifying the goals of education in formal, rational terms is recognized as a powerful way to change professional practice (Tyler, 1950; Mager, 1962). To recognize that objectives will change is not to argue that they should not be stated in advance of training. An awareness of purpose by both teacher and student is usually desired. Only occasionally will an educational experience be highly successful if there is no advance expectation as to what should occur. Usually the activity will be improved if the opportunity to learn is deliberately provided for. Often instruction will be improved if lesson plans focus on desired behaviors rather than entertain spontaneous interests and distractions.

Outside evaluation of the success of instruction is made much simpler and possibly more effective by the prespecification of objectives. Popham (1969) has identified these and other benefits that accrue to those who state their instructional objectives in advance and stick to them.*

* Popham discusses these teaching benefits in Sections 6 and 14.

SPECIFICATION COSTS. But each of these possible benefits carries with it a cost. Stating objectives properly is a lot of work. Some other possible costs are less obvious. . . .

To specify what is to be accomplished always fails to represent the sum total of what is desired. Language fails to portray exactly what we want. The error may be small and unimportant, or it may not. But to some extent there will be a misrepresentation of purpose. . . .

The schools presently pursue many more objectives than any educator can specify, more than he chooses to admit (Gooler, 1971). The results of a specification of objectives, for good or ill, is to increase substantially the emphasis on some objectives and to decrease substantially the emphasis on others. Some objectives are more easily specified and more easily measured than others. It is almost certain that easy-to-measure objectives will get increased emphasis when a statement of objectives is drawn up. . . .

The listing of trade-offs could go on. There are many things that happen when you try to state educational objectives in "simple, understandable terms." . . . Improved student performance *on the specified objectives* in some circumstances appear to be attributable to the specification itself. But Zahorik found that planning resulted in less attention to immediate concerns of the pupils. More research on the overall effects of specification is needed. For each effort to identify more specifically what will be learned, to identify it earlier, and to identify it formally as a statement of instructional objectives, it seems that there are both potential benefits and hazards for the ongoing instructional process.*

CRITERION TESTING PROCEDURES

Among test developers the most vexing problem has always been "the criterion problem," the problem of correlating test scores to a true criterion. For validating a new test, the developer needs to ascertain that at least for a small, carefully measured reference group of students there is a high correlation between what the test measures and what is already known about that group that the test is supposed to indicate.† A high correlation signifies that for that criterion chosen, the test is valid. The high scorers on a study-skills test, for example, would be the students who independently and by direct observation are judged to have the best study capabilities. True criterion observations — whatever the criterion might be — are not readily available on most students. Because of the difficulty and expense, any one standardized test will be validated against only one, or

---

* *Based on all you have read about behavioral objectives, which do you think are greater — the potential benefits or the hazards?*
† *Correlation is explained in the glossary.*

a very few, criterion variables. The most common criterion variable is a course grade given by a teacher or a grade-point average.

For performance testing, the standardized test — the right, already-validated, standardized test — is not likely to exist. The purposes of the contracted-for instruction are relatively sharp, e.g., to increase reading speed and comprehension — and the available tests have been validated against a more general criterion, e.g., grades in reading. The educator has a choice between using a not-quite appropriate available test and building an expensive and questionably valid test. The problem is a vexing one: how to select or construct the appropriate items, observations, or test to serve as the criterion of learning for the purpose of the contract.*

Three questionable aspects of the criterion test need careful thought. There is (1) a question about relying on performance as a criterion indicator of benefit from instruction, (2) a question about measuring complex performances with simple tests, and (3) a question of "teaching for the test." The first two are related to hazards in the choice of objectives as described in the previous sections. . . .

COMPLEX PERFORMANCES. It is unrealistic to expect that a project director [of a performance contract] can find or create paper-and-pencil test items, administrable to large numbers of students in an hour's interval by persons untrained in psychometric observation and standardized diagnostics, objectively scorable, valid for purposes of the performance contract, and readily interpretable. The more complex the training, the more unrealistic the expectation. One manner of compromise is to substitute criterion test items measuring simple behaviors for those measuring the complex behaviors targeted by the training. For example, the director may substitute vocabulary-recognition test items for reading-comprehension items or knowledge of components in place of actual dismantling of an engine.[2] The substitution may be sound, but the criterion test should be validated against performances directly indicated by the objectives. It almost never has been.

It would be unrealistic to expect that the benefits of instruction will be entirely apparent in the performances of learners at test-taking time.†
The tests to be used probably will evoke relatively simple behavior. Ebel (1971) said:

> most achievement tests . . . consist primarily of items testing specific elements of knowledge, facts, ideas, explanations, meanings, processes, procedures, relations, consequences and so on.

* Again, the cost of good measurement is an issue.
† Does this statement support Holt's contention that all testing should be eliminated?

He went on to point out that more than simple recall is involved in answering even the simplest vocabulary item.

Much more complex behavior is needed for answering a reading-comprehension item.[3] . . .

The success of Texarkana's first performance-contract year is still being debated. Late-winter (1969–1970) test results looked good, but spring test results were disappointing.[4] Relatively simple performance items had been used. But the "debate" did not get into that. It started when the project's "outside evaluator" ruled that there had been direct coaching on most, if not all, of the criterion test items. The criterion test items were known by the contractor during the school year. Critics claimed an unethical "teaching for the test." The contractor claimed that both teaching and testing had been directed toward the same specific goals, as should be the case in a good performance contract.* The issue is not only one of ethics, it deals with the very definition of education.

TEACHING FOR THE TEST. Test specialists have recognized an important difference between preparation for a test and direct coaching for a test (Anastasi, 1954, p. 52). To prepare an examinee, the teacher teaches the designated knowledge-skill domain and has the examinee practice good test-taking behavior (e.g., don't spend too much time on overly difficult items; guess when you have an inkling though not full knowledge; organize your answer before writing an essay item) so that relevant knowledge-skill is not obscured. Direct coaching is to teach the examinees how to make correct responses to the specific items on the criterion test.

This is an important difference when criterion test items represent only a small sample of the universe of items representing what has been taught or when the criterion test items are indirect indicators, i.e., correlates, rather than direct measurements, i.e., assessments (see Nunnally, 1959, p. 151).[5] It ceases to be an important difference when the criterion test is set up to measure directly and thoroughly that which has been taught. In this case, teaching for the test is exactly what *is* wanted.

The solution of the problem of teaching for the test probably lies in identifying for each objective a very large number (or all) of the items that indicate mastery or progress. Items from standardized tests, if used,[6] would be included as separate items, not as tests-as-a-whole. The item pool would need to be exhaustive in that, if a student could get a perfect score, there would be no important aspect of the objective that the student would not do well on. A separate random sample of items would be drawn for pretest and posttest for each child. Although attractive to a public concerned about the individual child, instructional success would

* *Key point; if you have behavioral objectives, teaching and measures of learning should emphasize the same goals.*

be based on the mean gain of all students of a kind rather than on the gain of individual students. (The use of individual gain scores will be discussed in the next section.) Finding a sufficiently large pool of relevant, psychometrically sound test items is a major chore; but if it can be done, this procedure will prevent "teaching for the test" without introducing a criterion unacceptable to the contractor.

Joselyn (1971) pointed out that the performance contractor and the school should agree in advance as to the criterion procedure though not necessarily to the specific items. To be fair to the contractor, the testing needs to be reasonably close to the teaching. To be fair to the school patrons, the testing needs to be representative of the domain of skills or abilities *they* are concerned about. A contract to develop reading skills would not be satisfied adequately by gains on a vocabulary test, according to the expectations of most people. All parties need to know how similar the testing is going to be to the actual teaching.

A DISSIMILARITY SCALE. Unfortunately, neither the test specialist nor anyone else has developed scales or grounds for describing the similarity between teaching and testing.[7] This is a most grievous failing. There is no good way to indicate how closely the tests match the instruction. Complete identity and uniqueness are recognizable by everyone, but important shades of difference are not even presently susceptible to good guessing. . . .

The problem is complicated by the fact that there are many ways for criterion questions to be made dissimilar. Here are some:

1. Syntactic transformation
2. Semantic transformation
3. Change in context or medium
4. Application, considering the particular instance
5. Inference, generalizing from learned instances
6. Implication, adding fast-taught information to generally known information

For examples of some of these transformations, see Table 1. Hively, Patterson, and Page (1968) and Bormuth (1970) have discussed procedures for using some of these transformations to generate test items.

The difficulty of these items depends on previous and intervening learnings as well as the thoroughness of teaching. A considerable difference in difficulty and perceived relevance might be found between the least and most dissimilar questions. It is apparent that performance contracting in the absence of good information about the similarity between test items and instructional objectives is scarcely an exercise in rationalism.

TABLE 1
An Example of Transformations
of Information Taught into Test Questions

Information taught:	Pt. Barrow is the northernmost town in Alaska.
Minimum transformation question:	What is the northernmost town in Alaska?
Semantic-syntactic transformation question:	What distinction does Pt. Barrow have among Alaskan villages?
Context-medium transformation question:	The dots on the adjacent map represent Alaskan cities and towns. One represents Pt. Barrow. Which one?
Implication question:	What would be unusual about summer sunsets in Pt. Barrow, Alaska?

ANALYSIS OF GAIN SCORES

The following hazards are present in any instruction, not just in performance contracting. The testing specialist sees not one but at least four hazards attendant to the analysis and interpretation of learning scores. They involve (1) grade-equivalent scores, (2) the "learning calendar," (3) the unreliability of gain scores, and (4) regression effects. All show how measures of achievement gain may be spurious.* Ignoring any one of them is an invitation to gross misjudgment of the worth of the instruction.

GRADE-EQUIVALENT SCORES. Standardized achievement tests have the very appealing feature of yielding grade-equivalent scores. Teachers and parents like to use grade-equivalent scores. Raw scores, usually the number of items right, are transformed to scores indicating (for some national reference-group population of students) the grade placement of all students who got this raw score. These transformed scores are called "grade equivalents." The raw scores are not very meaningful to people unacquainted with the particular test; the grade equivalents are widely accepted by teachers and parents. It is probably true that more of them *should* question the appropriateness of the distribution of scores made by the little-defined reference group as a yardstick for local assessment, but the grade equivalent does represent a piece of test information the public can readily put to use.[8] Grade equivalents are common terminology in performance contracts.

---

* *By this Stake means the measures may be superficial.*

Unfortunately, grade equivalents are only available from most publishers for tests, not for test items. Thus the whole test needs to be used, in the way prescribed in its manual, if the grade equivalents are to be meaningful, mean what they are supposed to mean. One problem of using whole tests was discussed in previous sections. Another problem is that the average annual "growth" for most standardized tests is a matter of only a few raw-score points. Consider in Table 2 the difference between a grade equivalent of 5.0 and 6.0 with four of the most popular test batteries.

Most teachers do not like to have their year's work summarized by so little a change in performance. Schools writing performance contracts perhaps should be reluctant to sign contracts for which the distinction between success and failure is so small. But to do so requires the abandonment of grade equivalents, at least until a large pool of appropriate items can be identified as to their grade equivalence.[9] . . .

THE SCHOOL CALENDAR. For most special instructional programs in the schools, criterion tests will be administered at the beginning of and immediately following instruction, often in the first and last weeks of school. There is a large amount of distraction in the schools those weeks, but choosing other times for pre- and post-testing has its hazards too. Getting progress every several weeks during the year is psychometrically preferrred (Wick and Beggs, 1971); but most instructional people are opposed to "all that testing."

Children learn year 'round, but the evidence of learning that gets inked on pupil-personnel records comes in irregular increments from season to season. Winter is the time of most rapid academic advancement, summer the least. Summer, in fact, is a period of setback for many youngsters.

TABLE 2
Gain in Items Right Needed to Advance
One Grade Equivalent on Three Typical Achievement Tests

	Grade equivalent		Items needed to improve one year G.E.
	5.0	6.0	
Comprehensive test of basic skills, Level 3: Reading comprehension	20	23	3
Metropolitan Achievement Test, Intermediate Form B: Spelling	24	31	7
Iowa Tests of Basic Skills, Test A1: Arithmetic concepts	10	14	4
Stanford Achievement Test, Form W, Intermediate II: Word meaning	18	26	8

Beggs and Hieronymus (1968) found punctuation skills to spurt more than a year's worth between October and April but to drop almost half a year between May and September. Discussing their reading test, Gates and MacGinitie (1965) said,

> in most cases, scores will be higher at the end of one grade than at the beginning of the next. That is, there is typically some loss of reading skill during the summer, especially in the lower grades.

The picture will be different, of course, depending on what the learners do in and out of school.[10]

The first month or two of the fall, when students first return to school, is the time for getting things organized and restoring general skill abilities lost during the summer. According to some records, spring instruction competes with only partial success with other spring attractions. Thus, the learning year is a lopsided year, a basis sometimes for miscalculations. Consider the results of testing shown in Table 3.

TABLE 3
Learning Calendar for a Typical Fifth-Grade Class

		Month							
	S	O	N	D	J	F	M	A	M
Mean achievement score	5.0	5.3	5.6	5.9	6.2	6.3			

The every-two-months averages in Table 3 are fictitious, but they represent test performance in a typical classroom. The growth for the year appears to be 1.3. No acknowledgment is made there that early-September standardized test results were poorer than those for the previous spring. For this example the *previous* May mean (not shown) was 5.2. The real gain, then, for the year is 1.1 grade equivalents rather than the apparent 1.3. It would be inappropriate to pay the contractor for a mean gain of 1.3.

Another possible overpayment on the contract can result by holding final testing early and extrapolating the previous per-week growth to the weeks or months that follow. In Texarkana, as in most schools, spring progress was not as good as winter. If an accurate evaluation of contract instructional services is to be made, repeated testing, perhaps a month-by-month record of learning performances needs to be considered.

Perhaps the biggest when-to-test problem arises from the common belief that schooling is not supposed to aim at terminal performance (at project's end) but to aim at continuing performance in the weeks and months and years that follow. . . .

UNRELIABLE GAIN SCORES. Most performance contracts pay off on an individual-student basis. The contractor may be paid for each student who gains more than an otherwise expected amount. This practice is commendable in that it emphasizes the importance of each individual learner and makes the contract easier to understand, but it bases payment on a precarious landmark: the gain score. . . .

Here are three ways of looking at [the problem of gain scores]:

Suppose that a contract student were to take a different parallel form of the criterion test on three successive days immediately following the pretest. The chances are better than 50:50 that on *one* of these tests the student would have gained a year or more in performance and would appear to be ready to graduate from the program.

Suppose that three students were to be tested with a parallel form immediately after the pretest. The chances are better than 50:50 that one of the three students — entirely due to the errors of measurement — would have gained a year or more and appear ready to graduate from the program.

Suppose that 100 students were admitted to contract instruction and pretested. After a period of time involving no training, they were tested again and the students gaining a year were graduated. After another period of time, another test, and another graduation. After the fourth terminal testing, even though no instruction had occurred, the chances are better than 50:50 that two-thirds of the students would have been graduated.

In other words, the unreliability of gain scores can give the appearance of learning that actually does not occur.

The unreliability also will give an equal number of false impressions of deteriorating performance. These errors (false gains and false losses) will balance out for a large group of students. If penalties for losses are paid by the contractor at the same rate bonuses are paid for gains, the contractor will not be overpaid. But according to the way contracts are being written, typified in the examples above, the error in gain scores does not balance out; it works in favor of the contractor. Measurement errors could be capitalized upon by unscrupulous promoters. Appropriate checks against these errors are built into the better contracts.

Errors in individual gain scores can be reduced by using longer tests. A better way to indicate true gain is to calculate the discrepancy between actual and expected final performances. Expectations can be based on the group as a whole or on an outside control group. Another way is to write the contract on the basis of mean scores for the group of students. Corrections for the unreliability of gain scores are possible, but they are not likely to be considered if the educators and contractors are statistically naive.

REGRESSION EFFECTS. Buried back here in this paper is probably the source of the greatest misinterpretation of the effects of remedial instruction. Regression effects are easily overlooked but need not be; they also are susceptible to correction.* For any pretest score the expected regression effect can be calculated. Regression effects make the poorest scorers look better the next time tested. Whether measurements are error-laden or error-free, meaningful or meaningless, when there is differential change between one measurement occasion and another (i.e., when there is less-than-perfect correlation), the lowest original scorers will make the greatest gains and the highest original scorers will make the least. On the average, posttest scores will, relative to their corresponding pretest scores, lie in the direction of the mean. This is the regression effect. Lord (1963) discussed this universal phenomenon and various ways to set up a proper correction for it.

The demand for performance contracts has occurred where conventional instructional programs fail to develop — for a sizable number of students — minimum competence in basic skills. Given a distribution of skill test scores, the lowest-scoring students, ones most needing assistance, are identified. It is reasonable to suppose that under unchanged instructional programs they would drop even further behind the high-scoring students. If a retest is given, however, after any period (of conventional instruction, of special instruction, or of no instruction), these students will no longer be the poorest performers. Some of them will be replaced by others who then appear to be most in need of special instruction. Instruction is not the obvious influence here — regression is. Regression effect is not due to test unreliability — but it causes some of the same misinterpretations. *The contract should read that instruction will be reimbursed when gain exceeds that attributable to regression effects.* The preferred evaluation design would call for control group(s) of similar students to provide a good estimate of the progress the contract students would have made in the absence of the special instruction.

THE SOCIAL PROCESS

The hazards of specific performance testing and performance contracting are more than curricular and psychometric. Social and humanistic challenges should be raised too. The teacher has a special opportunity and obligation to observe the influence of testing on social behavior.

At several places in the preceding pages I have referred to the *uniqueness* of making major personal and scholastic decisions on the sole basis of student performances. This is unique also because it puts the student in a position of administrative influence. Here he can influence what the

* *Regression effects are discussed in the glossary.*

instructional benefit would look like. He can make it look better or poorer than it really is (Anastasi, 1954, p. 56). More responsibility for school control possibly should accrue to students, but performance contracts seem a devious way to give it.

Even if he is quite young, the student is going to be aware that his good work will bring rewards to the contractor. Sooner or later he is going to know that, if he tests poorly at the beginning, he is able to do more for himself and the contractor. Bad performances are in his repertoire — he may be more anxious to make the contractor look bad than to make himself look good. He may be under undue pressure to do well on the posttests. These are pupil-teacher interactions that should be watched carefully. . . .

Still another hazard of performance contracting and many other uses of objectives and test items is that by using them as we do, without acknowledging how much they indirectly and incompletely represent educational goals, we misrepresent education. People inside school and out pay attention to grades and tests and monetary reimbursements. We may not value factual knowledges and simple skills proportionately to the attention they get, but we have ineffective ways of indicating what our priorities really are (Stake, 1970).

It is difficult for many people to accept the fact that in conventional classrooms a vast number of educational goals are simultaneously pursued (Gooler, 1971). Efforts to get teachers to specify those objectives result in a simplified and incomplete list. The performance contractor has an even shorter list. Even if performance contracting succeeds in doing the relatively small job it aims to do, adequate arguments have not been made that this job should be given the priority and resources that the contractors require. . . .

SUMMARY

Without yielding to the temptation to harass new efforts to provide instruction, educators should continue to be apprehensive about evaluating teaching on the basis of performance testing alone. They should know how difficult it is to represent educational goals with statements of objectives. They should know how costly it is to provide suitable criterion testing. They should know that the common-sense interpretation of these results is frequently wrong but that many members of the public and the profession think that special designs and controls are extravagant and mystical.

Performance contracting emerged because people inside the schools and out were dissatisfied with the instruction some children are getting. Implicit in the contracts is the expectation that available tests can measure the newly promised learning. The standardized test alone cannot measure the specific outcomes of an individual student with sufficient precision. This limitation and other hazards of performance measurement are applicable, of course, to the measurement of specific achievement in regular school programs.

EXERCISE

1. Many educators believe that tests cannot measure the emotions, higher cognitive processes, or interpersonal sensitivity. According to Stake, how do most test specialists respond to this criticism? (p. 601)

2. Why does Stake believe that complex instructional objectives will be underemphasized in testing done under a performance contract? (p. 604)

3. What is the difference between "preparation for testing" and "direct coaching for a test"? (p. 605)

4. According to Stake, why are grade-equivalent scores inadequate for measuring learning gain? (p. 608)

5. What does research indicate concerning student learning gain in winter compared to learning gain in summer? (pp. 608–609)

6. How do unreliable gain scores misrepresent learning? (p. 610)

7. Define the regression effect in testing. (p. 611)

NOTES AND REFERENCES

PART ONE

Section One

SKINNER
1. Skinner, B. F. *Science and Human Behavior.* New York: Macmillan, 1953.

BROWN
Bandura, A., and Huston, Aletha C. "Identification as a Process of Incidental Learning." *J. Abnorm. Soc. Psychol.*, 63, 1961, 311–318.

Bandura, A., and McDonald, F. J. "The Influence of Social Reinforcement and the Behavior of Models in Shaping Children's Moral Judgments." *J. Abnorm. Soc. Psychol.*, 67, 1963, 274–281.

Bandura, A., Ross, Dorothea, and Ross, Sheila A. "Transmission of Aggression through Imitation of Aggressive Models." *J. Abnorm. Soc. Psychol.*, 63, 1961, 575–582.

Bandura, A., Ross, Dorothea, and Ross, Sheila A. "Imitation of Film-Mediated Aggressive Models." *J. Abnormal Soc. Psychol.*, 66, 1963, 3–11. (a)

Bandura, A., Ross, Dorothea, and Ross, Sheila A. " 'Vicarious' Reinforcement and Imitative Learning." *J. Abnorm. Soc. Psychol.*, 67, 1963, 601–607. (c)

Bandura, A., and Walters, R. H. *Social Learning and Personality Development.* New York: Holt, Rinehart, Winston, 1963.

Brim, O. G. "Family Structure and Sex Role Learning by Children: A Further Analysis of Helen Koch's Data." *Sociometry*, 21, 1958, 1–16.

Hill, W. F. "Learning Theory and the Acquisition of Values." *Psychol. Rev.*, 67, 1960, 317–331.

Maccoby, Eleanor E. "Role-taking in Childhood and Its Consequences for Social Learning." *Child Develpm.*, 30, 1959, 239–252.

Whiting, J. W. M. "Resource Mediation and Learning by Identification." In I. Iscoe and H. Stevenson (eds.), *Personality Development in Children.* Austin: Univer. of Texas Press, 1960.

GAGNE
Ausubel, D. P. *Educational Psychology: A Cognitive View.* New York: Holt, Rinehart and Winston, 1968.

Bandura, A. *Principles of Behavior Modification.* New York: Holt, Rinehart and Winston, 1969.

Battig, W. F. "Paired-associate Learning." In T. R. Dixon and D. L. Horton (eds.), *Verbal Behavior and General Behavior Theory.* Englewood Cliffs, N.J.: Prentice-Hall, 1968, pp. 149–171.

Bloom, B. S. (Ed.) *Taxonomy of Educational Objectives. Handbook 1: Cognitive Domain.* New York: David McKay, 1956.

Bruner, J. S. "The Skill of Relevance and the Relevance of Skills." *Saturday Review*, Apr. 18, 1970, pp. 66–68, 78–79.

Bruner, J. S., Goodnow, J., and Austin, G. *A Study of Thinking.* New York: Wiley, 1956.

Fitts, P. M., and Posner, M. I. *Human Performance.* Belmont, Calif.: Brooks/Cole, 1967.

Gagné, R. M. *The Conditions of Learning.* (2d ed.) New York: Holt, Rinehart and Winston, 1970 (a)

Gagné, R. M. "Some New Views of Learning and Instruction." *Phi Delta Kappan,* 1970, 468–472. (b)

Gagné, R. M. "Instruction Based on Research in Learning." *Engineering Education,* 1971, 61, 519–523.

Hovland, C. I., Janis, I. L., and Kelley, H. H. *Communication and Persuasion.* New Haven: Yale University Press, 1953.

Jensen, A. R. "Social Class, Race, and Genetics: Implications for Education." *American Educational Research Journal,* 1968, 5, 1–42.

Krathwohl, D. R., Bloom, B. S., and Masia, B. B. *Taxonomy of Educational Objectives. Handbook II: Affective Domain.* New York: David McKay, 1964.

Leavitt, H. J., and Schlosberg, H. "The Retention of Verbal and of Motor Skills." *Journal of Experimental Psychology,* 1944, 34, 404–417.

Mandler, G. "From Association to Structure." *Psychological Review,* 1962, 69, 415–427.

Payne, D. A., Krathwohl, D. R., and Gordon, J. "The Effect of Sequence on Programmed Instruction." *American Educational Research Journal,* 1967, 4, 125–132.

Rosenberg, M. J., Hovland, C. I., McGuire, W. J., Abelson, R. P., and Brehm, J. W. *Attitude Organization and Change.* New Haven: Yale University Press, 1960.

Rohwer, W. D., Jr., and Levin, J. R. "Action, Meaning and Stimulus Selection in Paired-Associate Learning." *Journal of Verbal Learning and Verbal Behavior,* 1968, 7, 137–141.

Skinner, B. F. *The Technology of Teaching.* New York: Appleton-Century-Crofts, 1968.

Section Two

EBEL

1. In *The Aims of Education* (New York: Macmillan, 1929).

2. C. I. Lewis, *An Analysis of Knowledge and Valuation* (LaSalle, Ill.: Open Court, 1946).

3. Harry S. Broudy and John R. Palmer, *Exemplars of Teaching Method* (Chicago: Rand McNally, 1965).

BEREITER

1. The definition is from Thomas F. Green, "Schools and Communities: A Look Forward." *Harvard Educational Review,* 39 (Spring 1969), 235. The somewhat more descriptive but less familiar term "personalist education" is used by H. I. Marrou in his *History of Education in Antiquity* (New York: Sheed and Ward, 1956).

2. William Boyd, *The Emile of Jean Jacques Rousseau,* 3 (New York: Bureau of Publications, Teachers College, Columbia University, 1962), p. 19.

3. This estimate is probably too generous. Generally too little is known to permit the meaningful setting of minimum scores on personality tests, as was done with IQ. However, the Myers-Briggs Type Indicator (Isabell Briggs Myers. Manual: The Myers-Briggs Type Indicator, Princeton, New Jersey: Educational Testing Service, 1962), based on Jungian theory, provides a classification of people into types that is relevant to this issue. It seems reasonable that humanistic educators should be "intuitive" rather than "sense-perceptive" (fact-bound) types and that they should be "perceiving" (open to many possibilities) rather than "judging" types. A classification of nearly 4,000 students in highly-selective liberal arts colleges (who could therefore be presumed to meet the intelligence requirement) showed that only about a third of them qualify in both categories (ibid., p. 45).

4. U.S. Bureau of the Census, *Statistical Abstract of the United States: 1969* (Washington, D.C.: U.S. Government Printing Office, 1969), pp. 103 and 212.

5. Quoted in *The Futurist,* 3 (August, 1969), 100.
6. Green, pp. 235–236.
7. This is true, at least, of the first major experiment along these lines, the Parkway Project in Philadelphia. See D. Cox, "Learning on the Road: Parkway Project, Philadelphia," *Saturday Review,* 52 (May 17, 1969), 71.
8. I have in mind such possibilities as theater, music, and journalism produced by young people and youth participation in social action and scientific activities.

GUSZAK

Aschner, Mary June, Gallagher, J. J., Perry, Joyce M., Afsar, Sibel S., Jenne, W., and Farr, Helen. *A System for Classifying Thought Processes in the Context of Classroom Verbal Interaction.* Champaign, Illinois: Institute for Research on Exceptional Children, 1965.
Austin, Mary C., and Morrison, C. *The First R: The Harvard Report on Reading in Elementary Schools.* New York: Macmillan, 1964.
Bloom, B. S. (Ed.) *Taxonomy of Educational Objectives: Handbook I: Cognitive Domain.* New York: McKay, 1956.
Henry, J. "Reading for What?" *Teachers College Record,* 1963, 65.
Thorndike, E. L. "Reading as Reasoning: A Study of Mistakes in Paragraph Reading." *Journal of Educational Research,* 1917, 8, 323–332.

BANKS

1. *Report of the National Advisory Commission on Civil Disorders.* New York: Bantam Books, 1968, p. 1.
2. James Baldwin, "A Talk to Teachers," *Saturday Review,* December 21, 1963, p. 42.
3. Helen H. Davidson and Gerhard Lang, "Children's Perceptions of Their Teachers' Feelings Toward Them Related to Self-Perception, School Achievement, and Behavior," *Journal of Experimental Education,* 1960, pp. 107–18; reprinted in James A. Banks and William W. Joyce (eds.), *Teaching Social Studies to Culturally Different Children.* Reading, Mass.: Addison-Wesley, 1971, pp. 113–27.
4. For a review of this research, see James A. Banks, "Racial Prejudice and the Black Self-Concept," in James A. Banks and Jean Dresden Grambs (eds.), *Black Self-Concept: Implications for Education and Social Science.* New York: McGraw-Hill, 1972, pp. 5–35.
5. For a research summary and review, see Marcel L. Goldschmid (ed.), *Black Americans and White Racism: Theory and Research.* New York: Holt, Rinehart, and Winston, 1970.
6. Wilbur B. Brookover and Edsel L. Erikson, *Society, Schools, and Learning.* Boston: Allyn and Bacon, 1969, p. 3.
7. Robert E. L. Faris, "Reflections on the Ability Dimension in Human Society," *American Sociological Review,* December, 1961, pp. 835–42.
8. For a perceptive discussion of this point, see Barbara A. Sizemore, "Social Science and Education for a Black Identity," in Banks and Grambs, op. cit., pp. 141–70.

BESSELL

1. Acknowledgment is given to *Psychology Today* for permission to use passages from an article by the author which appeared in the January 1968 issue, entitled *The Content Is the Medium: The Confidence Is the Message.*
2. Bloom's contribution was his division of the educational process into three domains: the cognitive (thinking), the affective (feelings), and performance (behavior).

Bessell, H., and Palomares, O. H. *Methods in Human Development.* San Diego, Calif.: Human Development Training Institute, 1967.
Bloom, B. S. (ed.) *Taxonomy of Educational Objectives.* New York: McKay, 1956.
Freud, S. *The Ego and the Id.* New York: Norton, 1961.
Horney, K. *Neurosis and Human Growth.* New York: Norton, 1950.
Jowett, R. (ed.) *Plato: The Republic.* New York: Everyman, 1946, pp. 425–434.
Sullivan, H. S. *Conceptions of Modern Psychiatry* (2nd ed.). Washington, D.C.: William Alanson White Foundation, 1947.

PART TWO

Section Four

MAYESKE

1. Tetsuo Okada, Carl E. Wisler, Wallace M. Cohen, and Albert E. Beaton, Jr.

2. *Achievement (ACHV)*. A student with a high score on this composite tended to score high on all of the tests that entered into that composite: tests of verbal and non-verbal ability, reading comprehension, and mathematics achievement.

3. *Racial-Ethnic Group Membership (RETH)*. A student with a high score on this variable is white, a student with an intermediate score is Oriental-American, and a student with a low score is Puerto-Rican, Mexican-American, Indian-American, or Negro-American.

4. *Family Structure and Stability (FSS)*. A student with a high score on this index has both parents in the home, his father's earnings are the major source of income, his mother works part-time or not at all, and his family has not moved around much.

5. *Attitude Toward Life (ATTUD)*. A student with a high score on this index feels that people who accept their condition in life are not necessarily happier; hard work is more important than good luck for success; when he tries to get ahead he doesn't encounter many obstacles; with a good education he won't have difficulty getting a job; he would not sacrifice anything to get ahead nor does he want to change himself; he does not have difficulty learning nor does he feel that he would do better if his teachers went slower; and people like him have a chance to be successful.

Mayeske, G. W., et al., *A Study of Our Nation's Schools*. Washington, D.C.: U.S. Government Printing Office, 1969 (A Working Paper).

Mayeske, G. W., et al., *A Study of the Achievement of Our Nation's Students*. Washington, D.C.: U.S. Government Printing Office, 1971 (In Press).

JENSEN

Bereiter, C. "Genetics and Educability: Educational Implications of the Jensen Debate." In J. Hellmuth (ed.), *Disadvantaged Child*, vol. 3. *Compensatory Education: A National Debate*. New York: Brunner-Mazel, 1970, pp. 279–299.

De Fries, J. C. "Quantitative Aspects of Genetics and Environment in the Determination of Behavior." In E. Caspari (ed.), *Future Directions of Behavior Genetics*, in press.

Jensen, A. R. "How Much Can We Boost IQ and Scholastic Achievement?" *Harvard Educational Review*, 39, 1969, 1–123.

Jensen, A. R. "Race and the Genetics of Intelligence: A Reply to Lewontin." *Bulletin of the Atomic Scientists*, 26, 1970, 17–23.

Lewontin, R. C. "Race and Intelligence." *Bulletin of the Atomic Scientists*, 26, no. 3 (1970), 2–8. (a)

———. "Further Remarks on Race and the Genetics of Intelligence." *Bulletin of the Atomic Scientists*, 26, no. 5 (1970), 23–25. (b)

Lush, J. L. "Genetic Unknowns and Animal Breeding a Century after Mendel." *Transactions of the Kansas Academy of Science*, 71, 1968, 309–314.

Spuhler, J. N., and Lindzey, G. "Racial Differences in Behavior." In J. Hirsch (ed.), *Behavior-Genetic Analysis*. New York: McGraw-Hill, 1967, pp. 366–414.

DEUTSCH

1. In a recent discussion, Bernstein indicated that he was replacing the terms "public" and "formal" with the terms "elaborated" and "restricted." He feels that the latter offer better analytic distinctions and operate at a higher level of abstraction.

Bernstein, B. "Language and Social Class." *Brit. J. Sociol.*, 11, 1960, 271–276.

Bruner, J. S. "The Cognitive Consequences of Early Sensory Deprivation." In P. Solomon (ed.), *Sensory Deprivation*. Cambridge: Harvard Univer. Press, 1961, pp. 195–207.

Deutsch, M. "The Disadvantaged Child and the Learning Process." In A. H. Passow (ed.), *Education in Depressed Areas*. New York: Bur. Pub., Teach. Coll., Columbia Univer., 1963, pp. 163–179.

————. "Minority Group and Class Status as Related to Social and Personality Factors in Scholastic Achievment." *Monogr. Society for Applied Anthropology*, 1960, no. 2.

————, and Brown, B. "Social Influences in Negro-White Intelligence Differences." *J. Soc. Issues*, April 1964, 24–35 .

Harrington, M. *The Other America*. New York: Macmillan, 1962.

Hunt, J. McV. *Intelligence and Experience*. New York: Ronald Press, 1961.

Montessori, Maria. *Education for a New World*. Wheaton, Ill.: Theosophical Press, 1959.

Scott, J. P. "Critical Periods in Behavioral Development." *Science*, 138, 1962, 949–955.

White, R. "Motivation Reconsidered: The Concept of Competence." *Psychol. Rev.*, 66 (1959), 297–333.

Section Five

COHEN

1. *The IQ Argument*, The Library Press, 156 pp., $5.95.

2. It could be argued that the research I have summarized understates the influence of social and economic class, because dropouts were not included in the computations; but when they were included, the results barely changed. It could be argued that the role of intelligence is understated because a single test score can't summarize intelligence; yet when scores in four different tests were included instead of just one, nothing much changed either. And while there are plenty of other difficulties with the studies summarized here, none of them seems important enough to change the general pattern of results I have presented.

3. Occupational status is a term derived from studies of the prestige in which Americans hold different sorts of jobs. Generally, they think that professional and managerial jobs are very prestigious and that common labor is not. Indices of occupational prestige are very highly correlated with general indices of social and economic status.

GUILFORD

1. C. Spearman, *Am. J. Psychol.*, 15 (1904), 201.

2. For the benefit of the uninitiated, a (positive) correlation between any two tests means that if certain individuals make high (low) scores in one of them they are likely also to make high (low) scores in the other.

3. L. L. Thurstone, "Primary Mental Abilities," *Psychometric Monographs*, no. 1 (1938).

4. J. P. Guilford and J. I. Lacey, Eds., *Printed Classification Tests* (Washington, D.C.: Government Printing Office, 1947).

5. We are indebted to the Office of Naval Research, Personnel and Training Branch, for continued support, and for additional support at various times from the U.S. Office of Education and the National Science Foundation, Biological and Medical Sciences Division.

6. C. Burt, *Brit. J. Educ. Psychol.*, 19, 100, 176 (1949).

7. P. E. Vernon, *The Structure of Human Abilities* (New York: Wiley, 1950).

8. J. P. Guilford, *Psychol. Bull.* 53, 267 (1956).

9. F. Zwicky, *Morphological Analysis* (Berlin: Springer, 1957).

10. J. P. Guilford, *Am. Psychologist* 14, 468 (1959).

11. E. L. Thorndike, *Harper's Magazine* 140, 227 (1920).

12. J. P. Guilford, *The Nature of Human Intelligence* (New York: McGraw-Hill, 1967), chap. 14.

13. ———— and R. Hoepfner, *Indian J. Psychol.* 41, 7 (1966).

14. Expressional Fluency is the sentence-construction test illustrated earlier.

15. Guilford, *Nature of Human Intelligence*, p. 336.

Section Six

GAGE

American Educational Research Association, Committee on the Criteria of Teacher Effectiveness. (1953) Second report, *Journal of Educational Research*, 46, 641–658.

Ausubel, D. P. (1963) *The Psychology of Meaningful Verbal Learning: An Introduction to School Learning.* New York: Grune & Stratton.

Bowles, S., and Levin, Henry M. (1968a) "The Determinants of Scholastic Achievement — An Appraisal of Some Recent Evidence." *Journal of Human Resources*, 3, 3–24.

———— (1968b) "More on Multicollinearity and the Effectiveness of Schools." *Journal of Human Resources*, 3, 393–400.

Brim, O. G., Jr. (1958) *Sociology and the Field of Education.* New York: Russell Sage Foundation.

Bruner, J. S. (1966a) *Toward a Theory of Instruction.* Cambridge: Harvard University Press.

Coats, W. D., and Smidchens, U. (1966) "Audience Recall as a Function of Speaker Dynamism." *Journal of Educational Psychology*, 57, 189–191.

Cogan, M. I. (1958) "The Behavior of Teachers and the Productive Behavior of Their Pupils: I. 'Perception' Analysis. II. 'Trait' Analysis." *Journal of Experimental Education*, 27, 89–105, 107–124.

Coleman, J. S., et al. (1966) *Equality of Educational Opportunity.* Washington, D.C.: U.S. Government Printing Office.

Cook, W. W., Leeds, C. H., and Callis, R. (1951) *The Minnesota Teacher Attitude Inventory.* New York: Psychological Corp.

Dubin, R., and Taveggia, T. C. (1968) *The Teaching-Learning Paradox: A Comparative Analysis of College Teaching Methods.* Eugene, Ore.: Center for the Advanced Study of Educational Administration, University of Oregon.

Flanders, N. A. (1965) *Teacher Influence, Pupil Attitudes, and Achievement.* U.S. Department of Health, Education, and Welfare. Office of Education, Cooperative Research Monograph no. 12 (OE–25040). Washington, D.C.: U.S. Government Printing Office.

Flanders, N. A., and Simon, A. (1969) "Teacher Effectiveness." In R. L. Ebel (Ed.), *Encyclopedia of Educational Research*, (4th ed.) New York: Macmillan, pp. 1423–1436.

Gage, N. L., Leavitt, G. S., and Stone, G. C. (1957) "The Psychological Meaning of Acquiescence Set for Authoritarianism." *Journal of Abnormal and Social Psychology*, 55, 98–103.

Gagné, R. M. (1965) *The Conditions of Learning.* New York: Holt, Rinehart and Winston.

Getzels, J. W., and Jackson, P. W. (1963) "The Teacher's Personality and Characteristics." In N. L. Gage (ed.), *Handbook of Research on Teaching.* Chicago: Rand McNally, pp. 506–582.

Glaser, R., and Reynolds, H. H. (1964) "Instructional Objectives and Programmed Instruction: A Case Study." In C. M. Lindvall (ed.), *Defining Educational Objectives.* Pittsburgh: University of Pittsburgh Press, pp. 47–76.

Hickey, A. E., and Newton, J. M. (1964) "The Logical Basis of Teaching: I. The Effect of Sub-concept Sequence on Learning." Final Report to Office of Naval Research. Personnel and Training Branch, Contract Nonr-4215(00).

Mastin, V. E. (1963) "Teacher Enthusiasm." *Journal of Educational Research*, 56, 385–386.

McGee, H. M. (1955) "Measurement of Authoritarianism and Its Relation to Teachers' Classroom Behavior." *Genetic Psychology Monographs*, 52, 89–146.

Meux, M. O., and Smith, B. O. (1961) "Logical Dimensions of Teaching Behavior." Urbana: University of Illinois, Bureau of Educational Research. (Mimeographed.)

Orleans, J. S. (1952) *The Understanding of Arithmetic Processes and Concepts Possessed by Teachers of Arithmetic.* New York: Board of Education of the City of New York, Division of Teacher Education, Office of Research and Evaluation.

Rosenshine, B. (1970) "Enthusiastic Teaching: A Research Review." *School Review*, 78, 499–514.

Ryans, D. G. (1960) *Characteristics of Teachers*. Washington, D.C.: American Council on Education.

Sheldon, M. S., Coale, J. M., and Copple, R. (1959) "Concurrent Validity of the 'Warm Teacher Scales,' " *Journal of Educational Psychology* 50, 37–40.

Shulman, L., and Keislar, E. (eds.) (1966) *Learning by Discovery: A Critical Appraisal*, Chicago: Rand McNally.

Stephens, J. M. (1967) *The Process of Schooling*. New York: Holt, Rinehart and Winston.

Wallen, N. E., and Travers, R. M. W. (1963) "Analysis and Investigation of Teaching Methods." In N. L. Gage (ed.), *Handbook of Research on Teaching*. Chicago: Rand McNally, pp. 448–505.

Withall, J., and Lewis, W. W. (1963) "Social Interaction in the Classroom." In N. L. Gage (ed.), *Handbook of Research on Teaching*. Chicago: Rand McNally, pp. 683–714.

Yee, A. H. (1968) "Is the Minnesota Teacher Attitude Inventory Valid and Homogeneous?" *Journal of Educational Measurement*, 4, 151–161.

POPHAM

1. For a more extensive account of this research see W. James Popham, "Performance Tests of Teaching Proficiency: Rationale, Development, and Validation," *American Educational Research Journal*, January 1971, 105–117.

2. R. Glaser, "Instructional Technology and the Measurement of Learning Outcomes: Some Questions," *American Psychologist*, 18 (1963), 519–521.

3. I am indebted to the San Diego City Schools and several Orange County school districts for their cooperation in this project.

4. See, for example, the recently published volume by John D. McNeil, *Toward Accountable Teachers*. New York: Holt, Rinehart, and Winston, 1971.

5. Box 24095, Los Angeles, California 90024.

6. Vimcet Associates, P.O. Box 24714, Los Angeles, California 90024, distributes a series of teaching performance tests plus filmstrip-tape programs regarding how to build and use such tests.

FLANDERS, MORRISON, and BRODE

Flanders, N. A. "Helping Teachers Change Their Behavior." Terminal report, National Educational Defense Act, Title VII project, 1963.

Flanders, N. A. *Teacher Influence, Pupil Attitudes, and Achievement*. United States Office of Education Cooperative Research Monograph no. 12. Washington, D.C.: United States Government Printing Office, 1965.

Morrison, B. M. "The Reactions of External and Internal Pupils to Patterns of Teacher Behavior." Unpublished doctoral dissertation, University of Michigan, 1966.

Reiss, A. J., Jr. *Occupations and Social Status*. New York: Free Press of Glencoe, 1961.

Rotter, J. B., Seeman, M., and Liversant, S. "Internal versus External Control of Reinforcements: A Major Variable in Behavior Theory." In N. F. Washburne (ed.), *Decisions, Values, and Groups*, vol. 2, London: Pergamon Press, 1962.

BROPHY and GOOD

1. Janet Elashoff and Richard Snow, *Pygmalion Reconsidered* (Belmont, Calif.: Charles A. Jones, 1971).

2. Donald Meichenbaum, Kenneth Bowers, and Robert Ross. "A Behavioral Analysis of Teacher Expectancy Effect," *Journal of Personality and Social Psychology*, May, 1969, pp. 306–16.

3. W. Victor Beez, "Influence of Biased Psychological Reports on Teacher Behavior and Pupil Performance," *Proceedings of the Annual Convention of the American Psychological Association*, 1968, pp. 605, 606.

4. Myron Rothbart, Susan Dalfen, and Robert Barrett, "Effects of Teacher Expectancy on Student-Teacher Interaction," *Journal of Educational Psychology*, January–February, 1971, pp. 49–54.

5. Pamela Rubovits and Martin Maehr, "Pygmalion Analyzed: Toward an Explanation of the Rosenthal-Jacobson Findings," *Journal of Personality and Social Psychology*, August, 1971, pp. 197–203.

6. Gene Medinnus and Ronald Unruh, "Teacher Expectation and Verbal Communication," paper presented at the annual meeting of the Western Psychological Association, 1970.

7. Robert Rosenthal and Lenore Jacobson, *Pygmalion in the Classroom: Teacher Expectation and Pupils' Intellectual Development* (New York: Holt, Rinehart and Winston, 1968).

8. Elyse Fleming and Ralph Anttonen, "Teacher Expectancy or My Fair Lady," *American Educational Research Journal*, March, 1971, pp. 241–52.

9. Wilburn Schrank, "The Labeling Effect of Ability Grouping," *Journal of Educational Research*, October, 1968, pp. 51, 52; and "A Further Study of the Labeling Effect of Ability Grouping," *Journal of Educational Research*, April, 1970, pp. 358–60.

10. Jere Brophy and Thomas Good, "Teachers' Communication of Differential Expectations for Children's Classroom Performance: Some Behavioral Data," *Journal of Educational Psychology*, September–October, 1970, pp. 365–74.

11. Mary Budd Rowe, "Science, Silence, and Sanctions," *Science and Children*, September, 1969, pp. 11–13.

12. J. Michael Palardy, "What Teachers Believe, What Children Achieve," *Elementary School Journal*, April, 1969, pp. 370–74.

13. Wayne Doyle, Greg Hancock, and Edward Kiffer, "Teachers' Perceptions: Do They Make a Difference?" (paper presented at the annual meeting of the American Educational Research Association, 1971).

14. Thomas Good and Jere Brophy, *Looking in Classrooms* (New York: Harper and Row, 1973).

15. Jere Brophy and Thomas Good, *Individual Differences: Toward an Understanding of Classroom Life* (New York: Holt, Rinehart and Winston, in press).

Section Seven

TEMPLETON

Coleman, Peter. *Pupil-Teacher Ratios and the Use of Research Findings in Educational Policy-Making*, 1971. ERIC Document Reproduction Service ED 058 640.

Corey, Gerald F. *An Investigation of the Outcomes of Introductory Psychology*. Whittier, California: Rio Hondo Junior College, 1967.

Earthman, Glen L. *Study of Space Utilization*. Philadelphia: Philadelphia School District, 1969.

Edward W. Clark High School, *The Influence of Class Size on Academic Attainment and Student Satisfaction*. Las Vegas, Nevada; n.d.

Furno, Orlando F., and Collins, George J. *Class Size and Pupil Learning*. Baltimore: Baltimore City Public Schools, 1967.

Hopper, Harold H., and Keller, Helen. *Writing Skills — Are Large Classes Conducive to Effective Learning*. Fort Pierce, Florida: Indian River Junior College, 1966.

Johnson, Mauritz, and Scriven, Eldon, "Class Size and Achievement Gains in Seventh- and Eighth-Grade English and Mathematics." *The School Review*, 75, 3 (Autumn 1967).

McKeachie, Wilbert J. *Improving Teaching Effectiveness*. Washington, D.C.: U.S. Government Printing Office, 1971.

Olson, Martin N. "Ways to Achieve Quality in School Classrooms: Some Definitive Answers." *Phi Delta Kappan*, 53, 1 (September 1971), 63–65.

President's Commission on School Finance. *Schools, People, and Money. The Need for Educational Reform. Final Report*. Washington, D.C.: U.S. Government Printing Office, 1972.

Sitkei, E. George. *The Effects of Class Size: A Review of the Research. Research Study Series. 1967–68*. Los Angeles: Los Angeles County Superintendent of Schools, 1968.

Varner, Sherrell F. *Class Size.* Washington, D.C.: National Education Association, 1968.

Vincent, William S. "Further Clarification of the Class Size Question." New York: Institute of Administrative Research, Columbia University. *IAR Research Bulletin,* 9, 1 (November 1968).

Woodson, Marshall S. "Effect of Class Size as Measured by an Achievement Test Criterion." New York: Institute of Administrative Research, Columbia University. *IAR Research Bulletin,* 8, 2 (February 1968).

Section Eight

MONEY and EHRHARDT

1. Young, William C. "The Hormones and Mating Behavior." In W. C. Young (ed.), *Sex and Internal Secretions,* 3rd ed. Baltimore: Williams and Wilkins, 1961.

2. Ward, Ingeborg. "Prenatal Stress Feminizes and Demasculinizes the Behavior of Males." *Science* (1972), 1975:82–84.

SADKER

1. Quoted in the *Racine Journal Times,* December 12, 1972.

2. Eleanor Maccoby, "Sex Differences in Intellectual Functioning," in Eleanor Maccoby (ed.), *The Development of Sex Differences,* Stanford: Stanford University Press, 1966.

3. Stevenson Smith, "Age and Sex Differences in Children's Opinions Concerning Sex Differences," *Journal of Genetic Psychology,* 54, (March 1939), 17–25.

4. Patricia Minuchin, "Sex Differences in Children: Research Findings in an Educational Context," *National Elementary Principal,* 16, no. 2 (1966), 45-48.

5. Robert O'Hara, "The Roots of Careers," *Elementary School Journal,* 62, no. 5 (1962), 277–280.

6. Lynne Iglitzin, "A Child's-Eye View of Sex Roles." Paper presented at the American Political Science Association, Washington, D.C., 1972.

7. Patricia Cross, "College Women: A Research Description," *Journal of National Association of Women Deans and Counselors,* 32, no. 1 (1968), 12–21.

8. Peggy Harvly, "What Women Think Men Think," *Journal of Counseling Psychology,* 18, no. 3 (1971), 193–194.

9. "Facts About Women in Education," prepared by the Women's Equity Action League.

10. John McKee and Alex Sheriffs, "The Differential Education of Males and Females." *Journal of Personality,* 35, no. 3 (1957), 356–371.

11. Matinna Horner, "Woman's Will To Fail," *Psychology Today,* 3, no. 6 (1969).

12. B. J. Kemer, "A Study of the Relationship Between the Sex of the Student and the Assignment of Marks by Secondary School Teachers," Ph.D. diss., Michigan State University, 1965.

13. Arthur Thomas and Norman Stewart, "Counselor's Response to Female Clients with Deviate and Conforming Career Goals," *Journal of Counseling Psychology,* 18, no. 4, (July 1971), 352–357.

14. Phil Jackson and Henriette Lahaderne, "Inequalities of Teacher-Pupil Contacts," in Melvin Silberman (ed.), *The Experience of Schooling,* New York: Holt, Rinehart and Winston, 1971, pp. 123–124.

15. Ibid.

16. Robert Spaulding, "Achievement, Creativity, and Self-Concept Correlates of Teacher-Pupil Transactions in Elementary School," Cooperative Research Project No. 1352, U.S. Dept. of Health, Education, and Welfare, Office of Education, Washington, D.C., 1963.

17. Pauline Sears and David Feldman, "Teacher Interactions with Boys and Girls," *National Elementary Principal,* 46, no. 2 (1966), 13–17.

18. Jerome Bruner, *Toward a Theory of Instruction,* Cambridge, Mass.: Belknap Press of Harvard University, 1966, 123–124.

19. Eleanor Maccoby, "Woman's Intellect," in Seymour Farber and Roger Wilson (eds.), *The Potential of Woman*, New York: McGraw-Hill, 1963, 33.

20. Vaughn Crandall and Alice Rabson, "Children's Repetition Choices in an Intellectual Achievement Situation Following Success and Failure," *Journal of Genetic Psychology*, 97 (Sept. 1960), 161–168.

21. Lenore J. Weitzman, Deborah Eifler, Elizabeth Hokada, and Catherine Ross, "Sex-Role Socialization in Picture Books for Preschool Children," *The American Journal of Sociology*, 77, 61 (May 1972).

22. Quoted in "The Feminists on Children's Literature, A Feminist Look at Children's Books," *School Library Journal*, 17, 5 (1971), 19–24.

23. Women on Words and Images, *Dick and Jane as Victims*, 1972.

24. Marjorie U'Ren, "The Image of Women in Textbooks," in Vivian Gormick and Barbara Moran (eds.), *Woman in Sexist Society*, New York: Basic Books, 1971, 218–225.

25. Janice Trecher, "Women in U.S. History Textbooks," *Social Education*, 35, 3 (March 1971), 249.

26. Bernice Sandler, Women's Equity Action League, *Statement before the House Judiciary Committee*, Subcommittee no. 4, March 31, 1971.

27. Shirley McCune, *Proposal for a Resource Center to Combat Sexism in Elementary and Secondary Education*, 1972.

28. Patricia Sexton, *The Feminized Male*, New York, Vintage Books, 1969, pp. 141–143.

29. Norma Hare, "The Vanishing Woman Principal," *National Elementary Principal*, 45, no. 5 (1966), 12–13.

30. Thomas Lyles, "Grouping by Sex," *National Elementary Principal*, 46, 2 (1966), 38–41.

31. Excerpts of testimony quoted in Anne Grant West (ed.), *Report on Sex Bias in the Public Schools*. New York: Education Committee, NOW, 1971.

32. Emma Willard Task Force on Education, *Sexism in Education*, Dec. 8, 1971.

33. Marcia Federbush, *Let Them Aspire*, May 1971.

PART THREE

Section Nine

SHANE and NELSON

1. Respondents were selected from among five occupational categories: school administrators (72), subject matter specialists (42), curriculum professors (37), doctoral students (87), and a random sample of public school teachers (95).

2. This does not necessarily accurately reflect classroom teachers' attitudes. Only 95 of the 333 respondents were employed as teachers.

3. Most (76%) of the educators expect public schools to assume routine responsibility for identifying and treating incipient mental and psychological disorders or problems beginning in early childhood; 89% favor the idea.

Section Ten

HALL

1. S. Abrahamson, R. M. Wolf, and J. S. Denson, "A Computer-Based Patient Simulator for Training Anesthesiologists," *Educational Technology*, October 1969, p. 55.

2. W. Feurzeig, *Educational Potentials of Computer Technology*. Cambridge, Mass.: Bolt, Beranek and Newman, Inc., Report no. 1672, September 1968.

3. W. G. Harless et al., "Computer-Assisted Instruction in Continuing Medical Education," Journal of Medical Education, August 1969, pp. 670–674.

4. P. Suppes, "The Use of Computers in Education," *Scientific American*, September 1966, pp. 207–220.

5. C. F. Butler, "CAI in New York City — Report on the First Year's Operation," *Educational Technology*, October 1969, pp. 84–87.

RATHBONE

1. Portions of this description derive from my doctoral dissertation, "Open Education and the Teacher" (Harvard Graduate School of Education, 1970); I am indebted to Harvard University's Milton Fund and the Faculty Committee for Research and Development at Oberlin College for opportunities to visit British classrooms in 1968 and 1971.

2. Philip Jackson, *Life in Classrooms* (Chicago: University of Chicago Press, 1968).

3. William P. Hull, "Things to Think about While Observing," in *ESS Reader* (Newton, Mass.: Educational Development Center, 1971). The questions are his, the reordering of them, mine.

Section Eleven

GRAUBARD

1. Funded by HEW.

ILLICH

1. Documentation on the construction, testing, and use of such machines is now in preparation at CIDOC.

2. For a fuller discussion of these distinctions, see my book, *Deschooling Society* (New York: Harper & Row, 1971).

SULLIVAN

1. Maggie Scarf, "Brain Researcher José Delgado Asks — What Kind of Humans Would We Like to Construct?," *The New York Times Magazine*, November 15, 1970, pp. 44–47 ff.

2. Ibid., p. 170.

3. Gay Luce and Erik Peper, "Mind over Body, Mind over Mind," *The New York Times Magazine*, September 12, 1971, pp. 34–35 ff.

4. Ibid., p. 134; also Harold M. Schmeck Jr., "Control by Brain Studied as Way to Curb Body Ills," *The New York Times* January 10, 1971, p. 1 ff.

5. Luce and Peper, op. cit., p. 132.

6. Richard A. Knox, "Violence: As Likely from Faulty Brain as Faulty Upbringing," *Boston Sunday Globe*, November 29, 1970, p. 4-A.

7. The film *Titicut Follies*, a documentary, shows the shocking neglect and abuse of those who are confined to such institutions.

8. Aaron M. Altschul, "Food: Proteins for Humans," *Chemical and Engineering News*, November 24, 1969, p. 70.

9. Rita Bakan, "Malnutrition and Learning," *Phi Delta Kappan*, June, 1970, p. 528.

10. James D. Harmeling and Marshall B. Jones, "Birth Weights of High School Dropouts," *American Journal of Orthopsychiatry*, January, 1968, pp. 63–66.

11. Linus Pauling, *Vitamin C and the Common Cold*. San Francisco: W. H. Freeman and Co., 1970, pp. 20–22.

12. Bernard Agranoff, "Memory and Protein Synthesis," *Scientific American*, June, 1967, p. 115.

13. Ibid., p. 120.

14. Ibid., p. 121.

15. Small "Peptide Induces Fear of Darkness in Rats," *Chemical and Engineering News*, January 11, 1971, p. 27.

16. An excellent description of the hyperactive child can be found in Mark A. Stewart's article, "Hyperactive Children," *Scientific American*, April, 1970, pp. 94–98.

17. Randall Richard, "Drugs for Children — Miracle or Nightmare?," *Providence Sunday Journal*, February 6, 1972, p. B-13.

18. R. G. Edwards and Ruth E. Fowler, "Human Embryos in the Laboratory," *Scientific American*, December, 1970, p. 45.

19. Ellen L. Sullivan, "Test-Tube Baby Cloud Gathers," *Boston Sunday Globe*, January 3, 1971, p. A9.

ASTOR

1. James Evans, *Principles of Programmed Learning*, 3d ed. (New York: TMI-Grolier, 1962).

2. Milton H. Erickson, "Basic Psychological Problems in Hypnotic Research," in G. H. Estabrooks (ed.), *Hypnosis: Current Problems* (New York: Harper & Row, 1962), pp. 207–223.

3. George H. Estabrooks, "The Social Implications of Hypnosis," in *Hypnosis: Current Problems*, pp. 224–237.

4. Clark L. Hull, *Hypnosis and Suggestibility* (New York: Appleton-Century-Crofts, 1933), p. 127.

5. P. G. Bowers, "Effects of Hypnosis and Suggestion of Reduced Defensiveness on Creativity Test Performance," *Journal of Personality*, 35, 2:311–322 (June, 1967).

6. Estabrooks, op. cit., p. 228.

7. "Coping Through Hypnosis: Growing Practice in Japan," *Times Education Supplement*, 2616:71 (July 9, 1965).

8. Joseph Illovsky, "An Experience with Group Hypnosis in Reading Disability in Primary Behavior Disorders," *The Journal of Genetic Psychology*, 102:61–67 (1963).

Section Twelve

BORG, KELLEY, LANGER, and GALL

Acheson, K. A. "The Effect of Feedback from Television Recording and Three Types of Supervisory Treatment on Selected Teacher Behavior." Unpublished doctoral dissertation, Stanford University, 1964.

Joyce, B. R. "The Teacher-Innovator: A Program to Prepare Teachers." Final report on U.S.O.E. Project No. 8-9019, Columbia University, 1968.

Tuckman, B. W., and Oliver, W. F. "Effectiveness of Feedback to Teachers as a Function of Source." *Journal of Educational Psychology*, 1968, 59, 297–301.

Willis, D. E. "Learning and Teaching in Methods Courses, Part I: Current Practice." *Journal of Teacher Education*, 1968, 19, 39–46.

DUNNING and GALL

1. Of these teachers, 70 per cent reported that the Minicourse was better than any other inservice training they had received.

Bernstein, A. "Library Research — a Study in Remedial Arithmetic." *School Science and Mathematics* 59 (1959):185–95.

Borg, W. R., M. L. Kelley, P. Langer, and M. Gall. *The Minicourse: A Microteaching Approach to Teacher Education*. Beverly Hills: Macmillan Educational Services, 1970.

Brownell, W. A., and C. B. Chazal. "The Effects of Premature Drill in Third-Grade Arithmetic," *Journal of Educational Research* 29 (1935):17–28.

Brueckner, L. J., and G. Bond. *The Diagnosis and Treatment of Learning Difficulties*. New York: Appleton-Century-Crofts, 1955.

Glennon, V. J., and L. G. Callahan. *Elementary School Mathematics: A Guide to Current Research*. Washington, D.C.: NEA, Association for Supervision and Curriculum Development, 1968.

Roberts, G. H. "The Failure Strategies of Third-Grade Arithmetic Pupils." *Arithmetic Teacher* 15 (1968):442–46.

Ross, R. "Diagnosis and Correction of Arithmetic Underachievement." *Arithmetic Teacher* 10 (1963):22–27.

Tilton, J. W. "Individualized and Meaningful Instruction in Arithmetic." *Journal of Educational Psychology* 38 (1947): 83–88.

NASH and AGNE

1. Nash, Robert J. "Commitment to Competency: The New Fetishism in Teacher Education," *Phi Delta Kappan*, 52:240–243; December 1970.
2. Ryan, Kevin A. *A Plan for a New Type of Professional Training for a New Type of Teaching Staff*. The Teacher and His Staff, Occasional Papers no. 2. Washington, D.C.: National Commission on Teacher Education and Professional Standards, National Education Association, 1968.
3. Phi Delta Kappan. "Teacher Corps and Competency-Based Education." Newsnotes. *Phi Delta Kappan* 52:189; November 1970.
4. AACTE Bulletin. "15th School for Executives Draws Record Gathering: Teacher Educators Explore the Impact of Social Change." *AACTE Bulletin* 23: 1+; September 1970.
5. Silberman, Charles E. *Crisis in the Classroom: The Remaking of American Education*. New York: Random House, 1970, p. 472.
6. Heist, Paul. "Professions and the Student." *The College Student and His Culture: An Analysis*. (Edited by Kaoru Yamomoto.) Boston, Mass.: Houghton Mifflin, 1968, pp. 161–178.
7. Sanford, Nevitt. "The College Student of 1980." *Campus 1980: The Shape of the Future in American Higher Education*. (Edited by Alvin C. Eurich.) New York: Dela-Press, 1968, pp. 176–199.
8. Mullaney, Antony. "The University as a Community of Resistance," *Harvard Educational Review* 40:628–641; November 1970.
9. Jersild, Arthur T. *When Teachers Face Themselves*. New York: Teachers College Press, 1955, pp. 159–161.
10. Silberman, op. cit., pp. 373–525.
11. Wolfe, Alan. "The Perils of Professionalism," *Change* 2:51–54; September-October 1970.
12. Dreeben, Robert. *The Nature of Teaching Schools and the Work of Teachers*. Chicago, Ill.: Scott, Foresman, 1970, p. 34.

COHEN and HERSH

1. Nash, Robert J., and Agne, Russell M. "Competency in Teacher Education: A Prop for the Status Quo?" *The Journal of Teacher Education*, 22:147–156, Summer 1971.
2. Ryan, Kevin A. *A Plan for a New Type of Professional Training for a New Type of Teaching Staff*. The Teacher and His Staff, Occasional Papers No. 2. Washington, D.C.: National Commission on Teacher Education and Professional Standards, National Education Association, 1968. As cited by Nash and Agne, op. cit., p. 147.
3. Phi Delta Kappan. "Teacher Corps and Competency-Based Education." Newsnotes. *Phi Delta Kappan* 52:189; November 1970. As cited by Nash and Agne, op. cit., p. 148.
4. AACTE Bulletin, "15th School for Executives Draws Record Gathering: Teacher Educators Explore the Impact of Social Change." *AACTE Bulletin* 23: 1+; September 1970. As cited by Nash and Agne, op. cit., p. 148.
5. Ibid.
6. Nash and Agne, op. cit., p. 149.
7. Ibid., p. 153.
8. Ibid., p. 149.
9. Ibid., p. 150.
10. Ibid., p. 150.
11. For a discussion of value clarification, see Raths, Louis E.; Harmin, Merrill; and Simon, Sidney B. *Values and Teaching: Working with Values in the Classroom*. Columbus, Ohio: Charles E. Merrill Publishing Co., 1966.
12. Nash and Agne, op. cit., p. 151.
13. Ibid., p. 151.
14. For a discussion of children's strategies for learning the teacher, see Holt, John. *How Children Fail*. New York: Pitman, 1964.
15. Bloom, B. S., editor, *Taxonomy of Educational Objectives: The Classification of Educational Goals*, Handbook 1: *Cognitive Domain*. New York: Longmans, Green, and Co., 1956.

16. Nash and Agne, op. cit., p. 153.
17. Ibid., p. 153.
18. Ibid., p. 148.
19. Popham, W. James. "Performance Tests of Teaching Proficiency: Rationale, Development, and Validation." *American Educational Research Journal* 8:105–117, January 1971.

THELEN

1. The investigation reported here was partially supported by a grant from the National Institute of Mental Health for a study of "Small Group Methods to Adapt Problem Students."
2. "10-Year-Olds Are Tutoring 7-Year-Olds," *Education News*, January 22, 1968, p. 8.
3. *New York Times*, October 29, 1967.
4. "Underachievers in the Junior High," *Impact* (published by the School District of University City, Missouri) 4, no. 2 (1967):12–13.
5. "Evaluation Report: The Tutoring Program. A Comprehensive Remedial and Developmental Program for Disabled Learners at the Junior High School Level. July 5, 1967." University City, Mo.: Brittany Junior High School. (Provided by William R. Page.)
6. Ibid.
7. Marie J. Yerry, "Interage Classes in the Plainedge School District," planographed, illustrated (Bethpage, N.Y.).

NIMNICHT and BROWN

1. Toys in the Library are for children aged three through nine.
2. Although we designed most of the toys to meet our specific needs, we do use a few commercial toys.

Bowman, O. H., and Matthews, C. V. *The Motivations of Youth for Learning School.* U.S. Department of Health, Education, and Welfare, Office of Education, Report on Cooperative Research Project No. 200, Washington D.C.

Fowler, William. "Cognitive Learning in Infancy and Early Childhood." *Psychological Bulletin* 59: Chapter 2, 116–152; 1962.

Gray, Susan W., and Miller, James O. "Early Experience in Relation to Cognitive Development." *Review of Educational Research*, Vol. 37, No. 5 (December 1967).

Hess, Robert D., and Shipman, Virginia C. "Early Experience and Socialization of Cognitive Modes in Children." *Child Development* 36: No. 4, (December, 1965) 869–886.

McCandless, B. *Children and Adolescent Behavior and Development.* New York: Holt, Rinehart and Winston, 1961.

Norman, Ralph D. "The Interpersonal Values of Parents of Achieving and Non-Achieving Gifted Children." *Journal of Psychology* 64 (September, 1966), 49–57.

Rolcik, John W. "Scholastic Achievement of Teenager and Parental Attitudes Toward and Interest in Schoolwork. *Family Life Coordinator* 14 (October, 1965), 158–160.

Shaw, Merville C., and White, Donald I. "The Relationship Between Child-Parent Identification and Academic Underachievement." *Journal of Clinical Psychology* 21 (January, 1965), 10–13.

Wattenberg, William W., and Clifford, Claire. "Relation of Self-Concept to Beginning Achievement in Reading." *Child Development* 35: No. 2 (June, 1964).

Section Thirteen

HEATHERS

Abrahamson, David A. "The Effectiveness of Grouping for Students of High Ability." *Ed. Res. B.* 38:169–82; 1959.

Atkinson, John W., and O'Connor, Patricia. *Effects of Ability Grouping in Schools*

Related to Individual Differences in Achievement-Related Motivation. Project no. 1283. USOE, 1963. 175pp.

Borg, Walter R. *Ability Grouping in the Public Schools,* 2nd ed. Dembar Educational Research Services, 1966. 98pp.

Daniels, John C. "Effects of Streaming in the Primary School. II: A Comparison of Streamed and Unstreamed Schools." *Brit. J. Ed. Psychol.* 31:119–27; 1961.

Dean, Stuart A. *Elementary School Administration and Organization.* USOE Bulletin no. 11. HEW, 1960.

Deutsch, Martin A. "Dimensions of the School's Role in Problems of Integration," in Klopf, Gordon J., and Laster, Israel A. (Eds.) *Integration in the Urban School.* Teachers Col., Columbia University, 1963, pp. 29–44.

Dockrell, W. B. "Edmonton Junior High School Streaming Project," in *Studies in Grouping.* Alberta Teacher's Association, 1964.

Douglas, J. W. B. *The Home and the School: A Study of Ability and Attainment in the Primary School.* MacGibbon and Kee, 1964. 190pp.

Drews, Elizabeth M. *Student Abilities, Grouping Patterns, and Classroom Interactions.* Michigan State University Press, 1963.

Eckstrom, Ruth B. "Experimental Studies of Homogeneous Grouping: A Critical Review." *Sch. R.* 69:216–26; 1959.

Goldberg, Miriam and others. *The Effects of Ability Grouping.* Teachers College, Columbia University, 1969. 254pp.

Goodlad, John I. "Classroom Organization," in *Encyclopedia of Educational Research,* 3rd ed. Macmillan, 1960.

Heathers, Glen. *Organizing Schools Through the Dual Progress Plan.* Interstate, 1967, 228pp.

Husén, Torsten, and Svensson, Nils-Eric. "Pedagogic Milieu and Development of Intellectual Skills." *Sch. R.* 68:36–51, 1960.

Luchins, Abraham S., and Luchins, Edith H. "Children's Attitudes Toward Homogeneous Grouping." *J. Genet. Psychol.* 72:3–9; 1948.

National Education Association. *The Principals Look at the Schools.* NEA, 1962. 75pp.

Otto, Henry J., and Sanders, David C. *Elementary School Organization and Administration,* 4th ed. Appleton, 1964, 409pp.

Squire, James R. "National Study of High School English Programs: A School for All Seasons." *Engl. J.* 55:282–90; 1966.

Wilcox, John. "A Search for the Multiple Effects of Grouping upon the Growth and Behavior of Junior High School Pupils." Doctoral dissertation. Cornell University, 1961.

Willig, C. J. "Social Implications of Streaming in the Junior School." *Ed. Res.* 5: 151–4; 1963.

DOMINO

Domino, G. Differential prediction of academic achievement in conforming and independent settings. *Journal of Educational Psychology,* 1968, 59, 256–260.

Gough, H. G. *Manual for the California Psychological Inventory.* Palo Alto, California: Consulting Psychologists Press, 1957.

Guilford, J. P. Three faces of intellect. *American Psychologist,* 1959, 14, 469–479.

AUSTIN, ROGERS, and WALBESSER

Beggs, D. L., and Hieronymus, A. N. "Uniformity of Growth in the Basic Skills throughout the School Year and During the Summer." *Journal of Educational Measurement,* 1968, 5(2), 91–97.

Campbell, D., and Stanley, J. "Experimental and Quasi-experimental Designs for Research." In N. Gage (Ed.), *Handbook of Research in Teaching.* Chicago: Rand McNally, 1963.

Cohen, D. K. "Politics and Research: Evaluation of Social Action Programs in Education." *Review of Educational Research,* 1970, 40(2), 213–238.

Costa, T. "Second Annual Evaluation of Title I, Fiscal Year, 1967." Providence: Rhode Island State Department of Education, 1967. ERIC: ED 020256.

Fox, D. J. and Ward, E. "Summer Musical Talent Showcase for Disadvantaged High School Students." New York: Center for Urban Education, 1967. ERIC ED 029922.

Fox, D. J. and Weinberg, E. "Summer Schools for Junior High and Intermediate School Pupils." New York: Center for Urban Education, 1967. ERIC: ED 034010.

Fox, D. J., and others. "Summer 1967 Clinics for Speech Handicapped Children." New York: Center for Urban Education, 1967. ERIC ED 029921.

Hanson, W. E. "Aims and Purposes of Summer Programs." *Minnesota Journal of Education,* 1964, 44(8), 33, 48.

Hayes, E. M., and Kerr, T. H. "An Interdisciplinary Evaluation of a Summer Program for the Rural Disadvantaged Youth in Nelson County, Va." Final Report. Lovingston, Va.: Nelson Co. Public Schools, 1970. ERIC: ED 046599.

Iowa State Department of Public Instruction. "Annual Evaluation Report for Migrant Programs, Fiscal Year, 1969" (School Year 1968–1969). Des Moines: ISDPI, 1969, ERIC: ED 033809.

Medford Public Schools. "Evaluation Report for Operation 'RISE' (Recreation-Instruction-Service-Enrichment) in the City of Medford, Mass." Medford: MPS, 1969. ERIC: ED 041991.

Milwaukee Public Schools. "Evaluation of Elementary Summer School ESEA" (Title I). Milwaukee, Wis.: MPS, 1968. (a) ERIC: ED 028212.

Milwaukee Public Schools. "Evaluation of Seminar 1968 Program ESEA" (Title I). Milwaukee, Wis.: MPS, 1968. (b) ERIC: ED 028213.

Morris, G., and Wheater, J. "Born for Joy, A Unique Summer Program for Disadvantaged Children during July 1966." Lyons Falls, N.Y.: Board of Cooperative Education Services, 1966 ERIC: ED 020821.

National Education Association. "Summer School 1962." *NEA Research Bulletin,* 42(1), 1964, 18–23.

National Education Association. "The Rescheduled School Year." *NEA Research Bulletin,* 46(3), 1968, 67–70.

Roncour, L. E. "Summer School Programs in Minnesota." *Minnesota Journal of Education,* 43(10), 1963, 21.

Shaw, F. "Educating Culturally Deprived Youth in Urban Centers." *Phi Delta Kappan,* 45(2), 1963, 91–97.

Soar, R. S. and Soar, R. M. "Pupil Subject Matter Growth During Summer Vacation." *Educational Leadership,* 2(4), 1969, 577–587.

United States Office of Education. "Statistical report. Fiscal Year, 1968: A Report on the Third Year of Title I, ESEA." Washington, D. C.: USOE (DHEW), 1968. (OE-37021–68)

Wasik, B., and Sibley, S. A. "An Experimental Summer Kindergarten for Culturally Deprived Children." Durham, N. C.: Duke University, 1969. ERIC: ED 044174.

Williams, E. B. and Tannenbaum, R. S. "Educational Enrichment for Disadvantaged In-school Neighborhood Youth Corps Enrollees during the Summer, 1967." New York: Center for Urban Education, 1967. ERIC: ED 029938.

ROHWER

1. This study was conducted by Dr. Joan P. Bean, University of California, Berkeley.

Bugelski, B. R. "Presentation Time, Total Time, and Mediation in Paired-Associate Learning." *Journal of Experimental Psychology,* 63, 1962, 409–412.

Duncan, O. D., Featherman, D. L., and Duncan, B. "Socioeconomic Background and Occupational Achievement: Extensions of a Basic Model." Final Report, Project No. 5-0074 (EO-191), U.S. Department of Health, Education, and Welfare, Office of Education, Bureau of Research, May, 1968.

Elkind, D. "Piagetian and Psychometric Conceptions of Intelligence." *Harvard Educational Review,* 39, 1969, 319–337.

Evans, J. "Performance of Headstart Children in Early Grades of School" (National Impact Study). Symposium paper presented at the annual meeting of the American Psychological Association, Washington, D.C., 1969.

Flavell, J. H. "Developmental Studies of Mediated Memory." In H. W. Reese and

L. P. Lipsett (Eds.), Vol. 5. *Advances in Child Development*. New York: Academic Press. 1970.

Goodnow, J. J. "Cultural Variations in Cognitive Skills." *Cognitive Studies*. 1968, 1. prepub. draft.

Hoyt, D. P. "The Relationship between College Grades and Adult Achievement: A Review of the Literature." *American College Testing Program Research Reports*, 7, 1965, 1–58.

Husén, T. *International Study of Achievement in Mathematics*. Vol. 2. Uppsala, Sweden: Almquist and Wiksells, 1967.

Jensen, A. R. "How Much Can We Boost IQ and Scholastic Achievement?" *Harvard Educational Review*, 39, 1969, 1–123.

Jensen, A. R., and Rohwer, W. D., Jr. "Syntactical Mediation of Serial and Paired-Associate Learning as a Function of Age." *Child Development*, 36, 1965, 601–608.

Kohlberg, L. "Early education: A cognitive-developmental view." *Child Development*, 39, 1968, 1013–1062.

Martin, C. J., Cox, D. L., and Boersma, F. J. "The Role of Associative Strategies in the Acquisition of Paired-Associate Material: An Alternative Approach to Meaningfulness." *Psychonomic Science*, 3, 1965, 463–464.

Matz, R. D., and Rohwer, W. D., Jr. "Visual Elaboration and Comprehension of Text." Paper presented at the annual meeting of the American Educational Research Association, New York City, 1971.

Olton, R. M., and Crutchfield, R. S. "Developing the Skills of Productive Thinking." In P. Mussen, J. Langer, and M. Covington (Eds.). *Trends and Issues in Developmental Psychology*. New York: Holt, Rinehart, and Winston, 1969.

Rohwer, W. D., Jr. "Social Class Differences in the Role of Linguistic Structures in Paired-Associate learning: Elaboration and Learning Proficiency." Final report, U.S. Office of Education Basic Research Project No. 5-0605. Contract No. OE 6 10 273, November, 1967.

Rohwer, W. D., Jr. "Mental Elaboration and Proficient Learning." In J. P. Hill (Ed.), *Minnesota Symposia on Child Psychology*, Vol. 4. Minneapolis: University of Minnesota Press, 1970.

Rohwer, W. D., Jr., and Ammon, M. S. "Elaboration Training and Paired-Associate Learning Efficiency in Children." *Journal of Educational Psychology*, 62, 1971, 376–383.

Rohwer, W. D., Jr., Ammon, M. S., Suzuki, N., and Levin, J. R. "Population Differences in Learning Proficiency." *Journal of Educational Psychology*, 62, 1971, 1–14.

Rohwer, W. D., Jr., and Lynch, S. "Retardation, School Strata and Learning Proficiency." *American Journal of Mental Deficiency*, 73, 1968, 91–96.

Rohwer, W. D., Jr., Lynch, S., Levin, J. R., and Suzuki, N. "Grade Level, School Strata, and Learning Efficiency." *Journal of Educational Psychology*, 59, 1968, 26–31.

Runquist, W. N., and Farley, F. H. "The Use of Mediators in the Learning of Verbal Paired Associates." *Journal of Verbal Learning and Verbal Behavior*, 3, 1964, 280–285.

PART FOUR

Section Fourteen

POPHAM

Arnstine, D. G., "The Language and Values of Programmed Instruction: Part 2," *The Educational Forum*, 28, 1964.

Jackson, P. W., *The Way Teaching Is*. Washington, D. C.: National Education Association, 1966.

Komisar, P. B., and McClellan, J. E., "Professor Arnstine and Programmed Instruction." Reprint from *The Educational Forum*, 1965.

Mager, R. F., *Preparing Objectives for Programmed Instruction*, San Francisco: Fearon Press, 1962.

Munro, T., *The Creative Arts in American Education*, "The Interrelation of the Arts in Secondary Education," Harvard University Press, Massachusetts, 1960.

Section Fifteen

BLOCK

1. See Block (1971 or 1937a) for fuller description of Bloom's strategy.

Airasian, P. W. "The Role of Evaluation in Mastery Learning," in *Mastery Learning: Theory and Practice*. Edited by James H. Block, Holt, Rinehart and Winston, Inc., 1971.

Atkinson, R. C. "Computer-based Instruction in Initial Reading," in *Proceedings of the 1967 Invitational Conference on Testing Problems*. Princeton, New Jersey: Educational Testing Service, 1968.

Block, James H. (ed.). *Mastery Learning: Theory and Practice*. New York: Holt, Rinehart and Winston, 1971.

Block, James H. "Student Learning and the Setting of Mastery Performance Standards," *Educational Horizons*, 50 (1972), 183–191.

Block, James, H. "Mastery Learning in the Classroom: An Overview of Recent Research," in *Schools, Society and Mastery Learning*. Edited by James H. Block, Santa Barbara, California, 1973. (Unpublished manuscript).

Block, James H. "New Developments in Mastery Learning in Elementary and Secondary Schools." Paper presented at the annual meeting of the American Educational Research Association, New Orleans, Louisiana, February 28, 1973.

Bloom, Benjamin S. "Learning for Mastery," *Evaluation Comment*, 1, no. 2 (1968).

Bloom, Benjamin S. "Affective Consequences of School Achievement," in *Mastery Learning: Theory and Practice*. Edited by James H. Block. New York: Holt, Rinehart and Winston, Inc., 1971.

Bloom, Benjamin S. "An Introduction to Mastery Learning Theory," in *Schools, Society and Mastery Learning*. Edited by James H. Block. New York: Holt, Rinehart and Winston, in press.

Bloom, Benjamin S., Hastings, T. M. and Madaus, G. F. *Handbook on Formative and Summative Evaluation of Student Learning*. New York: McGraw-Hill, 1971.

Brown, George I. *Human Teaching for Human Learning*. New York: Viking Press, 1971.

Carroll, J. B. "A Model of School Learning," *Teachers College Record*, 64, 1963, 723–33.

Glaser, R. "Adapting the Elementary School Curriculum to Individual Performance," in *Proceedings of the 1967 Invitational Conference on Testing Problems*. Princeton, New Jersey: Educational Testing Service, 1968.

Keller, Fred S. "Goodbye, Teacher . . . ," *Journal of Applied Behavioral Analysis*, 1 (1968), 79–89.

Kifer, Edward. "Some Affective Traits Viewed as Consequences of School Achievement." Unpublished Ph. D. dissertation, University of Chicago, 1973.

Kim, Hogwon. "Mastery Learning in the Korean Middle Schools," *UNESCO Regional Office for Education in Asia*, 6 (Sept. 1971), Sec. I., 55–66.

Peterfreund, Stanley (ed.). "Innovation and Change in Public School Systems." Englewood Cliffs, New Jersey: Stanley Peterfreund Associates, 1970. (Unpublished manuscript.)

Peterson, Penelope. "A Review of the Research on Mastery Learning Strategies." Stockholm, Sweden: International Association for the Evaluation of Educational Achievement, 1972. (Unpublished manuscript.)

Postlethwait, S. N., Novak, J. and Murray, H. *The Audio-Tutorial Approach to Learning*. Minneapolis, Minnesota: Burgess Publishing Co., 1969.

Purkey, W. W. *Self-Concept and School Achievement*. Englewood Cliffs, N.J.: Prentice-Hall, Inc., 1970.

Romberg, T. A., Shepler, J. and King, I. *Mastery Learning and Retention*, Technical Report no. 151. Wisconsin R and D Center for Cognitive Learning, The University of Wisconsin, Madison, Wisconsin, 1970.

Suppes, P. "The Uses of Computers in Education." *Scientific American*, 215 (1966), 206–221.

Torshen, Kay P. "The Relation of Classroom Evaluation to Students' Self-concepts and Mental Health." Unpublished Ph. D. dissertation, University of Chicago, 1969.

Section Sixteen

FELDMESSER

1. Staff of the Office of Research, National Norms for Entering College Freshmen — Fall 1970 (Washington: American Council on Education, 1970), p. 43.
2. Melvin M. Tumin, "Evaluation of the Effectiveness of Education: Some Problems and Prospects," Interchange, 1 (1970): 96–109.
3. Burton R. Clark, The Distinctive College: Antioch, Reed, Swarthmore (Chicago: Aldine, 1970), p. 131.
4. William R. Torbert and J. Richard Hackman, "Taking the Fun Out of Outfoxing the System," in The Changing College Classroom, ed. Philip Runkel, Roger Harrison, and Margaret Runkel (San Francisco: Jossey-Bass, 1969), pp. 167–76; Robert A. Feldmesser, The Option: Analysis of an Educational Innovation (Hanover, N.H.: Dartmouth College, 1969), pp. 70–87.
5. Jonathan R. Warren, College Grading Practices: An Overview (Washington: ERIC Clearinghouse on Higher Education, George Washington University, 1971); Sidney B. Simon, "Grades Must Go," School Review, May 1970, pp. 397–402.
6. "The Relationship Between College Grades and Adult Achievement, A Review of the Literature," ACT Research Reports (Iowa City, Iowa: American College Testing Program, 1965), p. 46.
7. Howard S. Becker, Blanche Geer, and Everett C. Hughes, Making the Grade: The Academic Side of College Life (New York: John Wiley, 1968).
8. Norman F. Wallen and Robert M. W. Travers, "Analysis and Investigation of Teaching Methods," in Handbook of Research in Teaching, ed. N. L. Gage (Chicago: Rand McNally, 1963), p. 496.
9. "An Atmosphere to Breathe: Woodrow Wilson and the Life of the American University College" (New York: Woodrow Wilson Foundation, 1959), p. 19. See also Becker, Geer, and Hughes, Making the Grade, p. 140.
10. George R. Bramer, "Grading and Academic Justice," Improving College and University Teaching, Winter 1970, pp. 63–65.

MILLMAN

1. Benjamin S. Bloom, "Learning for Mastery," Evaluation Comment, May, 1968, 12 pp. (published by the UCLA Center for the Study of Evaluation of Instructional Programs); and Robert Glaser, "Adapting the Elementary School Curriculum to Individual Performance," in Proceedings of the 1967 Invitational Conference on Testing Problems, Benjamin Bloom, chairman, Princeton, N.J.: Educational Testing Service, 1967, pp. 3–36.
2. This point was made by Henry M. Brickell, who writes: "... If the innovation individualizes instruction in such a way that students begin to move through the same material at variable rates of speed controlled by their mastery of the material, report cards which tell parents about the student's degree of success in learning the content (usually expressed as letter grades indicating class standing) should have been replaced by new report cards which tell parents about the student's rate of progress." From "Appraising the Effects of Innovations in Local Schools," in Ralph W. Tyler, ed., Educational Evaluation: New Roles, New Means. Chicago: National Society for the Study of Education (68th Yearbook, Part II), 1969, pp. 301–02.
3. Robert L. Ebel, "Content Standard Test Scores," Educational and Psychological Measurement, Spring, 1962, pp. 15–25 and Robert Glaser, "Instructional Technology and the Measurement of Learning Outcomes: Some Questions," American Psychologist, August, 1963, pp. 519–21.
4. W. James Popham and T. R. Husek, "Implications of Criterion-Referenced Measurement," Journal of Educational Measurement, Spring, 1969, pp. 1–9.
5. "Reporting Pupil Progress," NEA Research Bulletin, October, 1969, pp. 75–76.
6. See, especially, Bloom, op. cit. The ungraded school, an administrative device to

facilitate adapting the curriculum and modifying instruction to the individual learner, is said to be based on the assumptions that "up to a certain point a 'slow learner,' if taught appropriately and given more time, can learn the same things that more capable students do" (an assumption of the Carroll Model of School Learning which was followed in the Bloom article) and that "up to that certain point all students *should* learn the same things." Mauritz Johnson, Jr., *Grouping in Graded and Ungraded Schools*, Cornell University Curriculum and Instruction Series, No. 4, pp. 15–16.

7. William W. Cooley and Robert Glaser, "An Information and Management System for Individually Prescribed Instruction," technical report, University of Pittsburgh Learning Research and Development Center, 1968.

8. W. James Popham, "Focus on Outcomes: A Guiding Theme of ES '70 Schools," *Phi Delta Kappan*, December, 1969, p. 208.

9. William Clark Trow, "On Marks, Norms, and Proficiency Scores," *Phi Delta Kappan*, December, 1966, pp. 171–73.

10. Elliot W. Eisner, "Instructional and Expressive Educational Objectives: Their Formulation and Use in Curriculum," in Robert E. Stake, series ed., *American Educational Research Association Monograph Series on Curriculum Evaluations*. Chicago: Rand McNally, 1969, pp. 1–31.

11. It is not my position that objectives need to be stated in behavorial terms and, indeed, the objectives shown in Figure 2 are not. Rather, I am arguing that what counts as evidence that the objectives have been met should be made explicit by the items constituting the criterion-reference tests.

12. There is the added question of college admissions. The school records will, under the system being proposed, contain information about *how much* a student has achieved — what he can and cannot do — rather than whether he earned higher grades than his classmates. This record, together with aptitude scores, letters of reference, the application form, and other items, should permit a sound basis for making admission decisions, especially in those institutions moving closer to an open enrollment policy.

13. Jane Loevinger, "Person and Population as Psychometric Concepts," *Psychological Review*, March, 1965, pp. 143–55.

STAKE

1. Examples of text items have been deleted here.

2. Tendencies to teach for the test in this situation must be checked.

3. An example of a reading-comprehension item has been deleted here.

4. The official evaluation report was written by Andrew and Roberts (1970). Summaries and commentaries have been written by Dyer (1970). Schwartz (1970), and Welch (1970).

5. The breech also represents the distance between an established teaching profession and challenging instructional technologists.

6. Publisher's permission is needed.

7. Richard C. Anderson and his colleagues at the Training Research Laboratory, University of Illinois, have been working on the problem (Anderson, Goldberg, and Hidde, 1971; Wittrock and Hill, 1968).

8. A shortage of understandable indicators is one reason the schools have not been accountable to the public. However, House (1971) claimed that it is unlikely that educators will use better report procedures even if available because there is much more risk than reward in doing so.

9. Then we would ask "At what grade level do half the students get this item right?" The score for a student would be the grade equivalents of the most difficult items he passes, with perhaps a correction for guessing.

10. A spring slowdown and summer setback sometimes occur in conventional school programs. If the instructional program began in March or in June, the results would not necessarily be the same.

Anastasi, Anne. *Psychological Testing*. New York: Macmillan, 1954.

Anderson, Richard C., Goldberg, Sheila M., and Hidde, Janet L. "Meaningful Processing of Sentences." *Journal of Educational Psychology*, 5(1971), 395–399.

Andrew, Dean C., and Roberts, Lawrence H. "Final Evaluation Report on the Texarkana Dropout Prevention Program," Magnolia, Arkansas: Region VIII. Education Service Center, July 20, 1970 (mimeo).

Beggs, Donald L., and Hieronymus, Al. Uniformity of Growth in the Basic Skills throughout the School Year and during the Summer. *Journal of Educational Measurement*, 5 (1968), 91–97.

Bhaerman, Robert. "A Paradigm for Accountability," *American Teacher*, 1970, 55 (3), 18–19.

Bloom, Benjamin S., Englehart, Max D., Furst, Edwin J., Hill, William H., and Krathwhol, David R. A *Taxonomy of Educational Objectives: Handbook I, The Cognitive Domain*. New York: David McKay, 1956.

Bormuth, John. *On the Theory of Achievement Test Items*. Chicago: University of Chicago Press, 1970.

Cohen, David K., "Politics and Research — Evaluation of Large-scale Education Programs." *Review of Educational Research*, 40, 2 (1970), 213–238.

Dyer, Henry S. "Performance Contracting: Too Simple a Solution for Difficult Problems." *The United Teacher*, November 29, 1970, 19–22.

Ebel, Robert L. "When Information Becomes Knowledge." *Science*, 171 (1971), 130–131.

Gates, Arthur I., and MacGinitie, Walter H. *Technical Manual for the Gates-MacGinitie Reading Tests*. New York: Teachers College Press, Columbia University, 1965, p. 5.

Gooler, Dennis D. "Strategies for Obtaining Clarification of Priorities in Education." Unpublished doctoral dissertation, University of Illinois at Urbana-Champaign, 1971.

Hastings, J. Thomas, Runkel, Philip J., and Damrin, Dora E. *Effects on Use of Tests by Teachers Trained in a Summer Institute*, Cooperative Research Project No. 702. Urbana: Bureau of Educational Research, College of Education, University of Illinois, 1961.

Hively, Wells, II, Patterson, Harry L., and Page, Sara H. "A 'Universe-defined' System of Arithmetic Achievement Tests." *Journal of Educational Measurement*, 5, 4 (1968), 275–290.

House, Ernest R. "The Conscience of Educational Evaluation." Paper presented at the Ninth Annual Conference of the California Association for the Gifted, Monterey, February 1971.

Joselyn, E. Gary. "Performance Contracting: What It's All About." Paper presented at Truth and Soul In Teaching Conference of the American Federation of Teachers, Chicago, January 1971.

Lennon, Roger T. *Testimony of Dr. Roger T. Lennon as Expert Witness on Psychological Testing*. New York: Harcourt, Brace and World, no date.

Lennon, Roger T. "Accountability and Performance Contracting." Paper presented at the annual meeting of the American Educational Research Association, New York, February 1971.

Lessinger, Leon. "Engineering Accountability for Results in Public Education." *Phi Delta Kappan*, 52, 4 (1970), 217–225.

Lieberman, Myron. "An Overview of Accountability." *Phi Delta Kappan*, 52, 4 (1970), 194–195.

Lord, Frederic M. "Elementary Models for Measuring Change." In Chester W. Harris (ed.), *Problems in Measuring Change*. Madison: University of Wisconsin Press, 1963, pp. 21–38.

Lord, Frederic. "A Theory of Test Scores." *Psychometric Monograph Number 7*, The Psychometric Society. Philadelphia: George E. Ferguson Co., 1952.

Mager, Robert F. *Preparing Objectives for Programmed Instruction*. San Francisco: Fearon Press, 1962.

Meacham, Merle L., and Wiesen, Allen E. *Changing Classroom Behavior: A Manual for Precision Teaching*. Scranton: International Textbook Co., 1969.

National School Board Journal Staff. "Two Out of Three Boardmen Buy Performance Contracting." *National School Board Journal*, November 1970, 35–36.

Nunnally, Jum C., Jr. *Tests and Measurements: Assessment and Prediction*. New York: McGraw-Hill, 1959.

Popham, W. James. "Objectives and Instruction." In Robert E. Stake (ed.) *Instructional Objectives*, AERA Monograph Series on Curriculum Evaluation, no. 3. Chicago: Rand McNally, 1969, pp. 32–52.

Schwartz, Ronald. "Performance Contracting: Industry's Reaction." *The Nation's Schools*, 86, 1970, 53–55.

Stake, Robert E. "Objectives, Priorities, and Other Judgment Data." *Review of Educational Research*, 40, 1970, 181–212.

Thorndike, E. L. *The Measurement of Educational Products*, Seventeenth Yearbook of the National Society for the Study of Education, Part II. Bloomington, Illinois: Public School Publishing Co., 1918. Also in Geraldine M. Joncich (ed.), *Psychology and the Science of Education*. New York: Bureau of Publications, Teachers College, Columbia University, 1962, p. 151.

Thorndike, R. L. *Educational Psychology*, vol. 1: *The Original Nature of Man*. New York: Teachers College, Columbia University, 1921, pp. 11–12.

Tyler, Ralph W. *Basic Principles of Curriculum and Instruction*. Chicago: University of Chicago Press, 1950, p. 83.

Wrightman, L., and Gorth, W. P. "CAM: The New Look in Classroom Testing." *Trend*, Spring 1969, 56–57.

Welsh, James. D. C. "Perspectives on Performance Contracting." *Educational Researcher*, vol. 21, October 1970, 1–3.

Wick, John, and Beggs, Donald L. *Evaluation for Decision-making in the Schools*. New York: Houghton Mifflin, 1971.

Wittrock, M. C., and Hill, Claude E. *Children's Preferences in the Transfer of Learning*. Final Report, Project no. 3264, U.S. Department of Health, Education, and Welfare, November 1968.

Yum, K. W. "An Experimental Test of the Law of Assimilation." *Journal of Experimental Psychology*, 14, 1931, 68–82.

Zahorik, John A. "The Effect of Planning on Teaching." *The Elementary School Journal*, December 1970, 143–151.

GLOSSARY

The following definitions are not meant to be technically precise, but to give the student without research training a general introduction to some of the techniques and statistical procedures mentioned in the readings.

ADJUSTED MEAN

A mathematical expression which is used to compare the final achievement level of two or more groups exposed to different instructional treatments and which takes into account differences in their initial achievement level. For example, suppose one group of students (A) is exposed to a new mathematics curriculum, while another group (B) receives the traditional curriculum. The following are their mean scores on mathematics tests administered at the beginning of the school year.

	Group A	Group B
September mean score	35.3	48.9
June mean score	47.1	61.5
Adjusted June mean score (hypothetical)	52.1	56.5

Group A seems to have a lower level of achievement at the end of the school year (47.1) than does Group B (61.5). However, this is not a fair comparison of the effects of the two curricula since the two groups did not start at the same achievement level in September (35.3 vs. 48.9). The adjusted mean uses the available test information to show what the scores of the two groups might have been had they started at the same achievement level. The difference between the adjusted June means of the two groups above would probably be fairly small, even though the actual June means differ substantially (*see also* Mean).

ANALYSIS OF VARIANCE

A mathematical technique enabling the researcher to draw certain conclusions about population characteristics, even though he has only studied a sample drawn from the population. Suppose that a researcher is comparing the effects of two curricula (A and B) on student achievement. He is also concerned that the students' reading ability may influence how much they learn from the curricula. Thus, he randomly assigns students of high and low reading ability to receive either Curriculum A or Curriculum B. After the students have finished the curriculum, they are given an achievement test. Their mean scores on this test are as follows:

	Reading Ability	
	High	Low
Curriculum A	88.2	40.8
Curriculum B	76.9	56.9

Analysis of variance can be used to test the statistical significance (*see* Test of statistical significance) of the difference between means of the high and low ability groups, independently of whether they received Curriculum A or B. Also, the same test can be made on the difference between means for students who were exposed to Curriculum A or B, independently of their reading ability level. Finally, analysis of variance enables the researcher to study interactions between several variables. In the above example, the researcher found that Curriculum A was better than Curriculum B for high ability students (88.2 vs. 76.9); however, just the reverse was true for low ability students (40.8 vs. 56.9). In other words, there was an interaction between the variables of curriculum and reading ability. Analysis of variance enables the researcher to test the statistical significance of this interaction.

CHOICE REACTION TIME, TEST OF

A measure of subjects' reaction time when they are presented with stimulus situations that convey different amounts of information. For example, a subject may be required to turn off a light as fast as possible after it goes on by pressing a button near the light. By presenting different numbers of light-button alternatives, researchers can increase the amount of information processing that the subject needs to perform before he can act. Thus, this test provides a simple measure of subjects' information-processing capacity.

CONCURRENT VALIDITY

The extent to which subjects' scores on one test are related to their scores on another test of the same construct (e.g., intelligence, anxiety, mathematics achievement) administered at the same time or within a short interval of time. This type of validity is most often relevant when there is a need to develop a shorter or more easily administered test than one which already exists. For example, the Stanford-Binet Intelligence Scale usually requires an hour or more of individual testing time. A test developer might undertake to develop a shorter, group-administered test measuring the same type of intelligence as the Stanford-Binet. After developing it, he then would administer the new measure and the Stanford-Binet to the same group of students within a short time interval. The concurrent validity of the new test is a function of how highly students' scores on it correlate positively (*see* Correlation) with their scores on the Stanford-Binet.

CONSTRUCT VALIDITY

The extent to which a test measures a psychological construct or trait, such as intelligence, authoritarianism, level of aspiration, or self-esteem. Suppose that someone told you that they had developed a new measure of positive self-esteem. One of the first questions you might ask this person is, "How do you know that your test measures self-esteem?" This would be a question about the test's construct validity. A test developer can use various methods to establish a test's construct validity. For example, he might hypothesize that students in counseling for school adjustment problems would have lower self-esteem than students not in counseling. If students in counseling do score significantly lower on his test than other students, this is evidence that the test is measuring positive self-esteem. Generally, the construct validity of a test increases as the test developer collects more and more supporting pieces of evidence that it indeed measures what it purports to measure.

CONTINGENCY

As used in Skinnerian learning theory, the set of conditions under which reinforcement is given. For example, a teacher may reinforce a child by saying "good" or some other verbal phrase only when the student gives correct answers to computational problems. In this case the behavior of giving correct answers is the contingency under which the teacher's reinforcement is given.

CORRELATION

A mathematical technique which can be used to determine the degree of linear relationship between two variables. For example, consider the relationship between height and weight. In a typical group of people, taller persons tend to be heavier than shorter persons. For each additional inch of height there is likely to be an increment in weight. When such a relationship between two variables exists, we say that they are positively correlated with each other. In education, IQ and achievement test scores usually are positively correlated with each other. It is also possible for two variables to be negatively correlated or to have a zero correlation with each other. Anxiety and achievement have been found to be negatively correlated with each other in some research investigations, that is, students with *higher* scores on a measure of anxiety tend to have *lower* achievement test scores. The correlation is not perfectly negative, though, since some students with high anxiety scores have high achievement scores, and some students with low anxiety scores have low achievement scores. (*See also* Correlation coefficient, Squared correlation.)

CORRELATION COEFFICIENT

A mathematical expression which can be used to indicate the degree of linear correlation between two variables. A correlation coefficient of zero (0) usually indicates that there is no correlation between two variables. A correlation coefficient of +1.0 usually indicates a perfect correlation between two variables: each increment in one variable (e.g., one point of an IQ scale) is associated with an increment in the other variable (e.g., one point on an achievement test). Coefficients with a value between zero and +1.0 indicate that two variables are positively, but not perfectly correlated with each other. Conversely, a correlation coefficient of −1.0 usually indicates a perfect negative correlation between two variables, and coefficients between 0.0 and −1.0 indicate varying degrees of negative correlation. (*See also* Correlation.)

COVARIANCE

Similar in meaning to the concept of correlation (*see* Correlation).

DEPENDENT VARIABLE

A variable which is measured after an instructional treatment has been administered. In educational research the dependent variable is usually a student's score on an achievement test, an attitude survey, or some other measure of his knowledge or skill. Teaching techniques and instructional materials are examples of instructional treatments which are introduced in hopes of producing changes in a dependent variable.

ENCOUNTER GROUP

A form of human relations training in which an experienced group leader helps participants to better understand interpersonal relationships, their impact on others, and how others perceive them. These groups differ from group therapy in that the personal pasts of participants are not discussed in any depth, and the leader does not attempt to treat emotional disorders that may be manifested by participants.

FACTOR ANALYSIS

A mathematical technique used to identify factors which several tests or test items share in common. For example, many tests of quantitative and verbal aptitude have been developed. If we administered these tests to a sample of students, we probably would find that the tests of quantitative aptitude are highly correlated with each other (*see* Correlation), and similarly the tests of verbal aptitude are highly correlated with each other. Also, each test of quantitative aptitude probably is correlated somewhat with each of the verbal aptitude tests, but not nearly to the same extent as the correlation between each test of quantitative aptitude and all the other tests of quantitative aptitude. Given this pattern of results, a factor analysis of the correlations probably would indicate that the tests measure two factors: quantitative aptitude and verbal aptitude. To measure one of these factors, then, it is not necessary to administer all the tests; the researcher need only administer one or two of the tests which "load" highly on the factor (i.e., are highly correlated with the factor). Factor analysis is also commonly used to determine which items on a test cluster together, that is, which items correlate highly with each other and thus define a common factor.

GENOTYPE

A class or group of individuals sharing a specified genetic make-up such as the gene structure producing blue eyes, brown hair, or some other genetically determined characteristic.

HEREDITABILITY

The capability of a particular behavioral disposition or physical characteristic to be acquired through genetic inheritance.

INTERMITTENT REINFORCEMENT

A reward that is administered occasionally, according to a schedule, rather than every time a given behavior occurs. (*See* Reinforcement.)

INVERSE RELATIONSHIP

Synonymous in meaning to negative correlation between two variables. (*See* Correlation.)

LAW OF EFFECT

A principle of learning formulated by E. L. Thorndike, stating that the association between a stimulus and a response is strengthened when the response leads to a reward. Correspondingly, the association is weakened when the response is unsuccessful or punishing to the learner. The law of effect is similar to Skinner's explanation of how reinforcement brings about learning. (*See* Reinforcement.)

MEAN (M)

The arithmetic average of all data of a particular type gathered from a sample of subjects. For example, the mean score on a reading achievement test for a sample of 50 students would equal the sum of the individual scores divided by the number of scores obtained (in this case 50).

MENDELIAN REVOLUTION

The change in the investigation of heredity following the development of Mendel's genetic theory of transmission of the neurological and physiological equipment of organisms. In the late 1800's Mendel theorized that organisms which are formed from the union of male and female germ cells receive an equal contribution of factors from both parents. Paired hereditary units representing various characteristics separate during gamete formation so each gamete has only one member of a pair. Uniting of the male and female gametes forms new pairs, which produce characteristics made up of a combination of both parents.

PREDICTIVE VALIDITY

The extent to which the predictions made by a test are confirmed by the later behavior of the subjects tested. For example, suppose that a foreign language aptitude test is administered to a group of eleventh-grade students prior to their entry into a two-year Spanish language program. At the end of the two years a test of Spanish language achievement is administered to the same students. Then the aptitude test scores are correlated (*see* Correlation) with the achievement test scores to determine whether there is a positive relationship. If the aptitude test has predictive validity, students with the higher aptitude scores will have higher achievement test scores; conversely, students with the lower aptitude scores will have lower achievement test scores.

PROBABILITY LEVEL (p)

See Test of statistical significance.

PURSUIT ROTOR LEARNING, TEST OF

A specialized learning task requiring the subject to use a jointed stylus to pursue a metal disc set flush with the surface of a turntable revolving at a relatively high rate of speed. The speed with which the turntable revolves may vary and the disc may move in a synchronous or asynchronous pattern. The subject is tested for his ability to follow the disc with the stylus. Learning generally is measured by the total time the stylus spends in contact with the disc.

QUANTITATIVE VARIABLE

A set of numerical values on a specific dimension. Yearly income, the number of correct items on a test, the number of years of school completed are quantitative variables. They can be counted and represented by a number. Mayeske (*see* Section 4) made membership in a particular racial-ethnic group into a quantitative variable by assigning a number for each group based on the group's mean score on the achievement composite.

REGRESSION EFFECT

The tendency for persons who score low on a test to score higher when a parallel form of the test is administered later, and, correspondingly, the tendency for persons who score high on the initial test to score lower upon retesting. The regression effect has a mathematical basis, but to explain it in nonmathematical terms, suppose that a student earns a very high score on a multiple-choice test. This is probably not his "true" score. In addition to using his ability, he probably made some lucky guesses, and also the test may have contained many items which he just happened to know. It is unlikely that these same chance factors will operate in his favor when he later takes a parallel form of the test. For example, he probably will not make the same number of lucky guesses as he did the first time. The result is that he earns a lower score on the second test. The reverse situation applies to the student who scored very low on the initial test. Part of his low score is probably due to bad luck in guessing and to a high proportion of items he happened not to know. The laws of probability dictate that it is likely his luck will improve on the second testing occasion, that is, it is quite unlikely that he will have bad luck twice in a row. Thus, even though the student may not have made any actual improvement in ability, his score is likely to indicate an improvement. The regression effect is especially important to consider when a researcher claims to have found that low-ability students make achievement gains on tests administered before and after they participate in a new educational program.

REINFORCEMENT

A term which has several technical meanings in the field of learning theory. In education, reinforcement usually refers to the practice of having a student learn a given response pattern by following an occurrence of that response with a reward. For example, if a student says "9" as a response to the question, "What is the sum of 4 and 5?", the teacher can "reinforce" that response by administering a reward such as saying, "Good; you got the right answer."

SQUARED CORRELATION

A simple computational procedure applied to a correlation coefficient for the purpose of obtaining a quantitative measure of the percentage of shared variance between two variables. Consider the following scores earned by a group of students on an aptitude measure and a school achievement test:

Student	Aptitude	Achievement
A	31	85
B	37	81
C	20	73
Mean score	19.2	65.3
D	16	67
E	12	50
F	9	36

Students' scores vary around the mean of each variable. One student's score is just above the mean; another's is just below it; and still another's is considerably below it. The squared correlation tells the researcher how well the variable in aptitude scores predicts the variance in achievement test scores, or vice versa.

STANDARD DEVIATION (SD)

One type of mathematical expression used to show the range and variability of a given set of scores. For example, suppose that students' scores on an achievement test have a mean of 50 and standard deviation of 10. Usually, one can deduce from these data that about two-thirds of the students earned scores between 40 (mean minus one standard deviation) and 60 (mean plus one standard deviation).

STATISTICAL SIGNIFICANCE

See Test of statistical significance.

TEST OF STATISTICAL SIGNIFICANCE

A mathematical technique enabling the researcher to draw some conclusions about a population, even though he only studies a sample drawn from the population. To illustrate, suppose that a researcher was interested in testing the hypothesis that independent students (identified by their high scores on a paper-and-pencil measure of independence) will learn more from individualized instruction than dependent students (identified by their low scores on the same measure). The researcher finds that a sample of 30 independent fifth-grade students earn an average achievement test score of 57.2 after a year of exposure to individualized instruction. In contrast, the mean score for a sample of 30 dependent fifth-grade students is 46.8. One might argue that this result could have occurred by chance: if the researcher had investigated all fifth-grade students in the United States with high or low scores on the measure of independence, he would have found no difference between them on the achievement test; even though there is no difference in the two populations of high and low scorers, he just happened to select two samples from these populations which differed on the achievement test. A test of statistical significance yields a probability level (p). If p is low enough (usually .05 or less), then the researcher rejects the alternative explanation that there is no difference between the two populations of independent and dependent fifth-grade students. Instead, he concludes that there is a real difference between the two samples and that he would also have found a difference if he had studied the entire populations.

VARIANCE

A quantitative measure of the extent to which persons' scores vary around the mean on a particular variable such as a reading achievement test. It is equal to the square of the standard deviation (see Mean, Standard deviation).

VICARIOUS REINFORCEMENT

A type of reward that increases the likelihood that a particular behavior pattern will occur. However, the reward is not given to the learner; it is given to another person who exhibits the desired behavior pattern. For example, a child might learn a certain behavior pattern because he observes other children being rewarded for this behavior.

Z TEST

One type of test of statistical significance. (See Test of statistical significance.)

INDEX

DATE DUE

NO 18 '92		
AP 5 '93		
NO 25 '93		
AP 11 '94		
APR 0 5 1999		
AUG 21 1999		

Demco, Inc. 38-293